W9-DIJ-660

Contents

Chapter 4 Profile of Aboriginal People II: Social Attributes   93

Chapter 5 The Canadian Justice System: The Tragedy and the Travesty   132

Chapter 6 The New Crucible of Aboriginal Revitalization: Urban Centres   161

Chapter 7 Indian Treaties and Métis Scrip: Old Promises and New Struggles   189

Chapter 8 Contesting Title and Ownership: The Modern Claims and Treaty Process   212

Chapter 9 Self-Determination and Self-Government: The Rights of Peoples   255

Figures and Tables

Figures

Tables

Preface

When I started working on the first edition of this book, little did I know that I would continue this venture for more than a quarter of a century. Over this time the global environment has changed substantially and new people have occupied positions of power. Old political figures are no longer recognized by young Canadians, and new institutions and new ways of operating have been created. While the process of devolution has continued to advance, many of the attributes of colonialism still remain. This new edition chronicles the changes that have taken place over the past century and how they have impacted upon Canadians and Aboriginal peoples. Dr. René Gadacz, my co-author, is a social anthropologist and has made a substantive contribution to the breadth and scope of the material presented.

Aboriginal Peoples in Canada provides the reader with an understanding of Aboriginal rights within the context of the Canadian Constitution. We begin with a historical discussion of Aboriginal–non-Aboriginal relations and then trace the evolution of these relations over time. The primary task of this book is to provide the reader with an understanding of the place of Aboriginal people within Canadian society. We provide this through a number of lenses. For example, the Supreme Court of Canada has dealt with Aboriginal rights and their links to British property law, and has clearly acknowledged that there is a new constitutional meaning and role for Aboriginal people. We also show how Aboriginal issues are viewed by politicians and representative Canadians.

We have tried to maintain our objectivity in presenting the material in this volume. However, we are all human beings with values and we admit that our personal experiences and points of view influence the approach taken in this book. Yet we have tried to state things as clearly as we can and not to let traditional or commonly accepted perspectives go unchallenged if they deserve to be challenged. We want readers to know that we do not have an "axe to grind," but we do have biases and we are sure they will show. Nevertheless, these are our personal views and should be assessed differently from those based upon solid social science research and careful public analysis.

The authors do not take a specific theoretical perspective in looking at Aboriginal–Euro-Canadian relations, although one could argue that the book is more focused on macro issues and looks at structural factors as shaping how Aboriginal people and the rest of Canada relate. We do not focus on micro (individual) factors although we understand that they operate in our society, e.g., prejudice, discrimination. But that is another story that deserves to be more fully articulated in another time and place. The book is steeped in an analysis of structural inter-group relations in which the two groups operate. We are convinced this approach is necessary for understanding the environment of Aboriginal–White relations and to make sense of the shifting landscape in which they take place.

For the first half of the 20th century, Canadians showed little interest in Aboriginal people. However, by the 1950s, government became embarrassed by international incidents that placed Canada and its treatment of Aboriginals on the global map. Through the commissioning of government reports, a small body of evidence emerged that suggested Aboriginal people were not benefiting from the growing economy. By the 1960s, academics began to write on the subject and to add to the growing knowledge base. However, it was not until the 1970s that an explosion of books, articles, movies, and other popular cultural and media representations occurred as a renaissance of Aboriginal identity began. By the mid-1980s, Aboriginal issues were dealt with by the mass media on a regular basis. Academics, including First Nation, Métis and Inuit scholars, now routinely teach in Native Studies programs or courses concerned with Aboriginal people. In the past two decades, a growing literature on Aboriginal people has been published in both scholarly journals and in the popular media by both Aboriginal and non-Aboriginal authors. These and other publications have a diversity of foci—legal, land claims, justice, deviance, health, housing, language, media and communication—from a variety of theoretical perspectives, e.g., Eurocentric, Aboriginal, feminist, Marxist, structural-functional. Aboriginal Studies is now a burgeoning area of study, regardless of its lack of boundaries and central focus, and 12 different universities across Canada now offer academic programs with advanced degrees in the area.

The eighth edition follows the general format of the original work. Nevertheless, the present volume comprises a considerable updating and revision of the last edition. While there have been many specific changes over the past five years, the overall position of Aboriginal people in our society has not appreciably changed. It is said that if you work on an enterprise long enough, you will eventually gain some perspective on it. But as noted elsewhere, failing eyesight sometimes offsets the gain in perspective. We have no doubt that as we write the eighth edition, both events have occurred. Nevertheless, even though our eyesight may have diminished, we are convinced that the perspective offered to the reader will illuminate his or her intellectual world and provide for a better understanding of Aboriginal people in Canadian society. We hope we are able to give the reader a lens through which to view our complex and diverse society and, in the end, we hope the reader will be able to develop a better appreciation of how historical events influence contemporary issues and thus have the intellectual tools to better analyze Aboriginal–Euro-Canadian relations.

Novelists, academics, and politicians have been inspired for years to write about their observations of Aboriginal people. While many Canadians have some knowledge or conception about Aboriginal people, most of us have few encounters with Aboriginal people directly. Yet, at a more abstract level, we speak about their plight and treatment. As you, the reader, go through this book, sometimes you will be in agreement, on other occasions your perspective will differ. Our goal is to write a book that provides a critical interpretation of the events that have shaped Aboriginal–Euro-Canadian relations and that thus have formed the structure of Canadian society. As we note in the text, many of the original works on Aboriginal people were written from the point of view of the dominant group. The material offered in this book tries to present ethnic relation from the position of "outsider," identifying both the majority and minority perspectives.

This eighth edition, like previous ones, has been written for individuals who are not experts in the area of Aboriginal Studies. It is primarily for the neophyte reader, but one who would like as panoramic a view as possible. More advanced readers will find it useful because it presents up-to-date statistical material and, where possible, the latest court decisions, current legislation as it impacts Aboriginal people, and the most recent research on Aboriginal issues. The list of reference material presents the reader with a cornucopia of citations that span the last century, and it will be a useful aid for covering the field. Instructors will benefit from the PowerPoint slides, which are a new feature of this edition.

Acknowledgements

Those who know the subject area will recognize that we owe a large debt to those who have already worked on and written about Aboriginal people. As such, regardless of what the copyright law says, this book is not the sole product of the co-authors. We have drawn heavily on the works of our colleagues across Canada and they have shared their thoughts and ideas with us—their understanding and criticism of old ideas made us search constantly for new conceptualizations and, hopefully, new solutions. We thank them for their insightful and analytical comments. We would also like to thank those Aboriginal people who have, over the years, shared with us their views and interpretations of Aboriginal–Euro-Canadian relations in this country. The citations at the end of this volume should be regarded as further acknowledgments of a number of scholars who have written on the subject.

At Pearson Education we are grateful to our Acquisitions Editor, Laura Forbes, and Marketing Manager, Sally Aspinall, for the strong support they have given this project. We owe special thanks to our Developmental Editor, Alexandra Dyer, for her endless good humour, patience, careful guidance, and outstanding contribution in preparing the manuscript for publication. John Firth deserves accolades for his very fine copyediting. We also thank Katie Hearn and Avinash Chandra for shepherding the text through production, as well as the team in Creative Services for their skillful design of the text. Lastly, we acknowledge Chris Andersen, Howard Doughty, David King, Sheldon Krasowski, Zahra Montazer, Rob Nestor, Janice Noël, and Eldon Yellowhorn, whose critical review comments helped shape this edition of *Aboriginal Peoples in Canada*.

ADDITIONAL THANKS

I owe a great deal to Dr. Roy Bowles, whose intellectual influence on me began when I first took a course from him while in graduate school. Don Whiteside (sin-a-paw), Tony Lussier, and Katie Cook have, over the years, shared with me their philosophical perspectives as well as the materials I requested, some of which were provided at considerable cost to themselves. Other scholars such as Tony Hall, George Calliou, Shawna Cunningham, Reg Crowshoe, Terry Wotherspoon, Marlene Castellano, Betty Bastien, Roger Gibbins, Cash Rowe, Leroy Little-Bear and Jim Webb have provided new interpretations to past events and given me the courage to challenge many previously accepted "truths."

J. S. Frideres
Calgary, Alberta

I would like to thank my students from the University of Northern British Columbia, Okanagan University College, the University of Victoria, and Grande Prairie Regional College for participating in the very difficult task of nation-building by questioning (and sometimes revising!) their personal assumptions and philosophies in the field of Aboriginal Studies. Special thanks to Ms. Leslie Fabriz, Nlaka'pumx Nation, for her very able research assistance on an earlier edition of this book, and to Ms. Ashley Prescott for research assistance on the eighth edition. I am also grateful to Michael I. Asch, the late Bruce G. Trigger, and James S. Frideres for opportunities, advice, insights, and encouragements over three decades of scholarship.

René R. Gadacz
Grande Prairie, Alberta

The Legacy of Canadian Colonialism

INTRODUCTION

How can you discover an inhabited land? This obvious point has eluded Canadians for the past five hundred years and yet we have built stories upon this myth that support the current view that Europeans discovered Canada and built what we have today through the efforts of hardworking immigrants. As Wright (2003) notes, these myths become maps by which succeeding generations navigate and make sense out of their world. Once the stories are told and re-told, they take on a sense of legitimacy and no one ever questions the veracity of such maps. As such, Canadians are loath to think that perhaps the past is not as they think.

Nevertheless, questions concerning the rights of Aboriginal people in Canada have taken a curious prominence in Canadian politics. The federal government has, for the past half-century, conveyed a message to Canadians that it has, or is just about to, resolve the issues that Aboriginal people are bringing forth (Churchill, 1999). Thus it is not surprising that most Canadians find it difficult to understand the demands being made by Aboriginal people. Moreover, Canadians find they are not prepared or able to link historical actions with contemporary events. In other words, it is difficult to see how historical events are causal agents of today's actions. Most people tend to see historical events as discrete events that have little or no bearing on today's events. One goal of this book is to show the reader how historical events, even though they may have happened one hundred years ago, have an impact on today's conditions.

The analysis presented in this book reveals both an active interference and a benign neglect on the part of both the federal and provincial governments as they deal with Aboriginal people over time. The marginalization that Aboriginal people experience today is no recent event but rather is rooted in historical circumstances. This political-economy approach will reveal the similarities among Aboriginal peoples around the world as they experienced similar fates in the past and face similar problems today. This suggests that there are similarities in settler societies with regard to the processes that affect Aboriginal peoples in historical times as well as in the present. These structural impacts began to affect Aboriginal people at the time of contact with Europeans and became increasingly influential as the immigrant population grew. As the world political economy began to integrate with the Canadian domestic economy, these structural effects relegated Aboriginal peoples in Canada and throughout the world to a peripheral position in society.

What are these processes? How have they impacted upon Aboriginal people? We wish to approach the problem from a perspective that involves social structural factors, e.g., the organization of the society, the alignment of social institutions, the change in demographic factors. While we will not deny that Aboriginal people are exposed to a great deal of prejudice and discrimination, their greatest obstacle is the very structure of our society itself, which prevents them from effectively participating in its social, economic, and political institutions. Furthermore, we feel that there is a linkage between the structural effects (the institutional arrangements of our society) and the behaviour of individuals.

Using a macro perspective allows us to present the Aboriginal community as an internal colony that is exploited by the dominant group in Canada. In this model, Canadians are seen as the colonizing people, while Aboriginal persons are considered the colonized people. By conceptualizing the Aboriginal community as an internal colony of a larger nation, it is possible to see beyond the individual factors involved in inter-group behaviour and focus on the structural arrangements. Indigenous peoples of Canada were unquestionably colonized (and continue to be) and their social and economic position in Canada today is a direct result of the colonization process.

Why was Canada so overwhelmed by European settlers? Europeans settling Canada argue that their own superiority in technology and the inferiority of Aboriginal society (e.g., they were primitive, too few in number, superstitious) contributed to the colonization. While these arguments are self-serving, they do not provide an adequate explanation.

It would seem that the major explanation for such a successful massive colonization effort came about through the introduction of disease—smallpox, yellow fever, measles, cholera, influenza, tuberculosis. With the introduction of such diseases, all unknown in Canada prior to the 16th century, the Aboriginal population was decimated. Because immunity had not been built up by Aboriginal peoples, when these diseases were introduced, a massive annihilation resulted. As Wright (2003) notes, " . . . the great death raged for more than a century . . . perhaps more than 90 million died . . . It was the greatest mortality in history" (Doybns,1983; Thorton, 1986). Regardless of the original number, we know that after nearly twenty new diseases were introduced to North America over the span of five generations, less than a tenth of the original population remained. In this catastrophic loss of people, leaders, intellectuals, military strategists and political leaders died.

Many will object to the numbers presented above, and while they are certainly controversial, much of the opposition to such large numbers is consonant with the myth of the "empty land" that has been created by the white settlers. Moreover, choosing a smaller figure for the number of Aboriginal people killed hides the genocidal depopulation of Aboriginal people by the actions of Europeans. At the same time, after being in Canada for over two hundred years, Europeans immigrants had not settled much of Canada; their presence was not noted in the interior but limited to a few major settlements along the coastal waters or major waterways.

Colonializing Canada's Aboriginal People

The colonization process can be considered in seven parts (Kennedy, 1945; Blauner, 1969). The first concerns the incursion of the colonizing group into a geographical area. This usually takes the form of forced-voluntary entry; acting in its own interests, the colonizing group forces its way into an area. In Canada, both French and English settlement followed this pattern. Lands and resources were taken from Aboriginal people and reallocated to settlers. At present, many Northern Aboriginal people argue that forced-voluntary colonization is still occurring in the North.

The second attribute of colonization is its destructive effect on the social and cultural structures of the indigenous group. In Canada's case, European colonizers destroyed the Native peoples' political, economic, kinship, and, in most cases, religious systems. The values and norms of Aboriginal peoples were either ignored or violated. For example, after the War of 1812, when a large number of European settlers arrived, the colonial government decided that Aboriginal persons should be forced to surrender their traditional lifestyles. Official programs were developed, and between 1830 and 1875 legislation was enacted to carry out this destructive policy (Surtees, 1969).

As Titley (1986) points out, the federal government's policies were in harmony with the demands of non-Aboriginal people. The creation of "trust authority" over Indian lands and assets demonstrates their commitment to dictating what resources would be exploited, in what quantities, and by whom. It also allowed the government to determine for what purpose and at what cost. As Wright (2003) argues, it was important that the reserves be made to look "self-governing" so that they would be exempt from normal business practices and thus subject only to the unique rules established by Indian Affairs. The protests of Aboriginal people were futile, and when they took action to support their claims in the late 1860s, harsh repression followed, including the bombardment of British Columbia coastal villages by British warships (Tobias, 1976). By the late 1890s, the federal government had amended the *Indian Act* (of 1876) so that "surplus" or "idle" Aboriginal land could be made available for the use of non-Indians. In 1911, amendments to the *Indian Act* gave even greater coercive powers to the federal government. For example, Section 46 allowed portions of reserves to be taken by municipalities or companies for roads or similar public purposes with the consent of the governor-in-council (today called the cabinet), but without a surrender (Carter, 1990; Imai and Hawley, 1995).

Canadian officials have, since the early 19th century, viewed Aboriginal people as inferior. Education and religious groups actively engaged in strategies to bring about Aboriginal social change in order to "civilize" and "Christianize" them. During this time, a symbiotic relationship emerged between various churches and the state. The best example of this was when the churches were being frustrated in their efforts to Christianize Native people. Church officials felt that because certain Aboriginal cultural components were incompatible with Christianity, they should be eradicated. They therefore convinced the state to pass legislation outlawing a variety of dances and other ceremonies that were an integral component of the Aboriginal culture—for example, the potlatch.

The third and fourth aspects of colonization are the interrelated processes of external political control and Aboriginal economic dependence. In the standard practice of colonization, the mother country sends out representatives through which it indirectly rules the newly conquered land. In our model, the representative ruler is the Department of Indian and Northern Affairs Canada (known as INAC). Until 1940, Indian Affairs decided which

Aboriginal people could and couldn't leave reserve lands. Aboriginal self-government has been effectively prevented. Until the latter part of the 20th century, band funds could not be used by Aboriginal people to develop social and political organizations of their own (Whiteside, 1972). In 2006 the federal court ruled on a case involving Indian monies that allowed a First Nations community in Alberta to control monies obtained from the development of natural resources. After ten years of litigation, the First Nations won, only to have the government appeal the decision to the Federal Court of Appeal and overturn the initial decision. A further appeal has now been launched by the Aboriginal communities.

The minister of Indian and Northern Affairs Canada can suspend almost any right set forth in the *Indian Act*. For example, Section 80 of the Act authorizes band councils to pass bylaws for public health and traffic regulation. However, to date, the minister has granted less than two-thirds of band councils the permission to do so.

Acting through cabinet, Indian Affairs can also veto any decisions of band councils. For example, Section 82 of the *Indian Act* allows a band to enact money by-laws. However, cabinet must first find that the band has reached a "high state of development" before allowing the band to pass such a by-law. At present, fewer than 50 bands have been so defined. Section 68 of the *Act* allows a band to "control, manage, and expand in whole or in part its revenue moneys." No band was actually permitted to do so until 1959, and to date fewer than 20 percent have received permission. Section 60 allows a band "the right to exercise such control and management over lands in the reserve occupied by that band as the Cabinet considers desirable." To date, cabinet has found this desirable for less than 15 percent of the reserves. Section 35 of the *Act* explicitly states that reserve land can be expropriated by the federal government at any time. Unfortunately, this provision has been implemented many times over the past half-century.

Aboriginal people remain economically dependent on the larger society because their reserves are treated as geographical and social hinterlands for Euro-Canadian exploitation. Initially Euro-Canadian settlers claimed sovereignty over the land. They then extended this to people and today they continue the process by claiming sovereignty over the resources on the land—all inanimate materials. Euro-Canadian–controlled businesses exploit non-renewable primary resources such as oil, minerals, water, and forest products, and ship them to urban industrial centres for processing. This practice has two important consequences for Aboriginal people on reserves: the development of Aboriginal-owned industries is pre-empted, and Aboriginal occupational activities remain at a primary level. As the treaties and the *Indian Act* show, federal policy has always tried to orient Aboriginal occupations toward agriculture and primary industries (Carter, 1990).

In the colonization process, a two-level system develops in which the colonizers own, direct, and profit from industries that depend upon exploitation of colonized peoples, who provide an unskilled, seasonal work force. On the reserves, the long-term result has been an Aboriginal population that lives at subsistence level, working at unskilled, seasonal jobs in primary industries, and practising subsistence agriculture to survive. Although the profits from raw material production are based on reserve resources and cheap Aboriginal labour, they disappear from the reserve into the pockets of non-Aboriginal entrepreneurs.

With few exceptions, Aboriginal communities across Canada are at a low level of economic development. Economic development is not the same as economic growth. Economic growth refers to an increase in the productive capacity of an area's economy, while economic development reflects a change in the structure of an area's economy, such as a movement from primary extractive or agricultural industries to secondary processing, or to knowledge industries. For example, some First Nation and Métis colonies within Alberta have experienced considerable short-term economic growth due to oil and mineral discoveries, but no real economic development. Most striking is the statistic relative to Aboriginal leaders who derive their influence from the economic sector. Not a single Aboriginal leader could be classified as exercising his/her influence in the economic sector. This provides evidence of the degree to which Aboriginal people generally have been excluded from the Canadian economic sector and hence the power structure.

The federal government has effectively discouraged the economic development of reserves, as the *Income Tax Act* and the *Indian Act* show. If Aboriginal people create a limited corporation to engage in business on reserves, they lose the benefit of exemption from taxation as individuals or as a band. As a result, income earned by a corporation wholly owned by Aboriginal people is subject to taxation the same as any corporation, even if the income is derived solely from activities on a reserve. While some provisions of the *Income Tax Act* have changed, the overall thrust continues the same today. The structural complexities involved in the payment of property taxes on reserve lands also prevent Aboriginal people from profitably leasing their lands.

A fifth attribute of colonization is the provision of low-quality social services for the colonized Aboriginal individuals in such areas as health and education. A survey by Indian Affairs confirms a desperate need for adequate health and social services (Canada, 2001). For example, the report points out a lower life expectancy than the general population, higher levels of support from social assistance organizations, and unhealthy lifestyles that are imposed by poverty. Although some housing conditions have improved, social problems, new diseases (e.g., diabetes, AIDS), alcohol abuse, welfare dependency, and water pollution have increased.

The sixth and seventh aspects of colonization relate to social interactions between Aboriginal and non-Aboriginal people and refer to racism and the establishment of a colour-line. Traditional racism is a belief in the genetic or cultural superiority of the colonizers and the inferiority of the colonized people. This pure form of racism, while alive and well in Canada, has transformed into what is called "structural" or "systemic" racism.

The Emergence of Whiteness: Structural Racism

As noted above, it is difficult to find a Canadian who will publicly state that some groups of people are racially inferior to others. What has happened over time is that overt biological racism has given way to a new form of racism. This new form of racism is covert, structural and is best described as the emergence of whiteness. All people other than whites are "raced." This embodies the assumption that white people are not racially seen or named and, as such, they function as the "human norm," i.e., white people are just people. It also conveys the message that others are something else. Over time this perspective has become part of the structure of Canadian society. This perspective was necessary for conquest, colonialization and enslavement to take place. As a result, an institutional set of structures and relations were put in place and still dominate how Canadians think about non-white people. Those who were white were able to dominate powerful positions in our organizations and institutions. Once a particular perspective (a white one) is built into the laws, norms and mores of a society, it becomes part of the "way things are" and remains an uncontested definition of normality. Most Canadians, rather than actively refusing to comply with the law, go along with the norm, particularly if they think the law doesn't affect them personally. In short, Whiteness functions as a large ensemble of practices and rules that give white people all sorts of advantages and privileges in life which they have trouble giving up. White privilege is the ability to make decisions that affect everyone without taking others into account. It is a standpoint, a location from which to see others, a product of history and it is a relational category. Whites have created the dominant images of the world and they don't see that they have constructed the world in their own image.

Today, white people don't see their white privilege and whiteness remains invisible. White culture and identity have, as it were, no content (e.g., no definable attributes or "ethnic markers"); consequently, white people can't see that they have anything that accounts for their position of privilege and power. Much of this ingrained privilege is not exhibited deliberately and maliciously, but the impact is the same—it stratifies society into whites and non-whites. Today the structural arrangements are seen as "normal" even though they disadvantage non-whites. Moreover, it is not always the intent of a white person to make use of the unearned benefits received on the basis of skin colour. In fact, many go through their day-to-day activities unaware that they are white or that it even matters. Nevertheless, throughout Canadian history, white power holders have made decisions that have affected white people as a group differently than groups of non-whites. White privilege allows white people *not* to see race in themselves and to be angry with others who do so. In the end, whites live in the centre, Aboriginals live on the margins.

Whites do not recognize their unearned privileges because whiteness operates by being invisible—so ubiquitous and entrenched as to appear natural and normative. Thus, whiteness operates as the unmarked norm against which other identities are marked and realized. On the other hand, while whiteness is invisible to whites, it is hyper-visible to Aboriginals. Whites never have to "speak for their race," nor are they viewed as the "white" teacher or lawyer. At the same time, Aboriginals seldom see themselves broadly represented in the media and educational curriculum, and when they do, it is usually not in a positive light. Aboriginal people have to deal with the above issues, which impose an important social and psychological cost. The advantage of being white is not to have to absorb this cost, or to even have to be aware of the benefits being received.

With a colour-line, indicators such as skin pigmentation and body structure are established as the basis for determining superiority and inferiority. Interaction then goes on only among members of the same group: non-Aboriginals interact with non-Aboriginals and Aboriginal people with Aboriginal people. In Canada, for example, Native people have the highest rate of marriage within their own ethnic group—almost 90 percent.

Consequences of Colonization

The ultimate consequence of colonization is to reduce the resistance of Aboriginal people to the point at which they can be controlled. Whether the motives for colonization are religious, economic, or political, the rewards are clearly economic. White Canada has gained far more than it has lost in colonizing its Aboriginal peoples. Over a ten-year period ending in 2005, Aboriginal groups in Alberta sued the federal government for more than $1.5 billion over non-payment of "Indian Monies" on the extraction of natural resources from land set aside for them. These battles have long histories but, with long-term profits estimated at $1–2 billion, the state and private enterprise are not about to give up easily.

In the initial stages of colonization, the colonized people generally accept their fate. Only later do they reject their powerless position. Aboriginal leaders on reserves today tend to be considerably more militant than those who initially signed treaties. But even if Aboriginal peoples no longer accept their subordinate status, there is little they can do to change it. Although, as Boldt (1980a) showed, many Aboriginal leaders view extra-legal activity as a viable method of pressing their claims, others have surrendered to a general apathy and dispiritedness, the long-term impact of colonialization. The process of acculturation and the demise of indigenous Aboriginal tribal associations have eroded Aboriginal self-identification. Communal bonds have broken down among individual Aboriginal persons and among bands, contributing to the continued failure of Aboriginal organizations. Leadership responsibilities on the reserves have become further divided and poorly defined, exacerbating the disorganization of Aboriginal groups. In the political arena, Aboriginal people have been ineffectual for several reasons. Most importantly, historically they have been prevented from voting or running for office. Aboriginal persons did not receive the right to vote in provincial elections until after World War II and they did not receive the federal franchise until 1960. Needless to say, this severely restricted their interest in political affairs and their ability to make political demands. Those with no voice in the political structure that governs their lives have few means of influencing or sanctioning the policies that affect them. Even after receiving the vote, Aboriginal people continue to be sceptical of their rights, although this attitude is changing.

There is a deprecation of identity by the dominant culture, with the result that Aboriginal people have a damaged sense of self. Aboriginal people are devalued by the dominant group and this brings about damage to their individual and collective identity. Aboriginal people have suffered a collective distortion in their relation to self and have internalized this negative self-image; this has prevented them from developing a healthy cultural identity of their own.

Limitations of Colonialization Model

Like any model, the colonization approach has certain limitations. The world is complex: people, social structures, and cultures change with time. Of necessity, however, a model is frozen in time, a static recreation of what occurs around us. In order to construct a portrait that corresponds closely to the real world, we select and incorporate certain variables, discard others as unimportant, and make assumptions about how people behave.

If the resulting model produces accurate explanations and predictions, it can be considered successful. It may then become a useful tool in finding solutions to social problems and in developing social action programs. If, however, a model proves incapable of providing accurate predictions or explanations, it must be revised or discarded. Our model suggests that historical colonialism has shaped the organization of our society and set in motion a number of factors that propelled Aboriginal people to the margins of our society.

First of all, Aboriginal participation in the Canadian economy has become economically redundant over time because of changes in the structure and technology of the national economy. After the buffalo hunts ended and the fur trade all but ceased, Aboriginal people were kept out of participating in the newly emerging economy. As Canadian society moved to agriculture and then to an urban-industrial base, Aboriginal peoples did not possess, and were not in a position to acquire, new technologies or skills. The result is that Aboriginal people found themselves operating a subsistence economy parallel to that of the more modern economy.

Today their lack of education, technical expertise and access to technology continues to keep them out of the new knowledge economy. This new knowledge economy focuses on the development of information rather than the production of goods. In other words, there are two economies in our society. The industrial, technological and knowledge-based modern sector of the economy is dynamic: change promotes further change. The traditional, subsistence sector of the economy, however, resists change: it clings to the old ways and is unable to adopt new technology (Wien, 1986). This of course suggests that, as our economy becomes more knowledge based, barriers continue to be created that hinder or prevent entrance of Aboriginal people into the knowledge era. Certain technical and social skills are now prerequisites for entering the labour force. People without these skills will be kept from participating as full-time members in a modern national, as well as international, labour market. Already researchers have noted the "digital divide" between Aboriginal and non-Aboriginal communities.

As individuals are prevented from entering the modern economy, a cultural ethos emerges that is quite different from the one expressed in the dominant sector. Anthropologists have referred to this distinctive ethos as the "culture of poverty." When the goals of higher status are denied to people, other forms of adaptation are created—for example, withdrawal and rebellion (often self-destructive)—in order to deal with the despair and hopelessness that are central to the culture of poverty. This encourages individuals to develop a different perspective on life and on how to deal with everyday occurrences.

Once an individual is placed within the traditional culture of poverty, it is almost impossible for him or her to get out. As we have seen, the lack of certain technical and social skills keeps Aboriginal persons from entering the modern labour market. And as that market becomes increasingly segmented into a primary and a secondary market, there is greater difficulty in moving from the secondary to the primary market.[1] As a result, Aboriginal persons are increasingly shut out of the primary market.

Aboriginal peoples played an important role in the development of Canada. However, as the 20th century emerged, their lack of technological skills relegated Aboriginal people to second-class citizens. While many history books acknowledge the interaction of Aboriginal people and Europeans, they tend to characterize Aboriginal persons as passive, always responding to actions taken by Europeans. In short, the interaction between the two parties usually portrays Europeans as the proactive agents, asserting their vision of Canada regardless of Aboriginal people. There are some exceptions to this general pattern (Miller, 2000), but the history of Aboriginal–Euro-Canadian relations in Canada has generally been told from the perspective of non-Aboriginal people. As Dickason (2002) points out, problems of interpretation become problematic when considering Europeans' accounts of their exploits in the new America. She notes, for example, that there can be differences in connotations of words as used in the 16th or 17th century and today. She also points out that in the case of historical published accounts, what appears in print may not be what the author wrote. Historically, publishers were more interested in the saleability of material than in its veracity.

The Clash of Two Cultures

When Aboriginal people and Europeans first encountered each other, two different cultures came into contact. Aboriginal people were hunters and gatherers (although there were some agricultural tribes) who lived in harmony with their physical environment. Their limited technological developments made few demands on the ecology, and the small numbers of people meant that population pressures were light (Miller, 2000). Europeans, on the other hand, were continually developing their technology to achieve control over nature. They were ethnocentric in outlook and had a mission to Christianize the world. The clash of these two cultures was resounding, and while there is no doubt that Native people have taken the brunt of this collision, they have, surprisingly, retained considerable elements of their culture. They have, when possible, taken a "controlled acculturation" perspective, adopting certain behaviours and ideas of Euro-American culture while retaining other valued mental constructs from their own culture. Perhaps the creation of reserves and the resulting high level of isolation of many Aboriginal people have allowed this selective retention to occur (Brown, 1980; Brown and Vibert, 2003).

The basis underlying Aboriginal–Euro-Canadian relations in our history is that Europeans have always assumed superiority over Aboriginal people. As was noted in the discussion of the characteristics of colonization, this is racism—the belief that one group is inferior to another group.

Although some people may object to this claim, racism is manifestly the ideology underlying the policies regarding Aboriginal–European relations throughout the history of Canada, and it continues to be prevalent today, albeit in a different form. For example, in a recent Ipsos-Reid survey, over 60% of adult non-Aboriginal Canadians believe that Aboriginal people are subject to prejudice and discrimination. In addition, following this premise of superiority, Euro-Canadians have taken it upon themselves to transform Aboriginal people both physically and culturally (dress, language and habits) into an image that is more acceptable to Euro-Canadians (Furniss, 2000).

The reader might claim that people are far more enlightened today. To be sure, most people today would not argue that one group of people are biologically inferior to another. However, this biological racism has been supplanted by a new form of social/cultural racism that focuses on the inferiority of a group's way of life, their ethos, and their assumptions about the world. In taking this view, people may escape being accused of "biological racism": they are prepared to accept the biological similarities of different groups of people. However, they are not prepared to accept cultural equality or the impact of historical structured inequality. As such, individual racism has given way to structural (systemic) racism. Examining structural racism allows one to focus on the way discrimination is built into systems of power and institutions in Canada (Nichols, 1998).

Some readers will be angered by these statements and indignant that Canada should be labelled racist. After all, they will claim, they do not engage in individual racist activities. They will point out that other history books do not make such claims. But history is humanity's way of recording past behaviour; historians are extremely susceptible to the political and social forces that prevail while they are writing their histories. What Aboriginal people have been encouraged to write histories? And when Aboriginal histories have been written, why have they been dismissed as fabrications?

The hostility and conflict established historically between Aboriginal people and political and legal enforcement bodies have contributed to the contemporary relationships between them, which are based on suspicion, disrespect, and mistrust on both sides. Through a history of enactments legislated through colonial parliaments, the institutions in this country have been used to segregate Aboriginal peoples from the dominant culture and to legitimize paternalistic control over all aspects of their lives. However, while being granted rights (in their own country) may have helped Aboriginal people to alleviate some of the consequences that emanated from the horrific colonial era, no attempts were made in political or judicial quarters to address the discriminatory and biased legal provisions that were used to deny them parity and equality with their dominant counterparts. The historical situation provided the initial conditions, and by apathy and indifference, rather than intentional exploitation, those conditions have continued to exist. While the introduction of the *Charter of Rights and Freedoms* in 1982 was assessed as a significant step toward enacting a degree of reform in this area, the Aboriginal population found little comfort in it because of the inadequacies that were attached to its legislative jurisdictional powers.

The old ways by which non-Aboriginal people look at and relate to Aboriginal people have been reflected in the way government has treated them. However, some of these old views are now coming under scrutiny and being challenged. Weaver (1981) points out that the *Penner Report* on Aboriginal self-government (Penner, 1983) and the *Coolican Report* on comprehensive land claims (DIAND, 1986) broke new ground in conceptualizing issues involving Aboriginal people. The Royal Commission on Aboriginal Peoples brought into focus what Aboriginal people were thinking and reflects their current view of how they should fit into Canadian society. What is this new conceptualization? First, a new idea about the relationship between Aboriginal and non-Aboriginal people is presented. Whereas non-Aboriginal people previously tended to view the linkages as eventually resulting in the "termination" of Aboriginal persons and/or their full integration into non-Aboriginal society, i.e., assimilation, these reports view the relationship as parallel over time, with the two cultures adjusting to each other as the time and context change. In other words, they see the relationship as equal, flexible, and evolving.

A second new conceptualization of Aboriginal–non-Aboriginal relations has been identified by Weaver (1981) and focuses on the notion of sanctioned rights, which she defines as those rights recognized by the state as justified claims against its actions toward a particular group. Related to this is a new political ethic developed in government with regard to how it deals with Aboriginal people. At the public level, there is a new commitment to being direct, honest, and honourable in government dealings with Aboriginal people. This new ethic has been brought to the forefront as a result of a number of court decisions that have gone against the government. This also means that the nature of the relationship government will have with Aboriginal people is one of partnership. Out of this partnership, jointly formulated policies will emerge that will lead to some form of Aboriginal empowerment (Weaver, 1981). However, the results of these limited judicial decisions have been negated when the application of these decisions are implemented in real life. Existing structural arrangements continue to neutralize the meagre impact of the courts decisions.

The Royal Commission on Aboriginal Peoples noted that if the social position of Aboriginal people is to change, then the relationship must be restructured. These new ideas have begun to challenge the old views, but before they become dominant in government thinking, old conceptualizations will have to be dropped. As the government reflects on possible changes, their agent, the Department of Indian Affairs, has undergone turbulent times in recent decades as proponents of each perspective try to make their position the basis for action. This is one reason why government seemingly takes contradictory stands in dealing with Aboriginal people. For example, Sanders (1990) points out that even the Supreme Court has not been consistent in its rulings with regard to Aboriginal people. In some cases the inconsistencies reflect the evolution of doctrine, while others defy explanation. Yet the changes seem to reflect the emergence of a new perspective and a new place for Aboriginal persons in Canadian society. However, whether or not this new view of Aboriginal people will become the dominant one remains to be seen.

Confrontations and Conflict

Press reports on confrontations between Aboriginal and non-Aboriginal people tend to focus on specific complaints, overlook broader issues, and reflect an old definition of Aboriginal people and their role in Canadian society. Hence, in many cases where conflict emerges, Aboriginal persons are labelled as malcontents, troublemakers, and opportunists—labels that can only be defended through a distorted and abbreviated view of history (Lambertus, 2004). For example, the Oka confrontation was defined by the media as a "law and order" problem which, once interpreted in this manner, required and justified the harsh and extraordinary measures that the federal government took. A similar definition has been applied to the more recent Caledonia conflict in Ontario. This conflict rages over the dispute between a housing developer and Aboriginals who claim that the land upon which houses are being built was illegally taken from First Nations many years ago.

As at Oka, the stage for clashes between Aboriginal and Euro-Canadian people has generally been set by historical facts and existing structural relations, though few people are interested in examining these. For example, the Lubicons in Alberta who have blockaded roads and shut down oil pumps have generally been depicted as irresponsible troublemakers. Yet surely the reasons for their protest were linked to the fact that the band has been fighting for land to be set aside for a reserve promised 50 years ago, and for compensation for energy and forestry development that had taken well over $5 billion of natural resources from the area. More broadly, they are protesting on behalf of the Aboriginal children who die before their first birthday, the Aboriginal people who are unable to get jobs, and the large number of Native people who are unable to secure adequate housing. Nevertheless, when confrontations erupt, the implication is that the fault (and the cause) lies largely with Aboriginal people. This assumption reveals a biased and short-term perspective. Such an assumption ignores the subtle violence that has been perpetrated against Aboriginal people since the arrival of the European explorers. It also serves those who want to remain in power and maintain the status quo that excludes Aboriginal people from a share in their country's bounty and that allows them to remain hungry, uneducated, and inadequately housed in the midst of plenty.

Writing a History

An author's explanation of social events depends on an individual point of view. Because overt social behaviour can be interpreted in many different ways, the historian must always infer the actors' motives. Historians infer motives for groups as well as for individuals. Unfortunately, until recently, our historians have largely been Euro-Canadians; as a result, they have largely based their inferences on the same primary assumptions and therefore have presented similar views of social reality (Trudel and Jain, 1970).

Throughout recorded time, empowered groups have been able to define history and provide an explanation of the present. A good example is the portrayal of wars between Aboriginal and European peoples by Canadian historians. Euro-Canadian historians have concentrated on these wars partly because of the "enemy concept": as Pelletier (1970) has pointed out, non-Aboriginal endeavours are continually described in terms of fighting an enemy, whether the war is waged against crime, inflation, or cancer.

In the history books, when Aboriginal people attacked a non-Aboriginal village or fort and won, the result was called a massacre. If Europeans attacked an Aboriginal village and won, it was described as a victory. Because the dominant group is able to make these interpretations and definitions, it is also able to keep others from initiating alternative explanations or definitions. History gives credence and legitimacy to a society's normative structure; to legitimize its power, the dominant groups must reconstruct social history whenever necessary. The early reconstructions of Canadian history were effective: today, most Canadians continue to associate "savage" and "heinous" behaviour with Canadian Aboriginal people. As Churchill (1999) points out, the standard European/Canadian depiction of Aboriginals has been one of a small number of people who wandered about in scattered bands, grubbing out an existence through hunting and gathering, never developing writing or serious appreciation of art, science, or mathematics. It has been believed that, aside from utilizing furs and hides for clothing and housing, there were few attributes that distinguished Aboriginal people from other higher orders of mammalian life.

As Patterson (1972) points out, alien history is pulled down and discredited, and national history replaces it. Continuity of tradition for any group is truncated when the communication channels are taken over by others who wish to transmit different information. How often have we known something to be true only to find out many years later that the government, or some other group, distorted information that might have led us to believe something quite different? Brown (1971) and Andrist (1964) have vividly portrayed American-Indian history from an alternative point of view. Their information concerning Aboriginal–non-Aboriginal relations is quite dissimilar to that provided by "established" historians. Recent histories by such authors as Miller (2000), Churchill (1999), Warry (2006) and Nichols (1998) portray a more balanced perspective of historical events and reveal the Aboriginal side to Canadian history.

Readers have reacted quite differently to books by Cardinal (1969), Pelletier (1970), and Waubageshig (1970) than they have to books by Morton (1963), McInnis (1959), and Lower (1957). The layperson typically rejects the conclusions of the first three authors as the products of bias. But the same person tends to accept the explanations provided by the second group of "established academic" authors. We are not suggesting that the first are right or the second wrong. But both groups deserve to be read and judged fairly. As a new generation of Aboriginal authors emerge (Waters, 2004; Cajete, 2000; Bastien, 2004), new data and views of history are being placed before readers. While some resistance to the new history still exists, many readers have responded with "I didn't know that," reflecting a grudging acceptance of the new perspective.

It is essential to realize that the history of Canada taught from Grade 5 through university has been written mainly by English-speaking Euro-Canadians, specifically of British/French ethnicity. The Ontario Education Commission, in a study of elementary Canadian history books, has discovered that many historical events involving Aboriginal peoples have not even been recorded. In fact, the commission found that many history books did not discuss the role of Aboriginal people in Canadian history at all.

Walker (1971) characterized Canadian historians in their analysis of Aboriginal people in Canada as ignorant, prejudiced, and, in some cases, dishonest. But we do not have to attribute deliberate falsification to historians. In any reconstruction of the past, the author shapes an interpretation of events according to individual perceptions, memories, analytical preferences, and social background. Whether deliberately or unconsciously, a reshaping of the past occurs. No historian is free of bias; no history is capable of presenting only the facts.

In writing a history, a Western perspective reveals that the history of North America begins with the arrival of the settlers. In short, there was no "history" before they arrived. Many will argue that there is no written history prior to the settlers' arrival and thus a history cannot be presented. Others will note that, while we have few written materials regarding many ancient civilizations, we are still able to use artifacts to reconstruct a history of a people. Nevertheless, in Canada, traditionally history begins with the arrival of European settlers. While certainly there is a history of Aboriginals presented as they come into contact with the settlers, there is a built-in assumption that as Aboriginals assimilated their history would disappear. As Dockstator (2005) points out, a Western historical perspective involves three factors regarding Aboriginal people: (1) they are a vanishing race, (2) they are a single homogenous group, and (3) Aboriginals are a mixture of what he calls simultaneous contrasts, e.g., noble yet savage, robust yet dying, existing but not really existing. For example, settlers had little interest in Aboriginal perspectives, and from the duality of their perspective, Aboriginal people were nations when it came to signing treaties but not nations once they were signed. In the end, from a Western perspective, Aboriginals are always placed at the margins of mainstream activity. There has been and continues to be a belief that Aboriginals will, through various legal acts (e.g., treaties, Indian Acts, federal bills) disappear and the end of their history will be written.

In contrast to the Western perspective, Aboriginal people know of their history. When contact occurred, they recognized Western culture as legitimate. And, while Aboriginals reacted as equals to the newcomers, settlers always viewed themselves as superior. Aboriginals viewed the negotiation of treaties as reflecting a principle of equality. As Dockstator (2005) concludes, Aboriginals believed in equality of the two nations although they certainly understood the indicators of equality would change over time. Aboriginals never viewed themselves as a vanishing race nor as a single homogeneous group. They were keenly aware of the cultural and linguistic differences among the various groups of Aboriginals. In the end, Aboriginal peoples have consistently maintained for over four centuries that their concept of nationhood originated long before the settlers came and it remains intact. They also argue that even after contact with the settlers, a balanced relationship between themselves and the settlers reflected two nations of equal status.

HISTORY OF RELATIONS BETWEEN EURO-CANADIANS AND ABORIGINAL PEOPLES

The balance of this chapter will provide an overview of the history of the relations between the two dominant Canadian groups and Aboriginal peoples. First the French policy will be considered, then the British. Conclusions have been based on documents and histories written (by both Aboriginals and non-Aboriginals) during the time of contact and since.

Before discussing Aboriginal–non-Aboriginal relations, we should point out that Aboriginal–Aboriginal relations are also an important component in the way Canada has developed. For those concerned with this issue, we suggest reading the work of Trigger (1985) and Dickason (2002), who point out that Europeans were able to establish themselves in Canada partially due to the fact that a large number of Native people allowed them to and supported them in doing so. They make it very clear that, since

Aboriginal people in the beginning controlled the fur trade and were militarily superior to the newcomers, European entry into the land could not have been accomplished without the cooperation of the Aboriginal groups (Coates, 1991).

In the study of Aboriginal–non-Aboriginal relations, there have been many critical historical periods that have shaped the structural linkages between them. These links determined the distribution of power, the opportunities to participate in the dominant structure, and the eventual position of subordination for the Aboriginal peoples (Nichols, 1998). In short, the actions of the government influenced the political development and incorporation of Aboriginal peoples. The most recent critical period was the 1960s, when the community development ideology began to emerge. At the turn of the 20th century, the political links between Aboriginal and European peoples had been extremely limited. Non-Indians had taken over Aboriginal communities and were accountable to other non-Indians. Power was unilateral in this relationship, which excluded Aboriginal people from participating in the larger socio-political structure. However, in the 1960s the federal government and other dominant agencies began to promote individualization as an antidote to what they saw as the problem of tribalism. This action would forever change the structure of the relationship between Aboriginal people and the government (Flanagan, 1983b, 2000).

Calls for reform in Aboriginal policy gained momentum after World War II. The new human rights awareness, the belief in social justice, and the interest in cultural diversity began to influence government policy. In the mid-1960s, the federal government commissioned a national study of the Aboriginal person's position in Canadian society—the *Hawthorn Report*. This document identified the appalling conditions under which Native people were forced to live. It suggested support for community development and promoted the implementation of major new initiatives in the areas of health and education. Nevertheless, the central assumption of the *Hawthorn Report* was that Aboriginal people should assimilate.

French–Aboriginal Relations

The French had developed strategies to deal with Aboriginal peoples many years before they began to settle New France. Four techniques were employed that had served them well in Brazil: providing presents of European origin; recognizing and providing Aboriginal leaders with goods and pay on an ongoing basis; encouraging their allies to kill enemies of the French government; and paying attention to the Aboriginal youth and socializing them to French culture and society (Dickason, 2002).

Initially, the French were interested in the New World as a source of wealth capable of financing wartime activities. It was hoped that the land would hold precious metals that would rival in worth those found in Spanish America (Trigger, 1985). Throughout the 16th century, fishing and whaling were the major economic activities that attracted more and more Europeans to North America. It was only at the end of the 16th century that the fur trade began to grow into an important economic activity (Brown and Vibert, 2003). The Canadian fur trade was important because, in 1583, the Swedes had captured the Baltic port of Narva through which Western Europe obtained furs from the Russians. Now that this port was closed, the French needed to find new sources.

French–Aboriginal relations must first be considered in the context of North America as a whole before we can turn specifically to Canada. A thorough review of the documents available on the attitudes of French settlers to the Aboriginal people reveals that no well-defined policy was established to govern French–Aboriginal relations. Generally, the French were attempting to exploit the land and to continue "pseudo-colonization" of North America. However, they did not initially intend to settle New France with any large stable population. Moreover, only a small number of French people wished to emigrate to New France; this fact, combined with France's mercantilistic philosophy[2] and the strong influence of Roman Catholicism, meant that no policy of cultural or physical genocide was invoked. Finally, the concept of "personal liberty" held by Aboriginal people in Canada was problematic for the French settlers. With different ideas of equality and individual freedom than those held by the French, Aboriginals were tenuous allies at best.

Initially, the French were totally dependent on the Aboriginal people, but the relationship between the two soon changed to a symbiotic one. Nevertheless, their policy toward Aboriginal people differed, depending upon the circumstances. At the international level, they argued that Aboriginals were sovereign nations, and thus France was not responsible for their behaviour. However, when the circumstances were focused on French settlements, they argued that they were subordinate to the French settlers.

With early settlements short of French women, intermarriage, or "wintering in," between French trappers and Indian women soon became common practice, and was encouraged by French authorities who wanted to strengthen Aboriginal relations so that the fur trade would continue. These marriages between French men and Indian women were not meant to be exploitative; the relationships were stable, and the man was considered legally responsible for his wife and offspring (Brown, 1980). However, the reader should understand that intermarriage was not a policy that originated in Canada. The French had used this technique when they colonized Brazil a century earlier. Moreover, intermarriage was eased for the French by the belief that Aboriginals were really white, turning brown because they ate certain foods and were out in the sun. If one looks at formal records of intermarriage, the incidence would indicate a small number. However, other documents suggest that the rate was quite high, supported by the missionaries as a form of concubinage. Thus both economic and religious institutions supported intermarriage between Aboriginal women and French men. Nevertheless, by the mid-18th century, intermarriage was not supported by the structures that had earlier facilitated the process.

In general, the French tried to expand their territories in North America by peaceful means (Francis, 1983). Usually they succeeded, because their agricultural style of life only minimally disrupted Aboriginal life.[3] After they had settled a territory, the French then asked the Indians to join in a treaty to acknowledge submission to the King of France. In this way, the French usually won territory without actually expropriating it. In 1611, Champlain sealed a pact of friendship with chief Anadabijou which allowed the French to establish themselves on Montagnais territory. In entering this alliance, the French were following a practice that they had developed a century earlier in Brazil and that was successful in establishing trade relations (Wright, 2003). The French had long come to realize that diplomatic protocol and negotiations (by means of gift distributions) were the process by which alliances were built with Aboriginal people. However, the process was not always so peaceful, and the French were certainly prepared to use force when they found it expedient to do so. When the Marquis de Tracy was placed in charge of Canada in 1663, his commissions included a provision for the use of arms to subjugate the Aboriginal peoples if necessary.[4]

The two strongest ideological influences in 17th century New France were Roman Catholicism and mercantilism, which was popular as an economic theory at the time. French policy, rather than treating Aboriginal people as distinct and inferior, tried to make them over into French citizens, at least in Canada.[5] This ideology of "Frenchification" is illustrated in various exchanges of letters between religious and state leaders of the day. For example, on April 6, 1666, Colbert wrote to Talon that:

> In order to strengthen the Colony in the manner you propose, by bringing the isolated settlements into parishes, it appears to me, without waiting to depend on the new colonists who may be sent from France, nothing would contribute more to it than to endeavour to civilize the Algonkians, the Hurons, and other Indians who have embraced Christianity, and to induce them to come and settle in common with the French, to live with them and raise their children according to our manners and customs. (O'Callaghan, 1856–1857: 184)

Talon replied, some seven months later, that he had tried to put Colbert's suggestions into practical operation under police regulations. Colbert then wrote, on April 9, 1667, as follows:

> Recommendation to mould the Indians, settled near us, after our manners and language.

> I confess that I agreed with you that very little regard had been paid, up to the present time, in New France, to the police [sic] and civilization of the Algonkians and Hurons (who were a long time ago subjected to the King's domination) through our neglect to detach them from their savage customs and to obligate them to adopt ours, especially to become acquainted with our language. On the contrary, to carry on some traffic with them, our French have been necessitated to attract those people, especially such as have embraced Christianity, to the vicinity of our settlements, if possible to mingle there with them, in order that through course of time, having only but one law and one master, they might likewise constitute only one people and one race.

Another exchange of letters from the period demonstrates that this policy of assimilation was expressly favoured by the king. Duchesneau, in his letter to de Signelay, November 10, 1679, writes:

> I communicated to the Religious communities, both male and female, and even to private persons, the King's and your intentions regarding the Frenchification of the Indians. They all promised me to use their best efforts to execute them, and I hope to let you have some news thereof next year. I shall begin by setting the example and will take some young Indians to have them instructed. (Cole, 1939: 864)

The French utilized the missionary zeal of the Catholic clergy to convert Aboriginal people. Thus, with the full support of the French monarchy and its colonial officials, the Catholic missionaries began the process of "civilizing" the Aboriginals but also converting them to Christianity. Both Jesuit and Recollet missionaries dealt with Aboriginal groups from the Gulf of St. Lawrence to Georgian Bay, encouraging them to take on a sedentary life as well as adopting the beliefs and values of Catholicism (Furniss, 2000).

Through a policy, then, of assimilation rather than genocide, the French were able to maintain relatively amicable relations with the Aboriginal population for quite some time. Moreover, throughout the history of New France, the French adopted a policy that treated Aboriginals with some consideration, avoided violence when possible, and assimilated them when possible (Dickason, 2002). As O'Callaghan (1856–1857) notes, the French had perfected the strategy of negotiation with Aboriginals through Indian diplomacy.

When war broke out with England in the 18th century the demand for fur decreased, and the French mercantilistic philosophy came to an end. War also brought a change in the French policy toward the Aboriginal peoples (Jaenen, 1986). Aboriginal land rights began to be systematically ignored (Harper, 1947: 131). Letters signed by Louis XV at this time gave companies headed for New France full ownership of the land, coasts, ports, and havens of New France, and full right to dispose of these properties in any way they desired (French, 1851). Similar provisions can be found in the privileges, power, and requirements given to the Company of One Hundred Associates by Cardinal Richelieu nearly a century earlier.[6]

The King of France understood that, if he was to colonize Canada, he would have to spend time, money, and energy in maintaining alliances with the Aboriginal peoples. He also realized that they were important allies in times of war, and that they would support the French if treated properly. Others have noted that the French used their Indian allies as "outposts" in the new world and thus reaped the benefits of low costs and accurate information. In the end, as Dickason (2002) points out, the French dealt with Aboriginal groups on a practical basis. It was a blend of give-and-take: giving when alliances were necessary, taking when the profits of the fur trade allowed. However, French domination in New France came to an end when the Treaty of Paris (1763) was signed and they handed over their vast territory to the British. Moreover, Aboriginal people found they now occupied a new niche in New France, devoid of any bargaining between the French and English, a loss of protection of their land and a halt to recognizing Aboriginal leaders or providing any gifts to recognized leaders.

British-Aboriginal Relations

As the French relinquished their control of North America to the British, Aboriginal people found themselves in a very different world. Their experience with the English was considerably more negative than that with the French. This was partly due to the operation of different structural variables, e.g., a new religious ideology, new racist philosophies, a different economy and the intrusion of thousands of new settlers on the land. Mercantilism as an economic theory had been discarded and the importance of the fur trade was dwindling; colonization in the true sense was now important. In addition, the religious ideology of the British had a very different basis than that of the French. As other religious denominations entered Canada, they continued the expansion of Christianity.

A review of the documents relevant to this early contact period between the English and the Aboriginals in Canada reveals that Aboriginal concerns were ignored. Little control was exerted over the British settlers as they expanded westward. As Thomas (1972) points out, Indians were not even mentioned in discussions when land was given to companies or settlers as they took over control of the United States and Canada.:

> For example, the letters patent of James I to Sir Thomas Gage and others for "two several colonies," dated April 10, 1606, although granting away two vast areas of territory greater than England, inhabited by thousands of Indians, a fact of which the King had knowledge both officially and unofficially, do not contain therein the slightest allusion to them. (Thomas, 1972: 550)

Although later charters recognized the existence of Aboriginal people, they did so in an extremely racist fashion. In the charters of Charles I, this statement, typical of several, authorizes the state to:

> collect troops and wage wars on the barbarians, and to pursue them even beyond the limits of their province and if God shall grant it, to vanquish and captivate them; and the captive put to death.

Until 1755 the English followed a policy of expediency they had developed and refined in dealing with Aboriginal people in the Thirteen Colonies (now the eastern United States). At first they chose to ignore the Aboriginal population. When allies were required, Aboriginals were courted and provided with resources. Later, when this was no longer necessary or feasible due to the need for westward expansion, the English chose to isolate Aboriginal people through the reserve system or to annihilate them, as with the Beothuk of Newfoundland. As far back as 1755 Indian agents, today called superintendents, were appointed, formally establishing Canada's policy of treating Aboriginal peoples as wards of the state. Significantly, the Indian agents initially placed in control of the reserves were always military men.

By 1830, the government questioned the value of the Aboriginal person in developing Canada's future. Although it remained a concern for some, invasion from the south by the United States was no longer an immediate and direct threat. Because there were no other potential attackers, Aboriginal people were not likely to be needed for support in military efforts. Without their status as military allies, Aboriginals had no value for a "white Canada." Thus, in 1830, Indian affairs were removed from military control and became a branch of the public service (Surtees, 1969). This change of jurisdiction allowed the British to adopt a more humanitarian attitude toward Aboriginal people (Doerr, 1974). This new humanitarian image of Aboriginals reflected a more general humanitarian ideology that arose through various social reform movements in Britain and the United States (Furniss, 2000). It also gained widespread popularity through the writings of individuals such as James Fenimore Cooper and George Grant as well as by the paintings of artists of the day.

By the mid-1880s, most areas in Canada were claimed by some religious denomination. Manifest destiny and the Hamite rationalization[7] pervaded the British secular way of life, exemplified in the Protestant ethic that hard work and no play would bring salvation. During this time the interests of the various settler groups (e.g., fur traders, missionaries, settlers, government officials) sometimes were in agreement, while at other times they conflicted. For example, missionaries and fur traders supported each other, although traders were more pragmatic in their dealings with Aboriginals than were the missionaries. Traders also saw disruptions to Aboriginal communities as against their interest, i.e., they would impact the effectiveness of gathering furs for trade. From the standpoint of the government officials, Aboriginals were, until the late 18th century, critical players as military allies.

POST CONFEDERATION ABORIGINAL-NON-ABORIGINAL RELATIONS

Under the terms of the *British North America Act*, the federal government took on legal responsibility for "Indians and Indian lands." The first *Indian Act* after Canadian Confederation was passed in 1876, bringing together a number of disparate pieces of legislation relating to Aboriginals. The intent of the Act was to control and manage the operation of reserves. It was first revised in 1880 (and placed under the Department of Indian Affairs), and received minor alterations in 1884 and 1885. For the next 65 years, the Act underwent annual minor changes. However, in 1951, a major revision was undertaken and, although there have been subsequent alterations, only one or two major changes have been made since that time. Interestingly enough, the 1880 version of the Act and the present one are remarkably similar, indicating that the Indian Affairs Department has not yet undergone any major ideological shifts in the past hundred years of dealing with the Aboriginal population.

In addition, Aboriginal affairs have long been thought of in terms of domestic affairs of little import in the operation of most of our institutional spheres, e.g., education, economics, and politics. However, during the latter part of the 20th century, it has become clear that they have taken on greater domestic importance and, as well, have entered the international scene. For example, in 1984, the Lubicon First Nation in northern Alberta approached the United Nations, claiming they were being denied the right of self-determination. Six years later, the Human Rights Subcommittee of the United Nations concluded that the Canadian government had not respected the civil and political rights of the Lubicons. The committee noted that the historical inequities and more recent developments threaten the way of life and culture of the Lubicons and constitute a violation of Article 27 of the International Covenant on Civil and Political Rights. Canada had first tried to get the case dismissed, but it was not successful; it now has found itself the centre of attention in the international arena. The UN committee's report, critical as it is of a member country, is embarrassing to Canada. Furthermore, the government, arguing that its $45 million settlement is sufficient, sees the Lubicons' rejection of its offer as solely an issue of money.[8] Lubicons, on the other hand, argue that the federal government is haggling over a few dollars, while they are fighting over the matter of their own future for all time.

From this example it is clear that, as we move into the 21st century, Aboriginal issues can no longer be viewed as unique to one community or area of Canada. What happens in one part of this country has substantive impacts on Aboriginal affairs in other parts. Unfortunately, it also demonstrates that the government of Canada has not taken any substantive action to resolve the issues. Moreover, it is clear that Aboriginal issues are no longer the concern solely of Aboriginal people. All Canadians are affected by a variety of issues—both directly and indirectly. For example, the settlement of land claims bears directly upon non-Aboriginal people in the area where the claims are being dealt with. Indirectly, land claim decisions have an impact upon businesses and potential land users. This has become painfully evident to Canadians when Aboriginal people have stopped pipelines from being built, forests from being cut down, and drilling for oil and gas or mining activities from taking place. In cases where non-Aboriginals are directly impacted, such as the housing development conflict in Caledonia, Ontario, they are more likely to take a great deal of interest in the conflict and actually become actively involved, sometimes trying to resolve the issue. On the other hand, when non-Aboriginals are only indirectly impacted, such as the "stand off" between a lawyer (Tony Merchant) and the federal government over the opening of Mr. Merchant's files for abused residential school attendees, they have little interest and are less inclined to become involved to "solve" the issue so that Aboriginal people who were abused in the residential schools can be paid compensation.

SUMMARY

Aboriginal policy of the French and English differed substantively. The French had a more practical approach, developed over years of Aboriginal diplomacy in Brazil, supported by an ideology that did not condemn Aboriginals to a position of subservience. Moreover, the French tried to understand the culture of Aboriginals and used that knowledge in negotiating with them. The results were positive and brought them benefits. English Canada, however, did not pursue the same policy. The English were more focused on domination and claiming the land for their expansion. For example, they were unwilling to accept verbal agreements and insisted on having written treaties. In addition, they held religious and ideological perspectives that convinced them of the inferiority of Aboriginal people.

Over time, we find that the policy governing Aboriginal–non-Aboriginal relations was administered differently throughout Canada. First of all, until 1830, Indians were viewed as military objects and were treated as such. If their presence would support the military campaign, they were given consideration. On the other hand, if their presence gave no military advantage, Aboriginals were ignored. By 1850 they would be defined as dangerous and dealt with accordingly. In Ontario and Quebec, until 1860, the imperial government handled all the affairs and expenses of Aboriginal people. As the British began to settle Canada, they devised a strategy by which land would be taken away from the Aboriginals and opened for settlement. As a result, treaties and pieces of legislation of all kinds and shapes were passed to legitimize the takeover of land once occupied and settled on by Aboriginals. At that time, a Crown Lands Department was established and a commissioner appointed to assume the role of chief superintendent of Indian Affairs. In other areas of Canada, the Indian Affairs office was administered directly by the various provincial or colonial governments (Hawley, 1990).

Included in the *British North America Act* of 1867 was a special provision allowing for the administration of Indian Affairs to come under the control of the government of Canada. Initially, Indian Affairs was the responsibility of the Department of the Secretary of State, but in 1873 it was transferred to the Department of the Interior. In 1880, a separate Department of Indian Affairs was formed. In 1936, it was shifted to the jurisdiction of the Department of Mines and Resources, and in 1950 it was shifted again to the Department of Citizenship and Immigration. From 1953 to 1966, Indian Affairs was handled by the Northern Affairs and National Resources Department. In 1966 it was called the Department of Indian Affairs and Northern Development. More recently the name has been changed to Indian and Northern Affairs Canada. Hence, the administration of Indian Affairs has been shunted from one department to another and has never been allowed to develop consistent, long-range policies.

KEY TERMS

political economy approach
colonization process
structural racism
whiteness

culture of poverty
Charter of Rights and Freedoms
Royal Commission on Aboriginal Peoples

"enemy" concept
Hawthorn Report
mercantilism

STUDY QUESTIONS

1. Discuss the seven stages of the colonization process. What impacts did each stage create?
2. What was the significance of the *Hawthorn Report*?

3. Compare and contrast French–Aboriginal and English–Aboriginal relations prior to Confederation.

4. How have Aboriginal–non-Aboriginal relations changed after Confederation?

5. What are the two key ways of establishing identity and how do they differ?

WEBLINKS

http://collections.ic.gc.ca/

The Canada Heirloom Series, Volume 2, includes extensive information (much of it historical) about various regional Aboriginal peoples in its online exhibit, "Canada's Native Peoples." Search for it by clicking on the Aboriginal Resources and Services menu choice.

www.ainc-inac.gc.ca

The Federal Department of Indian and Northern Affairs, discussed in this chapter, carries the institutional responsibility for "Aboriginal issues." Its website contains extensive resources, mostly from Ottawa's perspective.

NOTES

1. The primary labour market includes all those jobs that require skilled workers. The secondary market involves all unskilled labour.

2. Mercantilism was the economic theory that prevailed in Europe during the 18th century. Mercantilism held two basic tenets: the mother country was entitled to accumulate wealth in any form, and the mother country was entitled to exploit its colonies as a source for raw materials and a market for finished products, thereby maintaining a favourable balance of trade.

3. Because they used the seigneurial system of agriculture, the French always remained near major waterways and did not intrude into the interior of New France.

4. For a more thorough discussion of this issue, see Cumming and Mickenberg (1972).

5. Two additional factors contributed to the relatively peaceful relations between the French and the Indians: the military alliance of the Huron, the Algonkian, and the French; and the fact that the French settled in an area occupied by the Algonkian, who were migratory hunters (Jenness, 1937), who had no real tribal organization, and who were themselves recent arrivals in the area (Cumming, 1969).

6. See I.G. Shea, Charlevoix's *History of New France*, Vol. 2, 1879, p. 39.

7. Manifest destiny, though it varied considerably, was the belief that Europeans should control the world, or at least large parts of it. The Hamlite rationalization was the belief, taken from the Bible, that Ham was cursed by God and turned into a non-White person so that "he and his descendants should remain cursed and be subservient to Whites from then on." To the British, the Indians were clearly descendants of Ham.

8. The two parties agreed in 1988 that a 246-square-kilometre reserve with full mineral rights would be established.

chapter two

Aboriginal Canada:

Identity and Consciousness

INTRODUCTION

Before we can discuss Aboriginal issues or Aboriginal–non-Aboriginal relations, we must first identify who is an Aboriginal person. In answering this question, it is important that the reader appreciate the plethora of terms now used in identifying the original inhabitants of North America. Moreover, we will find that the indigenous population has undergone name changes that are not universally accepted—by either the indigenous population or the non-indigenous peoples. For example, since the 1970s, Eskimos have been referred to as Inuit in Canada, while in the United States they are still called Eskimos. Indigenous people have been referred to as Aboriginal or Native people although worldwide they often prefer the term "indigenous." The Métis are people of mixed ancestry—Indian and French, English, or Scottish background. Some Métis regard themselves as the only true Aboriginal or "original" peoples, since they alone emerged as a new ethno-cultural group in North America.

The term "First Nations" is a Canadian term that came about as a result of historical and political events. The National Indian Brotherhood first used the term in 1981 to address the Canadian rhetoric about the "two founding nations." In creating this term, they differentiated themselves from other Aboriginal groups and found that the new title was a powerful symbol that not only identified themselves but also has political cachet in dealing with legal issues as well as with identity. Terms such as "Aboriginal," "Native," and "First Nations" should be capitalized as they refer to a human group with respect to nation and nationality. Also, one does not use the phrase "Canada's First Nations," which assumes there are some. Given that there are many First Nations that have nation-to-nation relationships with the Crown, the independence of those relationships needs to be expressed. A more appropriate wording would be "First Nations in

Canada" or "First Nations citizens." This terminology reflects a meaning that, for First Nations, Canada is theirs, rather than that Canada "owns" First Nations. The term "Indian" has all but been removed from the discourse of today except for making specific legal statements. This chapter will define the various terms used to identify the growing number of Aboriginal peoples in our society (see Figure 2.1). The reader also will find that many Aboriginal groups have discarded the names given them by the settlers and have re-taken on traditional names they used before they were colonized, e.g., Sarcee now call themselves Tsuu T'ina, and Gleichen Blackfeet now call themselves the Siksika nation.

Nevertheless, Aboriginal people are in an identity crisis situation. After two centuries of oppressive colonialization, Aboriginal people are now beginning to have a clear vision of their own "heritage" culture as distinguished from "mainstream" society. Over the past half-century, Aboriginal people have started developing a new collective identity. As Taylor (1983) points out, collective identity arises when a culture is able to provide to its members a clear compliance ideology (a society's collective orientation through which all members make decisions and resolve dilemmas) upon which to build a strong unified ethos. One strand that links Aboriginal people is the general sense of betrayal and injustice they believe has been meted out over the past century. In other cases, political and economic issues have brought together various Aboriginal groups. Finally, a commonality in culture, e.g., spirituality, kinship, cultural ethos, has linked previously uncoupled groups together.

Aboriginal people also realize that the continued failure of government to deal with Aboriginal issues or to consult with them has contributed to their sense of isolation in Canada, but has also led to their resolve to create a better life. The inability of governments to act in a prudent manner to protect Aboriginal peoples continues to reinforce the belief that the achievement of any goals will have to come from within Aboriginal communities, and if they act in a collective manner they will have more impact to bring about the changes necessary. Nevertheless, there still remains an overall lack of Aboriginal identity, which has resulted in an inability to generate consensus on policy issues, chaos (with various segmented groups constantly vying for popular legitimacy), and an impotence felt by many members living in First Nations communities (Wilkins, 1999; Sawchuck, 1998).

In the Beginning

At the time when Europeans made first contact with the peoples of what is now Canada, they met Aboriginal peoples from a variety of cultural backgrounds, e.g., the Beothuk of Newfoundland and the Mi'kmaq of Nova Scotia, as well as a large number of indigenous peoples from the eastern regions of Quebec. There was a kaleidoscope of ethnic groups, each one unique in its economic organization as well as its language, religion, and values. Incoming Europeans found this ethnic diversity hard to deal with, and they quickly found a way to resolve the dilemma. Europeans quickly labelled all indigenous people as Indians. There would be some recognition of the different tribes, usually because of linguistic differences, but there was no real attempt to view Aboriginals as distinct cultural entities. When differences were acknowledged, they were considered minor attributes and were subsumed under the master trait of "Indian," which was a more meaningful and universal term from the Europeans' point of view (Hedican, 1995).

FIGURE 2.1 | Aboriginal Language and Cultural Divisions

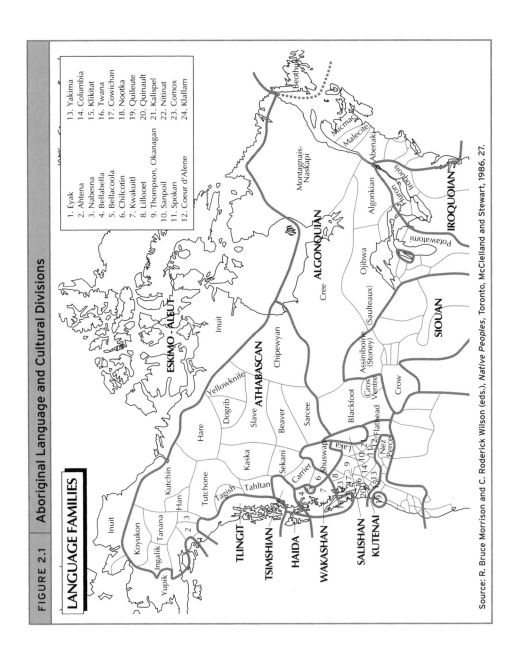

LANGUAGE FAMILIES

1. Eyak	13. Yakima
2. Ahtena	14. Columbia
3. Nabesna	15. Klikitat
4. Bellabella	16. Twana
5. Bellacoola	17. Cowichan
6. Chilcotin	18. Nootka
7. Kwakuitl	19. Quileute
8. Lillooet	20. Quinault
9. Thompson, Okanagan	21. Kalispel
10. Sanpoil	22. Nitinat
11. Spokan	23. Comox
12. Coeur d'Alene	24. Klallam

Source: R. Bruce Morrison and C. Roderick Wilson (eds.), *Native Peoples*, Toronto, McClelland and Stewart, 1986, 27.

Having noted the diversity among Aboriginal peoples, it must be pointed out that in a number of other ways there was some commonality. Aboriginal people interpreted life from a certain common perspective that was at variance with that of Europeans. For example, Europeans in the 16th and 17th centuries viewed science and religion as closely linked. They envisioned a rigid vertical hierarchical order of life with God on top; below God was a complex order of angels; below the angels, all other forms of life were ordered according to their descending levels of importance. These "natural" inequalities were fixed and ordained by God. Thus, poor people were not equal to rich people, and, it followed, ethical considerations appropriate for rich people did not need to be applied to the poor. Aboriginal people's view of their reality was quite different. They viewed all things (living and non-living) as having souls with a spiritual essence. Humans were no different than the trees, the lakes, or the bears. Humans did not have any predestined significance in the world; and while humans were different from other elements on earth, they were basically the same—having a spirit that gave them life. Again, while there may be some minor differences, the following illustration of the value system through life depicts natural law. (See Figure 2.2)

DEFINING AN ABORIGINAL PERSON

For the first 300 years after sustained contact was made with Aboriginal people, there was little difficulty in determining who was or was not an Aboriginal person. Nor was there any real need to establish a legal definition. Residents living in a small community were aware of who was Aboriginal or not. Ancestry, physiology, and way of life were the determining factors. This is not to say the question never arose, but rather, when it did arise, the answer was clear from the local residents' perspective. And it should be noted that there was not always consensus on the answer. But for the most part, local community residents understood who was and who was not Aboriginal.

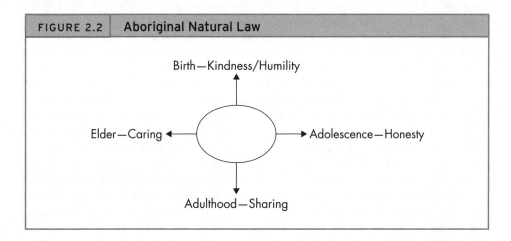

| FIGURE 2.2 | Aboriginal Natural Law |

Birth—Kindness/Humility

Elder—Caring   Adolescence—Honesty

Adulthood—Sharing

However, as the population of Canada grew and mobility became a fact of life, tension between Aboriginal people and the settlers intensified. It became apparent that a clearer demarcation as to who was an Aboriginal person would have to be established if social and legal relations were to be determined. However, it was not until 1850 that the first statutory definition of who was an Indian was enacted. This definition stated that an Indian was:

- First—All persons of Indian blood, reputed to belong to the particular body or tribe of Indians interested in living on specific lands, and their descendants;
- Second—All persons intermarried with any such Indians and residing amongst them, and the descendants of all such persons;
- Third—All persons residing among such Indians, whose parents on either side were or are Indians of such Body or Tribe, or entitled to be considered as such; and
- Fourth—All persons adopted in infancy by any such Indian, and residing in the Village or upon the lands of such Tribe or Body of Indians, and their descendants.

At this time the concept of Indian was a mixture of biology and culture. People of mixed ancestry were assigned either to Indian or Euro-Canadian society and did not constitute a separate category: only Indians and non-Indians existed (Hedican, 1991).

However, once the criteria were established to identify a legal/formal definition of an "Indian," individuals could then, when in question, revert to these attributes to categorize people. As the utility of such a categorization scheme became evident, this definitional strategy was employed by the dominant group without consideration of Aboriginal people. Nevertheless, changes to the definition of who is an Aboriginal have been made over time. In the case of defining an Indian by government, one of the first changes was to drop the blood quantum factor—that is, having a certain proportion of Indian blood. For many years this has not been part of a Canadian definition of who is an Indian. However, in the past decade, some bands have introduced "blood quantum" to determine who is a band member. This criterion has been one of the major attributes used in the United States to distinguish Indians from non-Indians.[1]

After contact was sustained for some time, phenotypical, cultural, and linguistic attributes became the master traits associated with "Indianness" and "whiteness." Thus, if a person evidenced a certain way of life, he or she was designated Indian or non-Indian, although in everyday life having evidence of visible biological traits of an Indian (e.g., dark skin colour, straight black hair) made it difficult to pass oneself off as a non-Indian. Nevertheless, if the individual gave ample evidence of being "white," he or she would normally be treated as one. For example, if individuals lived in a house rather than a tipi, wore cotton or wool clothes rather than clothes made out of animal hides, and had short hair, they may have been treated as non-Aboriginal; i.e., because the individuals followed a white or European lifestyle. Métis, for many years, were forced by the government to fall into one of these two categories. In some cases they were forcibly placed on the roll (a list of all people whom the federal government defines as Indians under the *Indian Act*), while at other times they were considered non-Aboriginal. The result of all this was that the early ethnic system was divided into two categories—Indians and non-Indians (Bartlett, 1980).

As the treaties were being established in the 1800s, mixed ancestry people often were forced to "take treaty" and became Indians under the *Indian Act*. However, some were declared non-Indian and were treated accordingly. Both before and after Confederation, it was possible to treat people of mixed ancestry, either individually or in groups, as Indians or non-Indians. However, even individuals initially defined as Indians were arbitrarily removed from the roll and made "non-Indians." The strategy for this action was that fewer individuals considered Indian at the time of signing of a treaty meant that the total cost of the treaty would be lessened. (Chartrand, 2004)

However, even early British and Canadian law did not distinguish Métis from Indians as representing two different people; as we have seen, mixed ancestry groups were forced to assimilate into Euro-Canadian society or to become Indian. At the time of treaty signing, negotiators made it clear that Métis could become Indians and thus participate in the bene-fits granted to status Indians under the treaty, or live as non-Indians on the reserve—if the Indians agreed. However, they would not be acknowledged as a separate legal entity. Why was this distinction so important? If land was to be given to Aboriginals, then Euro-Canadians had to know who the appropriate recipients were. Social mores also demanded that an individual's ancestry be public so that the community could respond accordingly (Dunning, 1972; Kaye, 1981).

As negotiations with Aboriginal people began over treaties, it became increasingly clear that more refined definitions would have to be determined. With the establishment of the *Indian Act* (1876) and the subsequent creation of an Indian roll, it became possible for the government to track and identify who was or was not Indian. By 1880, the federal gov-ernment excluded Métis from falling under the provisions of the *Indian Act*. And, as new legislation was passed, one could evaluate each person listed on the roll according to any new criteria that were enacted. Those who met the criteria remained on the roll and retained their Indian status (Chartrand, 2004). However, those who did not measure up to the new criteria were then dropped from the roll and by definition were no longer Indian. Whether their offspring retained their listing on the roll also varied according to the exist-ing legislation. Nevertheless, it is important to remember that those struck from the roll were not necessarily considered Métis, although a large number who were denied Indian status began to define themselves by that term. If people struck from the roll were not Métis, how were they defined? Formally, they were classified as non-status Indians, which meant they were neither Indian nor Métis. At the social level it was clear they were not "white" (Laing, 1967). Changes in definitions were continual, and the movement of large numbers of people in and out of categories is evident. Moreover, federal ministries in charge of keeping records were sloppy in documenting who was or was not Indian. Even when discrepancies were identified, federal ministries were more interested in reducing or limiting the number of people who would be labelled as Indian and were slow to change their records, if they ever did. This process continues today and, under *Bill C-31*, thousands of individuals who applied to be defined as Indian were denied their "Indian status."

Thus, since the late 19th century, there have been four major Aboriginal subgroups—legal or status Indians, non-status Indians, Inuit, and Métis. However, these four groups are not recognized in all parts of Canada. The legal status of each of these categories also varies as one goes across the country; e.g., in Quebec, Métis are not recognized by the provincial government, while in Alberta, there are formal Métis settlements with official rolls denoting the membership. Nevertheless, there has been a social, if not legal, recog-nition of the four groups since the late 19th century. The category of non-status Indians (sometimes calling themselves people of "Aboriginal ancestry") became diffuse as we moved into the 20th century, although these people have long lobbied for some official recognition and legal rights. As the 20th century unfolded, more and more attention was given to the legal category of "Indian" because of its financial and resource implications. The label "Métis" also began to recede in importance with regard to the federal and provincial governments (Moore, 1978), although with the inclusion of "Métis" in the *Constitution of Canada, 1982*, as a legal subcategory of Aboriginal, their prominence has become greater.

In censuses taken before 1941, ethnic origin was traced through the mother. Since eastern Indian tribes were matrilineal and matrilocal, this seemed a satisfactory means of distinguishing Indians from other ethnic groups. Before 1941, children whose mother was Indian were also defined as Indian. However, this was only true for those people who had been previously defined as Indian under the *British North America Act*.[2] Statistics Canada also still made a distinction between Indian and "mixed origin." In 1941 the definition was changed so that, for off-reserve Indians, the father's ethnic status determined that of his children. For those who lived on the reserve, both the mother's and father's lineages were used to classify a person as Indian (Romaniuc and Piche, 1972).

In 1951 a more complex legal definition was introduced, stating that only those individuals who fell under the *Indian Act* would be classified as Indians. Today, the federal (and some provincial) government(s) recognizes a legal and fiduciary obligation to legal (registered) Indians, Métis and Inuit. However, non-status Indians and those of Aboriginal ancestry, while given recognition in the census and other official government documents, are not considered a responsibility of Indian Affairs.

Culture and race no longer affect the definition of an Indian: today's definition is purely a legal one. If someone who exhibits all the racial and cultural attributes traditionally associated with "Indianness" does not come under the terms of the *Indian Act,* that person is not an Indian in the eyes of the federal and provincial governments. The following sections explain the categories in the government typology (Levine, 1970).

Registered Indians

The terms "legal," "registered," and "status" are generally used interchangeably to identify an Aboriginal person who is of federal concern. Registered Indians are defined in a legal manner and are different from other types of Aboriginal persons who do not have the same legal status. In short, "Indian" refers to a person who, pursuant to the *Indian Act,* is registered as an Indian or is entitled to be registered as an Indian. Put another way, the minister of Indian and Northern Affairs Canada has the unilateral right to determine who is and who is not an Indian. First Nation communities can decide who will be part of the band and who can live on the reserve but they cannot determine whether or not an individual is an Indian. Criteria for determining who is or is not an Indian are part of the *Indian Act* and remain firmly entrenched in the ministers' portfolio and are implemented through the content of the *Indian Act*.

Registered Indians are under the legislative and administrative competence of the federal government, as spelled out in the *British North America Act,* and are regulated by the contents of the *Indian Act*.[3] Today it is estimated that over 700 000 Canadians are defined as registered Indians. Being registered means that, with some exceptions, an individual is attached to a band and on the "roll" in Ottawa. As noted earlier, over the years, the federal government used a number of different criteria to decide who is and who isn't an Indian.

For example, between 1868 and 1985 the following groups of people have been defined at times as Indians and at other times as non-Indian:

1. Indian women married to non-Indian men;
2. Children of non-Indian mothers whose father also had a non-Indian mother;
3. Indians residing outside Canada for over five years;
4. Indians with a university degree;
5. Half-breed persons outside Manitoba who accepted scrip.

As identified in Figure 2.3, there are subtypes of legal Indians. First of all, legal Indians can be categorized according to whether or not they have "taken treaty"—that is, whether or not they or their ancestors signed a treaty with the federal government. As Figure 2.4 shows, Indians in British Columbia (with the exception of Vancouver Island), Yukon, Quebec, and the Atlantic provinces did not sign any treaties involving land transfers. Other groups, like the Iroquois of Brantford and Tyendingaga, who emigrated from the United States, are also considered non-treaty registered Indians.

Regardless of whether or not their ancestors signed a treaty, Indians are further subdivided into reserve and non-reserve, according to whether or not their ancestors were provided with reserve lands. For example, although a treaty (No. 11) was signed by Indians in the Northwest Territories, virtually no reserves exist. On the other hand, although British Columbian Indians have not taken treaty, many of them live on reserves.

In summary, the classification of a group of people as Indian arises from a legal definition. The concept "Indian" today does not solely reflect social, cultural, or racial attributes. The distinction between an Indian and a non-Indian is strictly a legal one.

Non-Status Indian

Although people in this group—i.e., people described as having some social or biological linkage to Indians—may exhibit all the social, cultural, and racial attributes of Indianness, they are not defined as Indians in the legal sense. Members of this group are not considered registered Indians because they were not defined as an Indian by the Crown. Included in this category are those Indians who have undergone "enfranchisement"—that is, they have lost their Indian status through changes in the definition of an Indian.

Enfranchisement (losing of Indian status) occurred in several ways. For example, until 1960 an Indian had to give up legal status in order to vote in a federal election. Until 1980, an Indian could choose to give up his or her Indian status by applying formally to Ottawa. In so doing, that person also surrendered status for all heirs (see Table 2.1). For years, one of the most common ways of losing Indian status was through intermarriage. Under the old *Indian Act,* any legally Indian female who married a non-legal Indian male lost Indian status for herself and for her children. On the other hand, if a legal Indian male married a non-Indian female, the female became legally Indian as did any offspring that may have resulted.[4] Other ways of losing Indian status included obtaining the right of title (fee simple) of land.

In general, a move from Indian to non-Indian status is made on the basis of legal criteria that are set forth by the *Indian Act.* However, informal changes to the Act also affect movement between categories; e.g., the minister of Indian Affairs, at the request of band

FIGURE 2.3 | Social-Legal Categories of Aboriginals Residing in Canada

Indians

	Registered				Non-Registered
	Band Membership			No Band Membership	Band Membership
Treaty		Non-Treaty			
Reserve	Non-Reserve	Reserve	Non-Reserve		
385 000	240 000	140 000	40 000	80 000	11 000

Métis

		Indian ancestry
Off-settlement	On-settlement	over 1 000 000
190 000	23 000	

Inuit

With disc number	Without disc number
15 000	41 000

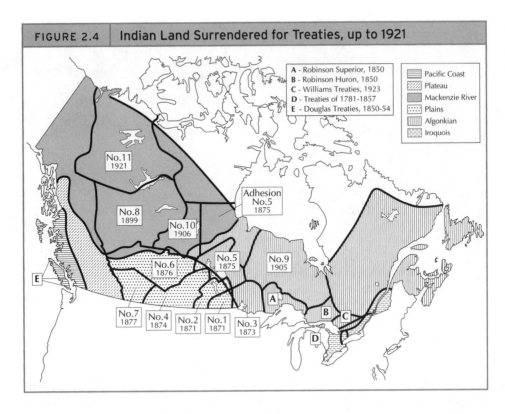

FIGURE 2.4 | Indian Land Surrendered for Treaties, up to 1921

A - Robinson Superior, 1850
B - Robinson Huron, 1850
C - Williams Treaties, 1923
D - Treaties of 1781-1857
E - Douglas Treaties, 1850-54

Pacific Coast
Plateau
Mackenzie River
Plains
Algonkian
Iroquois

councils, declared the government would suspend certain sections of the *Indian Act* that discriminated against Indian women who married non-Indians, as well as against their children. The government of Canada also has empowered the Department of Indian Affairs to declare that any portion of the Act may not apply to any Indian individuals, groups, or bands. These powers under Section 4(2) were recently invoked for members of certain bands in Quebec. Finally, as noted earlier, until the mid-20th century, Indian Affairs was notoriously lax in keeping accurate, up-to-date records about who was an Indian—using its own criteria. As Giokas and Chartrand (2002) point out, before the 1951 revision to the *Indian Act*, there was no well-organized or well-maintained manner of compiling a list of Indians who were to be on the Indian roll. The result was that many people who should have been on the list were omitted. When people's names were provided by the band for inclusion, Indian Affairs did not add the names to the list. Even after 1951, Indian Affairs did not exhibit "due diligence" in trying to establish an up-to-date and accurate list. Giokas and Chartrand (2002) suggest that there were several reasons: the very broad definition of "Indian," loose supervision of officials in the field, the pressures of trying to put a list together in a short time, and indifference to placing names on the roll. They also argue that irregular band members and non-treaty Indians were not considered by the registrar for inclusion on the roll at that time. The end result was the removal of many persons who would have legitimately been defined as Indian as well as the creation of the "non-status" Indian category.

TABLE 2.1	Accumulated Enfranchisements (1876–1985)
1876-1918	102
1919-1948	4000
1949-1968	13 670
1969	785
1970	714
1971	652
1972	304
1973-1975	467
1976-1985	94

Note: These figures include adult Indians enfranchised upon application together with their minor unmarried children as well as Indian women enfranchised following marriage to a non-Indian. Approximately 30 percent of the cases fall into the first category. The concept of enfranchisement is no longer considered operative since 1986, when further changes were made to the *Indian Act*.

Source: Adapted from Department of Indian Affairs, 1980, 1987.

Bill C-31

As noted above, until the late 20th century, the government focused on deleting Indians from the roll. However, in 1985, *Bill C-31 (An Act to Amend the Indian Act)* created new legislation that redefined who is and is not Indian. It also, for the first time, created the opportunity for First Nations to establish their own rules for determining membership. In short, it differentiates between registration as an "Indian" and First Nation membership. Three key provisions are part of this amendment to the *Indian Act*:

1. Reinstatement of Indians for those who lost their registration under earlier versions of the *Act* and the registration of their children.
2. New rules with regard to who could register as an Indian.
3. The ability for First Nations to determine their own rules for determining First Nations membership.

This amendment, for the first time, began to add people to the roll in a most peculiar fashion. The Bill was passed so that sexual discrimination would be eliminated, bringing the *Indian Act* into line with the *Canadian Charter of Rights and Freedoms*. It also abolished the concept of enfranchisement and provided for the partial reinstatement of those people who had lost their Indian status. Moreover, the Bill defined eligibility for various benefits that the federal government has provided for registered Indians. The overall effect of *Bill C-31* is to ensure that no one would gain or lose status through marriage.

The new Act identified four different types of Indians in addition to the differentiation between treaty and non-treaty: (1) status with band membership; (2) status with no band membership; (3) non-status, but with band membership; and (4) non-status, non-band. As a result, one may hold legal status and be on the roll but not be a member of a band. Previously, no such distinction was made. While people who lost their Indian status through marriage or enfranchisement may now reapply for status as a legal Indian, and also apply for band membership, those individuals whose ancestors (more than one generation removed) lost their status are not eligible. Those individuals applying to regain their Indian status are reviewed by Indian and Northern Affairs Canada (INAC) and a decision is made as to whether or not the individual has a legal right to claim Indian status. Almost 100 000 cases of adopted Indians were rejected by Indian Affairs on the grounds that the ethnic background of both the mother and father had to be known before approval would be given. In many cases this was not possible, or the mother was unprepared to name the father (or didn't know who the father was).

On the other hand, band membership is now determined by the band council. Bands were instructed by Indian Affairs to develop criteria for inclusion that had to be reviewed and approved by Indian Affairs officials. If the band did not state its criteria by the deadline (1987), the federal government would establish the criteria.

Others who are reinstated had to wait for two years to come under Sections 6(1) and 6(2) of the new *Indian Act*. Because acceptance into a band means that resources such as housing have to be shared, many band councils are reluctant to accept reinstated Indians onto their band membership lists. If a band failed to establish a membership code by the deadline, then all individuals who had been reinstated as Indians and had some historical basis for claiming membership to a particular band were automatically given band status. If, however, they did not meet the band criteria, they were counted as part of a new category of Indians (legal Indians with no band status).

At the time Bill C-31 was passed, most of those who applied early were reinstated. However, these were the easiest cases to document, and we find that later applicants had a much greater difficulty in "proving" their case. The Bill also addresses the issue of transmitting one's status (Section 6 of the *Indian Act*):

6. (1) Subject to Section 7, a person is entitled to be registered if

   (a) that person was registered or entitled to be registered immediately prior to April 17, 1985.

   (b) that person is a member of a body of persons that has been declared by the Governor in Council on or after April 17, 1985, to be a band for the purposes of this Act.

   (c) the name of that person was omitted or deleted from the Indian Register, or from a band list prior to September 4, 1951, under subparagraph 12(2)(a)(iv), paragraph 12(2)(b) or subsection 22(2) or under subparagraph 22(2)(a)(iii) pursuant to an order made under subsection 109(2), as each provision read immediately prior to April 17, 1985, or under any former provision of this Act relating to the same subject-matter as any of those provisions.

   (d) the name of that person was omitted or deleted from the Indian Register, or from a band list prior to September 4, 1951, under subparagraph 12(1)(a)(888) pursuant to an order made under subsection 109(1), as each provision read immediately prior to April 17, 1985, or under any former provision of this Act relating to the same subject-matter as any of those provisions.

   (e) the name of that person was omitted or deleted from the Indian Register, or from a band list prior to September 4, 1951.

      (i) under section 13, as it read immediately prior to September 4, 1951, or under any former provision of this Act relating to the same subject-matter as that section or

      (ii) under section 111, as it read immediately prior to July 1, 1920, or under any former provision of this Act relating to the same subject-matter as that section: or

   (f) that person is a person both of whose parents are or, if no longer living, were at the time of death entitled to be registered under this section.

6. (2) Subject to Section 7, a person is entitled to be registered if that person is a person one of whose parents is or, if no longer living, was at the time of death entitled to be registered under subsection (1).

6. (3) For the purposes of paragraph (1)(f) and subsection (2).

(a) a person who was no longer living immediately prior to April 17, 1985, but who was at the time of death entitled to be registered shall be deemed to be entitled to be registered under paragraph (1)(a); and

(b) a person described in paragraph (1)(c), (d) or (e) who was no longer living on April 17, 1985, shall be deemed to be entitled to be registered under that paragraph.

7. (1) The following persons are entitled to be registered:

(a) a person who was registered under paragraph 11(1)(f), as it read immediately prior to April 17, 1985, or under any former provision of this Act relating to the same subject-matter as that paragraph, and whose name was subsequently omitted or deleted from the Indian Register under this Act; or

(b) a person who is the child of a person who was registered or entitled to be registered under paragraph 11(1)(f), as it read immediately prior to April 17, 1985, or under any former provision of this Act relating to the same subject-matter as that paragraph, and is also the child of a person who is not entitled to be registered.

7. (2) Paragraph (1)(a) does not apply in respect of a female person who was, at any time prior to being registered under paragraph 11(1)(f), entitled to be registered under any other provision of this Act.

7. (3) Paragraph (1)(b) does not apply in respect of a child of a female person who was, at any time prior to being registered under paragraph 11(1)(f), entitled to be registered under any other provision of this Act.

Thus, Sections 6(1) and 6(2) serve to define who will be a status Indian in the future. Moreover, Section 6(1) identifies those who lost or were denied status as a result of the *Indian Act* prior to 1985. This includes such events as having married a non-Indian man, having been the child of a non-Indian man and a woman who was a status Indian at the time of birth, and enfranchisement. While at first reading it might seem as though the discriminatory aspects of the *Indian Act* had been removed, closer inspection will reveal that sex discrimination still remained, although it would not become evident for one generation. As Giokas and Groves (2002) and Loh and George (2003) point out, Section 6(1)(f) registers all those persons whose parents (living or dead) were registered or entitled to be registered under either Section 6(1) or 6(2). Section 6(2) registers only the child of one parent who was, or was entitled to be, registered under only Section 6(1).

As such, one can see that the children of a 6(2) parent are immediately penalized if that parent marries a non-Indian. At the same time, one can see that the penalty for a 6(1) person to marry a non-Indian does not have the same impact on the children of such a union. In summary, the changes to the *Indian Act* reveal that for 6(1) Indians, after two consecutive generations of marrying a non-Indian, Indian status will be lost. For 6(2) Indians, only one generation of marrying out will result in the children losing their Indian status. Similar issues arise when dealing with "illegitimate" Aboriginal children.

The above scenarios show that individuals who have obtained status through Section 6(2) and then marry a non-Indian will have children who are non-Indians. However, if they marry an Indian, then the child will be Indian. If those individuals who are registered under the conditions of Section 6(1) marry Indians, their children will be Indian. However, if they marry a non-Indian, the children will become Indians under Section 6(2) but will be unable to pass Indian status to their children. One final possibility would be to have two Indians under Section 6(2) marry. In this case, the children would be Indian under the provisions of Section 6(1). All children born "out of wedlock" will automatically be registered as Indians under Section 6(2) unless the mother can prove that the father was a status Indian, in which case they would be registered under Section 6(1).

An example provided by Giokas and Groves (2002) illustrates the point. Assume that a status Indian brother and his status Indian sister both marry non-Indians. The children of the sister who married out prior to the 1985 amendments will be "new status," since they all fall into the 6(2) category at the outset because they will only have one parent who was registered under *Bill C-31*. The children of the brother who married out prior to the 1985 amendments will be "old status" because both their parents already had status. They will therefore be 6(1) and will start off with an advantage over their similarly situated 6(2) cousins in terms of status transmission. The reader will recognize that this has nothing to do with the actual Indian ancestry since the brother and sister have exactly the same degree of Indian ancestry. In the end, this new bill may sow the seeds of discontent between factions of a community and bring further tension and conflict within the reserve.

Finally, the *Indian Act* also forces any enfranchised Indian who received more than $1000 of band funds (at the time of enfranchisement) to repay this money with interest before he or she can receive any band-fund disbursement or other band benefits (Joseph, 1991; Paul, 1990).

Figure 2.5 reveals the number of applicants for registration under *Bill C-31*. As of 2005, it is estimated that about 220 000 people applied for registration. Data from the

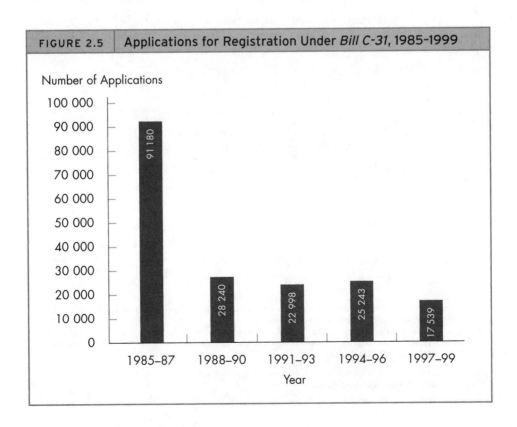

| FIGURE 2.5 | Applications for Registration Under *Bill C-31*, 1985-1999 |

Number of Applications

Year	Number of Applications
1985–87	91 180
1988–90	28 240
1991–93	22 998
1994–96	25 243
1997–99	17 539

Reinstatement of Status Information system has revealed that just over half of the applicants have been approved for registration (Joseph, 1991; Paul, 1990, INAC, 2002b).

Table 2.2 shows that the total number of *Bill C-31* registrants who were added to the Indian roll between 1985 and 2003 was nearly 120 000, nearly 17 percent of the total registered Indian population. At this time we are unable to determine how many are registered because of Section 11 in the old *Indian Act*. Nevertheless, we know that 72 percent of the *Bill C-31* registrants under the new 6(1) are female. The data also show that the average annual growth rate between 1985 and 1991 was three to seven times higher than the overall Canadian growth rate. Today, the pool of potential applicants is exhausted, and it is likely that *Bill C-31* will no longer have a substantial impact on the number of legal Indians. Nevertheless, it does show that the growth rate for Aboriginals is about twice that of the overall Canadian population.

The addition of *"Bill C-31"* people to the Indian roll has created substantial social and political problems for reserve Indians as well as financial problems for the federal government. A serious rift now exists between Indians who have spent their life on the reserve versus those who were enfranchised or otherwise forced to live off the reserve. The return of urban Indians to the reserves has brought about bitterness, jealousy, and factions within

TABLE 2.2	Registered Indians and Indians Registered Under *Bill C-31*, Average Annual Growth Rates, Canada 1981–2004				
	Registered Indians			Average Annual Growth (%)	
Year	Excluding *Bill C-31*	*Bill C-31* Population	Total	Excluding *Bill C-31*	Including *Bill C-31*
1981	323 782	0	323 782	2.59	0.00
1982	332 178	0	332 178	2.95	0.00
1983	341 968	0	341 968	2.00	0.00
1984	348 809	0	348 809	2.82	3.28
1985[a]	358 636	1 605	360 241	3.16	7.66
1986	369 972	17 857	387 829	2.40	7.24
1987	378 842	37 056	415 898	2.71	6.73
1988	389 110	54 774	443 884	2.65	5.06
1989[b]	399 433	66 904	466 337	4.20	5.11
1991	429 178	92 282	521 460	3.55	4.23
1996	506 005	104 869	610 874	2.83	3.01
2001	517 226	105 675	622 901	2.16	1.93
2004	527 570	106 456	637 227	2.00	2.03

a. In 1985, the *Indian Act* was amended to allow, through *Bill C-31*, the restoration of Indian status to those who had lost it due to discriminatory clauses in the *Indian Act*.
b. The high annual growth rate between 1989 and 1991 is due in part to the upward adjustments of the Indian Register for the purposes of the projections and to the Department's estimate of 86 000 *Bill C-31* registrants in 1990-91 plus the growth due to natural increase.

Sources: *Adapted from Basic Departmental Data*-1990, pp. 7, Indian and Northern Affairs Canada; Clatworthy, 2004; DIAND, 2004; Ram, 2004; Romaniuc, 2003.

the reserve community. In many areas, such as in educational institutions, a great deal of animosity exists between "traditional" Indians and *"Bill C-31"* Indians.

Because enfranchisement meant that Indians had to leave the reserve, most migrated to urban areas. Thus, many *Bill C-31* Indians have lived and raised their children in urban areas, and, over a generation of absence from the reserve, have been assimilated, taking on the attributes of non-Aboriginal culture. Under the new legislation, some of these Aboriginals are allowed to be reinstated, to claim their Indian identity (or what they have retained of it), and to benefit from the social and economic programs that are available to Indians. In some cases, this means access to a reserve and possible resettlement. Land allocation can be applied for and a share of the band profits will have to be allocated to these new Indians. In other cases, it means access to financial support to go to school. In still other cases, it provides an individual his or her birthright as an Indian. In these latter cases, the financial benefit is not at issue but rather the right to identify oneself with the group—Indians.

There are a number of complex problems involved in the implementation of *Bill C-31*. First of all, at a family level, it means that brothers and sisters may have different legal status. A second problem concerns band membership. Although some children (dependants— 6[2]) have a right to reside on the reserve, it is not certain that independent 6(2) children and their non-Indian fathers are allowed to reside on the reserve. A further problem of *Bill C-31* centres on band membership for reinstated women and their children. Bands have been given control over their membership, and some of these bands have adopted the old *Indian Act* band membership system and thus are able to exclude reinstated Indians from their membership.

Individuals reinstated through *Bill C-31* technically have the right to reside on a reserve. In the past, nearly all registered Indians were members of a band. However, because this new legislation allows for each Indian band to adopt its own rules governing membership, there are major differences between the number of people who are registered and the number who are members of bands. This difference may seem unimportant, but upon closer inspection several issues emerge. For example, if you are a band member, you are eligible to vote and to stand for band council membership. In addition, being a band member makes you eligible for a number of programs that are offered by the community, e.g., housing, social assistance, health. Moreover, if you are a band member you may be exempt from paying certain taxes. These are important considerations for any community, and they have not been taken lightly by First Nations.

However, the criteria of band membership criteria have been established by First Nations. Unfortunately, these criteria vary by band and do not have to be made public, and anyone wishing to review the criteria must apply to the band council. White, Maxim, and Beavon (2003) and Clatworthy (2004) have carried out a review of the membership rules of various First Nations and found four different types as depicted in Table 2.3.

The introduction of *Bill C-31* also has impacted the demography of the Aboriginal population. White, Maxim and Beavon (2003) show that substantial age differences exist between *Bill C-31* and pre-*Bill C-31* populations. For on-reserve populations, the average age of the *Bill C-31* population registered under 6(1) was 43.5 years, or about 15 years older than its pre-*Bill C-31* population. For those registered under 6(2), the difference was 24 years older on average. They note that age differences for those off-reserve were even greater. While the immediate impact of *Bill C-31* was to increase the Indian population, the long-term impacts are also of great interest. Clatworthy (2000) has developed a projection methodology that explores the future impacts of *Bill C-31* on the population entitled to

TABLE 2.3	Different Band Membership Rules by Number of First Nations and Population	
Type of Membership Rule	% of Number of First Nations Community	% of Population
Indian Act Rule	71.4	70.8
Unlimted One-Parent[a]	13.8	12.5
Two-Parent rule[b]	10.5	6.9
25-50% Blood Quantum	4.3	13.8
Total	609	725,700

[a]Unlimited one-parent rules, where eligibility requires that at least one parent be a member;
[b]Two-parent rules where eligibility requires that both parents be members of the band.

register under the *Indian Act*. His projections show that under the existing *Bill C-31* rules, the total population of survivors and descendants is projected to increase to slightly more than 2 million within four generations. However, the population entitled to be registered as "Indian" would grow for two generations to a peak of just over 1 million, and then an accelerating decline would take place over the next two generations. Thus, by the end of the fourth generation, only 750 000 would be registered as Indian, a number similar to today's population. After that, he projects a decrease in numbers such that, by the end of the sixth generation, there would be less than 100 000 individuals classified as "Indian" (White, Maxim and Beavon, 2003).

When *Bill C-31* was passed, the federal government argued that it had addressed the issue of sex discrimination. However, as Giokas and Groves (2002) point out, injustices remain. First, they observe that not all persons of Indian ancestry were included in the new registry. Second, they note that sex discrimination has not been eliminated because the effects of the earlier sex discrimination fall harder on Indian women and their descendants than on Indian men. Third, band membership codes do not deal with every person who has Indian status. Fourth, even where bands have been unable to exclude the new band members that the bill added, other ways are found to exclude them from the benefits of band membership—e.g., per-capita disbursements under the *Indian Act* were stopped and the funds moved to a band-controlled account from which new members were not provided with per-capita disbursements. Finally there are problems in how children are defined.

In the end, *Bill C-31* has probably created as many problems as it tried to solve. As White, Maxim and Beavon (2003) point out, how First Nations communities will deal with the different classes of citizens will indeed be daunting challenge.

Métis

The question of "Who is a Métis?" has long gone unanswered. And for most part of that time, the question was not really important. However, with constitutional recognition and affirmation of Métis as an Aboriginal people with rights, the question has taken on heightened importance. We must therefore provide a definition that has clearly articulated criteria. To begin to generate such a definition, we need first to provide a brief historical journey.

History reveals that a complex influence of the fur trade, the Hudson's Bay Company, the Roman Catholic Church, and Indian tribes all contributed to the development of Métis identity. They developed economic and social institutions and became a dominant economic force after 1750. By the 1820s many Métis had taken up residence at Red River, and thus it became their economic and social centre. It was at this time that they began to develop their own form of self-government. The Métis' sense of cohesiveness and political solidarity was evident by the late 1800s when they objected to the Hudson's Bay Company's decision to sell what is now Western Canada. Chartier (1988) notes that this same political consciousness was displayed in 1885 when the Métis fought the Canadian government. As Charlebois (1975) and Chartrand (1999-2000) point out, the Métis developed a separate culture and took on the characteristics of a separate nation. Living in distinct communities, they developed their own local laws and attempted to implement their own form of government. It is estimated that by the end of the 19th century Métis made up nearly three-quarters of the Hudson's Bay Company's labour force (Adams, 1975; Thomas, 1985). Within the economy of the 19th century, the Métis of Red River and Rupert's Land began to develop their identity and culture. Nevertheless, over time, many Métis were forced to become "Indian" (just as many Indians were forced to become Métis) in order for the government to create definitional boundaries that would reduce its financial liability for Native people.

While we know a considerable amount about the history and culture of the Red River and Rupert's Land Métis, we know little about the identity and culture of people of mixed ancestry elsewhere in Canada. As a result of sporadic and inconsistent approaches by government to mixed ancestry people, there is little known about how they were defined and how they defined themselves in the 19th and early 20th centuries (Giokas and Chartrand, 2002). For example, in Ontario, a Half-breed group was included in Treaty No. 3 as "treaty Indian" while others were not. In other cases, mixed ancestry people were explicitly excluded from the Robinson Huron and Robinson Superior Treaties. In other areas, Half-breeds were excluded from Treaty No. 9 because they were not living the Indian way of life.

The crystallization of a Métis identity was probably born out of the large influx of European settlers in the District of Assiniboia (Manitoba) in the early 1800s. In 1816, the Métis, in opposition to the Pemmican Proclamation (limiting the export of pemmican), raided a Hudson's Bay Company post, liberated the pemmican, and took it to the outskirts of Winnipeg. At a place called Seven Oaks, the Métis were challenged by government militia. At the end of the battle, the militia forces were killed and the Métis leader (Cuthbert Grant) was proclaimed the leader of the provisional Métis government until the emergence of the new leader, Louis Riel senior, in the 1840s. The continued importance of the Métis in this region of the country can be seen in the figures obtained in the 1871 Census: there were nearly 10 000 Métis counted (out of a total population of 12 000). However, a decade later, the Métis made up less than 2 percent of the Winnipeg population, and by the early 20th century the proportion was 3 percent.

In the late 1800s, the Métis of the Red River area objected to the government of Canada sending out land surveyors without the consultation of the Métis living in the area. Louis Riel, the leader of the Métis, objected, and he argued that the Hudson's Bay Company's trade monopoly did not include rights over the land and the people, and that before any transfer could take place, the government of Canada would need to negotiate with the Métis. The creation of the Province of Manitoba in 1870 was largely the result of the demands of the Métis and, under the provisions of the *Manitoba Act*, 500 000 hectares of

FIGURE 2.6 | Major Population Belts of Métis and Non-Status Indians

Source: L. Jantzen, "Reporting Métis in Urban Centres on the 1996 Census," *Canadian Ethnic Studies*, Vol. 35, 1 (2003), pp. 149-170; D. Newhouse & E. Peters (eds.), *Not Strangers in These Parts*, Ottawa, Policy Research Institute, 2003; J. Taylor & M. Bell, *Population Mobility and Indigenous Peoples in Australasia and North America*, London, Routledge, 2004; Correctional Service Canada, Aboriginal Initiatives Branch, Factors and Figures, Ottawa, 1999.

land were set aside for the children of the Métis. However, only 15–20 percent of the land was ever obtained by the Métis.

The continued influx of European settlers demanded that Métis and Indians be removed to make way for the settlement of the newcomers. However, land title began to become a serious problem and there was no agreement between the Métis communities across the Prairies and the government as to how it should be resolved. As Dickason (2002) noted, "Nothing seemed to work for the Métis, least of all getting Ottawa to listen" (p. 275). In the end, the conflict of 1885 between the Métis and the militia saw the Métis defeated at the battle of Batoche. The consequences were immediate and the Métis and Indians charged were imprisoned and, in nine cases (including Riel), hanged. The result was that the Métis, fearing for their lives, changed their names, fled to the United States or north to the Mackenzie River area, or declared themselves to be Indians and gained admittance to a reserve. In the end, a more dispersed Métis found themselves residing in an area between the Mackenzie and Red rivers.

Figure 2.6 locates the major belts of Métis and non-status Indians in Canada.

WHO ARE THE MÉTIS?

The term "Métis" refers to "in-between people"—those who are neither Indian nor non-Indian. The English term "half-breed" is less semantically correct than the French term "métis" because it does not imply a biological mix of "races" (Giokas and Chartrand, 2002).

Over time, the concept "Métis" has become highly politicized and the definition reveals the fact that the term has been used in different ways at different times. For example:

1. Treating Métis of either English or French mixed ancestry groups (from Rupert's Land) as the same;

2. Including any person of mixed ancestry as "Métis" even though they have no connection with the Red River or Rupert's Land Métis Nation; and

3. Identifying as Métis any person of mixed ancestry who has no Indian ancestry or may have lost it. (Giokas and Chartrand, p. 85)

Giokas and Chartrand (2002) have addressed this question in an attempt to provide an answer. They point out that when the *Manitoba Act* (1870) was passed, it applied to all residents of the original province of Manitoba. And since the *Manitoba Act* was passed, references in Canadian legislation have not distinguished between the two distinct groups of mixed-ancestry people. One year later, when the *Constitution Act, 1871* was passed, it also began to treat the Red River people (French speaking, Catholic) and the Rupert's Land Métis/Half-breed (English speaking, Protestant) as the same. Thus began a confounding of the term "Métis," and all subsequent legislation (until recently) failed to distinguish between the two distinct groups. As a result of this merging of the two groups into one, today no terminological distinction is made between the two historical groups. The Ewing Commission in Alberta (1935) took an initial theoretical approach in defining a "Half-breed/Métis" as a person of mixed blood, European and Indian, who lives the life of an ordinary Indian. However, by 1940 Alberta took a more narrow and applied definition requiring all "Métis" to have one-quarter Indian blood.

Under the 1870 *Manitoba Act*, Métis were given statutory recognition for the first time. One motive behind this recognition was the search for peace—and the establishment of government control—in the Red River area (Ens, 1996). This Act extinguished Indian title to the lands in the province of Manitoba and appropriated a portion of ungranted lands, to the extent of roughly 565 000 hectares for the benefit of the families of the Métis residents. Under the Act, the Governor General in Council would allow the Lieutenant-Governor to select lots or tracts of land in various parts of the province, as he deemed expedient, for Métis, and to divide the same lands among the children of the Half-breed heads of families residing in the province at the time of the transfer to Canada (Alberta Federation of Métis, 1978). In the end, the federal government allowed those who thought of themselves as Indian (and lived the Indian lifestyle) to be treated as Indians and allowed those who did not think of themselves as Indian to be treated as non-Indian. If a person accepted scrip (either land or money), they could not be considered Indian. This was formalized in the *Indian Act* that noted "no half-breed in Manitoba who has shared in the distribution of half-breed lands shall be accounted an Indian." If a person took scrip, they and their families and descendants could no longer be considered Indian. In short, not everyone who took scrip was a member of a Métis community (Groves and Morse, 2004). Nor was mixed ancestry an attribute that differentiated them from Indians. In all cases, Métis were offered the choice of taking treaty (as Indians) or taking scrip (as Métis/Half-breed.)

By the 1890s, the government began to implement its new policy of "civilizing" Indians. It began to promote individual enfranchisement and assimilation as well as to introduce and enforce the "out-marriage" provision in the *Indian Act*. The Half-breed/Métis who had "taken treaty" with the Indians were approached and requested to "take scrip," thereby removing them and their descendants from the Indian roll and saving the government money. Giokas and Chartrand (2002) point out that the 1885 Street Commission reported that one-third of the scrip claims allowed were issued to persons withdrawing from treaty. One year later, another Half-breed commission noted that nearly 90 percent of the individuals taking scrip were Half-breeds leaving treaty. They also point out that in the case of the treaty adhesion in the Lesser Slave Lake region, nearly 600 Indians were removed from the band list on the sole basis that they were of mixed ancestry. Although an inquiry was held and the presiding judge found that only about 200 people should have been removed from the roll, the department only reinstated about one-third of those recommended to be put back onto the roll. In the end, it can be seen that Métis do not necessarily have to be part of the historic Red River or Rupert's Land Métis nation. Nor is there any real distinction between Métis and Indians or non-status Indians other than the fact that the two groups seem to have chosen different ways of addressing their land claims: Indians took treaty and lived on a reserve, while the Métis took scrip. Giokas and Chartrand (2002) conclude that if judicial rulings continue the way they have in the recent past, scrip-takers may have an actionable claim to the restoration of Indian and band status as well as treaty and reserve land rights (p. 94). In the early 1950s, several bands asked the Department of Indian Affairs to expel "mixed ancestry" residents from the reserve. Changes to the *Indian Act* in 1958 effectively ended this attempt to expel members from the reserve. However, in the end, it created two different types of scrip-takers—those who were band members and status Indians prior to that date (1958) and those who were not.

Estimates of the number of Métis range from less than 500 000 to more than 1 000 000, depending upon the source. The lack of accurate information resulted, in 1941, from the deletion of "Métis" from the census. By 1980 government statistics (Canada, 1980) revealed the following figures:

- Métis and non-status Indian (core population)—300 000 to 435 000
- Métis and non-status Indian (self-identifying population)—400 000 to 600 000
- Métis and non-status Indian (noncore and nonself-identifying population)—1 to 2.5 million

However, after a lapse of several decades, the 1981 Census once again included Métis as a category of ethnic identification. The results were startling, since less than 100 000 people identified themselves as Métis. Today we find that, of persons who declared Aboriginal ancestry, nearly 175 000 identified themselves as Métis, with a further 26 000 status Indians identifying themselves as Métis. Some of these individuals are frustrated individuals who feel they are "Indian" but since they cannot obtain status, they settle for calling themselves "Métis."

Only Alberta has kept official records, and only for its Métis settlements. In 1980, approximately 4000 Métis resided on those settlements; estimates of Alberta's off-settlement Métis population range from 8000 to 15 000. (See Box 2.1)

The Métis have argued for many years that, as a special people, they are entitled to Aboriginal rights. The federal government has maintained that those Métis whose ancestors signed treaties or received scrip and land have had their Aboriginal rights extinguished (Cumming, 1973a). Presumably, others have not. However, once the Riel Rebellion was crushed (1885), the implementation of the provisions of the *Manitoba Act* (as it related to Métis) was not seriously undertaken (Daniel, 1980).

Métis Claims, Settlements, and Legal Issues

Over the years, the federal government has often recognized the existence of Métis claims. Under the *Dominion Act* and the *Manitoba Act,* the government provided scrip and land to Métis to extinguish their Aboriginal rights. The 1889 Treaty Commission was instructed to make treaty with the Indians and to investigate and extinguish any Half-breed titles (Cumming, 1973b). In the 1930s, the Ewing (Half-breed) Commission (1935) asserted the existence of Métis claims. As recently as 1969, the Indian claims commissioner also argued for the Aboriginal rights of Métis, stating that these were well established in Canadian law. According to the commissioner, various actions of the federal government, such as scrip allocation in Western Canada and the Adhesions to Treaty No. 3, have granted special status to the Métis, both morally and legally.

Even while recognizing Métis claims, the federal and provincial governments have tried to wish them away. The rights of the Métis in the Northwest Territories were ignored until rebellion was threatened in 1885. In the 1940s, as was mentioned above, the federal government deleted "Métis" from the census as a separate ethnic category. In 1944, Indian Affairs removed the names of nearly 1000 Indians from the roll, arguing that they were really Métis. Although a subsequent judicial inquiry forced the department to replace most of the names, clearly the government was hoping that the Métis would simply assimilate into Euro-Canadian society and disappear, along with their claims (Barkwell et al., 1989).

In their attempts to retain their ethnic status and to receive compensation for Aboriginal rights, the Métis, like the Indians and Inuit, have created complex and highly political organizations. The Native Council of Canada (NCC) was established in 1970 and became the political arm of the Métis. The NCC became known as the Congress of Aboriginal Peoples (CAP) in 1994. By the mid-1970s, there were 10 Métis organizations representing Métis in all regions of Canada. The overall mandate of the congress and its many provincial affiliates for these groups is to seek improved social conditions and a land base, and to deal with historical grievances (Purich, 1988; Sawchuck, 1998). The Métis argue that those whose ancestors did not take treaty or receive scrip or land still have Aboriginal rights.

At present, the relationship between the Métis and the federal and provincial governments varies from province to province.[5] In the Yukon, Métis demands have gone relatively unnoticed, or at least have been treated with less legitimacy than the Inuit or Dene demands (Coates and Morrison, 1986). On the other hand, in the Northwest Territories, the Métis are working alongside status Indians and Inuit to negotiate an agreement with the federal government. Until the 1990s, the British Columbia government refused to recognize the special rights of certain Aboriginal peoples in the province, including the Métis (Hatt, 1972).

Saskatchewan excludes Métis from any land claim registration now taking place with status Indians. In Saskatchewan, "farms" have been established for Métis, with land bases of less than four square kilometres each. Although Manitoba has historically recognized the Métis, it has recently refused to acknowledge their existence officially. The few monies that the Métis Association had been receiving from the provincial government for special education and cultural activities were cut off in 1982.

In Ontario, the Métis are recognized and are eligible to receive funds from a Native Community Branch. Although Quebec claims to define Métis and non-status Indians as Indians, it refuses to fund or implement programs for these special groups. In order to be officially recognized by the Quebec government, the Métis would have to reject the *Indian Act* and accept new terms outlined by the provincial government. Provincial policy with regard to Métis has been (with the exception of Alberta, which has accepted partial responsibility for Métis) one that claims that Métis fall under Section 94(21) of the Constitution and that they are thus a federal responsibility. Today there is no legislation in Canada that formally recognizes a group referred to as Métis prior to the acquisition of the Hudson's Bay Company in Rupert's Land in 1870. Nevertheless, Métis have been recognized as a people through the *Manitoba Act* and other pieces of legislation. However, there has not been a consistent or coherent national policy on Métis (Groves and Morse, 2004). Early in the history of Canada there was a belief that the Métis (however defined) would become integrated either into the Indian or non-Indian population and would thus no longer be a people. As such, the country wouldn't need a long-term policy with regard to this group.

Box 2.1 | Métis Settlements in Alberta

By the turn of the 20th century, the Métis of Alberta had begun organizing, and two decades later they were recognized by the provincial government. In Alberta, the provincial government's *Métis Betterment Act*, 1938, outlines its relationships with the Métis. The Alberta government does not acknowledge the legal existence of Métis off what were then called the colonies. Therefore, all Métis individuals who do not reside on a colony/settlement are considered regular Albertans with no Aboriginal or special rights. While most provinces argued that mixed ancestry individuals with Aboriginal backgrounds should be reinstated to Indian, Alberta took an alternative approach. During the Ewing Commission hearings, they took the position that Half-breeds/Métis were really Indians and took as a definition of Half-breed/Métis "a person of mixed blood, White and Indian, who lives the life of the ordinary Indian..." This definition was used in the 1938 *Métis Betterment Act*, which eventually established Métis settlements. Later, Alberta would revert to a blood quantum theory—e.g., a person had to have at least one-quarter Indian blood to reside on the colonies. This blood requirement remained in the Act until 1990.

Métis settlements located across the northern part of Alberta include the settlements of Paddle Prairie, Peavine, Gift Lake, East Prairie, Buffalo Lake, Kikino, Elizabeth, and Fishing Lake (see Figure 2.7). These eight settlements form the

only constitutionally protected Métis land base in Canada. They consist of 505 102 hectares, much of it covered by forest, pasture, and farmland.

The Métis are the descendants of European fur traders and Indian women who emerged as a distinct group on the Prairies towards the early part of the 19th century. Following the Northwest Rebellion of 1885, many Métis moved to the north and west. After a period of political activism among landless Métis in Alberta during the Depression, the provincial government passed the original *Métis Population Betterment Act* in 1938. Lands were set aside for Métis Settlement Associations, though four of the original settlements (Touchwood, Marlboro, Cold Lake, and Wolf Lake) were later rescinded by order of the Alberta government.

A distinct Métis culture, combining Indian and Euro-Canadian values and modes of expression, is practised in the Métis settlements. For example, jigging, a favourite form of dance, mixes the reels of Scotland and France with the chicken dance of the Cree. A distinct Métis language called Michif (combining Cree, French, and some English words) is still spoken alongside English. Most residents of Métis settlements retain Indian spiritual beliefs and customs.

The later 1955 and 1970 *Métis Betterment Acts* provided for settlement associations for each of the eight

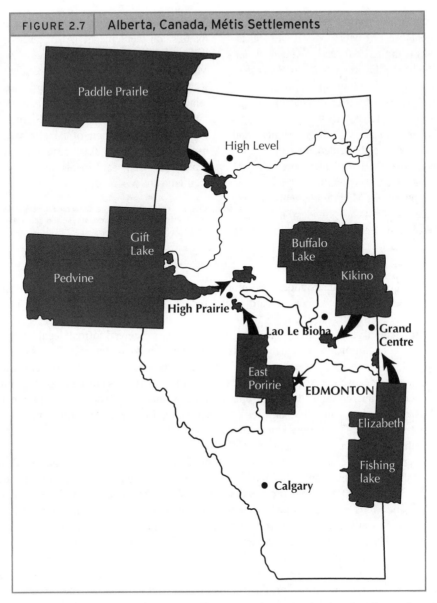

FIGURE 2.7 Alberta, Canada, Métis Settlements

Paddle Prairle

High Level

Gift Lake

Pedvine

Buffalo Lake

Kikino

High Prairie

Lao Le Bioha

Grand Centre

East Poririe

EDMONTON

Elizabeth

Fishing lake

Calgary

communities and laid the foundation for self-government. In each settlement, councils of five members are elected by settlement members to deal with matters affecting the settlements. In 1975 the Alberta Federation of Métis Settlement Associations was officially established to act as the political voice of the settlements and to pursue such goals as land security, local self-government, and long-term economic self-reliance. In 1985 the Alberta government passed what was known as Motion 18, a resolution committing the province to transfer title of the settlements to the Métis people and to provide provincial constitutional protection of the lands by means of an amendment to the *Alberta Act*. This paved the way for the historic 1989 Alberta Settlements Accord, which passed into legislation with the 1990 *Métis Settlements Act*. Replacing the previous *Métis Betterment Acts,* the *Métis Settlements Act* provides for the legal transfer of land title to the Métis people, as well as local municipal and traditional style self-government, and establishes eight settlement corporations and the Métis Settlements General Council as legal entities. The new Act establishes the Métis Settlements Appeals Tribunal, which provides a dispute resolution mechanism dealing with membership, land use, and resource matters on settlements. Also part of the Act is the Subsurface Resources Co-Management Agreement, an agreement whereby the settlements and the province jointly manage oil, gas, and other subsurface resources on the settlements. Significantly, the constitution of Alberta was itself amended in 1990 to recognize and protect the Métis settlements' interest in their land and resources.

Source: René R. Gadacz, *The Canadian Encyclopedia 2000*, World Edition. Toronto: McClelland and Stewart. Reproduced with permission.

In the Atlantic provinces, most governments simply refuse to acknowledge the existence of the Métis. Although Prince Edward Island recognizes them, it has no special policy because there are so few of them.

At the federal level, the Métis have only in recent years received formal, legal, and constitutional recognition beyond that established in the *Manitoba Act* of 1870. The Métis argue that, under this Act, they were recognized as a separate people with certain rights. Furthermore, because the Act cannot be changed without Britain's consent, the Métis and non-status Indians continue to have separate legal status. The federal government has established a cabinet committee on Métis and non-status Indians to investigate more fully the claims and issues put forward by them. Currently there is considerable debate about the legal status of Métis and their rights. (See Box 2.2)

In early 1981 the federal government recognized and affirmed the Aboriginal and treaty rights of Indians, Inuit, and Métis. These rights have been affirmed in the Constitution (1982, Sec. 35(1)), with the proviso that only "existing and treaty rights" are to be recognized. The Métis argue that their rights are a special case of Aboriginal rights, that they stem from the self-perception of the Métis people as an indigenous national minority (Daniels, 1981), and that they are derived from their Aboriginal ancestry and title—both of which constitute the national identity of the Métis.

In 1983, members of the Métis Nation created the Métis National Council, whose goal was to achieve a clear definition and defence of Métis rights. By the time the First Ministers' Conference on Aboriginal Affairs convened that same year, a separate invitation had been issued to the Métis National Council, thereby severing the formal relationship with the Native Council of Canada which had previously represented the Métis.

The Métis National Council has published material that identifies its criteria for determining whether a person is Métis:

The Métis are:

- an Aboriginal people distinct from Indian and Inuit;
- descendants of the historic Métis who evolved in what is now Western Canada as a people with a common political will; and
- descendants of those Aboriginal peoples who have been absorbed by the historic Métis.

Box 2.2	Establishing Métis Rights

To confirm their rights, Métis have taken their case to the courts. In the case of *R. v. Powley*, the Supreme Court of Canada made its first contemporary ruling about Métis and their Aboriginal rights. In 1993, the Powleys (father and son) killed a moose and tagged it. One week later they were charged with hunting without a licence and unlawful possession of moose contrary to Ontario's *Game and Fish Act*. Five years later the trial judge ruled that the Powleys had the "Métis right" to hunt, which is protected by Section 35 of the *Constitution Act, 1982* and the charges were dismissed. The Crown appealed the decision, and in 2000 the Ontario Superior Court of Justice confirmed the trial decision and dismissed the Crown's appeal. The Ontario Court of Appeal heard the case in 2001 and upheld the earlier decisions. Nevertheless, the Crown appealed to the Supreme Court of Canada. On September 19, 2003, the Supreme Court of Canada, in a unanimous judgment, upheld the lower court decisions and said that the Powleys can exercise the Métis right to hunt that is protected by Section 35. In summary, the court confirmed the existence of Métis communities in Canada and the constitutional protection of their existing Aboriginal rights.

The reader should note that the Supreme Court did not define who the Métis people are. The court set out three broad factors—self-identification, ancestral connection, and community acceptance—to be used in identifying who can exercise a Métis community's Section 35 right to hunt. This case is only about the Métis right to hunt and does not reflect on other rights Métis might have.

The Council goes on to point out that the Métis community comprises members of the above groups who share a common cultural identity and political will (Métis National Council, 1983). This is not to say that everyone accepts this definition. There is no single exclusive Métis people in Canada. Eastern Canadian Métis are different from Red River Métis. At a provincial level, the issue of who is or isn't Métis varies. In Alberta, recent changes to the *Métis Settlement Act* and the criteria set out by the Alberta Métis Nation Association have clarified the definition of a Métis. Both the government and the Association agree that a Métis is someone who declares himself or herself as a Métis, has traditionally held him- or herself as Métis, and is accepted by the Métis community as Métis.

In Manitoba, the Federation definition of a Métis remains a racial one that enables non-status Indians to join. The Saskatchewan Association of Métis and non-status Indians split in 1987, so the Métis Society of Saskatchewan defines a Métis in a manner similar to Alberta.

Today the term "Métis" has widespread usage. However, two different meanings have been given to the term. As the Métis National Council (1984) pointed out, written with a small *m,* "métis" is a racial term for anyone of mixed Indian and European ancestry. Nevertheless, the Métis National Council has objected to this distinction and argues that the acceptance of the latter (racial) definition undermines the rights of Métis people.

Today there is a distinction between the historical Métis and the Pan-Métis. "Pan-Métis" is a more inclusive term that includes historic Métis, people of mixed Indian-European ancestry, and non-status Indians. As Lussier (1979) points out, they gain their identity from a multitude of national roots.

The federal government has taken the position that Métis are a provincial responsibility, even though there are federal departments that provide funding for them—e.g., the Secretary of State. This position is based on the argument that Métis are not included in Section 91(24) of the *Constitution Act, 1867*. Provinces (except Alberta) contend that Métis are included under Section 91(24). The Métis National Council also maintains that Métis are a federal responsibility. Chartier (1988) claims that in 1984 the federal minister argued that, even if the Supreme Court ruled that Métis were a federal responsibility, the government could refuse to exercise its responsibility. Nevertheless, Chartier argues that Métis are covered within the term "Indian" (as are the Inuit) in Section 91(24). Others, such as Schwartz (1985; see also Sawchuck, 1998), view Métis as a people distinct from Indians and thus side with the federal government. However, he does offer a compromise in suggesting that small-*m* métis would be covered by Section 91(24) while capital-*M* Métis would not. What is suggested is that Métis may be entitled to be governed by some federal laws; however, even if this were the case, substantial co-operation among all the provinces would be needed to generate a uniform regime of Métis control.

While the federal government treats Métis as a provincial responsibility, certain interpretations of general programs provided to Canadians have allowed the Métis to benefit. In other areas of concern—e.g., constitutional negotiations—an informal agreement has been made whereby the minister of Justice is to act in a way that ensures that Métis interests are addressed and that the Métis have someone to listen to their concerns. Clearly, the inclusion of the Métis in Sections 35(1) and 35(2) of the Constitution is accorded legal significance. The recognition of the Métis as an Aboriginal people provides a constitutional base upon which negotiations for the recognition and compensation of their rights can fully begin. Finally, Section 25 also incorporates, by definition, a fiduciary relationship between the federal government and the Métis (Bell, 1991).

In 2002 the Métis Nation organization adopted a national definition of Métis and they have since been ratifying this national definition in the respective provincial jurisdictions. Their definition is that the Métis have a shared history, a common culture (song, dance, dress, national symbols), a unique language (Michif, with various regional dialects), extensive kinship connections from Ontario westward, a distinct way of life, a traditional territory, and a collective consciousness. The Métis Nation is represented through province-wide governance structures from Ontario westward; namely the Métis Nation of Ontario, the Manitoba Métis Federation, the Métis Nation-Saskatchewan, the Métis Nation of Alberta, and the Métis Provincial Council of British Columbia.

The question of who is a Métis will continue to be an issue as the boundary of inclusion and exclusion continues to shift. Aboriginal people also define themselves inconsistently and shift categories depending upon the situation and the changing definition of "who is an Indian" (Giokas and Chartrand, 2002). It is clear that the definition cannot be a biological one nor can it be dependent on kinship. The changing definition of who is or isn't an Indian also has clearly demonstrated that blood quantum is a fruitless strategy for defining the boundaries of a people. An equally fruitless strategy is kinship since out-marriage and enfranchisement have split families in many different ways. Self-identification is used by many Métis but this strategy has not had any political or legal support. Nevertheless, it is the only real choice people of mixed ancestry have in developing boundaries and political power. As Giokas and Chartrand (2002) have clearly noted, like much of our history, the basis for recognizing Aboriginal people is less a conscious policy and more of a shifting and haphazard strategy resulting from fiscal and political pressures over the years. As a result, no consistent basis for designating a person as Indian, Métis, or any other Aboriginal category has existed. In the end, there is no one single definition of the concept. As Peters, Rosenberg and Halseth (1989) point out, the term Métis is widespread in usage. It appears to have a well-accepted general meaning, reflecting the social aspect of Métis identity, and a reality that cannot be denied.

Inuit

The category of "Inuit" also has undergone a number of redefinitions. Until Confederation, there was no legal definition of Inuit, nor any real need to make such a distinction. And, since the issue was limited to local concerns, the government did not see fit to enter the debate. Immediately after Confederation the Inuit were placed under the control of the *Indian Act.* However, after a short time they were placed, and continue to be, under the direct jurisdiction of the federal government under the Canadian *Constitution Act, 1982.*[6]

When Canada began to think of developing the North in the early 20th century, the government decided that a census was needed to establish the actual number of Inuit. As a result, a "disc" number was allotted to each Inuk; for a time, only those with numbers were officially defined as Inuit.[7] However, other definitions of Inuit have developed since and will continue to be used. A more detailed profile and discussion on Inuit will be provided in Chapter 10.

SOCIAL DIVISIONS AMONG ABORIGINAL PEOPLE

The definitions of "Indian," "non-status," "Métis," and "Inuit" are far from being settled. Many of the decisions will rest with the courts. Indeed, it is clear that no single definition of Aboriginal peoples has been agreed upon. However, as Mallea (1994) argues, whatever the definition of "Indians," the legislation in place led to the government strategy of "divide and conquer" as well as assimilation. She contends that it allowed the government to create an apartheid system by placing Aboriginal peoples on reserves. Moreover, the changing definition of who is an Indian has an impact on who is defined as Métis and/or Inuit. Why have these legal distinctions been inflicted upon Canadian Aboriginal people? Those in power have surely been aware that such nominal distinctions have a "divide and conquer" effect. Aboriginal people became easier to control as they began to fight among themselves. The distinctions between the non-treaty and the treaty Indians are particularly divisive; the two groups received different privileges, different amounts of money from different sources, and different rights.[8]

The Lavell and Bedard Cases

Two legal cases from the early 1970s involving the sex-discriminatory status regulations in the *Indian Act* clearly illustrate the issue of definitions, the process of developing social divisions among Aboriginal groups, and the complexity of the Aboriginal women's sexual equality problem. The *Lavell* and *Bedard* cases also had a profound effect on the establishment of the Native Women's Association and on the way that organization manifested itself vis-à-vis national male-dominated Aboriginal organizations (King, 1972).

Jeanette Corbiere Lavell, a status Ojibwa from the Wikwemikong reserve in Ontario who was to marry a non-Aboriginal man in December 1970, had already declared before the date of her marriage that she intended to contest Sections 12(1)b and 14 of the *Indian Act* in court.

A precedent had been set in 1967 by a court case involving a liquor infraction in the Northwest Territories. An Indian man named Drybones was convicted under Section 94(b) of the *Indian Act* for being intoxicated off-reserve. Drybones successfully challenged his conviction before the Supreme Court in 1969 on the basis that this particular section of the *Indian Act* contravened Section 1(b) of the Diefenbaker *Canadian Bill of Rights* (1960) that prohibited racial discrimination. The *Drybones* case proved that it was possible for the *Indian Act* to be overruled by that Bill (Cardinal, 1979; Jamieson, 1978). The *Drybones* case and the report of the Royal Commission on the Status of Women, together with the withdrawal of the 1969 white paper on Indian policy, resulted in renewed pride in Indian identity (Krosenbrink-Gelissen, 1983) and an incentive to challenge the *Indian Act*.

In June 1971, an Ontario County Court dismissed Lavell's case on the grounds that, despite the loss of her Indian status, she had equal rights with all other married Canadian women. As such, it was found that she was not deprived of any human rights or freedoms contemplated in the *Bill of Rights*. The court did not find her inequality within her own class of people contrary to that Bill and, thus, overlooked the fact that the *Indian Act* reinforced an inferior position of Indian women vis-à-vis other Canadian women (Chapman, 1972; INAC 1983; Jamieson, 1978; Krosenbrink-Gelissen, 1984b).

In October 1971, Lavell made an appeal to the Federal Court of Appeals and won. The three judges concluded that the *Indian Act* resulted in different rights for Indian women than those of Indian men when women married non-status males or Indians from different bands. The court decided that Sections 11(1)f, 12(1)b, and 14 of the *Indian Act* contravened the *Bill of Rights* and should therefore be repealed in due course. Right after the decision from the Federal Court of Appeals, the federal government declared that it would bring the *Lavell* case before the Supreme Court of Canada (House of Commons, 1982). There it would be considered together with a second case, that of Yvonne Bedard, a non-status Iroquois woman from the Brantford reserve in Ontario.

Ms. Bedard had separated from her non-Aboriginal husband and returned to her reserve to live in the house that was willed to her by her parents. A year later, Bedard was evicted from the reserve by the band council, although DIAND had informed the council that on the basis of local control several other bands had decided not to implement that particular section of the *Indian Act*. Bedard successfully presented her case before the Supreme Court of Ontario on the same grounds that Lavell had used (Cheda, 1977; Jamieson, 1978; Weaver, 1978).

The *Lavell* and *Bedard* cases were brought before the Supreme Court of Canada in 1973. Both Lavell and Bedard received support from various women's groups, which recognized their cases as an opportunity to advance women's rights in general. Duclos argues that it was predominantly Euro-Canadian women who were spokespersons for the women's movement in Canada during the 1970s. They created "an image which constructs gender as the sole basis of women's oppression, cloaked in the privileges and power attached to being white" (1990: 38). Hence, feminist groups at that time focused on sex discrimination in the *Indian Act* as an example of the inequality of women, and did not recognize the dual discrimination operating in Indian women's situation. However, feminist groups were able to attract media attention. This way, Indian people across Canada were made aware of the significance of the *Lavell* and *Bedard* cases for the Indian movement (INAC, 1977, 1982).

The *Lavell* and *Bedard* cases led to considerable discussion among both Indian and non-Aboriginal people. Lobbying by both groups was complicated by a lack of consensus. Whereas non-Aboriginal groups focused on the matter of sexual equality per se, Aboriginal groups began raising the question of whether the federal government should continue determining Indian legal status and band membership. This awkward situation arose from the fact that Indian sexual equality rights were being discussed within the field of women's rights—a field which, as such, had nothing to do with the *Indian Act* (Roosens, 1986).

A significant reason for the divisiveness among Indians regarding the legal status issue in the *Indian Act* was that most Indians did not know what the *Indian Act* entailed and what it could or could not enforce (Silman, 1987). Status Indians found it hard to comprehend the problems that non-status Indians were confronted with. At the same time, a fundamental change of the *Indian Act* seemed inconceivable to many status Indians. A repeal of the *Indian Act,* according to them, would result in the loss of all Indian rights. Hence, those Indian persons who opposed Lavell and Bedard's actions in seeking an *Indian Act* amendment were not necessarily in favour of sexual inequality, but feared the loss of all Indian rights.

In February 1973 the *Lavell* and *Bedard* cases appeared before the Supreme Court of Canada. The Attorney General of Canada had made the appeal in response to suggestions from government officials who were afraid of the far-reaching implications if the lower court decisions in the *Lavell* and *Bedard* cases should be upheld. Most important, the appeal was also made in response to pressure from the National Indian Brotherhood. The federal government did not want a revision of the *Indian Act,* in view of the previous negative reactions by Indians when change was suggested, and because the abolition of sex discrimination in the *Indian Act* would bring about substantial financial liabilities (Murphy, 2001). The number of status Indians would increase dramatically if non-status Indian persons were to regain status and corresponding government services.

According to the National Indian Brotherhood, sex discrimination against women in the *Indian Act* was wrong, but the organization was afraid that if previous court decisions were upheld, the federal government would be given the ultimate power to change or even to repeal the *Indian Act* without the consent of Indian people. The white paper on Indian policy of 1969 was still fresh in the memories of those involved. The National Indian Brotherhood considered Section 12(1)b of the *Indian Act* as a strong lever to force the federal government to negotiate an *Indian Act* revision. It wanted to sidetrack the issue of sexual equality for Indian men and women in the interests of preserving Indian rights, either through the *Indian Act* or through other legal guarantees. Therefore, the National Indian Brotherhood wanted Indian women to wait for a redress of their rights in the interest of preserving Indian rights for (status) Indians as a group. Women were requested to subordinate their goal—Indian rights for Indian women—to that of Indian men; they were used as a political vehicle to pursue an *Indian Act* revision in the way that status Indian males saw fit.

While the National Indian Brotherhood's leading figures were against Lavell and Bedard primarily for political and strategic reasons, it appeared that the majority of its constituency—still not fully aware of the power and limitations of the *Indian Act*—was against these women's actions to regain their Indian rights for other and more far-reaching reasons. The constrained identity boundary mechanisms embedded in the status regulations of the *Indian Act* were largely internalized by Indian people and were therefore conceived of as Indian customary law. A good example of this is provided by the Association of Iroquois and Allied Tribes, of which Bedard's band was a member. The organization stated in a position paper of 1971 that the patrilineal and patrilocal status principles were in agreement with the traditional social organization of the Iroquois (Chapman, 1972). Anthropologists were aware that this claim was false. Furthermore, the National Indian Brotherhood's constituency in large part feared the influx of non-Aboriginal men on reserves if previous decisions in the *Lavell* and *Bedard* cases were upheld. This argument reflected an internalization of non-Aboriginal male sexism, since it indicated the Indian people's fear that non-Aboriginal men would take over political power. The presence of non-Aboriginal women on reserves (married, widowed, or separated from status Indian men) was not felt to be threatening, despite the increase in this trend. This argument also reveals a discrepancy between Indian ideology and practice (Malloy, 2001). Although Indian males and females unanimously acknowledged Indian women's crucial and continuing roles as mothers in retaining and enhancing cultural patterns, non-Aboriginal women were not perceived as a threat to the cultural survival of Indians (Krosenbrink-Gelissen, 1989). Many non-status Indian people argued that sex discrimination in the *Indian Act* is not a women's issue per se. Since Indian women were (and are) removed from the centre of life through the *Indian Act* regulations, the survival of Indian communities was actually at stake. They claimed that "Indian motherhood" is vital to the continuation of Indian nationhood (Holmes, 1987; Krosenbrink-Gelissen, 1984b; Meadows, 1981; Shkilnyk, 1985). Since the National Indian Brotherhood went so far as to determine Indian band membership in terms of cultural resourcefulness, the devaluation of women was perceived as detrimental to Indian cultural continuity (Weaver, 1978).

The Supreme Court decided, in a 5 to 4 vote, against Lavell and Bedard. The *Canadian Bill of Rights* was not considered effective to overrule the *Indian Act,* and the fact that Indian women were treated differently upon marriage to a non-status man or an Indian from another band was not considered relevant to the cases brought before the court (Eberts, 1985; Jamieson, 1978; Kerr, 1975). Both the federal government and the National Indian Brotherhood saw the decision as a victory. The National Indian Brotherhood saw it as a victory for Indian rights. The fact that Indian women were denied Indian rights was ignored, since it was not relevant to their political mandate.

The *Lavell* and *Bedard* cases had awakened both the Canadian public and the Indian people. The cases presented a moral dilemma over which the women's movement and the Indian movement collided; the Indian ideology of special status was perceived as irreconcilable with the equality ideology of the women's movement. However, to Indian women the issue had never been as described above. They had never asked for equal rights with other Canadians, but for equal rights with other Indians: "We can't begin discussing universal women's rights because at this time we can't even get Indian rights for Indian women" (*Indian Rights for Indian Women*, n.d.: 15). Misinterpretations of Indian women's political goals on the part of both the Indian movement and the women's movement were due to a lack of understanding of the true character of the Indian or Aboriginal women's movement, as the Native Women's Association of Canada was to argue in the 1980s.

SUMMARY

The organization of Indians into their present-day bands can be understood as a result of the draconian steps taken against Aboriginal people by government. The government, in a sense, forced Aboriginal persons to deal with them as a band, and, over time, this has become the basis upon which Aboriginal and non-Aboriginal people operate. Over time, Aboriginal people have accepted the band as the focus of their identity and organization. The indigenous institutional basis of the band is no longer evident. In other words, traditional forms of organization that were an integral part of Native culture have been replaced by a type of administrative structure designed primarily to serve the convenience of the federal and provincial governments. As Cornell (1988) points out, "Structures of authority and decision making, once embedded in the fabric of aboriginal society, are now attacked from the outside, institutionally separate from the culture of Natives" (pp. 101–102). Today the band no longer exhibits a sense of peoplehood but rather is a political–legal construct that has some legal relationship with other structures in our society.

Aboriginal identity has become complex and fragmented. For example, many people identify themselves as Bloods or Ojibwa, but this masks a multitude of meanings. For some it may mean a connection with the tradition of Bloods or Ojibwa, and for these people, maintenance of culture is of paramount importance. Others will identify with the local group experiences. Finally, some view their identity in terms of the legal definition of band membership. As a result, we find today that a sense of peoplehood is diverse, yet Aboriginal peoples are forced to act as a single political unit (Sealey, 1975).

Increasingly, for a large number of Aboriginal people, a Native identity that transcends bands, tribes, peoples and political borders is becoming an important basis for action and thought. The number of local and national (as well as international) Native organizations reflects the importance of such an identity. This Native consciousness has allowed for pan-Indianism to emerge along with the social and political organizations. This pan-Indianism is a kind of cultural synthesis of a number of different but related cultures. The resultant new identity (Indian consciousness) has created a linkage among groups that previously were viewed by others (and themselves) as distinct. While Aboriginal people are beginning to develop a consciousness of band and group solidarity, the process of establishing themselves as an ethnic entity is not yet complete. There are still major divisions between the various groups (e.g., Indians, Métis, and Inuit) but it is clear that the process of Aboriginal self-definition and identification has begun.

From the turn of the century to World War II, a collective Native identity began to emerge. The development of this identity was gradual and intermittent, varying from region to region. At the same time, however, government actions reduced the amount of intertribal interaction as well as political action. As a result, networks (small at first) among various groups of Aboriginal people focused on social and cultural affairs. Nevertheless, these activities promoted a sense of shared Nativism. For example, pow-wows began to become public, and they drew Aboriginal persons from other areas of the country for several days of socializing and learning cultural traditions.

KEY TERMS

First Nations	registered Indians	Métis
Indian Act	*Bill C-31*	Inuit

STUDY QUESTIONS

1. What was the result of the first statutory definition of who was an Indian in 1850?

2. What are the differences between treaty/non-treaty and reserve/non-reserve Indians?

3. What is *enfranchisement*?

4. Compare and contrast the benefits and downfalls of *Bill C-31*.

5. Explain the importance of Section 6(1) and 6(2) of the *Indian Act*.

6. What are the four types of membership rules for several First Nations?

7. What impact has taking treaty or scrip had upon members of the Métis community?

8. What is the distinction between the historic Métis and the pan-Métis?

9. Discuss the social impact of legal definitions of Aboriginal people.

10. What was the significance and outcome of the *Lavell* and *Bedard* cases?

WEBLINKS

www.bloorstreet.com/200block/sindact.htm

This website reproduces the entire *Indian Act*, with helpful notes explaining the provisions. It should be noted that this is the current version of the *Indian Act*, a piece of legislation that has been changed many times since its inception in 1876.

www.abo-peoples.org/programs/dnlsc-31.html

An argumentative essay by Harry Daniels of the Congress of Aboriginal Peoples on *Bill C-31* and its impact on Aboriginal identity. The author labels the legislation "the Abocide Bill."

www.metisnation.ca

The Canadian Métis National Council is a national organization representing Métis peoples across Canada. The site also provides current press releases, conferences, research, arts and culture, and links to regional and provincial councils.

NOTES

1. When discussions about who could be a member of a band took place between Government and First Nation communities, each community was given the opportunity to establish criteria to define who could be a member of a band. What is interesting is that at the beginning of the 21st century, the reintroduction of "blood quantum" would be used by First Nations' groups such as the Maliseet and Mi'kmaq to define an Indian.

2. In 1982 the *British North America Act* was changed to the *Constitution Act, 1867*. An attempt is made in this book to distinguish between the two names by using the *British North America Act* when citing legislation passed under the Act or references made to it before 1982, and by using the *Constitution Act, 1867* for any references thereafter.

3. *Indian Act*, R.A., c. 1–6, amended by c. 10 (2nd Supp.) 1974–75–76, c. 1/8. 1978 (Hull: Minister of Supply and Services Canada: 6–8).

4. One of the major concerns that DIAND had with regard to the changes in Section 12(1)(b) of the *Indian Act* was the financial cost. In a once-secret document of DIAND entitled "Amendments to Remove Discriminatory Sections of the *Indian Act*," the estimates ran from $312 to $557 million. These figures were based on estimates of the number of women who would be reinstated as Indian and the percentage who would return to the reserves; the low estimate allowed for a 30 percent reinstatement and a 30 percent return while the high estimate predicted a 100 percent reinstatement and a 70 percent return rate. In addition, approximately 57 000 children would be eligible for reinstatement.

A Cabinet discussion paper released in 1982 showed that settling land claims in the next 15 years could cost the government as much as $4.1 billion. About $1.8 billion of these claims concerns land in British Columbia, where the fewest treaties were signed; most of the rest would be divided between Aboriginals in the two territories. The $4.1 billion includes reparation for hunting and fishing rights, payment for land, and the implementation of various programs and other benefits. In addition, another $500 million could be spent by the government in the next 20 years to settle specific claims (*Indian News*, Vol. 22, No. 7, October 1981:7).

5. For a more thorough statement regarding the status of the Métis in Canada, the reader should consult "Native Rights: Policy and Practices," *Perception,* 4(2) (November/December 1981). Sawchuk (1998) provides an accessible and more contemporary account of Aboriginal—especially Métis—political organizing, lobbying, and activities. Much of the present information comes from this source.

6. In 1939 Quebec Premier Maurice Duplessis was able to get Northern Quebec Inuit redefined as Indians so that they came under federal, instead of provincial, control (Richardson, 1972).

7. Numbers were stamped on small metal discs that Inuit could carry with them for identification.

8. However, other groups have now decided that this is a politically useful term and it now has symbolic uses that far exceed its original definition (Siggner, 1998). In addition to the above, the reader should be aware that different definitions are presented by agencies collecting data on the ethnic makeup of our population. Statistics Canada, for example, makes a distinction between ethnic identity and ethnic origin when it collects data. On the other hand, when the Department of Indian Affairs collects data, it is only interested in those individuals who have legal status. Finally, individuals can have more than one ethnic affiliation or origin. This means that allowances in the data collection must be aware of single and multiple ethnic affiliations. Thus, again, some data collection agencies will take these aspects into consideration when collecting data (Eschbach, Supple & Snipp, 1998; Kreager, 1997).

chapter three

Profile of Aboriginal People I:
Population and Health

INTRODUCTION

Until the mid-1950s it was still believed that Aboriginal people were destined to disappear. Their numbers had decreased, they were marginalized and largely residing on isolated reserves. However, since that time, Aboriginal people have increased their population nearly five times. How did this happen? What were the mortality and fertility rates? Have they retained their traditional way of life? What is the future for this group?

To answer these and other questions, one needs to understand the demography of a population. Demography is the study of populations, their size, distribution and change. It provides us with an understanding of how societies and groups change over time. It examines how changes in a population act upon and change culture and society. It is also useful for helping us to understand enduring conflicts and competing interests within and among societies. Finally, demographic information will provide the context in which governments make policy and program decisions regarding Aboriginal people.

To ensure up-to-date information, every 10 years a census is undertaken that collects data from every Canadian. This systematic collection of data allows governments (federal, provincial, and municipal) to assess their policies as well as project into the future what programs will be required if they are to address the problems facing people. At the same time, the Department of Indian and Northern Affairs Canada (INAC) also collects information on Aboriginal people. Unfortunately the census data differ widely from the INAC data in their definition of an Aboriginal and their method of enumeration. As a result, statistics coming from one agency are not strictly comparable with statistics from the other. Needless to say, the lack of standardized data confuses policy makers and poses problems for short-term trend analyses while at the same time making future projections difficult. Moreover, because the definition of an Indian has changed over time, statistics reported by the same agency show wide discrepancies.

Our profile of Aboriginal people in Canada will begin with a discussion of residential patterns and then move to population size and growth, including births, deaths and migration. We also will look at the health factors that impinge upon population growth and will conclude with an analysis of infrastructure related to health issues (LaChance-Brulotte, 1984).

RESIDENTIAL PATTERNS

Where do Aboriginal people live? They reside in all parts of Canada, although they are not evenly distributed. Figure 3.1 reveals the geographical dispersion of First Nation communities across Canada. Tables 3.1, 3.2, and 3.3 reveal the regional dispersion of Aboriginal people over time. The data show that, while the overall status Indian population has increased all over Canada, the biggest gains were in Saskatchewan and Alberta. Approximately one-fourth live in Ontario, and another 16 percent in each of Saskatchewan and British Columbia. Other Western provinces show similar numbers, while much smaller numbers reside in Quebec and Atlantic Canada. Tables 3.2 and 3.3 identify the on- and off-reserve Indian population by region. In 1988, nearly 65 percent of status Indians lived on the reserve. The percentage living on reserves has decreased over the years, with just under 60 percent of the population remaining on lands set aside for First Nations people and held in trust by Ottawa. Less than half of the Yukon Indians live on reserves, Crown lands, or settlements, while in the Northwest Territories over 80 percent are "on reserve." Within the provinces, Saskatchewan reveals the lowest percentage, while Quebec shows nearly three-fourths of its Indian population on reserve. It is estimated that by 2017 there will be substantial increases in the on-reserve population for the Prairies.

When we focus on the off-reserve population, we see that all regions have experienced increases. However, the largest increases were in Saskatchewan and Alberta, with Quebec having the lowest. As we predict the future, the data suggest that Alberta as well as Manitoba will continue to have substantial increases in off-reserve Indians. When we focus on the geographical distribution of Métis and non-status Indians in 2005, we find that about 29 percent of the enumerated Métis live in Alberta while an additional 42 percent live in the other two Prairie provinces. Focusing on non-status Indians, we find that 40 percent live in Ontario while an additional 30 percent are in British Columbia.

Reserves

Canada has some 2720 reserves, though this number, like the number of bands (614), varies over time according to the policy of the federal government. Reserves also vary in size. Although there is no minimum area, 71.5 hectares per person is the maximum (the Blood reserve—900 square kilometres—in Alberta is the largest in the country) while some reserves in British Columbia cover only a few hectares. In Eastern Canada each band is generally limited to one reserve, while in the West one band may encompass several reserves. British Columbia has over 1600 reserves but fewer than 200 bands (Allan, 1943; Siggner and Locatelli, 1980).

Clearly, the reserve/settlement still provides security and roots for many Aboriginal people. These rural-based communities are where the majority of Aboriginals have grown

FIGURE 3.1 | First Nations Communities

First Nations Communities

First Nations Community

TABLE 3.1   Registered Indian Population by Region, 1966–2006

Region	1966 No.	%	1976 No.	%	1986 No.	%	1996 No.	%	2001 No.	%	2006 No.	%
Atlantic	8 494	3.8	10 891	3.8	16 460	4.1	21 835	3.8	23 398	3.8	41 800	5.3
Quebec	23 186	10.3	29 580	10.2	40 200	10.0	53 280	9.3	56 125	9.0	76 500	9.7
Ontario	52 408	23.4	64 690	22.4	91 250	22.6	126 755	22.1	134 372	21.6	175 600	22.3
Manitoba	31 000	13.8	42 311	14.6	59 064	14.7	84 684	14.8	93 020	14.9	112 200	14.2
Saskatchewan	31 362	14.0	43 404	15.0	62 232	15.5	93 250	16.3	105 830	17.0	107 100	13.6
Alberta	25 432	11.3	34 130	11.8	44 653	12.3	75 954	13.2	84 684	13.6	105 400	13.4
B.C.	46 543	20.8	53 342	18.5	69 822	17.3	96 472	16.8	102 552	16.5	146 500	18.6
Yukon	7 300	1.0	3 181	1.1	4 626	1.1	7 133	1.2	7 602	1.2	5 739	2.6
N.W.T.			7 409	2.6	9 735	2.4	13 906	2.4	15 318	2.5	13 700	1.9
Canada	224 164	100	288 938	100	403 042	100	573 269	100	622 901	100	786 400	100

(Note: In 1966 the figure 7 300 / 1.0 is a combined total for Yukon and N.W.T.)

Sources: Adapted from 1966–1989: *Indian Register*, DIAND; 1996–2001: *Population Projections of Registered Indians, 1986–2011*, DIAND, 1990; *Projections of the Aboriginal Populations, Canadian Provinces and Territories, 2001–2017*, Statistics Canada, 2005.

TABLE 3.2 — Registered Indian Population On-Reserve by Region, 1966–2005

Region	1966 No.	%	1976 No.	%	1986 No.	%	1996 No.	%	2001 No.	%	2005 No.	%
Atlantic	6 444	75.9	8 066	74.1	11 341	69.2	13 905	63.7	14 775	63.1	18 810	60.7
Quebec	18 720	80.7	24 198	81.8	32 137	79.9	38 238	71.8	40 223	71.7	46 709	67.9
Ontario	36 508	69.7	44 227	68.4	59 000	64.7	72 229	57.0	76 339	56.8	79 979	48.1
Manitoba	26 752	86.3	31 723	75.0	42 324	71.5	55 115	65.1	60 648	65.2	75 075	61.8
Saskatchewan	26 920	85.8	30 746	70.8	39 973	64.2	56 442	60.5	64 162	60.6	58 419	48.7
Alberta	22 573	88.8	26 841	78.6	35 798	72.1	48 656	64.1	54 630	64.5	59 788	61.8
B.C.	37 019	79.5	34 073	63.9	43 267	62.0	54 327	56.3	57 805	56.4	58 415	48.7
Yukon	5 482	95.5	2 620	82.4	3 023	65.3	3 905	54.7	4 182	55.0		
N.W.T.			7 143	96.4	8 978	92.2	11 562	83.1	12 750	83.2	–	–
Canada	180 418	80.5	209 637	72.6	275 891	68.5	354 379	61.8	385 514	61.9	397 980	53.2

On-reserve includes Crown lands and settlements. Percentages are based on regional totals shown in Table 3.1.

Sources: 1966-1989: *Indian Register*, DIAND; 1996-2001: *Population Projections of Registered Indians, 1986-2011*, DIAND, 1990; Statistics Canada, 2005.

TABLE 3.3	Registered Indian Population Off-Reserve by Region, 1966–2005														
	1966*		1976		1986		1996		2001		2005			
Region	No.	%	No.	%	No.	%	No.	%	No.	%	No	%		
Atlantic	2 050	24.1	2 825	25.9	5 069	30.8	7 930	36.3	8 623	36.9	12 141	39.2		
Quebec	4 466	19.3	5 382	18.2	8 063	20.1	15 041	28.2	15 902	28.3	20 503	29.8		
Ontario	15 900	30.3	20 463	31.6	32 250	35.3	54 526	43.0	58 032	43.2	84 581	50.9		
Manitoba	4 248	13.7	10 588	25.0	16 740	28.3	29 570	34.9	32 372	34.8	44 598	36.7		
Saskatchewan	4 442	14.2	12 658	29.2	22 259	35.8	36 809	39.5	41 669	39.4	59 730	49.7		
Alberta	2 859	11.2	7 289	21.4	13 855	27.9	27 298	35.9	30 054	35.5	34 033	35.6		
B.C.	9 524	20.5	19 269	36.1	26 555	38.0	42 145	43.7	44 747	43.6	61 263	51.0		
Yukon	257	4.5	561	17.6	1 603	34.7	3 228	45.3	3 420	45.0				
N.W.T.			266	3.6	757	7.7	2 343	16.8	2 568	16.8	–	–		
Canada	43 746	19.5	79 301	27.4	127 151	31.5	218 890	38.2	237 387	38.1	326 188	43.6		

Percentages are based on regional totals shown in Table 3.1. * In 1966, numbers include 274 individuals with unstated places of residence distributed as follows: Atlantic 5, Quebec 24, Ontario 51, Manitoba 12, Saskatchewan 33, Alberta 69, B.C. 56, Yukon and N.W.T. 24.

Sources: 1966–1989: *Indian Register*, DIAND; 1996–2001: *Population Projections of Registered Indians, 1986–2011*, DIAND, 1990; Statistics Canada, 2005.

up, among family and friends. Even for those who leave, it continues to provide a haven from the pressures of Euro-Canadian urban society. These factors, combined with the prejudicial attitudes of non-Aboriginal culture, create a strong internal pull and external push toward remaining or returning to the reserve. Even if an increasing number of Aboriginal people leave the reserve, the absolute population of those who remain will still show a sizeable increase. This could pose a number of issues for Canada. Reserves are potential hotbeds of political and social discontent. In addition, if First Nations on reserves become economically developed, they could pose a competitive threat to some Canadian corporate structures. Already, in Western Canada, First Nations have angered local businesspeople by building housing developments and strip malls, and by proposing casinos on reserve lands close to major cities.

Reserves are situated in a variety of geographical contexts that have significant implications for development potential, population mobility, and transportation routes. Indian and Northern Affairs Canada has characterized First Nations' communities in four ways: urban, rural, remote, and special access. Reserves/settlements within 50 kilometres of a service centre are considered urban. Rural is a zone where the reserve/settlement is located between 50 and 350 kilometres from a service centre. A remote reserve/settlement is located beyond the 350-kilometre limit but is accessible by a year-round road. The special access designation is for any First Nations community that has no year-round road connecting it to a service centre (Siggner, 1980).

Table 3.4 shows the distribution and proportion of Aboriginal people in each of the designated zones. While a majority of people live in urban and rural zones, considerable numbers live in remote and special access reserves. The data show that over one-third of

TABLE 3.4	On-Reserve Registered Indians by Region and DIAND Geographic Zone, 2001			
	Geographic zone			
Region	Urban & Rural %	Remote %	Special Access %	Total Number
Atlantic	100%	0.0	0.0	17 412
Quebec	71.2	17.9	10.9	44 856
Ontario	73.2	0.0	26.8	79 574
Manitoba	70.2	0.0	29.8	69 689
Saskatchewan	92.9	1.7	5.5	55 340
Alberta	93.0	0.0	7.0	58 026
B.C.	78.4	6.4	15.2	56 895
Yukon	60.4	32.5	7.0	3 908
N.W.T.	54.5	8.5	37.0	10 871
CANADA	79.4	3.7	16.9	396 571

On-reserve includes Crown lands and settlements. Excludes Cree and Naskapi bands in Quebec.

Sources: Adapted from *Basic Departmental Data*, 2002, pp. 40, Indian and Northern Affairs Canada.

TABLE 3.5 Registered Indian Population and Indian Lands, by Region, 2002

	Atlantic Provinces	Quebec	Ontario	Manitoba	Sask.	Alberta	B.C.	N.W.T.	Yukon	Canada
Total Indian population	28 819	65 496	159 107	112 430	111 635	89 812	114 120	15 586	7 846	704 851
% of total Indian population	4.0	10.0	22.3	14.8	15.6	12.6	17.2	2.3	1.1	100.0
% of total provincial/ territorial population	0.6	0.5	0.9	4.9	5.4	1.9	2.2	17.2	16.5	1.4
% living off-reserve	28.8	20.3	36.1	28.3	36.0	28.1	38.6	7.7	42.0	31.9
Number of Indian bands	33	39	126	62	70	44	198	16	26	614
% of Indian bands	5.2	6.6	21.3	10.1	11.5	6.9	33.1	2.4	2.9	100.0
Number of reserves and settlements	67	33	185	103	142	90	1610	29	25	2284
% of reserves and settlements	2.9	1.4	8.1	4.5	6.2	3.9	70.5	1.3	1.1	100.0
Approximate area of reserves (hectares)	31 800	85 450	736 210	235 120	645 010	725 010	372 300	–	–	2 830 900

Source: Adapted from *Registered Indian Population by Sex and Residence 2002*, Ottawa, 2003 (Ct. No. R31-3/2002E.).

the First Nations people in Manitoba and over one-quarter in Ontario live on reserves that have no road access to a service centre. A substantial number in Quebec and British Columbia reside in special access areas. On the other hand, fewer than 20 percent of Aboriginal persons in Alberta and Saskatchewan live in either remote or special access areas. Data gathered by Indian Affairs reveals that the pattern of residence has not changed substantially over the past two decades. When we look at just Inuit, we find that 90 percent live in remote areas and only 10 percent are considered urban although many live in small villages and towns.

The changes over time that are discernable reveal an increasing number of urban First Nations people (35 to 37 percent) and those living in rural areas (40 to 44 percent). At the same time there has been a decrease in the number living in remote and special access areas (5 to 2 percent and 21 to 18 percent respectively). These reserve lands make up a little less than 3 million hectares of land. The total area of reserve lands per capita has decreased over the past 20 years, although in the past five years, through major comprehensive land claims settlements, there has been an increase in the actual land base. For example, in the first five years of the 21st century, approximately 25 land claims have been settled, and additional lands added to the existing inventory. However, because of the high population growth, per capita allocations are less today than they were previously. In 1959, across Canada, there were 13 hectares per capita; but by 2001, there were only 12.6 hectares per capita (see also Table 3.5). The exceptions to this are in the North and in recent comprehensive treaty settlements, where Aboriginals have signed agreements with the federal government that give them control over vast areas of land.

Indian Bands

Nearly all registered (status) Indians are affiliated with one of the current 614 bands. A band is a group of Aboriginal people who share a common interest in land and money and whose historical connection is defined by the federal government (see Box 3.1). However, it is important to point out that the term "band" is also a political term; it is arbitrarily imposed on registered Indians, regardless of cultural differences, for the government's administrative purposes. The Ministry of Indian Affairs can create and do away with band designations, so that the number of bands often varies from year to year (See Table 3.6).

When the federal government first divided various Indian tribes into bands, it showed very little concern for the impact of these divisions on Aboriginal culture. For example, some tribes were matrilineal, tracing descent through the mother's side, while others were patrilineal. Yet, when the band system was established, tribes were arbitrarily thrown together, and all were treated as patrilineal. This produced serious social disorganization and a wide-ranging disruption of tribal culture.

At present, nearly 400 000 First Nations people live on reserves; the largest is the Six Nations band, near Brantford, Ontario, with a population of 8200. Each band is administered by one of 87 agencies across Canada; the Caughnawaga agency handles only one band, and the New Westminster agency handles 32. The average size of Indian bands in Canada has increased to approximately 500 people; in 1950 the average was 200. If we look at the size of communities of First Nations and Inuit south of the 60th parallel, we find that 43 percent live in communities of less than 400, 34 percent in communities between 401 and 1,000, 21 percent in communities between 1001 and 3000 people and only 2 percent living in communities larger than 3000.

Box 3.1	Bands

The band is a basic form of local residential group in traditional simple hunting and gathering societies all around the world. Before European colonization Canada had 26 band-organized societies: these included the Inuit, several Athapaskan (Dene) societies, several northern Algonquian societies, and the Beothuk. The local bands were essentially several families, usually from about 20 to 50 people, who lived and worked together in a co-operative and egalitarian way with extensive sharing of food. The size and composition of these local groups fluctuated according to such factors as availability of game and movements related to marriages. In the annual round of hunting, fishing, and plant gathering, it was common for several of these local bands to get together once or twice a year for festivals such as the powwow and sundance, involving several hundred people. Today the Canadian government uses the term "band" to describe the local unit of administration by Indian and Northern Affairs Canada. These units include the dozens of more complex Native societies that were traditionally organized not as bands but as tribes or chiefdoms. There are over 600 of these modern administrative bands, which function as small Native municipalities and are managed by elected band councils according to the laws of the *Indian Act* of Canada. These bands do not always coincide with the cultural and linguistic groupings of Native people.

Source: René R. Gadacz, *The Canadian Encyclopedia 2000*, World Edition. McClelland and Stewart: Toronto. Reproduced with permission.

Table 3.7 reveals the 20 largest bands in Canada and shows that while the size of the land base has increased slightly, the population base is increasing at a much faster rate. These figures also demonstrate that managing bands has become a major activity for First Nations as their size increases and the complexity of operating them is beginning to equal that of small towns.

POPULATION SIZE

It is crucial for policy and program analysts to have information regarding the size of the Aboriginal population they are dealing with. They must also be clear about the growth rate. The figures in Table 3.8 show a five-fold increase in the absolute size of the registered Indian population over the past century. During the same time period, however, the First Nations population has come to constitute a larger portion of the total population, increasing from 2.5 percent in 1881 to 3.8 percent in 2004. During the 1950s the natural rate of increase for registered Indians was 3 percent. While this rate increased to 3.4 percent by the late 1960s, it once again decreased to 2.8 percent in the early 1970s, where it remained until the mid-1980s (Canada, 1985b) when *Bill C-31* was implemented. Table 3.9 shows how the total Aboriginal population in 2001 broke down into various subcategories.

TABLE 3.6 | Numerical and Percentage Distribution of Indian Bands by Size and Geographic Location, for Regions

Region	Distribution of Bands by Population Size						Distribution of Bands by Geographic Location							
							Remote		Rural		Semi-Urban		Urban	
	100	100-499	500-999	1000-1999	2000+	Total	No.	%	No.	%	No.	%	No.	%
Atlantic	11	17	3	2	–	33	–	–	13	45	10	34	6	21
Québec	15	16	5	7	1	44	14	36	5	13	15	38	5	13
Ontario	39	54	20	5	3	121	34	30	52	45	21	18	8	7
Manitoba	11	27	12	11	1	62	25	44	26	46	5	9	1	2
Saskatchewan	7	44	16	2	1	70	10	15	43	63	13	19	2	3
Alberta	9	13	11	3	5	41	7	17	19	46	12	29	3	7
B.C.	98	85	14	2	–	199	53	27	77	40	41	21	23	12
N.W.T.	17	–	–	–	–	17	8	–	7	–	1	–	–	–
Yukon	14	–	–	–	–	14	13	–	–	–	–	–	1	–
Canada	221	256	81	32	11	601	164	29	242	42	118	21	49	9

Sources: Statistics Division, *Registered Indian Population by Sex and Residence, 1977* (Ottawa: Program Reference Centre, IIAP, 1979); Ponting and Gibbins, 1980, 35; Perreault, J., L. Paquette and M. George, *Population of Registered Indians, 1981-1986* (Ottawa: INAC, 1985).

TABLE 3.7	The Twenty Largest Bands in Canada, December 31, 2004	
Band	Region	Indian Register Population
Six Nations of the Grand River[1]	Ontario	22 924
Mohawks of Akwesasne	Ontario	10 013
Blood	Alberta	9 956
Kahnawake	Québec	10 201
Saddle Lake	Alberta	8,234
Lac La Ronge	Saskatchewan	7 965
Peguis	Manitoba	7 338
Mohawks of the Bay of Quinte	Ontario	7 720
Peter Ballantyne Cree Nation	Saskatchewan	7 589
Wikwemikong	Ontario	6 909
Fort Alexander	Manitoba	6 678
Cross Lake First Nation	Manitoba	6 214
Bigstone Cree Nation	Alberta	6 237
Samson	Alberta	6 249
Norway House Cree Nation	Manitoba	5 936
Siksika Nation	Alberta	5 785
Oneida Nation of the Thames	Ontario	5 013
Sandy Bay	Manitoba	4 933
Nisichawayasihk Cree Nation	Manitoba	5 013
Montagnais du Lac St-Jean	Québec	4 874

1 Six Nations of the Grand River consists of the following 13 Registry Groups: Bay of Quinte Mohawk, Bearfoot Onondaga, Delaware, Konadaha Seneca, Lower Cayuga, Lower Mohawk, Niharondasa Seneca, Oneida, Onondaga Clear Sky, Tuscarora, Upper Cayuga, Upper Mohawk, Walker Mohawk

Source: Updated and adapted from *Registered Indian Population by Sex and Residence, 2002*, pp. xiv, Indian and Northern Affairs Canada.

POPULATION GROWTH

With the introduction of *Bill C-31* in 1985, the registered Indian growth rate increased to over 7 percent and averaged well in excess of 6 percent until the 1990s, when it decreased to about 2 percent. These growth rates must be compared to the general Canadian growth rate of about 1 percent over the past decade. The overall Aboriginal population (Indian, Métis, and Inuit) is growing very fast; it is estimated that by 2017 it will be in excess of 1.3 million (See Figure 3.2). Figure 3.2 shows the age distribution of registered Indians in 2000 with an average growth rate. It shows that the proportion of males and females under the age of 18 is similar for both on- and off-reserve populations.

TABLE 3.8	Population of Registered Indians in Canada, 1881–2001
Year	Registered Indian Population
1881	108 547
1901	127 941
1929	108 012
1939	118 378
1949	136 407
1954	151 558
1961	191 709
1971	257 619
1981	323 782
1986	403 042
1991	521 461
1992	531 981
1996	573 269
2001	622 901
2006 (estimated)	713,100

Sources: Information Canada, *Perspective Canada I* (Ottawa: Queen's Printer, 1974), 240; *Perspective Canada II* (Ottawa: Queen's Printer, 1977), 282; Siggner (1986), 3; *Native Agenda News,* March, 1992; T. Courchene and L. Powell, *A First Nations Province,* Queens University, Institute of Intergovernmental Relations, Kingston, Ontario, 1995, 20; *Registered Indian Population by Sex and Residence,* 2002, Ottawa.

TABLE 3.9	Aboriginal Identity Population in 2001		
In the Census of 2001, the following figures were obtained			
Aboriginal Identity Population	Total	Male	Female
North American Indian	608 850	294 435	314 415
Métis	292 310	146 180	146 130
Inuit	45 070	22 560	22 510
Multiple Abor. Response	6 660	3 140	3 525
Abor. Response elsewhere	23 415	10 390	13 025
Registered Indian	558 175	268 430	289 745

Source: Adapted from information in *Aboriginal Peoples Survey, 2001,* Catalogue No. 89-592-XWE, Ottawa, Statistics Canada.

However, when we look at the 18–64 age group, there are significantly more registered women than men living off reserve (see Figure 3.3). We also find that projections for the number of Métis will increase substantially in the next decade, although for Inuit

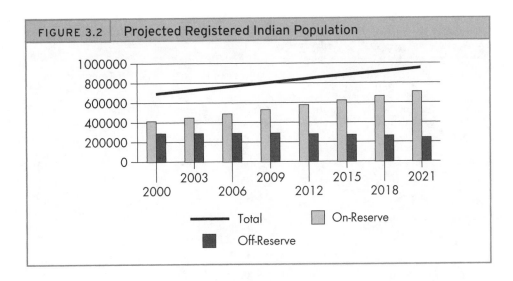

FIGURE 3.2 | Projected Registered Indian Population

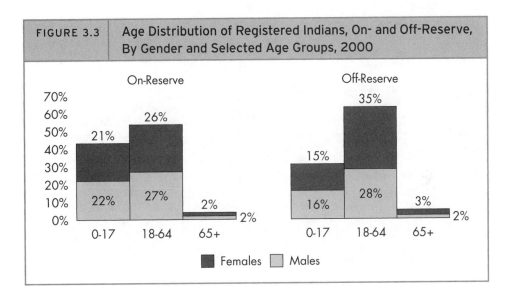

FIGURE 3.3 | Age Distribution of Registered Indians, On- and Off-Reserve, By Gender and Selected Age Groups, 2000

the increase will be larger. It has grown nearly twice the size since 1981 and similar increases are expected over the next decade.

In summary, demographers predict that status Indians and Inuit will continue to have higher growth rates than the Canadian population for several decades. Table 3.10 identifies the registered Indian population and average annual growth rates for both on- and off-reserve.

Other data show that the growth rates are extremely high, as the population more than doubled in size since 1966. The estimated registered Indian population as we entered the 21st century was nearly 700 000. These data also show that in 1966, 80 percent of the Indians lived on a reserve; by 1990, this had decreased to 60 percent (Piche and George, 1973; Basic Departmental Data, 2002).

TABLE 3.10	Population Growth of Status Indians: Total, On and Off Reserve, 1981-2001					
	Total Status Indians, Both sexes		On-Reserve Indians, Both Sexes		Off-Reserve Indians, Both Sexes	
Year	Total Population	Growth Rate	Total Population	Growth Rate	Total Population	Growth Rate
1981	336 900	–	237 600	–	99 300	–
1982	345 400	2.52	245 900	3.49	99 500	0.20
1983	354 400	2.61	253 300	3.01	101 100	1.61
1984	364 700	2.91	261 000	3.04	103 700	2.57
1985	376 400	3.21	268 000	2.68	108 400	4.53
1986	403 042	7.08	275 891	2.94	127 151	17.30
1987	431 439	7.05	282 671	2.46	148 768	17.00
1988	458 807	6.34	291 485	3.12	167 322	12.47
1989	485 186	5.75	299 869	2.88	185 317	10.75
1990	510 905	5.30	308 727	2.95	202 178	9.10
1991	521 461	2.07	316 273	2.44	205 188	1.49
1992	531 981	2.02	323 855	2.40	208 126	1.43
1993	542 426	1.96	331 457	2.35	210 970	1.37
1994	552 799	1.91	339 070	2.30	213 729	1.31
1995	563 082	1.86	346 711	2.25	216 371	1.24
1996	573 269	1.81	354 379	2.21	218 890	1.16
1997	583 356	1.76	360 599	1.76	222 757	1.77
1998	593 346	1.71	366 808	1.72	226 538	1.70
1999	603 271	1.67	373 027	1.70	230 245	1.64
2000	613 117	1.63	379 258	1.67	233 860	1.57
2001	622 901	1.60	385 514	1.65	237 387	1.51

Source: Adapted from the Statistics Canada "Aboriginal Peoples Survey," 2001.

The Federal *Bill C-31* restored Indian status and membership rights to individuals and their children who lost them because of discriminatory clauses—e.g., 12(1)(b)—in the previous *Indian Act*. Table 2.2 in the previous chapter showed the Indian population changes with and without *Bill C-31* additions. At the outset fewer than 2000 people were reinstated. However, by 1989 these new registrants represented nearly 15 percent of the total registered Indian population, and it is estimated that by 2010 they will make up nearly one-fifth of the total population. The data show that the natural annual growth rate has consistently exceeded 2 percent. However, when *Bill C-31* Indians are added to the figures, the growth rate increases to an astounding 6 percent (Paquette and Perreault, 1984; INAC, 2003).

Three factors affect the overall growth rate of the Aboriginal population: the birth and death rate, and the rate at which people lose or gain Indian status. The natural increase (births minus deaths) for the Aboriginal population has been declining over the past 30 years because of a rapidly declining birth rate and a reduced mortality rate. For example, in 1921 the crude birth rate for Aboriginal people was over 5.0 per 1000 population. By the 1970s this rate had decreased to 2.85, and by 2017 it is expected to be 2.35, but still nearly double the national average. Romaniuc (2003) has noted that the decline in the birth rate can be deduced from looking at the child:population ratio. The ratio of children under five years of age to the total Indian population fell from 19 percent in 1961 to 12 percent in 2001. Further evidence of fertility decline can be inferred from the average number of children born to never-married women 20–24 years of age. This was 2.3 in 1961 but fell to less than 1.5 in 2001. At the same time, the number of childless never-married women in the age category 20–24 went up from 11 percent in 1961 to 29 percent in 2001. When we compare fertility rates for on-reserve Indians and the general Canadian population for women aged 15–49, we find substantial differences. In 1986, on-reserve women had 3.2 children, while in the general Canadian population the number was 1.67. By 2004 Aboriginal women had decreased to 2.7 children while the overall Canadian number decreased to 1.57.

The birth rate is significantly influenced by the average age of marriage. Although, overall, the proportion of married Indians is lower than the national average, the proportion of married Indians in the highest-fertility age group of 20 to 24 exceeds that of non-Indians. Moreover, the fertility of Indians between 20 and 24 appears to be twice the Canadian average.

The average number of children by age group also reflects changes that have taken place in Aboriginal communities. In 2000 Aboriginal women had an average of 3.23 children, compared to 1.57 for non-Aboriginal women. When controlling for age, we find that the older Aboriginal women (65 and over) had 6.2 children during their child-bearing years (3.0 for non-Aboriginal women), with 6.0 children for Aboriginal women 45–64 (3.2 for non-Aboriginal women of this age). It is projected that in 2021, the fertility rate will decrease to 2.71 for on-reserve women (still twice as high as non-Aboriginal women) and 1.63 for off-reserve women (nearly equal to the non-Aboriginal women). There are, however, considerable regional variations in Aboriginal birth rates. Aboriginal women living in Eastern Canada have similar fertility rates to those of non-Aboriginal women, while Aboriginal women in the Prairies have much higher rates.

The second factor in determining the growth rate of a population is the mortality rate. Traditionally, the mortality rates for Aboriginal people have been very high, with life expectancy less than half that for a non-Aboriginal person. By 1960, an Aboriginal's expected life span had increased to 60 years (while for a non-Aboriginal it was 69) and it remained there until the 1980s.

Figure 3.4 shows the life expectancies at birth for status Indians and all Canadians by sex. It shows that the general trend of increasing life expectancy continues. Nevertheless, the data show that non-Indians still live longer than status Indians. While the gap remains, it is narrowing; and the data show that by the 21st century the life expectancy for Indian men was 70 versus 76 for non-Aboriginal men, and for women, 77 versus 83.

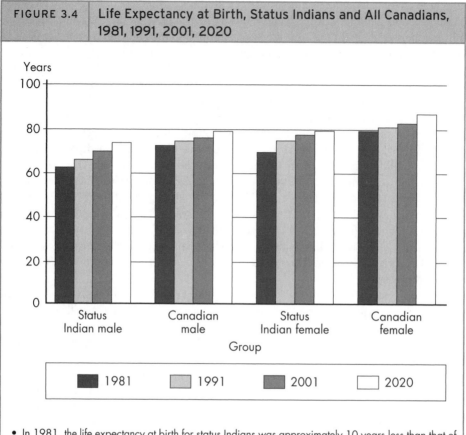

| FIGURE 3.4 | Life Expectancy at Birth, Status Indians and All Canadians, 1981, 1991, 2001, 2020 |

- In 1981, the life expectancy at birth for status Indians was approximately 10 years less than that of the national population, the same as it had been 20 years earlier. Projections for the next decade reveal similar gaps. However, life expectancy at birth for status Indians is increasing and will continue to increase. Between 1981 and 2020, the life expectancy at birth for status Indians is projected to increase by 5 years for both sexes. While the gap is narrowing it is projected that by 2020 the life expectancy for status Indians will still be 5 years less than that for other Canadians.

Sources: *Highlights of Aboriginal Conditions, 1981-2001, Part II, Social Conditions*, p. 5, Indian and Northern Affairs Canada, Statistics Canada, 2005; *Health Policy Research Bulletin*, Health Canada, 2003.

The average age at death is markedly lower for Aboriginal persons than the national average. As Table 3.11 shows, for Aboriginal persons the average age at death is 54, and for non-Aboriginal persons, 72. Recent data show that, while Aboriginal life expectancy has increased to 69 for males and 76 for females, it still remains over six years less than that for the average Canadian. Overall standardized death rates in 1981 show that for Indians it was 9.2 per 1000 compared to just 6 among the total Canadian population. In 2000, the Aboriginal mortality rates were up to almost 1.5 times higher than the national rates. Infant mortality (deaths of babies before the age of one) is perhaps an even more important factor in determining the growth rate of the population. The number of First Nations deaths per 1000 live births was nearly 80 in 1960. However, this decreased to 11.6 in 2003, while the Canadian rate was 6.5.

TABLE 3.11	Specific Measures of Mortality Among Registered Canadian Indians and Among Canadians as a Whole				
		A Crude Death Rate	B Infant Mortality Rate	C Average Age at Death	D Male Life Expectancy	E Female Life Expectancy
1960	Indians	10.9	79.0	–	59.7	63.5
	All Canadians	8.0	27.3	68.5	74.3	
1965	Indians	8.7	52.6	36.0	60.5	65.6
	All Canadians	7.5	23.6	64.0	68.8	75.2
1970	Indians	7.5	43.2*	42.0	60.2	66.2
	All Canadians	7.5	18.8	66.0	69.3	76.4
1976	Indians	7.5	32.1	43.0	–	–
	All Canadians	7.4	16.0	67.0		
1981	Indians	9.5	22.0	45.2	62.0	69.0
	All Canadians	6.1	10.0	69.0	72.0	78.0
1991	Indians	9.2	13.0	54.0	68.0	73.1
	All Canadians	6.0	8.0	72.1	74.0	80.0
2001	Indians	8.0	–	70.4	75.5	–
	All Canadians	5.3	6.5	82.1	–	–

Due to the difficulty of obtaining data, the data in any given cell may be for a different year than for that shown. The difference is never more than two years and usually only one, and in any such cases of discrepancy the data are more recent than the date shown.

* This figure is an average of the rates for 1969 and 1971, since the 1970 data are unreliable due to incomplete reporting that year.

A Death per 1000 population.
B Deaths of children in first year of life per 1000 live births.
C Sum of the age at death of all persons dying in a given year divided by the number of people dying that year.
D & E Age to which a person can be expected to live, calculated at time of birth. These figures are standardized death rates.

Sources: Medical Services Branch, *Health Data Book* (Ottawa: Department of National Health and Mortality Projections of Registered Indians, 1987 to 1996, INAC 1985); *Indian and Canadian Mortality Trends*, 1991, Ottawa, Health and Welfare Canada, *Basic Departmental Data*, 2002, pp.23, 26.

In 2000, Indian Affairs showed that the potential years of life lost by cause of death for First Nations and Canadians differed significantly. Potential years of life lost is the number of years of life "lost" from a death, when a person dies "prematurely." In the case of Aboriginals, it would be defined as dying before the average age of death of 75. For example, a person who commits suicide at age 25 has lost 50 potential years of life. For Aboriginals, suicide and unintentional injuries are the leading causes of potential years of life lost. These two causes of death are leading factors and contribute to nearly 40 percent of all deaths for youth. Suicide accounted for approximately 108 potential years of life lost per 1,000 population each year (This is three times the 2001 Canadian rate). Unintentional injuries to Aboriginals contributed to 257 (per 1,000) potential years of life lost in 2000 (four and-one-half times higher than the 2001 Canadian rate). However, there are some causes of death for which Canadians have higher rates than Aboriginals do—e.g., cancer, blood diseases, nervous system and sense organs, and circulatory system illnesses (Trovato,2001).

The above discussion shows that Aboriginal people, since the turn of the century, have gone through three stages of birth–death trends. During the first half of the century the Aboriginal population was characterized by extremely high birth and death rates. Then, after World War II, the death rate decreased substantially (because of medical advances and increased sanitation and housing), although the birth rate remained high. Today we see the third phase, which is a decline in both the fertility and mortality rates. What has confounded this profile is the introduction of *Bill C-31* that changed the definition of an "Indian." We now turn to the third component in population growth, migration. However, in/out migration of Aboriginal people does not refer to them leaving or entering the country. Rather, it reflects the different definitions and self-disclosure of who is and is not an Aboriginal.

ENFRANCHISEMENT AND *BILL C-31:*
A HISTORICAL NOTE

The number of registered Indians, as demonstrated earlier, is affected by external legislation that goes well beyond fertility and mortality. As noted earlier, people have been removed from and placed on the Indian roll over the past century at the will of the Crown. It is estimated that in the first half of the 20th century approximately 50,000 status Indians lost their status through government action and inaction. Given the family size this means that an additional 250,000 descendants also lost their status as legal Indians. Sloppy bookkeeping, concern about costs and unregistered births account for this loss. Moreover, when confronted with these issues, Indian Affairs ignored or rejected the claims without any serious investigation. Between 1955 and 1982 (when the general policy of enfranchisement was phased out), an additional 13 502 adults and children (as well as all their descendants) were formally enfranchised (removed from the Indian roll and no longer defined as Indians under the *Indian Act*). Most of the enfranchisements were Indian women who married non-Indian men. Under *Bill C-31,* some of these people and their descendants have recovered their Indian status, but in a most peculiar manner (IRIW, n.d.).

Both the enfranchisement rules and the "double mother" rule in the *Indian Act* have now been changed. As early as 1980, Indian and Inuit Affairs allowed bands that wanted to opt out of the conditions of 12(1)(b) and 12(1)(a)(iv) to do so. By 1984, 103 bands had opted out of the former section, while 309 acted on the latter. When *Bill C-31* was passed in 1985, new rules prevailed. This bill was introduced in order to comply with Section 15(1) of the Canadian Charter of Rights and Freedoms. In short, any individual who was registered as an Indian and subsequently lost status due to discriminatory sections of the *Indian Act* might be reinstated. This included women who were deleted from the register upon marriage to a non-Indian (Sections 12(1)(b) and 14), individuals deleted at the age of majority because their mothers and paternal grandmothers were not Canadian Indian by birth (Sections 12(i)(a)(iv)), individuals deleted due to husbands'/fathers' enfranchisement (Sections 10 and 109), and any illegitimate children of Indian women who were deleted from the register upon proof of non-Indian paternity (Subsection 12(2)).

However, under this new change, only the first generation of those listed above are eligible for registration. Applications were to be accepted (one must apply) until the year

2003. This means that minors could achieve the age of majority and then apply if before 2003. However, first-time registration is limited to first-generation children of a reinstated individual. If these children are themselves parents at the time of registration, their children cannot be registered. Once registered, however, these children have the capacity to transmit status to any children they have thereafter. In summary, projections for the Aboriginal population suggest that the overall registered Indian population will increase until 2041, at which time it will level off at around 1 million. After that time, it is expected to decrease, and the number of registered Indians will once again change because of a new definition that was established nearly 50 years earlier.

HEALTH

The health of any people determines its size and growth over time. While disease and genocide were important forces during the 17th, 18th, and early 19th centuries, they have not played an important role in the 20th century population dynamics of Canadian Indians. However, health has been an important factor this past century. Nevertheless, the federal government believes that, with certain exceptions, it does not have any legal or fiduciary obligations with regard to health care for Aboriginal people except in certain exceptional circumstances such as Treaty 6, which explicitly refers to the provision of a "medicine chest." Aboriginals disagree and claim the right to special treatment.

Disputes between the First Nations and the federal government revolve around three issues. First is the conflict in definitions of health. Second is how health policy is implemented for Aboriginal people. Third is the funding of First Nations health services, including the statutory, constitutional, or fiduciary obligations of the federal government regarding the provision of health services to Aboriginal people (Speck, 1989). The federal government has accepted some responsibility for Aboriginal health. Under Health and Welfare Canada, approximately $600 million is spent on six major health programs: Community Health Services, Environmental Health and Surveillance, Non-Insured Health Benefits, the National Native Alcohol and Drug Abuse Program, Hospital Services, and Capital Construction. While there is no direct federal government legislation for the provision of these services, custom and historical commitment provides the basis and rationale for covering the cost of these programs.

Until 1945, the Department of Indian Affairs was the sole provider of health care services to Indians on the reserve. However, in that year the Department of Health and Welfare was created and it took over providing services to First Nations and Inuit. In 1962, Indian Health Services (a division in Health and Welfare) was merged with six other federal health programs to form a specific branch: Medical Services. In 1964, Treaty Indians were defined as insured persons under provincial medicare. By 1970, the present structure of Indian Health Services was in place, although the 1974 *Lalonde Report* for the federal government first set the stage for the transfer of health care away from the federal government. This policy document reiterated that no statutory or treaty obligations exist to provide health services to Indians, but the federal government wanted to ensure that health services would be provided to Indians and Inuit when normal provincial services were not available. In 1979, a new Indian Health Policy was enacted to ensure that the needed community development would take place. It was at this time that the Medical Services Branch started to work toward transferring management of health services to First Nations. See Box 3.2 for a discussion of the Aboriginal Healing Foundation.

Box 3.2	The Aboriginal Healing Foundation

As part of the settlement of the residential school abuses, the federal government established the Aboriginal Healing Foundation in 1998 with a budget of $400M. Once the funds have been spent, there will be no additional funds provided by the federal government. Participants in the program include Métis, Inuit, and First Nations people. Over the past decade, the Foundation developed and supported programs to help Aboriginal people build and reinforce sustainable healing processes. These programs have taken different approaches (e.g., Aboriginal, Western) to "heal" those individuals who experienced abuse in the school system. Four volumes have now been published identifying the results of the work of the Foundation. For more details, the reader should consult the following: Kishk Anaquot Health Research, 2001, *An Interim Evaluation Report of Aboriginal Healing Foundation Program Activity*, Ottawa, Aboriginal Healing Foundation; Journey and Balance: *Second Interim Evaluation Report of the Aboriginal Healing Foundation Program Activity, 2002*; *Third Interim Evaluation Report of Aboriginal Healing Foundation Program Activity*, 2003; and L. Archibald, *Final Report of the Aboriginal Healing Foundation, 2006.*

By 1981, a proposal to transfer responsibility for health care services to Indian communities was approved, and by 1982 Indian Health Services standards were developed as a way of measuring the extent to which Aboriginal health needs were being met. The *Nielsen Report* was leaked in 1985 and focused on the federal government's insistence that it had no statutory or treaty obligations in this area, as well as on duplication of services.

In 1986 Health and Welfare (Medical Services Branch) announced a new policy initiative: The Indian Health Transfer Policy. This new policy, which was centred on the concept of self-determination, was to facilitate a developmental approach to transferring health care and services to Aboriginal communities. It was hoped that it would lead to First Nations autonomy and to community control of health care services (Speck, 1989). The transfer policy in health care is a continuation of the "devolution policy" developed by Indian and Northern Affairs Canada a decade earlier, in that it proposes that a larger share of the responsibility now allocated to the federal government be taken on by First Nations. In 2000, the Medical Services Branch was renamed the First Nations and Inuit Health Branch. Its mandate is to ensure the availability of and access to health services for Aboriginal people. They also have agreed to help First Nations address local health issues and to build strong relationships between Health Canada and the First Nations' communities. There is considerable conflict between the two parties with regard to how and under what conditions the transfer of management will take place and what the nature of the relationship will be.

Under the current policy First Nations are denied self-determination, which in turn denies them the opportunity to create conditions whereby Aboriginal health could be improved. For example, the federal government continues to administer health services as an isolated service that is separate from the political, social, and economic dimensions of life—a fact that Aboriginal and other people have consistently identified as one of the major problems in health care for Aboriginal people.

Today, in all but three of the provinces, insurance premiums are paid for everyone by provincial governments, which take payments from tax revenue. A variety of arrangements exist in these provinces for payment of premiums by registered Indians, ranging from bulk payments to general means tests. The specific features that differentiate Aboriginal from non-Aboriginal health services are the payment of medical and hospital insurance premiums by the federal government for three provinces, the provision of public health services by the federal government rather than the provincial, and the federal funding of additional non-insured services for Indians. Regardless of the source of funding, a full range of medical services is provided to First Nations, although the specifics of this care vary from one province to another depending upon the standards set by each province.

Medical Services Delivery

While the *Indian Act* itself says little about the specifics (see Section 73[1]) and its main focus is on the prevention of the spread of infectious diseases, there remains a strong financial commitment to Aboriginal health care through a variety of programs (Woodward, 1989). The mandate at the First Nations and Inuit Health Branch is to assist Aboriginal people in achieving levels of health comparable to that of other Canadians, to ensure their access to sustainable health services and to build capacity in the health field for all First Nations and Inuit communities. To ensure the achievement of these goals, the branch works with the Assembly of First Nations and the Inuit Tapiriit Kanatami, who have representatives sitting on the branch executive committee. In addition, each regional branch office has established joint committees with the regional First Nations and Inuit groups.

After the Indian Health Policy was created, First Nations and Inuit people could take over some responsibility for administering aspects of their community health programs. In 1989 the formal "transfer" process began. As of 2002, about 70 percent of eligible First Nations and Inuit communities have taken on some degree of administering their community health programs. Today, more than 80 percent of the funds for federal community health programs are channelled through agreements with First Nations and Inuit organizations.

Health and Welfare Canada operates a number of programs that also provide health care to Aboriginal people throughout Canada. The first major program is Community Health Services, which focuses on communicable disease control, health education, mental health, nursing, and the provision of medical advice and assistance. The second is the non-insured health benefits program. Through this program, Aboriginal people are provided general health care through access to the provincial medicare systems and supplemental programs. In addition, the program includes the transportation of patients, dental services, and other medical appliances and services. The third major program is one in which funding is provided to train and employ local health care workers under the aegis of the Community Health Services.

The provision of services for Aboriginal people is carried out through all three levels of government. Those services provided by provincial and municipal agencies are generally fully reimbursed by the federal government. At the federal level, the First Nations and Inuit Health Branch provides doctors and nurses. Over 500 community health workers are also contracted by the First Nations and Inuit Health Branch to provide health care for Aboriginal people. At the turn of the 21st century, there were almost 2000 Aboriginal health workers.

Approximately 800 were Aboriginal nurses and over 80 were Aboriginal physicians. On a per capita basis, the First Nations and Inuit Health Branch spends about $600 per year per Aboriginal person, approximately the same spent on non-Aboriginal people. Overall, Health Canada spent about $1.7 billion on health services to First Nations in 2003, compared to just over $1 billion in 1995. Just under half of these funds were allocated to non-insured health benefits. The remainder was spent on transfer agreements, management and support, and community health programs and community-based health services.

Health services also are provided through contributions and contract arrangements with Aboriginal organizations, bands, and post-secondary educational institutions. Community Health Services carry out this program through four main activities: health care and treatment services, public health services, involvement of Indians in the health care system, and the provision of physical facilities. One of the changes that has been implemented is the limitation of non-insured health benefits. All registered Indians were previously eligible to receive prescription medication, medical supplies, dental services, medical transportation, optometry services, and mental health services. This program now exceeds $550 million per year and has become the target for fiscal restraint. Specifically, off-reserve Indians have been cut off from such benefits (Adelson, 2005).

The overall structure for providing medical and health services to Aboriginal people is complex. At the national level, several government agencies interact to set policies, determine programs, and establish funding levels, e.g., deputy minister of Health and Welfare; director general, Policy and Evaluation, Treasury Board; and the directors of Indian/Inuit Policy, Planning, and Evaluation. At the provincial level, the regional director oversees implementation of the programs for each health zone, which involves doctors, nurses, and environmental health officers. At the local level, for those bands involved in health care delivery, band councils make decisions regarding training programs and who will be admitted to various health programs.

Research for the past quarter-century has noted that abuse of alcohol and other substances is a major problem in First Nations communities. In the recent Aboriginal Peoples Survey, nearly three-quarters of the respondents said that alcohol and drug abuse was a problem in their community. In this same survey, one in five Aboriginal youth reported having used solvents—and one in three solvent users is under the age of 15. One of the most widely known health services provided by Health Canada is in the area of substance abuse.

In the mid-1970s, a part of a pilot program, the National Native Alcohol and Drug Abuse Program, was put in place. This program still exists and has expanded its role as it deals with treatment, rehabilitation, and education. This program encompasses 52 treatment centres and 7 solvent centres located in First Nations and Inuit communities across Canada and has some 700 treatment beds. It has 550 prevention programs and over 700 employees with an annual cost of $35M. In-patient admissions have fluctuated between 4500 and 5000 patients a year. Over the past decade, the number of alcohol abuse admissions has decreased while, at the same time, the number of people being admitted for hallucinogens and other non-narcotic drugs has been on an upward trend. The program has been subject to a budget freeze over the past number of years and, as a result, the limited number of trained personnel available, the high turnover of staff and the dubious viability of smaller centres have all contributed to the difficulties of the program and the decreasing numbers. Nevertheless, the last review of the program carried out in the late 90s showed that the program was an unqualified success both for individuals and communities.

TABLE 3.12	National Age-Standardized Rate of Tuberculosis in the First Nations On-Reserve* and Overall Canadian Populations (1990–2005)	
Year	**First Nations**	**Canada**
1990	69.4	7.2
1991	59.5	7.2
1992	74.8	7.4
1993	54.3	7.0
1994	56.3	7.1
1995	53.4	6.5
1996	49.0	6.3
1997	53.3	6.6
1998	41.6	5.9
1999	61.5	5.9
2000	54.0	5.8
2005	53.3	5.6

* Data includes reported TB cases in the First Nations on-reserve populations of B.C., Alberta, Saskatchewan, Manitoba, Ontario, New Brunswick, and Nova Scotia.

Source: Adapted and updated from *Tuberculosis in First Nations Communities* 2002, Health Canada, www.hc-sc.gc.ca/fnihb/phcph/ tuberculosis/tb_fni_communities.htm; Health Canada, 2003. Reproduced with the permission of the Minister of Public Works and Government Services Canada, 2004.

Aboriginal Health

Many of the statistics about disease and illness among Aboriginal people have been published and are well known. Illnesses resulting from poverty, overcrowding, and poor housing have led to chronic and acute respiratory diseases, which take a heavy toll among Aboriginal people (for example, see Table 3.12 for Tuberculosis rates over the past decade). Overall, the crude mortality rate for First Nations is 354.2 deaths per 100 000. However, while the standardized death rate for the Aboriginal population was more than double that of the general Canadian population—15.9 versus 6.6 deaths per 1000 population during the 80s (Nuttall, 1982; INAC, 1988)—it is now similar to the general Canadian population (see Figure 3.5). The data reveal that the overall death rate among Aboriginal people has decreased by nearly one-half since 1978.

The data show that the First Nations' rate was similar to the national rate (662 versus 661 per 100 000 population). However, there is a gap between Aboriginals and the general Canadian population, particularly for ages 15 to 44; Aboriginals in this age group are more than twice as likely to die than the average Canadian. Moreover, the cause of death by age group varies. Figure 3.6 reveals the leading causes of death in First Nations by age group.

Infant mortality has a tremendous impact upon the population of all societies, since infants will (if they live) contribute to the growth of the population when they reach

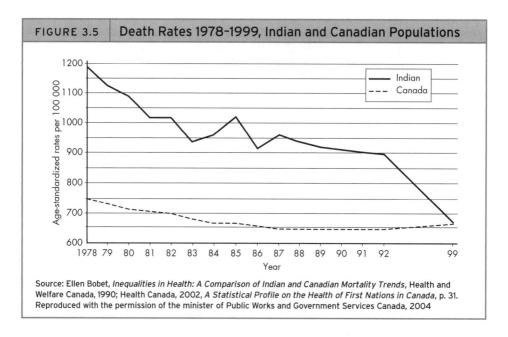

FIGURE 3.5 | Death Rates 1978–1999, Indian and Canadian Populations

Source: Ellen Bobet, *Inequalities in Health: A Comparison of Indian and Canadian Mortality Trends,* Health and Welfare Canada, 1990; Health Canada, 2002, *A Statistical Profile on the Health of First Nations in Canada,* p. 31. Reproduced with the permission of the minister of Public Works and Government Services Canada, 2004

childbearing age. Over the years, there has been a substantial decrease in infant mortality rates (see Figure 3.7). The data show that the infant mortality rate among Indian people is now less than one-sixth of what it was in 1960. However, it should be noted that, as late as 1990, it was double that of the general Canadian population: 7.9 versus 17.5 per 1000. Since 1988 a disturbing trend emerged, showing that while the infant mortality rate for all Canadians decreased, it increased for registered Indians. Fortunately this trend reversed in the late 90s and the gap has closed. However it is still 22 percent higher than the Canadian rate in 2001. A closer look at the infant mortality rate shows that Aboriginal rates of perinatal deaths (stillbirths and under one week of age) are twice as high as in the general population. On the other hand, neonatal (birth to one month) death rates for the two groups are very similar. Post-neonatal (one month to one year) death rates are more than three times higher for First Nations. These rates reflect the poor housing and other environmental conditions that Aboriginal children are born into (Canada, 1980).

The effectiveness of the Native health care system is related as much to the environmental conditions in which Aboriginal Canadians live as to the treatment and facilities provided. Health care provided is sometimes countered by social and economic problems such as overcrowding, poor nutrition, chronic unemployment, and community and family violence. For example, Figure 3.8 shows the relationship between overcrowding and the incidence of tuberculosis. Thus, an Aboriginal person, after receiving effective medical treatment, finds himself or herself returning to the social conditions that created the problem in the first place. In short, the causes of poor mental and physical health are not dealt with (Health Canada, 2003).

What are the specific causes of death? Over one-third of all registered Indian deaths (compared to 8 percent in the general population) are due to accidents and violence.

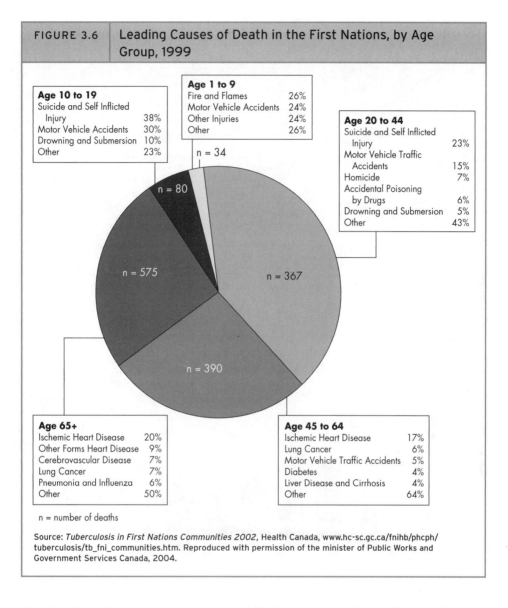

FIGURE 3.6 | **Leading Causes of Death in the First Nations, by Age Group, 1999**

Age 10 to 19
Suicide and Self Inflicted Injury	38%
Motor Vehicle Accidents	30%
Drowning and Submersion	10%
Other	23%

Age 1 to 9
Fire and Flames	26%
Motor Vehicle Accidents	24%
Other Injuries	24%
Other	26%

Age 20 to 44
Suicide and Self Inflicted Injury	23%
Motor Vehicle Traffic Accidents	15%
Homicide	7%
Accidental Poisoning by Drugs	6%
Drowning and Submersion	5%
Other	43%

n = 34

n = 80

n = 575

n = 367

n = 390

Age 65+
Ischemic Heart Disease	20%
Other Forms Heart Disease	9%
Cerebrovascular Disease	7%
Lung Cancer	7%
Pneumonia and Influenza	6%
Other	50%

Age 45 to 64
Ischemic Heart Disease	17%
Lung Cancer	6%
Motor Vehicle Traffic Accidents	5%
Diabetes	4%
Liver Disease and Cirrhosis	4%
Other	64%

n = number of deaths

Source: *Tuberculosis in First Nations Communities 2002*, Health Canada, www.hc-sc.gc.ca/fnihb/phcph/ tuberculosis/tb_fni_communities.htm. Reproduced with permission of the minister of Public Works and Government Services Canada, 2004.

Aboriginal people are up to 6.5 times more likely than the total Canadian population to die of injuries and poisonings. For all age groups up to 63, Aboriginal people are four times as likely as other Canadians to die from these causes. The most frequent are motor vehicle accidents, drowning, and fire. Although these rates are extremely high, they have been reduced by over 40 percent since 1980.

The other major causes of death (in order) are: diseases of the circulatory system, diseases of the respiratory system, cancer, suicide, and chronic conditions (e.g., tuberculosis and diabetes). Heart diseases, hypertension and AIDS are "new" diseases for Aboriginal people, although for each of the diseases listed, the incidence is much greater for Aboriginal people than for the general Canadian population.

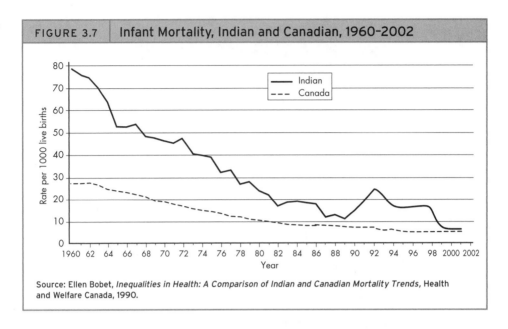

FIGURE 3.7 | Infant Mortality, Indian and Canadian, 1960-2002

Source: Ellen Bobet, *Inequalities in Health: A Comparison of Indian and Canadian Mortality Trends*, Health and Welfare Canada, 1990.

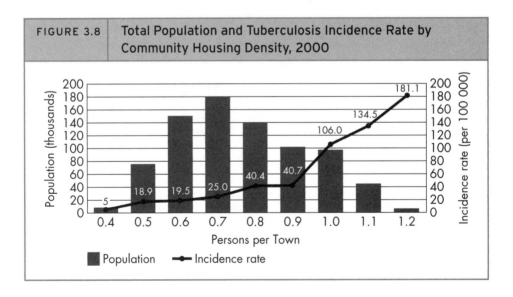

FIGURE 3.8 | Total Population and Tuberculosis Incidence Rate by Community Housing Density, 2000

New Diseases In the Aboriginal Community

Tuberculosis After treating tuberculosis (TB) in the Aboriginal community for nearly 50 years, by the end of the 1950s Canada had finally won the war. Unfortunately, TB began to return to First Nations communities in the mid-1980s, achieving near epidemic proportions. However, after a major TB elimination program that was implemented in 1992, the number of new and relapsed cases decreased until 1999, when they once again began to increase to 1990 levels. In 1992, the incidence per 100 000 people was 67.8, decreasing to 54.6 throughout much of the 1990s until 1999, when the rate went back up to nearly 64. As one can see in Table 3.12, these figures reveal a TB rate that is 10 times that of the entire Canadian population. It is important to realize that TB is not uniformly distributed across Canada. Saskatchewan has the highest incidence (ranging from 104.3 to 155.7 per 100 000) over the past decade, but Alberta and Manitoba also tend to experience higher rates than the national average. Mortality from TB is low due to aggressive case findings and effective treatment of the disease. In 2003 fewer than 50 individuals died from TB. However, what has emerged recently is the dramatic increase of HIV in First Nations communities and its primary and secondary (related to TB) contributions to death. A study in BC identified one-third of the identified HIV/TB patients as Aboriginals.

Diabetes Diabetes was virtually non-existent in the Aboriginal population before the 1940s. Today its incidence among Aboriginal people is estimated to be two to five times higher than in the non-Aboriginal population, and to be increasing rapidly (Wells, 1995). Its importance is heightened by the fact that it is increasingly showing early onset, greater severity at diagnosis, high rates of complications, lack of accessible services, increasing incidence, and increasing prevalence of risk factors for a population already at risk (Young et al. 1998). Health care officials in British Columbia report increases of 85 percent between 1992 and 2002. A comparison of life tables (length of life) between the Aboriginal and non-Aboriginal populations over the past 20 years shows that there has been little improvement in diabetes rates for Aboriginal people, and even a deterioration in the past decade (Nuttall, 1982; Young, 1984; Bobet 1997).

Based upon Statistics Canada data, it is estimated that between 80 000 and 120 000 Aboriginal people 15 years of age and over have diabetes (generally type 2). The latest First Nations and Inuit regional Health Survey conducted by the National Steering Committee estimates that the above figures are underestimates by 20 percent. Recent figures show that, among all First Nations people, the incidence of diabetes is 6.4 percent. For those living on reserves, the rate is 8.5 percent. Métis have reported a prevalence of 5.5 percent while Inuit report a 1.9 percent incidence. Age-standardized prevalence of diabetes for First Nations people is three to five times that of the general population, and this is true for all age categories. According to a regional health survey, 53 percent of the First Nations people with diabetes are 40 years old or younger and 65 percent are less than 45 years old. The onset of diabetes for Aboriginal people is now detected in those 30 to 35. This is in contrast to the general population where type two diabetes typically begins at age 40 and is highest for those 65 and older. Bobet (1997) found that approximately two-thirds of the First Nations people diagnosed with diabetes are women—a pattern that is not reflected in the general Canadian population. Aboriginal women have over five times the rate of diabetes compared to women in the general population, and Aboriginal men have over three times the corresponding rate for men in the general population. With the high rates of diabetes for Aboriginal people, it should not be surprising that health complications emerge. Secondary illnesses such as strokes, macro vascular disease, heart attacks, lower limb amputations, and high blood pressure are just some of the related health care issues for those who have diabetes. While national projections are not available, in Manitoba is has been estimated that the number of First Nations diabetes cases will increase three times over the next 20 years (Green et al., 1997). The impact of diabetes over the next decade is significant, and the disease will impose a high cost in resources if this problem is not addressed today. For example, the annual costs for diabetic drugs through the non-insured health benefits program are now in excess of $16M per year (Health Canada, 2000).

Related to diabetes is cardiovascular disease. While Canada is experiencing a decline in rates of cardiovascular disease, Aboriginal people have experienced a dramatic increase (Anand et al., 2001). The prevalence in First Nations communities is three times greater than for other Canadians. It is estimated that just over 40 percent of the First Nation population have metabolic syndrome, a primary cause of cardiovascular disease. Moreover, nearly three-quarters of the Aboriginal population are overweight, which is also a determinant of both diabetes and cardiovascular disease (First Nations Centre National Aboriginal Health Organization, 2004; Harris et al, 2002).

HIV/AIDS   Unlike the general population, where the number of AIDS cases has levelled off, the number of AIDS cases among Aboriginals has dramatically increased over the past two decades. From 1998 to 2001, over one-fourth of all reports of HIV-positive tests were from Aboriginal people. In cases where the ethnicity of the individual who has AIDS is known, the proportion of Aboriginal cases have increased from 1.5 percent to 5.6 percent. Smylie (2001) found in his study that more than 10 percent of those with AIDS are Aboriginal. Today we find the proportion of AIDS cases among Aboriginal persons has climbed from 1 percent of all cases in Canada before 1990 to over 7 percent in 2002.

A much higher proportion of Aboriginal people under 30 with AIDS are diagnosed than the general population (30 percent vs. 18 percent). Of those diagnosed with AIDS, 60 percent of the cases were a result of sex, 14 percent a result of both sex and injection drugs, and 20 percent from use of injection drugs only. Mobility between the city and rural communities has been identified as an important factor in the introduction and spread of HIV from infected individuals.

Unintentional/Intentional Injuries   The pattern of unintentional injuries among Aboriginal people is similar to that of the general Canadian population, with the exception that the rates are much higher for Aboriginals. The most common death resulting from injury was related to motor vehicle accidents, with a rate of 40 per 100 000 population, which is four times the national rate. Accidental poisoning is the second highest cause of accidental death (17 per 100 000), followed by drowning (9 per 100 000), both of which are four times the national rate. Accidental falls and death by fire/flames were the least common types of death for Aboriginals, but comparable data for the general population show that the Aboriginal rates are nonetheless three times higher.

When we look at intentional injuries leading to death, a similar picture emerges. Suicide accounts for up to one-quarter of all injury deaths in First Nations people. A majority of suicides occur in those aged 15 to 24, although in recent times there has been a doubling of suicides in the 1–14 age group. In 2001, suicide accounted for nearly 40 percent of all deaths in youth (ages 10–19) and nearly one-quarter of all deaths in ages 20–44. Overall, the First Nations suicide rate in 2001 was 27.4 deaths per million, which suggests that a sustained decrease has not occurred in the past quarter-century. Data show that suicides occur in "clusters" of specific areas and time periods, and in some areas the rates of suicide are extremely high. While the overall rate for young people is high, in areas such as Sioux Lookout, it is 50 times higher than the general Canadian population for the 10–19 age group. Overall, at ages 15–24, the suicide rate in First Nations women is almost eight times that of the same age group for all of Canada, while for men it is five times higher. While completed suicides are typically much higher among males, in general, females attempt suicide far more often than males—a pattern also seen in the general Canadian population (Whitehead et al., 1996). Homicide is the third most common cause of death by injury in First Nations communities: the rate is nearly five times higher than for the total population.

In conclusion, we find that suicide and self-inflicted injuries are three times higher (six times higher for the 15–24 age group), homicide rates are twice as high, congenital anomalies are 1.5 times higher, and pneumonia more than three times higher. Aboriginal people have five times the rate of child welfare, four times the death rate, three times the violent death, juvenile delinquency, and suicide rate, and twice the rate of hospital admissions of the average Canadian population. Aboriginal people have three times the rate of heart problems and hypertension compared to the general Canadian population. Figure 3.9 details the overall rate of death for Aboriginal peoples over the past quarter century.

Off-Reserve Indian Health

O'Donnell and Tait (2004) conclude that a majority of non-reserve Aboriginal people report excellent or very good health, and this is particularly true for young Aboriginals. Overall, the off-reserve Aboriginal population reported better health than their non-Aboriginal counterparts and, as incomes increased, the proportion of people reporting fair or poor health decreased. However, at the same time, on-reserve self-reported health was worse than that of the general Canadian population. In fact, the gap between the health status of older Aboriginals and Canadians widened over the past decade. The proportion of

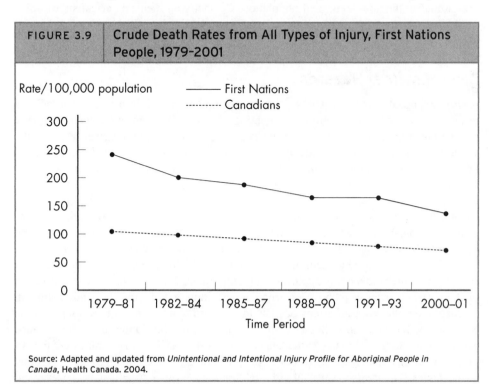

| FIGURE 3.9 | Crude Death Rates from All Types of Injury, First Nations People, 1979–2001 |

Source: Adapted and updated from *Unintentional and Intentional Injury Profile for Aboriginal People in Canada*, Health Canada. 2004.

Aboriginal people with fair or poor health is about double that of the Canadian population (O'Donnell and Tait, 2004).

However, when chronic conditions (health conditions lasting at least 6 months) were considered, over 60 percent of the off-reserve population reported at least one chronic condition, while less than half of the non-Aboriginal population reported this. Arthritis/rheumatism had the highest prevalence in the Aboriginal population (26 percent), followed by high blood pressure (15 percent) and diabetes (9 percent). When compared to the general Canadian population, these rates were much higher. For example, the diabetes rate was twice as high as that of the general population (Tjepkema, 2002). When long-term activity restrictions were assessed, over 16 percent of the off-reserve Aboriginal population reported such restriction, which was 1.6 times higher than in the non-Aboriginal population. When compared to Aboriginals living on-reserve, non-Aboriginal people reported similar levels of activity restriction. Surprisingly, middle-income off-reserve Aboriginals were more likely to report activity restrictions than other middle-income Canadians, while Aboriginals from high income groups report lower levels of restriction compared to high-income non-Aboriginal Canadians. The survey found that over 13 percent of the off-reserve Aboriginals had experienced a major depressive episode in the past year—nearly twice the level reported by the non-Aboriginal population. (Tjepkema, 2002).

Socio-economic status (income, education, job) are the major factors that determine the health status of both Aboriginals and non-Aboriginals. The second most important factor is physical activity, smoking status, and whether or not the individual was overweight or obese.

In terms of seeking health care services, over three-quarters of the off-reserve population had visited a general medical practitioner at least once in the previous year, and this was similar to the non-Aboriginal population. Contact with medical specialists was also similar between the two groups. However, when contact with dentists was assessed, Aboriginals were much less likely to see them than their non-Aboriginal counterparts.

Environmental Hazards

Aboriginal people are also exposed to severe environmental hazards: industrial and resource development have polluted water and disrupted fish and game stock for many reserve communities, seriously affecting quality of life. For example, residents of the White Dog and Grassy Narrows reserves in Ontario were found to have 40 to 150 times more mercury in their blood than the average Canadian (Bolaria, 1979). Various environmental disturbances have upset other Aboriginal communities, such as Cluff Lake (uranium pollution), Serpent River (acid discharge), and St. Regis (fluoride pollution). Obviously, Aboriginal lifestyles vary considerably from those of non-Aboriginal people (Ram and Romaniuc, 1984), as they are more likely to harvest and consume local game and plants. In the second diagnostic study of the health of First Nations and Inuit people, researchers found that 60 percent of Inuit children under the age of 15 and 40 percent of Inuit women of childbearing age on Broughton Island, Nunavut, have polychlorinated biphenyl (PCB) levels well above government definition of "tolerable." A similar study in Quebec found that concentrations of PCB in newborn children in Quebec Inuit and the Montagnais were four times higher than the concentrations in Southern Quebec infants. The concentrations of mercury in the Quebec and Northwest Territories Inuit were 6 to 14 times higher than the levels in the newborn Southern Quebec population. Another study in the James Bay area showed that although mercury levels exceeding the government levels had decreased over the past two decades, they were still higher than government standards.

In order to deal with escalating health care costs, the federal government has placed a cap on funding for Aboriginal health care for the past decade. This cap can be better understood when one realizes that it has been less than the annual increases in health program spending for non-Aboriginals.

HOUSING

The federal government also argues that it has no legal or treaty obligation to provide housing units or to repair existing ones for Aboriginal people. However, it does have a historical commitment to provide housing for Indians, which, so far, it has chosen to continue. With a birth rate double the national average, there is an ever-increasing demand for housing. To support this activity, the Department of Indian Affairs provides support to First Nation communities through the Capital Facilities and Maintenance Program.

Because of the geographical isolation and limited natural resources on reserves, most of them do not have the economic ability to meet the cost of various capital facilities. Therefore, funding by INAC is critical for these communities. One of the more important types of community facility that is being subsidized by Indian and Inuit Affairs is housing. Support for individuals and communities in order to provide adequate housing takes place through subsidies for the construction and renovation of houses on reserves. The subsidy levels for new construction vary from $19 000 to $50 000. Today, about 46 000 (out of a total of 91 600) housing units have been built on reserves under the Indian and Inuit Housing Program, at a cost of well over $250 million in 1999–2000. In addition to this, rural and Aboriginal housing programs have provided $123 million to subsidize housing for Inuit, Métis, and non-status Indians. Data relevant to the growth rate of the number of dwellings in relation to the growth rate of the population shows that between 1983–84 and 1989–90 an average of 3263 new dwelling units per year were built on reserves. In 1991 the number was slightly above 4000. However, since this time the number of new housing units each year has decreased, and by 2001 the number had decreased to fewer than 2000. Nearly 4000 homes per year since 1983 have been renovated, with an average subsidy of $8000 to $10 000. This activity also has decreased to fewer than 3000 homes per year. In the end, it is clear that these numbers are not keeping up with the demand. It is estimated today that the number of new housing units is approximately half the need.

The above figures must also be interpreted in the context of public housing standards. Aboriginal housing units, because of the standards employed by INAC, have a life span of 15 to 20 years—less than half the national average life span. Thus, even though there has been an increased number of housing units built on reserves, the poor quality of the houses and the increase in the number of people living on the reserves intensifies the competition for good housing. In the end, we find that the number of units in need of replacement has remained at about 5000 for the past five years, and the number of units in need of renovations has remained at about 30 000 over the past decade.

Figure 3.10 shows that the number of Aboriginal homes with more than one person per room is 200 to 300 times that of the overall Canadian population. The average number of Aboriginal persons per dwelling is 3.5, while for all of Canada it is less than 2. The average Canadian dwelling has 7.2 rooms, while the Aboriginal dwelling has 5.8. This overcrowding decreases the lifespan of a house and it worsens social and health problems in communities.

A more recent evaluation of the on-reserve housing program estimated that about three-quarters of all existing housing was inadequate in that it failed to meet some of the basic standards of safe and decent living. For example, while only 2 percent of the Canadian population live in crowded conditions, almost one-quarter of the Aboriginal houses were found to be overcrowded. In addition, the number of Aboriginal houses requiring major repairs nearly doubled between 1989 and 2001. By rating housing conditions as requiring regular maintenance, minor repairs, or major repairs, government officials determine the state of Aboriginal housing stock and provide an overview of housing conditions on reserves. Generally, slightly more than half the houses require major repairs.

Much of the housing on reserves is provided by the federal government, and because individual title is severely limited, most homes are not owned by individuals but by the band. The band councils "rent" the houses at a break-even point to keep the costs down. As a result, the absence of individual ownership reduces the chances that the occupant will maintain the unit in good repair. Houses on the reserves are also built almost exclusively as traditional single-family units, rendering the housing stock less suitable for single people and multigenerational families.

The above-mentioned program and philosophy have been unnecessarily restrictive and have partially contributed to the lack of Aboriginal housing. Some reserves in Ontario and Quebec have tried to combat the official rules and methods by investigating the feasibility of providing multi-unit buildings. A recent study carried out by INAC shows that nearly $1 billion would be needed to bring Aboriginal housing up to average Canadian standards. Despite this ongoing crisis in Aboriginal communities, the Canada Mortgage and Housing Corporation cut its funding in half for new First Nations housing, which means that the number of new houses will be reduced to 600 per year. This exacerbates the housing budget problem, as it has been frozen since 1988, when housing programs for off-reserve Aboriginals were also eliminated.

The federal government has not seriously dealt with the problem of housing until recently. A latent function of its policy of reducing the number of available housing units was to force more and more First Nations people to move off the reserve and into the city. By 2000, the total number of houses on reserves was nearly 80 000 and, of these, only about half were considered "adequate." But in 1996 the government introduced a new housing policy. This new approach gives Aboriginals control of their housing design, construction, and placement. Under this new First Nations Innovative Housing Initiative, new housing designs and types of construction—e.g., log houses—are being built in Aboriginal communities. In addition to the $138 million provided annually to support First Nations housing on reserve, Indian Affairs has committed another $220 million to support the 1996 policy. Between 1996 and 2002, the total number of houses on-reserve increased by more than 17 percent. During the same period, the number of houses considered to be in adequate condition increased by nearly 25 percent. In addition, the Innovative Housing Fund introduced in 1998 provides $2 million in annual funding for new building technology, alternative house designs, and energy sources. Finally, Indian Affairs provides ministerial loan guarantees and has increased the department's guarantee authority for these housing loans from $1.2 to $1.7 billion. Off the reserve, we find that less than 40 percent of Aboriginals own a home, compared to nearly three-quarters of the non-Aboriginal population. A study of homelessness in 19 urban areas across Canada revealed that over one-quarter of the homeless population was Aboriginal. In the end, core housing needs (i.e., lacking at least one dedicated room for each basic need like cooking, bathing, and sleeping) for Aboriginals is about 25 percent, while for non-Aboriginals it is less than 10 percent.

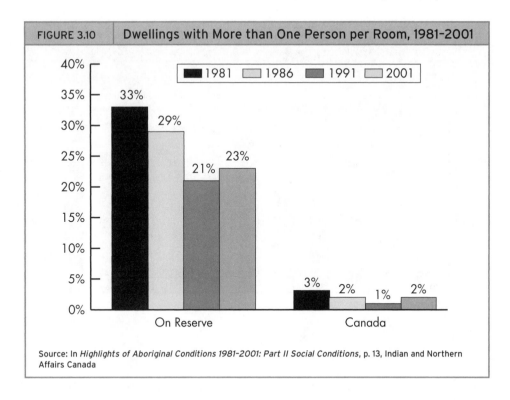

| FIGURE 3.10 | Dwellings with More than One Person per Room, 1981–2001 |

Source: In *Highlights of Aboriginal Conditions 1981–2001: Part II Social Conditions*, p. 13, Indian and Northern Affairs Canada

Infrastructure Services

The number and extent of government services available to Aboriginal people have a considerable impact on their quality of life. A major factor in the provision of services is accessibility by road or rail; without good transportation access, services are difficult and costly to provide. Yet only about one-third of the reserves even have year-round road access. Nearly half of all reserves and settlements are accessible only by water. And only 18 percent are accessible by both rail and road.

Figure 3.11 shows the average percentage of housing on Indian reserves with a sewer (or septic tank), and with running water. The data show that, on average, over 95 percent of reserve houses have an adequate water supply and sewage disposal. These figures show remarkable improvement when you consider that, in 1963, just over 10 percent of the Indian reserve population had adequate water supply and sewage disposal. Other data show that over 90 percent now have electricity. Recent statistics show continual improvement. However, just over one-quarter of the housing units on a reserve are now covered by fire protection services, and this figure reveals a slight decrease from a decade ago. Moreover, in 2006 a number of First Nations communities were confronted with water quality issues. In four cases, members were removed from the community and placed in a nearby town while the quality of the water was dealt with. A survey by INAC revealed that 17 percent of all First Nation communities had water quality issues that required immediate attention. One year later, only two of the communities were provided with new infrastructure to enhance the water quality. In Nunavut, over one-third of the people claimed that there were times of the year when their water was contaminated.

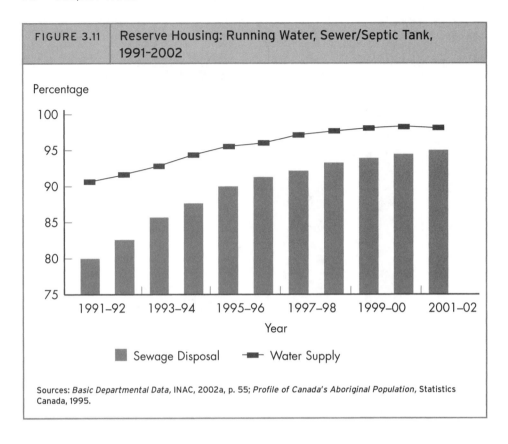

FIGURE 3.11 | Reserve Housing: Running Water, Sewer/Septic Tank, 1991-2002

Sources: *Basic Departmental Data*, INAC, 2002a, p. 55; *Profile of Canada's Aboriginal Population*, Statistics Canada, 1995.

While the infrastructure picture on reserves is better than it was in the past, when we compare these figures with the overall Canadian rate we find that Aboriginal dwellings are still far behind in having the basic necessities that most Canadians take for granted.

Less than three-quarters of Aboriginal homes have central heating, in contrast to over 90 percent of non-Aboriginal homes. As we have seen, crowding is also a problem for Aboriginal people. One in 43 non-Aboriginal homes was crowded, compared to the one in 4 proportion of Aboriginal homes. More than 15 percent of Aboriginal homes require major repairs. Overall, Aboriginal people have the least favourable housing conditions of any ethnic group in Canada.

The housing data released from Indian Affairs reveals a growing Aboriginal population with an almost static number of adequate houses now on the reserve. This reflects the aging housing stock, the slow construction (upgrading) of new housing, and the growing population.

Overall, the funded capital assets (excluding houses) across the reserves show that the average number of new assets was about 1300 per year for the past decade. Utilities accounted for 41 percent of new assets, buildings for 29 percent, and transport for 26 percent over the past decade. One specific facility that has increased over the past 10 years has been educational space. The total educational space on reserves has increased by 25 percent, and similar increases have been noted for increases in space allocated for schools.

SUMMARY

The above data reveal a profile that is unique in Canadian history. The Aboriginal population has taken dramatic twists from near extinction to impressive recovery. The conquest of Canada by the French and British combined to set off a depopulation of Aboriginals for the next two centuries. As we entered the 20th century, a slow journey toward demographic recovery began and accelerated as we ended the century (Romaniuc, 2003). Since the late 1980s, Aboriginal people have exhibited exceptionally high birth rates, decreasing death rates, and unprecedented "in-migration" rates. These changes have brought about phenomenal growth of the Aboriginal population. However, this has been moderated by the overall growth of the Canadian population. As a result, the proportion of the Aboriginal population in Canada has only decreased slightly over the past half-century.

KEY TERMS

Reserves   Enfranchisement   Aboriginal health
Indian Bands   *Bill C-31*

STUDY QUESTIONS

1. What is the significance of reserves within Canada? Describe the perceived benefits and downfalls.
2. What is a band?
3. Describe the impact on cultural and linguistic distinctions that migration has created.
4. Why are population size and growth rate important for First Nations?
5. In regards to health, what are the three issues in dispute between First Nations and the federal government?
6. What is the impact of social and economic problems on Aboriginal health?
7. Why is the quality of life experienced by Aboriginal people far worse than those who are non-Aboriginal?
8. In regards to environmental hazards, housing, and infrastructure services, what challenges do Aboriginal people living on reserves experience?

WEBLINKS

www.anac.on.ca

Founded in 1974, *The Aboriginal Nurses of Canada* recognizes that Aboriginal people's health needs are best met and understood by health professionals of similar cultural background. This site lists publications as well as a schedule of seminars and conferences on Aboriginal health issues and care.

www.inac.gc.ca/pr/sts/index_e.html

Despite the absence of an authoritative source for information about Aboriginal demographics, a good starting point is the Statistics page of the federal Department of Indian and Northern Affairs, which includes recent census data on Aboriginal people, information about social conditions, and more.

www.ainc-inac.gc.ca/ch/rcap/index_e.html

The 1996 Royal Commission on Aboriginal Peoples *Final Report* contains a wealth of information about living conditions of Aboriginal peoples across Canada. It includes information on demography and discusses Aboriginal relocation, housing, health, and other issues.

chapter four

Profile of Aboriginal People II: Social Attributes

INTRODUCTION

We now move to looking at the more general social profile of the Aboriginal population. While much of the data presented is from the Department of Indian Affairs and thus focuses solely on First Nations, data from other sources reveals that the profile is similar to that of other Aboriginal groups, e.g., Inuit, Métis. These statistics provide a mental image of the Aboriginal population and, when possible, comparisons with the average Canadian population are given. This will allow the reader to place the Aboriginal population in context within Canadian society. The profile will also allow policy analysts to better see the differences between Aboriginal and non-Aboriginal peoples and to understand the kinds of programs that need to be put in place to deal with the problems facing Aboriginal people. We will begin with a basic age–sex profile.

AGE

Figures 4.1, 4.2, and 4.3 show the distribution of Aboriginal Canadians by age, relative to the total Canadian population. The data reveal a very young population: well over one-third of the Aboriginal population is younger than 15 and over half is younger than 25. Of the total Canadian population, only about one-fifth of the population is under 15 and about one-third is under 25. Over 70 percent of the Aboriginal population is under 40 years of age, evenly divided between males and females. Thirty-seven percent of on-reserve Indians and Inuit are under age 15, while nearly two-thirds of them are under 25. Table 4.1 outlines the age/sex distribution for registered Indians in 2005.

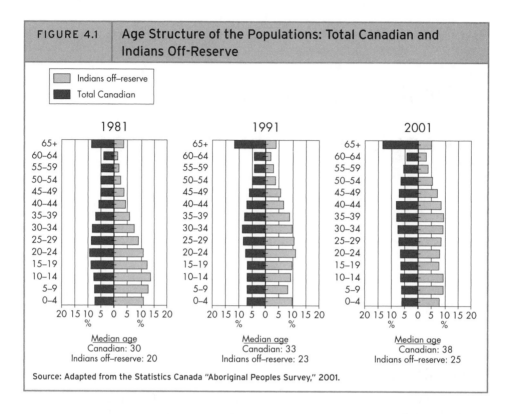

FIGURE 4.1   Age Structure of the Populations: Total Canadian and Indians Off-Reserve

Source: Adapted from the Statistics Canada "Aboriginal Peoples Survey," 2001.

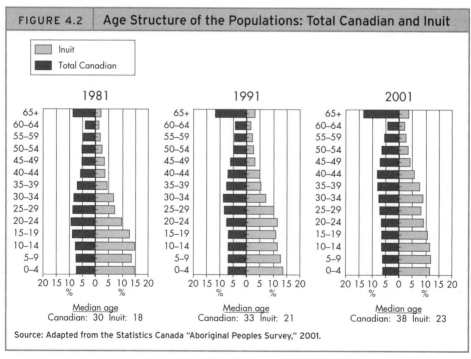

FIGURE 4.2   Age Structure of the Populations: Total Canadian and Inuit

Source: Adapted from the Statistics Canada "Aboriginal Peoples Survey," 2001.

| FIGURE 4.3 | Age Structure of the Populations: Total Canadian and Total Status Indians |

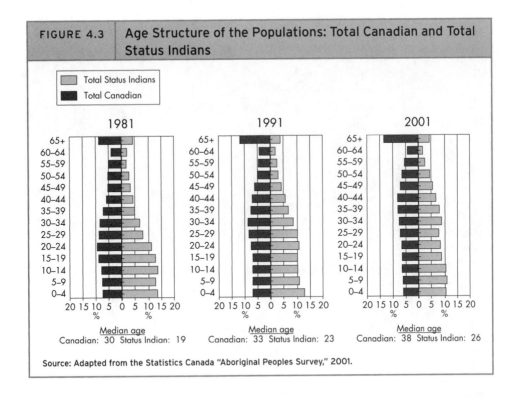

Source: Adapted from the Statistics Canada "Aboriginal Peoples Survey," 2001.

Thus far the evidence reveals that the proportion of young people in the overall Aboriginal population is growing. However, the growth is slowing down as the Aboriginal population ages. For example, in 1981 the median age for Aboriginal people was 19, while for the overall population it was 32. Today we find that the Aboriginal median age is 23, while the overall population has only increased to 34. Figure 4.4 reveals the Aboriginal and Canadian population by age for 2001 and 2017.

The dependency ratio is one way of assessing the burden of care placed on the working age population. The dependency ratios are outlined in Table 4.2. They show that, again, while the Aboriginal young dependency ratio is falling, it is substantially larger than that of non-Aboriginal people. At the same time, the aged dependency ratios have remained the same over the past decade. The overall dependency ratio for the Canadian population has remained stable over the past decade and will continue at this level well into the 21st century. On the other hand, the overall dependency ratio for Aboriginal people declined from 1981 to 2005. In the specific case of Inuit, it declined from 84 percent to 61 percent in 2001.

The above figures carry a number of implications. Clearly, there is a stable Aboriginal population-growth rate, meaning continued high growth, as well as a decreasing death rate. Unless birth rates also decrease, more and more Aboriginal people will be entering the prime employment category of 15–40, and the demand for jobs will increase. As Table 4.2 shows, the dependency ratios are already over twice as high for Aboriginal people as for the general population; this means that the working-age population must support a large number of non-productive people. Unemployment is already rampant among Aboriginal

TABLE 4.1 Registered Indian Population, by Type of Residence, Age Groups and Sex, December 31, 2005

Age	On Reserve				Off Reserve				Total			
	Male		Female		Male		Female		Male		Female	
	#	%	#	%	#	%	#	%	#	%	#	%
0-4	18 941	4.5	17 890	4.2	9 958	3.1	9 696	3.0	28 899	3.9	27 586	3.7
5-9	23 890	5.7	22 594	5.4	13 683	4.2	13 460	4.1	37 573	5.0	36 054	4.8
10-14	25 502	6.0	24 309	5.8	15 251	4.7	14 534	4.5	40 753	5.4	38 843	5.2
15-19	23 246	5.5	21 882	5.2	14 386	4.4	14 202	4.4	37 632	5.0	36 084	4.8
20-24	19 422	4.6	18 460	4.4	13 220	4.1	13 156	4.0	32 642	4.4	31 616	4.2
25-29	16 457	3.9	15 329	3.6	12 389	3.8	13 260	4.1	28 846	3.9	28 589	3.8
30-34	15 290	3.6	14 662	3.5	13 174	4.0	14 052	4.3	28 464	3.8	28 714	3.8
35-39	15 262	3.6	14 308	3.4	13 466	4.1	14 848	4.6	28 728	3.8	29 156	3.9
40-44	14 392	3.4	13 808	3.3	12 817	3.9	15 516	4.8	27 209	3.6	29 324	3.9
45-49	11 949	2.8	11 751	2.8	10 105	3.1	13 367	4.1	22 054	2.9	25 118	3.4
50-54	9 032	2.1	8 740	2.1	7 059	2.2	10 538	3.2	16 091	2.2	19 278	2.6
55-59	6 822	1.6	6 732	1.6	5 241	1.6	8 236	2.5	12 063	1.6	14 968	2.0
60-64	5 090	1.2	5 012	1.2	3 668	1.1	5 948	1.8	8 758	1.2	10 960	1.5
65+	9 862	2.3	11 549	2.7	7 522	2.3	13 436	4.1	17 384	2.3	24 985	3.3
Unstated	0		0		0		0		0		0	
Total	215 157	51.0	207 026	49.0	151 939	46.6	174 249	53.4	367 096	49.1	381 275	50.9
Total - both sexes	422 183 56%				326 188 44%				748 371 100%			

Note: On reserve includes on Crown land.

FIGURE 4.4	Distribution of the Canadian and American Aboriginal Population by Age Group, 2001 and 2017

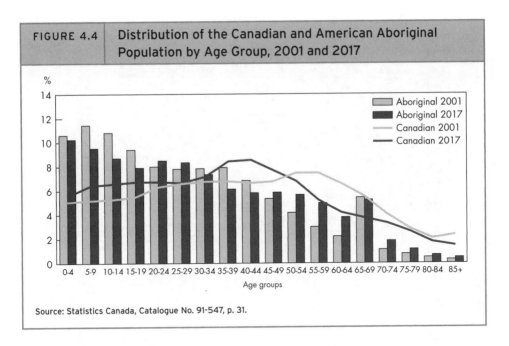

Source: Statistics Canada, Catalogue No. 91-547, p. 31.

Canadians, and, as more and more Aboriginals move into the prime employment category, greater competition for jobs is likely to take place. The data from Census Canada show that the number of people in the labour-force age range (15–64) has been increasing—from 46 percent in 1966 to nearly 65 percent by 2001.

LANGUAGE USE AND RETENTION

The language of any group is the repository of concepts, images, and history that allows individuals to organize their social environment. As Little Bear (2000) points out, language embodies the way a society thinks. And, through learning and speaking a language, the individual absorbs the collective thought processes of a people. Moreover, he notes that most Aboriginal languages are oriented toward process and action rather than objects (as are Western languages) and are free of dichotomies, e.g., black/white, either/or, animate/inanimate. Thus it is important to know the extent to which Aboriginal people use and retain their Aboriginal languages. Price (1981) and Norris (1998) have investigated the potential for the survival of Aboriginal languages in Canada. There are approximately 50 languages of Canada's Indigenous peoples, belonging to 11 major language families (Norris, 1998). Her research found that some language families are large and strong, others small and endangered. However, the three largest families are Algonquian (147 000), Inuktitut (28 000), and Athapaskan (20 000). Estimates are that long-term future viability has been secured for at least 18 Aboriginal languages (the three largest are Inuktitut, Cree, and Ojibwa) for which there are a minimum of 1000 speakers. An additional 16 languages are spoken by an estimated 100 to 1000 Aboriginal people and could be considered "endangered." The remaining 16 languages have less than 100 speakers and these are considered "near extinction," meaning that they are beyond the possibility of revival.

TABLE 4.2 | Age Distribution and Dependency Ratio of Aboriginal and Non-Aboriginal Population

| | Age Group | | | | Population | Dependency Ratio[a] | | | |
| | | | | | | Young | | Aged | |
	0-14 years (%)	15-64 years (%)	65 years and over (%)	No age given (%)		Indian	Non-Indian[b]	Indian	Non-Indian[b]
1924	32.2	51.2	5.9	10.7	104 894	62.9	56.5	11.5	7.9
1934	34.7	55.4	6.2	3.7	112 510	62.7	50.3	11.1	8.8
1944	37.5	55.9	6.6	–	125 686	67.0	42.4	11.8	10.2
1954	41.7	53.2	5.1	–	151 558	78.5	49.0	9.6	12.5
1964	46.7	49.1	4.2	–	211 389	95.0	58.1	8.6	13.1
1974	43.2	52.4	4.2	0.2	276 436	82.4	47.5	8.1	13.0
1981	39.0	57.0	4.0	–	323 000	68.4	48.8	7.0	12.8
1991	35.0	60.0	4.0	–	521 500	65.2	46.3	7.0	13.6
1999	29.5	65.3	5.2	–	604 400	59.5	29.4	6.3	17.9
2002	29.2	66.1	4.7	–	611 300	58.4	31.2	5.7	18.2
2005	28.0	66.3	5.7	–	748 371	43.2	29.5	8.5	18.4

a. The dependency ratios reflect the relationship between the groups least likely to be involved in the workforce (i.e., the young and the elderly), and the working-age population.
b. Data were not available for the corresponding year; the years represented are: 1921, 1931, 1941, 1951, 1961, 1971.

Sources: Information Canada, *Perspective Canada II*, (Ottawa: Queen's Printer, 1977), 287; *Census of Canada*, 1981; Indian and Northern Affairs Canada, *Quantitative Analysis and Socio-Demographic Research*, 1992; *Registered Indian Population by Sex and Residence*, 2002, INAC, Ottawa, 2003, Cat. No. R31-3/2002E; Health Canada, *A Statistical Profile on The Health of First Nations in Canada*, Ottawa, 2002.

While Aboriginal people still maintain a relatively high degree of adherence to their mother tongue,[1] this has diminished over time. In 1941, fewer than 10 percent of Aboriginal people claimed English as their mother tongue. The figure reached 15 percent in 1951 and over 25 percent in 1961; another 2 percent claimed French. By 2001, 71 percent claimed English and fewer than 5 percent were bilingual, i.e., spoke an Aboriginal language as well as either English or French. Of those who claimed Aboriginal dialects as their mother tongues, more than 40 percent were "somewhat" bilingual. Among non-reserve adults, one-third said they could speak or understand an Aboriginal language, although less than 15 percent said they were able to speak it. Of the three groups, Métis were the least likely to know an Aboriginal language. On the other hand, Inuktitut is spoken and understood by 90 percent of Inuit adults. Overall, the 2001 Census as well as data collected by Ipso-Reid, Ekos and Environics reveals that there is some evidence of an Aboriginal language revitalization through the efforts of parents as teachers (O'Donnell and Tait, 2004).

Home language reveals an equally skewed distribution, with almost 80 percent claiming English as the home language. However, 20 percent state that an Aboriginal language is used in their home. The data also show that 80 percent of Aboriginal people claimed to have a working knowledge of one official language.

Overall, 22 percent of the nearly 1.5 million Aboriginals in Canada speak an Aboriginal language at home. Of those who listed an Aboriginal language as their first language, 43 percent speak Cree, 14 percent speak Inuktitut, 13 percent speak Ojibwa, 3 percent speak Athapaskan, and 1 percent speak Sioux. Of those claiming to speak an Aboriginal language, we find that the average age is well in excess of 40. This suggests that it is the older segment of the population that still retains the language and not the younger generation. Norris (1998) found that the index of continuity was at 76 percent in 1981 but that 15 years later this had decreased to just below 65 percent. This means that for every 100 people with an Aboriginal mother tongue, the number who used an indigenous language most often at home declined from 76 to just under 65.

The overall diminishing of Aboriginal-language use is somewhat mediated by special schools and language instruction programs. Almost 34 000 students (or 42 percent of Aboriginal enrolment) received some Aboriginal language instruction in school during the year. In addition, the number of students taking courses in which an Aboriginal language is the medium of instruction over half the time increased by more than 60 percent during the 1980–84 period. However, like other ethnic minorities, Aboriginal people have learned that, to integrate into the larger society, they must learn to speak English or French. Thus, to a certain extent, the decreasing number of Aboriginal-language speakers reflects an increasing move away from the reserves and an increasing contact with non-Aboriginal persons. Nevertheless, the educational process has increased the number of Aboriginal-language speakers, through the provincial programs that have supported Aboriginal language at both the elementary and secondary levels. For example, In Alberta, Cree is taught in a number of public and private primary and secondary schools with an estimated 700 students enrolled.

Nearly all Aboriginal people who change language shift to English (96.8 percent). Inuit and other Aboriginal people living in the north of Canada were the most reluctant to change languages, while Métis were most likely to do so. We find that the young (under 14) and the old (65+) were least likely to take on English as their operating language. Younger children will, as they grow older, be more fully exposed to the larger society and will begin the process of linguistic shift. Thus, the fact that young people still retain their

Aboriginal tongue is no indication that they will be fluent in that language as they enter the labour force. The lack of shift in the older generation is due to the fact that they have spent their lives speaking an Aboriginal language and have been least exposed to the modern industrial society outside their community (Jarvis and Heaton, 1989).

Even though the number of persons reporting an Aboriginal mother tongue has increased by 25 percent over the last 15 years, proportionately fewer of these individuals used this indigenous language at home. As Norris (1998) points out, Aboriginal language vitality is decreasing at an alarming rate. At the same time, the link between the respondents' perceptions regarding children's grasp of Native culture and language is clear. Turcotte and Zhao (2004) show that nearly two-thirds of Aboriginal parents believe it is important for their children to speak and understand an Aboriginal language. We also know that parents are key language teachers for their children, but the question remains as to whether or not parents will be able to teach their children, since many of them have lost their ability to speak their Aboriginal language.

RELIGION

According to present statistics, 46 percent of Aboriginals in Canada are Catholics. This, of course, reflects the early Jesuit and Oblate missionary work among the Aboriginal people. Protestants make up an additional 36 percent, while "no religion" adds another 17 percent. The second-largest Aboriginal religious denomination is Anglican, with 18 percent. Another 10 percent of Aboriginal peoples belong to the United Church, and the remaining 8 percent are evenly distributed among the other Christian churches in Canada. However, no information has been gathered regarding the extent to which Aboriginal people still adhere to pre-Christian religious beliefs. Apparently, a significant percentage of Aboriginal persons have retained their indigenous religious beliefs. Nonetheless, Christianity has had a definite impact on Aboriginal culture during the past three centuries and its ideology of acceptance and obedience has contributed significantly to a widespread conservatism and fatalism among Aboriginal peoples.

MARITAL STATUS

Figures on the marital status of Aboriginal people do not support the stereotype of the broken Aboriginal family. Data shown in Table 4.3 reveal the marital status of the female Aboriginal population aged 15 and older. It shows that there are differences among the various Aboriginal groups and the non-Aboriginal population. For example, the proportion of married varies from 47 percent for off-reserve to nearly 60 percent for non-Aboriginals. Less than one-quarter of non-Aboriginals have never married, while on-reserve residents have the highest rate at 36.

Other statistics suggest that Aboriginal family patterns depart from non-Aboriginal norms. About 60 percent of Aboriginal people living together are officially married, as compared to 67 percent of the overall Canadian population. About one-quarter of registered Indian families are comprised of single-mother families. When we compare these figures to Inuit (20 percent) and Métis (15 percent) we find that Indians have a much higher rate. Non-Aboriginal families show the lowest rate of single-mother families, with 12 percent. The proportion of Canadian families headed by a single mother rose from 20 percent in 1981 to nearly 23 percent in 2002. Approximately one in three Aboriginal mothers in 2001 was a

TABLE 4.3	Marital Status of Female Aboriginal Population Aged 15 and older, Percentage Canada, 2001					
Registered	Total Abor.	On	Off	Métis	Inuit	Non-Aborig.
Married	49.3	50.6	46.6	50.1	55.7	58.4
Separated	4.4	3.1	5.3	4.9	2.0	2.8
Divorced	6.0	3.1	7.0	7.3	1.7	6.3
Widowed	5.2	6.6	4.9	4.7	4.9	8.9
Never Married	35.1	36.5	36.2	33.0	35.7	23.6

Source: Adapted from Hull, 2006; Department of Indian and Northern Affairs Canada, 2006.

lone parent, compared with one in six in the overall Canadian population. Young Aboriginal females between 15 and 19 are much more likely to marry than are other Canadian teenagers, and these young women are three times more likely to be single mothers than Canadian women of the same age. At the beginning of the 21st century, we found that lone-parent families headed by a single father were twice as common among on-reserve registered Indians as among the Canadian population. All of these statistics have implications for the high illegitimacy rate characteristic of the Aboriginal population (IRIW, 1979).

Related to marital status is the number and growth rate of Aboriginal families. In 2001 there were 143 000 families, a major increase from 1986. There is no question that *Bill C-31* had a significant impact on this growth rate: in 1987 the growth rate for families was 9 percent, six times that of the general Canadian family. However, even when the impact of this legislation is removed, the growth rate of Aboriginal families continues to be considerably higher than for the general Canadian population. The data show that the Aboriginal family is larger than the Canadian family, although there has been a decrease in family size from 1981 to 2001.

In looking at families, we must also assess the fertility rate of Aboriginals. Fertility over the past half-century has decreased although the tempo of this decline has varied over time. However the fertility pattern is not the same for all groups. In recent years, the Inuit have experienced a sharp decline in their fertility level, from over 4 children to about three (3.4). In contrast, Métis had the lowest fertility level and are now at the replacement level (2.2 children per family). First Nations families have about three children (2.9). We also find differences in fertility by region. Manitoba, Saskatchewan and the three Northern territories have high fertility rates (more than three children) while the rest of the country have lower levels (above two children per family) (Statistics Canada, 2005). The fertility rate for Aboriginal people over the next 20 years is a crucial demographic factor. The data show that the fertility rates will remain much higher than those for non-Aboriginal people. The projected fertility rate for registered Indians in 2017 will be 2.6, while for all Canadian women the rate will be 1.5. Projections for Métis will fall below replacement rates (1.95) and Inuit will drop marginally (3.02). These projections are not based upon changes in the definition of Aboriginality or the impact of such legislation as *Bill C-31*. If these factors are taken into consideration, it is estimated that the fertility rates provided above will be much higher (3.12 First Nation, 2.48 Métis, 3.47 Inuit).

SOCIO-ECONOMIC STATUS

Canada is an internally stratified, unequal society. This is to say that it can be divided into unequal or hierarchical categories that persist over time. Inequalities between categories thus become crystallized into social classes such that some groups perennially have more resources than others, which translates into a better quality of life. Those who rank high are able to enjoy the benefits of a modern industrial society with its enhanced educational, medical, and leisure activities. On the other hand, those who place low in our hierarchical system will not be able to benefit from the increased technological innovations to enhance their quality of life. In our social system, four factors influence one's ability to participate in modern industrial society: income, labour force participation, occupational status, and education.

Income

We begin our discussion by showing the change in income as well as the disparity between Aboriginal and non-Aboriginal incomes over time. In 1966 Hawthorn established that the per capita income per year for Aboriginal persons was about $300, and for other Canadians, about $1400. In 2004, the median family income for the general population was just over $64 000 per year, while for Aboriginals it was under $27 000.

When we review the average individual income by different Aboriginal groups, we find substantial differences (see Table 4.4). The data below (2002) provide the information for both males and females. They reveal dramatic differences in income among Aboriginal groups as well as between Aboriginal and non-Aboriginal.

Before discussing income further, it is important that the reader fully appreciate that income can be generated from a number of sources. The most general categories used in this review are those of wage (earned) and non-wage (unearned or transfer). The data from Statistics Canada show that earned income is the major source of income for all groups. They reveal that employment income makes up at least 60 percent of income for all groups. However, for on-reserve Aboriginals, 20 percent is from government transfer payments, in comparison to the 10 percent for non-Aboriginals. We also see that only non-Aboriginals have a substantial proportion of "other" income, e.g., interest, bonds, stocks. Another way of illustrating the income of groups is to look at the family income. Figure 4.5 reveals the total family income (regardless of source) for Canadians, compared to Aboriginal families. We see that 40 percent of Aboriginal families make less than $20 000 per year, compared to only 10 percent of non-Aboriginals. At the other end of the continuum, we find that 36 percent of non-Aboriginal people are making more than $70 000, while only 7 percent of Aboriginal families have that high an income.

TABLE 4.4	Income by Gender and Racial Group, 2002					
Registered	Total	On Res.	Off-Res.	Métis	Inuit	Non-Aborig.
Women	$16 519	13 968	16 483	18 144	18 721	23 065
Male	$21 969	14 907	22 849	26 634	21103	37 365

Source: www.ainc-inac.gc.ca/pr/pub/abw/t6-2_e.html.

We now move to the question of how many Aboriginal and non-Aboriginal people have an income. At least 75 percent of the total Canadian population (over the age of 15) has some income. However, nearly one-fourth of the Aboriginal population reported no income, while only 10 percent of the Canadian population reported no income.

The data show that the disparity between non-Aboriginal Canadian and Aboriginal individual income remained the same as it had been during the 1980–90 period. In 1980 the average income for status Indians was 70 percent of that for all Canadians, and by 1990 this had not changed. However, by 2002, this had decreased to just over 50 percent of the average Canadian yearly earnings, showing that the gap is growing over time. Family incomes show a similar pattern. Status Indian families have an average income of $21 800, which is about half that of the average Canadian family, at $38 000. Like individual incomes, family income disparity has increased, and recent information suggests that the increase continues.

To assess this pattern, we present Table 4.5, which reveals the average income by highest level of schooling. It reveals that, as the level of education increases, so does the income. However, it also reveals that the pay-off for increasing educational achievements is much greater for non-Aboriginal people ($14 249 for less than grade nine to $38 276 with a university degree for females) than for Aboriginal ($11 619 to $33 624). The difference is even more marked when comparing Aboriginal and non-Aboriginal male incomes by level of education.

A comparison of income over time shows that, while the absolute income of all Aboriginal people has increased over time, a gap between them and the rest of Canada continues to widen. The disparity in 1981 revealed that Aboriginal people made 67 percent of their non-aboriginal Canadian counterparts, but by 2001 the gap had widened and they only made 65 percent of the annual income of non-Aboriginals.

In summary, we find that the disparity of income between Aboriginal and non-Aboriginal Canadians noted by Hawthorn in the 1960s still exists. In addition, the data suggest that the gap between the two groups is getting larger. This startling fact emerges despite the large and complex structure we have put in place to help Aboriginal people find a niche in our society and integrate into the economic structure.

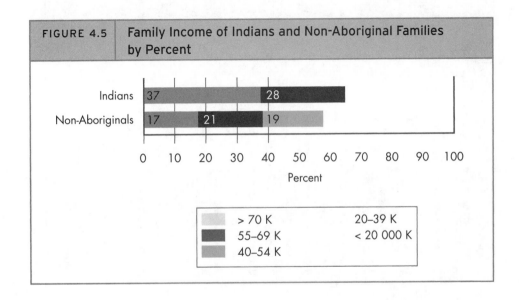

FIGURE 4.5 | Family Income of Indians and Non-Aboriginal Families by Percent

TABLE 4.5 Average Individual Income of the Population with Income by Gender, Highest Level of Schooling, Aboriginal Identity and Area of Residence, Canada, 2000

Gender and Highest Level of Schooling	Total Aboriginal	Registered Indian			Métis	Inuit	Other Aboriginal	Non-Aboriginal
		Total	On Reserve	Off Reserve				
Women–All Levels	**16 619**	**15 365**	**13 988**	**16 483**	**18 144**	**18 721**	**16 240**	**23 085**
Less than grade 9	11 619	11 175	10 989	11 480	12 157	14 179	10 470	14 249
Grades 9–13 without certificate	11 378	10 612	9 421	11 649	12 701	12 765	9 918	15 582
Grades 9–13 with certificate	16 041	15 174	13 692	15 984	16 826	19 063	15 888	20 363
Non-University without certificate	15 785	14 928	15 153	14 785	17 030	18 387	15 412	19 824
Trades certificate	13 360	17 329	17 273	17 375	19 277	24 835	18 422	21 574
Other Non-University certificate/diploma	22 408	21 624	20 652	22 191	22 484	31 080	22 526	26 324
University without degree	20 754	19 708	19 709	19 706	21 842	27 139	21 670	24 387
University degree	33 624	32 323	32 737	32 153	34 882	41 871	34 853	38 276
Men–All Levels	**21 958**	**18 724**	**14 907**	**22 849**	**26 634**	**21 103**	**23 827**	**37 285**
Less than grade 9	15 948	14 317	12 981	17 555	19 642	17 865	16 535	22 721
Grades 9–13 without certificate	16 365	13 708	10 948	16 872	20 855	14 000	16 320	25 531
Grades 9–13 with certificate	23 201	26 819	14 938	24 797	25 910	20 476	23 591	32 041
Non-University without certificate	20 676	18 118	16 231	19 738	24 333	21 444	23 521	29 456
Trades certificate	28 387	23 973	19 920	28 475	33 804	29 266	31 499	37 865
Other Non-University certificate/diploma	30 467	27 464	22 689	30 886	33 317	32 834	33 617	41 854
University without degree	26 299	23 871	21 147	25 482	28 321	35 825	30 205	36 583
University degree	43 752	41 185	34 458	34 458	44 629	43 199	48 056	63 255

Income Polarity While the data presented above reveal that, as a group, Aboriginal people are economically disadvantaged (consistent with the data presented by George et al. (2001) and Brunnen (2003), the question arises as to whether or not these disparities are increasing or decreasing. Walters, White, and Maxim (2004) noted that the Canadian population experienced a greater increase in family income during the 1990s than ever before. Maxim and White (2003) note that, on average, Canadian incomes increased 1.7 percent per annum during the last decade. Have Aboriginal people followed that trend? Data from Maxim and White show that, while the overall increase was just under 2 percent per year, the top quintile (upper 20 percent) of Canadian families experienced a 6.6 percent increase each year, while the lowest quintile experienced a 5.2 percent decrease each year in income. Given that we know that most Aboriginals have incomes in the lowest quintile, we can infer that they have experienced a decrease in income over the past decade, thus exacerbating the income polarity that existed a decade ago. Even when transfer payments—e.g., old age pension, disability, interest, dividends—are added to the total income of individuals, we find that there is no decrease in the income polarity but in fact an increase in disparity. This suggests that wealthy people are making more in government transfers than poor people are.

Another measurement strategy to determine social inequality has been undertaken by Armstrong (1999). He wanted to see how First Nations communities compared with communities in the rest of the country. He divided the country into five regions of "well-being" and identified the "best off" Aboriginal communities in terms of socio-economic indicators. He then compared the "best off" Aboriginal communities with the "worst-off" non-Aboriginal communities as identified in Figure 4.6. The results are dramatic, in that the "best-off" Aboriginal communities are not doing as well as the "worst-off" non-Aboriginal regions of the country (see Table 4.6).

Labour Force Participation

Participation in the labour force both impacts on the income of an individual or family, and provides an indicator of the degree of social integration in society. Participation in the

TABLE 4.6	Comparison of "Best-Off" Aboriginal Communities with "Worst-Off" Non-Aboriginal Communities	
Best-Off Aboriginal	Worst-Off Non-Communities	Aboriginal Communities.
Percent with less than grade 9	12	20
Percent Employed	58	57
Persons per home per home	0.7	0.6
Annual Income	18 200	18 900
Percent under 18 years	36	25

Source: Adapted from: Armstrong, R. 1999, "Mapping the Conditions of First Nations Communities," *Canadian Social Trends*, Winter, 14-18.

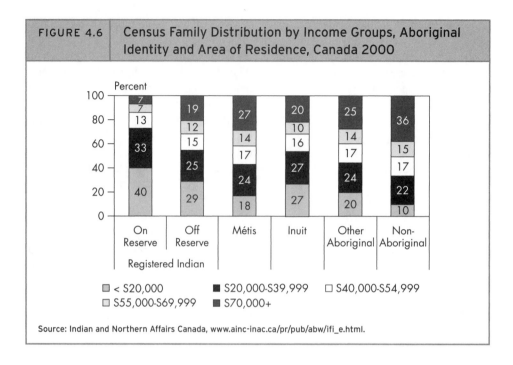

| FIGURE 4.6 | Census Family Distribution by Income Groups, Aboriginal Identity and Area of Residence, Canada 2000 |

Source: Indian and Northern Affairs Canada, www.ainc-inac.ca/pr/pub/abw/ifi_e.html.

labour force is highly differentiated as we look at comparisons between Canadians and Aboriginal Canadians. Data from Indian and Northern Affairs Canada (INAC) show that the gap between Aboriginal and Canadian labour force participation decreased between 1980 and 2005. One might argue that since many Aboriginal communities are small and isolated it would be inappropriate to compare their participation rates with the overall Canadian statistics. However, as the Royal Commission on Aboriginal Peoples points out, even when Aboriginals are compared with similar rural, isolated non-Aboriginal communities, their economic performance falls short. Table 4.7 reveals the labour force activity of the Aboriginal population. The results show that the involvement in the labour force by Aboriginals is much less than for non-Aboriginal people.

While an increasing number of Aboriginal people entered the labour force over the past two decades, their percentage of unemployed doubled, while for Canadians, the increase was minor. In 2001 the unemployment rate on the reserves was triple the official national rate of 7 percent. This disparity was larger on an age-specific basis. The gap between the First Nations and Canadians participating in the labour force was widest among the 15–24 age group, with a difference of 30 percent. We also found that the gap between the employment rates of First Nations people and Canadians is widening. For all age groups and sexes, the First Nations unemployment rates were at least twice as high, and the highest unemployment rate was in the 15–24 age group (Health Canada, 2003; see Table 4.7 below). These figures illustrate the degree of exclusion of Aboriginal people from the Canadian economy. To achieve parity with all Canadians, nearly 100 000 more Aboriginal people would have to be employed.

Participation in the labour force may be full-time or part-time/seasonal work. Data show that, in 2000, over 40 percent of Aboriginal women and 32 percent of Aboriginal men

TABLE 4.7	Labour Force Activity of Aboriginals Aged 15+ (percentage), Canada, 2001					
Total	Registered Abor.	On	Off	Métis	Inuit	Non-Aborig.
Women						
Part. Rate	57	47	55	65	60	61
Unempl Rate	17	22	19	12	19	7
Employ.Rate	47	37	45	57	48	56
Men						
Part. Rate	67	56	68	75	65	73
Unemp.Rate	21	33	21	15	25	7
Empl. Rate	53	38	53	64	49	68

Source: Adapted from Hull, 2006.

did not work during the year. This is compared to 36 percent and 25 percent for non-Aboriginal women and men. Looking at the other end of the continuum, we find that 36 percent of Aboriginal women and 40 percent of Aboriginal men worked more than 40 weeks (full time) during the year. This is in contrast to 47 percent and 59 percent of non-Aboriginal women and men for the same year. Table 4.8 reveals the labour market involvement

TABLE 4.8	Weeks Worked in 2000 by Sex and Aboriginal Identity (percentage)					
		Registered				
	Total	On	Off	Métis	Inuit	Non-Aboriginal
Women						
Not worked	41.4	50.6	43.8	32.7	35.7	36.8
1-9 weeks	2.9	3.5	2.8	2.4	4.9	1.5
10-20 weeks	8.5	8.0	8.5	8.9	11.2	6.1
21-39	9.0	7.4	9.0	10.1	11.0	7.5
40 plus	36.2	27.0	33.1	43.4	322	46.6
Males						
Not worked	31.7	42.0	31.5	23.4	29.2	25.0
1-9 weeks	3.3	4.3	3.1	2.6	5.7	1.4
10-20	10.2	12.2	9.8	8.8	12.5	5.9
21-39	11.7	11.2	11.9	12.5	11.7	7.9
40+ weeks	39.8	26.0	40.6	50.1	34.9	58.5

Source: Adapted from Hull, 2006.

differences among Aboriginal groups and between Aboriginal and non-Aboriginal groups. We also find that, even if level of education is controlled for, there is an increase in the labour force participation rate. However, the labour force participation rate for Aboriginal people does not match that of the non-Aboriginal population. Again this reveals that education does not "pay off" for Aboriginal people.

Turning now to the occupation of those labour force participants, Table 4.9 reveals the occupations of Aboriginals by group and sex.

The data show that over half of the jobs held by Aboriginal men were made up of skilled, semi-skilled, and other manual occupations (see Table 4.9). In fact, one-fourth of the jobs held by Aboriginal males were in manual labour. Just over 10 percent of the Canadian population were in the level D (manual labour) occupations. When we look at the upper scale of the occupational list (upper- and middle-level managers and professionals), we find over 25 percent of the total Canadian population, but less than half that percentage of Aboriginal people. Overall, compared to the total population, there are fewer Aboriginal persons in upper-status occupations and more Aboriginal persons in lower-status occupations.[2]

When we look at females in the labour force, we find a different distribution than that evidenced by the male population. At the upper ends of the occupational scale we find similarities between Aboriginal women and Canadian women, even though Aboriginal women are slightly underrepresented when compared to all females. The major differences between Aboriginal and all females is in two occupational categories—clerical and services. Nearly 30 percent of all female Canadians in the labour force hold jobs as clerks. For Aboriginal people it is less than 23 percent. On the other hand, one-fifth of the Aboriginal

TABLE 4.9	Occupations of Experienced Labour Force by Sex and Aboriginal Identity, 2001, (percentage)					
	Total Aboriginal	Registered On	Off	Métis	Inuit	Non-Aboriginal
Males						
Level A	12.9	13.3	12.5	12.7	14.5	26.2
Level B	33.2	30.8	33.5	35.3	29.2	33.0
Level C	30.4	27.6	30.8	31.5	29.9	27.6
Level D	23.5	28.2	23.1	20.6	26.4	13.3
Women						
Level A	17.9	20.0	18.0	16.5	22.2	24.8
Level B	252	27.6	26.4	24.9	24.9	25.9
Level C	36.5	324	36.5	39.7	27.2	36.1
Level D	20.4	20.0	21.1	18.9	25.8	13.1

Level A consists of senior and middle managers as well as professions. Level B are semi-professionals, supervisors, senior clerical and skilled sales, service crafts and trades. Level C are clerical personnel, intermediate sales and service and semi-skilled manual. Level D are other sales and service and other manual.

Source: Adapted from Hull, 2006.

females are in service occupations, compared to just over 10 percent of the total female population in the labour force.

In summary, Aboriginal people are participating more in the labour force over time. In 2003, 43 percent were employed, while a similar number (over the age of 15) were not part of the labour force. The remainder (14 percent) are officially considered unemployed. However, their participation continues to be at the margins and is not representative of the jobs that characterize a modern industrial society. In an attempt to further integrate Aboriginal people into the labour force, the federal government has introduced a number of programs to help Aboriginal people find jobs and relocate if necessary. These federal programs are attempting to raise Aboriginal people to the average Canadian standard of living. Unfortunately, the programs offer too little to be more than band-aid measures. They also operate only for short periods of time as pilot projects, which ensures that there is no commitment of funds beyond a one- or two-year period. In addition, the programs are generally designed only to meet the needs of middle-class Aboriginal people. Finally, the independent structure of programs reflects a lack of wide-ranging, integrated federal policy (Knight, 1978).

The Aboriginal participation rate in the labour force is about 20 percent lower than the national rate. And it has been estimated that, of those who do participate, over 12 percent will remain permanently unemployed. However, these figures should be approached warily. The criteria that define the active labour force are largely based upon white, middle-class values and include only those Aboriginal persons who have worked or looked for work during the past week. Moreover, because primary and unskilled jobs are extremely susceptible to seasonal factors, the time of year has a disproportionate impact on the Aboriginal employment rate. Nevertheless, even taking these factors into account, Aboriginal unemployment is still three times higher than the national average.

We also find that, because Aboriginal people usually work at seasonal or part-time jobs, they have little job security. And even in seasonal jobs, they are often discriminated against. We have shown that, even when education is entered into the equation, Aboriginals do not make as much money as non-Aboriginals with the same education, nor do they have similar occupations. Thus, the low income of Aboriginal workers reflects both the seasonal nature of their jobs and discrimination. The results show that if Aboriginal persons are able to enter the labour force they do quite well, although less so than the general population (Siggner, 1986). Many of them, after experiencing the "colour" bar in jobs, leave large organizations and begin their own companies.

EDUCATION

Canadian culture places a great emphasis on the value of education. Education is generally seen as essential to success; young people who do not show academic potential are usually regarded as early failures. Certainly, education has a great impact on lifestyle and life chances. Yet, for a variety of reasons, not all Canadians are able to use the educational system as effectively as possible. Aboriginal people in particular are excluded by several factors from the benefits of Euro-Canadian education.

At the financial level, the federal government appears to have fulfilled its responsibility to Aboriginal people in the area of education (Mendelson, 2006). Federal expenditures for Aboriginal education were $13.5 million in 1956; by 1980 they reached well over $270 million, or 39 percent of the total Indian–Inuit Affairs budget. In 2002, the Department spent $1.068 billion in elementary/secondary education and an additional $312 million on post-secondary education. However, today this represents less than 20 percent of the Department's total budget. During the 1970s, the number of students increased nearly 2 percent annually, to almost 100 000 students. (Today there are about 120 000.) In 2003, the government committed $35 million to deal with recommendations that were presented by the Indian Affairs National Working Group on Education. These figures demonstrate that expenditures per student more than doubled between 1981 and 1993 ($7212), representing an average annual growth rate of 7.1 percent. By 2002, the per capita average had increased to over $11 000 per year. (In comparison, over the past five years the federal government contributed over $7 billion to the education of non-Aboriginals, for activities that are not within the federal jurisdiction, i.e., Canadian research chairs, knowledge centres.)

However, less than 5 percent of this money has gone directly to Aboriginal communities to be controlled by Aboriginal people themselves. Most has been spent on the creation of various federal administrative and bureaucratic positions, or on capital grants to provincial and local governments to purchase "seats" in non-Aboriginal schools. Moreover, over the past decade, the federal government has kept Aboriginal education funding at a ceiling of 2 percent per year. An analysis of the enrolment increases in First Nations' schools demonstrates that it should have risen to 3 percent, which means that funding for education has decreased in terms of real, inflation-adjusted, per student dollars (Mendelson, 2006). In short, the fulfillment of the federal government's obligations to Aboriginal education has been only in the financial sector—and even then it has been inadequate.

What is troubling with the above picture is that, as the Auditor General pointed out in her 2004 report, "The Department of Indian Affairs does not know whether funding to First Nations is sufficient to meet the education standards it has set." An evaluation study of Aboriginal education in British Columbia (Postl, 2005) and Saskatchewan (QED, 2004) revealed that federal funding was not at the level of provincial funding and that federal funding did not cover "special needs" students or administrative support for teachers.

Educational Curriculum

People see and make sense of the world in many different ways; they also see their relationship to the environment in different ways. Since this is so, they approach problems looking for different solutions, and they may process information differently in arriving at those solutions. Hence, the educational process has an important impact on people exposed to it. For those who accept and are able to utilize the process to its fullest, the results are positive. However, there are others who do not accept it or are otherwise unable to take maximum advantage of conventional educational methods. This suggests that some people who are exposed to our particular type of educational system may be mismatched with the teaching process. Any discrepancy between learning style and instructional methods will lead to inefficiency and possibly to failure on the student's part (Pask and Scott, 1971). Until the 1970s, the educational curriculum was dominated by an assimilationist curriculum. Even today, the curriculum used in an Aboriginal school is regulated by the province's government and is the same as that designed for white middle-class students in all the other public schools. Under the current *Indian Act*, First Nations are not responsible for their own schools, although each band can enter into agreements with the Crown. Today, only one agreement, the 2006 agreement among Ottawa, the BC government and the BC First Nations Education Steering Committee, allows the First Nations Education Authority to function in the way of a school board, providing teacher and school certification and setting standards for curriculum and examinations for participating First Nations (Mendelson, 2006).

The present school system has been established on the premise that all members of our society are field-independent thinkers. To some extent, this may indeed be the predominant mode of thinking in our culture. However, some cultural groups do not promote this type of thinking and consequently find the present school system useless. Our best evidence suggests that Indian culture promotes a relational type of thinking (Weitz, 1971; see also the work of O'Meara and West, *From Our Eyes: Learning from Indigenous Peoples*, 1966). If such a statement is true, then the dismal educational record of Indian people should not come as a surprise.

Other experts in the field feel that the poor performance of Aboriginal students in formal education settings is a result of substandard schools and lack of reinforcement of education in the families. For example, it is argued that the Aboriginal community does not place a high value on obtaining an education, particularly for young males. Thus, these structural conditions make it extremely difficult for many Aboriginal young people to achieve success in the educational system.

History of Aboriginal Education

For many years after Britain took control of Canada, Aboriginal education was controlled by the military, acting for the Crown. Then, legislation was passed in 1830 transferring the responsibility to the provincial or local governments (Special Senate Hearing on Poverty, 1970: 14, 59).

In general, European settlers were indifferent to Aboriginal education: a public fund was not established for this purpose until 1848. In some cases, European settlers encouraged the school enrolment of Aboriginal children in order to pressure the province to establish more schools. As the density of the non-Aboriginal population increased, however, Aboriginal education was increasingly ignored. Later, the federal government was reluctant to operate schools for Indians, and passed the responsibility to other, mainly religious, agencies. With the passage of the *British North America Act, 1867,* Canada's parliament was given the power to administer Aboriginal affairs, including education. In 1876 the *Indian Act* was passed, providing the legal basis for federal administration of Aboriginal education. In addition, most treaties signed after 1871 contained an educational commitment to maintain schools on the reserve and provide educational services when required.

Federal and provincial government policy on Aboriginal education can be considered in two phases. The first, from 1867 to 1945, has been labelled the "paternalistic ideology" phase. Until 1945, Native schooling was "education in isolation." During this period, schools and hostels for Indian children were established, but scant attention was paid to developing a curriculum geared to either their language difficulties or their sociological needs. A few Indian bands established schools for their children on the reserves, but the majority of them had neither the financial resources nor the leadership to establish and operate their own schools. Provincial governments were too preoccupied with their own priorities to become involved in Indian education. Missionaries provided a modicum of services, but their "noble savage" philosophy effectively insulated the Indians from the mainstream of society (Special Senate Hearing on Poverty, 1970: 14, 59).

The second period, from 1945 to the present, has been called the "democratic ideology" phase (Hawthorn, 1967). The second phase simply refers to the "open door policy" that enabled Aboriginal students to attend school off the reserve.

The paternalistic policy whereby Aboriginal students were considered backward children was adopted and perpetuated by various religious orders in Canada. After Confederation, the first schools for Aboriginal children were quasi-educational institutions set up by religious orders. Under Sections 113 to 122 of the *Indian Act*, the federal government could legally arrange for provincial governments and religious organizations to provide Aboriginal education. Four churches—Roman Catholic, Anglican, Methodist and Presbyterian—began to educate Aboriginal children in denominational or residential schools.[3] Of these, the Catholics and Anglicans have had the greatest impact on Aboriginal people in Canada, and continue to do so.

Education was traditionally viewed by churches as the best way to assimilate Aboriginal people. The missionaries, who until the 1970s controlled Aboriginal education, were far more concerned with converting the students than with teaching useful, practical knowledge and skills. Because they felt that Aboriginal people would always live in isolation, the missionaries made no attempt to prepare them for successful careers in modern Canadian society. Instead, they concentrated on eradicating all traces of Aboriginal languages, traditions, and beliefs (Fuchs, 1970).

Because religious ideologies are fundamentally conservative, they discouraged protest and revolt on the part of the Aboriginal people. For example, Roman Catholicism holds that poverty is not a social evil, but is God's will. Instead of struggling against God's will, Catholics are encouraged to humbly accept their fates in order to ensure a place in heaven. Thus Roman Catholicism discourages social change, particularly that which involves force: in heaven "the first shall be last and the last shall be first" (Matt. 19:30).

Churches that operated schools were given land, per capita grants, and other material rewards for their efforts.[4] Often these grants resulted in the material exploitation of the Aboriginal peoples as churches pursued property and profits (McCullum and McCullum, 1975; Grant, 1996).

> As Hawthorn pointed out half a century ago, "We note that the greater the educational resources possessed by a church or the greater its investment in Indian education, the greater its anxiety to maintain the status quo. On the contrary, the faiths having the least material interests in Indian education are much more open to innovation." (1967: 61)

To accommodate the education of young Aboriginal students and facilitate their assimilation, residential schools were established throughout the country. Residential schools were almost all built in rural locations, far from non-Aboriginal settlements. These schools limited the contact between Aboriginal children and their parents to facilitate the transformation of the students from "heathens" to Christians. The schools were highly regimented and insisted on strict conformity. There were few adults, and most of these were non-Aboriginal persons; as a result, normal adult–child relations could not develop. (See Box 4.1 for a discussion of compensation being paid to former students of these schools.) Few of the teachers were well qualified; they neither stimulated the children nor acted as positive role models. The average annual staff turnover was never less than 21 percent and often higher, particularly after 1955.

In 1945, the "open door policy" was introduced, which allowed students to travel off the reserve to receive an education. This was a radical departure from the earlier policy of isolation, and residential schools began to decline in enrolment. Particularly since the early 1960s, the number of Aboriginal children attending residential schools has been drastically reduced. The unpopularity of these schools should come as a surprise to no one.[5]

Box 4.1	Residential School Compensation

For many years, Aboriginal people had stated that they were physically and sexually abused while in residential schools. However, it would not be until 1990 that the first Indian residential school claim was received. Six years later, the "Residential School Unit" at INAC was created and 200 claims were received. In 1998, the deputy prime minister delivered a statement of reconciliation and an apology to those people who experienced abuse while attending residential schools. The Aboriginal Healing Foundation was also established in this year. In 2001, the government of Canada began negotiations with the churches and bilateral negotiations were undertaken. In 2003 both the Presbyterian and Anglican Churches signed agreements with the government of Canada outlining how they would participate in compensating former abused residential students. In 2005, an Agreement in Principle was reached between the government and legal counsel for former students, the Assembly of First Nations and other Aboriginal organizations. The settlement Agreement was approved by the government and Aboriginal people of Canada in 2006. The settlement sets aside $2B for compensation. Payments are $10K for the first school year plus $3K for each school year after that. Those who suffered sexual or serious physical abuses will be able to apply for additional compensation between $5K and $275K. In addition, $125M for healing, $60M for research, documentation and preservation of the experiences of the survivors and $20M for national and community commemorative projects will be provided.

While there were over 85 000 students enrolled in residential schools over their history, less than 14 000 applications have been submitted. Over the past three years, nearly 3000 applications were not processed because the applicant had died during the time period. The settlement arrangements will not compensate children of abused students, but it has processed over 10 000 applications (mainly from aging Aboriginals) and paid out just over $80M.

As part of the settlement, the government will pay lawyers representing former students up to $100M in fees plus costs and taxes. This clause has led the minister of INAC to refuse further payouts until one legal firm (the Merchant lawyer group) provides detailed billing information for his clients. A stalemate has been reached. Once again, the people deserving of the compensation are being denied payment because of a difference between the government and a third party.

Types of Aboriginal Schools

Federal   Historically, Aboriginal students attended church-run, federally sponsored schools. Later, Aboriginal students could attend either federal schools or integrated (provincially/federally funded) joint schools. There were four types of federal schools: day schools; denominational (also called residential or religious) schools; boarding and hospital schools; and band schools. Day schools were the largest group under federal control.

They were located on the reserve and provided education only for those who lived there, including the non-Aboriginal children of teachers.

Denominational schools were those operated by religious groups. Since the late 1930s DIAND (now INAC) also operated residential schools, at first through the churches and then more directly. When day schools were established in 1950 for elementary education, residential schools began to provide secondary education only. Since the late 1960s the residential schools have been systematically shut down, the last one closing its doors in 1996.

Hospital schools provide classes for Aboriginal students in government hospitals, from the pre-school level through to adult education. Boarding schools are for Aboriginal orphans or children from broken homes, and may or may not be on the reserve.[6] All boarding schools are currently under government-financed church control, mainly Roman Catholic. Although these schools are technically integrated, they have a majority of Aboriginal students. At present, only five federal schools remain in operation. Thus, for practical purposes, all federal schools have been phased out of existence.

In 1961, over two-thirds of the Indian elementary and high school students went to federal schools. Five years later this had dwindled to 52 percent, and by 1980 it had further decreased to 44 percent. Today, less than 2 percent of Aboriginal students attend federal schools. If we look at the current Aboriginal population, we find that nearly 14 percent of those aged 55 years or older attended federal residential schools. This percent decreases to 11 for the 45–54 year category; and for the 15–34 age group, the number who attended federal residential schools is just over 2 percent.

Band   The creation of band schools emerged out of the political lobbying that Aboriginals participated in during the late 1960s and early 1970s. While these are technically federal schools, they have taken on an air of independence and largely manage themselves even though they receive federal dollars to operate. In 1973 the National Indian Brotherhood produced a document, *Indian Control of Indian Education,* which was later accepted by the federal government and adopted as official educational policy for Aboriginal education. This policy explicitly incorporated the principles of parental responsibility and local control. It was, for Indians, a time when they believed that they would become active participants in affecting their own educational experiences. The educational branch of Indian Affairs established guidelines and procedures for school transfers to bands and introduced a national formula-funding system for the allocation of resources for the band-operated schools.

By 1980, well over 100 band-operated schools were in operation. By 1990 the number had increased to 300 and today there are nearly 500. Band-operated schools make up an increasingly larger portion of the total Aboriginal student enrolment. Figure 4.7 shows the growth rate of First Nations schools. Table 4.10 shows the number of registered Indians enrolled in kindergarten to grades 12/13 by type of school. The information shows that over 60 percent of the primary and secondary school population attend First Nations (band) schools. Just over one-third attend provincial joint-integrated schools.

Provincial   Integrated joint schools are not controlled by the federal government. Essentially, these are provincial schools that allow Aboriginal students to attend and are paid a fee by Indian and Inuit Affairs for each student attending. The structure and curricula of

FIGURE 4.7	Number of First Nation Schools, Canada, 1992–93 to 2004–05

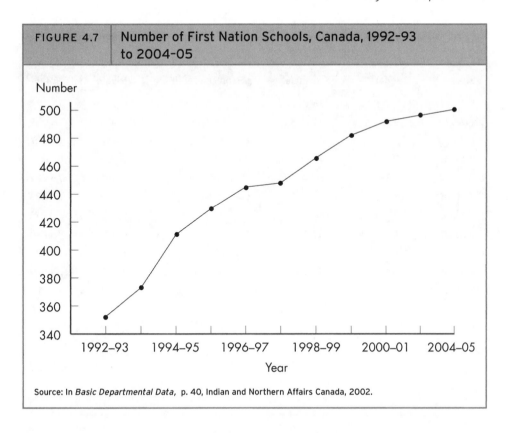

Source: In *Basic Departmental Data,* p. 40, Indian and Northern Affairs Canada, 2002.

these schools are not significantly different from those controlled by the federal government. The difference lies in the administration and financing. Although education is a provincial responsibility, the provincial governments argue that Aboriginal children are a federal responsibility and thus, if they attend a provincial school, the province must be compensated.[7]

Data from the Indian–Inuit Affairs Program (IIAP) show that, from 1964 to 1981, over 800 agreements were made between local school boards and the Department of Indian Affairs in order to secure positions for Aboriginal children in provincial schools. Table 4.11 shows the relative trends for Aboriginal enrolment by all types of schools. The data provided in Table 4.11 demonstrate the historical increase in Indian enrolment from 1961 to 2004. The data also show that the percentage of school-age children attending school has increased dramatically. In the early 1960s less than three-quarters of the potential student population was attending school. This increased to a high of 93.5 percent in 1980/81, but decreased over the following decades. The decrease noted from 1980 to 1989 was a result of the government's change in policy regarding the funding of off-reserve Indians and the elimination of funds for off-reserve urban students to buy books and supplies. The decrease from 1991 to 2001 is a result of the higher number of registered Indians due to *Bill C-31.* These young Aboriginals do not attend a federal, band, or provincial integrated school but rather a regular provincial urban school, not as an Aboriginal student but as a provincial citizen. Thus, while the rate looks low, if these additional students are counted, the school participation rate is about 89 percent.

TABLE 4.10	Enrolment by School Type, On-Reserve Population, Canada, 1975/76-2003/04				
Year	Federal	Provincial	Band-Operated	Private	Total
1975/76	29 581	38 079	2 842	1 315	71 817
1977/78	29 412	41 358	5 639	1 679	78 088
1979/80	27 742	45 742	6 311	1 442	81 237
1981/82	22 525	43 652	13 133	1 156	80 466
1983/84	21 893	39 474	16 715	n/a	78 082
1985/86	19 943	39 712	20 968	n/a	80 623
1987/88	17 322	40 520	26 429	n/a	84 271
1989/90	11 764	41 720	34 674	n/a	88 158
1991/92	6 180	43 092	45 665	1 657	96 594
1993/94	3 453	44 331	53 747	2 548	104 079
1995/96	1 794	43 787	63 000	2 534	111 115
1997/98	1 773	43 943	68 250	2 340	116 306
1999/00	1 708	43 775	71 823	2 064	119 370
2001/02	1 656	43 420	72 457	2 041	119 574
2003/04	1 685	43 509	72 469	2 757	120 421

Sources: In *Basic Departmental Data-1990, 2001, 2002, 2003.* p. 35, 37 38, 43. Indian and Northern Affairs Canada.

School Attendance: Primary and Secondary

Most Indian children used to attend federal schools until grade six and then switch to provincial schools for their secondary education. However, fewer than 10 percent continued in the federal school system; this was partially due to a lack of federal secondary schools. It also reflected the "culture shock" that students experienced when they moved from a school on the reserve to one outside. For example, in provincial schools, it was rare for the Aboriginal population to exceed 5 percent, and thus students were culturally and linguistically isolated from the rest of the school population.

The switch from one school system to another has a serious disruptive influence (both socially and academically) on the Aboriginal children. The change in social milieu has the greatest negative impact. Initially, Aboriginal children enter federal schools as a distinct cultural group with a minimal knowledge of English or French. Because they all share a similar social status, no one is at a disadvantage. However, when these students transfer, the cohort is usually broken up and the individuals are sent to different provincial schools, where they become outsiders among Euro-Canadian students for whom English or French is the mother tongue.

Aboriginal students at provincial schools face considerable discrimination. On the reserve these students have already met indirect, institutionalized racism; however, Aboriginal students in integrated schools are exposed daily to direct discrimination from teachers

TABLE 4.11	Enrolment in Kindergarten, Elementary, and Secondary Schools On-Reserve, Canada, 1960/61–2003/04		
Year	Enrolment[a]	Population 4-18 Years	Enrolment Rate
1960/61[b]	41 671	57 550	72.4%
1965/66[b]	54 670	73 632	74.2%
1970/71	68 449	81 531	84.0%
1975/76	71 817	88 660	81.0%
1980/81	82 801	88 581	93.5%
1985/86	80 623	92 080	87.6%
1986/87	82 271	94 169	87.4%
1987/88	84 271	95 336	88.4%
1988/89	85 582	96 606	88.6%
1989/90	88 158	97 751	90.2%
1990/91[c]	94 501	102 605	92.2%
2000/01[d]	95 358	79 967	83.9%
2003/04[d]	97 799	78 223	80.0%

Note: On-reserve includes Crown lands and settlements.
a. Total enrolment includes registered and non-registered Indians and Inuit in kindergarten to grade 13.
b. A breakdown of on/off-reserve Indian population was not available in 1960/61 and 1965/66. Based on 1975 Indian Register data, off-reserve was estimated to be 26 percent of the total population. Data also were not available for the 4-18 age population for 1960/61, estimated to be 42 percent of the total Indian population.
c. Data are based on population age 5-14, single response.
d. Data are based upon ages 6-16.

Sources: In *Basic Departmental Data 1990*, p. 35, *Basic Departmental Data 2001-02*, p. 36, *Basic Departmental Data 2002-03*, 37,. *Basic Departmental Data 2003-04*, Indian and Northern Affairs Canada, p. 45.

and other students. In the long term, racism results in a serious and permanent distortion of the Aboriginal children's self-image. The more short-term effects of discrimination include lower marks and a tendency to drop out at an early age.

The competition for achievement is also greater in integrated schools than in federal schools. Aboriginal children, not used to the intense competition that exists among non-Aboriginal middle-class students, may become psychologically uncomfortable and begin to lose academic ground. Usually they do not receive adequate counselling prior to or following placement in integrated schools. Not surprisingly, these social disruptions eventually result in a high drop-out rate among Aboriginal students.

The rate of Aboriginal students attending school has shown a general increase over the past two decades. This is particularly true for the younger ages. For example, in the late 1960s only about 43 percent of Aboriginal children aged four to five went to kindergarten. By the 2003–04 this figure had increased to nearly 80 percent. Total enrolment in elementary/secondary school has increased by over 8 percent during the past seven years and, as noted earlier, about 85 percent of the youth now attend school. Overall, about 39 percent of First Nations students aged 15 to 24 are attending school full time, while over 44 percent of the general population in that age group is doing so. Looking at the issue from another perspective, the differences are clearer: 16 percent of Canadians aged 20 to 24 had not completed high school, but among Aboriginal young adults 43 percent did not have a high school certificate. As Mendelson points out, in 2001, an astonishing 58 percent of young adults (age 20–24) living in a First Nations community did not complete high school. In the cities, we find that more than one-third of young Aboriginals failed to complete high school, more than double the rate of the total population (Mendelson, 2006).

Successful school completion to grades 12 or 13 is still much lower among Aboriginal students than among Canadians as a whole. In 1966 fewer than 5 percent of Indian students remained in school throughout the full 12 or 13 years. Although dramatic increases had occurred, the retention rates levelled off during the 1980s. However, since the mid-1990s the percentage of on-reserve students remaining until grade 12 for consecutive years of school increased to 74 percent in 1997–98. When we compare these retention rates for the general population, we find that the rate is about 30 percent less.

Nevertheless, the trend shows a steady increase in the number of Indian students remaining in school, although in the past 10 years (when large numbers of band schools were established) the retention rate has increased substantially. While these figures reflect a positive impact of education, the data do not provide information on the number of successful graduates. While Aboriginal students are technically attending school (so the school can collect their fees), they often do not receive a diploma or matriculation degree. The province of Alberta, for example, has had few First Nations graduates from the regular provincial school system over the past decade. Nevertheless, an increasing number of students are attending high school and graduating (see Table 4.12), although this rate is less than half the rate of graduation for the non-Aboriginal population.

The reasons for the high drop-out rate among Aboriginal students are complex but at the same time straightforward. Researchers in the area have noted that the distorted reflection of the Aboriginal student which is presented in the curriculum is not the chief source of the

TABLE 4.12	Percentage of High School Graduates Who Were Enrolled in Grade 12 or 13, On-Reserve Population, Canada, 1994-95 to 2003-04		
School Year	Enrolment	Graduates	Graduate Rate
1994-95	5743	1662	28.9
1995-96	5909	2001	33.9
1996-97	5618	1785	31.8
1997-98	5948	1975	33.2
1998-99	6036	1939	32.1
1999-00	6463	2072	32.1
2000-01	7063	2168	30.7
2003-04	7287	2203	30.2

Sources: In *Basic Departmental Data*-2002, p. 38. Indian and Northern Affairs Canada; Mendelson, 2006; Postl, 2005; QED Information Systems, 2004.

sense of incongruity which most Indian children experience in the white school system. Far more significant and handicapping is the fact that the verbal symbols and the theoretical constructions which the Indian child is being asked to manipulate bear little or no relation to the social environment with which he or she is most familiar. Students must acquire and accept a new form of consciousness, an orientation that not only displaces, but often devalues the worldviews they bring with them. (Castellano,1970; Hampton, 1993; Barnhardt, 2001)

The Canadian educational system has been developed and refined by and for a white, urban, middle-class culture. Universities do not train student teachers to enter the Aboriginal world. They ignore Aboriginal perspectives, values and issues and give little attention to the work environment in which students will use their professional knowledge and skills. In short, there is no affirmation of Aboriginal identity, and the university environment replicates the negative features that led students to drop out of school in the first place. The current educational system is somewhat alien and meaningless in the context of life on a reserve (Fisher, 1969). The subject matter is largely irrelevant to the Aboriginal child's everyday life. And the curriculum is set firmly within a white, middle-class system of values, which bears little relation to local Aboriginal concerns. Classes are taught by teachers who are almost always non-Aboriginal and who seldom become involved with the local Aboriginal community. Furthermore, the competitive hierarchical structure of the schools is foreign to Aboriginal values. Not surprisingly, Aboriginal students are alienated from their educational system at a very young age.

Aboriginal students also have to contend with the poor image of themselves projected by the mass media, including films and books used in the schools. A study of social studies texts for grades one through eight revealed that Aboriginals were generally portrayed, if at all, as nonentities, evil-doers, or savages (Vanderburgh, 1968). These portraits have a serious impact on the personal development of Aboriginal children. As Kardiner and Ovesey (1951) have pointed out, people to whom negative traits are continually assigned will eventually begin to incorporate them into their identities. Someone who is continually called inferior will eventually believe it to be true.

Others have argued that lack of parental support is an additional factor in the drop-out rate. However, there are many structural reasons for this. Not surprisingly, because Aboriginal parents have had no control over curriculum, textbooks, or staff, until recently they have come to regard the educational system as an "outside," racist institution, to be tolerated but not supported. Parents who have had no education, or negative experiences with the educational system as children, are reluctant to endorse such as system.[8]

Active adult community support for education will only develop when Aboriginal people who live on the reserve are allowed to control the curriculum, hold teaching and administrative positions and determine the teaching techniques. To blame parental neglect for the high drop-out rate is naive: when all the structural variables are considered, the reaction of Aboriginal parents to the educational system is not apathetic but actively and understandably hostile (Battiste and Barman, 1995).

Quality of Aboriginal Education

The quality of Aboriginal education is determined by a variety of factors, including operation and maintenance costs, pupil–teacher ratios, teacher qualifications, the proportion of Aboriginal teachers, community involvement, educational expenditures, and overall per-student education costs. For example, the pupil–teacher ratio provides some evidence as to the amount of time teachers can spend with individual students. Teachers in charge of a class of 27 have less time to deal with students than those operating in a class of 17. Federal schools have pupil–teacher ratios that are higher than in provincial schools— approximately 20 percent higher. In addition, the educational qualifications of teachers in federal schools are lower than those evidenced in provincial schools. This partially reflects an unwillingness of teachers to teach on reserves and the ability of outstanding teachers to move to large urban areas. In addition, reserve schools do not have the professional backup resources—for example, curriculum development specialists and language consultants— which are present in most provincial schools. Finally, there is no Teachers Association that federal teachers can join to increase their teaching and educational skills. In the end, while all teachers have to meet minimum standards, many teachers on the reserves are consid- ered unable to secure jobs elsewhere in the school system. In addition, since the creation of the band schools, teachers and the curriculum have been increasingly subjected to political battles that take place in the community. While the proportion of Aboriginal administrators and teachers in federal schools more than tripled between 1966 and 2001, to over 36 per- cent, there is considerable turnover. Moreover, the number of Aboriginal students in post- secondary institutions planning to become teachers has plummeted over the past decade. It is also worth noting that, even though 90 percent of the teachers in Aboriginal schools have formal teaching credentials, only about 23 percent of the teachers are university graduates.

More recently, Indian Affairs commissioned a national working group on education to look at ways to improve education for First Nations children and youth. The report, *Our Children—Keepers of the Sacred Knowledge,* made several major recommendations, and the department has set aside funds to implement the recommendations. The question remains as to whether the funds set aside will be allocated to implement the recommenda- tions or whether other priorities will take precedence.

Educational Attainment

In 1981 (when systematic data was first collected), there was evidence of a major gap between Aboriginals and non-Aboriginals in every level of educational attainment. For example, 17 percent more non-Aboriginals graduated from elementary school than Aboriginals. Ten years later, this gap had been reduced to 10 percent. However, since this time, the gap has remained unchanged. An even larger gap existed between Aboriginal and non-Aboriginal people for high school graduation. In 1981 the gap was 23 percent, and by 2001 it was reduced to just under 20 percent. Gaps between the two groups for successful completion of post-secondary education also remain, although not as large as those above. In 2001, 23 percent of registered Indians attained a post-secondary certificate, diploma or degree. For non-Aboriginals, the rate was 38 percent. These data show the changes (or lack thereof) that are taking place within both the Aboriginal community and all of Canada. Unfortunately, current data reveals a gap that is as wide as that evidenced 20 years ago (see Table 4.13).

The data show that, when compared to the overall Canadian rate, the educational attainment of Aboriginals is substantially less. The data show that the bulk of Aboriginal women have either a secondary or non-university post-secondary school attainment. When compared to Aboriginal men, Aboriginal women have been relatively successful. They have higher levels of attainment than their male counterparts, particularly in terms of uni- versity attainment (14 percent vs. 10 percent). When we look at the educational attainment levels of different Aboriginal groups, we see that Inuit women and registered women on

TABLE 4.13	Level of Education by Aboriginal Group and non-Aboriginal, 2004					
Females						
Education Level	Total Aboriginal	On Reserve	Off Reserve	Métis	Inuit	Non-Aboriginal
‹ Grade 9	16.2	26.6	13.5	10.0	32.7	11.2
Grade 9-13	39.5	36.7	40.9	40.4	31.2	34.8
Non-Univ.	30.3	25.3	30.0	34.6	29.5	29.1
University	14.0	11.4	15.7	15.0	6.6	29.9
All Post-Sec.	44.3	36.7	45.6	49.7	36.0	54.0
Males						
‹ Grade 9	17.6	27.5	12.8	12.2	31.2	10.3
Grade 9-13	41.8	39.2	44.0	42.6	31.5	33.0
Non-Univ.	30.6	26.8	30.6	33.3	33.3	30.7
University	10.1	6.5	12.6	11.9	4.0	26.0
All Post-Sec.	40.6	33.3	43.1	42	37.3	56.7

reserves have the lowest levels of education. Finally, when we compare Aboriginals with non-Aboriginals, we find that the educational gap continues, with Aboriginals have a greater proportion in the "less than grade nine" category and less (16 percent) in the university and all post-secondary categories. If a historical approach were presented, we would find that Aboriginal peoples have increased their educational attainments over the past quarter century. However, so have the non-Aboriginal people, and thus the gap between the two continues and, in some cases, has increased.

The highest level of education for Aboriginal Canadians and all Canadians is presented in Table 4.14. It shows the educational attainment for those above 15 years of age, as well

TABLE 4.14	Aboriginal Education and Employment Income, Ages 15+, 2001		
INCOME			EDUCATION
	Percent	Percent	
Less than $10 000	10	31	Less than Grade 8
$10 000-$19 000	21	32	Some high school
$20 000-$29 000	20	6	High school graduate
$30 000-$39,000	19	24	Tech/vocational diploma
$40 000+	34	8	University degree

Note: The importance of education is seen by the nearly linear relationship between education and income. With one exception (college without a certificate), the average income increases with additional educational attainment.

as their income. The data show that Aboriginals have entered the educational arena, although there is still a sizeable proportion of the population with less than a grade nine education. However, looking at the category of high school, Aboriginal people show a higher rate than other Canadians. But as the educational attainment level rises, the gap between Aboriginal and all Canadians increases.

Post-Secondary School Attendance

In 1960, 200 status Indians enrolled at a college or university. By 2001, this had increased to almost 30 000, but it has levelled off for nearly a decade. Several factors explain this profile. First Nations' increasing control over their own education and the provision of funds by Indian and Inuit Affairs account for the dramatic increase. However, the failure of Indian and Inuit Affairs to increase the funds to support Aboriginal people accounts for the lack of increase since the late 90s.

Because of the increased number of high school graduates, more and more Aboriginal students are attending post-secondary educational institutions. By 2004 this number had increased to approximately 30 000. From a modest $2.5 million budget in 1981, the post-secondary budget increased to over $315 million in 2005. Bands, or their educational authorities, administer more than 80 percent of the primary/secondary education budget. The number of Aboriginal students receiving assistance more than quadrupled since 1981. In addition to helping individual students, the post-secondary education program funds the Indian Studies Support Program and special institutions such as the Saskatchewan Indian Federated College (now called the First Nations University of Canada, in Regina). Recognizing the importance of post-secondary education, the federal government committed an additional $1.2 billion for a five-year (1991–1996) period. In 2003, the government created a $12 million endowment for scholarships for Aboriginals who want to go on to post-secondary schools.

As noted above, these figures show the Aboriginal post-secondary enrolment has increased from 200 to nearly 30 000. This reflects an increase from less than 1 percent to about 6 percent in the past two decades for those in the 17–34 age group. Nevertheless, this is still considerably lower than the overall national rate of over 12 percent.

With regard to supporting post-secondary education, INAC allocated $304 million in the 2002–03 budget. While this reflects a major increase in expenditures from 1984 (only $50 million), the data shows that this represents about 6 percent of the total INAC budget, and this proportion has not changed for the past two decades (see Figure 4.8). Beyond the elementary school level, and particularly beyond the secondary level, the pattern of Aboriginal student enrolment diverges sharply from the Canadian norm. In 2001, less than 1 percent of Aboriginal persons attended university, as compared with nearly 8 percent of the general Canadian population. It seems clear that nearly all Aboriginal people who enrol in post-secondary education are being prepared for jobs at the semi-skilled level or lower.

While there has been a dramatic increase since the early 1960s in the number of Aboriginal students attending college and/or university, most of these students are in a college program, working toward a certificate or diploma. It is estimated that about 80 percent are college registrants and 20 percent enrolled in a university degree program. Within universities, Aboriginal students generally make up less than 2 percent of the student population, while at colleges, they make up in excess of 10 percent. To deal with the lack of Aboriginal enrolment, a number of universities have tailored special programs to meet the interests

FIGURE 4.8	Registered Indians and Inuit Enrolled in Post-Secondary Receiving INAC Funding, Canada, 1975-76 to 2003-04

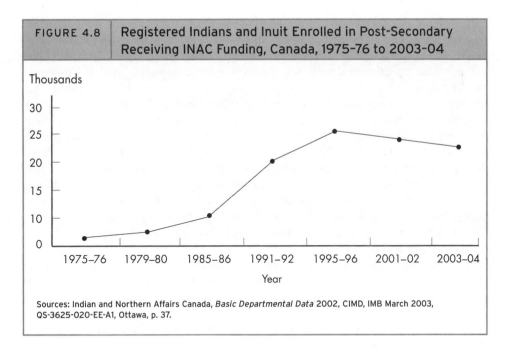

Sources: Indian and Northern Affairs Canada, *Basic Departmental Data* 2002, CIMD, IMB March 2003, QS-3625-020-EE-A1, Ottawa, p. 37.

and needs of Aboriginal students, while others have provided remedial services to assist Aboriginal persons who are entering university. However, even though the increase in Aboriginal enrolment has been rapid, the Aboriginal participation rate is still less than half the national level. For example, in 1975, 20 percent of the Canadian population between the ages of 18 and 24 was enrolled in universities, while only 8 percent of the same-aged Aboriginal population was. Today we find that less than 10 percent of the Aboriginal population between the ages of 18 to 24 is enrolled in universities, while 31.2 percent of the non-Aboriginal youth population are enrolled. Even more dismal than the enrolment figures are the statistics that reflect the rate of graduation from post-secondary educational institutions. It is estimated that about 28 percent of the Aboriginal students enrolled in university programs graduate. These figures have remained constant for the past decade and there is no evidence that they will change in the near future. Clearly, an Aboriginal student's chances of finishing university are still quite small. For individuals having attended university, non-Aboriginals are about 2.4 times as likely as registered Indians to earn a degree. However, while the success rate for registered Indians is lower than that of the general population, it is increasing. Language and cultural differences, as well as the effects of discrimination, have not been adequately addressed and continue to place Aboriginal students at a serious disadvantage in the university system.

To deal with the lack of success in post-secondary educational institutions, Aboriginal organizations have recently entered the arena. Several major agreements have been signed in Western provinces. For example, the Nisga'a have contributed $250 000 to the University of Northern British Columbia to offer courses in the Nass Valley, the traditional home of the Nisga'a. To implement the program, the Wilxo'oskwhl Nisga'a Post-Secondary Institute was created. The University of Manitoba also began offering social work classes to isolated First Nations communities. The University of Calgary's Virtual Circles Program is a similar arrangement that has been established for distance education in Alberta. In this program, instructors go to various First Nations communities to teach and students can obtain a degree in Social Work. The creation of First Nations Adult Higher Education Consortium, made up of several First Nations community colleges in Western Canada, is another strategy being employed. These community colleges are working out partnership agreements with nearby public educational institutions so that students completing their program in the Aboriginal college will be able to seamlessly enter the university system. For example, in Hobbema, Alberta, the community is investing $7.5 million in an attempt to provide Aboriginal people the first two years of a degree program. This move replaces the existing Maskwachees Cultural College and expands the course offerings. Red Crow College, in Cardston, Alberta, has linked with the University of Lethbridge to provide students with courses in the community and to offer the college's own courses, which can be transferred to the university for credit. The University of British Columbia is working with First Nations communities to initiate professional development and support services to First Nation schools.

The challenge facing Aboriginal communities today is to take control of the formal education process; however, there is nothing in the *Indian Act* that would give them any leverage in doing this, although Indian and Northern Affairs Canada has demonstrated a willingness to revise the *Indian Act* when it signed an agreement with British Columbia First Nations giving them control over the content and delivery of the curriculum. Until specific sections of the Act are changed, the minister of INAC has complete control over which schools students attend and over the nature of the contents of any education agreement. Aboriginal people have no right of appeal or review. However, it is unlikely that the Act will be changed in the near future to allow for greater Indian control in matters of education, as there have been no consultations with Aboriginal people as to what the changes might be.

Even if the Act were changed, it is unlikely that Aboriginal people could take control of the education process unless other structures and processes in place are changed. In the first place, the federal government has more trust in provincial school authorities (with regard to finances) than in Aboriginal people. Second, because the federal government does not operate an educational system, it relies on the provincial curricula and standards. Thus it is not interested in developing new approaches to education that would be appropriate or relevant to the diversity of Aboriginal communities (Longboat, 1987). Finally, INAC's education policy is developed and carried out by department officials; it is not a cooperative effort between Aboriginal people and the government. For example, even though the government adopted a stance acknowledging Indians' right to control education in the early 1970s, it added an important condition: any agreement that had already been signed with provincial officials would be honoured until its term expired. In other words, local control of education would not be discussed until the terms of any federal–provincial agreement had concluded. Because most of the capital agreements (agreements to pay a percentage of the school board's capital and building costs) are 20- to 25-year contracts, Aboriginal communities will have to wait an entire generation before they can begin to discuss local control of their schools (Longboat, 1987).

Since 1980 there have been some major policy developments. Changes were made to the K–12 guidelines in 1987,[9] and the publication in 1988 of the Assembly of First Nations' National Review of First Nations Education brought about substantial changes in government programs. Earlier changes (1983) made it possible for Aboriginal students to obtain preparatory study prior to full-time entry into university. Aboriginal Studies programs were created in the late 1980s at various universities, which allowed Aboriginals to gain entrance to the schools under conditions different from those of non-Aboriginal students. These programs started small but they have grown in size over the years. Nevertheless, as universities continue to experience budget cuts, they are currently under review as "untraditional programs." Their vulnerability is exacerbated by the fact that few academic administrators are prepared to lobby for their continuance.

Overall, the educational attainment of Aboriginal people has increased over the past 50 years. These increases are a result of several factors. First, they are due in part to the increased number of band-operated schools: almost all of the schools on reserves are administered by First Nations themselves, and many are secondary schools. Second, there has been an increase in federal funding for post-secondary education. Third, there has been a major expansion of Aboriginal studies programs in Canadian universities. Finally, universities are starting to implement policies that will render the institutions more welcoming to Aboriginal students.

LIVING CONDITIONS AND QUALITY OF LIFE

The term "living conditions" refers to specific objective factors that affect an Aboriginal person's ability to maintain a quality of life commensurate with that of other Canadians. This includes such considerations as the availability and quality of housing, and the provision of community services such as health care and welfare. As pointed out previously, the life expectancy of Aboriginal people is still much lower than the national average. Other indicators, such as the rates of suicide, violent death, and alcohol abuse, demonstrate a general increase in social problems and a lowering of the quality of life, especially among reserve Indians.

Social Assistance

Aboriginal people rely upon social assistance more than any other ethno-cultural group in Canada. Participation in social assistance programs is just one indicator of poverty. The data examined show that this reliance is increasing, even though a variety of economic development projects have been implemented. The extent of social assistance provides a negative indicator for both the quality of life of Aboriginal people and how well the economic programs are working. Table 4.15 shows the total social assistance expenditures for Indians from 1973 to 2003. The results show that the amount of expenditures has doubled over this time. In the past decade, the expenditures have nearly doubled again. However, even though the budget has doubled, the expenditure per recipient increased only by one-third. The average annual number of recipients per month has increased by nearly 30 percent over the past 10 years, and is now nearly 75 000 people. When dependants of these recipients are added to the figures, we find that over 146 000 Indian people are receiving social assistance, at a cost of over $600 million per year. This expenditure represents a 30-percent increase over the 1990 level and stands at about 3 percent of the overall total Canadian social assistance budget. In addition, $600 million is allocated for social support services and an additional $225 million is earmarked for Aboriginal welfare services. Child and Family Services (78 percent) and Adult Care (22 percent) make up this program's budget. Expenditures per child in care increased at an annual average

TABLE 4.15	Social Assistance Expenditures, Registered Indian Population, Canada, 1973/74–2002/03				
Fiscal year	Per Number of Recipients[a] (current $)	Total Expenditures (current $)	Per Recipient (current $)	Total Expenditures[b] (81 constant $)	Per Recipients (81 constant $)
1973/74	n/a	53 319 000	n/a	112 014 706	n/a
1975/76	n/a	73 023 000	n/a	124 825 641	n/a
1977/78	n/a	85 753 000	n/a	126 293 078	n/a
1979/80	n/a	122 004 400	n/a	151 182 652	n/a
1981/82	39 146	165 030 100	4 216	165 030 100	4 216
1983/84	43 750	216 157 600	4 941	184 434 812	4 216
1985/86	48 494	255 288 200	5 264	200 698 270	4 139
1987/88	54 170	314 446 000	5 805	227 529 667	4 200
1989/90	59 680	390 017 600	6 535	258 289 801	4 328
1997/98	70 927	–	–	–	–
2000/01	72 465	–	–	–	–
2002/03	74 481	624 000 000	8 432	–	––

a. Excludes Indians residing in N.W.T. and Newfoundland.
b. The expenditures in constant dollars have been calculated using the Consumer Price Index based the year 1981 from Statistics Canada

Source: Adapted from *Basic Departmental Data*, 1990, 2001, 2002, 2003, 2004 Indian and Northern Affairs Canada.

rate of 17 percent over the past decade, while adult care increased annually at 10 percent, from $12 000 to $28 250. Recently a family violence initiative was created, with a budget of $36 million. The funds are to be used to provide services to families on the reserve and for training of health and social service personnel. These increases prompted the Assembly of First Nations to argue for massive spending in the education and economic spheres to enhance the social and economic position of Aboriginal people. With the Federal government resisting additional investments in these spheres, the above figures demonstrate that social assistance costs will continue to increase at levels well above the investments suggested by the Royal Commission on Aboriginal Peoples. Their analysis reveals that investments made today would be repaid in 28 years. In addition, an investment today would result in fewer First Nations youth placed in correctional facilities that cost the judicial system $616M per year and the social services system $1.2B.

In addition to the above expenditures for social assistance, in 2003–04, over 700 adult registered Indians were in institutional care, with a cost of over $23 million per year. This represents a ratio of 3.2 per 1000, which has decreased only slightly from 1971, when the ratio was 3.7 per 1000.

Since the late 1970s, when the number of Indian children in care peaked at 6.5 percent of the total child population (age 16 and under), there was a decrease until the mid-1990s, when dramatic increases were once again evident. Nevertheless, today, just under 6 percent

TABLE 4.16	On-Reserve Children in Care, Registered Indian Population, Canada, 1966/67–2003/04						

Fiscal Year	Children in Care*	Children aged 16 and under	Percent	Fiscal Year	Children in Care*	Children Aged 16 and Under	Percent
1966/67	3 201	93 101	3.4%	1978/79	6 177	94 866	6.5%
1969/70	4 861	94 698	5.1%	1981/82	5 144	94 608	5.4%
1972/73	5 336	94 906	5.6%	1984/85	3 887	97 586	4.0%
1975/76	6 078	96 493	6.3%	1987/88	3 836	101 537	3.8%
				1990/91	4 352	109 165	4.0%
				1997/98	6 220	139 564	4.5%
				1999/00	7 762	148 664	5.2%
				2001/02	8 828	150 646	5.9%
				2003/04	8 846	154 632	5.7%

* The total number of children in care calculated by Social Development Branch is obtained by dividing the total number of case-days by 365. Child care cases do not include preventive and alternate approaches to child and family services (e.g., homemakers). Excludes Indians residing in the N.W.T. and Newfoundland.

Sources: Adapted from the Statistics Canada publication, "Social Security, National Programs," Catalogue 86-201, 1978, and Catalogue 86-511, 1981/82, 1989/90, and the Statistics Canada *Aboriginal Peoples Survey*, 2001, *Basic Demographic Data*, 2003-04, INAC, p. 61.

of Aboriginal children are under state care. As Table 4.16 shows, this represents about 9000 children in care facilities. The cost of child care has risen from just under $2 million in the mid-1960s to well over $100 million today—a sevenfold increase. Even with this increase, provincial agencies provide 22 percent more funding per child than First Nations agencies receive from the federal government. In 2005, INAC announced a $25M yearly increase for First Nations child welfare funding. However, it held back $16M to offset their increasing maintenance budget costs and to address other internal costs. In the end, only $8M was provided to child and family service agencies. INAC also argues that it has provided an 11 percent increase in funding for the First Nation Child welfare program. Again, this is only for the maintenance portion of the budget and the funds allocated have been drawn from other essential INAC funded programs such as capital, housing, and income assistance. Some of the increase has subsequently been allocated to emergency water measures in some regions. In short, there has been *no* cost-of-living or population-based increases beyond a 2 percent cap for the program for over a decade.

Today, there are more than 27 000 First Nations children in state care. This means that one out of every 10 First Nations children is in care compared to 1 in 200 for non-First Nations children. It will be noted that in Table 4.16 only 9000 children are listed. These refer to First Nations children in the care of First Nations agencies only and *not* First Nation children in care throughout provincial agencies. Moreover, there has been a total increase of 65 percent in the number of First Nations children in care since 1996.

The number of First Nations children receiving social assistance has increased since the early 1980s. While the increase between 1981 and 1986 was from 16.5 to 17.8 percent, the corresponding increase for non-Aboriginal people was from 6.2 to 7.9 percent. These figures reflect the fact that the rate of poverty for First Nations children is twice as high as for the general population.

The funds provided through social assistance enable Aboriginal people to maintain basic levels of health, safety, and family unity. They provide Aboriginal recipients with food, clothing, and shelter, as well as counselling to enable them to achieve independence and self-sufficiency. In addition to the social assistance program, Indian Affairs also offers welfare services to ensure that Aboriginals who need protection from neglect or who need help with personal problems have access to a variety of services (Canada, 1979b).

Overall, over half of the total Aboriginal population received social assistance or welfare payments in 2000. An even more astounding fact is that nearly 90 percent of Indians, at one time in their lives, have received social assistance/social support. These figures compare with 14 percent for non-Aboriginal people in 1999, and a lifetime non-Aboriginal experience with social assistance of 22 percent. There are regional variations in the numbers of social-assistance recipients. Both Aboriginal and non-Aboriginal people in the Maritimes have required social assistance and social welfare at much higher rates than elsewhere in Canada. Finally, it should be pointed out that most of the Aboriginals who have received welfare payments were employable. These facts suggest that social assistance to Aboriginal people is offered as an alternative to employment, not as a measure to help them enter the labour force and obtain wage labour. As the data show, there are an increasing number of Aboriginal people who seek social assistance and social welfare. These conditions have not reversed, which suggests that economic dependency will continue well into the 21st century.

Unemployment creates a need for social assistance that goes beyond simply providing funds for food and housing. A considerable number of studies have shown that an indirect effect of unemployment is its negative impact upon self-esteem and interpersonal relationships. Unemployment places considerable strain on individual relationships, including relations within the family. These interpersonal problems do not appear immediately, but develop slowly and come into full play when a person feels emotionally battered and unable to cope with other stresses (Lauer, 1989). As a result, neglect occurs when a child's parents are not able to provide the essential support for a child's emotional and physical development. Neglect remains the form of maltreatment most closely associated with poverty (Assembly of First Nations, 2007).

In summary, social assistance is a far more serious problem for Aboriginal people than for other social groups in our society. Structural factors have produced the problems that have forced Aboriginal people to become dependent on social assistance; yet most Canadians engage in a form of personal attack, implying or asserting that Aboriginal people themselves are the cause of their need for social assistance. Maintaining that Aboriginal people, as a group, have brought on their own problems draws our attention away from dealing with the structural problems preventing them from fully participating in Canadian society.

At the same time, Canadians appear to be largely in agreement that our "social charter" requires that we provide assistance to people unable to attain an adequate quality of life. Yet we provide that assistance grudgingly and not without comment, without trying to solve the underlying conditions that brought about the problem.

SUMMARY

As we have seen, Aboriginal people in Canada reside in scattered communities and are divided by geographical boundaries, cultural differences, and legal distinctions. However, Aboriginal Canadians do share one common feature across Canada: they lead marginal lives characterized by poverty and dependence. Indeed, many people argue that Aboriginal people are members of a culture of poverty. They are alienated from middle-class Canadian society not only through Euro-Canadian racism but also through the destructive mechanisms whereby one class profits at the expense of another.

The position of Aboriginal Canadians in today's society is not the result of any single factor but of complex historical and contemporary events. The alienation of Aboriginal Canadians began with historical subjugation and subsequent economic displacement. This was followed by a failure to recognize and guarantee certain inalienable Aboriginal rights.

The subjugation and control of Aboriginal Canadians has been continued through a process of individual and institutional racism. The federal government has neglected to consult with Aboriginal peoples concerning their welfare, has failed to develop and finance effective programs to assist Aboriginal persons, and, at times, has actively prevented Aboriginal people from becoming organized in pursuit of their rights. The political organization of Aboriginal people has also been hindered by the factionalism that has developed within different segments of Aboriginal society. All these factors, and others, have led to the marginality of Aboriginal people in Canada.

Both Aboriginal people and government officials decry the poverty and associated ills that currently face Aboriginal people. Throughout the 1990s, the federal and provincial governments cut funding for programs dedicated to Aboriginal children aged 6 to 12, funding for friendship centres and funding for Aboriginal language programs. Today is the time for all levels of governments to collaborate with Aboriginal organizations to increase social investments that enable young and old Aboriginals to succeed. As then Prime Minister Paul Martin noted in his speech to parliament (February 4, 2004), "The continuing gap in life conditions between Aboriginal and other Canadians is intolerable. It offends our values and we cannot remain on our current path. We will not allow ourselves to be caught up in jurisdictional wrangling, passing the buck and bypassing their needs." Unfortunately the new government has not taken up the challenge and continues to cut programs for Aboriginal people. In early 2007, the Assembly of First Nations and the First Nations Child and Family Caring Society of Canada lodged a complaint with the Canadian Human Rights Commission regarding lack of funding for First Nations child welfare. The Assembly noted that it has been negotiating with INAC for years and they have taken no action on recommendations made by the Assembly, the Society or a host of other experts.

There seems to have been little done to redress or correct the social inequality problem in any significant manner. It should not come as a surprise, then, that Aboriginals feel hostile toward our value system. Aboriginal people's contact with the various institutional orders has brought about an experience that not only denies them their self-esteem but also contributes to their dysfunctional state, leaving them unable to cope with the industrial/technological structure we have put in place and with mainstream Canadian society in general.

KEY TERMS

dependency ratio   labour force participation   living conditions
language families   band schools

STUDY QUESTIONS

1. What are the implications of the aging of the Aboriginal and Canadian populations?
2. What impact has Christianity had upon Aboriginal culture?
3. What are the four factors which influence an individual's quality of life? How do each relate to Aboriginal people within Canada?
4. Compare and contrast paternalistic ideology and democratic ideology.
5. How does the *Indian Act* affect the Aboriginal education process?
6. What are Aboriginal living conditions and how do they affect their quality of life?

WEBLINKS

www.ayn.ca/AYNHome.aspx

The Aboriginal Youth Network is an organization dedicated to the creation of a dynamic community nationwide.

www.afn.ca/residentialschools/index.html

The legacy of residential schools for Aboriginal students is documented on a special part of the Assembly of First Nations' website. It includes discussion of ongoing court cases and an analysis of the needs of victims of abuse.

NOTES

1. Statistics Canada defines "mother tongue" as the language a person first learns in childhood and still understands.

2. The data show how many percentage points each group is over or under its representation in the general labour force. That is, if ethnicity were not a factor in occupational placement, the proportion of each ethnic group in every occupational category would be the same proportion of that group to the total population. For example, if Aboriginals made up 1.2 percent of the total population, they would make up a similar percentage in each occupational category. Ideally, the over-/underrepresentation should hover around zero.

3. Denominational schools are founded and operated by a particular religious group. Residential schools are also denominational.

4. Religious schools receive a fixed amount, proportional to the number of pupils, for the administration, maintenance, and repair of their buildings.

5. See Caldwell (1967) and the *Canadian Superintendent* (1965).

6. All of these schools were funded by the federal government but operated by religious orders.

7. In certain provinces, such as Nova Scotia, the Department of Indian Affairs has a master agreement with the province concerning payment for Aboriginal students in provincial schools.

8. This policy of exclusion is now under review. Aboriginals now use school committees to communicate their desires and objections. These committees are set up by the band council and authorized to act on behalf of the Aboriginal community, but under regulations drawn up by Indian Affairs.

9. These are written documents produced by the government of Canada outlining the policy and programs designed to deal with Indian educational issues, such as funding, building of schools, eligibility of students, etc. (for kindergarten to grade 12/13).

chapter five

The Canadian Justice System: The Tragedy and the Travesty

INTRODUCTION

Justice must not only be carried out; it must be perceived by all constituents that the justice carried out is fair. Living in a society where justice has been imposed by the dominant society without concern for Aboriginal culture or tradition, many Aboriginal people have rejected "white" law and have little faith that it will serve them well. Does the current system resolve disputes or simply commit more and more Aboriginal people to jails across the country? Do our courts fairly deal with Aboriginal issues such as treaty rights, land claims, and resource rights? Again, it would seem that the scales of justice are tipped in favour of the dominant group, and even when the courts make decisions that support Aboriginal people, the politics and policies of the dominant group negate those court decisions.

ABORIGINAL-WHITE DISPUTES

With their domination of Aboriginal peoples in the 18th century, Euro-Canadians began to define right and wrong behaviour. As they solidified their control over the social character of Canadian society, some of their definitions became paramount and took on the status of "law." In short, conceptions and discussions of right and wrong were based upon a Euro-Canadian perspective, and all behaviour was defined and dealt with in terms of this definition. Moreover, those conceptions also would define the responses toward "correct" and "wrong" behaviour. Once a social issue was characterized in one particular way, the institutional order of the dominant culture established appropriate organizations and structures to maintain and legitimize that characterization. For example, as the Law

Commission (Canada, 1999a) points out, once the police define behaviour as a criminal offence, the individuals behaving in such a manner are powerless to change that definition. The decision on how to proceed to resolve the "conflict" has been built into the structure of society, with rules established as to how to conduct the resolution. For many years, the definition of right and wrong was a fixed assessment by Canadians, as they took their Euro-Canadian perspective as the only one to be used in judging people's behaviour. It has only been in the recent past that Canadians have begun to accept the idea that definitions of right and wrong are not fixed, and that other cultural perspectives may have some validity (Robertson, 1988).

We begin our discussion by noting that not all conflict is dysfunctional; conflict can also play an important positive function for society. First of all, it establishes what behaviour is acceptable. Second, it allows minorities to take on roles that they normally would not be able to assume, and thus formalizes the process by which they are able to publicly articulate their concerns, i.e., they can interact with the dominant group as equals. Finally, conflict situations bring social issues to the public foreground and force people to address them (Schmeiser, 1974).

As Black (1998) points out, conflict emerges whenever anyone provokes or expresses a grievance—whenever someone engages in conduct that another individual or group defines as inappropriate and that requires an agent of society to respond. This relational concept reveals that conflict is not the opposite of order, nor should these two concepts be viewed as opposite ends of a continuum. Moreover, the responses to conflict may vary from polite admonishments to more harsh responses, such as prison or death. (Nielsen and Silverman, 1996).

From an Aboriginal perspective, the current definitions of deviance are a means by which the relationships of unequal power are maintained by Euro-Canadians (Canada, 1999a). Moreover, many Aboriginal people believe that the law has been ineffective in controlling or reducing the amount of crime committed by or toward Aboriginal people. They believe both that, once Aboriginal people are defined as criminals or charged with an offence, they will re-offend, and that the justice system will fail to deter or rehabilitate offenders. In fact, some would argue that prisons make some offenders more prone to commit crimes when they are released (Canada, 1999a).

EURO-CANADIAN VIEW OF JUSTICE

When Europeans first set foot on what is now Canadian soil, they found a rich and complex Aboriginal culture. While social and formal norms were part of this society, the settlers refused to acknowledge indigenous values or social structures. As Jefferson (1978) points out in his history of legal concepts among Aboriginal peoples, most Aboriginal societies had well-developed rules with regard to "deviant" behaviour in their community. While the definition might vary from one group to the next and the penalties for violating social norms varied, the concept was in force. Children were instructed in the customs and rules of their society, and violations were dealt with in an appropriate manner. Justice was most refined in the Iroquois Confederacy (Five Nations) and was formalized by a constitution recorded on wampum belts to preserve the social relations over generations. If this society had such a well-developed system of justice, how was it that the early immigrants were unable to see it or to understand it? As noted earlier, with pre-determined definitions, the settlers defined Aboriginal values and organizations as inappropriate or irrelevant. Moreover, with the lack of understanding of the culture or the language, it is unlikely that many settlers fully understood the full range of the Aboriginal justice system.

From the earliest contact between the settlers and the Aboriginal people, it was clear that settlers' rule would prevail (Jefferson, 1978). As such, representatives of the government such as Indian agents, superintendents, and commissaries were given power to act as legal magistrates in dealing with Aboriginal issues. By the late 1800s, the North West Mounted Police was created to maintain law and order. To effectively enforce the dominant view of reality, the police were given the right to arrest, prosecute, judge, sentence, and confine persons residing in the Northwest Territories. While the police implemented these actions, they had not created the laws or regulations. Nevertheless, by this time, it was evident that no other view of reality mattered, as only actions condoned by the dominant society could be defined as acceptable behaviour. In short, the social transformation had occurred!

ABORIGINAL INVOLVEMENT

While there are virtually no differences between Aboriginal and non-Aboriginal people with regard to their contact with the police for things such as seeking information or traffic violation, Aboriginal people are more likely than non-Aboriginals to have contact with the police for what are considered to be more serious reasons. For example, they are more likely to come into contact with the police as victims of crime (17 percent vs. 13 percent), as witnesses to a crime (11 percent vs. 6 percent), and by being arrested (4 percent vs. 1 percent). The Department of Justice notes that while Aboriginals make less than 4 percent of the population, they make up 15 percent of victims of crimes and 28 percent of those accused of crimes. Moreover, they project that the proportion of Aboriginal victims (and those accused of crimes) will increase at a 20 percent rate (compared to 4 percent for non-Aboriginals) over the next five years.

The Office of the Correctional Investigator in 2006 noted that Correctional Services does have a constitutional and statutory obligation to manage sentences in a culturally responsive and non-discriminatory manner. It went on to note that Aboriginal offenders were less likely to be granted temporary absences and parole, were granted parole later in their sentence, were more likely to have their parole suspended or revoked, and were more likely to be classified at a higher security level, outcomes that had already been evident two decades ago.

It has been argued for many years that Aboriginal people need to be involved in the administration of justice. Today, after more than a quarter-century since the first self-help program was implemented, the dominant bureaucracy still maintains control of the policy, direction, and staff of the justice system (Office of the Correctional Investigator, 2005–2006) even though a substantial number of Aboriginals are working for Correctional Services Canada.

Aboriginal Police

Early programs such as the band constable policing system lasted only a few years. A small program to encourage Aboriginal people to join the Royal Canadian Mounted Police, it was implemented but was phased out by the late 1980s. Although national data are unavailable, detailed information about Alberta was made public in *The Report on the Task Force on the Criminal Justice System and Its Impact on the Indian and Métis People of Alberta* (Alberta, 1991). This report showed that only 2.5 percent of the RCMP employees were Aboriginal (1 percent for the nation). The representation of Aboriginal people in municipal police forces was even less—1 percent. In provincial jails, only 2.7 percent of the employees were Aboriginal, while at the federal level Aboriginals made up 4 percent of Correctional Services of Canada employees. Today, 10 years later, the profile has changed significantly as the numbers have increased to over 7 percent. The special Indian constables (as part of the RCMP) are the only major vehicle by which Aboriginal persons come into contact with other Aboriginal persons in the context of justice. Even under such a program, band councils are not involved in the operation of the program. Governments and Native organizations have failed to show interest in incarcerated Aboriginal people or in dealing with them once they are released (Canada, 1973).

However, in 1991 the First Nations Policing Policy was announced by the federal government, and it gave First Nations communities the opportunity to participate in the development of policing services in their communities (Brzozowski, Taylor-Butts and Johnson, 2006). First Nations communities may develop and administer their own police service or they may choose a police service that is delivered by members of their own community but within a provincial or federal police force. In 2006 Alberta shut down its Aboriginal provincial police force serving six northern communities after nearly ten years of operation. Lack of due diligence by the force was the reason given by the provincial solicitor general.

ABORIGINAL-EURO-CANADIAN CONCEPTIONS OF JUSTICE

The differences in the principles involved in the administration of justice between Canadians and Aboriginal society are vast. The dominant society bases its laws upon a modified version of the British tradition of common law and principles. Aboriginal society reveals that the exercise of power was tempered by the expression of public opinion and that the family was the basic social, economic, and political unit for inspiring and restoring peace. Table 5.1 identifies the highlights of the two systems. Aboriginal people have a desire for community harmony, and they try to avoid confrontation and adversarial positions. While these are certainly broad generalizations and are not true for all Aboriginal people, the attributes reflect the overall culture. And, while it is true that Aboriginals have experienced the dominant society for well over 200 years, they have maintained aspects of their culture that differ from mainstream society. They have traditionally used ridicule, avoidance, shaming, and teasing to maintain order and community harmony. Conflicts arise when Aboriginal values mix with the Canadian justice system. For example, Judge Murray Sinclair noted that the legal concept of innocence/guilt is not granted the same importance by Aboriginal culture as it is in the Canadian criminal justice system. In an Aboriginal community, guilt is usually secondary to the central issue that something is wrong and has to be fixed. The main concern in Aboriginal communities is not to punish a wrongdoer but to restore the harmony and balance that existed before the violation of the norm.

While not all of the above cultural elements have the same salience today, there are still enough differences in the two cultures to pose problems for Aboriginal people who come into conflict with the law. The legal philosophy, the offences, and the court procedures are

TABLE 5.1	Canadian vs. Traditional Native Justice

Anglo-Canadian Justice	Traditional Indian Justice
• laws formulated by elected representatives	• laws formulated by the community through tradition and consensus
• laws tied to man-made economy	• laws tied to the natural environment, only a few universally condemned actions
• Protestant ethic and Christianity the moral foundation of the law	• traditional Native religions the foundation of Native codes of behaviour
• personal offences seen as transgressions against the state as represented by the monarch	• personal offences seen as transgressions against the victim and his/her family; community involved only when the public peace threatened
• law administered by representatives of the state in the form of officially recognized or operated social institutions	• law usually administered by the offended party, e.g., the family, the clan
• force and punishment used as methods of social control	• arbitration and ostracism usual peacekeeping methods
• individualistic basis for society and the use of the law to protect private property	• communal basis for society, no legal protection for private property. Land held in trust by an individual and protected by the group

often the root of the problem, and this is compounded when Aboriginal people find themselves in an urban context. In addition, language difficulties, ignorance of the law, poverty (particularly the inability to pay fines), and lack of education add to the disadvantage of Aboriginal people when facing the justice system (Hylton, 1981). When the laws have benefited the dominant society, they have been relentlessly applied; when the laws have not been to the advantage of the dominant group, they have been openly ignored. Such is the case when one group has power (Hagan, 1974). For example, in a recent court decision the verdict was that government has to consult with Aboriginal people when they plan an activity that will or might have an impact on them. The Alberta Government has redefined the decision and concluded that it does NOT have to consult with Aboriginal people except in specific instances.

When asked how they evaluated the behaviour of the police, the courts, and prisons, Aboriginal people were less satisfied and more critical of police than their non-Aboriginal counterparts. They were less likely to rate the police as doing a good job in a number of areas: being approachable and easy to talk to, ensuring the safety of citizens, enforcing the laws, supplying information on ways to reduce crime, and responding promptly to calls (see Box 5.1 below). On the other hand, they were more likely than non-Aboriginals to assess the courts positively. With regard to the prison and parole system, there were virtually no differences in the opinions of Aboriginal and non-Aboriginal people, although both were generally not very positive in their assessment. For example, approximately one-quarter of the sample felt that the prison system was doing a good job of supervising and controlling prisoners and only 14 percent felt that the system was doing a good job at helping prisoners become law-abiding citizens. Again, Aboriginals and non-Aboriginals were similar in their assessment of the parole system. Only 16 percent felt that it was doing a good job at releasing offenders who are not likely to re-offend (Johnson, 2005).

ABORIGINAL VICTIMIZATION

Nearly half of the Aboriginal people in Canada have claimed to have been victims of a crime at least once over the past year while just over one quarter of non-Aboriginal people made such a claim. In addition, compared to non-Aboriginals, Aboriginal people were nearly twice as likely to be repeat victims of crime. Overall, we find that. in 2004, Aboriginal people experienced violent victimization at a rate that was nearly three times greater than non-Aboriginals

Box 5.1	Justice Denied

Seventeen-year-old Neil Stonechild's frozen body was found in a field on the outskirts of Saskatoon in 1990. The teen's body was found five days after a witness saw him in the back of a police cruiser. This case was all but forgotten for ten years until the RCMP reopened it after two other Aboriginal men were found frozen outside the city. For years the Saskatoon police service insisted that picking up Aboriginal men in the city and dropping them off in the country during winter never happened. Then, after 2001, when two police were convicted of dropping an Aboriginal youth in the countryside in -30-degree weather, the police chief finally conceded that this was a practice of the police in dealing with Aboriginal people. In 2003 the province established an inquiry into the death of Neil Stonechild. The inquiry found that the police did not seriously investigate the circumstances surrounding the death of Mr. Stonechild, prematurely destroyed all the records of the case and ignored important information relating to Stonechild's disappearance and death. It also found that, in the years that followed, the chiefs and deputy chiefs of police rejected or ignored reports that

cast serious doubts on the conduct of the Stonechild investigation. It was noted that the same attitudes were shown by members of the Saskatoon Police during the inquiry ten years later. The Commissioner, Justice David Wright, concluded by noting that the Saskatoon Police Service's submissions regarding the improvements to the Service did not contain any reference at all to attempts to ameliorate their interaction with Aboriginals and other racial groups.

In addition to being victims of violence, Aboriginal people also view their neighbourhood as exhibiting "socially disruptive" conditions, e.g., drug trafficking, public drunkenness, and high levels of vandalism. What is surprising is that the fear levels of crime and violence among Aboriginal people are relatively low. When asked whether or not they felt safe walking alone in their neighbourhood after dark, over 90 percent of Aboriginal people said that they did. Nor were they worried about becoming a victim of a crime while alone in their homes in the evening. Sixty percent were not worried when using public transportation alone in the evening.

(Brzozowski, Taylor-Butts and Johnson, 2006). (See Figure 5.1) In summary, being an Aboriginal person significantly increased the probability of experiencing victimization. In fact, as Brzozowski, Taylor-Butts and Johnson (2006) conclude, when all other factors are held constant, the odds of being a victim of a violent crime are about three times higher for an Aboriginal person than they are for a non-Aboriginal person. When we review the profile of violent incidents against Aboriginals, we find that most of the perpetrators were known by the victim, while for non-Aboriginals this was not the case. We also find that over all in Canada most violent crimes occur in a commercial or institutional establishment, while for Aboriginals most violent incidents were likely to occur in or around the victim's home.

ABORIGINALS INVOLVED IN CRIME

Table 5.9 on page 147 shows the federal statute applying to incidents reported to police on First Nations communities for 2004. It reveals very different profiles between Aboriginals and non-Aboriginals with regard to being charged with a crime. We find that 50 percent of the cases against Aboriginal people are considered violent crimes (e.g., assault, sexual assault), while only 39 percent of non-Aboriginals are charged with such a crime. On the other hand, 37 percent of incidents of the non-Aboriginals charged with a federal statute offence involve a property crime (e.g., break and enter, mischief), while just over one-fifth of the Aboriginal population face such a charge.

Just as we noted that Aboriginals are overrepresented as victims of crime, we also find that they are overrepresented as persons accused of crime. However, as Wood and Griffiths (2000) point out, there is considerable variation in crime rates among Aboriginal communities and groups throughout Canada. Nevertheless, over all, this overrepresentation is evident in the number of Aboriginal persons accused of homicide. In 2004, of all Canadians accused of homicide, nearly one-quarter were Aboriginal. In comparing data from 1997 to 2004, we find that Aboriginal people were ten times more likely to be accused of homicide than were non-Aboriginal people. Even the type of homicide charges differ between Aboriginal and non-Aboriginal people. For example, Aboriginal people were most likely to be charged with second-degree murder (66 percent) followed by first-degree (20 percent) and manslaughter (14 percent). By comparison, non-Aboriginals were most likely to be charged with first-degree murder (46 percent) followed by second-degree (39 percent) and the remainder with manslaughter.

We now turn to the nature and extent of crime that takes place within First Nations communities. Quan and Trevethan (2000) have demonstrated that both the crime rates and the nature of the crimes in First Nations communities are worse than rates outside reserves. Four percent of all crimes reported were committed in First Nations communities, which reveals that crime rates in First Nations communities were about three times higher than crime rates elsewhere in Canada (29 000 per 100 000 population compared to 8500 per 100 000). We also find that the rate of violent crime committed in First Nations communities is higher than elsewhere in the country; eight times higher for assaults, seven times higher for sexual assaults and six times higher for homicides. Only the incidence of robbery was lower in First Nations communities than elsewhere in Canada. When the nature of the crime is property-related, crimes in First Nations communities still have rates that are much higher than off-reserve areas. For example, break-and-enter rates in First Nations communities were three times higher, and possession of stolen goods is twice that of off-reserve rates. Other types of crime such as disturbing the peace or offensive weapons

TABLE 5.2	Percent Adult Aboriginal Offenders by Province, 2004-2005				
	Sentenced Custody	Remand	Probation	Conditional Sentence	Aboriginal Total Adult Population
NL	13	14	-	-	3%
PEI	-	-	-	-	1
NS	7	7	5	6	2
NB	7	10	7	6	2
QU	2	4	7	6	1
ON	9	8	7	9	1
MN	70	64	53	48	11
SK	77	75	66	72	10
AB	38	27	22	16	4
BC	20	20	20	18	4
Yukon	74	73	60	83	20
NWT	85	88	-	-	45
Nunavut	97	96	95	95	78
Provincial jails	22	17	17	19	-
Federal jails	17	N/A	N/A	N/A	-

Source: Adapted from: Beattie (2006), Johnson (2005).

had rates 7 to 12 times higher than the rest of Canada. In summary, the rate of criminal activities in First Nations communities is much higher than the rest of Canada.

When we look at the incidence of youth (12–17) crime in First Nations communities we find that the rate is three times higher than the rate of youth crime elsewhere in Canada. Young offenders in First Nations communities were accused of homicide at 11 times the rate of young people off-reserve. Rates of crime for Aboriginal youth were also much higher than for non-Aboriginal youth in other types of crime, such as break and enter and disturbing the peace. Nevertheless, most of the crimes committed in First Nations communities by youth were not serious crimes, and were most often associated with "mischief" offences. Nevertheless, these charges place a "record" on the individual and thus predispose police and the courts to define the individual as a "petty criminal." In the end, the "record" of the individual will be noted if the individual is charged with another crime later in life.

Incarceration

Canada is one of the most frequent users of imprisonment as a means of punishment, compared with other Western, Asian, and Pacific countries. In Canada, members of minority groups are 7 to 16 times more likely than the overall non-Aboriginal population to be imprisoned. One explanation is that these groups commit more imprisonable crimes than members of the dominant group. An alternative explanation, offered by Frideres and Robertson (1994), is that the justice system is racially discriminatory. Their data clearly show that Aboriginals are disproportionately suspects for homicides in every major city in Canada. At the same time, Aboriginals are victims of homicides well beyond their national representation within each of the cities.

There are two competing explanations for the rate of incarceration of individuals within a society. On the one hand, it is suggested that the agents involved in the administration of justice are the responsible forces. For example, if police bring fewer charges against individuals, the courts will have fewer individuals to deal with. And, if the courts are not content to send people to jail, there will be fewer individuals incarcerated. An alternative explanation is that social structural factors produce variations in the crime rate. For example, economic recessions are linked to an increased rate of crimes committed. Thus, this explanation argues that, when there are structural changes in the society, more (or fewer) crimes will be committed. We suggest that both explanations together form a more complete explanation as to why individuals commit crimes and why they are (or are not) sent to jail. It is important to point out that, for those Aboriginals sentenced to a federal jail, over half of the Aboriginal population have had at least one previous jail sentence. In comparison, only 25 percent of non-Aboriginal offenders have had one or more previous sentences, and less than half of the non-Aboriginal male population has had more than one previous jail sentence.

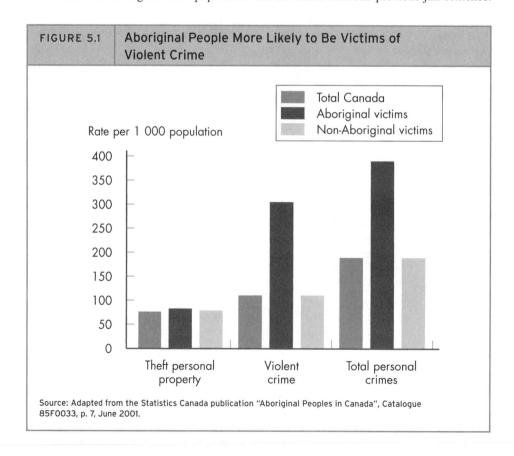

FIGURE 5.1   **Aboriginal People More Likely to Be Victims of Violent Crime**

Source: Adapted from the Statistics Canada publication "Aboriginal Peoples in Canada", Catalogue 85F0033, p. 7, June 2001.

In 1996 the *Criminal Code* was changed to require a court to consider all available sanctions other than imprisonment that are reasonable in the circumstances for all offenders, with particular attention to the circumstances of Aboriginal offenders. The *Youth Criminal Justice Act* (2003) has similar provisions. Despite these changes, Aboriginal people are still highly represented in our jails. Moreover, Aboriginal people admitted to federal jails are increasingly younger. Aboriginal people are placed in prison at levels higher than their proportion in the general population. The Office of the Correctional Investigator noted in his 2006 report that 18 percent of the federal prison population is Aboriginal, even though they represent less than 4 percent of the population. He goes on to note that Canada has an overall (provincial and federal) incarceration rate of 130 per 100,000 adults. For Aboriginal people, 1024 per 100,000 are sent to prison, while for non-Aboriginals the rate is 117 per 100,000. In 2004/05, Aboriginal people accounted for over one-fifth of the admission to provincial jails. In addition they made up nearly one-fifth of the remand cases in Canada. What is more disturbing is that these figures reveal a 2 percent increase over the previous three years. The data show that Aboriginal overrepresentation in prisons is greatest in the Prairies for both federal and provincial correctional institutions.

Table 5.3 reveals the 2001 inmate population in Canada, classified according to prison security level.

When the Aboriginal–non-Aboriginal ratio of sentenced admissions in provincial jails is reviewed, we find that Saskatchewan is nearly 25 times higher than the overall average; Manitoba is nearly 10 times higher, and Alberta is more than 7 times higher (see Table 5.4). Aboriginal women are also disproportionately represented in admissions in comparison to non-Aboriginal women in all provinces. In 1997 it was found that females accounted for 25 percent of inmates in Canadian provincial/territorial correctional facilities. By 2004 this had increased to 29 percent. For federal correctional facilities, Aboriginal women make up nearly 4 percent of the inmate population. In the specific case of fine defaults, we find that Aboriginals are disproportionately more likely than non-Aboriginal offenders to serve time. This simply reflects the poverty of Aboriginal people and their inability to pay fines imposed by the courts. Table 5.5 reveals the percentage of Aboriginal intake for both provincial and federal prisons. These numbers are to be compared to the overall population of Aboriginal people, which now stands at less than 4 percent.

In 2003–04 we find that 14 percent of all adult Aboriginals faced with court sentencing were sent to remand, 19 percent to provincial/territorial custody, 18 percent to federal custody, and 13 percent to probation. Sixteen percent were given a conditional sentence, and

TABLE 5.3	Level of Security of Prison Inmates by Sex, 2001		
Security	Men %	Women %	Aboriginals %
Maximum	14	9	16
Medium	59	40	62
Minimum	21	44	17
Not yet classified	6	7	5

Source: Adapted from www.csc.gc.ca/text/facts/facts07-content05. shtml, Correctional Service of Canada, 2003.

TABLE 5.4	Percent Remand and Sentenced Admissions and Total Aboriginal Population		
Province	Total Number of Offenders	Percent of Total Population That Is of Aboriginal Descent	Total Number of Provincial Offenders That Are of Aboriginal Descent
Newfoundland	890	10	89
Prince Edward Island	650	3	20
Nova Scotia	1 507	7	105
New Brunswick	1 555	7	109
Quebec	14 372	2	287
Ontario	31 980	9	2 878
Manitoba	3 025	69	2 087
Saskatchewan	3 410	77	2 626
Alberta	15 164	38	5 762
British Columbia	9 263	21	1 945
Yukon	280	76	213
Northwest Territories	562	90	506
Nunavut	217	98	213
Total Incarcerated population	82 875		16 840

Source: "Breakdown of Provincial Aboriginal Offenders (Admissions for 2001/2002)" adapted from the Statistics Canada publication, *Juristat*, Catalogue 85-002, Vol. 23, No. 11, Adult Correctional Services in Canada, 2001-2002.

TABLE 5.5	Aboriginal Inmates in Correctional Institutions by Region		
Region	Aboriginal Inmates in Provincial Institutions (% of all inmates)	Aboriginal Inmates in Federal Institutions (% of all inmates)	Off-Reserve Registered Indians (% of all Registered Indians)
Atlantic Provinces	3	3	33
Quebec	2	1	22
Ontario	8	4	46
Manitoba	49	39	34
Saskatchewan	68	52	46
Alberta	34	31	34
British Columbia	18	14	47
N.W.T.	91	37	21
Yukon	63	94	54

Sources: Boe (2000);, Johnson (2005), Wood and Griffiths (2000) and Beattie (2006).

the remainder had other forms of sentences. These figures are remarkably similar to those found in 1994–95. We can debate the value of prisons and the appropriate amount of jail time for an offence. However, the data today do not show an association between prison time and deterrence. In other words, a greater reliance on imprisonment does not reduce crime rates. The results of today's research suggest that prisons are merely warehouses for the socially undesirable and that they focus on punishing the disadvantaged and marginalized.

Aboriginal Inmates

Figure 5.2 reveals the percentage of Aboriginal inmates in both federal and provincial jails. Aboriginal inmates are younger, have less education (48 percent in provincial correctional institutions and 56 percent in federal ones had less than Grade 9), are more likely to be unemployed (50 to 70 percent for Aboriginals compared to 40 to 47 percent for non-Aboriginals), and are from more dysfunctional families than non-Aboriginal inmates. The median age of Aboriginal provincial inmates is three years less than non-Aboriginal inmates (29 vs. 32), while in federal prisons, they are four years younger (31 vs. 35). On the other hand, Aboriginal inmates are similar to non-Aboriginal offenders in that they have drug and alcohol addiction problems, poor upbringing/poverty, abuse and violence in their lives, as well as a lack of education, and are similar in the types of offences committed. Table 5.6 reveals a profile of persons involved in adult correctional services for three provinces. Aboriginal offenders reflect the "revolving door" syndrome. Many are admitted to a prison several times in their life time and it is estimated that 90 percent of all adult male Natives have been in jail at least

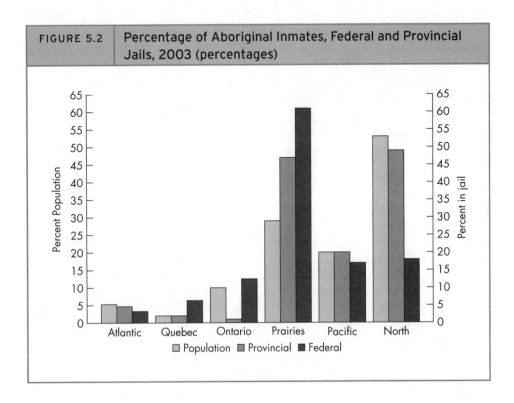

| FIGURE 5.2 | Percentage of Aboriginal Inmates, Federal and Provincial Jails, 2003 (percentages) |

TABLE 5.6	Characteristics of All Persons Involved in Adult Correctional Services, Nova Scotia, New Brunswick, Saskatchewan, 2004/05

	Aboriginal		Non-Aboriginal	
	#	%	#	%
Total Number	4878	100	9885	100
Sex M		82.4		87.5
F		17.6		12.5
Age at First Admission				
18-19		11.3		8.3
20-29		42.1		34.7
30-39		27.9		25.1
40-49		14.4		21.0
50+		4.2		10.8
Mean Age:		30.4		33.9
Marital Status				
Single, Never Married		54.4		58.6
Married		7.2		10.9
Common Law		29.7		16.8
Separated/Divorced		8.2		13.2
Widow		0.6		0.5
Education				
No Formal Education		0.0		0.1
Some Primary		11.4		4.5
Completed Primary/Some Secondary		58.3		27.1
Completed Secondary/Some Post-Secondary		27.6		57.9
Completed Secondary		2.7		10.3
Employment Status				
Unemployed		45.9		47.6
Employed		35.7		44.8
Not employable		5.5		1.8
Student		6.0		4.0
Retired		0.0		0.7
Other-not employed		7.0		1.1

	Aboriginal	Non-Aboriginal
Need Indicated		
Substance Abuse	92.7	74.5
Attitude	79.4	63.3
Family/Marital	58.7	47.8
Personal/Emotional	13.7	18.4
Social Interaction	81.5	61.0
Employment	66.8	39.0
Most Serious Offence, First Involvement		
Violent Offences	34.8	30.3
Property Offences	26.3	24.8
Traffic Offences	9.6	11.6
Other Criminal Code	10.3	7.1
Other, Drug, Justice	26.5	26.2

once. Jackson (1992) found three kinds of Aboriginal inmates: traditional, bicultural, and assimilated. These groups differed in terms of their facility with the English language, time spent on the reserve/in the city, mobility, Aboriginal identity, and beliefs and practices (Métis

TABLE 5.7	Profile of Prison Inmate Population, 2000–2001			
	Aboriginal		Non-Aboriginal	
	Male %	Female %	Male %	Female %
< 3 years	21	39	19	36
3–6 years	33	22	31	27
6–10	17	17	15	12
10+	9	7	13	5
Life	20	16	21	19
Offence				
Murder–1st	4	1	5	4
Murder–2nd	13	13	13	15
1 (no sex)[a]	67	56	59	44
1 (sex)[b]	21	1	16	2
2 (drugs)	4	22	9	24

Note:
a. Schedule 1 excluding sexual offences
b. Schedule 1 including sexual offences

Source: Adapted from Correctional Service of Canada, 2003.

TABLE 5.8	Adult Correctional Services Survey, 1989-2004. Percent Admissions to Custody by Aboriginal Status, by Selected Province

	% Aboriginal						
Province	1989	1992	1994	1996	1998	1999	2004
Newfoundland	11	6	7	9	6	6	13
Nova Scotia	5	4	3	4	5	4	7
Quebec	3	4	5	5	6	8	2
Ontario	4	3	5	7	7	7	9
Manitoba	43	43	55	47	47	n/a	70
Saskatchewan	56	58	58	56	61	63	77
Alberta	21	24	23	22	24	20	38
B.C.	15	17	15	16	16	17	20
Yukon	60	71	79	69	96	80	74
N.W.T[a].	91	93	n/a	n/a	n/a	n/a	85
Total Canada		13	12	13	14	14	13

a. In Nunavut, the admission rate for Natives was 97%

Source: Adapted from the Statistics Canada publication, "Aboriginal Peoples in Canada," Catalogue 85F0033, June 2001; Beattie, 2006.

and Non-Status, 1977). Table 5.7 reveals the attributes of the Aboriginal and non-Aboriginal inmate population in 2000–2001.

Table 5.8 reveals the admissions to custody over a 15-year time period. What is particularly disturbing is that the pattern of the percentage of Aboriginals in custody shows an increase over time. The data show that the problem of Aboriginal overrepresentation in correctional institutions and the criminal justice system seems unlikely to disappear.

Types of Offences   Given the social and economic position of Aboriginal people, it is not surprising to find that they are overrepresented in offences involving fine defaults, failure to appear for court, and breaches of probation. Upon analysis of data we find remarkable similarities in types of offences between Aboriginals and non-Aboriginals, although there are some crimes unique to each group. With their lack of monetary resources, it is not surprising to find that Aboriginal offenders would run the risk of defaulting on their fines. With cultural differences and lack of resources, it also is no surprise that Aboriginal persons would find it difficult to deal with the urban courts. How does a poor person find his or her way from a reserve to an urban centre for a precise appointment the court has set without consulting the accused? On the more "serious" side of offences, we find that about 14 percent of Aboriginal people were charged with some form of murder and 16 percent of non-Aboriginal people were similarly charged. However, when comparing the two groups on the crime "assault causing injury," we find that nearly twice as many Aboriginals have been found guilty as non-Aboriginals. The 2004 General Social Survey study found that

TABLE 5.9	Characteristics of All Persons Involved in Adult Correction Services, 1990–00 to 2003–04, Saskatchewan	
	Aboriginal	Non-Aboriginal
Violent Offences	50.6	38.5
Serious Violent Offences	18.0	9.0
Sexual Offences	4.4	5.2
Robbery	3.3	2.5
Common Assault	19.6	21.4
Other Violent Offences	5.2	10.4
Property Offences	19.8	37.2
Break and Enter	7.0	11.8
Theft	8.0	19.3
Fraud	2.7	18.8
Other Property Offences	2.0	7.1
Offences Against Administration of Justice	7.9	14.4
Other Criminal Code (No Traffic)	4.6	13.5
Criminal Code (Traffic)	10.7	37.0
Drug Offences	3.4	20.7
Other	3.0	11.5

Aboriginal inmates were incarcerated more often than non-Aboriginal inmates for crimes against a person (43 percent compared to 33 percent in provincial facilities, and 78 percent vs. 70 percent in federal ones). On the other hand, the percentage of Aboriginal people charged with a "firearms" offence is about half that for non-Aboriginal people. Hann and Harman (1992) found that the charge against an Aboriginal person was most likely to be for a crime against a person, while for non-Aboriginal suspects the charge would involve a property offence. Data in Table 5.9 reveals the pattern of charges against Aboriginal and non-Aboriginal adults for Saskatchewan, which is typical of most provincial statistics. It shows that in Saskatchewan, over half of the Aboriginal people in jail were charged with a violent offence while for non-Aboriginals, it was just over 38 percent.

Sentence Length In both federal and provincial cases, Aboriginal sentences are less severe than those of non-Aboriginals (Motiuk and Nafekh, 2000). This difference comes about due to the types of crimes committed and the seriousness of them as viewed by the courts. We find that the average federal sentence (excluding life sentences) for Aboriginal offenders is 3.57 years, while for non-Aboriginal offenders it is 3.72. What is more pronounced is the range of sentences exhibited in the two groups. Aboriginal people receive shorter sentences (average 3.4 years), but the range is 33 years. For non-Aboriginal persons the average is 4.3, with a range of 75 years. Thus, the variability of sentences for non-Aboriginal offenders is nearly twice that of Aboriginal persons charged with a crime. The data also reveal a pattern that shows a larger percentage of Aboriginal people receiving

TABLE 5.10	Average Sentence Length by Aboriginal and Non-Aboriginal			
Population	North American Indian	Métis	Inuit	Non-Aboriginal
Admissions	3.57	3.24	3.92	3.72
Releases	3.94	4.11	4.12	4.41
Institutional	5.06	5.16	4.95	5.75
Conditional Release	4.07	4.43	4.28	5.47

Source: ©Her Majesty the Queen in Right of Canada. Motiuk and Nafekh, 2000, p. 13, Correctional Service of Canada, 2000. Reproduced with the permission of the Minister of Public Works and Government Services Canada, 2004.

short-term sentences (nearly always greater than non-Aboriginal persons), and this trend reverses as we move to the 10-year and longer sentences (Solicitor General, 1985). The data in Table 5.10 reveal the average sentences under different conditions.

No discussion of crime would be complete without a comment on the recidivism rate of offenders. A study by Johnson (2005) looked at the recidivism rates of Aboriginals for the province of Saskatchewan. She found that 60 percent of Aboriginals released from jail in 1999 returned to a correctional facility at least once over the next five years, in comparison to less than 30 percent of non-Aboriginals. She found that one-quarter of Aboriginals released from jail had been returned within one year and one-third within two years.

Aboriginal Youth and the Law   Aboriginal youth face many obstacles as they grow up. They live below the poverty line and their families have experienced violence, illness, and substance abuse. They have limited access to education facilities and occupational choices. On top of all this, they have to adapt to mainstream Canadian society while at the same time trying to learn and retain their traditional culture (Mount Pleasant-Jette, 1993).

Young Aboriginal offenders have a history of offences. Nearly 60 percent of the males and 40 percent of the females admitted to correctional facilities have had at least one prior offence. Moreover, nearly half of the males and one-quarter of the females have been under community supervision when admitted to correctional facilities. This leads us to question to what extent young Aboriginals are exposed to the justice system. Are young Aboriginals who come into contact with the police diverted to alternative measures of a non-judicial type? Alternative programs include such actions as financial compensation to a victim, community service, educational programs, and apologies that are related to the offence. In 1999, 4 percent of the youth population were Aboriginal, but they are involved in 15 percent of the alternative measures that were implemented—an increase of 3 percent from the preceding year. Aboriginal youth participation in alternative measures was particularly noticeable in Saskatchewan (making up nearly half of the cases involving alternative measures) and in Alberta and the Yukon.

Today Aboriginal youth admissions make up over one-quarter of the total admissions to remand although they make up 7 percent of the youth. This is particularly noticeable in Western Canada. For example, in Manitoba, nearly 70 percent of youth admissions into remand were identified as being Aboriginal, while these youth make up only 16 percent of the total population. In Alberta, one-third of the admissions were Aboriginal, while they make up only 6 percent of the total youth population.

Table 5.11 reveals the extent of youth (12–17) crime on reserves for 2004. It shows that common assault is the single largest crime that youth are charged with. Compared to non-Aboriginal youth, Aboriginal youth are nearly six times more likely to be charged with assault. When comparing Aboriginal and non-Aboriginal youth with regard to property crimes (e.g., breaking and entering, motor vehicle theft), we find that Aboriginal youth are more than twice as likely to be charged with one of these offences. Examining other types of Criminal Code offences shows that Aboriginal youth are five times more likely to be charged with offences such as mischief, disturbing the peace, and bail violation, than non-Aboriginal youth. When we compare Aboriginal youth with regard to all federal charges with their non-Aboriginal counterparts, we find that they are more than three times more likely to be charged with a crime.

We also find that Aboriginal youth are overrepresented in sentenced custody admissions. The data from the General Social Survey (Reitano, 2004) revealed that Aboriginal youth admissions accounted for over one-quarter of the total admissions to sentenced custody. In almost every province in the country (P.E.I. being the exception), Aboriginal youth were overrepresented in custody facilities. For example, in Manitoba, where 16 percent of the youth are Aboriginal, over 75 percent of the sentenced custody admissions were Aboriginal. When we look at probation, we find that Aboriginal people account for 14 percent of youth on probation.

We find these high rates a function of both the behaviour of the police as well as the courts. Police are less likely to use discretionary powers when confronting Aboriginal youth. For example, if a youth has offended previously and is once again in contact with the police, he/she will be construed as resisting rehabilitation and deterrence, and as such will not be a recipient of discretionary behaviour by the police. Moreover, the Crown is subject to pressures as it deals with information provided by the police.

Today, governments have recognized the importance of proactive approaches to crime, and they have tried to develop new policy designs and programs to meet the needs of First Nations youth. For example, diversion programs, bush camps, and Aboriginal youth justice committees have been established to deal with Aboriginal youth offenders as an alternative to their entering the criminal justice system. However, as Figure 5.3 reveals, their admission to all types of correctional facilities is nearly five times greater than their representation in the population.

TABLE 5.11	Youth Crime On/Off Reserve, 2004	
	On Reserve Rate per 100,000 population	Off Reserve Rate per 100,000 Population
Homicide	15	1
Attempted Murder	2	2
Robbery	124	151
Assault	5 773	1 196
Sexual Assault	358	112
Other Sexual Offences	35	12
Abduction	2	0
		(Continued)

TABLE 5.11	(Continued)	
	On Reserve Rate per 100 000 population	Off Reserve Rate per 100 000 population
Total Violent Crimes	6 310	1 474
Break and Enter	4 384	609
Motor Vehicle Theft	1 170	247
Theft over $5 000	50	13
Theft under $5 000	2 087	1 667
Possession	261	296
Fraud	52	109
Total Property Crimes	8 004	2 941
Offensive Weapons	427	134
Arson	204	58
Bail Violations	1 461	483
Disturbing the Peace	1 772	265
Property Damage	3 815	939
Other	2 397	729
Total Other Criminal Code Offences	10 077	2 608
Total Criminal Code Offences	24 391	7 023

FIGURE 5.3	Aboriginal Youth Highly Represented in Admissions to All Types of Correctional Services, 2003/04

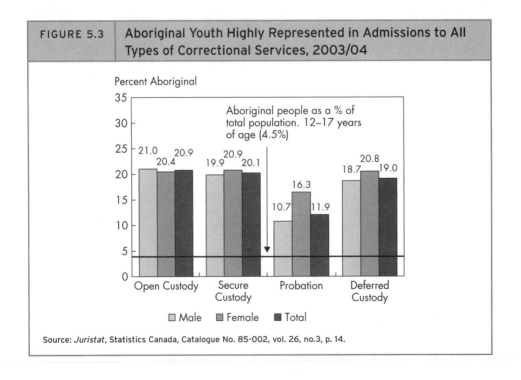

Source: *Juristat*, Statistics Canada, Catalogue No. 85-002, vol. 26, no.3, p. 14.

Explanations   Why are Aboriginal people overrepresented in our prisons? Braithwaite (1990, 1993) argues that a lack of social integration is the best explanation for why Aboriginal people seem to violate the law. He notes that the degree to which an individual is linked to significant people and institutions, such as schools, jobs, and family, will determine the extent of deviant behaviour exhibited. These structural factors impinge upon an individual's social conscience and are an external source of direction in regulating an individual's behaviour. Since individuals of lower socio-economic status or those operating in an anomic state are not as linked to the middle-class structures, they have less control. In addition, lower-class individuals or those experiencing anomie are more likely to experience dysfunctional families, lack steady employment, and be more marginalized than any other group. Aboriginal people living in the inner core of large major urban centres are characterized by this lack of structural linkages (Canada, 1978b).

Braithwaite notes that the greater the degree of interdependency and integratedness of people, the lower the levels of deviant behaviour. As Aboriginal people continue to be marginalized and anomic, their level of integratedness with either their own community or that of the dominant society has decreased over time and continues to block the effects of integration. The result is that the Aboriginal offender is unable to find a community into which he or she can integrate. Aboriginal people have lost their social sense of community; even reserves reflect trends of the dominant society in that they are becoming communities that reveal extreme social and economic cleavages, preventing the development of a caring, integrative social unit. This social dislocation and economic stratification within Aboriginal communities does not allow for either formal or informal social control mechanisms to be effectively implemented. In addition, the diminishment of the family and group authority on the reserve has created social and economic divisions between individuals and families, and has had a profound impact on the socialization of the young (LaPrairie, 1996).

Is there a difference in the number of urban and rural Aboriginal people committing criminal offences? The Cawsey Inquiry (1991) showed that about 6 percent of the Aboriginal persons charged with a criminal offence in Alberta were living on a reserve at the time they were charged even though two-thirds of the Aboriginal population reside on reserves. McCaskill (1985) found that over two-thirds of the federal and provincial prisoners from Manitoba lived in urban areas when they were charged with an offence. Johnston (1997) found that, for federal prisoners, at the time of offence about one-quarter were from a reserve or remote rural area, 44 percent were from a rural area, and 30 percent were from urban areas. Why? It may be as simple as the level of police coverage. In rural areas there is far less coverage than in urban centres and thus offenders are more likely to be caught in urban areas. Other explanations are that crimes in urban areas are more likely to be reported or detected, e.g., public disturbance (Nuffield, 1998).

LaPrairie (1998) points out that reserves are not the peaceful and cohesive communities that are sometimes portrayed. Many reserves are characterized as high-crime areas that have high unemployment and demonstrate many other indicators of social disorganization. In some cases, violence (domestic and gang) has become accepted behaviour if the circumstances are understood by the community. However, when the individual moves into an urban centre, there is a major change in the level of tolerance by residents, and thus many Aboriginal persons who exhibit normative behaviour on the reserve are called to the attention of the police in urban areas. Moreover, in urban centres, young Aboriginals are more likely to come into contact with gang members and participate in their activities.

REHABILITATION

What happens to the individual once he or she is placed in jail? Are Aboriginal and non-Aboriginal inmates treated differently? Are there differential rates of correctional rehabilitation? Overall, the impact of rehabilitation in prison seems minimal, irrespective of the individual's ethnicity. Antonowicz and Ross (1994) point out that their research finds only 20 effective programs implemented over the past two decades. Others argue that methodological issues such as measuring "success" are problematic and need to be reconceptualized. For example, if recidivism is a measure of success (or lack thereof), it does not measure any other increases in the individual's "well-being" that might have been brought about through the program, e.g., community reintegration, family interaction.

Nevertheless, correctional institutions are notoriously poor in implementing rehabilitation programs for any inmates, Aboriginal or not. Why is this so? Correctional officials are security conscious, so any program that compromises or potentially compromises this issue will be viewed negatively. Other reasons include a general distrust of the inmates by prison officials, a disbelief that the program will help inmates and a lack of resources to implement programs of rehabilitation. Bonta, Lipinski and Martin (1992) argue that other factors, such as the nature of the programs and the population identified to be part of the program, also are responsible for low success rates.

On the other hand, there have been some successes, and these seem to have focused on linking the prisoner with his or her community, e.g., school, family, social service agency, neighbourhood organization. This involves significant community input and participation in the programs directed toward the inmates. LaPrairie (1996) finds that programs taking a social cognitive approach are the most effective.

It is ironic that the first Aboriginal self-help social movements in Canada were developed within prisons. Prisoners of Aboriginal descent were acutely aware of their minority status, and they realized that the only people who would help them were other Native inmates. The development of these social organizations drew inspiration from the American Indian Movement as well as the Black prison organizations that were operating in the United States. The First Indian Brotherhood was formed in Stoney Mountain Penitentiary in Manitoba and was comprised of status Indians (later, all inmates of Aboriginal ancestry could join). It was not until 1975 that the commissioner of penitentiaries officially recognized it as a viable self-help program. The central focus of activities for this and other groups was on cultural awareness and pride in Aboriginal identity. As Jefferson (1978) points out, the Brotherhood focused on leadership training, public speaking, cultural pride, and self-awareness. It also provided Aboriginal inmates with some protection against discriminatory treatment, either by other inmates or by the staff of the institution. While the role of alcohol has been a major force in Aboriginal people coming into contact with the law, it was not until the mid-1970s that alcohol counselling programs were supported by the government.

Today, almost every federal and provincial correctional institution has Aboriginal Brother/Sisterhood organizations operating. While these organizations work within the correctional system, there is little outside the system to help Aboriginal people integrate into the larger society once they leave the correctional system. This problem arises due to jurisdictional wrangling as to who has responsibility—federal or provincial governments.

The Native Liaison Support System was the precursor of today's Native Liaison Program, which operates in both the provincial and federal correctional institutions. Now evident in prisons are programs that are cultural and/or spiritual in nature, with a focus on reintegrating the offender into the home community. In 1987 a federal policy on "Native Offender Programs" was instituted, and the federal government also established the Task Force on Aboriginal Peoples in Federal Corrections to examine how an Aboriginal person is processed through the correctional institution. Today, the policy objectives related to Aboriginal offenders in prison focus on each institution developing Aboriginal-specific programs to replace "regular" programs for Aboriginal inmates and take into account both the culture and language of the Aboriginal people. The *Corrections and Conditional Release Act* notes that all prisons should provide a range of programs to deal with the needs of Aboriginal prisoners and contribute to their successful reintegration into the community. Under the new policy, Correctional Services Canada can transfer care and custody of Aboriginal offenders to an Aboriginal community or organization. Today we find that many Aboriginal inmates are involved in the Pathways program (a traditional environment for Aboriginal offenders who wish to follow a healing path) and healing lodges (institutions that offer culturally appropriate services and programs in an environment that incorporates Aboriginal peoples' traditions and beliefs) that have been developed by Correctional Services Canada. There has also been the transition of four minimum security facilities to Aboriginal communities. Advisory committees that counsel federal bodies on Aboriginal issues have also been created. Finally, the Act established the office of the Corporate Advisor, Aboriginal Correctional Programs, to act as a catalyst for Aboriginal programs and to liaise with Aboriginal communities (LaPrairie, 1996).

While most provincial correctional institutions have the same programs and policies as noted above, Ontario, Alberta, and British Columbia have gone one step further by identifying Aboriginal justice branches to support provincial correctional institutions. Programs such as traditional spiritual practices, Aboriginal literacy, Aboriginal cultural skills, sacred circles, Native awareness, sweat lodge ceremonies, and Aboriginal language programs are evident as one moves from one institution to another. In this respect, provincial jails do not have the consistency that is found in federal jails, but they do consider regional variations in developing specific programs for Aboriginal people. In addition, provincial correctional institutions have hired Aboriginal people and require staff to take courses on cross-cultural training. Specific programs that have been developed include the Search of Your Warrior Program, developed by the Native Counselling Services of Alberta. This program focuses on violent criminal behaviour and is implemented in the Prairie, Pacific, and Quebec regions. The Mama Wi Program is a family violence treatment program that is currently being implemented in the Prairie region. A national Aboriginal offender pre-orientation program has been developed to increase inmates' preparedness to benefit from other programs offered by Correctional Services Canada. Pre-orientation also determines cultural and criminogenic needs, and starts the education of Aboriginal offenders about corrections, Aboriginal heritage, and healing opportunities. Finally, a national Aboriginal healing program that identifies traditional cultural methods of living in balance is being developed in collaboration with Native court workers and the Aboriginal Healing Foundation. By the end of the 1990s, 23 Aboriginal-specific programs had been identified (13 federal, 10 provincial) (Epprecht, 2000).

The Aboriginal justice strategy is a federal program intended to address the over-representation of Aboriginals in our justice system. It is comprised of community-based programs that are cost-shared with provincial and territorial governments. The goal of this program is to support Aboriginal communities as they take greater responsibility for the administration of justice, and to help reduce crime. Currently there are four different programs supported by this strategy: diversion or alternative measures, community sentencing circles, mediation and arbitration in family and civil cases and court community/justice programs.

Correctional Services Canada has now taken a position that it is committed to providing reintegration programs that are responsive to the needs of Aboriginal offenders. However, it is agreed that, while the Aboriginal-specific programs are successful, there are many other social and economic factors that need to be dealt with if the prisoner is to successfully integrate into his or her community or larger society. Solving a specific problem is the outcome of the program, but securing the total "well-being" of the individual once released from prison is more than the specific program deals with. The results of evaluations of this program also demonstrated that Aboriginal inmates have fewer personal and social skills than non-Aboriginal inmates on a number of dimensions (Ellerby, 1995).

RETURNING TO SOCIETY

We now turn to the issue of what happens when the inmate is being considered for release. First of all, prison officials carry out a risk assessment, if the inmate is not up for statutory release, to determine if an individual can be released into community supervision. The data show a difference between Aboriginal and non-Aboriginal offenders applying for release on full parole. Twelve percent more Aboriginal offenders who were released on parole were defined as high-risk, compared to non-Aboriginal offenders. Because Aboriginals are considered a higher risk of re-offending than non-Aboriginal inmates, fewer Aboriginal offenders are eligible to be released to community supervision than non-Aboriginal offenders.

Who actually gets released or paroled? It has been argued that the reason for the high rate of Aboriginal incarceration is that Aboriginal offenders do not get early release from prison. The Task Force on Aboriginal Peoples in Federal Corrections assessed their data and found that Aboriginal inmates are indeed less likely to be released on parole than non-Aboriginal inmates are. The data show that non-Aboriginals are twice as likely as Aboriginal inmates to be given parole. However, a more detailed analysis by LaPrairie (1996) shows that the difference arises because of the type of crime committed. The fact that Aboriginal offenders are more likely to have committed violent person-type crimes seems to explain the difference—and not racial bias in the system. In the end, Aboriginal people spend more time in prison even though they may have received shorter sentences than non-Aboriginal offenders. Welsh's (2000) study compared Aboriginal and non-Aboriginal offenders at two stages of the full parole review process and found that 6.3 percent of Aboriginals were given day parole, compared to 4.8 percent of non-Aboriginal inmates. On the other hand, only 18.3 percent of Aboriginals were given full parole, in comparison with 44.7 percent of non-Aboriginal inmates. Welsh (2000) also found that Aboriginal offenders are far less likely to apply for full parole than non-Aboriginal offenders are. This probably reflects Aboriginal distrust of the correctional system. Second, he found that when Aboriginal offenders apply for full parole, they are less likely to be granted release.

One major factor in parole release is that Aboriginal inmates are considered to be at higher risk to re-offend than non-Aboriginal prisoners and to have greater needs than non-Aboriginal inmates. Nearly 60 percent of Aboriginal inmates in provincial facilities were classified as a high risk to re-offend, as compared to only 44 percent of non-Aboriginal inmates. In federal facilities, almost 70 percent of Aboriginal inmates were classified as

TABLE 5.12	Risk and Need Levels of Aboriginal/Non-Aboriginal Inmates	
	Aboriginal	Non-Aboriginal
Risk level		
Low	37.5	54.6
Medium	34.7	23.7
High	27.7	20
Need level		
Low	20.7	39.6
Medium	47	37.7
High	32.3	20.9

Source Adapted from Welsh, 2000, p. 62, Correctional Service of Canada, 2004.

high-risk, as compared to less than 60 percent of non-Aboriginal inmates. As for needs, each prisoner is assessed in terms of his or her needs when released. Seven needs are assessed in the conditional releases that take place. Overall, about half of the Aboriginal inmates are shown to have employment, personal/emotional, and marital/ family needs. In addition, about one-quarter to one-third of these inmates have needs involving substance abuse, unsavoury associates, and lack of community functioning (see Table 5.12).

The last step in the justice process is reintegration. How do offenders reintegrate into the community? In looking at the reintegrative process, we must note that there are two components to the equation: the offender and the community. Unless the community is prepared to accept the offender into the community, it is clear that the process will be difficult. At the same time, the offender must be prepared to take on the necessary skills in order to achieve reintegration. This, of course, is complicated by the type and nature of the crime committed by the offender. Less serious crimes are less problematic for community members, while serious crimes leave the community members apprehensive and concerned about their own and their family's safety and security. In the end, a lack of reintegration assures that the offender will become a repeat offender, and the process leads to further offences.

What happens to the offender once he or she is released into the community? The answer depends upon how well the individual has been integrated into his or her community. Do recidivism rates between Aboriginal and non-Aboriginal people differ? A growing body of evidence suggests that Aboriginal recidivism tends to be higher than for non-Aboriginal groups. Hann and Harman (1993) show the recidivism rate for Aboriginal people in federal jails (66 percent) was about one-third higher than for non-Aboriginal people. However, such a trend was not evident in a limited study of Ontario provincial jails.

ALTERNATIVES TO IMPRISONMENT

Is there an alternative to prison? What is the value of imprisonment? What are the costs to society? Many Canadians are uneasy with the tendency to impose prison sentences on more and more people, particularly young offenders. Moreover, with the cost of incarceration escalating (currently estimated at $400 per day for provincial inmate and over $500 per day for federal inmates), individuals are questioning the value of such action.

Three possible strategies have been offered to deal with the growing prison population and the increasing tendency to deal with offenders by placing them in prison. The first is the use of alternative sanctions. These include fines, community service, home detention and electronic monitoring, close supervision, and boot camps. In the case of Aboriginal youth to be considered for extrajudicial measures, they must present themselves as willing and able to comply with the expectations of the proposed measures. This assumes a level of sophistication and competence that is well beyond the capacity of most Aboriginal youth. And as such, they will not be considered for extrajudicial measures (Vandergoot, 2006). Moreover, a majority of young Aboriginals who come into contact with the law have little knowledge about their rights and their ability to exercise them, e.g., rights to counsel and silence. As a result, in a majority of cases involving Aboriginal youth, they waive these rights without understanding what they have done. It has been argued (Junger-Tas, 1994) that these alternative sanctions ensure that the offender faces real punishment and retribution while, at the same time, society is attempting to keep the individual from repeating his or her crime. While such alternative sanctions have their supporters, there are many who are critical. They argue that these new sanctions widen the net of correctional controls over an increasing number of people. In the end, more people will be captured in the "net" and be labelled criminals. In addition, the cost of administration will far outpace the costs of maintaining prisons. They also argue that the fact that these types of social control mechanisms exist does not mean the courts will use them. These individuals argue that many young Aboriginal suffer permanent social and emotional consequences as a result of their involvement in the criminal justice system. They are stigmatized and this has an impact on their self-concept. As Vandergoot (2006) points out, encounters with the law may create "blocks" or "snares" in the youth self-concept that effectively arrest their psychological and emotional development. With a lowering of confidence and motivation, depression and anger may take over with negative consequences that become self-fulfilling.

The second alternative to prisons is to increase the use of the existing community-based correctional resources. There are a number of different types of resources that are now being used: attendance centres, bush camps, home detention, and community correctional centres. Today, there are only two Aboriginal-specific community correctional centres in Canada: the Stan Daniels Centre in Edmonton and the Wasekun House in Montreal. However, Aboriginal people may use the services of other centres that are not Aboriginal-specific.

A third and highly controversial alternative is the use of local justice systems. While there is some acceptance of the community's role in the criminal justice process, there is no consensus as to what this role might be. Focusing specifically on Aboriginal systems, there are several examples across the country. Sentencing circles in the North, the Western provinces, and Quebec have proven to be highly controversial (LaPrairie and Roberts, 1997). This community-based program is a good example of a culturally sensitive approach to justice. Sentencing circles, which are Aboriginal forms of dispensing justice, gained the attention of the Canadian criminal justice system in the early 1900s within the Yukon Territorial Court. The concept involves the community hearing the evidence of an alleged crime and seeking input from all sectors of the community (defendant, perpetrator, and others in the community who have been affected by the alleged crime), after which the community decides on the appropriate sentence. This method is used only when the community requests such "court proceedings," the Crown gives permission, and the presiding judge gives permission to invoke this form of justice. At the same time, the entire process is monitored by a Canadian judge. The Community Holistic Circle Healing project in Hollow Water, Manitoba, has been defined by both Aboriginal and non-Aboriginal people as a success. Other examples of local justice in Aboriginal communities are the Indian Brook Diversion project in Nova Scotia, the Toronto Aboriginal Legal Services project, and the Family Group Conferencing in Newfoundland (Jackson, 1992).

The right to counsel upon arrest is another issue of concern for Aboriginal people. For many Aboriginal people in remote communities, this right is meaningless because counsel

Box 5.2 | Conflict Incidents

The following two episodes are reflective of the conflict that has erupted over the past decade. They also demonstrate the inordinate time span and legal wrangling required before resolution of cases are pronounced.

Ipperwash Crisis: In 1995, members of the Stony Point Ojibway band occupied Ipperwash Provincial Park claiming the land was theirs. It had been appropriated by the federal government in 1942 under the War Measures Act. While the Department of National Defence said it would give the land back after the war, 50 years later this had not happened and no compensation had been offered. In 1993, Stony Point members began moving on to the land and the military withdrew in 1995. The band members built barricades to underline their land claim and to protest the destruction of the burial grounds. After several days of confrontation between First Nations and the police, several vehicles driven by Aboriginals approached the police and the police opened fire on the vehicles, killing Mr. Dudley George. The original land claim was settled in 1998 when it was agreed that the land would be cleared and returned to the Kettle and Stony Point First Nation. As well, every member of the band was to receive between $150 and $400K. An inquiry was held between 2003 and 2006 but the final report has yet to be released.

Burnt Church Crisis: In 2000, after the Supreme Court ruled that a Mi'kmaq had the right to fish for eels out of season, other First Nations members interpreted this as meaning they could catch lobsters at any time during the year, and therefore set out traps. The Government of Canada signed "fishing agreements" with most of the bands in Atlantic Canada, but the Burnt Church Band was not one of them. Over the next three years, considerable conflict (e.g., boat burning, destroying of a wharf, arrests) was carried out between the Aboriginal and non-Aboriginal community in the area. In 2002, the Burnt Church Band signed an agreement in principle with the federal government which allows Aboriginal people to have a number of lobster traps (previously they had none), and gave them compensation worth $20M.

is not easy to obtain. And, although police have the duty to advise people of their rights to silence and to consult a lawyer, they do not have to make counsel available. A recent study in an urban Canadian centre noted that over 60 percent of the Aboriginal defendants had legal counsel. Thus, in urban areas, legal counsel is widely available and used, while in rural areas it is almost nonexistent. And, when legal aid is available for Aboriginals in these isolated communities, it doesn't begin until the actual court appearance. Our research has also found that, regardless of his or her criminal record or the type of offence with which he or she has been charged, an Aboriginal is more likely to be held in custody than to be released with a summons to appear.

The 1999 Supreme Court decision (*R. v. Gladue*) was a recognition of the plight of Aboriginal people and their contact with Canadian law. They noted in their decision that years of dislocation and economic development have translated for many Aboriginal people into low incomes, high unemployment, lack of opportunities and options, lack of education, substance abuse, loneliness and community fragmentation. These and other factors contribute to a higher incidence of crime and incarceration (Green and Healy, 2003). See Box 5.2 for some examples of the sort of conflicts that have taken place in recent years between Native people and the law.

SUMMARY

The data reveal that Aboriginal people are more likely to come into contact with the Canadian judicial system than non-Aboriginals. In addition, once they become involved with the legal system, they are more likely to be sentenced, spend greater time in jail and are less likely to be released on parole.

While most Canadians hold the court system in high regard, Aboriginal people tend to see the courts as a tool of oppression. Aboriginal people do not experience the courts as being accountable to their communities, nor do they see them as resolving disputes between parties. For Aboriginal people, justice can only be obtained thorough the establishment of alternative dispute resolution processes such as day courts and justices of the peace. These courts would be staffed by Aboriginal people and would be a suitable compromise, allowing justice to be more equitably distributed. This arrangement would allow Aboriginal people to become more involved in the system, and the participation of people like Aboriginal elders and laypersons would lend greater legitimacy to the process. And, in the end, their involvement would be more effective in resolving problems in the community (Royal Commission on Aboriginal Peoples, 1996a).

Because of the difference in world view, Aboriginals cannot fully comprehend our dominant society's court process, nor can the courts fully understand the Aboriginal world view. For example, the difficulties of language incompatibility have been included in many Aboriginal claims that the court system does not adequately represent Aboriginal people. As the Alexander tribal government pointed out in its submission to the Task Force on the Criminal Justice System and Its Impact on the Indian and Métis People of Alberta, some members of the courts suffer from "cultural blindness." They are unable to see and hear the Aboriginal victims, the accused, and the witnesses who appear before them; Aboriginals lack a voice in the process (Cawsey, 1991).

Aboriginal people also have pointed out that, because of the isolation of many Aboriginal communities, the provision of justice by our courts is viewed by them as serving the convenience of the judges and lawyers while inconveniencing community people. Aboriginal people have argued that, in isolated communities, the courts rush the process of justice so officials can return to their homes. Postponements of court appearances are also based upon their convenience to the courts, not to the community. In short, few court hearings are held in Aboriginal communities, which supports the Aboriginal view that the courts are foreign institutions (Elias, 1976).

Through persistent dialogue with various levels of government, Aboriginal communities across Canada have gradually begun to explore the possibility of administering various components of the criminal justice system. While this has been a slow process and many problems still exist within the current relationship between Aboriginal offenders and the judicial system, some progress is being made.

KEY TERMS

Euro-Canadian justice   Cawsey Inquiry
traditional Native justice   sentencing circles

STUDY QUESTIONS

1. Define *conflict*. From an Aboriginal perspective, what impact does this definition have?

2. What is the First Indian Brotherhood?

3. Compare and contrast Aboriginal–Euro-Canadian conceptions of justice.

4. What are the two explanation for why individuals commit crimes and why they are (or are not) sentenced to jail? How do these relate to Aboriginal and non-Aboriginal offenders?

5. Explain the *revolving door syndrome* and how this relates to Aboriginal people within Canada.

6. Compare and contrast types of offences and sentence length for Aboriginal and non-Aboriginal people.

7. Discuss social integration in relation to Aboriginal people and crime.

8. How has Correctional Services Canada responded to the over-representation of Aboriginal people within the Canadian prison system?

9. What impact can a community have upon an offender during the reintegration process?

10. Discuss the concept of *sentencing circles*.

WEBLINKS

www.usask.ca/nativelaw/publications/jah/circle.html

Often hailed as the example par excellence of adapting the conventional European model of justice to an Aboriginal context, "sentencing circles" often involve the offender, victim, and members of the community in determining the penalty for a crime. This is an excellent collection of information about sentencing circles.

www.usask.ca/nativelaw/publications/desc/justice.html

Justice as Healing is a newsletter that focuses on Aboriginal concepts of justice based upon Aboriginal knowledge and languages, and rooted in Aboriginal experiences and feelings of wrongs and indignities. It is published in an online format by the University of Saskatchewan Native Law Program.

www.fncpa.ca

For some Aboriginal communities, the face of justice is literally changing. Policing is, increasingly, managed by Aboriginal peoples. The First Nations Chiefs of Police Association website promotes First Nations police services.

chapter six

The New Crucible of Aboriginal Revitalization: Urban Centres

INTRODUCTION

Over the past half-century, the number of Aboriginal people taking up residence in urban areas has increased substantially. As we begin the 21st century, we find that nearly half the Aboriginal population live in large urban centres across the country. Nearly 3 in 10 Aboriginal people live in one of Canada's 27 census metropolitan areas and a further 25 percent live in 11 other urban centres. All demographic projections show that this number will continue to grow for the foreseeable future.

As the presence of Aboriginals in urban areas becomes increasingly visible, new relationships between Aboriginals and non-Aboriginals are emerging. While this visibility has been evident for some time in some Western cities, it is now increasingly evident across the country. The increase in visibility is not just due to increasing numbers but is a result of the emergence of Aboriginal communities, businesses, institutions, and networks in urban centres. Members of different First Nations who meet in the city serve as a communications link for their respective Aboriginal communities back in the rural areas (Levesque, 2003). As a result, new ties are being forged between city and rural Aboriginal communities. The Aboriginal presence in Western urban centres is particularly important, as it is estimated that in 10 years one-sixth of the labour force in Winnipeg, Saskatoon, and Regina will be Aboriginal (Mendelson and Battle, 1999).

Why Aboriginal people have come to the urban centres is now a major concern to all levels of government, social agencies, and Aboriginal leaders. However, governments at all levels have been hesitant to develop policy with regard to urban Aboriginal people. The central reason for this reluctance is that that there has been and continues to be a jurisdictional dispute as to which level of government has legislative authority and responsibility for urban Aboriginal people. The federal government is quick to agree that it is responsible for all registered First Nations people who live on reserve or Crown land. However, the authority and responsibility for other Aboriginal people is subject to disagreement, and the federal government argues that the provinces have a primary (but not exclusive) responsibility for other Aboriginal people. The provinces, in turn, have argued that all Aboriginal people are the primary responsibility of the federal government, and that provincial responsibility is limited to serving Aboriginal people as part of the larger provincial population. The provincial governments have therefore not developed inclusive policy with regard to urban First Nations people (Hanselmann, 2001). The consequence is a "policy vacuum" that has resulted in urban Aboriginals being ignored (Canada, 1996d, p. 538).

Despite the concern expressed by various levels of government, there is a paucity of research focusing on why Aboriginal people move to the city, their experiences once they enter the city, and why they stay or leave after a period of time. Because urban Aboriginals are hypermobile and tend to blend into the general population of the urban poor, statistics are particularly difficult to obtain; politicians, as well as academics, tend to concentrate their efforts elsewhere. Moreover, the Royal Commission on Aboriginal Peoples did not forcefully address the issue of urbanized Aboriginal peoples, and thus further marginalized their participation in the political and legal processes now being employed by more traditional "land-based" Aboriginal communities (Anderson and Denis, 2003). However, the issue of Aboriginal urbanization has recently been brought to the attention of municipal, provincial, and federal governments by such indirectly related issues as social services, unemployment, and urban crime. The growth in the numbers of Aboriginal people now living in urban centres have produced a major crisis for federal, provincial, and municipal governments (Hanselmann and Gibbins, 2002). In short, Aboriginal urbanization has been defined as a "social problem" that needs to be dealt with.

When the federal government commissioned a study on Aboriginal people in the 1960s, the results suggested a major influx of reserve Aboriginals into major urban centres (Hawthorn, 1966–67). It also went on to point out that, when this happened, special facilities would be needed to deal with the process of social adjustment. This migration has been as massive as Hawthorn predicted, and as Figure 6.1 identifies, the proportion of on-reserve registered Indians has decreased from 71 percent in 1960 to only 58 percent in 2001. What is equally remarkable is that, after 50 years, neither the federal nor provincial governments have developed strategies or programs that would facilitate the integration of Aboriginal people into urban centres.

In the mid-1980s this migration movement slowed down, and Siggner (1986) noted that, at the time, the mobility patterns of Aboriginals and non-Aboriginals were almost identical; nearly one-fifth of both groups lived at a different location than the one they had lived at 10 years previously. However, more recent data shows that the Aboriginal population is more mobile than the non-Aboriginal population. For example, Norris et al. (2002) observe that, between 1991 and 1996, well over half of the Aboriginal population moved (compared to just 40 percent of the non-Aboriginal population). They note that the Aboriginal population living in urban centres is particularly mobile, and between 1991 and 1996, 70 percent of Aboriginal residents moved, compared to just under 50 percent of the non-Aboriginal population.

After Aboriginal people had been forced onto reserves, their social and economic structures became incapable of supporting a growing population. In addition, the process

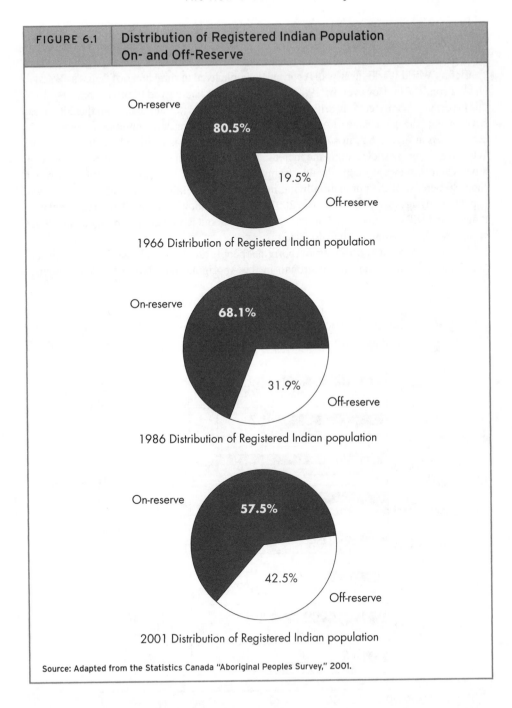

| FIGURE 6.1 | Distribution of Registered Indian Population On- and Off-Reserve |

On-reserve
80.5%
19.5%
Off-reserve

1966 Distribution of Registered Indian population

On-reserve
68.1%
31.9%
Off-reserve

1986 Distribution of Registered Indian population

On-reserve
57.5%
42.5%
Off-reserve

2001 Distribution of Registered Indian population

Source: Adapted from the Statistics Canada "Aboriginal Peoples Survey," 2001.

of enfranchisement moved individuals off the reserve and into urban centres. Then, after World War II, Canada itself shifted from a rural, agricultural economic system to an urban, industrialized one. As a result of this transition, Aboriginal people found themselves migrating to urban centres in larger numbers than before, looking for employment or better services or simply for a way of leaving the reserve. For example, in Manitoba the urban Aboriginal population jumped over 300 percent between 1966 and 1986.

Before World War II, nearly all Aboriginal people lived in rural areas of Canada (Waddell and Watson, 1971). However, by 1960 about 15 percent had moved to urban areas. By 1986 this percentage increased to nearly one-third (see Figure 6.1). Later data from the 2001 Census show that the percentage of Aboriginal people living off reserve continues to increase. As can be seen in Figure 6.2, in some provinces the proportion is nearing half the population. While these figures show a dramatic increase in the proportion of Aboriginal people living in urban centres, they vary considerably from the statistics for the general population, which show 80 percent of the population living in urban centres. Table 6.1 reveals the off-reserve population by age group from 1981 to 2001. The results show that the off-reserve population is aging and will continue to get older; e.g., in 1981 about 3.5 percent were in the 45–49 age group; by 2001 that number had doubled.

Nearly 80 percent of off-reserve Aboriginal people are living in large metropolitan centres. Table 6.2 shows the rate of growth in the Aboriginal population for selected cities

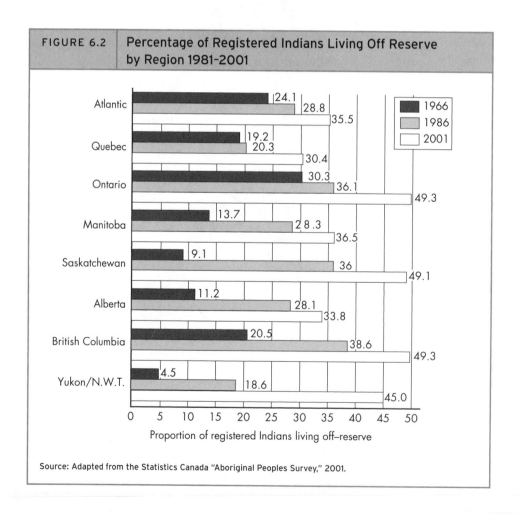

FIGURE 6.2 | **Percentage of Registered Indians Living Off Reserve by Region 1981-2001**

Proportion of registered Indians living off–reserve

Source: Adapted from the Statistics Canada "Aboriginal Peoples Survey," 2001.

TABLE 6.1	Population by Age Group, Aboriginals Off-Reserve, 1981, 1991, 2001					
Age	1981 Population	% Total Pop.	1991 Population	% Total Pop.	2001 Population	% Total Pop.
0-4	10 908	10.99	19 252	9.38	18 934	7.98
5-9	12 651	12.74	16 535	8.06	22 320	9.40
10-14	13 294	13.39	18 701	9.11	22 116	9.32
15-19	12 205	12.29	19 791	9.65	17 261	7.27
20-24	10 559	10.64	21 395	10.43	17 632	7.43
25-29	8 751	8.81	21 083	10.27	19 399	8.17
30-34	7 491	7.55	19 902	9.70	21 827	9.19
35-39	5 985	6.03	17 313	8.44	22 282	9.39
40-44	4 401	4.43	13 781	6.72	20 079	8.46
45-49	3 407	3.43	10 650	5.19	15 997	6.74
50-54	2 599	2.62	7 994	3.90	12 136	5.11
55-59	2 079	2.09	6 046	2.95	9 042	3.81
60-64	1 428	1.44	4 373	2.13	6 590	2.78
65+	3 523	3.55	8 373	4.08	11 772	4.96
Total	99 281	100.00	205 188	100.00	237 387	100.00

Source: Adapted from *Highlights of Aboriginal Conditions*, 1981–2001, *Part I, Demographic Trends* p. 27, Indian and Northern Affairs Canada, 2002.

between 1951 and 2001. Clearly, rapid growth has taken place in the number of Aboriginals moving to the city. However, Table 6.2 does not reflect the number of Aboriginals who have entered the city as other than full-time residents, or whose lifestyles have frustrated the attempts of an enumeration agency to count them. The most dramatic increases from 1966 to 2001 have been in the West and North, where off-reserve rates have doubled and, in the case of Saskatchewan, have quadrupled. However, projections suggest that the urban migration has now stabilized and only marginal increases will take place.

Only a few cities in Canada have tried to gather up-to-date and dependable data, with often surprising results: on the basis of its own figures, Regina predicts that by 2011 over one-third of its population will be Aboriginal.

Migration is a reciprocal process, referring to the movement of Aboriginal people both into and out of the city. In some cases, Aboriginal people who move off the reserve settle permanently in the city; others only sojourn in the city, remaining for a while, then moving back to their reserves. Even though urban areas are the recipients of large numbers of Aboriginal people, they also contribute to the total number of out-migrants among Aboriginal people. The end result in the past few decades was that for the period of 1976–81, compared to 1966–71, urban areas showed a 6 percent increase in the influx of Aboriginal *migrants* but a net loss of 2 percent in their *total* Aboriginal population. Focusing just on registered Indians, we find that the five-year net migration flow between 1991 and 1996

TABLE 6.2	Growth of Aboriginal and Métis Population in Urban Centres, 1951-2001			
	1951	1971*	1996	2001
Calgary	62	2 265	23 450	21 915
Edmonton	616	4 260	44 150	45 930
Halifax	–	–	7 795	8 100
Hamilton	493	1 470	11 020	12 200
London	133	1 015	8 200	8 200
Montreal	296	3 215	43 875	43 875
Ottawa-Hull	–	–	29 915	30 915
Regina	160	2 860	14 570	15 760
Saskatoon	48	1 070	18 160	20 275
Toronto	805	2 990	39 380	39 580
Vancouver	239	3 000	48 805	50 805
Winnipeg	210	4 940	52 525	55 760

* Does not include Inuit.

Source: Canada, Government of, *Perspective Canada I* (Ottawa: Queens Printer, 1974), 244; Canadian Metropolitan Areas, *Dimensions*, Statistics Canada, Table 9, 1986; Newhouse and Peters, 2003; INAC, *Registered Indian Population Projections*, 1998-2008, 2000; Siggner & Costa, 2005.

reveals an important pattern: on-reserve communities have had an increase of nearly 15 000 people (coming from rural and urban areas). This influx is partially due to the changes in definition of an "Indian," but it also demonstrates that there is considerable migration between rural, urban, and reserve contexts. Figure 6.3 elucidates this flow.

Before examining the process of urbanization, a brief characterization of the Aboriginal people who currently live in Canadian cities will be useful.

URBAN ABORIGINAL PROFILE

The proportion of Aboriginal people in urban areas increased substantially from the early 1950s until the early 1970s, when it began to decrease. Table 6.1 showed that in 1981 more than one-fourth of the Aboriginal population who lived off the reserve were between the ages of 25 and 44. By 1991 well over one-third of the urban Aboriginal population was in this age category. These figures support the observation that urban migration is stabilizing as fewer Aboriginal people enter the urban setting and more return to the reserve. When age groups of Aboriginal migrants are compared, however, no substantial difference emerges in migration patterns. This suggests that members of all age groups migrate in almost equal numbers to urban centres, although somewhat fewer Aboriginals over 50 migrate. The high proportion of children up to 14 years old shows that many Aboriginal people bring their children with them as they enter the city. For example, as early as 1970 Vincent found that in Winnipeg over half the Aboriginal people were younger than 30;

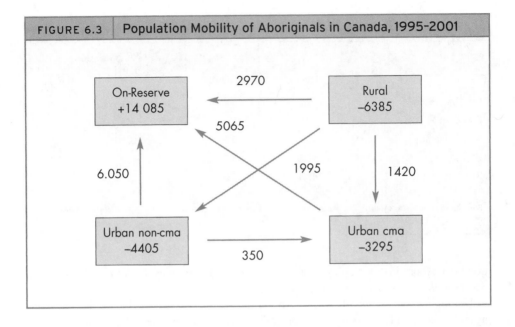

FIGURE 6.3 | **Population Mobility of Aboriginals in Canada, 1995–2001**

other studies have since supported this finding, with slightly different figures (Siggner and Costa, 2005). Today, nearly 30 percent of all aboriginal people in Canada in the age group 0–14 live in urban centres. Forty percent of Aboriginals between the ages of 25 to 54 also live in urban centres, while less than 7 percent of those over the age of 55 live in urban centres (Siggner and Costa, 2005). Vincent also found that 60 percent of urban Aboriginal people were married, though not necessarily living with their spouses. According to the male–female ratio, there are about 10 percent more Aboriginal women in urban centres than men. This figure does not include women who have been forced off the reserves through marriage to non-Aboriginal men.

While levels of education for off-reserve Aboriginal people are significantly lower than the national average (Federation of Saskatchewan Indians, 1978; Hanselmann, 2001), when these figures are compared to those of 1981, we find that school attendance among urban Aboriginal youth increased substantially. However, we also find that non-Aboriginal urban youth are staying in secondary school at higher rates, so that the difference between the two groups is even widening. When comparing the educational levels of on- and off-reserve Aboriginal people, the difference is not significant (see Table 6.3). In other words, there is no "brain drain" operating on the reserves. Nevertheless, Table 6.4 reveals major differences in educational achievement between urban Aboriginals and urban non-Aboriginals for specific urban areas in Canada.

A number of surveys over the past two decades have been undertaken to assess the labour-force involvement of urban Aboriginals (Stanbury and Fields, 1975; Norris, 2000; Norris et al., 2002; Frideres and Ryan, 1980; Wotherspoon, 2003; Norris and Jantzen, 2003). All the data show that the unemployment rate for off-reserve Aboriginals is five to six times higher than for non-Aboriginal people living in the urban area. Not only are unemployment rates higher, but the length of time that Aboriginals have held jobs is also much shorter than for non-Aboriginal people. Only about one-fifth of the urban Aboriginal population have held jobs for more than a month (Hanselmann, 2001). Unemployment rates

TABLE 6.3	Highest Level of Schooling by Gender, Percent, 2001			
	Off Reserve		On Reserve	
	Male	Female	Male	Female
Less than Grade 9	12.8	13.5	10.3	11.2
Grade 9-13	44.0	40.9	33.0	34.8
Non-University	30.6	30.0	30.7	29.1
University	12.6	15.7	26.0	24.9
All Post-Secondary	43.1	45.6	56.7	54.0

Source: Adapted from J. Hull, *Aboriginal Women: A Profile from the 2001 Census*, Indian and Northern Affairs Canada, 2006, pp. 42-43.

reveal that Aboriginal unemployment rates are two to three times that of non-Aboriginals. (See Table 6.5, for selected urban centres).

Unemployment among off-reserve Aboriginal people is generally due to a lack of training and a need to attend to family responsibilities. However, Siggner (2001) also found that discrimination in employment contributed significantly. Because of the low labour-force participation rate, high unemployment, and low educational attainment, the income levels of urban Aboriginal people were very low. Well over half of the Aboriginal people in urban centres had incomes well below the poverty level, compared with less than one-fourth for the non-Aboriginal population. Hanselmann (2001) reviewed the population 15 years and older and found that between 40 to 51 percent of urban Aboriginals made less than $10 000

TABLE 6.4	Proportion of Total Aboriginals and Non-Aboriginals Aged 20–24 not Attending School, Having Less than High School Education, by Gender, in Selected Cities, 2001			
	Aboriginal Population		Non-Aboriginal Population	
	Males	Females	Males	Females
Montreal	20.7	12.6	14.1	8.9
Ottawa-Hull	24.0	12.6	11.0	6.2
Toronto	25.6	18.9	10.6	8.1
Sudbury	25.9	18.9	10.6	8.1
Winnipeg	37.3	32.4	14.5	7.9
Regina	27.2	34.3	14.5	7.9
Saskatoon	42.9	30.0	15.4	10.3
Calgary	32.4	30.6	16.1	10.4
Edmonton	42.1	33.3	18.7	11.5
Vancouver	33.1	22.2	10.8	7.2

TABLE 6.5	Unemployment Rate by City, 2001	
	Aboriginal	Non-Aboriginal
Montreal	21.0	9.8
Toronto	15.7	9.3
Ottawa-Hull	16.3	8.7
Vancouver	20.4	8.4
Calgary	14.3	6.5
Edmonton	22.5	7.8
Saskatoon	25.1	6.6
Regina	26.8	6.4
Winnipeg	25.1	7.1

Source: Hanselmann, 2001. © Copyright Canada West Foundation.

per year, while for non-Aboriginals in the same cities only about 25 percent made less than $10 000 (see Table 6.6).

Because of their difficulty in obtaining employment and their low incomes, many Aboriginal people in urban centres have a lower standard of living than their non-Aboriginal counterparts. Siggner and Costa (2005) show that, while the number of Aboriginal people with employment incomes of $40 000 or more increased by nearly 300 percent between 1980 and 2001, the number of Aboriginals making less than $14 000 grew faster. As a result, their lives require extensive social assistance, e.g., housing, child care, and food. Their lower

TABLE 6.6	Median Employment Income for Aboriginal and non-Aboriginal Population Aged 15+ in Selected Cities, 2000	
	Aboriginal	Non-Aboriginal
Montreal	20 033	25 216
Ottawa-Hull	26 080	30 802
Toronto	26 040	29 990
Sudbury	20 043	25 068
Thunder Bay	18 449	27 598
Winnipeg	16 918	24 796
Regina	16 932	25 556
Saskatoon	15 000	22 953
Calgary	20 061	28 026
Edmonton	17 925	26 026
Vancouver	20 038	27 836

standard of living also leads to an increased risk of family and social problems and an increased risk of homelessness. We find that Aboriginal people who live in urban centres attempt to utilize more services than those living on reserves. However, because of legal disputes between the federal and provincial governments, they are not able to gain access to this multitude of services. Their lack of access is also a result of their poor understanding of their rights as Canadians and their unwillingness to press for services that they might need. Consequently, urban Aboriginal people continue to live in poverty, as they did on the reserve. Jantzen (2003) has carried out an analysis of Métis residing in urban areas, and her work confirms this finding. She concludes that Métis—especially those reporting a single Métis origin—are not faring as well as the non-Aboriginal population.

In summary, our analysis of urban Aboriginals reveals a profile that is different from non-Aboriginals living in major urban centres. The data confirm that Aboriginal people (1) are more likely to have low levels of education, (2) have low labour force participation rates, (3) have higher unemployment rates, (4) have low income levels, (5) have high rates of homelessness and greater housing needs, (6) are overrepresented in the criminal justice system (both as victims and offenders), (7) have poor health status (particularly in areas such as diabetes, HIV and AIDS, suicide, and substance abuse), and (8) are over twice as likely to be lone-parent families and to experience domestic violence. These results portray a sub-population in the urban context that needs special attention as they try to integrate into the larger social and economic structure of the industrial economy.

Decision to Migrate

Most studies of Aboriginal migration have focused on the individual, i.e., on the factors that lead individuals to migrate to the urban centres from their reserves. Moreover, their focus has been on the economic motivation factors. At the same time, the effect of the structure of the reserve community upon migration has seldom been investigated, except as a place of destination for returning migrants. The work of Gerber (1977, 1980) is an exception to this and merits an extended discussion in any analysis of Aboriginal urbanization, since both levels of variables need to be discussed if we are to clearly understand the process of Aboriginal urbanization (Neils, 1971).

The structures of particular reserves have an important influence on Aboriginal migration patterns. Gerber found that Prairie reserves are very communally oriented, while Eastern reserves tend to be much more individualistic. For example, Eastern Aboriginal people are more likely to hold location tickets (a legal document entitling an individual to the right to occupy and use a piece of land) that they can bequeath or sell to other Aboriginals. This cultural variable has considerable impact on an individual's decision to migrate to or from the city.

The specific structural factors of reserves that Gerber found important in affecting Aboriginal urbanization were proximity of the reserve to an urban centre, road access, the size of the band, the degree of community development, and the retained use of Aboriginal languages. As Gerber's research shows, high-migration bands were small, located outside the Prairies, and largely English-speaking. In addition, the sex ratio of high-migration bands was, on average, 141 men to 100 women.

Gerber also found that the development of personal and group resources was particularly important in determining migration patterns. Table 6.7 shows the typology she

TABLE 6.7	Gerber's Typology for Migration Patterns		
		Level of Community Development	
		Low	High
Level of personal resources	Low	1[a]	2
	High	3	4
a. Numbers are for identifying the cell, i.e., the type of band.			
Source: Based on Gerber, 1979.			

developed to indicate potential migration patterns. Bands in cell 1 are "inert," in that they are not adapting to the larger dominant culture or attempting to develop internally. Those in cell 2 are "pluralistic." They are high in community development yet low in personal resources; even though considerable economic and social development has taken place, individuals have not participated in the education system or labour force to any great degree. In contrast, the bands in cell 3 are "integrative." Through education and job experience they have prepared individuals to enter the dominant culture, but they have not created opportunities within the community. As a result individuals must move to the outside world. Finally, the "municipal" Aboriginals have a high rate of migration, but opportunities exist on the reserve for those who choose to remain.

In short, as one moves counter-clockwise from cell 1 in Table 6.7, the likelihood of urbanization increases. Apparently the band itself provides the basic structural context that determines the rates of and reasons for urban migration. Those bands with high community development provide opportunities for their members to remain on the reserve. Those communities with high personal-resource development encourage their members to migrate to the city; when, in addition, community development is low, individuals are forced off the reserve but can compete successfully in the urban context. However, as Gerber argues, an increase in off-reserve residence also results when community development stimulates out-migration to compensate for a lack of personal-resource development (Ryan, 1978).

Clearly, the structural conditions that govern life determine, more or less, the decisions of individual Aboriginal people to migrate off the reserve. Denton (1972) also points out that, in addition to social factors, cultural factors come into play. According to Denton, reserves are governed by strong "village norms and social control mechanics which encourage work, independence, and earning one's own money" (1972: 55). Thus, from an early age, children are socialized into work roles and, as they grow older, make increasing contributions to family maintenance (Honigman, 1967). Often conflicts result between children and parents; children are taught to be self-reliant and independent, but at the same time must bend to the will of their families. These factors continue to influence Aboriginals' decisions to migrate (White, Maxim and Beavon, 2003). Finally, human capital (e.g., education, job market experience and age) also enter the matrix of decision making.

These structural, individual, social and cultural conditions, then, are instrumental in pushing/pulling the Aboriginal off the reserve and into the urban context. Moreover, a decision to return to the reserve is also influenced by these factors (Ablon, 1965, Peters, 2000).

As we have pointed out, social, structural and individual factors determine the migration process. However, most Aboriginal people tell investigators that they have come to the city to participate in the labour force. This provides a legitimate explanation to non-Aboriginal people and allows Aboriginal people to apply for welfare aid more easily. However, Aboriginal people are very much aware of the poor opportunities for steady employment in the city. What, then, are the real reasons for urban migration?

First of all, as pointed out previously, an increase in population has created overcrowding on the reserve, specifically in the areas of housing and employment. Most reserves are rural-based and can only provide jobs for a limited population. As Deprez and Sigurdson (1969) pointed out many years ago, because the economic base of most reserves is incapable of supporting the existing Aboriginal population, out-migration is essential. This continues to be a major factor in out-migration from the reserves. Second, the availability of housing on reserves is limited due to the increase in population and the low level of new or renovated housing being made available to residents. Third, the level of violence that may be occurring in the community may precipitate movement into the city. And finally, changing legal definitions as to who is a status Indians may force some people off the reserve.

Each Aboriginal person must assess the chances of obtaining work and housing on the reserve. Because both are scarce, a great deal of competition exists among reserve residents. As in most social organizations, access to housing and employment is partially controlled by a relatively affluent elite on the reserve. For example, the housing needs of young, single males and females are not considered high priority; since young singles are seen as capable of entering the world outside the reserve. If they have not been able to develop a social network that includes older relatives in official positions of power in the community, they cannot expect help in finding housing on the reserve when they approach community leaders. In particular, unmarried females, with or without children, receive low priority in housing allocation. This means that if an unmarried woman wants to remain in the community, she will have to live with a relative who currently has housing. Hence, a decision about living in crowded conditions or opting for urban housing becomes a calculated risk. This partly accounts for the high ratio of males to females on certain reserves, as well as for the high proportion of children under 15 who have moved off the reserve.

Migration away from the reserve is as much a result of push factors as it is pull factors. The urban setting, as a permanent residence, is attractive only to those who are qualified to participate actively in it; few Aboriginals are able to do so. However, most Aboriginal people decide to leave the reserve only when they are forced to by an absence of housing and employment opportunities or by other factors, e.g., domestic violence.

Entering the City

The first Aboriginal institutions to emerge in a city are bars with large Aboriginal clienteles. From these first interactions, cliques then emerge and create a social network in the urban environment for Aboriginal people to enter and leave at will. Through these cliques, the second stage of urbanization evolves; Aboriginal social and cultural centres develop, along with more extended social networks. J. Price (1979) calls these centres "second-stage institutions." The centres inhibit integration into the urban milieu, yet increase the odds for urban survival. In addition, they promote and facilitate a chain migration of Aboriginals to the cities (Johnson, 1976).

The third stage of urbanization, institutional completeness, has not yet been reached. Institutional completeness is the creation and maintenance of a set of institutions, such as schools, churches, and employment agencies, that meet most social, cultural, and economic needs of the ethnic group. Aboriginal institutional completeness has failed to develop in the urban centres for a number of reasons. The leaders of Aboriginal bands generally remain on the reserve, even though regional, provincial, and national government offices are located in urban areas. Aboriginal political organizations continue to focus on rural issues such as band claims and treaty rights. Due to internal rivalries between Aboriginal factions, urban Aboriginal leaders have failed to gain political momentum. Moreover, because urban Aboriginal organizations, such as friendship centres, are not able to offer employment, they have not been able to address the general social and economic needs of urban Aboriginal people.

Clearly, few Aboriginal persons enjoy the stable social networks in cities that would permit institutional completeness to develop. Aboriginal urbanization will not be complete until agencies are developed and staffed by Aboriginals to provide employment and services to the Aboriginal community. At this time, Aboriginal people have become heavily involved in social and cultural centres, provincial political associations, and local and Aboriginal political organizations. Each urban area is developing somewhat differently, however, and according to varying schedules. Nevertheless, as more Aboriginal institutions are established and a number of "middle class" Aboriginals reside in the urban centres, the social fabric of the community may allow for the beginning of institutional completeness.

Aboriginal city-dwellers have been classified as transients, migrants, commuters, and residents. The transient moves continually from one place to another without establishing full residence in any urban area (Nagler, 1971). The migrant simply transfers a social network from a rural base to an urban one, moving to the city but only interacting with other Aboriginal people. The commuter lives close enough to an urban centre to spend large amounts of time there, yet retains residence on the reserve. The resident has been born in the city and spends most of his or her time in an urban context (Brody, 1971).

What happens after the Aboriginal enters the city? What kinds of experience take place? Why are some transients while others become commuters? The answers to these questions largely depend on the lifestyle of the individual and spatial factors such as distance of the reserve from the urban centre. For the purposes of this discussion, urban Aboriginal people can be divided into transients and residents.

Transients are those individuals who are unable or unwilling to integrate into non-Aboriginal society because of their high mobility patterns or continued linkages with rural-based communities. Because they retain a rural orientation and possess few job skills, transients are not able to participate in the social or economic fabric of Canadian society. As a result, they become more and more dependent on the same social-service organizations that, ironically, encouraged them to migrate in the first place.

Table 6.8 lists some of the value differences that exist between Aboriginal and non-Aboriginal people. Of course, both value systems are in a state of flux and neither is as straightforward as it appears. For example, the introduction of social welfare, combined with Aboriginal people's lack of control over their destiny, has led to a dependency ethos that did not exist before contact with European culture. Moreover, Aboriginal people have been in contact with white society for well over two hundred years, so they are acutely aware of the dominant society's values. In addition, some of these values may have been incorporated into the Aboriginal value structure.

TABLE 6.8	Cultural Differences between Non-Aboriginals and Aboriginals
Aboriginal Values	**White Values**
Group emphasis	Individual emphasis
Cooperation (group concern)	Competition (self-concern)
Present-oriented	Future-oriented
Non-awareness of time	Awareness of time
Elder	Youth
Harmony with nature	Conquest of nature
Giving	Saving
Practical	Theoretical
Patience	Impatience
Extended family	Immediate family
Non-materialistic	Materialistic
Modest	Overstates (over-confident)
Silent	Noisy
Low self-value	Strong self-value
Respects other religions	Converts others to own religion
Religion a way of life	Religion a segment of life
Land, water, forests and other resources belong to all, and are used reasonably	Land, water, forests and other resources belong to the private domain, and are used in a greedy manner
Equality	Wealth
Face-to-face government	Representative democracy

Source: Based on Tanner, 1983.

A basis for some of the differences that exist between Aboriginal and non-Aboriginal people lies in the philosophical assumptions made about human beings and society. The basis of present Western thought can be found in the liberal political philosophy of Rousseau, Locke, and Hobbes, which stressed that individual self-interest should take precedence over group rights. However, it was argued, individuals must operate in a collective unit so that all individuals can survive. To further this aim, a state apparatus was created in which individuals voluntarily agreed to subordinate their self-interest to the common good. Nevertheless, the individual is considered to be morally prior to any group, and the individuals within a state are to be viewed as acting for themselves, not as members of any collectivity (Boldt and Long, 1985a).

Contrary to this Western philosophical position (which emerged out of feudalism), Aboriginal people have a cosmocentric view of the universe (in contrast to homocentric) that focuses not on the individual but on the "whole." Individuals, then, are to be subordinate to the whole. Human beings are just part of the whole, which also includes animals, plants, and inanimate objects. All of these parts must exist in harmony and balance and the parts as well as the whole can only survive if each works in harmony with the others. Therefore, all the parts are forced to interact with each other and to take the others into consideration. Human beings, in Aboriginal culture, are viewed as just another limb in the body of life, but a limb with certain additional responsibilities. As a result, individual self-interest is defined as group-interest and the group and the individual are seen to share a common identity. Laslett (1963) uses the onion-skin analogy to illustrate the relationship of the individual to the whole. The entire onion represents group-orientation attributes. Each person has more or fewer of these group attributes as he or she moves through society over time. However, if all oriented attributes are removed, there is no core of self or individual remaining. While not all Aboriginal people fully subscribe to this perspective, there are remnants of this philosophy present today in varying degrees.

Non-Aboriginal society can be characterized as using "linear and singular" thinking. A good example of this is the concept of time as defined by non-Aboriginal Canadians. First, time is conceptualized as a straight line. What is immediate in time is present; what is behind is the past and the future is yet to be achieved. Time can be viewed as a row of similar units that can be divided into separate and different units. Thus, for example, Europeans think in terms of minutes, hours, and days, and implicit in this linear thinking is the view that time flows one way and you cannot recapture time from the past. Linear thinking also lends itself to singular thinking; that is, linear thinking propels individuals toward values that imply "one answer," "one way." Linear thinking can be either horizontal or vertical, but the general principle remains the same. This linear worldview also leads to specialist activity in that one moves toward "one thing." You can only be good at one thing, not a number of things.

In contrast to the linear worldview, the Aboriginal worldview can be characterized as cyclical or holistic. This view begins with the premise that everything is interrelated. It is a generalist perspective rather than the specialist one that characterizes Canadian non-Aboriginal culture. As many Aboriginal people note, their view of the world is more circular; there is no beginning, no end. There are phases and patterns to the world, but they are repetitive and cyclical. Since all parts are interrelated, each part is equal to all others. The system could not continue with a missing part. In addition, when the world is viewed as a whole there is a tendency to see the whole or group as more important than the individual. Being part of the group is better than being alone. The interrelated whole results in harmony and balance (Waters, 2004; Bol, 2003).

Aboriginal Canadians find a great deal of discontinuity between life on the reserve and life in the city. As they reach the city they enter a world that is generally alien, frightening, frustrating, and hostile. Many Aboriginal people express total confusion as to "how whites work." Of course, the reaction of individual Aboriginal people to Euro-Canadian society varies: some find it extremely bizarre and hostile, while others quickly adapt to the Euro-Canadian ethos. The extent to which Aboriginal people can reconcile the "two solitudes" of reserve life and city life depends on early socialization experiences and past interactions with non-Aboriginal society as well as the level of expertise and skills they have. Insofar as the structure of Canadian society plays a large role in socialization experiences, it has a profound effect on the ability of Aboriginal people to integrate into urban life. We now turn to examining the processes that affect and influence the Aboriginal's foray into urban life. We will show how the various organizations impinge upon the Aboriginal's attempts to deal with life in an urban area.

Social Organizations and Aboriginal Urbanization

Over the years, various levels of government have established agencies to provide support for Aboriginals entering the urban centres, trying to encourage Aboriginal people to abandon their reserves and treaty rights, mobilizing them as Canadian citizens but not as "citizens plus" (Canada, 1969; Weaver, 1981). "Citizens plus" refers to the view that, since Aboriginal people were the first inhabitants of Canada, they should be afforded special status and rights. By curtailing services on the reserves, most noticeably in the area of housing and economic development, the government has tried to push Aboriginal people into the city. In addition, by transferring the provision of services from the federal to the provincial system, the federal government has attempted to reduce its constitutional and treaty obligations.

However, the federal government does not have jurisdiction over many of these social services, particularly education and social welfare, that have been used to expand citizens' rights and to urbanize members of the lower classes. In Canada, these services are generally provided by provincial agencies. While the provincial educational system has made some effort to increase Aboriginal levels of literacy and formal certification, the welfare system has not been expanded to incorporate Aboriginal people into urban society. Although the number of Aboriginal persons on welfare has increased in cities, they generally receive only short-term services that relieve temporary problems of urban subsistence (Stymeist, 1975).

The lack of educational and job qualifications continues to prevent full urban integration for most Aboriginal people. As stated earlier, Aboriginal people who claim a desire for employment as the primary reason for moving to the city generally do so because of the requirements of the welfare system, rather than because they perceive actual employment opportunities for themselves. For some, such as single mothers with children, provincial welfare services allow a higher standard of life in the city than on a reserve or in a Métis settlement. For most, however, government social services are not sufficient to encourage Aboriginal people to remain in cities. As a result, an increasing number of urban Aboriginal persons can be classed as transient.

More and more young Aboriginal people are moving back and forth between urban and rural residences, generally on a seasonal basis. Faced with an inability to secure employment, or even to understand and use various government and private agencies, they commute into the city for short periods of time and then leave, their frustrations intact (Frideres and Ryan, 1980). Even though these Aboriginal people may spend large amounts of time in the urban context, they retain their social ties in the rural area.

A second group of Aboriginal people, migrants, has succeeded in establishing residence, if not employment, in the cities. This group is predominantly female with young dependants. If these individuals do not have long-term employment, they rely on the support of relatives and friends in addition to government services. For example, from an Edmonton sample, 76 percent of urban Aboriginal persons had relatives in the city when they first entered and 65 percent had friends.

A third, much smaller group of Aboriginal people, residents, appears to have successfully settled into urban society. Members of this group most closely approximate the white, middle-class, urban family: they live in single-family units as married adults with children; they have full-time employment; and they live in acceptable housing. Successful entry into urban society appears to be contingent upon attaining a level of education, health, and well-being as well as actively participating in the labour market.

The Transition

Aboriginal people move into the urban context in a series of stages.[1] Although these stages are serial, they are not necessarily "step-wise sequential"; that is, all of the steps are not essential in order to achieve the final stage. Also, progression through the stages is usually not completed in one continuous linear sequence.[2] As Figure 6.4 indicates, Aboriginal people are exposed to a funnelling effect: although most have some contact with service organizations, few become independent of the organizations, and even fewer are successfully placed in the city.

Aboriginal people move from Stage 1 to Stage 2 largely as a result of the recruitment procedures of service organizations. The type of service organization and its policy plays an important role in determining the rate of rural-to-urban transition (see Table 6.9) although service organizations have little influence on the degree to which Aboriginal people can successfully adapt to the urban centre.

The issue of whether government or voluntary agencies should deal with Aboriginal problems has long been debated in Canada. Although the provincial governments recognize a partnership between the two sectors, they have tried to maintain the primacy of government both in policy formation and in program maintenance. Private agencies do not have the complex network of contacts and services that government programs can provide. Nonetheless, a policy of subsidiarity, whereby governments refuse to duplicate the services offered by private citizens, has taken precedence. As a result, the government has become essentially a financier, relying upon the private sector to provide primary services to those in need.

Aboriginal Policy

The development of policy provides a guide for governments as to how to spend money, develop programs, and set priorities in terms of action. In another sense, policy is a statement of responsibility on the part of government. As Hanselmann (2001) points out, a policy reflects an overarching public written statement that sets out a government's approach to an issue. In the case of Aboriginals, most policy related to them emanates from the federal Department of Indian and Northern Affairs Canada (INAC). Unfortunately, there are

| FIGURE 6.4 | Stages of Advancement of Aboriginal People in Final Adaptation to Urban Milieu |

1. Entering the city.
2. Becoming a client of a service organization.
3. "Graduating" from the service organization.
4. "Final" placement in the city.

TABLE 6.9   Attributes of Types of Service Organizations

Organizational Type	Organizational Effectiveness	Value Representative	Selected Attributes of Organizations			
			Membership Recruitment	Extent of Services	Ethnic Comp. of Staff	Ability to Place Clients
Public Service	High	Middle-class	Mass[a]	Singular	Middle-class; White	High
Acculturating Service	High	Middle-class	Very[b] selective	Multiple; integrated	Middle-class; White	High
Accommodating Service	Low	Aboriginal	Mass	Singular	Mixed-Aboriginal; middle-class; White	Low
Member	Moderate	Aboriginal	Mass; Aboriginal	Singular	Aboriginal	Low

a. Recruitment is selective, yet the services offered are considered the right of all citizens.
b. Recruitment is usually on a sponsorship basis.

Source: J. Frideres and W. Reeves, 1981.

few government-wide policies with regard to urban Aboriginals. The reader should note that policy is quite different from programs, which are specific actions taken by a department. While programs generally implement the policy, they may also be unique and "one off" in design. In addition, just because there is no policy with regard to a field, this does not mean that there are no programs. In fact, this has been one of the problems that urban Aboriginals have faced. Various levels of government have funded programs but have no policy to link them to. As a result, within short periods of time, these programs are stopped and other "ad hoc" programs emerge. The chart in Figure 6.5, developed by Hanselmann

FIGURE 6.5	Comparative Policy Landscape					
	Vancouver	Calgary	Edmonton	Saskatoon	Regina	Winnipeg
Education	P	P	P	P	P	M
Training	F P	F	F	F P M	F P	F M
Employment	F M	F P	F P	F P M	F P	F M
Income Support					M	
Econ. Development		P	P	P	P	M
Family Violence						
Childcare						
Health	P	P	P	P	P	M
Addictions						
Suicide						
Homelessness	F	F P M	F P	F M	F	F
Housing				P M	P	M
Justice	F	F P	F P	F P	F P	F
Human Rights				M		
Urban Transition	P	P	P			
Cultural Support		P	P	P M	P	M
Other	F P	F P M	F P M	F P M	F P	F

F   Federal policy   P   Provincial policy   M   Municipal policy

Urban Aboriginal policy

Source: Hanselmann, 2001, p. 18. © Copyright Canada West Foundation.

for Western Canada, shows the comparative policy landscape for six urban areas with regard to urban Aboriginal policies across 17 fields of action.

Hanselmann's data show that issues regarding Aboriginal urbanization are not systematically being addressed. Rather, as Hanselmann (2001) points out, the responses to the challenges facing urban Aboriginal people are taking place in a "differentiated policy environment." His analysis shows that the urban Aboriginal-specific policy landscape ranges from comprehensive government-wide strategies to specific departmental programs. Governments are not responding in a consistent manner, although all levels of government seem to have implemented some urban Aboriginal policy. The existing policy environment (disagreement between the federal and provincial governments as to who has primary responsibility for urban Indians) continues to thwart any system of policy development with regard to urban Aboriginals.

Moreover, the analysis shows that there are major gaps in the policy fields. For example, there are no policies in the areas of child care and family violence, and only partial coverage in areas such as income support, housing, and human rights. We also find that the policies that exist are not well linked to the everyday experiences of urban Aboriginals. For example, housing is a major concern for urban Aboriginals, and yet only half of the cities surveyed have a policy with regard to urban Aboriginals. Finally, the data reveal considerable overlap in policies among the three levels of government. While some of the overlap may be complementary, some is simply duplicative. While this multiple-level policy suggests that different levels of government agree that this field is important, these different levels have yet to coordinate their activities to ensure efficiency and effectiveness.

Models of how urban Aboriginals might organize and meet the needs and aspirations of their constituency have not been well developed. These models need to understand that Aboriginal people in urban areas may participate fully in the local, provincial, and federal arenas, but in other matters—such as those related to cultural survival—Aboriginal people may develop their own services and institutions (Wherrett and Brown, 1994). The problems faced by Aboriginal people in Canadian urban centres have led them to try to develop services and institutions to suit their unique needs. The forms of organization and scope of services provided by existing institutions reveal the weaknesses and strengths of the current political and institutional framework. For example, the institutions in place today have been limited by a lack of autonomy and inadequate and inconsistent funding. Aboriginal organizations also have to align their activities with the municipal, provincial, and federal programs that are in place but not specifically directed toward Aboriginal people (Wherrett and Brown, 1994).

Aboriginal Organization Contact

Aboriginal people entering the city usually find the process difficult and problematic. Most find that they must utilize the services of a variety of organizations in order to remain. Although some Aboriginal people on reserves or in Métis settlements find that some form of sponsorship is necessary to remain in an urban centre, most of them are poorly prepared for urban life.

Even disregarding social and cultural factors, the vast majority of Aboriginal people entering cities do not have the qualifications necessary to get work, obtain social services, or succeed in school. Most cannot even qualify for employment insurance. Their poverty, combined with their unconventional lifestyles, exposes them to much higher-than-average levels of detention and arrest by the police. In the end, most Aboriginal people are not successful in adapting to city life.

Because of their unique position, urban Aboriginal people are much more likely than non-Aboriginals to come into direct contact with service organizations that regulate and monitor social behaviour. Aboriginal people have consistently posed problems to those organizations in their attempts to establish public order and provide various services. Organizations that attempt to deal with Aboriginal urban problems can be broken down into four categories: public service, acculturating service, accommodating service, and member organizations. Table 6.9 outlined the attributes of each type.

Public service organizations provide a single, specific service, such as justice, education, or welfare, to the general public. They work within the prevailing Canadian system of values and beliefs and are typically staffed by middle-class executives, clerical workers, and members of service-oriented occupations. Public service organizations are designed to provide certain minimum levels of service to the general public. As a citizen, each individual has the right to a basic education, a basic standard of living, and equal treatment before the law. Public service organizations, especially education and justice systems, also are important mechanisms for encouraging the participation of individuals in society. For example, educational achievement draws individuals out of their immediate locales and moves them into a socio-economic framework through entry into the labour force. Similarly, the basic requirements of public health and order encourage normative social behaviour.

In Canada, public services have failed to integrate Aboriginal people into urban society. Aboriginal persons who have come into contact with these organizations have tended to become virtually permanent clients, as evidenced by recurrent patterns of detention and arrest, high rates of hospitalization and premature death, and the inability of most Aboriginal people to leave the welfare rolls. In the educational system, where permanent subsistence is not permitted, Aboriginal students tend to drop out before achieving the minimum standards of attainment for success in the labour force. In short, public service organizations do not assist most Aboriginal people to live in the city as competent citizens. Indeed, as currently constituted, these organizations more often present a barrier that denies Aboriginal citizens entry into the mainstream of urban Canadian life.

A second type of service organization is the acculturating organization. Like the public service, acculturating service organizations draw their staff from the middle class and act to promote or maintain the assimilation of Aboriginal people into Euro-Canadian culture. Acculturating service organizations include post-secondary institutions, such as colleges and universities, provincial apprenticeship branches, the Central Mortgage and Housing Corporation and the Alberta Opportunity Fund (a source of credit for small business). They usually obtain many, if not most, of their clients through a system of referrals from the public service organizations. Whenever possible, they exercise discretion when accepting prospective clients, taking only those who have a good chance of succeeding in their programs. Once accepted, their clients typically do succeed: formal and informal counselling services, along with other sources of support, minimize the drop-out rates. For example, a few Aboriginal people on Aboriginal reserves or Métis settlements who display a potential for academic achievement are supported through secondary school and then referred to a post-secondary institution, usually a college or a university. Once sponsored, these people have a high incidence of success in the system.

Acculturating service agencies also have few Aboriginal clients, as most simply do not have the minimal qualifications necessary to be referred to or accepted into such programs. Furthermore, Aboriginal people have found it difficult to obtain services from these organizations because they have difficulty understanding and coping with non-Aboriginal rules and procedures.

A third type of service organization, accommodating, attempts to compensate for the lack of preparation revealed by Aboriginals in their contacts with Euro-Canadian society. These agencies are often funded by public service organizations to deal with problematic clients. For example, the Special Constables Program of the RCMP, the Courtworkers' Program, and the race relations units of municipal police forces all attempt to handle the problems that have arisen among Aboriginal citizens, the public, and the courts. These agencies try to protect the rights of Aboriginal people and, at the same time, render the legal system more efficient. Also, several acculturating service organizations support the work of accommodating service organizations; examples include the Aboriginal counselling and Aboriginal studies programs on the campuses of various universities.

The ability of an accommodating service organization to actually alter the fate of its clients is extremely limited. These agencies support the work of public and acculturating service organizations and generally operate within a white, middle-class value system. They have managed to attract Aboriginal clients by hiring a greater proportion of Aboriginal staff members and by modifying some operating procedures to reflect their clients' cultural background. However, because funding is short term and often depends on enrolment figures, this "accommodation" of Aboriginal interests is not entirely altruistic. Programs offered by these organizations usually lack scope and continuity. Accommodating agencies are generally expected to simply direct their clients to existing services provided elsewhere. Indeed, accommodating service organizations are often limited simply to registering, screening, and referring their clients to other organizations. Moreover, they are unable to offer any real assistance to Aboriginal people in their dealings with those other organizations.

Unlike the other three types of service organizations, member organizations tend to work against the assimilation of Aboriginal people into the mainstream of Canadian society. Member organizations represent the interests of Aboriginal people as members of a distinct ethnic group. They provide some employment for Aboriginal persons, promote the revitalization of Aboriginal culture, and attempt to provide the broad range of social support necessary to allow people to lead an Aboriginal lifestyle. Some organizations, like provincial Aboriginal associations, are working to develop and document a case for entrenched Aboriginal economic and political rights. Others, like the Aboriginal friendship centres, are attempting to promote an Aboriginal lifestyle in the cities. These organizations also function to encourage the emergence of a Aboriginal elite that has not been co-opted into the staff of various other types of public service organizations.

Although member organizations successfully provide services to urban Aboriginal people, their effectiveness is weakened by a virtual absence of employment for Aboriginal people as Aboriginal people. Member organizations have tried to promote the institutional completeness needed for in-group cohesiveness and solidarity. However, this institutional completeness cannot be achieved without the creation of jobs for their members. To remedy this problem, Aboriginal people need to establish and run their own businesses and organizations.

At present, an inability to establish jobs for their memberships stymies the success of Aboriginal member organizations. Like those who rely on public service organizations, Aboriginal persons who belong to member organizations continue to be excluded and stigmatized by non-Aboriginal, urban society. Unlike the clients of public service organizations, however, Aboriginal people in member organizations are less likely to regard themselves and their fellows as failures (McCaskill, 1981).

How has mainstream society reacted to the inability of public service organizations to help Aboriginal people adapt to urban life? As more and more Aboriginal people moved to the city in the late 1960s, public and acculturating service organizations came under increasing pressure. In coping with this influx, public service organizations experienced a disproportionate decrease in effectiveness and a disproportionate increase in costs. Although the schools experienced some problems in assimilating Aboriginal children, the brunt of this problem was felt by the police and courts. Moreover, young Aboriginal people who migrated to the cities lacked the prerequisite skills for employment and were unable to cope in a conventional fashion with the demands of urban society. Frustration and unemployment combined with divergent values to produce a style of life that frequently deviated from the social norms and laws in the cities. While greater expenditures on law enforcement increased the number of Aboriginal persons being processed (and reprocessed) in the system, they did not reduce the threat to public order. This simultaneous decrease of effectiveness and increase in costs was underscored by social scientists, who pointed out that nearly half the inmates in provincial jails were Aboriginal.

Managers of acculturative service programs were also faced with escalating costs accompanied by decreased effectiveness. Their programs were sporadic, unevenly implemented, and made little attempt to find standardized solutions to Aboriginal problems. In addition, they were under pressure to debureaucratize existing legitimate programs. Acculturating service organizations were also criticized on a different ground. Because Aboriginal people as a group were systematically undercertified, exceedingly few of them enrolled in university, entered unionized occupations, or qualified for credit assistance in purchasing a home or establishing a business. With greater urbanization, Aboriginal people became a more visible minority, demonstrably denied access to many of the avenues to success in Canadian society. Aboriginal member organizations publicly questioned the legitimacy of training programs and assistance agencies that failed to recruit proportionate numbers of Aboriginal people into their publicly funded programs.

Like the public service organizations, then, the acculturative service agencies were faced with a credibility problem: those Aboriginal people most in need of their services were clearly not receiving them. Both in public and acculturative service organizations, middle-level managers, who were responsible for day-to-day internal administration, funding, personnel, and clientele, felt that some action was necessary. Although the issue of legitimacy did not actually threaten their budgets, it did increase public scrutiny of funding and internal administration, reducing managerial discretion and hindering the management of day-to-day operations.

In order to reach a greater number of Aboriginal people, middle-level management in public and acculturating service organizations began to fund new projects proposed by accommodating service organizations.[3] In some cases, existing Aboriginal member organizations were co-opted to run these programs, e.g., Plains Indian Cultural Survival School, Native counselling services, Native employment transitional services, and Native alcoholism services. In other cases, funding was provided for the formation of new Aboriginal-oriented service organizations.[4]

Whatever their origins, accommodating service organizations tend to enhance the legitimacy of existing service organizations. Accommodating service programs essentially deal with the problem clients of public service organizations, and leave other operations intact. For example, Aboriginal students unable to complete their secondary education in the public high schools are referred to an "alternative" public school run by Aboriginal personnel.

By registering, screening, and referring problematic clients, accommodating organizations can forecast or even regulate the number of clients they deal with, and accommodating agencies can tailor specific projects to particular problematic groups. These special programs justified their high costs and provided a rationale by which public service organizations could

offer special treatment to—and acculturating service organizations could relax entry and performance standards for—certain preferred groups, such as Aboriginal people. Over the
years, as Newhouse (2003) points out, a number of member institutions have been established by urban Aboriginals. However, over time, these institutions have ceased to function
due to a lack of funding, or they have evolved into accommodating service organizations and
are not distinguishable from other non-Aboriginal accommodating service organizations.

Essentially, by offering a bicultural program, the middle-level managers of service
organizations shifted some of the responsibility for problem clients onto the shoulders of
those operating the accommodating and member organizations. The bicultural program
could accommodate both non-Aboriginal and Aboriginal values. Moreover, accommodating
service organizations could attract increasing numbers of clients without seriously affecting
either the service standards of acculturating organizations or the cost-effectiveness of public
service organizations.

Ironically, the accommodating organizations inherited the same problems of legitimacy
that plagued the public and acculturating service organizations. Accommodating organizations are generally small, independent, voluntary associations that undergo major program
and staff transformations every few years. Their instability is partly due to the nature of
their financial support. They face serious problems establishing a permanent source of
funding and, therefore, a clearly defined mandate. Usually their budgets are mostly made
up of grants from public service organizations. These grants are generally earmarked for
specific projects designed to last for a limited period of time, often one to three years. In
addition, they are aimed at protecting the rights of individual clients, and do not attempt to
address the general problems of Aboriginals. As a result, accommodating service agencies
generally offer services for Aboriginals that are far too restricted in focus to address adequately the low quality of life experienced by Aboriginals in the city.

To get funding, the accommodating organizations orient their programs toward Aboriginal culture in hopes of attracting Aboriginal clients. However, the placement of these
clients then becomes problematic. Because non-Aboriginal businesses generally refuse to
hire them, Aboriginal people become perpetual clients of the agencies and are locked into
a limbo between the reserve and the city. As a result, a large number of them enter these
accommodating organizations, but few graduate. Also, because the organizations to some
extent encourage Aboriginal values and lifestyles, they do not prepare Aboriginal people
for white, middle-class society; at best, they produce marginal Aboriginals.

Because the federal and provincial governments desire to provide social services on an
equal basis to individual members of the general public, they have been unwilling to
address the problems of particular groups or communities. The current political climate
exacerbates this problem. At the constitutional level, the provincial government has refused
to accept sole legal responsibility for the social support of status Indians off the reserve. To
avoid giving even de facto recognition to the collective rights of Aboriginal people, these
governments have restricted their support of organizations for Aboriginal persons to nar-
row-range, small-scale, temporary projects. As a result, the precarious status of accommodating agencies undermines their effectiveness. Overly specific short-term programs
discourage the regular, full-time participation of Aboriginal people. Moreover, remedial
programs are often too narrow to ensure continued Aboriginal participation without a
broad range of additional social support to counteract the effects of poverty and unemployment. To obtain this support, accommodating organizations must refer their clients to the
system of social services offered by public and acculturating organizations, despite the fact

that their own projects often run counter to, and are not integrated with, these social services. Clearly, whatever the efficiency of accommodating organizations under ideal conditions, the absence of wider social support sabotages their effectiveness and undermines what few gains they manage to achieve.

URBAN RESERVES

With increasing numbers of Aboriginals living in urban areas, many are beginning to push for the creation of an urban reserve. For these individuals, city life is now an integral attribute of "urban" Indians. Moreover, this urban migration was brought about because of an aggressive federal policy started over half a century ago.

Aboriginal people in cities are not homogenous with respect to status or culture. Today, urban Aboriginals can participate in self-determining organizations either by participating in activities on a reserve or through urban Aboriginal organizations. Only the Congress of Aboriginal Peoples, as a national or provincial organization, has been active with respect to urban Aboriginal issues. The Assembly of First Nations has not had an interest in urban issues until recently and it only represents "registered Indians." Hence only local Aboriginal organizations such as the Friendship Centres have been an advocate for urban Aboriginal peoples.

Aboriginal people now make up a part of the urban landscape and will remain there for a long time. However, rather than assimilating into the larger society, these residents maintain close ties to their communities of origin and desire a quality of life that maintains a distinctive culture as well as exercising self-governance. Newhouse and Peters (2003) point out that, for Aboriginal people in the city, maintaining their identity is an essential and self-validating pursuit. Contemporary urban Aboriginal people see their communities in urban centres as real and as no different than rural reserve communities. These residents have a growing interest in self-determination and self-government in cities, and there are attempts to coordinate all levels of government to support their urban communities. This new view sees urban Aboriginals as part of their communities, with goals and needs that they want to attain within an urban landscape (Peters 2001).

The Royal Commission on Aboriginal Peoples addressed this issue, suggesting that an approach to urban governance might be exercised through the "extra-territorial jurisdiction" of an Aboriginal nation with jurisdiction over a land-base providing programs for its members living off the land base. When the Supreme Court of Canada brought down its *Corbiere* decision, it gave band members living off the reserve the right to vote in band elections and referenda. This means that reserves must be required to respond to the priorities of their members living off the reserve. While this may resolve the needs for "status" First Nations living in the city, it does not address the concerns of other Aboriginal peoples, e.g., Métis, non-status Indians, or Inuit. And data show that between 40 to 60 percent of Aboriginals living in urban areas are not band members.

While there are currently over 20 urban reserves in Saskatchewan and other Canadian cities, two recent initiatives to establish urban reserves have drawn the ire of non-Aboriginals. In Winnipeg, a 40-hectare area has been purchased by a First Nation with the intent of developing it for commercial outlets. Similarly, in Regina property in the city's north-central area has been purchased by a First Nations group. In both cases, servicing agreements between the First Nation and the city have been agreed upon, but in neither case would the band be required to pay property taxes. With urban reserve status, which has to be approved by Ottawa, band members would be able to buy products on the new property without paying provincial or federal sales tax. Opponents of the developments have charged that this arrangement would create an "uneven playing field" between urban reserve businesses and those non-Aboriginal businesses in the area. Aboriginal people argue that such arrangements will in fact provide for a "level playing field" that has, up until now, been tipped in favour of the non-Aboriginal businesses.

As diverse urban Aboriginal people become an "urban community of interest," they may develop a social organization that "creates" itself so that it spawns specific organizations to each deal with a single policy sector, or they may create a single city-wide body that exercises self-government in a range of policy sectors through a number of different organizations. However, given the diversity of Aboriginal groups in any city, fragmentation of the population may emerge as the various groups compete for limited resources. As such, before such organizations can be created, the diverse groups residing within the city will need to resolve their differences and engage in collaborative activities. In some cities, e.g., Winnipeg, there is an impressive array of urban Aboriginal service organizations that are now in the process of developing an integrative structure.

SUMMARY

The number of Aboriginal people entering urban centres, either as transients or permanent residents, will continue to increase over time. Nevertheless, a sizeable proportion of the population will remain on the reserves. This split population, along with the hypermobility they exhibit, makes it difficult to develop policy to deal with the urban sector of the population. The consequence of this increased urbanization will be greater demands placed on service organizations to deal with Aboriginal people, demands which most urban service organizations are unable to fulfil. As a result, few urban Aboriginal persons are fully participating members of the modern industrial society. They are marginal in their own country.

In recent years, some urban areas have attempted to develop strategies to circumvent the policy vacuum and jurisdictional disputes. Hanselmann and Gibbins (2002) have shown that several urban centres have been able to develop programs without a macro policy framework. They have identified the development of multilateral agreements (memoranda of understanding) as an instrument through which federal and provincial governments work together, and with third parties (Wong, 2002). An example of this is the city of Winnipeg, which has formal agreements with Aboriginal organizations and two levels of government. These agreements have resulted in significant investments by the three levels of government in partnership with Aboriginal organizations. Another example of informal partnerships is the Saskatoon Community Partnership Table, in which the Aboriginal community identifies certain social issues as a priority (e.g., housing and homelessness), and the three levels of government and the First Nations and Métis come to the table for discussion of the issues as equal partners. All participants have equal voice regardless of the resources they bring to the table. This approach has required the federal and provincial governments to modify their practices in dealing with Aboriginal communities. These and other strategies are being developed to address the lack of impact that traditional organizational structures have had with regard to urban Aboriginals. The slow acceptance of an intergovernmentalist approach has opened new ways of dealing with urban Aboriginal issues.

Others (Wherrett and Brown, 1994) have identified alternative strategies for exercising self-government within an urban context. If the traditional reserve exists within the urban area, governing would simply become an extension of how governance is applied on any reserve. Examples here are the Mi'kmaq in Halifax, the Algonquians in Ottawa–Hull, and the Sarcee in Calgary. Another way in which urban Aboriginals might exercise governance would be to use Section 35 of the *Constitution Act, 1982* to develop a National Treaty that covers all Aboriginal people, no matter where they live.

In developing models, Aboriginals will need to explore alternatives. For example, some may wish to use a "community of interest" model in instances where Aboriginals are dispersed throughout an urban area. In this case, the "territory" would be cultural rather than geographic. In this instance, they would need to develop their own school system as the Catholic and charter schools have done. Wherrett and Brown (1994) point out that another possibility exists where there is a concentration of Aboriginals in a particular area of the city: here, a "neighbourhood" model might be more appropriate. This is not a new idea, as Dosman (1972) proposed this type of model well over a quarter-century ago. This model would see a community take over various institutions in the neighbourhood to provide support for Aboriginals attempting to integrate into the urban setting and to help meet their economic, political, and psychological needs.

KEY TERMS

urban reserves

aboriginal values

institutional completeness

"citizens plus"

"comparative policy
   landscape"

acculturating service
   organizations

accommodating service
   organizations

STUDY QUESTIONS

1. What challenges do Aboriginal people within Canada face when living in major urban centers, as compared to non-Aboriginal people?

2. What structural, social and cultural factors affect Aboriginal urbanization?

3. Discuss the three stages of urbanization.

4. Compare and contrast Aboriginal and non-Aboriginal societies. How are these differences viewed by Aboriginal Canadians?

5. Define "citizens plus."

6. What are the four stages that Aboriginal people experience when moving to an urban area?

7. What is "policy environment"?

8. Compare and contrast two of the four types of organizations that attempt to address Aboriginal urban problems. What are the benefits and downfalls?

WEBLINKS

www.nafc-aboriginal.com

The National Association of Friendship Centres site provides valuable links to provincial and territorial centres and their websites, press releases on various topics of interest, history, and links to aboriginal urban youth centres across Canada.

http://www.ainc-inac.gc.ca/ch/rcap

Volume 4 of the *Royal Commission on Aboriginal Peoples Final Report* discusses urban Aboriginal issues, including identity in an urban context, governance, and urban Aboriginal women, elders, and youth. Click on each of the seven chapters and two appendices listed for Volume 4 at this site.

http://scc.lexum.umontreal.ca/en/index.html

The Supreme Court of Canada, in the *Corbiere* case, recently ruled that off-reserve band members must be allowed to vote in band council elections. The decision, which is based on the equality guarantee in the Charter of Rights and Freedoms, may have political implications both for bands and urban Aboriginal people. This link takes you to the Supreme Court's decisions website, where you can search for "Corbiere" in the search box.

NOTES

1. Some of the material presented has been previously published by Reeves and Frideres in *Canadian Public Policy* (1981).

2. The length of time between stages varies and should not be seen as equal. Movement to the next stage is not automatic and several starts may be needed before it takes place.

3. At the same time, Aboriginals on the reserves and in the city lacked an elite to promote a rediscovery and resurgence of Aboriginal culture. They also lacked service organizations to encourage participation in the larger society. The end result was the creation of a very passive and apathetic population that remained on the reserve or in rural areas. Those who became "active" were generally co-opted and acculturated out of Aboriginal culture and into mainstream society.

4. These organizations screen potential clients and sort them into appropriate homogeneous streams before providing services. In essence, accommodating service programs stream special problems away from the general program. The bicultural program can accommodate Euro-Canadian and Aboriginal values, thereby rendering acculturating service organizations more effective while increasing the clientele of accommodating service organizations. This new composite organization has allowed an increasing number of Aboriginal people to stay in urban areas.

chapter seven

Indian Treaties and Métis Scrip: Old Promises and New Struggles

INTRODUCTION

When William Robinson was sent to deal with Indian complaints about the intrusion of whites looking for minerals on land along the eastern and northern shores of Lake Superior, a new era in Indian–white relations emerged. Robinson met with the Ojibwa leaders and the first land-based treaties were established (the Robinson–Superior and Robinson–Huron treaties of 1850). These treaties provided a template that would be used by Robinson's successors and would forever change the social landscape of Canada. Later treaties were intended to give recognition to Indian interests in the land, to provide compensation, and to establish an orderly transition of land ownership from one group to another. The treaties also established the rules of the relationship between Indians and the federal government once land was transferred (Daniel, 1980).

While the land rights of Aboriginal peoples in Canada have not been treated uniformly, there did develop in British North America a consistent body of precedent and tradition that was utilized on new frontiers where fairly rapid settlement or resource exploitation took place. This involved negotiations by which Aboriginal peoples surrendered most of their territorial rights and in return gained various forms of compensation. Although numerous land surrender treaties had already been made in the Thirteen Colonies, it was not until after the American Revolution that surrender/compensation was first systematically used in Canada (Ray, 1974).

Nevertheless, many Canadians feel that treaties are no more than outdated contracts between a group of Indians and the federal government. There is also a belief that, since the treaties are old, the agreements within them can be breached. However, in a Supreme Court decision concerning hunting rights (*Simon* v. *The Queen,* 1985), the court held that treaties were neither contracts nor international instruments. They are to be regarded as agreements *sui generis*, that is, existing, in force and binding.

ORIGIN OF THE TREATIES: COLONIAL STRUGGLES AND THE MAKING OF CANADA

Some of the earliest agreements between the Indians and government have been called "Peace and Friendship" treaties, and were carried out primarily in the Maritime area.[1] These pre-Confederation treaties generally dealt with military and political relations and did not involve specific land transfers, annuities, trading rights, or compensation for rights limited or taken away (Sanders, 1983a). Yet by no means are these early treaties unimportant even today. A good example of "Peace and Friendship" treaties are those signed between the Mi'kmaq and the governor of Nova Scotia in 1760–61. It was these treaties, and specifically the right within them to catch and sell fish for profit (including lobster), that were at the centre of the controversial and highly publicized Marshall case, argued in the Supreme Court of Canada (*R. v. Marshall*, 1999; Coates, 2000). Pre-Confederation agreements continue to be reinterpreted and to generate new court rulings over access to different resources.

By the Treaty of Utrecht (1713), France ceded Acadia (excepting Cape Breton Island) to Great Britain, recognized the British sovereign's suzerainty over the Iroquois people, relinquished all claims to Newfoundland, and recognized British rights to Rupert's Land. When the charter for exploitation of Rupert's Land was granted by Charles II to the Hudson's Bay Company in 1670, it is doubtful that even the claimants were aware of the vast territory involved: all the land draining into Hudson's Bay from the tip of Ungava on the northeast to the headwaters of the Saskatchewan River in the southwest. For the next century and a quarter, the western boundaries of Rupert's Land were to remain the firmest delineation of British North America's western extent.

With the fall of the French fortress at Louisbourg, Cape Breton, and by the Treaty of Paris in 1763 which ended hostilities, France ceded all its North American possessions to Great Britain, with the exception of St. Pierre and Miquelon Islands (which it still retains) and Louisiana (which it later ceded to Spain). In the spring of that year the crystallization of Indian misgivings gained expression through the activities of Chief Pontiac,[2] although particular provisions in the *Royal Proclamation* concerning the protection of Indian-occupied lands were designed to allay such fears. The *Royal Proclamation* of 1763 did indeed define lands that were to remain, at the sovereign's pleasure, with the Indians as their hunting grounds, but Rupert's Land and the old colony of Quebec were specifically exempted. In what was to become Canada, the hunting grounds in the east comprised a relatively narrow strip between the northern bounds of Quebec and Rupert's Land, along with all of what was to become Upper Canada; in the northwest, they comprised an amorphous area bounded by Rupert's Land, the Beaufort Sea, and the Russian and Spanish claims to the west and south.

In 1769, St. John's Island (renamed Prince Edward Island in 1798) became a colony separate from Nova Scotia. By the *Quebec Act, 1774,* in what has been described as a statutory repudiation or breach of *Royal Proclamation* policy, Quebec's boundaries were extended to encompass all the land described in the preceding paragraph as the eastern Indian hunting grounds.

With the Revolutionary War of 1775 to 1783, the emphasis in the colonies of Nova Scotia and Quebec changed irrevocably to settlement, development, lumbering, fishing, and trade; dissolution of the 200-year-old partnership between Indian and fur trader was well on the way. The most immediate effect was a 50-percent increase in population in the two colonies occasioned by the influx of United Empire Loyalists, who were primarily interested in farming, homesteading and business. These were followed, particularly in Upper Canada after 1791, by a steady stream of settlers with like interests from the south. They brought with them the desire for peace, law, good order and the other concomitants of settled living.

The Treaty of Paris, 1783, signed between Great Britain and the United States, established the boundary from the Atlantic to the Lake of the Woods. At one stroke Canada lost the entire southwestern half of the vast inland domain that French and British adventurers had discovered, explored and exploited with the help of the Indian people. Along with it went that portion of the Indian hunting grounds, established in 1763, that was bounded by the Great Lakes and the Ohio and Mississippi Rivers. A natural point of departure for the future boundary at the 49th parallel of latitude was also ensured. The inevitable dissension with the Indian people that followed, however, was reaped by the United States rather than Great Britain.

In 1784, as a result of the large-scale influx of United Empire Loyalists into the Saint John River area the year before, New Brunswick was separated from Nova Scotia. Cape Breton Island also became a separate entity.

By the *Constitutional* (or *Canada*) *Act* of 1791, the British Parliament divided Quebec into the provinces of Upper Canada and Lower Canada, abolished the conciliar form of government that had existed in Quebec for two centuries, and established representative government in both provinces. Land was to be granted in freehold tenure in Upper Canada and could be so granted in Lower Canada, if desired.

In 1796, by the terms of the Jay Treaty, the fur-trading posts of Niagara, Detroit, Michilimackinac and Grand Portage—which were still in British hands—were handed over to the United States in accordance with the boundary provisions agreed to in 1783. In order to facilitate what remained of the fur trade, an article in the *Jay Treaty* provided for the free passage of Indian trappers back and forth across the boundary with "their ordinary goods and peltries"; it is on the basis of this provision that the present-day Iroquois claim duty-free passage across the international boundary (Innis, 1970).

In 1803, by the Louisiana Purchase, the United States acquired that vast, vaguely defined territory west of the Mississippi that had been ceded back to France by Spain in 1800. The consequent push westward, and the inevitable rivalries arising, would once again raise the contentious question of the boundary between British America and the United States.

On the Pacific coast, the leading protagonists changed over the course of time from Russia, Britain, and Spain to Russia, Britain, and the United States, but it was not from the sea that this contest was to be settled. Indeed, although Captain Cook had made his landfall at Nootka Sound in 1778, the traders who followed him lost their vessels and furs to the Spanish, who were engaged in a last endeavour to enforce their claims to the northwest coast. In 1791, Captain George Vancouver arrived to officially acknowledge the restoration of British rights after the Nootka Convention with the Spanish; the Russians were concurrently pushing down from the north, following the seal and the sea otter.

The only firm and lasting links with the Pacific coast, however, would have to be established by land, and these were provided through Alexander Mackenzie in 1793, by way of the Peace River canyon to Dean Channel; Simon Fraser in 1808, by the tumultuous river that bears his name; and David Thompson in 1811, down the Columbia to its mouth. These Canadian Scots were all members of the North-West Company, and they were rivals, not only of the Spanish, Russians, and Americans, but also of the Hudson's Bay Company. With their exploits the chain of discovery and exploration, whose initial links were forged in the quest for furs along the Atlantic coast over the preceding two centuries, was complete from ocean to ocean—all in the name of the fur trade. In each instance, the ubiquitous Scot was accompanied, guided and sustained by Aboriginal companions (Wildsmith, 1985). For the United States, Lewis and Clarke had, of course, paced the Canadians, reaching the Columbia River in 1805. John Jacob Astor established the western headquarters of his fur company at the mouth of the Columbia in 1810, a year before Thompson arrived there.

In 1809, by the *Labrador Act,* Anticosti Island and the coast of Labrador from the St. Jean River to Hudson Strait were transferred from Lower Canada to Newfoundland. Not even the eastern provinces, however, were to be allowed to engage in such peaceful organizational exercises much longer. The improvement in relations that the Jay Treaty appeared to herald had not resolved the border ambiguities at the centre of the continent, and the animosities of the American Revolution were by no means exhausted.

The outbreak of war in 1812 saw 500 000 British Americans (of whom fewer than 5000 were regular troops) confronted by a population of 8 million in the United States. Great Britain was not only at war with the United States but had its strength committed to the struggle with Napoleon. Through a combination of dogged determination on the part of the British Americans (aided by several hundred Indians under Chief Tecumseh) in throwing back invasion forces and ineffective planning on the part of the enemy, Canada managed to hold out until the defeat of Napoleon in 1814, allowed Britain to bring all its forces to bear in America. Having thus gained the initiative in no uncertain manner, it is hard to understand why the British did not seek more equitable boundary terms by the Treaty of Ghent in 1814, but both parties appeared content to settle the controversy through a mutual return of conquered territories. Thus were Canadian interests sacrificed to ensure American cordiality.

The United States considered the Jay Treaty of 1796 to be abrogated by the War of 1812–14; but the Convention of 1818 settled the outstanding boundary matters by confirming the border to the Lake of the Woods and extending it along the 49th parallel to the Rocky Mountains. The Treaty of Ghent reinstated the provisions of the Jay Treaty affecting Indian people, but, as the conditions of the former were not considered to be self-executing, it became the individual responsibility of each of the governments concerned to give effect to the relevant provisions by appropriate legislation (Leslie and Maguire, 1978).

In terminating the international boundary at the Rocky Mountains, the Convention of 1818 left one major area subject to contention with the growing neighbour to the south—the so-called Oregon Territory, jointly occupied by Britain and the United States. The first large-scale movement of American settlers into Oregon in 1842 naturally created a clamour for annexation to the United States. Fortunately, the contention was resolved through the Treaty of Washington in 1846, by which the boundary was continued to the sea along the 49th parallel, and Vancouver Island was confirmed as a British possession. With the agreement of 1825 between Britain and Russia on a description of the Alaska boundary, to all intents and purposes Canada's external boundaries now were fixed and its attention could be concentrated on consolidation.

Early Ontario Treaties

Algonkian-speaking peoples formed the Indian population of southern Ontario when the European claim to territorial sovereignty passed from the French to the British in 1763, but European settlement did not occur there to any degree until 20 years later. In those post-Revolutionary years, the separation of the Thirteen Colonies from British North America created an urgent need for land on which to settle disbanded soldiers and other Loyalists. The unsettled areas of British North America provided a ready solution to the problem.

About 10 000 United Empire Loyalists moved into the area of the St. Lawrence–Lower Great Lakes. In presiding over this settlement, the Imperial government did not simply grant land to these newcomers without regard for the Indian inhabitants. As has been seen, the *Royal Proclamation* of 1763 declared that Indian land rights could only be ceded, or given up, at a public meeting or assembly of the Indians called for the purpose, and then only to the Crown. Although often honoured only in the breach, the Proclamation's principles were respected through a complicated series of formal treaties and surrenders in what became Southern Ontario.

To the government, treaties were little more than territorial cessions in return for once-for-all grants, usually in goods. However, there is evidence that some of the Indians involved felt that the government was assuming broader trusteeship responsibilities as part of the bargain. Annuities, or annual payments for the ceded land rights, first appeared in a treaty in 1818 and thereafter became routine. At this stage, the provision of land for Indian reserves only occasionally formed part of the surrender terms. Similarly, the right to continue hunting and fishing over ceded territories was very rarely mentioned in the written terms of surrender. Not until 1850, when cessions of land rights were taken by William Robinson along the northern shores of Lakes Huron and Superior, were treaties made that granted to the Indians all four items: once-for-all expenditures, annuities, reserves and guarantees concerning hunting and fishing. It was for this reason that Alexander Morris, the most widely known of the government's negotiators, noted in the early 1870s that the Robinson Treaties constituted the "forerunners of the future treaties" to be made by the recently created Dominion.

The provisions of many of the southern Ontario treaties and surrenders are quite discordant with more modern agreements conveying far greater benefits to Aboriginal peoples elsewhere. Most cessions made in Ontario after 1830 were concluded in trust. The government assumed responsibility for disposing of the ceded lands on the Indians' behalf, with the proceeds of sales usually going to the particular Indians involved. As with land cessions made earlier, which were at times outright surrenders with the government as purchaser, there are strong arguments that inadequate compensation was given. Surrenders concluded prior to 1818 provided for a lump-sum payment along with a nominal yearly rent; in one 1816 surrender of Thurlow Township, for instance, the yearly rent was fixed at one peppercorn. In an 1836 surrender, it was considered sufficient to promise the Chippewa claimants agricultural and educational aid in exchange for their surrender of 1.5 million acres south of Owen Sound. The Robinson–Huron and Robinson–Superior Treaties also supplied only minimal payments to the Indians, although they contained provisions for a limited augmentation of annuities in the future. One oversight in the Huron Treaty presumably left Aboriginal rights intact at Temagami.

TREATIES AND TREATY MAKING AFTER 1867

Pre-Confederation treaties were made with the Crown through representatives of the British government. Later, after Confederation, treaties would be made through the Canadian government. All the terms of the pre-Confederation treaties were turned over to the Canadian government at the time of Confederation. When the *Royal Proclamation* of 1763 was issued, Indian rights were specifically referred to for the first time in Canadian history. The *Royal Proclamation* confirmed that Aboriginal rights existed. However, the question still remains as to how much of what is now Canada is covered by the proclamation. Driben (1983) pointed out that it is difficult today to determine the boundaries of what the *Royal Proclamation* referred to as "Indian territory."

When the Hudson's Bay Company (HBC) surrendered Rupert's Land in 1869, Canada inherited the responsibility for negotiating with the resident Aboriginal tribes. Prior to the transfer, the *Royal Proclamation* had established the "equitable principles" governing the purchase and surrender of Aboriginal lands. The Imperial order-in-council that transferred this responsibility is stipulated in Article 14:

> Any claim of Indians to compensation for lands required for the purposes of settlement shall be disposed of by the Canadian government in communications with the Imperial government; and the Company shall be relieved of all responsibility in respect of them.

The administrators who were subsequently appointed to negotiate federal treaties with the Indians were inexperienced and unfamiliar with Aboriginal customs. Lacking first-hand knowledge, these administrators fell back on the legacy of the Hudson's Bay Company's treatment of Aboriginal people, as well as on some sketchy reports of the negotiations behind the Robinson Treaties of 1850 and 1862 and the Manitoulin Island Treaty, also of 1862.

Preliminary negotiations between the Indians in Manitoba and the representatives of the government began in 1870. By 1871, Treaties Nos. 1 and 2 were signed, and in 1873 the lands between Manitoba and Lake Superior were ceded in Treaty No. 3. Northern Manitoba and the remainder of the southern prairies were surrendered by the Aboriginal peoples between 1874 and 1877 in Treaties Nos. 4, 5, 6, and 7.

The land taken by the Canadian government under Treaties Nos. 1 through 7 provided sufficient land for the mass settlement of immigrants entering Canada for the time being. However, by 1899 the pressures of settlement and mineral development again caused the government to negotiate for new lands from the Aboriginal peoples. Although these later treaties, Nos. 8 through 11, differed in many respects from the earlier ones, they were also clearly modelled upon earlier treaties. Subsequent modern agreements may, in turn, be modelled upon and indeed even replace these numbered treaties, as is the case for Treaty 11 (see later in this chapter and chapter 8 for some details on the 2003 Tlicho [Dene/Dogrib] Agreement).

The federal government decided to negotiate with the Aboriginal peoples largely because its own agents foresaw violence against European settlers if treaties were not established. However, this perception was not based on particular threats or claims on the part of the Aboriginal peoples, who simply wished to carry out direct negotiations with the government for compensation for the lands they occupied prior to European settlement. After the first treaty was signed, neither the government nor the Aboriginal people attempted to find alternative means to deal with "Indian claims." Government officials based future treaties on prior ones, and Aboriginal groups insisted on treatment similar to that received by those who had signed earlier treaties.

Despite specific differences, the contents of all the treaties are remarkably similar. Treaties Nos. 1 and 2 set the stage. They created reserve lands granting 160 acres per family. Annuities of $3 per person, a gratuity of $3 per person, and a school on each reserve were agreed upon. Other promises were also made orally during the negotiations; some of these were later given formal recognition by an order-in-council.[3] Treaty No. 3 contained the same provisions as Treaties Nos. 1 and 2, except that its reserve allotment was increased to 640 acres per family of five.[4]

The federal government desired treaties that were brief, simple and uniform in content. Nonetheless, although constrained by these government-imposed limitations, negotiators were often forced to make minor additions to a treaty; sometimes these took the form of verbal promises, presumably to avoid deviations from the standard written form. For example, the government negotiators for Treaty No. 6 were forced to add several benefits such as medicine chests and provisions for relief in times of famine.

In general, however, the government negotiators had by far the best of the bargaining. Indeed, most treaties were written by the government and simply presented to the Indians for signing. The terms of Treaty No. 9, for example, were determined by the Ontario and Canadian governments well in advance of discussions with Aboriginal people. Moreover, there is evidence that, in many cases, hard-won oral promises have never been recognized nor acted upon by the government.

In their negotiations with the Aboriginal people, treaty commissioners always avoided discussing the nature or extent of Aboriginal land rights. Although the commissioners obscured the issue, the Aboriginal people clearly surrendered rights to land by signing the treaties. In many cases, the commissioners argued that the Indians had no land rights at all; if the Aboriginal negotiators objected to this argument, the commissioners would enlist support from missionaries or traders whom the Aboriginal people trusted. In the end, however, no Indian treaty was ever brought before parliament. Instead, the treaties were presented to cabinet and ratified by an order-in-council. This suggests that they were accepted by the government of Canada, both as a recognition of Aboriginal land claims and as a means of their negotiation and resolution.

British Columbia: A Special Case

British Columbia was a special case in its handling of treaties. Between 1849 and 1854, James Douglas, the governor of the colony, negotiated a series of treaties with the Indians on Vancouver Island. After 1854 this policy was discontinued; although the Colonial Office in England supported the treaties, it would not provide Douglas with monies to continue them. British Columbia settlers refused responsibility for negotiations with the Indians and would not release public funds to settle land claims.

As Berger (1981: 222–23) points out, British Columbia's House of Assembly had initially recognized Aboriginal land titles. However, when told by London that it would have to provide the funds to settle those titles, the House of Assembly withdrew recognition of Indian land claims. This meant that, technically, the Aboriginal peoples were not entitled to any compensation by the province.

No further treaties were made in British Columbia until recently. (The only exception was the northeastern part of the province, which was later to be covered by Treaty No. 8.)

With the entry of British Columbia into Confederation in 1871, the administration of Indians and Indian lands in the province fell under the jurisdiction of the federal government. However, the federal government's interpretation of this jurisdiction has remained controversial up to the present (Duff, 1997).

When British Columbia entered Confederation, the actual terms concerning the treatment of Aboriginal people were unclear. The terms of union clearly stated that all public lands were to be the property of the provincial government; this meant that the federal government owned no land outright in the province to give to the Aboriginal people. Some provision was made, however, for Aboriginal lands. The province agreed to relinquish to the federal government "tracts of land of such extent as it had hitherto been the practice of the British Columbian government to appropriate for that purpose" (Berger, 1981: 224).

Unfortunately, the practice of the British Columbian government was to supply considerably less land than did the federal government. When allotting land, non-Aboriginal settlers had received 320 acres of land per homestead from the province; Aboriginal people had been granted considerably less. In 1887 the federal government asked the province to determine the size of the reserves by relinquishing 80 acres per Indian family. The province set aside only 20 acres per family, a much lower acreage than that set aside for other Aboriginal peoples by the Canadian government. Understandably, Indians in British Columbia objected strongly and insisted on their Aboriginal rights.

The British Columbian Aboriginal peoples continued to oppose the establishment of reserves and to argue title to their own lands. The federal government dissolved its commission in 1910 after the provincial government refused to sanction any more reserves. In the early 1900s, Indians sent delegations to Victoria and to England in an attempt to argue their claims for Aboriginal rights. The federal government partly supported these claims and tried unsuccessfully for a hearing before the Supreme Court of Canada. The province refused to participate in the legal proceedings and thus thwarted the efforts of the federal government.

In 1913 a royal commission was established by the federal government, partly to adjust the acreage of the reserves in British Columbia. In 1916 the commission produced a report detailing lands to be added to and removed from existing reserves. The added land was to be twice the size of the land taken away; however, the land to be taken away was, at that time, worth twice as much money.

As the federal government tried to implement this report it met increased opposition from the provincial government and from the Aboriginal peoples. The province finally confirmed an amended version of the report in 1923, but the Aboriginal peoples never accepted it. The Allied Indian Tribes of British Columbia emerged to become a powerful political force uniting Aboriginal opposition to the decision. In 1923 the Allied Indian Tribes of British Columbia presented a list of far-reaching demands to the federal government and agreed to relinquish their Aboriginal title claim only if the demands were met. These demands were remarkably similar to those met by previous treaties in other provinces, namely, 160 acres per capita, hunting rights, and the establishment of reserves.

The Allied Indian Tribes of British Columbia demanded that either a treaty be negotiated or that their Aboriginal title claim be submitted to the judicial committee of the Privy Council. In essence, they argued that, contrary to the beliefs of the federal and provincial governments, there had been no final settlement of their claims. As a result of the Indians' petition, a special joint committee of the House and Senate was convened to hear evidence and make a decision. This committee decided that the Indians had not established any claims to land based on Aboriginal title; however, it did recommend that an annual sum of $100 000 be spent for the good of Indians in British Columbia.

In order to prevent an appeal of this decision, the federal government passed an amend-ment to the *Indian Act* that prohibited the collection of funds by Aboriginal people for the advancement of a land claim. This amendment remained law until the middle of the 20th century. As a result, Aboriginal groups became powerless to press their claims, and were successfully ignored by the federal government throughout the Depression and World War II. Of necessity, local issues replaced larger concerns during this time: the Native Brotherhood of British Columbia was established in 1931 and, in 1942, became prominent in its fight against income tax for Aboriginal fishermen. But Aboriginal claims in British Columbia (McGhee, 1996) did not emerge again as an issue until the 1960s, when they played an important role in, amongst other things, the creation of the Indian Land Com-mission. Chapter 9 will detail 21st century developments in British Columbia, from the 2002 Referendum on Aboriginal Treaties to major treaties signed in 2006.

The Historical, or Numbered, Treaties

Treaties Nos. 1 to 7 were made during the 1870s in the territory between the watershed west of Lake Superior and the Rocky Mountains, in what was then Canada's newly acquired northwest. These treaties utilized many features of the earlier transactions, but were far more comprehensive in their provisions and more uniform and consistent with one another. Their characteristics and relative similarities were not due to a broad policy worked out in advance by the federal government. Indeed, immediately before the first of these treaties was made, the government had little information about the Indians of its new territory, let alone a policy. It proceeded to deal with the Aboriginal occupants in an ad hoc fashion as necessity dictated. Almost inevitably the patterns of earlier Canadian experi-ence were adapted to a new time and place. The seven treaties that emerged were partly shaped by the Indians themselves and were indirectly influenced by United States policy and practice.

The government's purpose in negotiating treaties in the Northwest was to free land for settlement and development. A corollary of this was the urgent desire to satisfy the Indians sufficiently so that they would remain peaceful. The nature and extent of Indian rights to the territory were not discussed at the negotiations, nor were they defined in the treaties themselves. It is evident from the texts, nevertheless, that the government intended that whatever title the Indians might possess should be extinguished, since the opening clauses of all seven agreements deal with land surrender. This emphasis was not reflected in the preliminary treaty negotiations. There, the stress was on what the Indians would receive rather than on what they were giving up. The commissioners gave them assurances that the Queen understood their problems and was anxious to help them (Henderson, Benson and Findlay, 2000).

The loss of control over land use and the diminishing game supply threatened the traditional Aboriginal way of life. While the Indians attempted to retain as much control as possible over their own territory and future, a secondary desire was the attempt to gain sufficient compensa-tion and support to ensure their survival amidst rapidly changing conditions. As a result of hard bargaining, Indians did manage to have some additional provisions included in the treaties beyond those the government had originally intended. These included agricultural aid and certain liberties to hunt and fish (Rotman, 1996).

Aboriginal people today make several points in relation to these treaties. The major one is that the treaty texts do not reflect the verbal promises made during the negotiations and accepted by a people accustomed to an oral tradition. They state that their ancestors understood the treaties to be specifically designed to protect them and help them adapt to the new realities by developing an alternative agricultural base to complement their traditional livelihood of hunting and fishing. An excellent example and discussion of the Aboriginal view of treaties, their intent, expectations and interpretation, is presented in a study by Treaty 7 Elders and Tribal Council (1996).

Aboriginal associations strongly deny that the treaties obligate the government only to fulfil their terms as they appear in the essential treaty texts. They uniformly insist that the written versions must be taken together with the words spoken by the government's agents during the negotiations. In a submission to the commissioner on Indian claims, the Federation of Saskatchewan Indians states that:

> In his various addresses to Chiefs and Headmen at treaty meetings, Commissioner Morris had a single message for the Indians: The Queen was not approaching the Indians to barter for their lands, but to help them, to alleviate their distress and assist them in obtaining security for the future. "We are not here as traders, I do not come as to buy or sell horses or goods, I come to you, children of the Queen, to try to help you. The Queen knows that you are poor: the Queen knows that it is hard to find food for yourselves and children: she knows that the winters are cold, and you(r) children are often hungry: she has always cared for her Red children as much as for her White. Out of her generous heart and liberal hand she wants to do something for you...."
>
> These verbal assurances and statement of Crown intent, and the many others like them given by Morris in his address to Chiefs and Headmen, cannot be separated from treaty documents because they were accepted as truth by the assembled Indians.

The nature and extent of the implementation of treaty provisions are another source of grievance in this area. The government's open policy of detribalization, which held as its goal the assimilation of Indian people into the dominant society, motivated a number of specific policies that were destructive of Indian efforts to develop within the context of their own cultures. The field of education is one of the most conspicuous examples of this process, since it is easy to appreciate the effects of isolating children in residential schools where they were taught that their parents' language and culture were inferior, and where a set of alien customs and values were instilled in them (Pennekeok, 1976).

In the Aboriginal peoples' view, during the late 19th and early 20th centuries the government failed to provide the expected agricultural assistance and unduly restricted Indian agricultural development. It encouraged the surrender of some of the best agricultural land from the reserves when its efforts failed to turn the Indians into farmers.

All of the Prairie Aboriginal organizations, along with the Grand Council of Treaty No. 3 in northern Ontario, think the treaties should be reworded in terms that will embody their original spirit and intent. As in the area of Aboriginal title, the results of such settlements could, they say, provide the basis for revolutionizing the future development of Aboriginal peoples and reserves on Aboriginal terms. The treaty Indians' organizations have outlined some specific objectives and proposals for an approach to development. A primary characteristic of these is their rejection of the concept of assimilation or detribalization, and, stemming from this, the conviction that the Aboriginal people must initiate and control the development effort themselves.

Only at the turn of the 20th century, when mineral exploitation provided the impetus, were treaties made to the north of the areas surrendered during the 1870s. Treaty No. 8 was concluded in the Athabasca District, Treaty No. 9 in northern Ontario, and Treaty No. 10 in northern Saskatchewan. In addition, adhesions to Treaty No. 5 were taken in northern Manitoba to extend the limit of ceded territory to the northern boundary of the province. Finally, in 1921, following the discovery of oil at Norman Wells, Treaty No. 11 was made in the Northwest Territories.

The numbered, or historical, treaties between the Indians and the Dominion thus began in the mid-1800s (in southern Ontario) and moved westward, eventually encompassing all of Manitoba, Saskatchewan, and Alberta. The treaty period ended in 1921 with the signing of Treaty No. 11, which encompasses almost all of the Mackenzie Valley of the Northwest Territories. Today, only British Columbia, the Yukon, parts of Quebec, and Newfoundland have not "treatied" with the Indians. It should be emphasized that, where treaties have not been made, Aboriginal title is said to still exist, thus providing the basis for subsequent land claims and the modern-day treaty-making process (McGhee, 1996).

CLAIMS REGARDING TREATIES

As we pointed out earlier, the treaties have been the focal point for specific claims that have been pursued by Indians. Their claims with regard to treaties focus on several aspects. First of all, Indians argue that the treaty texts do not include the verbal promises made by the government during the negotiation period prior to the actual signing. Hence, they argue that the treaties oblige the government to keep promises made in both verbal and written contexts—e.g., Treaties Nos. 8 and 11 (Melville, 1981). Secondly, inequality among the various treaties' land provisions has provoked specific claims—for example, Treaty No. 5 provides for 71 hectares per family while other treaties provide 285 hectares.

One example of a "modern" settlement involving a treaty concerns the Peter Ballantyne Band in Saskatchewan. To fulfil its remaining outstanding land entitlement claim, the Peter Ballantyne Band has selected approximately 81 000 hectares of land, including the site of the Prince Albert School student residence. With the exception of the residence land, the rest is provincial Crown land. Remaining transfer settlements are now to be made between the province and the band. Under the terms of the Saskatchewan Formula of 1976, which is the federal–provincial agreement under which outstanding treaty land entitlements in Saskatchewan are being settled, the Peter Ballantyne Band's outstanding entitlement is 92 860 hectares. The selection of these lands must deal satisfactorily with the interests of affected third parties. The transfer to reserve status means that the land will continue to be federal Crown land; however, it will be set aside as a reserve for the use and benefit of the Peter Ballantyne Band. The minister has approved the band's request that the land be set aside under the authority of Section 18(2) of the *Indian Act* for Aboriginal educational use. The band has stated that the current use of the land will not change in the foreseeable future.

The Prince Albert School is the only parcel of federal Crown land in Saskatchewan within a major urban area that has historically been administered by Canada, through the department of Indian Affairs, for the benefit of the Aboriginal people. In this respect the selection is unique and its transfer to reserve status is now viewed as a precedent for future land selections.

The 1991 settlement between the Alberta Stoney Indian tribe and the federal government is the second-largest specific claim ever settled in Alberta. It provides nearly $20 million in compensation to the tribe for loss of mineral rights on land surrendered in 1929 for hydro development.

In 1999, Canada's oldest Indian person (aged 106) launched a suit against the federal government for $1.5 billion and access to a few square kilometres of land in Alberta's tar-sands country. Mr. Raphael Cree and others have been pressing their claim to the Little Clearwater River Reserve for decades (first in 1921) without success. The claim stems from the failure of Treaty 8 to include all Indian groups in portions of Alberta's north.

Treaties have three possible interpretations. In one sense they can be viewed as agreements between two or more *nations*. Most Aboriginal people claim this interpretation when they refer to the various treaties with the federal government. On the other hand, it is clear that the Canadian government (as evidenced through certain legislation and court decisions) does not interpret the treaties in the same manner (Weaver, 1983).

Secondly, treaties have at times been interpreted as contracts. While there is some legal support for this interpretation, the nature of the jurisprudence dealing with this issue is so specific that one must be cautious in interpreting treaties from this perspective. Nevertheless, former Prime Minister Pierre E. Trudeau publicly stated that treaties are analogous to contracts.

Finally, treaties can be viewed as pieces of legislation. This interpretation is plausible, since many Indian treaties were made before such legislation as the *Indian Act*. Hence, any legal means that attempts to establish an orderly relationship between people could be viewed as analogous to legislation (Marule, 1977).

Even today, it is unclear which interpretation prevails. Nevertheless, the courts have viewed treaties as enforceable obligations, which has required the federal government in large part to live up to those obligations; indeed, both section 25 of the Canadian Charter of Rights and Freedoms as well as section 35, or Part 2, of the Canadian Constitution (1982) have enshrined "existing" treaty rights.

Treaties are therefore legal arrangements between Aboriginal peoples and the government of Canada. Moreover, treaties confer benefits upon successors even though at times it is difficult to identify who those successors are. The Supreme Court of Canada has identified a number of conditions to determine if a document is a treaty. It listed five considerations:

1. continuous exercise of a right in the past and at present;
2. the reasons that the Crown made a commitment;
3. the situation prevailing at the time the document was signed;
4. evidence of relations of mutual respect and esteem between the negotiators; and
5. the subsequent conduct of the parties.

If, after reviewing the above, ambiguity still remains, the court decided that one could look at extrinsic evidence, such as the historical context, information about what went on at the time the document was signed, and the subsequent conduct of the parties. In all instances regarding the interpretation of treaties, the Supreme Court encourages and supports interpretations in favour of, and for the benefit of, Indian people as part of fiduciary doctrine (see Box 7.1). The court's and the federal government's reasoning extends even to the "Peace and Friendship" treaties of the 18th century, as shown by the Marshall decision in September 1999.

Box 7.1	"Scope of Aboriginal Ruling in Dispute"

Natives, federal minister say forestry and mining, as well as fishing rights must be discussed

By Heather Scoffield

Indian Affairs Minister Robert Nault says he would be able to resolve the Mi'kmaq fishing dispute on the East coast if only the provinces would cooperate....

The federal government has appointed a chief negotiator to lead talks between the Aboriginal groups, the maritime provinces and the federal government. The object is to settle on how to interpret the Sept. 17 Supreme Court decision, which ruled that maritime Natives have the right to fish, hunt and gather for a "moderate livelihood."...

Mr. Nault says the negotiations must involve more than fish. The Supreme Court decision that set off the dispute between Native and non-Native fishermen on the East coast, applied broadly to Aboriginal rights in all natural resources, he said.

But the Maritime provinces, which met with Mr. Nault earlier this week, say the negotiations with the Natives of the East coast should be limited to dealing with the lobster fishery.

Nova Scotia's minister of Aboriginal Affairs said the lobster dispute must be settled before there can be any discussion of extending the treaty right.

"People here are extremely frustrated that more than one month after the Supreme Court of Canada ruling there is still too much uncertainty over management of the lobster fishery," Michael Baker said in a statement. "We've said it before, but what we need here is some real leadership."

New Brunswick Aboriginal Affairs Brad Green has insisted that his province does not accept the federal view that the treaty right extends to logging.

But since the decision, several loggers in the northern New Brunswick Bands of Big Cove and Red Bank have resumed logging operations....

On Thursday, the Mi'kmaq of Nova Scotia won another court battle over natural resources. The federal court of appeal ruled that the National Energy Board did not deal adequately with Aboriginal people when it granted construction rights for a $1.7 billion pipeline for the Sable Island project.

And another key case about Aboriginal rights over natural resources is expected soon.

"We keep going back to the whole theme of Aboriginal people having the right to share in resources," Mr. Nault said.

Source: Excerpted from *The Globe and Mail*, October 23, 1999, p. A5. Reprinted with permission from *The Globe and Mail*.

MÉTIS SCRIP

Related to the issue of treaties are the concerns Métis people have regarding their Aboriginal and/or land rights. While not called treaties, several acts were passed by the federal government that provided land for Métis, e.g., the *Manitoba Act* and *Dominion Lands Act,* in exchange for their Aboriginal rights. The conditions for the transfer of land to Métis are outlined in these various acts. In the case of the Métis, the allocation of land (or money) was through the process of scrip. Scrip is a certificate giving the holder the right to receive payment later in the form of cash, goods, or land (Sawchuk, Sawchuk, and Ferguson, 1981). This process differed from Indian treaties in that it involved grants to *individuals*; it did not purport to set up the Métis as a continuing corporate entity. For over 30 years (1885–1923) there was a series of scrip allotments to Métis. Each time that a new part of the prairie provinces or the Mackenzie Valley was ceded by Indians, persons of mixed blood who did not participate were allocated scrip redeemable in land (Flanagan, 1983a).

Prior to 1870, Métis had not been dealt with as a separate group. However, expediency or perhaps humanitarian reasons led to a change; under Section 31 of the *Manitoba Act, 1870,* a proportion of 623 000 hectares originally calculated as unoccupied land was set aside for the children of Métis families in Manitoba. This land was reserved for "the benefits [sic] of the families of the half-breed residents." It was to be divided "among the children of the half-breed heads of families" residing in the province at the time of its transfer to Canada. Initially, the amount of land set aside was thought to provide each child with 290 acres (116 hectares). However, due to miscalculations, the government also had to issue money scrip in lieu of land. In 1874 the heads of Métis families were also provided with scrip (71 hectares or $160). Under the *Dominion Lands Act* in 1885, all Métis resident in the Northwest Territories outside the limits of Manitoba in 1870 were granted 107 hectares. By this time, the government had allotted 579 264 hectares of land and $509 760 to Métis in Manitoba. Four years later this would be extended to Métis resident in the area ceded by the adhesion to Treaty No. 6 (Taylor, 1983). In 1899 Métis in the Athabasca and Peace River areas were given scrip, and in 1906 all Métis permanently residing in the territory ceded at the time of making Treaty No. 10 were provided with 107 hectares. Finally, in 1921 each Métis of the Mackenzie River district received $240 to extinguish their Aboriginal rights (Sealey and Lussier, 1975). In all, the government handled more than 24 000 Métis claims (14 000 in the Northwest Territories, Saskatchewan, and Alberta, and 10 000 in Manitoba). These claims involved over one million hectares of land and in excess of $3.6 million.

The use of scrip was not confined to Métis. Non-Aboriginal settlers in 1873, veterans after 1885 (e.g, of the Boer War), and officers of the North West Mounted Police were also given land scrip. Scrip came in two forms and looked as follows.[5]

A typical land scrip certificate read:

Dominion of Canada

Department of the Interior

This Scrip note is receivable as payment in full for ONE HUNDRED and SIXTY ACRES of Dominion Lands, open for ordinary Homestead only if presented by _____ at the office of Dominion Lands of the District within which such lands are situated in conformity with Scrip Certificate form _____ granted by the North West Half Breed Commission this _____ day of _____, 18 _____.

A typical money scrip certificate read:

Dominion of Canada

Department of the Interior

In conformity with Certificate form No. _____ granted by the North West Half Breed Commission, it is Hereby Certified that under the authority of an order of the Honorable Privy Council dated _____ day of _____, 18 _____ as amended by the order of _____ of _____,

18 _____, and in accordance with the provisions of subsec. (e), Sec. 81, 46 Vic. Cap. 17 _____, a Half-Breed is entitled to TWO HUNDRED AND FORTY DOLLARS IN SCRIP. The coupons attached to this will be accepted in payment of Dominion Lands on presentation at the office of Dominion Lands of the District within which such lands are situated.

Issued at the Department of the Interior, Ottawa, this _____ day of _____, 18 _____.

After passage of the *Manitoba Act* of 1870, which set aside lands for Métis, the government began a systematic process of amending the Act so that land set aside would not actually be allotted. From 1873 to 1884, 11 amendments were passed, referred to as Manitoba Supplementary Provisions. Nearly half of these amendments altered substantive portions of the original law. The effect of all of the amendments was the dispersal of the original Métis people in Manitoba. Only about 20 percent of the claimants received and made use of their land allotments. A similar percentage of river-lot occupants obtained patents and remained on the land they occupied in 1870. Over half the potential recipients were denied their land through a number of government manoeuvres (Sawchuk, 1978, 1998).

Perhaps the single most important factor that prevented Métis from reaping the potential benefits of land claim settlements was the 1874 amendment to the 1870 Act, which restricted eligibility for the initial allotment. It should be noted that even in the original allotment many children were omitted from participating in the benefits of the Act. The 1874 amendment, which declared that heads of families were entitled to the same benefits as children, excluded the heads from receiving any part of the original 1.4 million acres set aside. Instead they were awarded $160 in scrip that could be used to purchase Crown land (O. Dickason, 1992). As Dickason points out, "Fortunes were made at the expense of the Métis—half-breed scrip millionaires" were created (1992, p. 317). Scrip was sold to land speculators (bankers and wealthy individuals) for as little as half its face value. In some cases, accepting scrip left Métis poorer than before.

Children who received an allotment were not adequately protected. For example, their allotments were subject to payment of local taxes from the moment the allotment was drawn. Thus, even if they were minors and had no way of paying the tax, they were expected to do so. Failure of tax payment meant the loss of the property.

Finally, Métis river-lot claimants were not compensated by the government for railway or other public expropriation. However, homesteaders were. The federal government acted in many other ways that placed the Métis in a disadvantageous position (Peterson and Brown, 1985).

Some writers, such as Flanagan (1983a), claim that Métis only wanted money scrip and thus were not interested in obtaining land scrip. He also notes that some Métis insisted on receiving their entitlements in as liquid a form as possible. He points to the Métis of Lesser Slave Lake, who refused to accept scrip until it was rewritten "payable to the bearer." He also argues that Métis were good negotiators and that they operated in a "willing buyer–willing seller" market. We would acknowledge that some Métis preferred money scrip and we would concur that some were skilful negotiators. However, the structural conditions under which Métis operated did not allow for the exercise of choice, nor did they fully understand the implications of not having land deeded to them. For example, nearly 60 percent of the Métis were illiterate, a definite liability when dealing with banks and lawyers. The Métis Association of Alberta also pointed out in its study, *Métis Land Rights in Alberta: A Political History* (1981), that the use of land scrip came about because Métis opposed money scrip and wanted land grants. Métis of the Qu'Appelle Lakes refused to accept money scrip. Thus, land scrip was considered a compromise. There is also no doubt that most of the land scrip issued to Métis was eventually owned by banks and financial agents.

Evidence today is clear that when fraud was committed in obtaining these certificates, the government did little or nothing about it. For example, in 1900 two federal commissioners found that many powers of attorney were signed without the forms being completed. In other cases, Métis who anticipated receiving scrip were asked to sign power of attorney to brokers hoping to make money out of scrip settlements (Purich, 1988). Other evidence shows that land owned by minors was not safeguarded and was lost to non-Aboriginal land speculators for much less than it was worth. It is clear that large-scale land transfer from Métis to land agents and banks took place. What has been problematic is how the government resolves these fraudulent transfers and their consequences (Pelletier, 1974, 1975).

The scrip claims being pursued today by the Métis centre on several charges: (1) that scrip was unjustly and inefficiently administered, (2) that the compensation was inadequate, (3) that Métis in British Columbia, Southern Alberta, and the Yukon received no compensation, and (4) that in certain areas most of the scrip issued was in the form of cash, not land (Hatt, 1983). Driben (1983) argues that since the government agreed to make scrip available to Métis in Western Canada as compensation, it was a *de facto* admission that they held Aboriginal title. Furthermore, he argues that the legal definition until just after Confederation did not distinguish between Métis and Indians; they were both considered "Aboriginal." Scrip takers and their descendants are now challenging the legality of the issuance of scrip to many people, which forced them to lose their Indian status and treaty rights. Giokas and Chartrand (2002) note that court cases filed focus on "Canada's breach of their treaty rights as well as instances of duress, undue influence, fraud, bribery, and *non-es factum*" (p. 94). Finally, Driben points out that Métis were, on occasion, included in the treaties, and he cites Treaty No. 3 as an example. Indeed, a Supreme Court landmark decision of September 19, 2003, finally recognized Métis peoples as Aboriginal peoples under the Canadian Constitution, granting them status on par with Native Indians and Inuit (see Box 7.2).

TREATIES TODAY

Are treaties signed years ago still valid? Canadians woke up on September 17, 1999, to find they are indeed. A Supreme Court decision (the Marshall decision) on that day upheld a 240-year-old treaty between the King of England and the Mi'kmaq Indians. The Supreme Court ruled that the treaty gave Mi'kmaq the right to fish for daily needs and/or to obtain a moderate livelihood, including food, clothing, and housing, supplemented by a few amenities. This decision has forced the federal government to reassess its position on the over 800 outstanding treaty cases now before the department of Indian Affairs (as of November 2006). The impact of this decision is far reaching, and Aboriginal people on the West Coast have argued that they also have fishing and hunting rights under the 150-year-old Douglas Treaty. Russel Barsh has noted that the high court's ruling includes a "way of life" provision that will have a dramatic effect on provincial hunting and fishing regulations in Canada. For example, he noted that members of Treaty 7 could hunt legally in the national parks and on unoccupied Crown land.

Box 7.2	Métis Win Landmark Ruling

Supreme Court decision grants status on par with native Indians and Inuit

By Kirk Makin

The Métis people are a distinct aboriginal group with a constitutional right to hunt for food, the Supreme Court of Canada said in a landmark ruling yesterday.

The unanimous judgment vaulted the approximately 300,000 Métis across the country from their lowly station in Canadian constitutional limbo to a rank that equates them with native Indians and Inuit.

If their overtures are rejected, the Métis would be in a position to return to court clutching the court's powerful ruling as ammunition.

A jubilant roar filled the Supreme Court's vast marble lobby as the ruling was released. Dozens of Métis people wearing colourful traditional sashes hugged and wept. The decision caps a 130-year battle dating back to the rebellions led by Louis Riel.

The court's judgment stressed that the existence in the Constitution of the Métis—of mixed native and European descent—"protects practices that were historically important features of these distinctive communities, and that persist in the present day as integral elements of their Métis culture."

Highlights of the Supreme Court ruling on the Métis:

- The development of a more systematic method of identifying Métis rights-holders for the purpose of enforcing hunting regulations is an urgent priority.
- In addition to demographic evidence, proof of shared customs, traditions and a collective identity is required to demonstrate the existence of a Métis community that can support a claim to site-specific aboriginal rights.
- As Métis communities continue to organize themselves more formally and to assert their constitutional rights, it is imperative that membership requirements become more standardized so that legitimate rights-holders can be identified.

Source: Excerpted from *The Globe and Mail*, September 20, 2003, pp. A1, A4. Reprinted with permission from the *Globe and Mail*.

As a result of the treaties, the government of Canada received millions of acres of land from the surrender of First Nations while, in return, 0.32 percent of Canada's land mass was set aside for reserves. Many irregularities emerged in the allocation of this land and, in many cases, treaty land entitlements could be claimed. While these entitlements are complex and complicated, they are legal obligations recognized in the Constitution that must be dealt with by the government of Canada. The term *treaty land entitlement* is used to document land claims that flow from Treaty Nos. 1 through 11. There are two forms. The first is called initial or "late" entitlement, which reflects the fact that the First Nations did not receive the land promised under the treaty. The second is a shortfall, which refers to the situation in which a calculation for the amount of land to be set aside did not include all the eligible population. To resolve these *specific claims* requires considerable time and money to ensure that all factors are taken into consideration when evaluating the claim.

One of the major recommendations presented by the Royal Commission on Aboriginal Peoples (Canada, 1996d) was that the federal government develop a trilateral relationship with regard to establishing new treaties. These new treaties would establish integrated processes on a regional level to deal with governance and jurisdictional issues. This recommendation has been accepted and is now in force in several provinces. With a new federal policy emphasizing a renewed partnership with Aboriginal peoples and an agreement that land claims need to be settled, it comes as no surprise that considerable activity has focused on land and land compensation. British Columbia is by far the most active in establishing new treaties and, by 2003, 51 Aboriginal groups, representing over 70 percent of B.C.'s First Nations, were active in treaty negotiation through the tripartite lands commission. Setting the stage, the province established a Treaty Negotiation Advisory Committee in 1996 to provide input and advice to the government with regard to establishing treaties in the province and settling outstanding claims by Aboriginal peoples. Progress is equally dramatic in other jurisdictions, as shown by the example of the Tlicho final agreement (August 25, 2003), which effectively replaces the 82-year-old Treaty No. 11 from the Northwest Territories (see Box 7.3).

By far one of the most important settlements that has taken place over the past five years is the 2000 Nisga'a Treaty. This treaty is the first British Columbia treaty since 1899 and is the 14th modern-day treaty in Canada. This settlement was approved amid considerable

---

Box 7.3	N.W.T. Natives Granted Control of 39 000 sq. km

PM signs land claim the size of Belgium

By Nathan Vanderklippe

About 3000 aborginal residents of the Northwest Territories entered a new era of self-determination yesterday as federal, territorial and aboriginal leaders signed the Tlicho [Dogrib] final agreement....

The Tlicho final agreement creates the first aboriginal government in the N.W.T. It gives the Tlicho $152-million over 15 years, year-round hunting and fishing rights and control over 39 000 square kilometres....

Negotiations on the Tlicho final agreement began in 1992, 17 years after the N.W.T. Indian Brotherhood issued a controversial statement saying that the government of the Northwest Territories was not the government of the Dene.

The new agreement creates two new land and water management boards, giving the Tlicho regulatory authority over their land. It also gives the Tlicho the ability to assess royalties on any mining or oil and gas activity within the newly created region....

The Treaty 11 Council has already developed an extensive network of band-owned companies that build roads and houses, operate an airport, run a sporting-goods store, haul diamond ore, fight forest fires and match southern companies with northern workers.

The agreement leaves administration of key programs such as health care and education with the territorial government for the next 10 years, while the Tlicho prepare to run programs.

political controversy and over 500 public events and consultations have taken place in the negotiations between the Nisga'a and the provincial Treaty Negotiation Advisory Committee, composed of 31 individuals representing various third-party interests. The treaty has been accepted by the Nisga'a council and the B.C. legislature. Once parliament ratifies the treaty, it cannot be amended by parliament according to the provisions of the treaty itself.

The Nisga'a treaty took 111 years to be settled and represents a milestone in treaty settlements in British Columbia. It will also give the Nisga'a a central government with the authority to make laws concerning social services (including child and family issues), adoption and health services, as well as tribal jurisdiction over education. While laws can be established by the Nisga'a, they must be in agreement with the existing provincial and federal statutes. Laws established by the Nisga'a will have standing in any court dispute. In addition, the Nisga'a will administer and deliver federal and provincial social services. How this will take place will be agreed to by both the provincial and federal governments. Under the treaty, the Nisga'a will continue to provide the services they have been taking over and will then have full jurisdiction over them. These services will be funded through a federal transfer of funds. However, as soon as the Nisga'a begin to generate their own income, perhaps through taxation, the transfer funds will be reduced commensurately. On the face of it, the treaty seems to give the Nisga'a municipal status. However, the fact that they will be in control of their social services, health, and education makes their system different from a mere municipal structure. For example, the treaty notes (Section 27) that, in the event of an inconsistency between the Nisga'a laws and federal and provincial laws of general application, Nisga'a law will prevail. Finally, the treaty stipulates that voting rights on Native territory will be restricted to people of Nisga'a descent.

Several criticisms of the treaty have been identified. First of all, critics claim that the treaty is "race based" and thus it gives the Nisga'a rights that other "races" do not have. A closer look at the treaty characterizes the Nisga'a as a linguistically and culturally identified group, not a race. Others claim that the treaty is an example of modern day apartheid. As Foster (1998–99) points out, there is something hypocritical about stripping a people of their resources in one generation and then describing a complex and careful attempt by the next generation to restore some of those resources as "apartheid" or as a violation of equality before the law. A second criticism is that the government "gave it all away." In truth, the Nisga'a will only be getting about 10 percent of the land they are able to demonstrate as their traditional territories. In British Columbia, Indian reserves make up about 0.35 percent of the province and the treaty will add little to this figure. Surely this cannot be viewed as an exorbitant land settlement. Other critics claim that the treaty amends the Constitution because it requires a referendum by both the provincial legislature and the federal House of Commons. On the contrary, the treaty does not amend the Constitution but rather ensures that both levels of government confirm the treaty and take it seriously (section 25 of the Charter of Rights and Freedoms, and section 35 of the Canadian Constitution). Finally, it is argued that it is not prudent for Canada and British Columbia to sign a final agreement with the Nisga'a when it is still not clear whether or not the 1997 *Delgamuukw* decision has given the Nisga'a more or fewer rights than the Nisga'a will get in the agreement. According to federal and provincial authorities, they, along with the Nisga'a, reviewed the decision before deciding to carry on negotiations and they have agreed that the treaty is a final settlement of the Nisga'a land claims. Behind these criticisms, one suspects that the real reason for objecting to the Nisga'a treaty is that it sets a "benchmark" for all others now being negotiated. No Aboriginal negotiator will take less than the Nisga'a, and that might be a real problem—or one that simply leads to unrealistic expectations. Whichever the case, the treaty has definite implications for future negotiations (Gibson, 1998–99).

In addition to non-Aboriginal people criticizing the treaty, other Aboriginal groups have raised questions (Sterritt, 1998–99). They argue that the Nisga'a do not have a claim to the entire Nass watershed (based upon the critics' own evidence) and thus the treaty violates the rights of other nearby Aboriginal groups. They go on to point out that the failure of the provincial and federal governments' response to the claims made by the Gitksan and Gitanyow submissions has serious consequences for their "overlapping" claims (Rotman, 1997).

SUMMARY

Indian treaty activity in Canada began with the Maritime "Peace and Friendship" agreements during colonial struggles, in which the principals agreed to aid each other in conflict or to remain neutral. There was no mention of land title, and, invariably, the Indian people were assured that they would not be disturbed in their traditional pursuits (hunting, fishing, and trapping). Between 1725 and 1779 there were as many as eight agreements of this type; the Mi'kmaq treaties of 1760–61 are examples which have become the basis for modern-day treaty interpretations and negotiations.

The most significant date in Canadian Indian treaty matters is October 7, 1763, when, by *Royal Proclamation*, the British sovereign directed that all endeavours to clear the Indian title must be by Crown purchase. In practice, the proclamation applied to lands then west of the settled areas, "Old" Quebec and the Maritimes having been passed over as if they had been adequately dealt with. The influx of settlers was accelerated by the American Revolutionary War (1775–83) and then by the War of 1812; hence, the half-century between 1775 and 1825 witnessed a comprehensive land surrender scheme to extinguish Indian title, involving most of what is now southern Ontario. Compensation to the Indian groups deemed to be *in situ* was sometimes in cash, sometimes in goods. The land so cleared or ceded was considered freed of all encumbrance, with plenty of room for Indians and non-Indians alike.

Thereafter, the exigencies of Canada's growth westward and northward dictated the pace and direction of treaty activity. The discovery of minerals north of Lakes Superior and Huron precipitated the negotiation of the Robinson Treaties in 1850 with the Ojibwa. Plans to settle the region of the Fertile Belt in the prairies exerted similar pressures as the Indian peoples, and the Crown in right of Canada signed Treaties Nos. 1 through 7 between 1871 and 1877. Subsequent treaty activity continued ad hoc—the discovery of gold at the Klondike River (1897) led to Treaty No. 8 in 1899, thus clearing the access route from Edmonton to the Pelly River; plans for construction of roads and railways precipitated the signing of Treaty No. 9 in 1905; Treaty No. 10 in 1906 immediately followed the attainment of provincial status for Saskatchewan and Alberta; the discovery of oil at Norman Wells in 1920 preceded Treaty No. 11 by one year.

The commissioners saw the treaties in one way; the Indians in quite another. A reading of the reports of the commissioners and of Lieutenant-Governor Morris's book (1880, 1971) shows that the two groups came together with radically different expectations. The Indians sought to be protected from land-grabbing settlers and from the evils they sensed. Buffalo herds were diminishing—the railway was projected; they sought wide ranges that they could call their own and over which they could live much as they had in the past. The commissioners saw Indian reserves as places where Indians could learn to be settlers and farmers. Some Indian spokesmen appeared to accept the idea of farming, but it is unlikely that they fully understood all that was entailed (Maybury-Lewis, 1997).

There has been little treaty activity in Canada since the 1923 Chippewa and Mississauga Agreements in Ontario (agreements that involved compensation for surrender of Indian hunting, fishing, and trapping rights).

In the 1970s, loss of "traditional livelihood" through hydroelectric power development (James Bay) and oil-producing schemes (northern pipelines) precipitated a strong dialogue between Aboriginal groups and government. By combining a higher degree of research with consultation and negotiations on both sides, compensatory agreements have been or are being worked out in many non-treaty areas of Canada. In those areas already covered by treaties, the federal government has stated that it will honour its "lawful obligations"; to this effect it has provided research funding for Aboriginal bands and organizations in order to investigate claims or grievances relating to the fulfilment or interpretation of Indian treaties.

Box 7.4 | Native Group to Give Ottawa Failing Grade for Treaties

Royal Commission's recommendations still being ignored 10 years later, AFN says

By Bill Curry

Native leaders will mark the 10th anniversary of the Royal Commission on Aboriginal Peoples today, with the release of a report card that shows Ottawa has failed to act on the vast majority of its recommendations.

The Assembly of First Nations gives Ottawa an F in all areas dealing with the respect of treaties, which the commission argues are key to giving natives enough power and land to lift most out of poverty . . .

The main recommendations called for a royal proclamation affirming aboriginal and treaty rights, and the regrouping of natives as self-governing nations that would manage a larger land base.

Phil Fontaine, the national chief of the AFN, will play host at a reception this evening marking the anniversary at the Museum of Civilization in Gatineau . . . After 10 years of federal inaction on the commission's recommendations, Mr. Fontaine will argue that it is now a key moment for the country. "Canada is at a crossroads between the path of cooperation and conflict," the text of his speech states. "We can move forward or we can move backward."

Indian Affairs Minister Jim Prentice seized on the AFN's report card yesterday . . . "Frankly, I agree with the AFN, the Auditor-General and virtually every other independent commentator who has remarked on the terrible Liberal F for their failure and their disgraceful, shameful abandonment of Aboriginal Canadians," he said.

Source: Excerpted from *The Globe and Mail*, November 22, 2006, pp. A6. Reprinted with permission from *The Globe and Mail*.

Aboriginal people see more advantages than disadvantages in the treaty process, and consider it the preferred manner in which to handle future negotiated settlements—if only the government of Canada would live up to its promises and agreements (see Box 7.4).

The disadvantages of the treaty process stem from issues of interpretation that have often led to disagreements between the two parties. When trying to resolve treaty issues, governments have insisted on looking only at the written documentation, not often reflecting on the oral arrangements that led up to and included the written document. On the other hand, when the courts have been asked to render an interpretation, the more recent cases (but not all) have favoured the Indian position. This has raised some concerns about using treaties as the strategy for resolving land/treaty claims for Aboriginal groups (Perry, 1996).

Aboriginal people feel that the terms set out in each treaty need to be fulfilled and dealt with immediately. They also feel that there must be reconciliation between the spirit and intent of the treaties and the rights of Canadians as a whole.

KEY TERMS

Peace and Friendship
   treaties
Royal Proclamation
   of 1763

post-Confederation treaties
the numbered treaties
fiduciary doctrine

Métis scrip
treaty land entitlement
specific claims

STUDY QUESTIONS

1. What did pre-Confederation treaties attempt to accomplish?
2. Explain the importance of the Jay Treaty of 1796.
3. Discuss the significance of the *Royal Proclamation* of 1763.
4. How can treaties be interpreted and what role has the Supreme Court of Canada represented within these interpretations?
5. What is *scrip* and how does it differ from a *treaty*?
6. Discuss the four foci of scrip claims.
7. Define and discuss the term "treaty land entitlement."
8. Discuss the significance of the Nisga'a Treaty of 2000.

WEBLINKS

www.bloorstreet.com/200block/brintro.htm

"A Brief Introduction into Aboriginal Law in Canada," by Bill Henderson, is an ideal point of departure for learning about various historical treaties between Aboriginal peoples and European-settler governments.

www.bloorstreet.com/200block/rp1763.htm

The *Royal Proclamation* of 1763 is reproduced in full, with an annotation giving some context and interpretive assistance. The treaty is known as the "Magna Carta of Indian Rights."

www.inac.gc.ca

This link is to the Indian and Northern Affairs site, which provides current highlights, access to regional offices, programs and services, publications and research, and important internal links to news releases and information on Aboriginal status and treaties. A related site is

www.inac.gc.ca/bc/ftno

which is the Federal Treaty Negotiation Office; this site provides information on progress in treaty negotiations, FAQs, and links to many treaty-related sites across Canada.

NOTES

1. Portions of this chapter are from *Indian Claims in Canada and Indian Treaties in Historical Perspective* (Ottawa: Minister of Supply and Services, 1981). Permission has been received from the Minister of Supply and Services Canada to reproduce the material.

2. Pontiac was an early leader of a Nativistic movement directed against the intrusion of missionaries into the area. He was also a firm believer in uniting Indian tribes and had led several successful engagements against the English, including such unorthodox Indian war strategies as laying siege to Fort Detroit.

3. In 1981, the Ontario Supreme Court decided that Aboriginal peoples who have treaty rights can legally hunt and fish out of season on Crown land in eastern Ontario. The decision, involving the 1818 treaty with the Mississauga Indians, was partially based upon oral records of the day. The decision states that the minutes of a council meeting between the deputy superintendent of Indian Affairs and the Indians in 1818 recorded the oral portion of the 1818 treaty and are as much a part of the treaty as the written articles of the provincial agreement.

4. The increased allotment of 640 acres (260 hectares) in Treaty No. 3 became standard for all future treaties except for Treaty No. 5, which reverted to the 160-acre (65 hectares) allotment. Other changes that became standard included assurances of continued hunting, fishing, and trapping rights, an annual budget for ammunitions, and the provision of agricultural supplies, such as cattle, seed, and farm implements.

5. Over time the specific words were changed, but the overall structure and legal effect remained the same.

chapter eight

Contesting Title and Ownership: The Modern Claims and Treaty Process

INTRODUCTION

Aboriginal land claims today involve much more than legal questions about the collective title and property rights of Aboriginal peoples. They are also not simply concerned with determining an appropriate amount of financial compensation (Moss and Niemczak, 1991). Land claims are a balance between negotiation and litigation, between government action and inaction, as well as being subject to passive and active resistance by both Aboriginal people and governments (Hodgins, Heard and Milloy, 1992). They are perhaps the most sensitive and socially volatile issues now confronting Aboriginal peoples and governments (Mallea, 1994).

In the 19th century, Aboriginal land fuelled Canadian and American economic growth. However, dispossession had an opposite effect on the Indian nations. It contributed to their underdevelopment to the extent that Aboriginal peoples were unable to sustain themselves. Within a century this process had destroyed the Aboriginal economic base, wherever their societies were. In addition, the land base was unequally distributed: the most fertile land was taken for European settlers, control over water went to the government, and the environment was altered to the disadvantage of Aboriginal people. As Cornell (1988) points out, they struggled to adapt, but their economies were falling apart and they had no way of entering the new emerging capitalist structure. The result was the spiralling towards economic marginalization and dependency. Today many Aboriginals remain among the most marginalized and poorest communities, discriminated against and often exposed to grave abuses of their fundamental rights. While the Canadian government has publicly stated that it wants to make indigenous rights a reality (despite its actions and, just as frequently, its failure to act) the results have not changed First Nations' status in over a century. This lack of commitment is most clearly demonstrated by the way government has been dragging its feet with regard to land claims. Large-scale projects for the construction of infrastructure or the extraction of natural resources on indigenous lands have been, until the late 20th century, pursued without consultation or thought as to how they will impact the lives and health of Aboriginal people.

The reactive stance that Aboriginal people have typically adopted can be seen in a variety of institutional settings—religious, economic and educational. Often, the inability to coordinate their actions, the lack of funding, and the lack of understanding of the political process have led to this failure to control the agenda when dealing with the federal/provincial governments. The emergence of various factions within the Aboriginal community has also hindered their planning and political strategies. Attempts to establish any sense of community and/or compromise amongst Aboriginal groups have been lacking—a situation ostensibly at odds with the traditional Aboriginal "consensus" model of decision-making.

This lack of consensus has been exploited by agencies and organizations dealing with Aboriginal people. It has allowed them to act in any way they wanted to, justifying their actions through the inability of Aboriginal people to agree. However, conditions have changed over the past several decades and Aboriginal people are beginning to act in a concerted and proactive manner. They have come to realize that, if they do not, decisions will be enacted that will seal the fate of Aboriginals as peoples relegated to a marginal position in the political economy of Canada (Cultural Survival Quarterly, n.d.).

Aboriginal people have begun to think in proactive terms, not constrained by existing bureaucratic rules in their dealings with provincial and federal governments. However, over a century of control and marginalization has had its impact; a dependency mentality has been created, and it is this sense of limited capacity to act, or lack of agency, that must be overcome. They are also prioritizing the goals that they are prepared to pursue. Boundaries are being established in order to determine when and how they will take action. Agendas are being clearly spelled out, and strategies planned. Community divisiveness is being dealt with and ranks are being closed to ensure a unified response to government. Finally, fiscal issues are being considered as only one component in a highly complex matrix of decision-making. If decisions are always based on financial considerations, then the process of consultation and negotiation is reduced to economic choices, a substantial handicap for any group trying to advance its agenda (Sanders, 1983a, 1983b).

One issue about which Aboriginal people have become more proactive is their concern over land. They have, after many years, realized that they can successfully pursue land claims even though results are not easily achieved. The early, disappointing outcome of their land claims slowed their initiatives. However, as they have become more skilled at legal confrontation, their successes have increased. They have also more fully appreciated the connectedness of land and their culture. As Altman and Nieuwenhuysen (1979) point out, the special relationship that Aboriginal people have with the land seems best described by the word "spiritual." Having fully reclaimed this perspective, Aboriginal people have now taken on the challenge of reclaiming land that they feel rightly belongs to them. As Mallea (1994) and Isaac (1995) have pointed out, the law on this subject has developed rapidly, and concepts and precedents have even travelled across international borders.

EARLY LAND CONFLICTS

Aboriginal peoples of Canada have come under European influence in various ways, to differing degrees and at different historical periods. For example, little impact was made on Aboriginal peoples in the Arctic until this century, and most of that has occurred since World War II. On the other hand, the Indians of the Atlantic coast and along the shores of the St. Lawrence River encountered Europeans early in the 16th century. As a result of this contact, the Beothuk of Newfoundland became extinct. Overall, Aboriginal people in the more southerly parts of the country have, since contact, moved toward a Euro-Canadian way of life, while in northern areas more continuity has been preserved with traditional patterns of living. However, nowhere has Aboriginal life been entirely unaffected by the advent of the European settlers and their domination of territory that was once the exclusive domain of Aboriginal peoples (DIAND, 1978, 1981.

Early relationships between Aboriginal peoples and Europeans were both positive and destructive, sought after and rejected, rewarding and penalizing. However, for Aboriginal peoples, the positive outcomes of contact were outweighed by the negative consequences. The acquisition of metal tools allowed them to hunt and gather in a more efficient manner, which probably improved the quality of their lives. However, at the same time, this acceptance of "modern" technology meant the destruction of their habitat, their way of life and eventually their ideology, that is, the belief system that structures their relationship with nature and the cosmos. On the other side, as Miller (2000) points out, Europeans benefited from the contact through profit and expansion; the fur trade was the most obvious advantage.

European–Aboriginal interaction has taken many forms. The fur trade significantly altered the way of life of much of the Indian population, economically, politically and socially. While the fur trade introduced European goods and commercial values, it also brought with it Western moral and religious persuasions. At the same time, social interaction brought into being people of mixed ancestry, known as the Métis people. The later occupation of land for settlement was further instrumental in modifying the economic and socio-cultural bases of Aboriginal societies. Resource exploitation in almost every part of the country also disturbed the lives of Aboriginal peoples both directly and indirectly through its environmental effects. Such activity continues today, with similarly disruptive results.

From an early period, the government of the colonizing society made itself specifically responsible for the relationship between the immigrants and the Aboriginal people. In law, the Aboriginal interest in land and other natural resources could not be acquired directly by the newcomers, but only through the agency of their government. In addition, the government assumed much of the direction of Aboriginal societies, particularly those whose traditional way of life was most disrupted. The historical relationship of the government to Aboriginal groups accounts for Aboriginal insistence on their continuing special status as the original people of Canada (Shewell, 2004). As a result, the federal government has become the target of Aboriginal grievances in regard to land, natural resources and the management of Aboriginal affairs. These claims are based on Aboriginal rights or on agreements made with the government that were based on the Indians' position as unconquered indigenous occupants of the land.

TYPES OF CLAIMS

There are three general categories of claims: *Aboriginal rights* (which includes "title" and self-government), *treaty and scrip settlement grievances*, and *land claims*. Chapter 7 has already focused specifically on treaty and scrip issues (also called specific claims), so this chapter will deal with Aboriginal rights and land claims (also called comprehensive claims). Chapter 9 will deal with self-determination and self-government.

The notion of Aboriginal rights is the prime rationale underlying all Aboriginal claims in Canada. Aboriginal people assert that their rights to land derive from their original occupancy, and they point out that Aboriginal title has been recognized by the dominant society through numerous judicial decrees and actions of the government going back to the *Royal Proclamation* of 1763. It is important to note that no treaties were ever made for about half the territory in Canada where Aboriginal people surrendered their lands. On this basis alone, both status and non-status Indians, as well as Inuit, are now developing or negotiating treaty terms.

Treaty Indians have a number of claims that relate to the agreement for the cession of their lands. Some of these rest on an insistence that specific treaty terms have not been fulfilled, or that the broader spirit of the treaties has not been acknowledged by the government. A frequent claim is that verbal promises made at the time of the negotiations were not included in the written texts. In some areas, Indian people also emphasize in their treaty claims that these transactions constituted inadequate settlements, even if all their terms were fulfilled (for example, treaty land/reserve entitlement claims, noted in Chapter 7). These claims involve assertions about the way in which treaties were negotiated, the disparities between the two contracting parties, and the alleged unfairness of the terms.

Most status (or registered) Indians have rights to reserve lands held in common for their band. Most bands, whether in treaty or non-treaty areas, usually have specific claims to make. The most numerous and widespread are those stemming from reserve land losses. Reserve land was sometimes lost through squatting by non-Aboriginal people, or through error, or by being re-surveyed. Most typically it was lost as a result of formal surrenders to, and expropriations by, the federal or provincial governments. Claims may be based on the dubious legality of these occurrences or on the propriety of certain methods of land alienation. Claims based on such land (reserve) losses are sometimes called "surrender claims," involving either a technical breach (of the *Indian Act*), or a fiduciary breach in the case of a surrender that was not in the First Nation's best interests (Indian Claims Commission, 2005). Management of band funds, reserve resources and the administration of band affairs, particularly with regard to economic development, are also the bases of band claims.

Land is an extremely important element in Aboriginal claims in general. As mentioned above, Aboriginal peoples are becoming more articulate about their unique relationship to the land, both past and present, and about the meaning it has for them. They are also aware that the material standard of living that has been achieved generally in Canada derives ultimately from the land and its resources. As a consequence, they seek not only a role in determining the way in which the land and other resources are used, but also an equitable portion of the substantial benefits derived from their exploitation. This theme is basic in Aboriginal rights claims, but it also appears in treaty claims where the original land agreements may be in question, and in band claims concerning lost reserve land or other natural resources.

For the Aboriginal people, *trusteeship,* a fundamental element in their claims, involves both protection and assistance. When the federal government assumed political control over Aboriginal people it undertook responsibilities for reserve land and band finances, and it imposed special limitations on Indians as a feature of Indian status. It adopted a protective role over Indians and their affairs analogous to that of the duty of a guardian or trustee toward a ward or beneficiary (Rotman 1996). From this *fiduciary relationship* (or duty) flow grievances and claims that pertain to the government's management of Indian resources (DIAND, 1982a, 1985).

ABORIGINAL-GOVERNMENT RELATIONS

Canadian jurisprudence has taken the position that Canada was acquired by discovery or settlement (Bartlett, 1984) and, although the concept of "existing Aboriginal rights" (from which it is assumed that Aboriginal title flows) is now entrenched in the Canadian Constitution (see Sections 25 and 35), it is unclear what the words "existing Aboriginal rights" actually mean (W. Henderson, 1983; Sanders, 1985b, 1990).

One of the first legal rulings on the issue of Aboriginal title was handed down in 1885 (*St. Catharines Milling and Lumber Company* v. *The Queen*). This ruling characterized Aboriginal title as a possessory right, a right to use and occupancy similar to a usufructuary right, that is, a right based on *traditional* use and occupancy (R. Thompson, 1982). The Privy Council in 1888 changed this interpretation slightly when it characterized Aboriginal title as a personal usufructuary right, dependent upon the goodwill of the sovereign. It would not be until nearly a century later, when in 1973 the *Calder et al.* v. *Attorney General of British Columbia* case came before the Supreme Court of Canada, that the basis of this right was re-examined. Even though the Nisga'a Indians did not win this case, three of the seven Supreme Court justices ruled that Aboriginal title did exist in common law irrespective of any formal recognition—that is, independent of the *Royal Proclamation* of 1763. These justices argued that once Aboriginal title has been established it is presumed to continue until the contrary is proven (making it an inherent right), and that the onus is upon the government to prove that it intended to extinguish Indian title through various legislation ordinances. Since no specific legislation was enacted that provided for Indian title to be extinguished, these judges concluded that the Indians may indeed still be in possession of Aboriginal title.

Prior to the Nisga'a case, the federal government held that Aboriginal land rights were so general and undefined that it was not realistic to view them as claims capable of remedy through law. However, after the Calder case the government announced a change in its policy with regard to legal obligations to legitimate claims being pursued by Indians. The government indicated that it was willing to negotiate settlements with Native groups where Native rights based upon usufruct had not been explicitly extinguished by treaty or otherwise superseded by law (Bankes, 1983; Asch, 1993).

Other writers, such as Driben (1983), Cumming and Mickenberg (1972), T. Clark (1994), and Asch (1993, 1997) have gone beyond the Supreme Court's ruling and have suggested that Aboriginal interest rests on a solid legal foundation. They point to the *Royal Proclamation* of 1763, which pledged, in a legal context, that Aboriginal title would be respected. The surrender or extinguishment of title could only take place if Indians approved of the action at a public meeting with public officials. When the surrender took place, it could only be to the Crown. Today, according to the courts, Aboriginal rights are vested in Native people by virtue of both the *Royal Proclamation* of 1763 and by the fact that they were the sovereign inhabitants in Canada before the land was considered French or English property (Indian Claims Commission, 1975).

Land Claims Before 1969

The modern Specific Claims process traces its roots to 1947, when the federal government struck a special joint committee of the House and Senate to investigate matters relating to Indian Affairs. This committee operated for one year and heard presentations from Aboriginals across the country. The committee recommended the creation of an independent administrative tribunal to adjudicate claims, but this did not come to pass. Ten years later another joint committee was created. It made the same recommendation as the previous committee but, as before, nothing came of the recommendation (Prentice and Bellegarde, 2001). Similar recommendations were made for the next 20 years, but a "lack of political will" was demonstrated in that no such tribunal was ever established. As such, prior to the establishment of the Indian lands commissioner (1969) and the Office of Aboriginal Claims (1974), Indian claims were handled on an individual basis. The processing of a claim was dealt with either by the Department of Indian Affairs and Northern Development or by the Department of Justice. There was a dual filing system utilized by DIAND through which all claims were sorted. One was labelled "petitions and complaints," the other "claims and disputes." The former label was interpreted by government officials as representing grievances and as such did not require any legal action on their part. However, the claims in the latter file were interpreted as legitimate and thus required the department to respond (Daniel, 1980; Wright, 1995).

By 1969, the federal government decided to take a different course and it offered its infamous white paper to deal with such thorny issues as land claims, Aboriginal rights, and other disputes between Aboriginal and non-Aboriginal peoples. This, of course, would have solved the issue of Indian claims in that Indians would have, in a legal sense, no basis upon which to bring claims forward (McNab, 1999).

As Daniel (1980) points out, the 1969 white paper on Indian policies was vigorously repudiated by Indian leaders. They were joined in their opposition by a number of non-Indian social and political organizations, and the policy soon became the *bête noire* of government–Indian relations. However, one recommendation of the white paper was for the appointment of an Indian claims commissioner. In late 1969 Dr. Lloyd Barber was appointed Canada's first and only Indian claims commissioner, a position he would hold until 1977 when the office was terminated. The commissioner's mandate was to receive and study grievances and to recommend measures to adjudicate any claims. He himself did not have powers of adjudication since his role was only advisory. Nevertheless, he played an important role in educating government officials and the public at large (Morse, 1991). The Indian Claims Commission and the Indian claims commissioner's office had divergent aims, and this was partially a result of the government's insistence that Indians had no legal basis on which to make claims. The creation of the commissioner's office was an interim structure developed by the government that was meant to be phased out once a new policy could be drafted (Sanders, 1983c, 1985a).

The government also established funding programs to help defray the costs to Aboriginal groups of researching and presenting their claims. Funds were provided by the Privy Council from 1970 to 1973, by the Indian claims commissioner from 1972 to 1973, and mainly by the Rights and Treaty Research Program (DIAND) from 1972 to 1976. In 1974 the federal government created the Office of Native Claims (within DIAND) to deal with specific grievances. While the Indian claims commissioner and the Office of Native Claims (ONC) overlapped between 1974 and 1977, their roles were very different. The Indian claims commission was established to receive and study grievances presented by Indians as well as to suggest the process by which particular claims could be adjudicated. On the other hand, the Office of Native Claims accepted the legitimacy of Aboriginal land rights. Its function therefore was to coordinate federal negotiations regarding claims that Indians presented to the federal government.

GOVERNMENT LAND NEGOTIATIONS

Since Confederation, the Canadian government has shown a reluctance to negotiate with Aboriginal people over land issues. Each time the federal government has developed a land claims policy, Aboriginal people have denounced the content. As Mallea (1994) points out, on the whole, Aboriginal people have found negotiating with the government to be a frustrating exercise. In most cases the government itself has been viewed as an obstruction to achieving justice.

In approaching land claims, Aboriginal groups have been required by the courts to meet four conditions to establish proof of Aboriginal title. This is referred to as the "Baker Lake Test" (*Baker Lake* v. *Minister of Indian Affairs and Northern Development,* 1980) The requirements are:

1. that they and their ancestors were members of an organized society;

2. that the organized society occupied the specific territory over which they assert the Aboriginal title;

3. that the occupation was to the exclusion of other organized societies; and

4. that the occupation was an established fact at the time sovereignty was asserted by England.

In 1990 the Supreme Court of Canada, in a landmark decision, set specific guidelines for determining Aboriginal rights in general. This decision (*R.* v. *Sparrow* [1990]—see below) held that an Aboriginal right could be claimed even though it was not otherwise supported by a treaty. The court also ruled that existing Aboriginal rights should not be subject to Section 33 of the Charter (the "notwithstanding" clause) and the decision goes on to say that any proposed legislation negatively affecting Aboriginal people may only be enacted if it meets a strict legal test that justifies such an interference.

Sparrow and *Delgamuukw:* A Turning Point

Aboriginal land rights were given a serious blow in the *Delgamuukw* v. *British Columbia* (1991) case when the B.C. Supreme Court judge, Alan McEachern, ruled that the 8000 Gitksan and Wet'suwet'en British Columbian Indians do not hold Aboriginal rights to the land. He stated that the *Royal Proclamation* of 1763 has never applied to the province of British Columbia, and that Aboriginal interest in the land did not include ownership of or jurisdiction over the territory. He also ruled that pre-Confederation colonial laws, construed in their historical setting, show a clear intention to extinguish Aboriginal interests in order to give unburdened titles to the settlers, and that the Crown extinguised all Aboriginal rights implicitly (because no specific extinguishment act was passed) even before the province entered Confederation in 1871. Therefore, he argued, since Confederation the province has had title to the soil of the province and the right to dispose of Crown lands unburdened by Aboriginal title. However, the judge did acknowledge that the Indians could use vacant Crown land, but that this is not an exclusive right—their use of Crown land is subject to the general laws of the province.

The trial took more than four years, during which communities and forestry and mining companies fought the Aboriginal land claims. Their $1 billion investments were deemed at risk until the judgment was made. Uncharacteristically, the judgment ended with a stern lecture from the judge. He insisted that only political negotiations could solve the land issue, and questioned the focus on legal and constitutional matters such as ownership, sovereignty and rights. He also noted that the issues now facing Aboriginal people could not be solved by continuing the reserve system, which, he argued, had created "fishing footholds and ethnic enclaves." He concluded his judgment by arguing that enlarging the reserves is not in the best interest of anyone, and suggested that Indians must leave the reserve and enter the urban centres of Canada so that they can participate in the economic activities found there. The Gitksan-Wet'suwet'en nation appealed the decision and the case eventually went to the B.C. Court of Appeal.

Before discussing the appeal, it might prove instructive to discuss the Supreme Court's decision. First of all, the judge (McEachern) assessed Aboriginal society using a very ethnocentric perspective, e.g., since Aboriginal people did not use the wheel, have a written language, or use domesticated animals for food production, he claimed that they did not have an organized, integrated society. In fact, he argued that early Aboriginal life was "nasty, brutish and short." He concluded that "many of the badges of civilization, as we of European culture understand them, were indeed absent" (p. 31). In short, the judge introduced highly ethnocentric and biased perspectives about what constitutes "civilization" and/or "development" and concluded that, since Aboriginal people did not have many of the cultural artifacts of Europeans, they could only be considered "primitive."

The findings of McEachern were puzzling and without precedent. He rejected testimony from certain experts out of hand and without adequate justification, while allowing testimony from others. For example, he rejected testimony from anthropologists but accepted it from historians and linguists. Furthermore, there are well-accepted principles that the judge did not follow. For example, all testimony must be understood by the judge (since he/she must make a ruling); otherwise, the judge must simply accept the conclusions of the experts unless those are successfully challenged by information from other experts. Nevertheless, the transcripts of the trial show that the judge openly acknowledged that he did not understand the logic or the argument of certain witnesses, yet he accepted their conclusions unquestioningly, even when the illogical and uninterpretable arguments were questioned by others. The judge's insistence on seeing himself as a social scientist was without precedent. Much of the data presented to him by anthropologists were rejected with no good explanation. He then proceeded to develop his own biased and ethnocentric explanation about Aboriginal people, totally devoid of evidence or logic (Elliott, 1991).

The *Delgamuukw* Appeal

In 1993 an appeal of the *Delgamuukw* decision was heard by the British Columbia Court of Appeal. A majority of the judges agreed with the trial judge that certain Aboriginal rights were in force when British sovereignty was established. Moreover, the Appeal Court agreed that these rights were *not* ownership rights. However, it disagreed with McEachern in finding that the Aboriginal rights had not been extinguished, basing its decision on a test much less stringent than that adopted by the *Sparrow* court (see below).

This B.C. Court of Appeal decision modified the meaning of the *Sparrow* decision in that it redefined what it thought the Supreme Court meant when it delivered that judgment. There have been few comparable cases since the *Delgamuukw* appeal, so it is difficult to interpret the impact of this case. Subsequent well-known cases that have variously expanded upon *Sparrow,* mostly in favour of Aboriginal people, and that have served as important precedents for the final 1997 *Delgamuukw* Supreme Court of Canada decision (1997) include *R.* v. *VanDerPeet* (1996), *R.* v. *NTC Smokehouse* (1996), *R.* v. *Gladstone* (1996), and *R.* v. *Côté* (1996), among others.

In the *Guerin* v. *Regina* (1984) and *Sparrow* (1990) cases, the Supreme Court acknowledged and reinforced the fiduciary relationship between the Crown and Aboriginal people. These precedent-setting judgments forcefully noted that the government has a responsibility to act in a fiduciary capacity with respect to Aboriginal people. They went on to point out that the relationship between the government and Aboriginal people is trust-like rather than adversarial, and contemporary recognition and affirmation of Aboriginal rights, as reflected in the (1997) *Delgamuukw* decision, must continue to be defined in light of this historic relationship (see Box 8.1).

Beyond its fiduciary obligation toward Aboriginal people, the federal government is also required to guarantee the rights and freedoms found in the Charter. Actions by government toward Aboriginal people reveal that there are numerous violations of Aboriginal civil liberties. For example, the presentation by the Indigenous Bar Association to the Standing Committee on Aboriginal Affairs regarding the events of Kanesatake and Kahnawake during the summer of 1990 noted that the most serious violation of Aboriginal civil liberties was when the minister of Indian Affairs signed an agreement on preconditions to negotiations with Aboriginal peoples!

The pivotal *Sparrow* (1990) case in B.C. attracted the attention of all individuals interested in Aboriginal–non-Aboriginal affairs. The case involved an Indian who was fishing at the mouth of the Fraser River. In 1987, in what amounted to a sting operation, agents working on behalf of the Fisheries Department acted as individual Canadians who wanted to buy fish illegally from band members. While the "sting" resulted in 25 Indians being charged, none were convicted of illegally fishing. It was at this time that the Fisheries Department implemented another procedure to reduce the number of fish caught by Aboriginal people; i.e., they reduced the net depth from 38 to 25 fathoms so that the Indians would not catch as many fish.

After the new regulations were in place, Sparrow, an Indian fisherman, was caught fishing with a net over 25 fathoms and was subsequently charged under the new regulations. Even though historical data showed that Indians had fished this area since time immemorial, the provincial court found Sparrow guilty. The court ruled that Aboriginal rights had been extinguished at the beginning of the century. This was appealed to the county court, then to the Court of Appeal of British Columbia and eventually to the Supreme Court of Canada.

Box 8.1	*Delgamuukw*—"We Are All Here to Stay"

The claim by Gitksan and Wet'suwet'en was originally for "ownership" and "jurisdiction" over separate portions of 58 000 square kilometres of northern British Columbia. The following are some of the significant finds from the decision (Supreme Court of Canada, December 11, 1997):

- The court found that Aboriginal title is an exclusive communal interest or a right to the land itself, encompassing more than hunting and fishing rights.
- The court emphasized that Aboriginal title encompasses the right to choose what happens on traditional lands. First Nations can now expect to be included in decisions involving the allocation of such lands and resources.
- The court found that Aboriginal title can be held jointly by more than one First Nation—two or more First Nations may jointly hold title if their joint use of the land meets a test of exclusive possession (i.e., an ability to exclude others).
- The court sent a strong message to trial courts to be more open to evidence in the form of oral histories and other forms of traditional knowledge used in establishing First Nations' use and occupancy of their traditional territories.
- The province does not have the authority to extinguish Aboriginal title. Only the federal government has that power and authority.

- First Nations wishing to use lands under Aboriginal title in ways that conflict with that title must first surrender their title and convert the lands into non-title lands. Maintaining title requires that use of land and resources does not destroy the unique value of the land.

The court identified Aboriginal title at one end of the spectrum of Aboriginal Rights protected under Section 35(1) of the *Constitution Act*. At the other end are activities integral to their culture, as well as their right to engage in traditional activities such as hunting and fishing. The rights First Nations have over lands in their traditional territories will therefore vary from a right to the land itself to the right to use the land for traditional practices. With this decision, the Supreme Court of Canada sent a message that Aboriginal title requires a process of good faith negotiation and reconciliation between the Crown and First Nations. Aboriginal rights and title can no longer be ignored in the general economic development of the province. The resolution of this case and other outstanding issues and competing interests is, as the court suggested, best achieved by negotiation and not litigation. As the chief justice observed, "Let us face it, we are all here to stay."

The Supreme Court ruled that, while the provincial regulations were legal and forced Indians out of their fishing activities, the province could not extinguish Aboriginal rights through the application of provincial or federal regulations. The regulations would have to specifically (explicitly) state that Aboriginal rights were to be extinguished. Moreover, the Supreme Court ruling also stated that, in cases where regulations are ambiguous or vague, the interpretation would favour of Aboriginal people. This reasoning was upheld specifically in such similar cases as *Gladstone* (1996) and *NTC Smokehouse* (1996).

Comprehensive Claims

There are two major categories of claims now being pursued by Aboriginal peoples in Canada, as mentioned before. The first is referred to as comprehensive claims or Aboriginal title claims, while the second is called specific claims and will be discussed later. Progress in some jurisdictions has been significant, as examples in Chapter 7 show. In British Columbia, for example, these claims make up nearly 75 percent of the province.

These claims take two different forms which are, to some extent, regionally based. In the North, the claims focus on a demand for formal legal recognition of Aboriginal land title and all the rights that are derived from it. In the South, comprehensive claims place more emphasis on the cooperation between Aboriginal peoples and the government for the extinguishment of Aboriginal title and the restitution of specific rights—e.g., hunting and fishing rights (Canada, n.d.).

The map in Figure 8.1 identifies the major areas in Canada that are under comprehensive claims processing at the present time. As one can see, almost the entire Canadian North is claimed by Aboriginal groups, and various Aboriginal associations are actively pursuing their cases. Areas in the Arctic are being pursued by the Inuit, while the Métis and Indians in the Mackenzie Valley area of the Northwest Territories and in the Yukon have filed several claims.

Comprehensive claims are not negotiations about grievances related to the interpretation and the shortcomings of previous treaties. Rather, they are land claims that deal with areas of the country where various Aboriginal people continue to live and where treaties were never entered into (and where presumably Aboriginal title still exists and has not been extinguished or surrendered). An exception to this is the Dene/Métis claim in the Northwest Territories, where Treaty 8 encompasses some of the land but no reserves were ever established. The policy of establishing comprehensive land claims began in 1973, and has subsequently been revised and updated several times. As Harry Swain, then Deputy Minister of Indian Affairs, pointed out in 1988, comprehensive claims are a unique arrangement in which Aboriginal people can finally settle outstanding land issues.

The process is one through which Aboriginal groups agree to exchange their Aboriginal title over all or most of the land covered in return for land, money, certain rights and other conditions designed to protect and enhance their social, cultural and economic well-being.

The comprehensive land claims agreements that emerge from these negotiations are formal, legal and binding documents. Also known as modern-day treaties, they have to be ratified by the Aboriginal groups and communities concerned and by the federal government, and are then enacted into law by parliament. They now constitute a substantial body of law and have helped to redefine the relationship between the government of Canada and many of its Aboriginal citizens. Since 1982 these agreements have also been protected constitutionally; future agreements will also be protected.

The first of these landmark comprehensive land claims agreements was the James Bay and Northern Quebec Agreement, which was reached between the federal and provincial governments and the Cree and Inuit communities of Northern Quebec in 1975 (Niezen, 1998). This was followed by the Northeastern Quebec Agreement in 1978, and later by an agreement with the Inuvialuit of the Mackenzie Delta and the Beaufort Sea region in 1984.

By March 2002, 53 First Nations were participating in modern land claim negotiations. There were also 18 other comprehensive land claims taking place throughout Canada

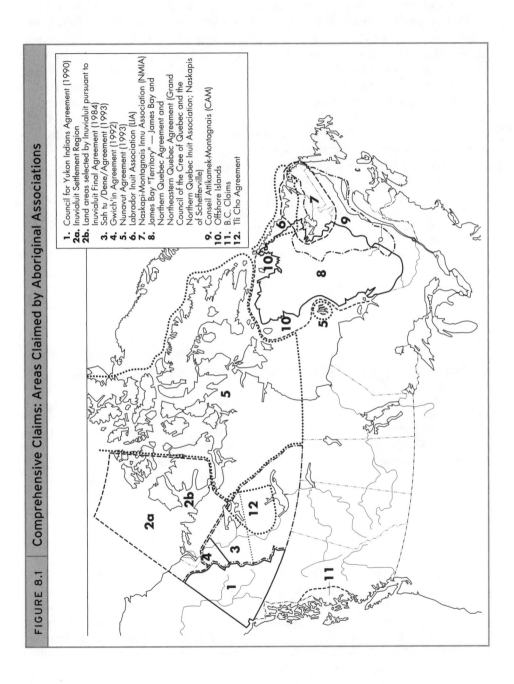

FIGURE 8.1   Comprehensive Claims: Areas Claimed by Aboriginal Associations

1. Council for Yukon Indians Agreement (1990)
2a. Inuvialuit Settlement Region
2b. Land areas selected by Inuvialuit pursuant to Inuvialuit Final Agreement (1984)
3. Sah tu /Dene/ Agreement (1993)
4. Gwich'in Agreement (1992)
5. Nunavut Agreement (1993)
6. Labrador Inuit Association (LIA)
7. Naskapi-Montagnais Innu Association (NMIA) James Bay "Territory" — James Bay and Northern Quebec Agreement and
8. Northeastern Quebec Agreement (Grand Council of the Cree of Quebec and the Northern Quebec Inuit Association; Naskapis of Schefferville)
9. Conseil Attikamek-Montagnais (CAM)
10. Offshore Islands
11. B.C. Claims
12. Tli Cho Agreement

involving 78 communities. Since the inception of the program (1973), 15 final land claim agreements had been completed (Indian and Northern Affairs Canada website, July 17, 2003); by 2006 several more important agreements were completed (see Box 8.2 for an example).

Each of these land claims is distinctive and has taken into consideration the unique conditions of history, geography, culture and economic circumstances that exist in the particular region and communities concerned. Still, there is a similar pattern to all of these claims—a pattern set initially in 1973 and reinforced in the government's revised comprehensive land claims policy of 1986. As a result, while there are individual differences, a considerable body of precedent has been established in the terms and conditions provided in these settlements.

When faced with the decision to cede, or surrender, in whole or in part, their Aboriginal title to certain areas, Aboriginal Canadians are naturally concerned that in return they receive benefits that will enable them to prosper and survive as distinct and definable groups. The most basic concern is of course for land. All the agreements are, at heart, land settlements. All designate specific lands that the claimant group will own outright, as well as land-related rights in areas where they have certain interests in perpetuity. But Aboriginal concerns go beyond mere ownership of land. Essentially they seek, through these agreements, terms and conditions that will allow them to:

- continue to maintain to the greatest degree possible their traditional lifestyle and culture;
- participate in the decision-making process regarding land and resource management within their claim area; and
- receive a fair share of the economic opportunities and economic benefits that may exist in the claim area.

Box 8.2   Maa-Nulth First Nations Sign Historic B.C. Land Treaty

After years of little progress and costly negotiations, five Vancouver Island First Nations signed a treaty Saturday worth almost $500 million, a treaty that includes more than 24000 hectares of land.

The Maa-nulth First Nations live on the west coast of Vancouver Island with some of the land bordering the scenic Pacific Rim Park near Tofino. Five Maa-nulth chiefs, B.C. Premier Gordon Campbell and federal Indian Affairs Minister Jim Prentice gathered Saturday for a ceremony in Victoria . . .

The deal must still be ratified by the 2,000 Maa-nulth people and the federal and B.C. governments. Once ratified and enacted as legislation, Prentice said

the treaty benefits both the province and First Nations . . .

The Maa-nulth are part of Vancouver Island's 14-member Nuu-chah-nulth Tribal Council, but the five bands decided to negotiate a treaty as a separate group . . . The financial component of the Maa-nulth treaty includes cash in lump sum and timed payments. The First Nations will receive $90 million in cash, up to $45 million over 25 years for potential revenue sharing projects, and $150 million over eight years for program financing. Estimates for the value of the treaty lands range between $100 million and $200 million.

As a result, these comprehensive claims agreements cover a range of issues besides land and basic compensation. The issues include surface and sub-surface resource provisions, guaranteed rights for wildlife harvesting and fishing, resource revenue sharing, participation in renewable resource management, and environmental protection measures. An excellent example of a modern-day treaty, or comprehensive claim, wherein these issues are paramount, is the 2000 Nisga'a Treaty (see pages 251–252). Six major issues are present in comprehensive claims resolved to date. They include:

- *Land:* All agreements confer on the beneficiaries' primary interest over extensive areas of land.
- *Cash:* In consideration for certainty of title over their settlement regions, all signed agreements provide significant financial compensation packages. These are considered payments in exchange for rights.
- *Wildlife:* Wildlife management and Aboriginal control over wildlife harvesting are usually negotiated. These are an important part of traditional Aboriginal lifestyles. The agreements in principle or sub-agreements also provide for harvesting rights, priorities, and privileges. For instance, some provide for the right to harvest all species up to the full level of economic, social, and cultural needs. And, if there are residual surpluses, Aboriginal organizations have harvesting priority. Should surpluses still exist, a limited entry system gives preference to local residents in the allocation of commercial licences. Various rights and privileges under these agreements include permit or tax exemptions; the right to sell, barter, exchange, and give freely the harvested wildlife; the right of first refusal for new hunting, fishing, and tourism lodges over settlement regions; and the right of first refusal for the marketing of wildlife, and wildlife parts and products.
- *Environmental protection:* All agreements have provisions for the protection of the environment and of the Aboriginal societies in the settlement areas; these provisions spell out the terms and conditions of any future development, and subject all developers to specific duties and responsibilities. For instance, before approval of a project, a developer may be required to conduct prior consultation with local communities, offer compensation, and negotiate employment of contractual opportunities.[1]
- *Economic participation:* The agreements recognize the necessity to preserve Aboriginal cultural identity and values, in part through enabling Aboriginal people to become more equal participants in Canada's economy. The comprehensive claims policy provides for resource royalty sharing. For example, the Dene/Métis agreement in principle provides that the Aboriginal claimants will annually receive 50 percent of the first $2 million and 10 percent of the balance of resource royalties from the settlement area.

  All agreements in principle and sub-agreements contain various similar provisions to support the beneficiaries and businesses under their control. These cover such items as access to information relating to business ventures and opportunities, tax exemptions, incentive measures, contract splitting, and financial and technical support measures.

- *Interim protection:* The present policy permits the negotiation of interim measures to protect Aboriginal interests while the claim is being negotiated. They are identified in the initial negotiating mandate. These measures operate over the claimed territory and remain in effect until a final agreement has been signed. They can impose general or specific obligations on the parties that relate to land and its future development; the protection of traditional hunting, fishing, and trapping activities, and the other rights that are generally negotiated in a comprehensive claim.

The measures enable negotiations to proceed in good faith, thus lessening the need for court intervention that could have the effect of freezing any type of development in a claimed area. It must be said, however, that an agreement on interim measures does not affect the rights of any party to seek judicial recourse should they consider their interests to be endangered.

- *Other provisions:* There is a whole range of other provisions in the agreements, covering in substantial detail areas such as access to Aboriginal lands, establishment of protected areas, fisheries, social protection, and the incorporation and management of local governments. These are positive measures intended to provide a genuine opportunity for Aboriginal economic and cultural progress.

The terms and conditions of the agreements are established in Canadian law and, under the Constitution, cannot be unilaterally changed. They are not subject to override by other existing laws nor by any future legislation that may be enacted. The comprehensive claims process has resulted in long-term agreements between Canadian governments and Aboriginal peoples, agreements that have in fact redefined in a truly unique way the relationship between Aboriginal people, the Canadian government and other Canadians.

By 1990 the government had come under attack because of its handling of comprehensive claims. Aboriginal people accused the government of pursuing a goal of extinguishing the "burden" of Aboriginal rights and minimizing its legal obligation. A working group composed of Indian leaders representing Aboriginal interests across Canada was established to identify problem areas and recommend change. Later in the year, the policy of restricting the number of comprehensive claims being investigated to six was removed. Amendments to the comprehensive claims policy removed the idea of "blanket extinguishment" of all Aboriginal rights, including title, and allowed for the retention of Aboriginal land rights, provided these rights do not conflict with the negotiated settlement agreement.

The Assembly of First Nations (1990a) has claimed that the existing comprehensive claims policy excludes self-government provisions. The federal government has argued that this claim is untrue. Yet when the *Delgamuukw* case was appealed to the Supreme Court of Canada after 1993, Chief Justice Lamer rejected "the respondents' submission with respect to the substitution of Aboriginal title and self-government for the original claim of ownership and jurisdiction." Aboriginal negotiators have consistently sought to settle their land claims and to establish the right of self-determination through the process of self-government. The government has been prepared to give "advanced" bands some legal powers similar to those of a municipality, but not additional powers.

Specific Claims

A specific claim deals with treaties and scrip (discussed in Chapter 7) and band claims. It is, as the term implies, specific to a particular concern; for example, a clause in a treaty, or land withdrawn from a reserve. Between 1970 and 1981, 250 specific claims were presented to the Office of Native Claims for adjudication. During this 11-year period, only 12 were settled, for a total cost of $2.3 million. By 2002, 117 specific claims were under negotiation, with a further 491 under assessment. By late 2006, the number of outstanding and submitted claims rose to well over 800 (see Box 8.3).

Table 8.1 identifies the number of specific claims that had been submitted by the early 21st century. As is clear from the low number of claims that have been settled, the Office of Native Claims and subsequent agencies have not substantiated all of the Native claims. Clearly, this is unacceptable and has sparked protest, often violent, across the country.

Box 8.3	**Backlog of Unsolved Land Claims Nears 800 As Minister Plans Overhaul**

More conflicts like that happening in Caledonia, Ontario, may occur as the number of unresolved native land claims nears 800, where the wait time for settlements may exceed nine years. Difficult and more complicated cases may even take longer. In fact the federal Justice Department may take as long as five years to just draft a legal opinion on the basic merits of a particular case. Jim Prentice, Indian Affairs Minister, has been quoted by the Canadian Press as saying that he plans an overhaul of the whole claims system that is blamed for rising tensions and over-all lack of progress.

Prentice told CP that his department is considering such changes as increased mediation, the use of more skilled negotiators and other ways to simplify an exceptionally bureaucratic process. Not surprisingly, more funding may also be needed for a system that has already cost Ottawa in excess of $500 million to negotiate, settle and implement land claims between 2004 and 2005. Indian Affairs Minister Jim Prentice's background includes leading over 50 public inquiries into native land claims when he served as co-chairman of the federal Indian Claims Commission.

Prentice has acknowledged the high levels of frustration experienced by aboriginal people because of the lack of progress.

Conflict erupted in 2006 in Caledonia, near Hamilton, in a series of violent confrontations over a subdivision claimed by Six Nations members. In mid-2006 about six bands in Manitoba also threatened to block rail traffic around the province as part of a 24-hour protest over delayed land claims.

Most specific claims are filed by First Nations who say that the federal government misused traditional lands or breached historic treaties. Audrey Stewart, director general of specific claims for Indian Affairs, told the Canadian Press that, in financial terms, cases have been settled ranging from $12,000 to $150 million. Stewart stated that about 20 specific claims are settled each year—compared to 55 new cases that are filed every year. Stewart suggested that without major changes and serious progress, more conflict and confrontations like those at Oka and Ipperwash are inevitable.

Source: Adapted from Bailey, S. 2006, "Backlog of Unsolved Land Claims Nears 800 as Minister Plans Overhaul," The Canadian Press.

TABLE 8.1	Specific Claims in Canada, 2001

Specific claims are concerned with unfulfilled or disputed treaty obligations.
The specific claims that have been submitted can be subdivided into the following statuses.

Under review[a]	408
Resolved	251
Rejected	89
In negotiation	115
Before the ICC	61
In active litigation	47
Total	1071

a Includes 56 treaty land entitlements in the Prairie provinces.

During the late 1980s and until the turn of the millennium, the government spent less than $5 million per year on the Indian Claims Commission for mediation services, public education, and ongoing inquiries with regard to Aboriginal land claims. Since then, there has been a slight increase to nearly $6 million per year. During the decade that the Indian Claims Commission existed, it facilitated the process by which First Nations would enter negotiations with the federal government. For example, in 2002–03 the Indian Claims Commission handled nearly 60 cases. They recommended that the government accept 42 of these for negotiation. The government accepted most of these recommendations. On the other hand, the commission recommended that seven cases not be sent to negotiation. The remainder of the cases considered by the commission were dealt with in different ways. Some were sent back to the First Nations community for additional work, others were actually settled, and still others continued to be reviewed by the commission.

The history of Aboriginal claims shows that that there had been sustained pressure on the government of Canada to reform the Specific Claims process and establish an independent claims body. Yet this did not happen until 2003. It takes the government of Canada five to eight years to complete its validation process in assessing any particular First Nations' claim. Then, it takes another five to seven years to negotiate the resolution of a claim. On average, since 1973, the government of Canada has resolved only 7.5 claims per year. This means it will take the next 50 years to settle existing claims without adding the new ones that emerge. From 1991 to 1999, Canada settled 23 specific claims, totalling nearly $33 million and involving the return of nearly 15 000 acres of land back to Aboriginal people.

In 2003, the government of Canada passed the *Specific Claims Resolution Act*, creating the Canadian Centre for the Independent Resolution of First Nations Specific Claims. It replaced the Indian Claims Commission, which had been created in 1991 as an interim structure to deal with Aboriginal land claims. The new centre has two separate components: a commission and a tribunal. In addition, the commission facilitates negotiated settlements using mediation, negotiation, and other means of dispute resolution. It provides these services for all claims, regardless of the potential amount of a claim, although there is a $10 million ceiling on settlements. The tribunal is a quasi-judicial body able to make final decisions on the validity of claims that were not reached through a negotiated settlement.

Band Claims

A special type of specific claim encompassing the multifarious, scattered claims of individual Indian bands is called a band claim. Several categories of these can be identified at present, including claims relating to the loss of land and other natural resources from established reserves, as well as issues pertaining to the government's stewardship of various bands' financial assets over the years. Underlying all these claims is the difficult question of trusteeship.

The full story of the government's management of reserve resources and band funds across Canada is only gradually being pieced together from the files of the Department of Indian and Northern Affairs, from the accounts of missionaries and other Euro-Canadian sources, and from the oral testimony of Indian people themselves. Reserve resources include not only land but also minerals, timber and water. Band funds in most cases derive from land and other resource sales. Where land was surrendered or sold off from reserves, the capital went into band funds to be administered in trust by the federal government.

Land losses from established Indian reserves account for by far the majority of band claims (or surrender claims) brought forward to date. Groups of them are probably sufficiently similar to be classified on a regional and historical basis. Grievances arising in New France have certain elements in common, as do Indian claims in the Maritimes, in Ontario, in the southern Prairies and in British Columbia. The problem of pressure for reserve-land acquisition by speculators and settlers is central to all.

The French, who were the first European power to control the northern half of North America, were the first to establish any sort of Canadian Indian policy. Their approach was dictated by several factors, including geographical distance from the mother country, overwhelming Aboriginal military strength, a fur trade economy, and negligible European settlement. They sought, if unsuccessfully, the Indians' assimilation into French-Canadian society and saw the converted Aboriginal people as equal in civil and legal status to France's European subjects.

There are conflicting interpretations of whether Indian territorial rights were affirmed or extinguished under the French regime; treaties were never concluded for territory either in New France or in Acadia. Land was given to Indians through imperial grace, just as it was to European colonists. However, the Crown, instead of granting such tracts directly to the Aboriginal people, handed them in trust to the religious orders, the most efficient civilizing and Christianizing agencies then known. Six Indian reserves were formed in this manner.

At the time of the British takeover in 1760, France's Indian allies had been given land for their exclusive use. By 1851, 230 000 acres (92 000 hectares) were set aside as Indian reserves and a further 330 000 acres (132 000 hectares) were similarly appropriated by the Quebec *Lands and Forests Act* of 1922. Additional reserves were created through the transfer of land from the provincial to the federal government by letters patent issued by Quebec, through direct purchase by the Dominion from a private party, or through private leases.

The Aboriginal peoples of Quebec have, over the years, sought increased compensation for land lost from these reserves; settlement of disputes between bands and tribes over reserve ownership; restitution for damages done through logging, fishing, and canal construction; and compensation for questionable band-fund management. The existence of these grievances suggests a basic difference in perspective on the part of the Indians and the federal government, which has historically tended to judge the issues solely on their legal merits as determined by the Department of Justice.

In the 19th century, for instance, the complaints of the Hurons of Lorette and the Montagnais of Pointe-Bleur against European squatters went unnoticed. Charges that the municipality near the Iroquois Oka reserve had unjustly taken over land to allow for the construction of three roads were only briefly considered, as was the Caughnawaga claim for land sold as a clergy reserve. The St. Regis Iroquois protests against the Quebec government's unilateral renewal of leases to, and sale of, islands in the St. Lawrence, along with their claim to compensation for the flooding of additional islands by the Cornwall Canal, were to no avail. Dozens of claims to islands, first voiced in the 18th and 19th centuries, remained unsettled, and many of the current disputes over expropriation, whether by settlers, clergy, or the Crown, go back to these earlier years. At the root of most of this lack of responsiveness is the government's and the courts' persistent denial of the Indians' contention that they owned the land initially granted to the religious orders. The denial is based on the grounds that title thereto had been given directly to those orders and not to the Indians themselves.

The arrival of the British in New France, so far as the Indian people were concerned, did not favourably alter their condition. The same could be said for the Maritimes. As British settlement and power increased, large tracts were set apart for Indian use and occupation. Although these lands were called Indian reserves, they were not guaranteed to the Indians through treaties and were subsequently reduced as more land was required for settlement. Further pressures on these reserves in the Maritimes in the early 19th century, coupled with problems in dealing with flagrant non-Aboriginal squatting, motivated the colonial governments to appoint commissioners to deal with and supervise reserves. These officers apparently had, and certainly exercised, the right to sell reserve lands without Indian consent. With Confederation, the existing reserves were transferred to the jurisdiction of the federal government, though for a long time the underlying title lay with the respective provinces.

Claims have been presented to the federal government for past reserve-land losses. Within this category several main types of claims are emerging. A large number contest the legal status of surrenders of reserve lands. These include submissions on surrenders processed without proper Indian consent, uncompleted sales of surrendered land, sales of lands prior to their being surrendered, lack of letters patent for completed sales, and even forged Indian signatures or identifying marks on surrenders. In Nova Scotia, a general claim had also been presented contesting the legality of all land surrenders between 1867 and 1960. This is based on the argument that the Mi'kmaq Indians of that province constituted one band; and that under the *Indian Act* and its subsequent amendments throughout the period, surrenders could only be obtained at a meeting of a majority of all band members of the requisite sex and age. Another group of Maritime band claims against the federal government arose from the contention that several reserves transferred to the federal government after Confederation were subsequently listed or surveyed by the Department of Indian Affairs as containing smaller areas than the original acreages listed, or were simply never surveyed and registered as reserves at all.

There are also Maritime Indian claims against the federal government's handling of its trusteeship role. The Union of Nova Scotia Indians put forth a number of claims concerning mismanagement by the government of its obligation to ensure adequate and proper compensation for reserve lands surrendered or expropriated for highway rights-of-way, utility easements and other public purposes.

The sources of Aboriginal claims in Southern Ontario are similar to those in Quebec and the Maritimes. Probably the bulk of them have not yet been disclosed; at any rate, no formal comprehensive claims statement has emerged. In common with Quebec, though, past cases or recorded claims for such losses abound. Some have been rejected by the Departments of Indian Affairs and Justice or by the courts; many, however, lie dormant. It would not be unreasonable to expect these cases, and new contentions based on them, to be advanced in greater numbers over time.

Indian people have claimed that unjust cessions and legally questionable government expropriations of reserve lands were common. Government initiatives, along with pressure from non-Aboriginal speculators and settlers, were, as usual, dominant factors. The Six Nations' Grand River surrender in 1841, the Mohawks' cession of Tyendinaga Township in 1843, the Moore Township surrender made by the Chippewa later that year, and the 1847 cession by the St. Regis Iroquois of Glengarry County are prime examples of cases where surrenders were attained under pressure. All these lands were ceded in trust, although there is evidence that the trust provisions were not always upheld. Similar grievances pertain to the government's acquisition of unceded islands. Equally familiar was the variety of expropriation that allowed the sale of individual lots from Indian reserves for clergy and state purposes. Disputes over the status of territory were also prevalent. These were generally related to squatter infiltration and occasionally extended into inter-tribal conflicts for reserve lands and, accordingly, for annuities.

The social and economic factors underlying the loss of Indian reserve lands in central and eastern Canada soon found expression on the Prairies. In the years following the making of the treaties and the setting aside of the reserves, the southern Prairies were gradually settled. Towns and cities sometimes grew on the very edges of reserves or even around them, and railways ran through them or along their boundaries. As in Ontario, Prairie reserves located on good farming land were coveted by settlers. For all these reasons, political pressure frequently developed for the surrender of all or a portion of a reserve. In many cases Indian Affairs responded by obtaining a surrender of the reserve land in question; proceeds from the sales of such land were credited to the particular band's fund and administered under the terms of the *Indian Act* (Hall, 1991).

In the last few decades of the 20th century, the bands and Aboriginal associations of the Prairies have clearly articulated several claims arising from previous government policies in relation to land surrenders. They have re-examined both the justification for these surrenders in general, and the legality and propriety of specific cessions, such as those involving Enoch's Band near Edmonton. In this case, three surrenders took place. The entire Passpasschase Reserve was ceded shortly after most of the band members left treaty and took Métis scrip. The remaining members moved elsewhere and subsequently the band and its assets were amalgamated with Enoch's Band, residing on the Stony Plain reserve. In 1902 and 1908, political forces largely supported, if not generated, by the minister responsible for Indian Affairs compelled the surrender of portions of this reserve. In taking the surrenders, government officials used approaches that appear to have been morally and legally dubious. Such questions surround many other surrenders in the Prairie region and also in northern Ontario (Sanders, 1983b).

At the heart of many Indian grievances in the Prairies is the issue of unfulfilled treaty entitlements to land. Complex in themselves, such claims have been further complicated by the need for provincial assent to any proposed transfer of lands to Indian reserve status. Under the 1930 Natural Resources Transfer agreements, the three Prairie provinces obliged themselves to transfer to the federal government, out of the unoccupied Crown lands, sufficient area to meet unfulfilled treaty obligations. Aboriginal people have felt that there has been provincial reluctance to comply with this, and disputes have arisen over the exact nature of the commitments. The Island Lake bands in Manitoba, for instance, have raised the matter of what population base should be utilized in the granting of unfulfilled treaty entitlements. A substantial proportion of the bands' allotments under Treaty No. 5 were made in 1924, but the land assigned was approximately 1200 hectares short, if based on the populations at the date and on the treaty terms. The bands maintain that their total entitlement should be computed using a recent population total, with the 1924 allotment simply subtracted from the new allocation.

In addition, this case points to the inequality among the various treaties' land provisions throughout the Canadian West. In common with other treaties in Manitoba, Treaty No. 5 provides for 160 acres (65 hectares) per family of five, compared with the 640-acre (260-hectare) figure for treaties elsewhere. Since the land in this region of Canada cannot be farmed, an additional inequity is present relative to more southerly fertile regions. The bands contend that a fair solution, satisfying the twin criteria of population data and uniform treaty terms, would be an allocation of almost 120 000 hectares.

In British Columbia the history of Indian reserves is substantially different from those recorded in the other provinces. During the 1850s, when Vancouver Island was still provisionally governed by the Hudson's Bay Company, certain minor surrenders were concluded by the company's chief factor, James Douglas, for several parcels of land there. But these, along with the territory in the northeastern corner of the mainland part of the province included in Treaty No. 8, are the only areas covered by treaty. The dual governorship of the two colonies of Vancouver Island and British Columbia under Douglas in 1858 was soon accompanied by the establishment of comparatively liberal reserves both within and outside the treaty areas. But then, expanding European settlement motivated Douglas's successors to reverse his policy of allowing the tribes as much land as the Indians themselves judged necessary and, accordingly, to reduce the reserves wherever possible. Only with great reluctance did the colonial government allot new reserves in areas opening to settlement (Flanagan, 1983a).

By 1871, when the colony entered Confederation, Indian complaints concerning the failure to allot adequate reserves and reserve land reductions were already numerous. The Terms of Union that year did nothing to allay these grievances. Fundamentally, the terms provided for the transfer of responsibility for reserves to the Dominion, and for the conveyance of land for new reserves from the province to the Dominion. Since no amounts were agreed upon, a dispute immediately arose between the two governments over the appropriate acreage to be allotted per family. The province declared 10 acres sufficient; the federal government proposed 80. An agreement establishing an Indian reserve commission was concluded in 1875 to review the matter, but there continued to be provincial resistance against attempts to liberalize reserve allotments.

This is just one more source of Indian claims in British Columbia. A report by the Union of British Columbia Indian Chiefs, entitled *The Lands We Lost* (1974), details others. They include the by now familiar pattern of encroachment by non-Indian people, together with questions about various government surveys and commissions, federal orders in council, and reserve land surrenders. The primary cause of such losses and the major grievance expressed in this regard were the work of the federal–provincial McKenna–McBride Commission, set up in 1912 to resolve the outstanding differences between the two governments respecting Indian land in British Columbia. The commissioners were appointed to determine the land needs of the Indians and to recommend appropriate alterations to the boundaries of Indian reserves. All reductions were to require the consent of the bands involved, but in practice this stipulation was not followed. The recommendations were subsequently ratified by both governments under legislation that authorized these reductions irrespective of the provisions of the *Indian Act* controlling the surrender of reserve lands. Eventually, some 35 cut-offs totalling 36 000 acres were made, while lands of far less value, although of larger area, were added to the reserves.

In summary, most of the band claims now being dealt with by the federal government have come primarily from the Maritime provinces and the Prairies, with a lesser number from Quebec, Ontario and British Columbia. Some of these claims have been submitted to Indian and Northern Affairs, while others have been channelled through the Claims Commission.

CLAIMS POLICY TODAY

After the 1973 Supreme Court decision with regard to the Nisga'a Indians in British Columbia, the federal government developed new land claims policy. The new policies on comprehensive and specific claims identified the procedures and limitations of negotiating. The policies also provided the philosophical assumptions (on the part of the government) underlying these policies. These new policies divided land claims into the two types discussed above—comprehensive and specific. Furthermore, it suggested that the comprehensive claims (British Columbia, northern Quebec, the Yukon, and parts of the Northwest Territories) would receive more favourable treatment than comprehensive claims from southern Quebec and the Atlantic provinces. However, this policy also specified that Aboriginal claims would be dealt with through direct negotiations between Indian and Northern Affairs and the Aboriginal claimants. The government felt that, in Southern Quebec and the Atlantic provinces, historical negotiations had taken place between the government and the Indians, however imperfect those negotiations had been. There was some evidence that the government had taken treaty with these Indians. However, in British Columbia, northern Quebec, the Yukon, and areas of the Northwest Territories, it was clear that no negotiations had ever taken place.

The comprehensive claims policy was adopted in 1981 with the publication of the document *In All Fairness: A Native Claims Policy, Comprehensive Claims* (Canada, 1981). The policy stated that the federal government was willing "to exchange undefined Aboriginal land rights for concrete rights and benefits" (1981: 19). Some of these benefits would entail land, wildlife, sub-surface rights and monetary compensation. With regard to land rights, the document stated that lands to be selected by Aboriginal peoples would be limited to traditional lands that they currently use and occupy. It also stated that "third parties" would be fairly dealt with on the issue of sub-surface rights and that the government was prepared to grant some sub-surface rights in certain areas. Finally, the compensation (in whatever form) was to be "specific and final." However, the policy paper adopted the use of the term Aboriginal "interests" rather than "rights" (Iverson, 1990; Swain, 1988).

The process for resolving these comprehensive claims is to follow a negotiating procedure culminating in a compromise settlement. In summary, Aboriginal people are limited in (1) the scope of what they can negotiate, (2) their standing in relation to other "interests," and (3) the extent of their involvement in trying to settle their claim (Hatt, 1982). The actors involved in the process usually consist of the federal government, the Aboriginal group, and a provincial/territorial government. Because of the scope of such undertakings, the federal government earlier had limited to six the number of separate negotiations that may proceed at any time. For example, in the 1990s it negotiated with the Council for Yukon Indians, the Dene/Métis of the Northwest Territories, the Tungavik Federation of Nunavut, the Conseil Attikamek–Montagnais, and the Labrador Inuit Association.

In 1982 the government published its policy with regard to specific claims in a document titled *Outstanding Business* (DIAND, 1982a). This policy reaffirmed the government's commitment to resolving specific claims and in some respects expanded on the previous role it played in settling claims. As noted previously, specific claims relate to the administration of land or other Indian assets under the *Indian Act* and to the fulfilment of treaties or other agreements. Box 8.4 is an excellent example of a specific claim/band claim grievance other than a land dispute.

Under the terms of the policy for specific claims, the process of handling the claims is a combination of adjudication and negotiation. Claims are first submitted to the minister of Indian and Northern Affairs, acting on behalf of the government of Canada. After the claim is submitted, the Office of Native Claims (ONC) reviews the case and analyzes the material. The claim and supporting materials (both *for* or *against*) are referred to the Department of Justice for advice. On the basis of the Department of Justice's advice, the ONC (1) negotiates a settlement with the claimant, (2) rejects the claim, or (3) returns the claim for additional documentation. If the claim is accepted, the ONC and the claimant negotiate the

---

| Box 8.4 | First Nations File Claims for Bullets and Twine Never Received from Ottawa |

About 14 First Nations in Canada are waiting to settle claims for compensation with the federal government that they filed because they allege they did not receive bullets and fishing twine from Ottawa a century ago. Sixteen First Nations originally filed ammunition and twine claims, but two were settled in the 1970s, and the rest are still waiting for the claims to be resolved. Many of the claims are under review.

Bradford Morse, a law professor at the University of Ottawa, said he thinks the federal government is reluctant to resolve these claims because, even though they involve some relatively inexpensive items, the cost to settle them now is high due to inflation. "You start thinking this is just a little bit of string, a couple of bullets. The small item of thinking in terms of 10 dollars

[sic]. Now you're talking ten of millions of dollars."

The First Nations, which include the Driftpile First Nation in Alberta, say Ottawa failed to give them the ammunition and twine they needed when hunting for food as a key to their survival in Canada.

Christopher Devlin, a Victoria, B.C., lawyer representing the Driftpile First Nation, said its members did not get ammunition and twine from 1899 to 1952. It's not a question of Canada showing up with a tractor trailer of bullets and spools of twine, and saying, "OK, sorry for not giving it to you earlier, but here it is now." Devlin says it was a treaty violation and the people deserve compensation.

terms of settlement; for example, land, cash or other benefits. Once the claim has been settled it represents final redress, and a form release is obtained from the claimant so that it
cannot be reopened at some later time.

Because Aboriginal peoples do not have their own financial resources to carry out
research in order to document their claims, the federal government has made substantial contributions to various Aboriginal organizations that are engaged in this research process. Since
1973 the federal government spent in excess of $100 million on negotiations, but has produced
only three agreements. For example, between 1972 and 1982, more than $22 million in contri-
butions were made for research into Aboriginal rights, treaties, and claims, plus an additional
$94 million in loans between 1974 and 1982. Since the creation of the ONC in 1974, more
than $26 million has been spent on the operation and management of the claim process (both
specific and comprehensive). If the claim being submitted by the Indians is substantiated and
compensation paid, part of the "contribution" portion given to the Indians is repaid. Thus far
about $15 million has been repaid by Aboriginal groups who have signed final agreements.
On the other hand, if the claim is dismissed, no repayment is necessary. This infusion of money
into Aboriginal organizations has enabled them to pursue vigorously many claims which,
without the funds, would never have been researched and brought forward.

Research contributions and loans are provided to Aboriginal people for both specific
and comprehensive claims. Funding for both specific and comprehensive claims in the late
1970s was about $8 million. However, in the early 1980s this was increased to about $14
million, where it remained until 1989. However, as we entered the 1990s, major expenditures were provided to settle a growing backlog of both comprehensive and specific claims.

In 1985 a task force that had been struck to review comprehensive claims policy
reported to the minister of Indian and Northern Affairs. The report noted that the negotiating process used up until then to resolve Aboriginal claims had tried to incorporate two
principles: (1) to encourage the cultural development of Aboriginal people, and (2) to provide a climate for the overall economic growth of Canada. The government, in dealing with
Aboriginal peoples, had argued that Aboriginal goals could be best pursued by settling
claims through an extinguishment of all Aboriginal claims once and for all. Aboriginal
peoples have not accepted this philosophy. As a result, negotiations stalled and settlements
of various Aboriginal claims had been few. The task force recommended that a blanket
extinguishment of all Aboriginal rights was unacceptable. Furthermore, it made the following noteworthy recommendations:

1. Agreements should recognize and affirm Aboriginal rights.

2. The policy should allow for the negotiation of Aboriginal self-government.

3. Agreements should be flexible enough to ensure that their objectives are being
   achieved. They should provide sufficient certainty to protect the rights of all parties in
   relation to land and resources, and to facilitate investment and development.

4. The process should be open to all Aboriginal peoples who continue to use and to
   occupy traditional lands and whose Aboriginal title to such lands has not been dealt
   with either by a land-cession treaty or by explicit legislation.

5. The policy should allow for variations between and within regions based on historical,
   political, economic, and cultural differences.

6. Parity among agreements should not necessarily mean that their contents are identical.

7. Given the comprehensive nature of agreements and the division of powers between governments under the Canadian Constitution, the provincial and territorial governments should be encouraged to participate in negotiations. The participation of the provinces will be necessary in the negotiation of matters directly affecting the exercise of their jurisdiction.

8. The scope of negotiations should include all issues that will facilitate the achievement of the objectives of the claims policy.

9. Agreements should enable Aboriginal peoples and the government to share both the responsibility for the management of land and resources and the benefits from their use.

10. Existing third-party interests should be dealt with equitably.

11. Settlements should be reached through negotiated agreements.

12. The claims process should be fair and expeditious.

13. An authority independent of the negotiating parties should be established to monitor the process for fairness and progress, and to ensure its accountability to the public.

14. The process should be supported by government structures that separate the functions of facilitating the process and negotiating the terms of agreement.

15. The policy should provide for effective implementation of agreements. (DIAND, 1985: 31–32)

Previous claims were settled through one of two options: (1) by the signing of a final agreement extinguishing all Aboriginal rights, or (2) by doing nothing and maintaining the status quo. Contemporary policy does not see a settlement as a final agreement but rather as an agreement that will settle immediate issues and define the context for issues that emerge later on. It argues that there is no need to insist on extinguishment of Aboriginal rights, including title, when a voluntary surrender of rights has been obtained from the Aboriginal peoples. This procedure has been made more acceptable by all parties because of the difficulties that emerged after the signing of the James Bay Agreement, when DIAND found that there were problems of implementation, unresolved disputes, and in some cases a failure to fully implement the agreement in both its spirit and intent (DIAND, 1982a; Mendes and Bendin, n.d.).

The task force suggested several alternatives to the claims process. One alternative is to return to the legal technicalities used in pre-Confederation treaties. Specific rights such as land and wildlife harvesting would be subjected to extinguishment or retention. However, the loss or retention of one right would not affect other rights; each would have to be subjected to a court of law (Dyck, 1990).

A second option is to separate land rights from all other rights. Thus, land rights could be dealt with by negotiations or through the courts but would be separate from other Aboriginal rights such as culture and religion. Finally, a third option would be to set aside the issue of Aboriginal rights altogether when discussing land rights. Although this would not produce an answer with regard to the existence of Aboriginal rights, it would allow Aboriginal groups and other parties to continue to carry out economic activities. An example of this approach in another area is that of the federal and Nova Scotia governments' approach to the ownership of offshore rights: the issue of ownership of offshore oil has been set aside for now so that development of the natural resource can proceed.

Regardless of the option(s) pursued there will have to be some flexibility in their application, since Aboriginal groups come from different regions, have different interests, and operate in different political contexts. The task force recommended that negotiations continue to be the major mode of settling claims. The force's members felt that litigation fosters an adversarial approach that is not conducive to settling claims and to developing a true social contract between Aboriginal and non-Aboriginal people. The task force's report goes on to suggest that, prior to negotiations, the process of "scoping" be undertaken. This process, in which important issues and alternatives are dealt with by both parties prior to actual negotiations, is now used in social impact assessments. The task force also felt that negotiations must deal more expeditiously with Aboriginal claims and that Aboriginal interests should be protected during the negotiations.

In summary, the task force felt that new approaches to settling Aboriginal claims must be undertaken. Contemporary policies have not really been effective, either in social or economic terms. If Canada is to continue to develop as a nation these issues must be resolved. At the same time, if Aboriginal people are to retain their identity and self-worth by developing communities that will actively participate in Canadian society, settlements must be negotiated. As the members of the task force so eloquently stated in their report:

> Much is at stake in working towards consensual settlements with those Aboriginal peoples who have never entered into agreements concerning the destiny of their traditional lands within Canada. In the deepest sense, what is at stake is our identity as a nation that resolves its internal differences not through coercion or domination by the majority, but through agreements based on mutual consent. (Canada, 1985a: 101)

In April 1991 the prime minister announced plans to establish a royal commission on Aboriginal affairs. There was also a promise by the federal government to ensure Aboriginal participation in the constitutional process and to put more money toward resolving the land claims disputes. Specifically, the government made a commitment to spend $355 million on resolving land claims between 1991 and 1995, four times the amount spent in the late 1980s. The government also developed "streamlined" procedures to deal with land claims under a half-million dollars. In addition, DIAND was given complete authority to approve settlements of up to $7 million without the Treasury Board having to review and accept the proposal. There was a belief that more than 250 outstanding claims could be settled within the first few years of the new millennium. However, as we near the end of the first decade of the 21st century, fewer than 30 land claims have been settled, and thus the backlog continues to grow.

The White Paper and the Indian Claims Commissioner: A History Lesson

The first of a series of contemporary responses to Indian claims started with the 1969 white paper on Indian policy. This event marked the beginning of a new era of unprecedented claims activity. The government proposed an approach that it said would lead to equality of opportunity for Aboriginal peoples. This was described as "...an equality which preserves and enriches Indian identity and distinction; an equality which stresses Indian participation in its creation and which manifests itself in all aspects of Indian life" (Canada, 1969). To this end, the *British North America Act* would be amended to terminate the legal distinction between Indians and other Canadians, the *Indian Act* would be repealed, and Indians would gradually take control of their lands. The operations of the Indian Affairs branch would be discontinued, and services that had previously been provided on a special basis would be taken over by the federal or provincial agencies that serve other Canadians. Economic development funds would be provided as an interim measure. In short, Indians would come to be treated like all other Canadians: special status would cease.

In laying out these proposals the government continued to recognize the existence of Indian claims, and proposed the establishment of an Indian claims commission, but solely as an advisory body. It was made clear that the government was no longer prepared to accept Aboriginal rights claims: "These," the paper said, "are so general and undefined that it is not realistic to think of them as specific claims capable of remedy except through a policy and program that will end injustice to Indians as members of the Canadian community. This is the policy that the government is proposing for discussion." Treaty claims, while acknowledged, were also placed in a dubious light:

> The terms and effects of the treaties between Indian people and the government are widely misunderstood. A plain reading of the words used in the treaties reveals the limited and minimal promises which were included in them.... The significance of the treaties in meeting the economic, educational, health, and welfare needs of the Indian people has always been limited and will continue to decline.... Once Indian lands are securely within Indian control, the anomaly of treaties between groups within society and the government of that society will require that these treaties be reviewed to see how they can be equitably ended.

The government apparently felt that while the central Aboriginal and treaty claims had little virtue and were directly at odds with the proposed policy, there were instances where claims might be accepted. Lawful obligations would be recognized.

Rather than proceeding with the kind of commission discussed in the 1960s, it was decided that further study and research were required by both the Indians and the federal government. Accordingly, the contemporary form of commission was established under the *Public Inquiries Act* to consult with the Indian people and to inquire into claims arising out of treaties, formal agreements, and legislation. The commissioner would then indicate to the government what classes of claims were judged worthy of special treatment and would recommend means for their resolution.

Given the nature of Indian views on their rights and claims as we understand them, it is not surprising that their reaction to the 1969 white paper was strongly negative. The National Indian Brotherhood (NIB) immediately issued a statement declaring that:

> the policy proposals put forward by the Minister of Indian Affairs are not acceptable to the Indian people of Canada.... We view this as a policy designed to divest us of our Aboriginal, residual and statutory rights. If we accept this policy, and in the process lose our rights and our lands, we become willing partners in cultural genocide. This we cannot do.

In the following months Aboriginal groups across the country forcefully and repeatedly echoed this response. When the commissioner, Dr. Lloyd Barber, was appointed in December 1969, the National Brotherhood rejected his office as an outgrowth of the unacceptable white paper, viewing it as an attempt to force the policy on Aboriginal people. Indians saw the white paper as the new articulation of a long-resisted policy of assimilation. The proposal was denounced as a powerful, threatening extension of traditional Indian policy in Canada.

In rallying to oppose this apparent challenge to their rights, the Aboriginal peoples in turn produced extensive statements of their own positions. While difficulties were encountered in arranging for research funding, sufficient government monies were made available to finance some of this work. The resulting statements, together with concerted legal and political action on the part of Indians, led to significant changes in the government's approach.

An early response occurred in August 1971, when, in reply to submissions from the commissioner and Indian leaders, then Prime Minister Pierre E. Trudeau agreed that the commissioner would not be exceeding his terms of reference if he were to "hear such arguments as the Indians may wish to bring forward on these matters in order that the government may consider whether there is any course that should be adopted or any procedure suggested that was not considered previously." The commissioner took this to mean that he was free to look at all types of grievances and claims, including Aboriginal rights issues.

In August 1973, the government made a substantial change in its position on Aboriginal rights by announcing that it was prepared to negotiate settlements in many areas where these had not been dealt with. Then in April 1975, on the basis of proposals developed through consultations between Indian leaders and the commissioner, the government accepted an approach to the resolution of Indian claims based upon negotiation.

This new policy would take the issue of land claims out of the legal arena and provide an alternative forum to solve problems. This also meant that there could be greater flexibility in introducing and using certain documents—for example, historical and anthropological ones—in the negotiating process. In addition, the government felt that this process would also provide a forum that would take into account the interests of non-claimant groups who reside (or have an interest) in an area that could be affected by a settlement. Finally, and perhaps most importantly, it was believed that the process would allow for transforming the Aboriginal-rights concept into concrete and lasting benefits. In addition, the process would be final and not subject to being reopened at some later time.

This procedure had been attempted in 1890–91, when a three-person board of arbitrators was appointed to settle disputes between the Dominion and the provinces of Ontario and Quebec. Claims were presented by the Department of Indian Affairs on behalf of the Indians. Twenty cases were heard by the board, but few were resolved since the cases generally became embedded in federal–provincial conflicts. In addition, because the board had no final adjudicator, its power, by the turn of the century, waned into insignificance. With few exceptions, the Indians derived no benefit from this board of arbitrators.

To facilitate the process of negotiation and to stem the tide of Aboriginal opposition to DIAND, the government formed a joint NIB–cabinet committee in 1974. Its role was to identify and address issues that Indian people felt had to be resolved. As Morse (1989) explains, in order to facilitate this, the Canadian Indian Rights Council was established as an independent body to act as a secretariat for the joint committee. Four years later, the joint committee was dissolved because of lack of progress.

Not all Indians, however, were prepared to give up this process. Four Ontario Indian associations approached DIAND with a proposal to create a new structure that would be applicable to Ontario. As a result, new tripartite councils were created. The Indian Commission of Ontario, for example, assists the three parties (federal, provincial, and Indians) in resolving Indian claims. As Daniel (1980) points out, the functions of the commissioner included arranging mediation to resolve issues that have been authorized by the tripartite councils. However, the commission lacked the institutional structure that could facilitate the processing of a large number of claims; for example, it had neither the authority to bring legal pressure to bear on recalcitrant parties nor the legal powers necessary to provide an incentive for compromise.

While coercion was widely used in the late 18th and early 19th centuries, the process of resolution of Aboriginal claims has changed over time. Negotiation has become the accepted strategy, even though it presupposes that the two disputants are of equal power. But since Aboriginal peoples are not equal in power to the government, it has become clear that this important precondition for negotiation would have to be met (Dyck, 1981). In certain cases the government has tried to equalize that power—for example, through the provision of loans to Aboriginal groups so that they can research their claims. Nevertheless, a new strategy for resolving Aboriginal claims, one of mediation, has emerged. Modern-day claims, therefore, are not to be viewed solely in a legal context. Many legal experts and politicians agree that the issues are more of a political than a legal nature. As former Justice Minister Otto Lang stated long ago:

> We have legal questions raised about [claims] and non-lawyers particularly love the legal questions; love to think that the caveat of the court will decide the issue. But probably it is not so. The important questions are political ones. (From personal correspondence with the author, 1974)

As Watson (1979, 1981) points out, each group (non-Aboriginal and Aboriginal) attributes to the other a failure to redeem debts. Aboriginal tradition states unequivocally that non-Aboriginal people owe them for the land they provided, which permitted European settlement to proceed unhindered. Non-Aboriginal people, on the other hand, have viewed treaties as a thing of the past and of small consequence. As a result, they do not acknowledge a debt to Aboriginal people. However, these positions are not inflexible, and they are modified and abandoned when opportune. The negotiating of claims, then, is not carried out by a strictly reasoned legal argument, but by public bargaining over symbolic provisions.

The Oka Crisis of 1990: Another History Lesson

No other situation in the recent history of Aboriginal–Euro-Canadian relations has brought the complexity of the issue of comprehensive and specific claims into sharper relief than the Oka standoff of the summer of 1990, as this section explains. For 78 days the Oka standoff kept Canadians wondering how this armed conflict would be resolved. The events of Oka have remained fresh in our minds as we remember the barricades, the tanks, the low-flying aircraft, and the nightly interviews with municipal, provincial, and federal officials recounting the events of the day. After watching these events Canadians were convinced that this conflict would produce substantive changes in our treatment of Aboriginal people.

There are six Mohawk communities in Canada—Kanesatake, Kahnawake, Akwesasne, Tyendinaga, Wahta, and Six Nations at Ohsweken—totalling about 40 000 persons. The following discussion focuses on Kanesatake, since it was central to the events at Oka. Other groups in the Six Nations were involved in the resolution of the Oka dispute, but they played a more supportive role in the events.

In the 17th century the Mohawks were located in the northern part of New York State (from the Adirondacks in the east to the five Finger Lakes in the west). By the middle of the 17th century, following the arrival of the Europeans, a number of Mohawks converted to Catholicism and joined settlements of New France. The origin of land disputes between Aboriginal and non-Aboriginal people in the region of Kanesatake and Oka can be traced to the 1717 land grant by the king of France to the ecclesiastics of the Seminary of St. Sulpice of Montreal. Around 1721, the Sulpicians established a settlement of religious converts, composed of Iroquois (Mohawk), Nipissing, and Algonquin people, within the

1717 seigneurial grant at Lac-des-Deux-Montagnes. The original grant was subsequently enlarged by the King of France in 1735. It is generally acknowledged that these tracts of land were granted to the Sulpicians for the purpose of protecting and instructing the indigenous people (a policy reflecting the ethnocentrism and paternalism of that time). However, the precise nature of the obligations of the Sulpicians to the Aboriginal people has remained a point of controversy ever since. (Later, seigneuries were granted to the Jesuits and the Sulpicians for the benefit of the Indians living in the Montreal area, at Kahnawake and Oka respectively. By the mid-18th century, a portion of the Mohawks of Kahnawake settled in St. Regis, where the Akwesasne reserve was later created.)

Although the *Royal Proclamation* of 1763 recognized that Indian lands had to be purchased by the Crown before settlement could occur, it was not applied in the St. Lawrence Valley or Atlantic colonies. Thus the Sulpicians' claim at Kanesatake was accepted, even though the claim made by the Mohawks in neighbouring Kahnawake against the Jesuits of Sault St. Louis had been recognized. After 1787, the Mohawks publicly protested the Sulpicians' claim several times, but to no avail. They continued their protest well after the mid-19th century.

Conflicts between the Aboriginal people and the Sulpicians over the land were frequent, particularly over the issue of sale of the land to third parties. In response to petitions from Indians of Oka during the 1800s for title to the land granted to the seminary, the legislature of Lower Canada enacted a statute confirming the full proprietary title of the seminary to the disputed land while retaining the somewhat vaguely defined obligations to the Aboriginal population. *An Act Respecting the Seminary of St. Sulpice* incorporated the members of the seminary, and provided that the corporation "shall have, hold, and possess" the "fief and seigneury" of Lac-des-Deux-Montagnes as proprietors in the same manner and to the same extent as the seminary did under the original land grant. Local Mohawks continued to dispute the right of the seminary to sell the land and complained about the manner in which the land was managed.

In the early part of this century, the federal government attempted to resolve this issue by initiating a court action on behalf of the indigenous people at Lac-des-Deux-Montagnes to determine the respective legal rights and obligations of the seminary and the Aboriginal population. In determining the nature of the land rights of the seminary, its ability to sell the land unencumbered to third parties would also be clarified. This legal action culminated in the 1912 decision of the Judicial Committee of the Privy Council (then the final court of appeal for Canada). The court stated that the effect of the 1841 legislation "was to place beyond question the title of the respondents [the seminary] to the Seigneury; and to make it impossible for the appellants to establish an independent title to possession or control in the administration." The Privy Council also said that the Mohawks could not assert title over the land because they had not been in the area from time immemorial. Furthermore, it was accepted that the French had extinguished whatever title the Indians might have had. The Indians had not taken treaty, nor had the land been set aside for them in trust. The Privy Council went on to suggest that there might be the possibility of a charitable trust, but that the issue was not argued in this case. In essence, the court held that the Mohawk people had a right to occupy and use the land until the Sulpicians exercised their unfettered right to sell it.

The conflict between the seminary, which continued to sell off parts of the original grant, and the Aboriginal people continued. In 1945, in another attempt to end this controversy, the federal government purchased what was left of the Sulpician lands and assumed whatever obligations the Sulpicians had toward the Mohawks, but without consulting the Mohawks about this agreement. This was the beginning of a process that continues today of assembling land under federal jurisdiction for a reserve at Kanesatake.

In the 1960s the Mohawks pursued further legal action. However, resistance at the departmental level prevented the claim from being acted upon. One of the obstacles to creating a reserve base under the *Indian Act,* or any future legislation, was that the land purchased in 1945 consists of a series of blocks interspersed with privately held lands within the municipality of Oka. Both the community of Kanesatake and the municipality of Oka were faced with the dual problems of making decisions regarding land use and management that may affect the other community, and of dealing with the effects of decisions made by the other community. The question of coordinating land-use policies had been a source of friction between the two communities for some time.

In 1975 the Mohawks of Kanesatake presented a joint claim under the federal comprehensive land claims policy with the Mohawk people of Kahnawake and Akwesasne, asserting Aboriginal title to lands along the St. Lawrence and Ottawa Rivers in southern Quebec. Comprehensive claims, as we have seen, involve claims to an existing Aboriginal title, and presume the need to negotiate a range of matters such as land to be held under Aboriginal control, lands to be ceded, compensation, and future legislative regimes to be applied to the territory in question (see Figure 8.2). The Mohawk comprehensive claim includes the southwestern part of the province of Quebec, encompassing the area along and adjacent to the St. Lawrence and Ottawa rivers stretching south and east to the U.S. border and north to a point near the Saguenay River, and including areas to the north and west of the St. Lawrence and Ottawa Rivers.

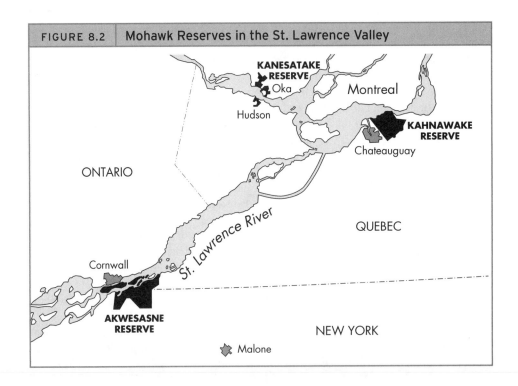

FIGURE 8.2   Mohawk Reserves in the St. Lawrence Valley

The federal government rejected the Mohawk 1975 comprehensive claim on the following grounds:

1. The Mohawks could not assert Aboriginal title, as they had not maintained possession of the land since time immemorial. The land had been alternately and concurrently occupied by the Nipissing, Algonquin and Iroquois.

2. Any Aboriginal title that may have existed had been extinguished first by the kings of France with respect to the land grants made by them, including the seigneurial grant to the Seminary of St. Sulpice, and by the British Crown through the granting of title to others when lands were opened to settlement.

3. Mohawk presence in the region did not pre-date European presence; the Mohawks came to settle at Oka only after the mission was established in 1721.

The Department of Indian Affairs restated its view that the fundamental weakness of the Mohawk land claim in the area of Oka is that the historical record, as the department viewed it, failed to demonstrate exclusive Mohawk use of the territory since time immemorial—relative to both other Aboriginal peoples, and non-Aboriginal people such as the Sulpicians. From the Mohawk perspective, the claims of Canadian governments and non-Aboriginal settlers are at least equally flawed.

The Mohawk claim was also been expressed another way. Since the department had described the Mohawks at Oka as descendants of the Iroquois, Algonquins, and Nipissings, then the indigenous people of Kanesatake could demonstrate traditional use and occupancy of the land not just as Mohawks but also as descendants of all Aboriginal peoples who used that territory prior to and since the arrival of Europeans.

As an alternative argument to the comprehensive claim, Mohawks say that the Sulpician land grant was intended for the benefit of the indigenous people. Accordingly, the Sulpician Order was not free to sell any of this land without the consent of the Aboriginal people concerned. If this argument was used, then this ought to be regarded as a *specific claims* issue, since specific claims arise from allegations of government mismanagement of particular Indian lands. With respect to any specific claim in this region, the federal government took the position that the 1912 Privy Council decision fully answered the question of any outstanding legal obligation of the federal government. The answer was *none*.

The Mohawks then submitted a specific claim in June 1977, which was ultimately rejected in October 1986. The Department of Justice advised that a lawful obligation on the part of the federal government did not exist. However, in a letter to the band informing them that no outstanding lawful obligation on the part of Canada existed, then minister of Indian Affairs Bill McKnight expressed the federal government's willingness to consider proposals for alternative means of redress of the Kanesatake band's grievance.

In summary, Mohawk claims to land have been advanced on a number of grounds, each representing a separate legal argument but also related to one another:

1. territorial sovereignty flowing from status as a sovereign nation;

2. treaty rights;

3. the *Royal Proclamation* of 1763;

4. unextinguished Aboriginal title under common law;

5. land rights flowing from the obligations imposed on the Sulpician order in the 18th-century land grants to the order by the king of France.

From the viewpoints of the federal, provincial and municipal governments, these issues were decided against the Mohawks as a result of the 1912 decision of the Judicial Committee of the Privy Council in *Corinthe* v. *Seminary of St. Sulpice*. However, it is important to note that the issue of Mohawk sovereignty was not directly before that court.

Mohawk land rights issues at Kanesatake are distinct from many other indigenous land rights issues because they are one of a handful of Aboriginal title cases to have reached a final court of appeal (this is not to suggest that there are not other legal issues relating to land that could be litigated); and the Mohawks are one of a few groups to have worked their way through *both* the specific and comprehensive claims processes. Both claims were rejected by the federal government. Despite these setbacks, Mohawks continue to argue that they have land rights based on all the grounds set out above.

The Mohawk people today argue that, independent of the arrival of Mohawk religious converts in 1721 at the Sulpician mission at Lac-des-Deux-Montagnes, the Mohawk nation used and occupied that territory and exercised sovereignty over it long before the land grants by the king of France. The Mohawk people make reference to a number of treaties with European powers (Holland, France, and England), which they say acknowledge the sovereign status of the Mohawk people throughout their territory in Canada and the United States. They also question the legality, under international law, of the land grants. For example, if these lands were unoccupied by non-Aboriginal people before 1717 but were occupied and used by indigenous people (whether Mohawk, Nipissing, or Algonquin), by what international legal principle could a European power assert sovereignty over the territory in the absence of conquest or cession?

Contrary to this position, the municipality of Oka, the federal and provincial governments, and persons claiming a clear title through the seminary argued that the Aboriginal people have no proprietary rights outside the federally purchased lands, and that this issue had been conclusively settled by legislation and litigation. In 1936 the Sulpician order sold nearly all of the land to a Belgian real estate company. The company began to sell the land in parcels for agricultural development. In 1945 the Department of Indian Affairs purchased the seminary's unsold lands plus some additional surrounding land. The seminary retained a small parcel, which is used for religious purposes. The land question continued to be important to the Mohawks, but the government felt that the issue had been resolved. Lacking funds and legal expertise, the Mohawks were unable to further pursue their claims. It would not be until the 1990s, in the face of the Oka affair, that the federal government would act on the claim.

The conflict was over 39 hectares of land. The municipality wanted to use this land to expand an existing nine-hole golf course. This land included an Aboriginal cemetery and parts of a pine forest that the Mohawks consider theirs. Ottawa has since purchased the land for $5.2 million and turned it over to the Mohawks.

In early 1991, one year after the Oka crisis, a Quebec judge ruled that the federal government could hold a referendum to determine the method of local government in the Kahnesatake community at Oka. The chief and council at Kahnesatake are not elected but instead are selected, following Mohawk custom, by clan mothers of the Turtle, Wolf, and Bear clans. In June of 1991 the community elected an interim chief and band council. The new interim band developed a Kahnesatake Mohawk election code that was acceptable to the community.

In 1992 the grand chief of the Mohawk Council of Kahnawake and the minister of state for Indian Affairs and Northern Development signed a framework agreement to start negotiations on a new relationship between the government and Kahnawake. In the long term, the Mohawks are proposing to revive the structures, institutions, and principles of the Great Law of the Iroquois of Six Nations. In the meantime, they intend to change their existing relationship with the federal government in order to get recognition of their juris-diction in a variety of areas—e.g., policing. Negotiations include the nature and scope of Mohawk government, justice, land management, land control, environment, social serv-ices, health, education, and cultural matters. But just as one crisis is settled, others loom on the horizon. The early new millennium has seen its share of standoffs and confronta-tions; seemingly the more things change, the more they stay the same (see Box 8.5).

LATE 20TH- AND EARLY 21ST-CENTURY CLAIMS

Since the establishment of a federal policy for the settlement of Aboriginal land claims in 1973, a significant number of major comprehensive claims agreements have come into effect in Canada. An American claim in Alaska (1971) became the model for subsequent Canadian settlements—e.g., in James Bay (1975) and the Western Arctic (1984). These include the Northeastern Quebec agreement (1978), the Inuvialuit final agreement (1984), the Nunavut land claims agreement (1993), the Sahtu Dene and Métis agreement (1993), the Selkirk First Nation (1997), the Nisga'a Treaty (2000), and the Tli Cho Agreement

---

Box 8.5	Talks Resume in Caledonia (Ontario) Stalemate but Fears of Violence Not Gone

Talks resumed in June [2006] in a bid to settle the land-claim stalemate in Caledonia but those observing the situation and with information from abo-riginal protesters and local residents fear there could be more violent out-bursts if the claim isn't resolved soon.

Ontario's Premier McGuinty called off talks after several confrontations near the occupied land. He warned that "protesters had just about exhausted our goodwill and patience." The Cana-dian Press quoted Cynthia Wesley-Esquimaux, an instructor in aboriginal studies at the University of Toronto, who said that the violent setback was symptomatic of what's been a stressful and exhausting ordeal for everyone involved, and tensions could very easily explode again. CP quoted Wesley-Esquimaux as saying that "the majority of the aboriginal population is under the age of 25 and the potential for another violent incident triggered by frayed nerves is very real . . . So I'm obviously really concerned about it because I'm afraid it's going to create a further rift in relations between the Canadian public and aboriginals and it's going to be harder to fix."

"There have been land claims griev-ances for the last 400 years, many of which have not been resolved to any-one's satisfaction," Wesley-Esquimaux told CP. "So is it realistic to assume this particular one is going to be resolved [soon] when there are [dozens of] out-standing claims that need to be addressed?"

Source: Adapted from Oliveira, M. 2006, "Talks Resume in Caledonia Stalemate," The Canadian Press, June 15.

(2003), and others since then. These settlements involve three major components: land cession to the Aboriginal groups, financial payment for cession, and the creation of corporate structures to deal with land, money or environmental issues. Aboriginal corporate and political structures were also established. A more detailed description of a selection of these settlements can be seen in the "Prime Examples" section below.

In British Columbia, direct action by Aboriginal people in the 1970s and 1980s prompted the federal government to re-evaluate its policy and programs. Although the provincial government continued to deny the existence of Aboriginal title, by the late 1980s it became more responsive to Aboriginal concerns. The Ministry of Native Affairs and the Premier's Council on Native Affairs were created to meet with Aboriginal groups regarding a range of Aboriginal issues. In 1990 the British Columbia government agreed to establish a process by which Aboriginal land claims could be received and placed on the negotiating table. In August 1990, the province of British Columbia agreed to join Aboriginal groups and the federal government in negotiating land claims settlements. This meeting resulted in the creation of a tripartite task force to develop a process for negotiations. By late 1990 this task force was created, and in June 1991 it submitted its report.

The British Columbia Claims Task Force was established in the early 1990s to provide advice to parties involved in negotiating a land claim. Members of the task force include provincial and federal authorities as well as representatives from the First Nations community. In addition the province created a land claims registry, which receives and provides an initial assessment of a claim once it has been accepted for negotiation by the federal government. Finally, a land claims implementation group was established in an attempt to help coordinate the activities of general inter-ministry committees and other groups involved in data collection with regard to land claims being pursued by Aboriginal groups.

There are currently over 60 comprehensive land claims being negotiated in British Columbia by various Aboriginal groups. The total land area being contested represents nearly three-quarters of the total land area of the province. An example of one major claim that has been settled is that of the Nisga'a: In early 1996, the Nisga'a in the B.C. Nass River Valley settled a land claim well over 100 years old. The 2400 people, living in four communities, received almost $200 million and over 2000 square kilometres of land.

It is estimated that British Columbia land claims (both specific and comprehensive) will cost in excess of $10 billion when they are all settled. Under provincial–federal agreements, land claims are equally shared by both parties. The federal government will contribute most of its share in cash while the province will pay most of its share in land. As shown in Chapter 7, British Columbia is indeed a special case in that Aboriginal title in most of the province still exists except in the northeast (where title was extinguished by virtue of Treaty No. 8) and the small reserves established on Vancouver Island. There has thus been pressure on the provincial government to accelerate the treaty process and settle claims quickly. In 2002 the British Columbia government proposed a province-wide referendum to determine both support for and direction of treaty negotiations, perhaps in the hopes of ending the process entirely. Ultimately the referendum and its results were rejected on the basis that the process itself constituted an attack on the agreements between the Crown and Aboriginal people, and on decisions of the courts that have established Aboriginal rights; besides all of this, there was a significant lack of voter support. The referendum was considered a shameful act for the B.C. government to have carried out by First Nations and their supporters (including the Canadian Jewish Congress, the B.C. Federation of Labour, and the David Suzuki Foundation), who argued that the rights of a minority should not be determined by a vote of the majority. Voters were asked to consider and vote "yes" or "no" to some eight principles, including the following:

1. Private property should not be expropriated for treaty settlements.

2. Hunting, fishing, and recreational opportunities on Crown land should be ensured for all British Columbians.

3. Parks and protected areas should be maintained for the use and benefit of all British Columbians.

4. Province-wide standards of resource management and environmental protection should continue to apply.

5. The existing tax exemptions for Aboriginal people should be phased out.

Notwithstanding the fact that these were "loaded" statements in the first place, it was the potential precedent of specifically targeting minority group rights that angered First Nations and most citizens. The 2002 B.C. referendum provides a clear example of how strong feelings are in relation to treaties and claims, and how far some governments are willing to go to deal with them.

In 1991 the federal government formed the Indian Claims Commission to examine claims rejected by the federal government, to review compensation awards, and to help mediate disputes between government and Aboriginal claimants. This commission can only recommend actions to the federal government, and there have been several occasions when the government has rejected its advice. In 1996 the members of the commission resigned after the federal government refused to act upon their recommendations. However, today the commission still operates and continues to mediate claims brought forward by Aboriginal groups.

An argument for Canada to reopen the historical (numbered) treaties might be made. The white paper introduced by the government in 1969 brought to the collective attention of Canadians the problems of Aboriginal groups and their claims. This was buttressed by the Supreme Court decision in 1973 (*Calder* case) and the Berger Commission (1974), which both gave some credence to Aboriginal claims.[2] However, by the late 20th century public interest and support had waned somewhat (Ponting, 1987). The issue of land claims is still being overshadowed by other concerns such as employment, the environment, constitutional reform, health care, energy policies and Quebec secession. Settling land claims has faded somewhat into the background (except perhaps in British Columbia and in parts of northern Canada), and this means reduced interest in and support of Aboriginal claims on the part of Canadians. National surveys carried out at the close of the 20th century showed that less than 5 percent of the people questioned felt that Aboriginal–Non-Aboriginal problems should be the first of our national priorities. The environment, senior-citizen issues, "Quebec independence," and women's issues were cited as having higher priority. It would seem, then, that the government's commitment to settling claims is a one-time deal. Aboriginal people are consequently well aware that failure to achieve a settlement now may mean that the issue will be shifted to an even lower priority and require a heavier investment of time, money and energy in the future. On the other hand, to settle now, under existing conditions, may mean that their land and culture might be lost.

COMPREHENSIVE LAND CLAIMS: PRIME EXAMPLES

1. James Bay

The James Bay and Northern Quebec Agreement (1975) and the Northeastern Quebec Agreement (1978) required the federal and Quebec governments to enact special legislation in respect to local government and land administration for Aboriginal people in the area. Between 1976 and 1979 a number of bills were passed to enact the agreements. Thirty-one boards, committees, commissions, and councils were established in order to deal with the organizational structure that resulted from the agreements; for example, the Cree School Board, the Income Security Board, and the Cree Trappers Association (see Figure 8.3). The agreements also required that the traditional financial arrangements between Aboriginal groups in the area and the federal government be changed as bands began to take on more and more political control and accountability. The new agreements (confirmed in the *Cree/Naskapi Act, 1984*) provided for:

1. funding for local government, safeguarding of community infrastructure and delivery of essential services;

2. the determination of funding needs;

FIGURE 8.3 | **The James Bay Hydroelectric Project**

3. the principle of local autonomy and the elimination of unnecessary central administration;

4. unconditional grant funding; and

5. grants that will be submitted to Parliament annually based on five-year agreements. (Indian and Aboriginal Program, 1985; 261–262)

In return for the Cree allowing Phase I to proceed, they received $136 million from the Quebec and federal governments. This money was invested in the Cree Regional Economic Enterprises (CREECO) and the Cree Regional Authority Board of Compensation. CREECO dominates the Aboriginal economy, by means of its $36 million in revenues and through its control of the airways and housing projects. Both companies have expanded and created hundreds of jobs. However, profit was slow to come, and CREECO registered a $5.2 million deficit in 1989. In addition to the above revenues, CREECO obtained over $30 million in Hydro-Quebec contracts in 1989 and over $50 million in 1990. This created permanent jobs for the Cree and changed their lifestyle considerably. With assets of over $140 million, the Cree have invested in Quebec government bonds, debentures and blue chip stocks (they were required under the terms of the agreement), thus generating over $11 million revenue. Other monies received were used by communities to build infrastructure and develop creative investments; e.g., Waskaganish Enterprises Development Corporation entered into a joint venture with Yamaha Motors Canada to build fibreglass freighter canoes.

Proponents of Hydro-Quebec's James Bay development, which diverts and stores the waters that flow into James Bay and Hudson Bay, feel that the production of 26 000 megawatts of power is reason enough for its existence. The original project altered the flow of several rivers in the region. When the water from the Caniapiscau River was first diverted to a reservoir, the volume (19 billion cubic metres) was so great that a minor tremor was felt.

The battle over this $50 billion-plus project once again came to the foreground as the first phase reached completion (in 1984) and the provincial government moved into the second and third stages. For over two decades the Cree (10 000 of them) fought against development, but eventually agreed to allow the project to proceed after the provincial and federal governments agreed to compensation (Raunet, 1984).

As Phase II continued, the Cree asked the court to declare the original settlement "null and void" because the agreement was based upon the assumption that hydroelectric power development was compatible with the Cree way of life, and this, the Cree argued, is not true. In Phase I Hydro-Quebec erected 215 dams and dikes, and more than 10 000 square kilometres of new lake were created. Some consequences were not anticipated; for example, flooding released mercury from the bedrock and thus contaminated certain fish. But the more dramatic and significant consequences are the social impacts. The sudden modernization and urbanization of a previously nomadic society will continue to have immediate and long-term effects (Wertman, 1983), and has prompted both a re-examination of the original treaty and additional lawsuits (see Box 8.6).

After the completion of Phase I, the Province of Quebec and Hydro-Quebec began planning the Great Whale phase to enlarge the hydro generating capacity of the region. After ten years of legal wrangling, the province dropped the project. However, after 1990, Hydro-Quebec and the provincial government developed plans for a new hydro dam project in the region and, in 2002, secured the support of the Cree. That project is now moving forward. The agreement with the Cree will see them receive $70M a year for the next 50 years as well as timber rights in a large area of northern Quebec.

Box 8.6	Quebec's Innu Launch $11 B Lawsuit

The Pessmit Innu are relaunching an $11-billion lawsuit against Quebec, the federal government and Hydro-Quebec, saying 13 dams were built on their ancestral land 50 years ago without their consent. Innu Chief Raphael Picard says the three parties violated his people's rights by building the hydroelectric dams. He figures $11 billion is about the amount that Quebec society has made from the development of the land.

The suit was first launched in 1998 for $500 million, but Picard suspended it when he became chief four years ago. Now he says that was a mistake, and that negotiations with the government are going nowhere. "The first goal for my community: that the two governments respect our title and native rights on the territory because 50 years ago, the Quebec government (did) not respect our rights and title," Picard said Tuesday.

Source: © Canadian Broadcasting Corporation, June 27, 2006. Reprinted with permission.

Almost 50 percent of the people in northern Quebec, including the Cree, remain unemployed. The tradition of community food is no longer part of their customs. Alcoholism, substance abuse, and spouse abuse are rampant, as are suicide attempts. On the other hand, the villages established now have water, sewage, electricity, and schools. Children no longer have to be sent to southern schools to be educated in English.

2. Council of Yukon Indians (CYI) Claim

The Yukon Indians had pressed to settle their land claims for nearly a quarter-century. And, while the federal government accepted their claim for negotiation in 1973, no final agreement had been put in place. An initial agreement was signed in 1984, but this agreement was eventually rejected by the Council of Yukon Indians General Assembly. Two years later a new federal comprehensive claims policy was announced that dealt with many of the concerns raised by the Council. In 1988 a new agreement in principle was accepted.

In 1989 the federal government approved the negotiation of self-government agreements for the Yukon First Nations Final (land claim) Agreements. Four Yukon First Nations signed self-government agreements and no longer have to function under the *Indian Act*. Each group will exercise law-making powers on settlement lands with regard to land use, hunting, trapping, fishing, licensing and the regulation of businesses. They will also have the right to pass laws in the areas of language, culture, health care and services, social and welfare services, training programs, care and placement of children, educational programs and licences to raise revenue. These self-government agreements will not affect any Aboriginal claim or right and will still allow them to participate in government programs for status Indians.

In 1993 a comprehensive settlement was made with the Yukon First Nations. The Council of Yukon Indians Umbrella Final Agreement is a framework agreement that sets out the terms for final land claim settlements and self-government agreements with each of the Yukon's 14 First Nations. Ten other Yukon First Nations are to be included in the agreement.

The umbrella agreement is composed of two parts. First are the land claim agreements, and second are the self-government agreements. These agreements involve about 8000 Yukon Indians. Under the Umbrella Final Agreement, each of the 14 First Nations will conclude their final claim settlement agreement. Overall, the agreement provides for over 41 000 square kilometres of land, including category A land (which is controlled solely by Aboriginal people) with surface and sub-surface rights, and category B land (controlled by the federal government subject to input by Aboriginal communities) with surface rights only, but including rights to materials such as sand and gravel. In addition, $243 million will be divided among the 14 First Nations and paid over 15 years. Yukon First Nations also receive full rental revenues from surface leases, and royalties from the development of nonrenewable resources. First Nations are guaranteed at least one-third representation on the land use planning bodies, Yukon water board, and other agencies. Individual First Nations in Yukon continue to pursue final land claim agreements.

3. The Nisga'a Treaty

Canadian history was made on August 4, 1998, at the initialling of the Nisga'a Final Treaty Agreement. Ratified first by the Nisga'a and the province of British Columbia and then by parliament in Ottawa, the final agreement came into effect on May 11, 2000. It was British Columbia's first treaty since 1899—some 112 years after the Nisga'a first went to Victoria to attempt to settle the land issue. By this agreement, the Nisga'a Aboriginal rights under Sections 25 and 35 of the Constitution are modified into both treaty rights and a land claims agreement. To the extent that any Aboriginal rights or title that the Nisga'a have, or may ever have, differ from those set out in the treaty, those rights are released by the Nisga'a. The treaty also reaffirms the Nisga'a Nation as an Aboriginal people of Canada, while acknowledging that the Canadian *Charter of Rights and Freedoms*, the Canadian Criminal Code, and other federal and provincial laws of general application apply to Nisga'a government.

The Final Agreement sets aside approximately 2000 square kilometres of the Nass River Valley as Nisga'a lands (of the original land claim of 24 000 square kilometres) and establishes a Nisga'a central government with jurisdiction and powers similar to those of other local municipal-style governments, including law making, policing, corrections services, and establishment of a Nisga'a court. The 56 Indian reserves cease to be reserves and become instead Nisga'a communal and fee simple property. Under the terms of the treaty, the Nisga'a will own surface and subsurface resources on Nisga'a lands and have a share in the Nass River salmon stocks and Nass area wildlife harvests.

The treaty also provides for a financial transfer of $190 million (with a formula for how the cost will be shared between British Columbia and Canada), payable over 15 years, as well as $21.5 million in other benefits. These payments will support economic growth in the region and should help to break the cycle of dependency. In addition, the Final Agreement specifies that personal tax exemptions for Nisga'a citizens will be phased out. Other provisions in the treaty specify that, after a transition period of 12 years, the Nisga'a will cease to be administered under the *Indian Act*, will become subject to all provincial and federal taxes, and will become responsible for an increasing share of the cost of public services as the Nisga'a develop their own sources of revenue.

Despite continued opposition and criticism from some federal and provincial political parties, some resource companies, and some non-Aboriginal people, the Nisga'a treaty set a new precedent for settling the approximately 100 outstanding Aboriginal land and rights claims in British Columbia. The treaty is considered a milestone, particularly considering that between 1890 and the 1960s Nisga'a negotiators were banned from the legislature in Victoria and prohibited from publicly raising their claims.

4. Tli Cho Agreement

In 2003, the Tli Cho Agreement transferred control of the largest block of land in Canada to the Dogrib First Nation, covering an area from the Great Slave Lake to the Great Bear Lake and into Nunavut (39 000 square kilometres). The transfer includes both surface and sub-surface rights. Three levels of government are involved, as this land covers the Northwest Territories and Nunavut and includes the Tli Cho First Nation government. Highlights of the agreement include a public government for each of the four communities in the area—Behcho Ko (Rae-Edzo), Wha Ti (Lac La Martre), Gameti (Rae Lakes), and Wekweti (Snare Lake). The new Dogrib government will have the power to tax Dogrib citizens on Dogrib land but also be tax exempt regarding its government activities, as are other governments in Canada. A Dogrib community government will comprise an elected chief and an even number of councillors, and no more than half of the council seats can be filled by persons who are not Dogrib citizens. The Dogrib Nation will control hunting and fishing as well as industrial development. This new government also will have entitlement to royalties on resources from its land and waters.

5. The Prince George Treaty

Fish, land and cash are the highlights of this British Columbia land-claims treaty that is likely to become the first agreement reached under a government and Aboriginal negotiation process since the late 1990s. This would also be the first B.C. treaty since the historic Nisga'a deal signed in 1998. Should it be successfully concluded, the treaty will represent a final agreement between the 315-member Lheidli T'enneh Band and the federal and B.C. governments.

The major components of the treaty, as so far negotiated among the three parties, will include a sockeye salmon fishing agreement, rights to 43.3 square kilometres of land in and near the central B.C. city of Prince George, and more than $13 million in cash. The fish component of the treaty would provide the Lheidli T'enneh with a one-time grant of $3 million to monitor and assess salmon stocks in the Upper Fraser River area. A significant amount of the land parcels in the treaty are within Prince George city limits. The treaty will include an agreement among the band, the city and Prince George regional district which would harmonize property taxes, land-use plans and municipal services. In exchange for the salmon, land and cash, the Lheidli T'enneh Band would agree to give up their income-tax–free status, just as the Nisga'a did.

As is sometimes the case, however, ratification votes can return the parties to the bargaining table. On March 30, 2007, the band rejected the claim settlement in a 53 percent vote. This means that the treaty is still in the process of negotiation, and illustrates the difficulties, frustrations and challenges facing all parties.

SUMMARY

Land and other title claims continue to be a major focal point of discussion between Aboriginal groups and government. They also represent a growing crisis for both Aboriginal and non-Aboriginal people. Aboriginal groups continue to press for compensation, whether it be through a reinterpretation of treaties, restitution for errors in land transfers, or comprehensive land claims. The Mi'kmaq of Nova Scotia and Prince Edward Island illustrate the first case, whereby they are trying to force the government to compensate them for land taken under the Treaty of Utrecht (1713, 1725, and 1752). They continue to seek other Aboriginal rights under this treaty that they feel have been taken away. The Mississauga First Nations claim is a good example of "error" compensation. In the mid-1990s they signed a compensation package for $13.7 million plus 16 000 hectares of land because of an error made in 1852. In the new millennium, the Cree of James Bay have taken the federal and provincial governments to court in an attempt to get them to implement the agreement they signed over two decades ago. Interpretation of the agreement has been under question, and a second generation of court cases aimed at both renegotiating the original agreement and implementing aspects of the agreement has emerged.

Given the large number of claims still before the courts and the slow pace at which they are resolved, land issues will remain an important "flash point" between Aboriginal and non-Aboriginal Canadians for some time to come.

KEY TERMS

Aboriginal rights

Aboriginal title

treaty and scrip settlement
    grievances

trusteeship

fiduciary relationship (or
    duty)

usufructory rights

land claims

surrender claims

Baker Lake v. *Minister
    of Indian Affairs and
    Northern Development*

Delgamuukw v. *British
    Columbia*

comprehensive land claims

specific claims

band claims

white paper (1969)

Oka crisis

STUDY QUESTIONS

1. What are land claims?

2. Discuss the basis for claims against the federal government.

3. What are the three types of claims?

4. Explain the importance of land to Aboriginal people.

5. In regards to claims, what is the *Baker Lake Test*?

6. Compare and contrast comprehensive, specific and band claims.

7. Discuss the significance of the 1969 white paper on Indian policy.

WEBLINKS

www.bctreaty.net

The British Columbia Treaty Commission has been at the heart of the recent treaty process in that province, discussed in this chapter. Its website explains its work and offers updates on recent developments.

www.bloorstreet.com/300block/ablawleg.htm

This is an excellent general website on issues in Aboriginal and First Nations law. It includes a discussion of major cases in the area, including a number dealing with treaty and Aboriginal rights like *Delgamuukw* and *Sparrow*. It also includes links to those decisions (at the Supreme Court's website).

www.gcc.ca/index.php

The Grand Council of Cree website on the James Bay and Northern Quebec Agreement, including the text of the agreement.

NOTES

1. The Canada–U.S. free trade agreement does not change the negotiated rights of Indian and Inuit people. The responsibility for determining the pace and conditions of exploration and development remains in Canada.
2. In 1974 the federal government appointed Mr. Justice Thomas Berger to conduct a social and environmental impact assessment on the proposed pipelines that would cut across the Mackenzie Valley, where they would eventually connect with the existing pipeline system. Soon after his appointment, Berger declared that he would visit all communities in the North that were likely to be affected and solicit their assessments and recommendations. He also held hearings in major urban areas in southern Canada. After more than two years of hearings, he submitted the first of two volumes of his report to the minister of DIAND—*Northern Frontier, Northern Homeland.*

    His recommendations were straightforward. He did not recommend against building the pipeline, but rather concluded that a ten-year moratorium be placed on its construction in order for the Aboriginal people to prepare themselves for such a project, to settle the land claims they had with the federal government, and to allow further testing of some "state of the art" technology being proposed in the construction of the pipeline.

    In the end, the federal government accepted Justice Berger's recommendation not to build the pipeline at that time, and chose an alternative route. However, due to hydrocarbon finds in British Columbia and Alberta, the decline in the price of oil and gas, as well as other social, economic, and political factors, the entire idea of transporting hydrocarbons from the North to the South was dropped.

chapter nine

Self-Determination and Self-Government: The Rights of Peoples

INTRODUCTION

The quest for self-determination by Aboriginal peoples has gone on for many years. It was not until the 1973 *Calder* case, when the judges ruled that Aboriginal title existed prior to Confederation, that self-government would be put back onto the negotiation table and a new era of discussions would take place between Aboriginal groups and the government (Dyck, 1996). Aboriginal peoples continue to make choices that maximize economic and social activities while, at the same time, struggling to maintain their group identity and political self-sufficiency. Aboriginal groups across Canada agree that the right to self-determination requires control over one's life individually and collectively (Fontaine, 1998).

All of this takes place in an ethos of Canadian society which seems to accept the premise that Aboriginal cultures are doomed and that no human efforts can save them from extinction. This philosophy was put into action over the past two centuries as vigorous measures were designed to undermine tribal authority and extinguish tribal ways of life (Laselva, 1998–99). Aboriginal people are unquestionably victims of colonialism and have been treated as an inferior culture in their own homeland. As Laselva points out, when equality has been offered to them, the condition for it was a renunciation of their identity. In the end they have rejected assimilation, exhibited the will to survive, and insisted on their right to self-government (Bell, 1998).

After World War II, many Canadians believed that we had become a "class-based" society, and that ethnicity or cultural affiliation were no longer important as a basis for identifying oneself or defining social relationships. Canadians felt sure that as Aboriginal people became exposed to modern society and the industrial-technological complex, Aboriginal identity (both individual and collective) would wane. The fact that more and more Aboriginal people were migrating to the city seemed to underscore this belief. However, a series of important political and legal events occurred in the 1960s and early 1970s that gave tremendous impetus to a growth in Aboriginal identity. The publication of the *Hawthorn Report,* the establishment of the Bilingual and Bicultural Commission, and the Supreme Court's ruling that Aboriginal rights existed, all contributed to a resurgence of Aboriginal self-determination (Chretien, 1969).

For ideological and practical reasons, governments have always argued against Indian self-determination. From an ideological perspective, Canadians argue that all legal authority had been delegated to either the federal or provincial government and that there was nothing left to delegate (from the point of view of the *BNA Act*, for example). Furthermore, there was a belief by policy makers and government officials (evidenced by their support of the *Indian Act*) that Aboriginal people have not yet become sufficiently "developed" to make major political and economic decisions. Finally, it was argued that Aboriginal people, as Canadian citizens, are subject to the federal and provincial levels of government. From a practical standpoint, few people could envisage over 600 (band) mini-governments (even the Royal Commission on Aboriginal Peoples suggested there might be as many as 60 First Nations); the economic implications of such an arrangement alone were mind-boggling (Mickenberg, 1971).

On the other hand, Indians began to demand the right to be recognized as distinct cultures with all the rights afforded to sovereign nations. They argued that when the existing Constitution was put in place Aboriginal people were excluded and treated as a racial minority, rather than as a political community with full collective rights (Chartrand, 1993). They demanded that the two levels of government recognize them as a collective "distinct society" with political rights (Deloria and Lytle, 1984). Aboriginal people began to demand policies and programs that would support indigenous institutions, and they wanted the freedom to adopt (or not!) whatever non-Aboriginal institutions they thought were compatible with Aboriginal values. Aboriginal people have not merely asserted their rights or claimed that their goal was to "oust" the colonizers, but have pushed for what they see as their legitimate entitlement of self-government.

Aboriginal people want a new order of government that would be set within the Canadian Constitution and that would guarantee the inherent right of Aboriginal people to be self-determining and self-governing (Bell, 1998). This new order of government would have the right to opt out of parts of the Canadian *Charter of Rights and Freedoms* under certain conditions. In the end, Aboriginal people want to be assured that they have the authority to make their own choices as to how they are governed (Hutchins, Hilling and Schulze, 1999). For example, *Bill C-49* (Statutes of Canada, 1999 – *First Nations Land Management Act*) gives signatory bands the power to expropriate land for community use and draft land codes. Aboriginal people argue that the Supreme Court has supported their basic objective of self-government. In the *Delgamuukw* case, the chief justice (of the Supreme Court of Canada) noted that the Crown is under a moral, if not a legal, duty to enter negotiations with Aboriginal people in good faith with the objective to achieve reconciliation of the pre-existence of Aboriginal societies with the sovereignty of the Crown (Laselva, 1998–99).

Cultural resurgence and the defence of territory are but two overt expressions of Aboriginal self-determination. The concept of self-determination was born during the French Revolution, though it has roots in earlier times. Our (and the Aboriginals') use of the term refers to the right of Aboriginal people to determine their political future and to freely pursue their cultural and economic development (Umozurike, 1972). Politically, this idea is expressed through independence, self-government, local autonomy, or some other defined form of increased participation in the governing process. In Canada, federalism and minority rights are fundamental constitutional principles and have acquired increased importance over the past several decades. Aboriginal people seek independence in order to ensure their self determination and limit the extent of external domination. Unfortunately, the concept of self-determination has been variously defined and interpreted. This has made cross-cultural communication between Aboriginal people and those non-Aboriginal people who discuss the issue rather problematic. Whatever unifying factors are used to define a people—e.g., ethnicity, nationality, class, or race—are in the end simply arbitrary symbols, though profoundly meaningful for the people using them. The basis for unifying people may change over time or may contain more than one of these factors. It may also lead to different strategies being employed by different Aboriginal people to achieve the common goal of self-determination (Miller, 1991).

Self-determination must involve a new respect for Aboriginal culture and a commitment to its survival. This, in turn, will enhance self-concepts and validate the positive aspects of Aboriginal culture (Elliott, 1980).

Aboriginal peoples have taken a seemingly contradictory position in regards to federal trust. They feel that they have a "trust relationship" with the federal government that must be honoured. As Cornell (1988) points out, the demands for self-determination and a continued relationship of entrustment—independence vs. paternalism—seem contradictory. However, closer inspection of this position reveals that most Aboriginal people feel that they will be better able to achieve self-determination if they dealt solely with the federal government rather than provincial officials. They are clearly aware that linkages with the federal government mean that they are dependent upon it both politically and economically. However, Aboriginal people believe that through this linkage they will be able to obtain some long-term base financial support that will allow them to become economically independent.

As the issues confronting Aboriginal people have increased in number and scope, policy making (for both Aboriginal people and the government) has become increasingly complex and challenging. Many more government departments (besides Indian Affairs) have become active participants in the process. As Weaver (1985) noted, this has led to central government agencies playing the role of referee when different departments disagree over policy creation, change or implementation. Overall, this has somewhat reduced the ability of Indian Affairs to carry through with its own policies. In short, Aboriginal policy is no longer the exclusive role of one department, but results from a collaboration by a number of departments and agencies.

CONSTITUTIONAL PATRIATION

Before we begin discussing sovereignty and self-determination, we need to place these ideas in their philosophical and political context. The federal government's desire to patriate the Constitution facilitated the efforts of Aboriginal people to discuss their concerns and bring several new issues to the foreground. The discussion of constitutional issues provided a national and international forum for Aboriginal people to air their concerns about their inability to participate in Canadian society. The average Canadian could no longer claim to be ignorant of the issues, nor could the elected representatives hide behind such a facade. The issues became public and were forcefully articulated by the Aboriginal leaders, who also managed to convey a sense of urgency (Morse, 1991).

Until the late 1970s, the federal government's attempts to patriate our Constitution were vague and episodic. Eventually, however, constitutional reform won national attention because of (1) Quebec's threats to secede from Confederation, (2) the increasing alienation of the West, and (3) conflict between the federal and provincial governments (Gibbins, 1986b). Constitutional reform was not initiated by Aboriginal people's concerns or by lobbying efforts exerted by Aboriginal organizations. Nevertheless, Aboriginal people had become interested in the constitutional issue and had been active in the arena since the mid-1970s, when northern Aboriginal people developed and presented the *Dene Declaration*. This was followed by the Inuit's *Nunavut Proposal* and the Federation of Saskatchewan Indians' *Indian Government* proposal. In line with these new political philosophies, Indian organizations adapted to the new realities of the time; for example, the National Indian Brotherhood reorganized during the 1980–82 period and created the Assembly of First Nations. These political activities by Aboriginal groups were made possible through increased government funding and by the 1973 Supreme Court ruling in the Nisga'a land-claims case, which acknowledged (albeit indirectly) the existence of Aboriginal rights.

When the first constitutional amendment bill was introduced in 1978, only vague references were made to Aboriginal issues. This suggested that Aboriginal people were not considered an important element in Canadian society by the federal and provincial governments. It also seemed to imply that the 1969 white paper (which would have done away with the legal concept of "Indian") was being implemented through the back door. Because of pressure brought to bear by a variety of non-Aboriginal groups, the federal government agreed to allow the three major Aboriginal organizations to attend the first ministers' meetings as observers. Aboriginal people responded by claiming that this was exclusion in disguise. They preferred to sit at the conference as equals and be given voting privileges when matters pertaining to Aboriginal people were discussed.

Late in 1979 the Continuing Committee for Ministers on the Constitution (CCMC) met to decide how to handle further challenges and protests from Aboriginal people. They created a steering committee to meet formally with the three Aboriginal organizations representing the status Indians, Inuit, and non-status Indians and Métis—the National Indian Brotherhood (NIB), the Inuit Committee on National Issues (ICNI), and the Native Council of Canada (NCC). The Federal–Provincial Relations Office (the federal body dealing with Aboriginal people on this issue) met both formally and informally with Aboriginal groups through the remaining months of 1979 (Bartlett, 1984).

When the 1980 First Ministers' Conference was held, specifically "Aboriginal" concerns were not on the agenda and Aboriginal peoples were invited only as observers. However, many matters under discussion did (and do) directly affect Aboriginal peoples even though they were not distinctly "Aboriginal" issues; for example, provincial versus federal jurisdiction. Feeling completely left out, Aboriginal people chose to act in a more visible political manner, not just nationally but internationally as well (Sanders, 1983b). This increased international activity on the part of Aboriginal people and produced some coalitions among the three major Aboriginal groups, as well as among non-Aboriginal organizations. By early 1981, the federal government relented and added two sections to the constitutional proposals that (1) protected the rights of Aboriginal peoples, and (2) required that future first ministers' meetings be held to deal with Aboriginal issues. However, further amendments were introduced by the government that would have permitted it and any provincial government to come to a bilateral agreement nullifying the protection of Aboriginal peoples (Zlotkin, 1983). As a result, Aboriginal people, with the exception of the Inuit, withdrew their short-lived support of the first constitutional conference.

In late 1981, the Supreme Court ruled that a unilateral request by the federal government to the parliament of United Kingdom to amend the Constitution was legal but not in keeping with tradition. But since the federal government wanted the provinces' support, it agreed to delete the clause affording protection to Aboriginal people from the final form of the November Accord of 1982. When it was announced, the Accord did not contain any clause recognizing or affirming Aboriginal or treaty rights. The Aboriginal groups strongly objected to this and created the Aboriginal Rights Coalition. In addition, they began to intensify their international lobbying (Sanders, 1983a). It was also at this time that media support began to materialize on behalf of the Aboriginal people; for example, *The Globe and Mail* supported the entrenchment of Aboriginal rights. As a result of both domestic and international concern, the premiers agreed to reinstate the Aboriginal-rights clause with one change: "rights" was changed to "existing rights."

Aboriginal rights were finally entrenched in Section 35, which is Part II of the *Constitution Act,* and came into force April 17, 1982. In addition, Section 25 of this Act ensures that Aboriginal rights are not adversely affected by the *Charter of Rights and Freedoms* (which is Part I of the Constitution) *and* recognizes the *Royal Proclamation* of 1763. Finally, Section 32 requires that the federal government convene additional constitutional conferences to deal with Aboriginal peoples. The first conference, held in 1983, resulted in minor changes to Sections 25(b), 35 and 37 of the Constitution. Since then, three additional first ministers' meetings have been held to deal with Aboriginal issues. None of these meetings produced any substantive results. (For a thorough review of the first two conferences, see Schwartz, 1986).

Between the first conference in 1983 and the last one in 1987, the *Penner Report* was released, *Bill C-31* was passed,[1] the task force reviewing comprehensive claims policy released its report, and *Bill C-43* (the *Sechelt Indian Band Self-Government Act*) was introduced. A new political climate was evident as the participants prepared for the last conference, but internal discord emerged on the Aboriginal side, and a lack of political will was apparent in the preliminary statements released by the premiers. The talks, therefore, were doomed to failure before they began.

Provincial officials had quietly agreed among themselves to take a stand against the form of Indian self-government being promoted by the Assembly of First Nations. The premiers were not prepared to be innovative in their approach to Aboriginal issues, nor were they in any mood to propose new policy directions themselves. In short, their chief concern was to maintain the status quo while still fulfilling the requirement to hold this conference, as was set out in the Charter in 1982 (Assembly of Manitoba Chiefs, 1994).

Aboriginal involvement in the constitutional patriation process had been based on several premises. First, Aboriginal people saw the Constitution as a symbolic statement about what is important in Canadian society. They also viewed the document as a potential lever for use in future political action. As Gibbins (1986a) pointed out, the inclusion of Aboriginal people and their concerns in such important documents as a country's constitution legitimizes the group's interests and claims. In short, Aboriginal people felt that, if they could be recognized as an important group in Canadian society, they could use this as a stepping stone to further such aspirations as settling land claims. They also wanted to influence the government in regard to Aboriginal and treaty rights. Finally, they hoped that through their involvement in the patriation of the Constitution, they would be able to exert pressure on the federal government to discuss issues of sovereignty and self-government.

The initial involvement in the constitutional talks by Aboriginal groups was minimal because of a lack of organization and funds. Also, they did not offer any stance of their own in regard to Aboriginal rights, but merely reacted to the federal and provincial governments' vague pronouncements. It was only after debate had been initiated that Aboriginal groups put forth more specific proposals with regard to Aboriginal, treaty and land rights. Federal and provincial officials reacted to these proposals by asking for more information and clarification. The governments did not put forth any new proposals, but simply used this strategy of stalling to maintain a benevolent image by never having to say "no" (Schwartz, 1986). It was also during this time that Aboriginal people began to discuss the issues of sovereignty and self-government. Although their concerns were initially dismissed by government officials, their persistence paid off. Slowly these issues entered the public arena of discussion, and when the *Constitution Act, 1982,* was finally enacted, Aboriginal rights had been entrenched.

The preamble to the *Constitution Act, 1982,* makes a significant statement on the nature of Canadian culture: "Canada is founded upon principles that recognize the supremacy of God and the rule of law." This assumption is implicitly insensitive to cultural differences and inappropriate for Aboriginal groups, e.g., the rule of law is not an integral component of Aboriginal culture. Furthermore, the Charter does not support a collectivist idea of rights for culturally distinct (non-European) peoples. Turpel (1990) notes that the Charter largely expresses the values of a liberal democracy on the European model. With the exception of sections dealing with language and education rights, gender, multiculturalism and Aboriginal rights, the Charter, arguably, favours individualism and assumes a highly organized and impersonal industrial society. The paradigm of individual rights is antithetical to the understanding of the individual's relationship to society that is widely shared by First Nations peoples.

SOVEREIGNTY AND ABORIGINAL RIGHTS

The concept of sovereignty[2] as defined by Indians implies that they have the right of self-determination. This right, they argue, arises not only out of the various treaties, the *Constitution Act, 1867,* the *Royal Proclamation* of 1763, and assorted other federal acts, but also (and perhaps more importantly) as a gift from the Creator. This gift has never been, nor can it ever be, surrendered (Nadeau, 1979). Aboriginal people also argue that there are certain federal statutes (or documents that have the force of statutes) that specify that the federal government has a special trust relationship with them and is responsible for providing the resources that will enable them to achieve their goal of self-sufficiency.

Indian organizations formally established their positions on this issue; but, partially because the various Aboriginal groups cannot agree and partially because the issue has not been fully analyzed, no precise statement on sovereignty, self-determination, or self-government has ever been articulated by Aboriginal groups or organizations. The Royal Commission on Aboriginal Peoples has presented some options but concludes that the specific form will vary from one First Nation to the next (Fleras and Elliott, 1992).

Aboriginal Rights

With the patriation of the Constitution in 1982, Aboriginal peoples finally had their Aboriginal and treaty rights recognized and affirmed. Section 32 of the Constitution explicitly states that all laws and policies in Canada must be consistent with these rights. While the federal government has accepted these guidelines in principle, in practice it continues to develop policy and programs that often run counter to the Constitution. Despite some progress, this is most clearly seen in the area of land rights. Aboriginal people feel that their land rights should be recognized and that actions should be taken to reaffirm those rights. On the other hand, the government has taken the position that it really would like to extinguish the "burden" of Aboriginal rights (ONWA, 1983).

Needless to say, the government's position was found wanting by Aboriginal people and was finally called into question by the courts with the 1973 *Calder* v. *Attorney General of British Columbia* and the 1974 *Cardinal* v. *The Queen* rulings. Ten years later *Nowegijick* v. *The Queen* (1983) and *Guerin* v. *The Queen* (1984) would reaffirm these earlier decisions and fundamentally alter the relationship between Aboriginal people and the government (both federal and provincial). Since these rulings, both parties have continued the process of trying to resolve the question of rights and responsibilities; however, by the beginning of the 21st century the assumptions have changed yet again (Anaya, Falk and Pharand, 1995).

During the 1980s and 1990s, because of international pressure and domestic concern, the Canadian government tried to deal directly with the issue of Aboriginal rights. Specifically, the patriation of the Constitution led to a sense of urgency in resolving outstanding problems and issues. In the end, the government entrenched Aboriginal rights in the Constitution without really knowing or specifying what they entailed. The inclusion of the phrase "existing rights" has done little to clarify the meaning of the concept, although as Flanagan (1983a, 1985) points out, it may at some point provide a legitimate (legal) basis for excluding Métis Aboriginal rights claims—or certainly making it more difficult for the Métis to claim their rights.

The existence of Aboriginal rights in Canada must be seen through the lens in which they are presented. On the one hand, there are a number of academics, historians and some legal advisors who are convinced of their existence based upon their assessments of the law and of history (Wilkins, 1999; Davies, 1985). On the other hand, when one considers case law, it appears that many trial judges are not of the same opinion. Past and current court decisions suggest that, if Aboriginal rights do exist, they take the form of personal usufruct—the right of an individual to occupy and use a piece of land—not collective, group rights. The *Baker Lake* decision (1980) is one notable exception to this rule.

The *Hamlet of Baker Lake* v. *Minister of Indian Affairs and Northern Development* decision arose out of a dispute between the Inuit around Baker Lake and the private corporations that were attempting to exploit the mineral potential in the area. In this case, Justice Mahoney ruled that the original Inuit had an organized society. He stated that they did not have a very elaborate system of institutions but that theirs was a society organized to exploit the resources available in the area. He also recognized the existence of Aboriginal land use rights *and* that these rights belonged to the Aboriginal collectivity. It follows that, if the collectivity has rights, it must also have the right to determine how it will exercise those rights.

An Aboriginal tribe, however, has no status as a legal entity under international law. It is generally accepted that, even though Indians were "sovereign and independent" societies before Europeans entered North America, this status was lost through the operation of European international law. The British and American claims tribunals have stated that an Indian tribe is not subject to international law and is a legal unit only insofar as the law of the country in which it lives recognizes it as such (Bennett, 1978; Gibbins, 1986b; Anaya, 2000).

International law has a more direct influence on how Canada deals with its Aboriginal people through the international treaties that have been signed and ratified by Canada (see Box 9.1). Breach of these treaties could bring international censure, judgment by the International Court of Justice, or an arbitration tribunal. Again, however, one must remember that Indians have no international standing and thus cannot sue Canada for breach of its obligations toward them. It should also be noted that Canada is not legally bound by many international treaties because it has not signed them. The rationale for not signing them has two bases: (1) many of the matters involved are not under federal jurisdiction but provincial, and (2) a concept of written codes of human rights seems to be contrary to common law and to the doctrine of parliamentary sovereignty (Culhane, 1998).

The Concept of Right

The word "right" seems to mean that one person has an affirmative claim against another—that is, the other person has a legal duty to respect that right. Thus, the concepts of right and duty go hand in hand. However, the concept of right is not to be confused with

---

Box 9.1	Historic Talks on Native Rights to Be Held in Hobbema

UN looks to establish international standards

Historic United Nations discussions about indigenous treaty talks will take place this week in Hobbema [Alberta]. The meeting that starts on Tuesday comes on the heels of a new poll that suggests Canadians want their government to support international standards for aboriginal human rights. "I'm not surprised by that poll, actually," said Willie Littlechild, regional chief for Treaties 6, 7 and 8 for the Assembly of First Nations . . . Amnesty International's poll was released last week and indicated that more than 70% of Canadians feel the UN should do more to protect the human rights of indigenous people around the world . . .

Littlechild was among a group of experts on indigenous people from around the globe who gathered at the Enoch Cree Nation on Sunday to prepare for the UN meeting in Hobbema. The Hobbema meeting will be the first time a UN expert seminar on indigenous peoples has been held outside the UN buildings in New York City or Geneva, Switzerland . . .

The ultimate goal of the Alberta meeting is to help the United Nations establish international standards that will guide governments around the world in dealing with treaty agreements. No real international rules around treaty rights exist right now.

Source: Material reprinted with the express permission of "Edmonton Journal Group Inc.", a CanWest Partnership. November 2006.

that of privilege. The difference seems to lie in the fact that it is the absence of duty that identifies a privilege. Thus, the privilege to do a certain act arises where the privileged person has no duty to refrain from doing the privileged act. When people assert that they have a right, it means that they are confirming that they have a legal interest in an object, such as land. But whether or not someone else can change the nature of that legal interest depends on the powers and the immunities associated with that object. Powers are created by statute and involve the ability to change the nature of the interest. Anyone who tries to deny another's interest in an object but does not have the power to do so can be accused of acting *ultra vires*—that is, beyond the scope of the powers granted them by law (Henderson, 1978; Barsh and Henderson, 1982; Dupuis and McNeil, 1995).

In the end, the best we can offer for a definition of Aboriginal rights is the one suggested by Cumming (1973b): "those property rights which Aboriginal people retain as a result of their original use and occupancy of lands" (p. 238). This is not to suggest that this is an official or even legal definition used by litigants or governments. It is simply a definition that captures the very essence of Aboriginal rights (Weaver, 1985).

What legal or political conditions would be necessary for Natives to convince others that they have Aboriginal rights? Elliott (1991) has noted three ways in which it could be argued that such rights exist. One of the most easily recognized ways is through reference to royal prerogatives. These are statements issued by a government in the name of the sovereign with regard to some issue; they have the force of statutes. In Canada, the *Royal Proclamation* (1763) is an example of a royal prerogative. The *Royal Proclamation* was issued by King George III of Britain, and one section of it deals with Indian people. It suggests that Indians had a pre-existing title to lands. Some would argue, therefore, that it supports Aboriginal claims to Aboriginal rights. The section that deals with Indian people has never been repealed and thus still remains part of our legal system (Henderson, 1985).

A second way in which the existence of Aboriginal rights can be argued in Canada is by reference to the decisions of the courts—that is, common law. As Elliott (1991) points out, two conflicting notions about Aboriginal rights have emerged out of common law. One was that the *Royal Proclamation* of 1763 gave Indians Aboriginal title, and the other was that Aboriginal title was derived from their use and occupancy of the land from time immemorial.

The courts' interpretation that Aboriginal title derives from royal prerogative was based on one of the few court cases dealing with Aboriginal rights. This case, *St. Catharines Milling and Lumber Company v. The Queen, 1885,* influenced the court's interpretations of Aboriginal rights for nearly 100 years. The key component of the decision, handed down by the Privy Council, was the recognition of the existence in law of an Indian interest in the land in question, and the Council attributed the interest solely to the provisions of the *Royal Proclamation* of 1763 (Elliott, 1991).

In 1973, Canadian common law on the issue of Aboriginal rights would change from an exclusive basis in royal prerogative to include a possible basis in use and occupancy. This new interpretation was based on the *Calder v. Attorney General of British Columbia* (1973) case. In this case, the Nisga'a Indians (represented by Calder) lost their land claims but won judicial recognition of the crucial issue that their claim to the land was based on their ancestors' occupation and use of it from time immemorial (Gibbins and Ponting, 1986).

Today, both arguments are used to support Aboriginal claims of Aboriginal rights. However, the question remains as to whether the *Calder* case stands as a general legal recognition of the validity of occupancy-based claims. The answer, unfortunately, is both yes and no. Some courts have recognized and accepted this argument, while others have not. A review of court decisions would suggest that lower Canadian courts have accepted occupancy-based title as a legitimate argument, while higher courts have not always given clear legal recognition to occupancy-based Aboriginal title (Elliott, 1991: 81; Federation of Saskatchewan Indian Nations, 1985; Green, 1983).

The third support for Aboriginal rights comes from the constitutional framework of a country (Henderson, Benson and Findlay, 2000). While there has been no general legislation passed by the Canadian parliament that explicitly recognizes Aboriginal title, there are some pieces of legislation that implicitly apply to Aboriginal rights—for example, the *Manitoba Act, 1870*; the *Dominion Lands Act,* from 1872 to 1908; land cession treaties; and, of course, Sections 35 and 37(1) and (2) of the *Constitution Act, 1982.*

As noted above, Aboriginal title, until lately, was interpreted as resting solely upon royal prerogative. However, occupancy-based arguments are being re-evaluated and put forward. Finally, issues emerging out of the patriated Canadian Constitution have come to the foreground in the last twenty years. However, because our court system approaches law from a positivist framework, the courts have been slow to change their interpretation. Henderson (1983) and Elliott (1991) have noted that the Canadian courts have looked at the legal system as a closed system, and thus evaluate laws on procedural or technical issues rather than undertaking a substantive examination of Aboriginal rights.

The second issue arising from the concept of Aboriginal rights is the question of content. In other words, assuming that Aboriginal rights exist, what do they entail and what exactly are they? How long do they exist and under what, if any, restrictions? Elliott (1991) looked at land rights and provided a concrete example. He began his analysis of these rights by setting fee simple interest in land as a base line. Fee simple, he pointed out, gives the owner an unlimited right to use and occupy the land for an indefinite period of time. In addition, there are no restrictions on owners who want to alienate (sell) the land. Using fee simple as a comparative construct, we can see the variations that are possible. For example, do Aboriginal peoples hold title to the land? How can Indians alienate (sell, or dispose) of their land? Although a few of these concerns have been dealt with by lower courts, previous experience suggests that higher courts tend to reverse these decisions. Finally, the very fact that so few cases have come before the courts has also created uncertainty as to the content of Aboriginal rights.

Then there is the issue of changing or extinguishing Aboriginal rights. Here the question is whether or not these rights can be legally terminated or otherwise changed so that they are not as comprehensive as previously thought. The law has provided for this possibility. Again, using Elliott's example of land title, one can point to treaties that were negotiated for the express purpose of obtaining land rights from Indians. The issue becomes more problematic, however, when actions taken by the government seem to extinguish Aboriginal rights (land title) while not explicitly saying so. This was one of the reasons why the Supreme Court justices differed in their decisions with regard to the Nisga'a in the *Calder* case.

Finally, there is the question of compensation for Aboriginal rights. As Elliott (1991) noted, although many statutes provide for compensation when property is expropriated, there is no constitutional right to compensation. Even though the Canadian *Charter of Rights and Freedoms* provides for the right of the individual to life, liberty, security of person, and the right not to be deprived of any of these except by due process of law, it does not deal with compensation when these rights are infringed upon or taken away. In other words, if private property is expropriated, there is no legal statute that forces the government to compensate one for it (but see Mainville, 2001).

Regardless of the tentativeness, vagueness and lack of clarity of the above issues, the *Constitution Act, 1982*, section 35(1), recognizes and affirms the *existing* Aboriginal rights. What these rights are has been the subject of intense debate. Aboriginal people argue that they include a number of general concerns—e.g., education, self-government, and housing. But others feel that the list needs to be more specific. The task that has been before the courts and politicians is to define and outline exactly what "existing" Aboriginal rights entail.

Noteworthy court cases have supported interpretations long held by Aboriginal people but which are reluctantly accepted by government officials. For example, the landmark decision of the Supreme Court in 1973 in the Nisga'a land claim case forced Canadians to change their views about Aboriginal land claims. Recall that the Supreme Court decision in 1990 (*Sparrow* v. *The Queen*) ruled that Indian rights could only be removed if there was explicit legislation to that effect. Thus, unless specific legislation was passed to divest Aboriginal people of their land claims and right of self-government, the rights remain theirs. The prerogative legislation that confirmed Aboriginal self-government has never been repealed, and thus one has to conclude that other rights also exist.[3] This has become more compelling since the inclusion of the statement that "existing Aboriginal and treaty rights of the Aboriginal peoples of Canada are hereby recognized and affirmed," in Section 35(1) of the *Constitution Act, 1982*. This means that if these rights existed prior to 1982, it is not possible, unless the Constitution is changed, to do away with Aboriginal rights—e.g., land and self-government.

If the evidence overwhelmingly points to the existence of Aboriginal rights, why have these not been acted upon? First, for a number of years government officials simply refused to acknowledge that Aboriginal people had specific claims or rights beyond that of ordinary Canadian citizens. Government officials also acted in a unilateral fashion to suspend certain rights through a variety of procedures. For example, it would not be until the second half of the 20th century that Aboriginal persons had federal voting rights. In other cases, historical documents were not released, kept hidden or were ignored as not relevant to the case at hand. Still other procedures were implemented to keep Aboriginal groups from pursuing various claims—e.g., preventing lawyers from accepting monies to act on behalf of Indian peoples. The end result was that Aboriginal claims, whatever they were, were defined by Canadians as not of sufficient importance for federal or provincial officials to pursue; Aboriginal claims were considered to be a myth perpetuated by Aboriginal people.

After the 1973 *Calder* Supreme Court decision, both levels of government had to face the legitimacy of Aboriginal claims. The government's initial reaction was to claim that these rights had been repealed, rendered inoperative, or extinguished. Still others claimed that Aboriginal rights had been "superseded" by federal and/or provincial legislation. As Clark (1994: 149) pointed out, this might have been appropriate if Aboriginal self-government had been constituted as domestic common law instead of being confirmed by imperial legislation. In other cases, provincial governments claimed that the 1763 *Royal Proclamation* did not apply to them; others suggested that the *Quebec Act*, 1774, repealed the *Royal Proclamation* and, thus, that it was not operative. And so on. Whatever the basis, they argued that Aboriginal claims had been extinguished, or at least derogated, from the constitutional character of the protection identified by the *Royal Proclamation*. However, it soon became clear enough that the number of court rulings in favour of Aboriginal peoples' claims increasingly supported the Aboriginal position. As a result of these court decisions and a concurrent change in the public's attitude toward the rights of Aboriginal people, the federal government embarked upon a new policy for Indian affairs.

One might also ask why Aboriginal people didn't pursue their claim of Aboriginal rights more vigorously. In other words, if the case is clear that Aboriginal people have certain rights (e.g., land and self-government), why did they not directly challenge the federal government? The answer lies in the practical realities of implementing these rights. The federal government has to anticipate the administrative and financial costs involved in attempting to implement many different Aboriginal governments; for example, assuming that each band achieved self-government, there would be over 600 different Aboriginal governments (Ponting and Gibbins, 1980). Government officials would be concerned with the cost of operating such a structure. Finally, there would be the cost of reparation to Aboriginal peoples by the Canadian government—that is, if the federal government accepted the inherent right to self-government, under the rulings outlined in many recent court cases compensation would have to be made to those bands that expressed a desire to achieve self-government in the past but were thwarted by the federal government. As a result, government officials have steadfastly rejected the idea of Aboriginal rights, irrespective of the court decisions. Nevertheless, as legal decisions continue to uphold and reinforce Aboriginal claims—e.g., claims to self-government, to land, and to the government's fiduciary responsibility to Aboriginal people—the federal government has been held accountable to deal publicly with these ideals.

The question still remains as to why Aboriginal people have not "forced the hand" of government to recognize their specific claims. First of all, this would mean pursuing additional court cases and running the risk of not having their cases upheld. The *Delgamuukw* v. *British Columbia* case, for example, supported their suspicions. Even though that decision was later reversed by a higher court, the claims of Aboriginal groups remained in suspension until a higher court ruled. Second, Aboriginal people have always viewed the courts as foreign institutions that they do not fully understand and trust. But perhaps even more important is the issue of money. It is all very well to force the government, through the courts, to admit to the existence of such rights as self-government. However, even if such rights were publicly recognized, the government is not obligated to bear the cost of resulting administrative structures—it would be a pyrrhic victory for Aboriginal people.

Because of these issues, both the Aboriginal people and the federal government have tried to establish a common ground for dealing with Aboriginal rights claims from which a compromise acceptable to both parties would result. The federal government developed its first strategy to deal with this problem in the 1973 Indian Affairs Policy Statement. This document noted that the government was determined to find the most effective way of giving Aboriginal peoples control over their affairs. It clearly stated that the government was aware of the problem of Aboriginal claims and was prepared to do something about it. However, the statement was equally clear in developing a policy that preserved the government's view of its reality. For example, while the federal government acknowledges the Aboriginal right of self-government, the only form of self-government defined as acceptable seems to be the delegated-municipal style. This position was buttressed by the federal government's concurrent policy that self-government would be dealt with in all comprehensive land claims. This strategy for enticing Aboriginal people to accept self-government under these conditions focused on providing Aboriginal people with funds if they were willing participants in the process of negotiating their claims, whatever they were. The acceptance of negotiations as a mode of decision making meant that the government would not have to relinquish decision making to an independent third party—e.g., the courts. And, by not allowing the courts the right to make decisions, the government avoided the possibility of any (in its view) unacceptable decision confirming Aboriginal rights—e.g., inherent traditional self-government. Aboriginal people caught between the confirmation of rights and the lack of funds to implement them then sought to enter the negotiation process in the belief that they could achieve both goals. They did so on the basis of past actions they had undertaken with regard to the federal government and the belief that they could replicate the results. For example, the gains Quebec Cree achieved when they dropped their court case—for a guaranteed annual income, a land base and funds to operate Aboriginal businesses—gave some support to this view. In other cases, bands were able to negotiate specific claims that they felt were in their favour, instead of taking the long, expensive route through the courts.

After this period of unprecedented development (the 1970s and 1980s), the leadership of major Aboriginal organizations became further removed from Aboriginal communities—a trend that unfortunately continued until recently. For example, the National Indian Brotherhood began to act in much the same manner as any other large political organization that is funded by an outside agency and thus no longer feels responsible to the people it ostensibly represents. Most Aboriginal organizations were established in large urban areas where few of the people they represented actually resided. It was difficult to maintain communications with the grassroots, especially when representatives of Aboriginal organizations began to sound like the federal bureaucrats with whom Aboriginal people had dealt for so many years. Aboriginal staff placed in departments that dealt with Aboriginal people (e.g., Indian and Northern Affairs) were subject to the constraints of federal policy. As a result, they found themselves ineffectual, and they were increasingly ignored as positive and effective agents of change. By the 1980s the federal government also began to cut back on funding. A call for a decentralization of Aboriginal organizations subsequently led to the creation of the Assembly of First Nations and the phasing out of the National Indian Brotherhood. However, by this time the effectiveness of the NIB had been substantially reduced anyway; first by the funding cuts implemented by the federal government, and then by Aboriginal perceptions of the organization as ineffective. The inability of Aboriginal people either to thwart or to change the content of the *Constitution Act, 1982,* further weakened their effectiveness. The end result was that by the mid-1980s Aboriginal organizations were disorganized, demoralized and without effective leadership. It was at this time that the federal government publicly revealed its new policy regarding Aboriginal rights.

THE CONCEPT OF SELF-GOVERNMENT

Until the late 1970s, the federal and provincial governments' response to demands for Indian self-government was an adamant "no." They took the position that they could not recognize Indian sovereignty because the only sovereignty that existed in Canada was vested in the Crown. Therefore, if any group claimed sovereignty on any other basis—such as use and occupancy from time immemorial—governments were not prepared to discuss or even consider it. It was only since the constitutional debates of the early 1980s and the first ministers' conferences in the mid-1980s that the federal government agreed to act on the issue. The Supreme Court's ruling in the *Musqueam* case (1985) persuaded the two levels of government to rethink their position. In that case, the Supreme Court recognized that Indian sovereignty and Indian rights were *independent and apart from the Crown.* The court ruled that these rights flowed from Indian title and Indian occupation and from no other source (Cardinal, 1986). Nevertheless, provincial governments remained highly skeptical of such a change, although they did not overtly challenge the issue. Their concerns about Aboriginal self-government and their willingness to discuss the issues emerged out of their growing recognition of the increased role they might play in Aboriginal affairs. They were also acutely aware of the federal government's thinking on this issue. For example, Indian Affairs published its *Directional Plan of the 1980s,* in which it argued that Indians, instead of using so many federal programs and resources, should take advantage of more provincial programs and resources. Other federal documents, such as the *Nielsen Study Team Report* (1986) and the *Indian and Native Sector* (1986), reiterated these strategies (Harvey, 1996).

Although these federal policies have only selectively been implemented, they certainly influenced the provinces' perception of how the federal government planned to act in the future and have forced them to develop strategies to deal with the possible changes in policy. Because there are significant differences in political philosophies among provinces, there would be both constitutional and practical implications to consider. As a result, there are several different stances taken by the individual provinces: Alberta insists that Indians are a federal responsibility, while Quebec's position is more ambiguous (Calder, 1986; Gadacz and McBlane, 1999).

From the other side, there has never really been a single position among Aboriginal groups as to what self-government means or how it is to be implemented (Cardinal, 1986). Indians have insisted that their inherent sovereignty defines and formalizes them as a fourth level of government. Inuit, on the other hand, prefer to develop a provincial-type government because they occupy a large land base and make up nearly all of the population of that area. Finally, the non-status Indians and Métis have publicly accepted the fact that any government for them will have to be delegated by either the provincial or the federal government. Clearly, because of different historical experiences, the evolution of Aboriginal–non-Aboriginal relationships has not been the same for the three major Aboriginal groups (Hawkes, 1985).

Nevertheless, there is some agreement on what is embodied in the concept of self-government. In general terms, Aboriginal people agree that the concept of self-government (or autonomy) implies that for important national issues they will remain within the territorial jurisdiction of the provincial or federal government but that they will enjoy the freedom to regulate certain of their own affairs without interference from outside (Kulchynski, 1994; Hylton, 1994). While no list of issues has been drafted, general (universal?) principles of democracy, justice and equality would be supported. Other rights such as freedom of speech, the right to be judged by one's peers, and equal access to educational and economic institutions would also be supported. By granting autonomy to Aboriginal peoples, the government would acknowledge that certain rights are to be given to a specific segment of the country's population, which needs protection in view of the way that many of its characteristics differ from those of the majority of the population. Autonomy would also allow the people inhabiting a local area to exercise direct control over important affairs of special concern to them, while allowing the larger entity, which retains certain powers over the local area and other areas, to exercise those powers that are in the common interest of both Aboriginal and non-Aboriginal people (Umozurike, 1972). In order to preserve Aboriginal culture, language and religion, Aboriginal people would prefer to have complete control over their own schools, and they are also interested in preventing the federal and provincial governments from interfering with their traditional way of life. Because they perceive that they are different from the majority of Canadians, they simply insist on different rights to maintain their uniqueness (Englestad and Bird, 1993).

Indian leaders would like to have a fourth order of government—one that fits with their notion of Indian sovereignty. Indians see self-government as a means of allowing them to achieve three central goals: (1) to increase local control and decision-making; (2) to recognize and respond to the diverse needs and cultures of Indians throughout Canada; and, (3) to provide accountability to local electors rather than to a federal bureaucracy. This new order of government would have powers similar to those of the federal and provincial governments. It would, for example, have full jurisdiction over such areas as resources, education, social development, and taxation (McMahon and Martin, 1985).

Over time, the federal government contemplated an amendment to the *Indian Act* in order to establish a more solid legislative basis for an anticipated future Indian self-government. This response was a result of the fact that Aboriginal spokespeople never fully articulated what the concept of self-government ought to entail. While the concept has been discussed for several decades in a variety of contexts (Weaver, 1984), the full organizational structure and its implications continue to be worked out. However, most federal government initiatives have consistently been challenged and criticized by First Nations. A case in point is *Bill C-7*, known as the *First Nations Governance Act*, which passed first reading in parliament in October 2002. More than 50 amendments were subsequently recommended by the House of Commons Standing Committee on Aboriginal Affairs and Northern Development. Criticized on a number of grounds by First Nations and non-Aboriginals alike, the Act proposed to remove sections of the existing *Indian Act* pertaining to elections, governance, and administration, and to replace them with a new set of rules. *Bill C-7* also proposed that First Nations communities become corporations and municipalities. From January through March 2003, the House Committee held approximately 60 Ottawa and cross-country meetings on Bill C-7, hearing from over 500 witnesses, including First Nations organizations, community leaders and individuals, as well as other interested participants from various spheres such as legal and church communities. Bill C-7 was not debated further when parliament resumed in September of that year and so died on the order paper with the prorogation of parliament in November 2003.

LEGAL AND POLITICAL ISSUES

Within our federal system we have different levels of government. As Rieber (1977) pointed out, each level of government relates directly to the immediately superior level, from which it receives its enabling organizational act. However, when Aboriginal government is introduced into the argument, a potential new structure emerges (see Figure 9.1). In this organizational structure, Aboriginal people would not only relate to the federal government (in its trust relationship) but also to lower levels of government.

The major problems confronting Aboriginal groups in attempting to establish self-government are diverse and extensive (see the papers in Hylton, 1994). For example, the issue of jurisdiction remains a basic problem. The issue of subrogation must also be resolved. This is the process whereby, as a consequence of a change of territorial sovereignty, there is a legal transfer of liabilities or of rights and duties arising from treaties and other international agreements. Added to this problem is the level of government that Aboriginal people have to deal with on any specific issues. For example, Aboriginal people are part of the

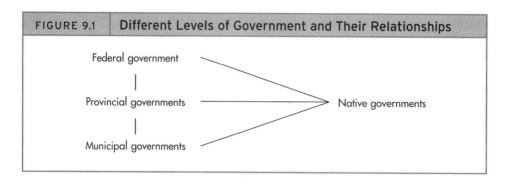

FIGURE 9.1 | Different Levels of Government and Their Relationships

Federal government

Provincial governments — Native governments

Municipal governments

tripartite (Aboriginal–federal–provincial) structure in which jurisdictional issues can arise in any one of the three relationships: Aboriginal–federal, Aboriginal–provincial, and provincial–federal. In some cases, issues fall clearly along one of the arms of this triangle. For example, reserves are clearly in the Aboriginal–federal arm of the triangle, except under certain circumstances. Other issues that have confronted Aboriginal people and that must be dealt with are domain (jurisdictional specification over property), fishing and hunting rights, law enforcement, financing, economic development, community development, and off-reserve Indian rights (Paton, 1982). Are these Aboriginal–federal or Aboriginal–provincial?

We also find that, according to the *Indian Act,* neither the band nor the band council can be incorporated for the purpose of establishing a band government. Since Aboriginal peoples are pressuring the federal government for local self-government, this problem must be resolved. Any solution must include both the legal and political issues at stake. For example, a municipal government might act in a fashion appropriate to a province, or it might act in a fashion appropriate to itself as a municipality. This means that, in part through social necessity, even though municipalities are created by the province, they are able to control their own affairs, e.g., pass bylaws, levy taxes, create policy and programs. The federal government would like Aboriginal self-government to be modelled on municipal government. Aboriginal people, on the other hand, reject this proposal and wish to establish their own form of government that would not be dependent on the provincial governments for some issues and on the federal government for others (Cassidy and Bish, 1989; Ponting, 1997).

A Historical Backgrounder: The Federal Government's Early Response–Optional Indian Government Legislation

By 1986 Ottawa had introduced its community-based self-government policy and began negotiating with specific Aboriginal communities.[4] Aboriginal people have long argued that they require an authority base that would allow them, collectively, to advance their own interests. Furthermore, this authority had to derive from their Aboriginal title and not from parliament (Tennant, 1984). They claimed that they originally had a system of self-government that regulated their internal and external relations (Boldt, Long and Little Bear, 1985). As Aboriginal organizations lobbied for self-government during the 1970s, DIAND developed a policy (without consulting Aboriginal people) to create band government. This devolutionary process was to lead to an entirely new relationship between Aboriginal people and the government. Each band would be given the opportunity to choose the form and structure of a type of self-government that it saw fit for itself. This policy was rejected by Aboriginal people because it failed to recognize the Aboriginal source of authority (Tennant, 1984).

The rejection of DIAND's proposed self-government policy led to the creation of a special federal committee that was charged with reviewing all legal and related institutional factors affecting the status, development, and responsibilities of band government on Indian reserves. Weaver (1984) showed that the committee became a vehicle for articulating Indian interests to the public. After a cross-country hearing, the committee submitted its report in 1983.

The *Penner Report*, produced by the special committee, listed 58 recommendations designed to integrate Indians into Canadian society. The most relevant for our purposes are the recommendations that Indian people should have self-government and that this should be recognized as an Aboriginal right. As Tennant (1984) observed, the committee recommended that the Indian governments should derive their existence and legitimacy not from parliament or legislation, nor even from the Constitution, but from a pre-existing (inherent) right. The committee proposed legislation that would have the federal and provincial governments recognize Indian governments, author federal–Indian agreements, and allow Indians to govern themselves (Tennant, 1984). The committee also recommended that DIAND be phased out of existence as its functions were taken over by Indians. This particular recommendation was also in line with the average Canadian's thinking about DIAND at the time.[5]

Finally, the committee recommended that the Indian band-government legislation proposed by DIAND be rejected and that new legislation be implemented to clear the way for a different form of Indian self-government. It was felt that the proposed legislation by DIAND simply involved a delegation of powers rather than a true recognition of the sovereignty of Indian First Nations.

The committee felt that Indian self-government could be implemented under the existing constitutional structure, and many of its recommendations were set forth within this context. However, committee members were also aware that other changes could take place outside the constitutional structure. To this end, the committee recommended that the government become involved in the creation of new legislation, increased funding, and administrative arrangements.

In summary, the *Penner Report* called for a new order of government to be established in order to incorporate Aboriginal people into Canadian society. The primary unit of self-government would be the band. Thus each Indian governing body would then be related to the other two higher levels of government through the band government.

DIAND and the Assembly of First Nations (AFN) quickly responded to the recommendations of the committee. By the end of 1983 a draft policy, *Indian Nations Recognition and Validating Act,* was completed by DIAND officials. This proposed act formally recognized Indian First Nations and allowed each nation to enact legislation independently of Canada as long as it did not conflict with the laws of parliament. The federal government responded in early 1984. It refused to accept self-government *as an Aboriginal right.* Nevertheless, it agreed to drop the band-government legislation and began investigating the possibility of implementing the spirit of the *Penner Report.*

The result was the creation of a new committee consisting of a number of people from the constitutional unit of DIAND and the public-law unit of the Ministry of Justice. Their job was to draft new legislation that would incorporate the recommendations of the *Penner Report* but would also be palatable to parliament. The first draft was rejected by the Priorities and Planning Committee of the cabinet. New officials were then added to the committee trying to draft the legislation. In June 1984, *Bill C-52, An Act Relating to Self-Government for Indian Nations,* was introduced. While some of the recommendations of the *Penner Report* were part of this bill, it was little more than a reformulation of the old band-government legislation. As parliament dissolved, so did the bill and the policy alliance that had formed between AFN and the government in the workings of the special committee. *Bill C-93* (discussed below), a revision of *C-52,* was then introduced and became the basis for establishing a negotiating stance with regard to self-government for Indians.

By proposing this legislation the federal government tried to (1) develop Aboriginal self-reliance rather than dependency, (2) develop grassroots programs rather than Ottawa-built programs, and (3) develop community control and participation. To achieve these ends, more local control and decision-making had to be made possible. The new policy also had to be flexible in order to deal with the diverse needs and cultures of Aboriginal people. It was hoped that self-government would make Aboriginal officials more accountable to their own electors rather than to the federal government (Rawson, 1988). Finally, it was felt that structural changes in DIAND would have to occur in order to facilitate these program goals. For example, the department would have to be regionalized into four new sectors, and the Corporate Policy and Native Claims sectors would need to be dismantled and absorbed into the new organization.

To reiterate, self-government for Aboriginals means that they, as First Nations, will govern their own people and their own affairs, including land and its use. Self-government flows from Aboriginal rights, which provide for the right of a people's cultural survival and self-determination (Leonard, 1995). Specifically, this would exempt them (or at least protect them) from the application of laws of another jurisdiction (Ahenakew, 1985; Plain, 1985). The Aboriginal proposals for self-government call for a new order of government with powers similar to those of a province. In fact, some proposals have even suggested that the Indian First Nations would have the right to sign international treaties and to issue valid passports (Dalon, 1985). These proposals have been summarily rejected by both levels of government. There was a great fear that until all the implications of self-government were clear, it could not be entrenched in the Constitution or given even tentative support (Dalon, 1985; Long, Boldt and Little Bear, 1983).

Nevertheless, the federal government's proposal did not suggest that each band's authority would come from its status as a sovereign entity. Rather, the authority was seen to exist because the federal government chose to delegate it to the band. Aboriginal people have objected vociferously to this stance. They are adamant that self-government is an inherent right, not a contingent right (i.e., "at the pleasure of the Crown"). They pointed out that an all-party committee (the Special Committee on Indian Self-Government, 1983) endorsed their constituency's right to self-government. At the same time, as Dyck (1991) pointed out, there must be no illusions about the difficulties that would be encountered in trying to implement the process. Anderson, Benson and Flanagan (2006) note that over time, Aboriginal people have become more adept at resisting authority than exercising it, and this will have to change if self-government is to succeed.

Indians wanted to entrench their rights in the Constitution by establishing a form of Indian government outside the framework of the *Indian Act* (Weaver, 1984, Tennant, 1984). One year after *Bill C-52* was introduced, the Mulroney Conservatives having replaced the Turner Liberals in office, the government presented new legislation in parliament to allow for the recognition of Indian government, *Bill C-93*. The proposed legislation was not meant to displace (or act as a substitute for) constitutional processes and initiatives. It was explicitly noted that it would not detract from existing Aboriginal and treaty rights affirmed in the Constitution (Long, Boldt and Little Bear, 1982).

This proposed legislation (*Bill C-93*) was not really what Indian people had in mind when they raised the matter of self-government. (See, for example, the Assembly of First Nations' *Proposed 1985 Constitutional Accord Relating to the Aboriginal Peoples of Canada*, First Ministers' Conference on Aboriginal Constitutional Matters, 1985.) Aboriginal peoples believe that, in order to survive as a cultural entity, they must have a land base and self-government. The government, although agreeing with the sentiment that self-government would be helpful, would first like to see the broad parameters as it maps out its response. For example, is it land-based? If so, this might be an appropriate model for Indians and Inuit but not necessarily for Métis. In addition, neither the provincial governments nor the federal government were prepared to include in the concept of self-government the notions of full independence or sovereignty. Although Aboriginal people do view self-government as an inherent right, they have always pictured its expression as taking place within the Canadian political system (Hawkes, 1985). They also believe that self-government could be attained even without a land base if there were guaranteed representation for Aboriginal peoples in the House of Commons, the provincial legislatures, and the Senate.

The First Nations' Position: The Point of Departure

How did Aboriginal peoples react to the legislation and initiatives dealing with Aboriginal self-government proposed early on by the federal government and DIAND? And what is their overall position (despite the fact there has never been a single position among all Aboriginal groups) as to what self-government means or entails? In 1975, the National Indian Brotherhood passed a resolution that in part stated a need for a phased approach to revision of the *Indian Act*. It also put forth the principle of optional adoption by bands of any revised provisions of the Act (Hawkes, 1985). However, Indians today argue that, because the political scene is radically different than in 1975, this resolution is no longer applicable; they consider it obsolete. They further argue that if the federal government had consulted with them, they would have long ago realized that this was no longer a viable position for Aboriginal people to hold.

The general principles of Indian government might be summarized as follows. These principles may not be fully endorsed by all Aboriginal people, but they would seem to be those that are most consistently advocated. Aboriginal people argue that *sovereignty exists in and of its own right*. It is a gift from their Creator, which has never been and can never be surrendered. In pre-contact times Aboriginal people formed a variety of political units, with their own governments and other institutions. They claim that, with colonization, their right to exercise their sovereignty was unjustly abrogated and ignored, and their political institutions were systematically dismantled. But, as in the past, they continue to assert their sovereignty and the right to create their own unique institutions of self-government.

In accordance with the principle of self-determination, Aboriginal people want to exercise their right to make and administer decisions on all matters pertaining to themselves and their lands. Aboriginal government is the expression of this inherent right of sovereign nations to self-determination. Aboriginal people continue to anticipate a new order of government within Confederation, and they have been renegotiating the terms of their relationship in the hope that the Constitution will recognize not only federal and provincial governments, but also Indian governments that will exercise full internal sovereignty.

First Nations claim to have exclusive legislative, executive, and administrative jurisdiction over Indian lands and resources and over the people within their territories. Indian territory would have three components: (1) land and territory as presently recognized; (2) territory to which there is a valid claim; and (3) those hunting, fishing, trapping and gathering territories not included in the first two components. Indian governments would have jurisdiction over all persons on Indian land and exclusive jurisdiction in determining Indian citizenship. They would be responsible for peace, order, and good government within Indian territory and for the maintenance and well-being of Indian people. Indian jurisdiction would not be limited to Indian territory when matters of social and cultural responsibility for its citizens extend beyond it (Hodgins, Heard and Milloy, 1992). In point of fact, where First Nations have successfully negotiated comprehensive land claims agreements, there has also been the successful establishment of Aboriginal governments with wide-ranging jurisdictions and powers (see Chapter 8).

Indian people would continue to develop their own constitutions. They themselves will determine whether they choose to be single units or to amalgamate to pursue common goals as Indian nations. The actual form that these political units take would be based on the needs and aspirations of the Indian people involved. Aboriginal people feel that the rights confirmed by the *Royal Proclamation,* the *British North America Act,* the treaties, and the trust relationship between Indians and the federal government mean that the government of Canada is responsible for providing the resources, including land, that would enable Aboriginal governments to attain their goal of economic self-sufficiency. Of course, self-government *in practice* might end up looking quite different.

SELF-GOVERNMENT IN THE NEW MILLENNIUM

Despite significant progress, Aboriginal rights in Canadian law are still being defined ("a work in progress"), but several basic points are now clear. These rights are collective rights, which derive legal force from common-law recognition of the legitimacy of the prior occupancy and use of certain territories. The essence of the common-law view of these rights is that they protect whatever it was that the organized society of Aboriginal peoples did before coming into contact with Europeans. To date this has focused Aboriginal concerns mainly on land use and occupancy (usufruct), but, logically speaking, Aboriginal rights could include many other social activities, such as the determination of descent, family and kinship matters, and ceremonial practices. And this, of course, is what is now being discussed under the rubric of self-government.

The *St. Catharines Milling* case, decided in the late 19th century, was regarded as the precedent-setting case with respect to Aboriginal rights until 1973. The general import of the decision was that the source of Indian rights in Canada was the *Royal Proclamation* of 1763. However, in 1973, the *Calder* case in British Columbia tentatively ruled that Indian rights were not dependent upon the *Royal Proclamation* but could be viewed as independent rights, that is, as rights independent from anyone's ruling or document. However, it was not until 1984, with the *Guerin* case, that the Supreme Court ruled that Aboriginal rights were derived from the original possession of the North American continent—that is, that

Indian interest in the land was a pre-existing legal right not created by the *Royal Proclamation,* by statute, or by executive order. This important ruling set the stage for the federal government's willingness to begin discussions with Aboriginal people with regard to self-government (Canada, 1983).

The Chrétien government's *Creating Opportunity: The Liberal Plan for Canada* (the Red Book, as it was then called) outlined its commitment to act on the implementation of this fundamental right for Aboriginal peoples. In 1995, the federal government established a policy and a process by which it would be able to accept the principles of Aboriginal self-government. In developing the policy, the federal government consulted widely with Aboriginal people from across the country and included the provincial and territorial governments in the discussions. Today the government's position is that it recognizes the inherent right of self-government as an existing right within Section 35(1) of the *Constitution Act, 1982.* As such, it feels that negotiations with Aboriginal peoples are the preferred way to establish self-government, and litigation should be a last resort. In addition, because the form of self-government may take many different forms, the federal government feels that provincial governments are a necessary party to the negotiations. However, there are limits to the recognition of Aboriginal self-government: Aboriginal self-government does not include a right of sovereignty in the international law sense, nor will it result in sovereign independent Aboriginal nation states. As such, any agreement and form of self-government stipulates that the *Charter of Rights and Freedoms* will apply to Aboriginal governments and institutions. Negotiations with Aboriginal groups will include a wide array of issues, including membership, marriage, education, social services, policing, property rights, taxation, hunting, housing, local transportation, and a host of others. Any arrangement will have to harmonize with existing Canadian laws (Daugherty, Wayne and Magill, 1980).

How will these agreements be implemented? There are a number of ways in which these agreements could be put in place. Thus far, new treaties and agreements, parts of comprehensive land claims, and addenda to existing treaties continue to be the favoured strategies. However, other mechanisms have been identified by which self-government arrangements will be implemented. These include actual legislation, contracts, and non-binding memoranda of understanding (MOU) or of agreement (MOA). There also is recognition that the form and process of achieving self-government may be different for the various Aboriginal groups, and these have been identified. For example, in the policy paper, there is an explicit recognition of the different groups—First Nations; Inuit communities; Métis and Indian groups off a land base; Métis with a land base; and Aboriginal groups in the western Northwest Territories, just as some examples. Finally, the policy recognizes that Aboriginal self-government may have an impact upon third parties. As such, the process of negotiating self-government has become public, and provinces, municipalities and other interest groups will become party to the negotiations. The 1999 Sechelt treaty is a good example of how the community can be part of the overall process, but it is not the only one. In July 2000, Westbank First Nation (WFN) in the central Okanagan concluded a self-government agreement with the federal government, the fifth self-government agreement for a Native community in Canada. The WFN agreement covers all aspects of band management and accountability; introduces special land, resource, and development codes; and removes the community from the jurisdiction of the *Indian Act*. The agreement was ratified in May 2003 and received royal assent in May 2004.

The reader, having finished the material presented thus far, has probably found it very difficult to ascertain the specifics of what is involved in the notion of Aboriginal self-determination or Aboriginal rights. Here is a summary of the central tenets of self-government from the perspective of Aboriginal peoples. We think that four factors constitute the overall Aboriginal thinking on self-government:

1. *Greater self-determination and social justice.* Protection of and control over one's own destiny, rather than subordination to political and bureaucratic authorities based outside the group.

2. *Economic development to end dependency, poverty, and unemployment.* Economic justice, in the sense of a fair distribution of wealth between the Aboriginal and non-Aboriginal populations.

3. *Protection and retention of Aboriginal culture.*

4. *Social vitality and development that will overcome such existing social problems as ill health, the housing crisis, irrelevant and demeaning education, and alienation.*

In order to achieve these aspirations, Aboriginal self-governments would need (1) political institutions that would be accountable to the Aboriginal electorate, (2) a territorial base, (3) control over group membership, and (4) continuing fiscal support. This would mean control over a number of areas that deal with or affect Aboriginal people—for example, citizenship, land, water, forestry, minerals, conservation, environment, economic development, education, health, cultural development, and law enforcement (Peters, 1987).

There are several different forms of Aboriginal self-government that now exist in Canadian society. All of these arrangements have focused on Aboriginal people with "status." Seven current strategies that have been established for achieving self-government for Aboriginal peoples are:

1. band government under the *Indian Act, 1876*;

2. the *Sechelt Indian Band Self-Government Act, 1986*;

3. community-based self-government;

4. the *Cree/Naskapi* (of Quebec) *Act,* Yukon First Nations Agreements;

5. the *Act Concerning Northern Villages and the Kativik Regional Government* (Inuit);

6. municipal-style government; and

7. "regional"- or "territorial"-style government, which includes Nunavut (1999) and the 2003 Tlicho Agreement (Dogrib/Dene).

What follows is a brief discussion of four of these alternatives that illustrate the differences among them; the last, Nunavut, is discussed in detail in Chapter 10.

The *Indian Act*

Critics of band government under the *Indian Act* suggest that this is not really a form of self-government but rather a form of self-administration. Nevertheless, under the *Indian Act,* band councils were created to implement the principles of democracy and to assure the existence of self-government. Under this form of government, a chief and band council are elected; the council has one chief, and one councillor is elected for every 100 band members. The powers held by the band council are wide-ranging—for example, providing for the health of band members, destroying and controlling noxious weeds, removing and punishing persons trespassing on the reserve, providing for entry permits to band lands, and regulating the residence of band members. Certain other bylaws can be passed if the government of Canada feels that the band has the ability to understand and implement the regulations. However, at the same time, the minister of Indian and Northern Affairs can carry out activities on the reserve without band consent—for example, issuing permits for the use of reserve land and determining the location of roads on the reserve (DIAND, 1982c, 1982d).

Most provincial laws of a general nature apply to Indian people. Under these regulations, a province, municipality, or corporation can expropriate reserve land for public use if it has the consent of the federal government. Certain federal laws take precedence over the *Indian Act,* although the exact relationship between laws is sometimes up for discussion. Each year bands receive money from Indian Affairs for the administration of their own and government programs. Today, over half of the budget allocated to Indians is controlled by band councils. These funding arrangements encompass areas such as education, housing, governance support, economic development, and other activities taking place on the reserve. In terms of actual dollars, First Nations now control well in excess of $4 billion each year. Other data show that Indians and Inuit now control 82 percent of the DIAND's Indian and Inuit Affairs program expenditures through band councils, tribal councils, or other First Nations organizations. These data confirm that First Nations' control of program expenditures has steadily increased over time, within the operation of the *Indian Act* (Hylton, 1994).

The above brief summary illustrates that, under the *Indian Act,* Aboriginal people do enjoy some powers of self-government. However, Aboriginal people argue that, under the *Indian Act,* almost all actions taken by band councils can be disallowed by the minister. Furthermore, under these circumstances, Aboriginal people can only be reactive, not proactive. Finally, Aboriginal people argue that the structural arrangements between them and the government are paternalistic and contribute to the continuing dependency of Aboriginal people (Fisher, 1977). Even the proposed *First Nations Governance Act* (*Bill C-7,* 2002–2003, mentioned above), proposed by the federal government to radically remake the *Indian Act*, has been criticized for its alleged effect of actually reinforcing the federal government's control of reserves and band governments.

The federal government's attempts to strike a new relationship with the Aboriginal communities seems to always revolve around the *Indian Act.* There is a sense that if the content of the *Indian Act* can be further revised, amended, rewritten, and reconceptualized, a new partnership between Aboriginal peoples and the government can somehow be established. This assumption is being contested by First Nations.

The *Sechelt Act*

In an attempt to change the existing structural and institutional arrangements between Aboriginal people and the government, the *Sechelt Indian Band Self-Government Act* was passed in 1986. The Sechelt Indian band consists of 33 reserves located approximately 50 kilometres north of Vancouver along the coastline. Through this legislation, under which the Sechelt assumed the rights of self-government, the Sechelt band was established as a legal entity. A written band constitution was put in place under the Act, and the band council became the governing body of the band. According to these legal conditions, the band could enter into contracts and agreements, acquire and hold property and spend, borrow, and invest money. The council also had additional powers under the *Sechelt Act.* Not only does it enjoy all the powers identified under the *Indian Act,* it can also carry out actions that were previously entrusted to the minister—for example, the construction of roads, the granting of access to and residence on Sechelt lands, and the zoning of land.

The organizational structure created under the *Sechelt Act* is contained within the confines of each of the reserves. However, the possibility exists that if the provincial government were to give its approval for a referendum, the federal government could potentially recognize a Sechelt Indian government district, which could then exercise jurisdiction over land outside the Sechelt reserves (i.e., between the 33 reserves). If this were to happen, the Sechelt Indian government district council would be the political organization over the entire district. Under the *Sechelt Act,* both federal and provincial laws of general application would be in effect with regard to the band and its members, except those laws that are inconsistent with the *Indian Act* (Peters, 1987). The financing arrangements under the *Sechelt Act* are quite different from those of the *Indian Act.* Under the Act, the band has powers to tax local residents and businesses for maintaining the local infrastructure. Furthermore, the band may seek external financing with regard to any projects it wishes to take on. In addition, the band received a single lump sum of money to be held in trust for its own use.

In 1999, the Sechelt First Nation signed an agreement with the federal and provincial governments (a tripartite process) after five years of negotiation. This agreement was the first one signed by the B.C. Treaty Commission that was then negotiating with some 50 other Aboriginal groups. The new treaty gave the Sechelt $42 million in cash, 933 hectares of provincial Crown land, and an additional 288 hectares of non-Crown land. Other resources include commercial fishing licences, management of forest resources, and additional property within the coastal community. Band members lost their tax-exempt status and began paying provincial goods and services taxes eight years after the treaty came into effect, and income tax after 12 years. This new treaty incorporated self-government into the language and allows the communities to develop self-sufficiency. Since then, several other treaties have been signed or are currently being negotiated across the Canada. The Westbank agreement mentioned above is one example; the Prince George treaty mentioned in Chapter 8 is another.

Community-Based Self-Government

It was in 1978 that federal bureaucrats first proposed community-based government. This early "pre-policy," unannounced and invisible, was put into action as they forced Aboriginal peoples to separate the land claims issue from self-government. Focused on land claims, Aboriginal people were unaware that there was a new thrust. They were flushed with victory in winning new sources of funding and seemingly greater influence over the spending of monies earmarked for them. However, the economic recession of the early 1980s dealt a crippling blow to economic development and control by Aboriginal people. By the time the recession ended in the mid-1980s, Aboriginal people were once again economically dependent. And, by this time, government officials had firmly entrenched the policies and operating procedures for developing municipal-style self-government.

Early in 1982 the *Optional Indian Band Government Legislation* was introduced and was incorporated into federal legislation. Those bands that did not want to participate (either then or in the future) could remain under the *Indian Act.* However, the *Indian Act* would be revised and new alternative funding arrangements would be implemented for those bands remaining under the jurisdiction of the Act. This new alternative allowed Aboriginal groups to apply to the federal government in order to assume greater control over various facets of reserve life; e.g., management of lands, monies, and definitions of who is a member of the band. If, at some future time, the "less advanced" bands wanted to further develop their own form of self-government, they would have had the experience of exercising control over financial matters and other concerns (DIAND, 1982d).

In 1985 the federal cabinet began to discuss constitutional and non-constitutional initiatives that would enable Aboriginal peoples to directly take on some form of self-government. In 1986 the federal government publicly announced its community-based self-government policy. This new policy was intended to circumvent parts of the *Indian Act.* Under this policy, a community could be composed of individual bands, groups of bands, tribal councils, treaty groupings, or other regional entities. The government recognized that not all bands are the same and that a great diversity of Aboriginal communities exists. As a result, the policy of self-government could be achieved through a number of avenues, each to be negotiated by the local community. After the 1987 First Ministers' Conference, cabinet reaffirmed its commitment to the constitutional process and continuation of a community self-government policy. One year later, cabinet authorized up to 15 sets of self-government negotiations with individual bands.

The community-based self-government process was divided into four phases: (1) development: the building of community awareness and consensus with regard to goals; (2) framework: design of proposals that are more specific in terms of goals and structure of government; (3) substantive negotiations: negotiations of the two parties over specific issues proposed by the community; and (4) implementation: moving the proposal from paper to action in the community (DIAND, 1982h).

The policy guidelines delineated the boundaries of the demands the policy was designed to accommodate, as well as the contents of the negotiations. As noted by the policy:

- Negotiations are to be conducted without prejudice to Aboriginal rights, existing or future land claims, or future constitutional developments;
- The extent and division of powers between the federal and provincial government will not be changed through self-government negotiations;
- There will be an attempt to accommodate Aboriginal governments within the existing constitutional framework;
- The resultant self-government structures must conform to the established principles, jurisdictions, and institutions of Canadian jurisprudence; and
- All financial arrangements will be consistent with the historic levels provided to that community.

There are limits to what can be negotiated. For example, there are some areas the federal government refuses to negotiate with Aboriginal people—e.g., labour relations, immigration—and so these are not on the bargaining table. Other provisions, such as the government's insistence that criteria for band membership be established and retained, limit the nature and type of discussion. Each of the guidelines has been unilaterally established by the federal government with little consultation with Aboriginal people. At the same time, the government reserves the unilateral right to change the guidelines without prior notice or to introduce retroactive policy guidelines. Aboriginal people have pointed out that, in negotiations, federal agents have added guidelines that are not part of the written guidelines.

Nevertheless, once a community decides to pursue self-government, it must begin to put together a proposal that sets out, in as much detail as possible, the community's overall goals and aspirations in the area of self-government. The options range from exercising more of the authorities currently available under the *Indian Act* to new arrangements beyond the limits of the Act. Different parts of the Department of Indian Affairs are responsible for assisting communities in a variety of areas. Hence, once a decision is made by the community to proceed, the proposal is sent to the appropriate departmental officials for action. In point of fact, proposed agreements require virtually unanimous community agreement. Even the Westbank First Nation Agreement (2004), mentioned above, only passed on its third band ratification vote.

The federal government is very much aware of the control it can exert under this style of government. It is cognizant of the controls that go along with this type of self-government; this control makes Aboriginal decision-making processes more transparent and thus reviewable by the non-Aboriginal system. This, in turn, allows for a greater probability of subjecting Indian political and legal processes to the non-Aboriginal processes (Clark, 1994). Aboriginal people, of course, would prefer a more traditional form of government under which they could develop a measure of cultural and political autonomy.

Municipal Government

A newer form of self-government has been offered to Aboriginal people. This new form of self-government is similar to the existing Canadian municipal government structure. Under the policy, the unit (which could be a band, community, a number of reserves, etc.) would take on the political, economic, and social privileges and responsibilities of a normal municipal government in Canada. The unit would be able to establish residence lists, invoke taxation, create by-laws, own land, and carry out a relationship with the other two levels of government.

This option is enticing to Aboriginal people. It would, on the face of it, lead to greater self-control. It would also make Aboriginal leaders accountable to the local population they represent. And acceptance of this controlled style of self-government would result in the financial support of the federal government. However, this form of municipal self-government is not the fourth level of government envisioned by some Aboriginal leaders. The structure of municipal government, however, ensures that local Aboriginal leaders would provide a buffer between individuals living on the reserves and the federal government. Concern and hostility would be deflected to local leadership, not Indian Affairs personnel. On the downside, the acceptance of the municipal style of government by Aboriginal people could lead to acceptance of the dominant society's culture and values, thus ensuring the further assimilation of Aboriginal persons. The implications of this policy have not gone unnoticed by Aboriginal people; yet they are in a position in which they must make a decision.

Aboriginal people once again find themselves at the crossroads of their destiny. Despite great strides, they are clearly cognizant that they will remain, for some time, economically dependent upon government for the implementation of various programs and services. At the same time, they are determined to develop greater self-control and self-reliance. Their task is to develop one or several workable systems within the context of the Canadian federal system by which they can achieve this goal—unfortunately there can be no "one size fits all" solution.

SUMMARY

The creation of many tribes/nations has led to the use of tribalism as a tool for Aboriginal people negotiating with the federal government and with other special-interest groups. For example, being able to speak for a particular nation gives leaders some credibility and enhances the leaders' ability to achieve specific goals. This has on occasion led to coalitions of several Aboriginal groups in their quest for a particular goal. However, the same structure also leads to inter-tribal conflict. As past experience has vividly shown, coalitions are notoriously unstable, and, as a result, they are usually unable to build long-lasting relationships.

One would assume that, as Aboriginal Canadians continue their urbanization process, tribalism would lose some of its impact, since they would be forced to live in a heterogeneous environment. This should weaken tribal identity. However, evidence suggests that this is not necessarily happening. Competition for political power and jobs in the urban areas has tended to increase rather than decrease the incidence of tribalism (Uchendu, 1970).

In their quest for self-government, Aboriginal people have created a fiction of statehood—a myth that they traditionally had hierarchically structured governments and a ruling elite. As Boldt and Long (1985b) noted, these two factors have not been part of traditional Aboriginal society. The basis of Aboriginal social order, they maintain, was not built on hierarchical authority wielded by a central political organization. Their analysis of Aboriginal culture suggests that these values are essentially irreconcilable with Native history and experiences.

Nevertheless, Aboriginal people have claimed that they have always had some form of statehood and, thus, should also have self-government. The acceptance of this new-model form of European government by Aboriginal people has ushered in a new era with regard to Aboriginal and non-Aboriginal relationships. It also signifies a break with traditional Aboriginal culture and may ultimately mean that the forced assimilation employed by the Canadian government has been successful.

The implementation of municipal self-government, which has become the accepted norm, requires massive ideological and structural changes in the Indian–Inuit Affairs Program. Historically, DIAND was an integrated agent–client organization. During the 1960s it changed to a highly differentiated, but also highly centralized, organizational structure with a number of divisions delivering programs or services to Indians and Inuit (Paton, 1982: 20). Today, both the process of devolution (decentralization) and the concurrent implementation of the policy of band control have adjusted the program's focus. This is discussed in more detail in Chapter 12. The administrative and budgetary control held by DIAND has remained highly centralized throughout its relationship with Canada's Aboriginal peoples.[6]

The different and varied approaches to Aboriginal self-government have been a response to dealing with the unwieldy and confused state of affairs that has prevailed in the Indian–Inuit Affairs Program for many decades (Paton, 1982: 34). This policy has given program authority to Aboriginal communities and established a system of funding that has placed bands in a position of direct responsibility to their constituencies.

KEY TERMS

section 35 of the *Constitution Act*

section 25 of the *Charter of Rights and Freedoms*

Royal Proclamation of 1763

Constitution Act, 1867

Constitution Act, 1982

Calder v. *Attorney General of British Columbia*

Penner Report

Aboriginal self-government

Sechelt Act

STUDY QUESTIONS

1. Define self-determination.

2. What significance did the constitutional patriation hold for Aboriginal people?

3. What three goals could self-government allow Indians to achieve?

4. What are the general principles of Indian government?

5. Discuss the four focuses of Aboriginal self-government and the required action to ensure success.

6. Discuss the significance of the *Sechelt Act*.

7. Discuss the four phases of the community-based self-government process.

8. Discuss the implications of an Aboriginal municipal government for self-government.

WEBLINKS

www.ainc-inac.gc.ca/pr/agr/index_e.html

This Indian and Northern Affairs website is devoted to final agreements, treaties, comprehensive and specific claims, land governance agreements, status of claims, maps, implementation plans, and much more, including self-government agreements. An important related web link is www.aboriginalcanada.gc.ca, which is the government of Canada's Aboriginal Canada Portal, a gateway to links to all major national Aboriginal organizations, economic development, self-government, language and heritage, health and social services, and more.

www.inac.gc.ca/ps/sg/index_e.html

The federal government has collected a number of documents relating to self-government issues at this website, including a statement of Ottawa's policy.

www.gov.bc.ca/arr/treaty/default.html

The B.C. treaty process led to the conclusion of the Nisga'a Final Agreement, which includes substantial self-government powers for the Nisga'a. The agreement is the final settlement of the Nisga'a Aboriginal rights, title, and interest.

NOTES

1. The unilateral imposition of *Bill C-31* by the federal government suggests that neither side has been able to establish a sympathetic relation with the other. *Bill C-31* changed the *Indian Act* with regard to band membership. Under this Bill, bands will control their own membership, and Indian women will no longer lose their status by marrying non-Indians. In addition, Indians who lost their status because of Section 12, 1(b) of the *Indian Act* can now be reinstated and allowed to return to their reserve (see Chapter 2).

2. When the concept of sovereignty is applied to a particular region or people, it suggests that a political state exists. As Nadeau (1979) points out, in order for a state to exist, three conditions have to be present: population, territory, and government. Indians argue that since they possess these three attributes, they should, in turn, have sovereignty.

3. As Clark (1994) points out, the concept of self-government must be distinguished from self-management/administration. These latter terms refer to managing or administering laws that have been created and put in place by other legal entities.

4. The information that follows is taken from published documents of DIAND, personal correspondence with DIAND officials, and from other internal documents produced by DIAND.

5. A series of national surveys showed that Canadians feel that the federal government has become too involved in Aboriginal affairs and that more and more responsibility should be taken over by the Aboriginal people themselves. The surveys also revealed that Canadians feel that Aboriginal people should become more involved in the national economy and that special rights should not exist for them.

6. Throughout the country there are wide variations in the organizational structure of DIAND programs. For example, in British Columbia the program and the budget are almost completely decentralized, while in Manitoba, Indian communities are taking over as DIAND is phasing itself out of existence.

chapter ten

The Inuit of the North: Recognition in the 21st Century

INTRODUCTION

Inuit inhabit vast areas of the Northwest Territories, Yukon, Nunavut, the coast of Northern Labrador, and over one-quarter of Northern Quebec. Inuit origins in Canada go back nearly four millennia and, through their intimate knowledge of the land and its life forms, they have developed skills and technology uniquely adapted to one of the harshest and most demanding environments in Canada.

At the same time, there are Inuit all across the northern region of Canada and they, like other ethnic groups, represent different cultures, languages, and people. (See Figure 10.1) While there are some cultural and historical similarities between the peoples within each of the four regions of the North (See Figure 10.2), each is distinct from the other. Nunatsiavut is the region along the northern coast of Labrador, home to just 5 percent of all Inuit. Nunavik, which is primarily north of the 55th parallel in Quebec, has about one-fifth of the Inuit population. The territory of Nunavut, comprised of many islands, has about one-half of the Inuit in Canada. Finally, the Inuvialuit region in the north-western part of the Northwest Territories has about 7 percent of the Inuit population. The remainder live outside of these regions, including urban areas of southern Canada.

Contact with the outside world came at different times and in different ways as one reviews the history of each of these groups. An analysis of Canada's Inuit provides a revealing look at such issues as class formation, assimilation, the sources and uses of power, community building, and intergenerational differences, just to mention a few. It also allows us to assess how Canadians have dealt with an ethnic group similar to but different from First Nations.[1] Finally, it allows us to gain insights into the successes that Inuit have had in the past two decades over issues such as land claims—successes that First Nations peoples have not had (Brody, 2003). We begin with a brief history of how contact came to be made with Inuit and then look at the social processes and change they have had to deal with. We also look at the issue of identity and how it has changed over time.

In Inuktitut, the word *Inuit* means "the people." It replaces the previous term, *Eskimo,* which is an Indian word used to identify these Arctic people. As Euro-Canadians entered the North they continued to use this term. It would not be until the 1970s that Inuit would ask others not to identify them as Eskimo. Nevertheless, today there are many Canadians who continue to call them Eskimo; and equally important, there are many residents of the Arctic who define themselves as Eskimos, continuing to use the labels attached to them more than a century ago. We also find that many Canadians view and treat Inuit as a homogeneous population and fail to recognize the different ethnic groupings of Inuit in the Arctic and the cultural differences between them. There are many recognized Inuit communities, language groups, and delineated cultural areas. Readers who are going on to specialize in Aboriginal Studies will see that the level of generality in this introductory text requires refinement and specificity as they begin to look at the micro structures of communities and individuals. For example, the Caribou Inuit traditions and interaction patterns are quite different from those of the Baffin Island Inuit, which in turn are different from those of the Netsilik. Nevertheless, it is possible to discuss some common and fundamental aspects of Inuit society in an introductory text. Hence, the more macro perspective will be adopted as we develop a portrait of Inuit in Canada.

FIGURE 10.1	Approximate Location of Indian and Inuit Peoples in Northern Canada Before A.D. 1500, by Language and Dialect Groups

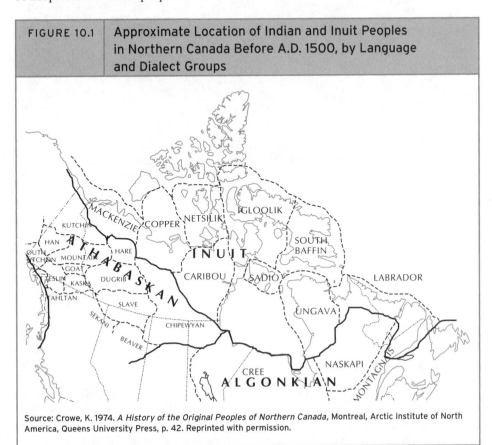

Source: Crowe, K. 1974. *A History of the Original Peoples of Northern Canada*, Montreal, Arctic Institute of North America, Queens University Press, p. 42. Reprinted with permission.

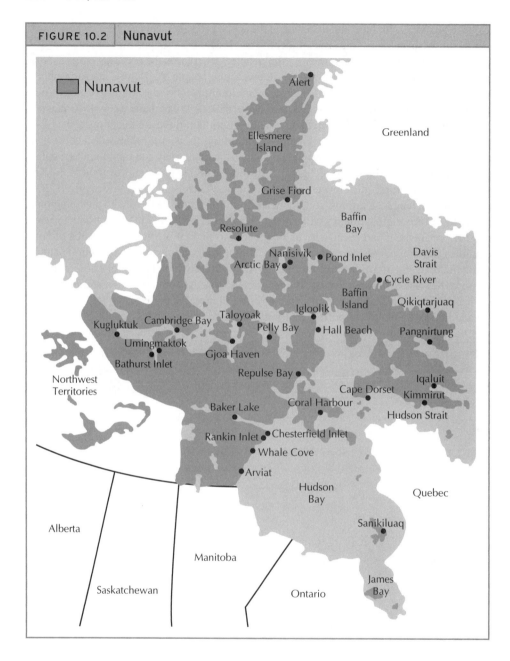

FIGURE 10.2 | Nunavut

A BRIEF HISTORY

Few Canadians realize that the Arctic has been the residence of many different peoples over the past centuries. It is estimated that approximately 10 000 years ago the People of the Small Knife entered the valleys and plateaus of Alaska and Yukon. They were replaced by the Long Spear People some 7000 years ago as they moved north into the lands vacated by the ice. This group was followed by the Denbigh People who, about 5000 years ago, moved into the east shore of the Bering Strait. A fourth prehistorical group in the North were the People of the Old Rock. These residents of northern Quebec and Kivalliq remained in the North until about 3000 years ago, when the climate grew colder and pushed the people southward. This group was replaced by the People of the Arrowhead (3000 years ago) and the Harpoon People, who entered the region approximately 2000 years ago (Crowe, 1974; Richardson, 1993).

Modern-day Inuit emerged from recent groups living in the North. In about 1000 B.C. the Dorset People moved to Baffin Island and spread rapidly across the Arctic. They moved down the Labrador coast and around the coast of Newfoundland by 500 A.D. Between 800 and 1300 A.D. new immigrants from the western Arctic migrated to the east. The new immigrants were better organized and equipped than the Dorset, and within a few years the Dorset People disappeared. This new group (the Thule Inuit) are the direct ancestors of modern Canadian and other Arctic Inuit. It is thought that the original home of the Thule people was in Alaska. The Inuit of Northern Labrador are the most southerly and easterly of Canada's Inuit. They are descendants of Thule Eskimo and it is believed that they have lived in this area since the mid-15th century. They speak Inuktitut, but it is a unique dialect (Fossett, 2001).

The contact period between Inuit and Europeans began around 1500 in the East and the late 1800s in the West. During the 1500s, various nations of Europe were exploring the world, wishing to conquer and spread the Christian faith to all. These European explorers first came into contact with Inuit on the eastern coast of Canada, and later in the central Arctic as they made inroads into the archipelago. For example, the explorer Frobisher kidnapped Inuit both to confirm his landings in a new country and to set up exhibitions for Queen Elizabeth I. The extent of contact is evident by the fact that, during the 17th and 18th centuries, major conflicts between the English and the Inuit of southern Labrador were taking place.

In addition to the explorers, European ships began to hunt whales in the eastern Arctic; most were Scottish and American, although ships from around the world came to these fertile grounds. In the beginning, the contacts between whalers and Inuit on the east coast were peaceful and symbiotic. The Inuit were able to trade for goods not otherwise available to them, and the ships' captains were able to obtain information about whales held only by the Inuit. There was a clear trade between information and material artefacts. By the early 20th century whaling ships were carrying on a brisk trade with the eastern Inuit. However, the influence of the Euro-Canadians went beyond the material and social artefacts brought by the whalers; they also transmitted diseases that decimated many Inuit communities (e.g., scarlet fever and whooping cough) and introduced such goods as alcohol. Within a few years most of the baleen whales in the eastern Arctic had been harvested, and land animals—e.g., caribou and muskox—were close to extinction as a result of the hunting efforts of the whalers and Inuit.

Inuit and outsiders in the western Arctic did not come in contact until later. American whalers entered the western Arctic waters through the Bering Strait around the mid-19th century. Many whaling ships leaving San Francisco in the spring didn't arrive in the Arctic until the summer, and had to "winter over" in order to complete their catch. During this period they remained in the western Arctic, bartering with local Inuit. Bartering was extensive, and the drawing power of the goods being offered by the whalers—e.g., guns and metal tools—was significant. The trade was so pervasive and lasted for so long that large numbers of Inuit migrated to the Beaufort Sea coast in order to participate in the exchange of goods.

The cultural impact of the American whalers was substantial, both in material artefacts and way of life. Over time, many of the species in the area were reduced to the point where they would not support human habitation. In addition, the introduction of influenza and other epidemics decimated the Inuvialuit population, forcing the whalers to bring in Alaskan Inupiat to help them. So great was the social impact that, when the whale market collapsed in the early 1900s, Inuit who were still alive were so integrated into the barter trade that they were unable to return to their former independent rural life (Alunik, 2003).

Another major impact on the North followed the emergence of the fur trade, as new agents of control from southern Canada entered the Arctic. The first, back in the 1600s, were the French Compagnie du Nord and the free traders. These voyageurs were major influences on Inuit as they developed the fur trade. The establishment of forts along water-ways and coastal areas as the centres of trade encouraged Inuit to engage in the fur trade and remain in localized areas. The voyageurs also established the beginning of an unequal trade relationship with the Inuit. Soon after, the Hudson's Bay Company began to dominate the fur trade and extend its sphere of influence into other domains of life.[2]

On the Labrador coast, beginning in the 1750s, the Moravian missionaries and traders began to have sustained contact with Inuit which lasted for over 200 years. Other mission-aries from various religious denominations were to enter the North and attempt to convert Inuit to Christianity.[3] Their impact on the social and cultural way of life of the Inuit was substantial. While their influence was directed toward religious activities, they struck at the basic norms and values of Inuit life. For example, religious groups destroyed the social sol-idarity of Inuit groups by insisting that sexual liaisons between men and women who were not married must stop.

Yet another group to have a deep influence on the Inuit was the Royal Canadian Mounted Police. This group was sent into the North to establish a Canadian presence as well as to enforce Canadian law. Any behaviour by the Inuit that did not meet the minimum conditions of Canadian law was subject to immediate and harsh sanctions.

The fur traders, the missionaries, and the police would influence the lives of the Inuit across the Arctic for half a century (Crowe, 1974).[4] As this triumvirate of Canadian insti-tutions imposed its will, it was able to influence every institutional sphere and network of the Inuit. By the mid-20th century, much of the traditional Inuit way of life had changed (McGhee, 1996).

The traditional way of life of Inuit in the eastern Arctic underwent even more dramatic changes after World War II. As the fur trade collapsed there was a concurrent decline of caribou and fox, which led to a greater dependency on imported goods—e.g., clothes and food, from the South. The collapse of the fur trade also meant that the productive activi-ties of Inuit—e.g., hunting and trapping—did not produce a wage or saleable goods. After World War II the federal government continued its centralization policy to "urbanize" the North, with most of the Inuit population leaving the tundra, the sea, and the sea ice to live in small, serviced communities. At the same time, improved educational and medical facilities in the small towns of the Arctic attracted Inuit. There was also the possibility of wage jobs in these settlements. As a result, for the next two decades there was a steady migration of Inuit from the tundra to the settlements. This movement was supported by government bureaucrats, since it meant that their charges would be in easy reach at all times. Thus, permanent residence in the settlements began, and a social, economic, and transportation infrastructure was put in place in order to service the communities (Lu and Emerson, 1973).

For many years after Confederation the federal government's concern with the North and its people was solely directed toward establishing a physical presence and thus establishing sovereignty over the area. The reader also should remember that the boundaries of the Northwest Territories have changed significantly over the past one hundred years. In the early 1900s, Quebec, Ontario and Manitoba were extended north at the expense of the Territories, while Alberta and Saskatchewan were carved out of their original boundaries, followed by the creation of Yukon. More recently, Nunavut has been established as a new territory out of what was formerly the Northwest Territories.

It was believed that if Canada were to lay claim to the Arctic, it would have to demonstrate to the world that it had permanent residents upon the soil it claimed as part of Canada. While the placement of Royal Canadian Mounted Police stations in various parts of the North went some way toward establishing sovereignty, there was also a belief that "other" Canadians would also have to be physically present. Moreover, there was a belief that the Canadian government would have to provide support to these residents. Thus, effective occupation was the initial and prime consideration for government officials as the 20th century emerged.[5] It was also incumbent upon the Canadian government to make sure that Canadians were living in the Arctic on a year-round basis. As such, relocation programs were invented in order to move Inuit to areas not previously inhabited. For example, families from Inukjuak would be relocated to the high Arctic such as Grise Fiord (in 1953), and later Inuit would be moved to Resolute Bay. Other Inuit relocations were put in place throughout the 1950s.[6] The placement of Inuit into permanent residences also demonstrates the push by government to urbanize the Arctic. Finally, the creation of communities in the Arctic was also justified on the basis that they would afford Inuit an opportunity to pursue their traditional lifestyle (Tester and Kulchyski, 1994).

When the potential of natural resource development emerged in the 1960s, Canadians once again looked to the North to solve their problems. By the end of the 1960s, Inuit were dominated economically, politically, and ideologically. The influence of the traders, missionaries, and police had been supplanted by the presence of the state and multinational corporations. Social programs were extended to Inuit, and housing and medical programs were expanded as the government took a lead in the economic and social development of the North. D'Anglure (1984) argues that the 1960s marked the end of the traditional culture of Inuit and the emergence of the modern economy in the North.

During the 1960s major economic development projects were carried out in the North. The underlying assumption in all these developments was that southern Canada had needs that subordinated those of the indigenous population of the Arctic. There was also a belief that Inuit culture was inferior, and that the standard of living for Inuit needed to be enhanced. Nevertheless, the ambivalence of the federal government's policy toward Inuit showed through. On the one hand it was sure that Inuit culture was doomed, but at the same time it wanted to allow Inuit to "live off the land" if that was what Inuit wanted to do.[7] The result was a compromise: it was decided to create cooperatives as a tool that would allow Inuit integration into the economic structure of Canada, while at the same time allowing them to retain their traditional cultural patterns in other spheres of life. While there was no overall economic plan, there was a logic to the policy (Mitchell, 1996).

If there is a lesson to be learned from this short history of the Arctic, it is that the entry of southern Canadians has always created a crisis for Inuit. As Moss (1995) points out, their presence has always been so intrusive that it displaced and disrupted Inuit culture. Thus, it should not come as a surprise that Inuit are less than enthusiastic about any plans that southern Canadians have about the North, and that they wish to achieve some level of self-government that aligns with Inuit culture and cosmology.

It is important for the reader to understand the Inuit cosmology that guides their thinking and behaviour. While the following is a broad generalization for all Inuit, we believe the five central tenets of Inuit culture are:

1. Everyone must contribute (the principle of communality).
2. Life may have to be sacrificed in order for others to survive (the life principle).
3. Every being contains its whole ancestry
4. There is no hierarchical classification of human and non-human creatures
5. Each form contains multitudes (no form is stable) (Dybbroe, 1996)

While Inuit recognize that their traditional conceptions of sex and leadership have changed, when externally imposed structure did not fit into their culture, they do not adopt it. As one Inuit spokesperson noted:

> No individual makes or enforces law. No group of individuals can speak on behalf of other individuals. No group of individuals constitutes an assembly or equivalent to government. The individualism of the culture is a barrier against any form of organized domination; the egalitarianism a barricade against competitive individualism.

As Dybbroe (1996) points out, the impact of urbanization on Inuit culture may take more time to make itself felt. The relations among Inuit take place within the confines of the family. Although the family is affected by urban life, as a private affair it allows Inuit to maintain a semblance of control over their lives. Nevertheless, Inuit recognize that change is occurring and that they must adapt their beliefs and behaviours to the new way of life.

TABLE 10.1	Inuit Population by Province, 2001		
	Number	Percent Inuit-only Ancestry	Percent Mixed Inuit and Non-Inuit
Canada	55 700	65.7	34.3
Nunavut	27 560	89.2	10.8
Northern Quebec	11 700	88.8	11.2
Newfoundland and Labrador	5 750	52.8	47.2
Northwest Territories	4 350	71.3	28.8
Ontario	1 725	14.8	85.2
Rest of Canada	3 900	25.4	74.6

Source: "Population Reporting an Inuit Identity, Canada and Selected Provinces and Territories, 2001," adapted from the Statistics Canada publication *Aboriginal Peoples of Canada, A Demographic Profile*, Catalogue 96F0030, January 2003; Inuit Tapiriit Kanatami, *Determining the Inuit Population*, December 2006, INAC, 2006, Statistics Canada, 2005.

POPULATION AND SOCIO-DEMOGRAPHIC PROFILE

The total Inuit population in 2001 was nearly 56 000, an increase of 14 percent from 1996. The national distribution of this population is seen in Table 10.1. Sixty-five percent of the population are "Inuit-only" ancestry with the remainder being mixed Inuit and non-Inuit ancestry population. Nearly three-quarters of Inuit live in coastal communities in the North, not accessible by road. Perhaps what is even more important than the small numbers and isolated villages is the linkages that the Inuit have established with other Arctic groups—e.g., Chukotka (Russia), Alaska (United States), and Greenland (Denmark). These groups have formed an international alliance and have become politically active over the past quarter-century.

The age distribution (see Table 10.2) reveals that the Inuit population is very young, with nearly 60 percent under the age of 25. The median age for Inuit is 20.6, 17 years below the median of the non-Aboriginal population. Less than 3 percent of the Inuit population is 65 or older while over 13 percent of the Canadian population is 65 or older. The birth rate for Inuit is estimated to be 4 percent, one of the highest in the world. If this rate were to continue, we could expect the population to double every 18 years. The high birth rate means that Inuit communities are "young" and will continue to exert pressure to integrate into the labour force for some years to come. Nevertheless, the Inuit life expectancy is the lowest in Canada, at 67.7 years for males and 70.2 years for females. In summary, the Inuit population has grown rapidly over the past decade and estimates suggest that, if the present trends continue, there will be nearly 100 000 Inuit in Canada by 2016. The mobility status of Inuit reveals that over 50 percent of Inuit residing in Nunavut did not live at the same address five years ago. Eighty percent of Inuit are Protestant, with only 18 percent Catholic. The remainder are "other" or have no religious affiliation.

Unemployment is high in Inuit communities; unemployment rates of 60 to 80 percent are not uncommon. In 2001 only slightly more than two-thirds of adults reported employment income.[8] An estimated unemployment rate for all Inuit in the North is 21 percent. However, when you compare the discrepancy between Inuit and non-Inuit in Nunavut, Inuit unemployment was 36 percent compared to non-Inuit at 3 percent. Inuit between the ages of 15 to 24 have had an average unemployment rate of 48 percent over the past five

TABLE 10.2	Inuit Age Distribution, 1996 and 2001			
	2001		1996	
	Number	Percent	Number	Percent
Age Group				
0-14	17 460	38.7	16 510	41.0
15-24	8 260	18.3	7 605	18.9
25-64	17 950	39.8	15 095	37.5
65 and over	1 405	3.1	1 015	2.5

Source: "Population Reporting an Inuit Identity, and Age Groups, 1996 and 2001," adapted from the Statistics Canada publication *Aboriginal Peoples of Canada, A Demographic Profile*, Catalogue 96F0030, January 2003; Inuit Tapiriit Kanatami, *Determining the Inuit Population*, December 2006, INAC 2006, Statistics Canada, 2005.

years. The depressed economy of the Arctic is the major structural reason for its high unemployment, and this is not likely to change in the near future.

Table 10.3 identifies Inuit placement in the occupational structure for 2001. The data show that most of the Inuit within the labour force are found in semi-skilled and manual-labour types of jobs (52%). There are some skilled craftspersons and semi-professionals (29%), but these are limited. Even fewer are in positions of power and decision making. It is also important to note that, regardless of the field, many of the jobs in the Arctic are in government (federal, territorial, and municipal) as opposed to the private sector.

While employment is related to income, the most recent data show that 17 percent of the Inuit adult population claimed no earned income for 2004.[9] Ten percent made under $2000 per year, and another 30 percent made between $2000 and $10 000 per year. This means that well over half of the Inuit population made less than $10 000 per year. Twenty percent made between $10 000 and $20 000 while 16 percent made between $20 000 and $40 000 per year. Only 7 percent made more than $40 000 per year. Overall, we find that Inuit working full time had a median income in 2004 of $19 900 while for non-Inuit living in the North, it was $58,100.

While standard measures of employment and income may not be as appropriate for Inuit living in the north as for other Canadians, the data show that over the past two decades labour force participation has increased for both Inuit men and women.[10] At the same time, the unemployment gap between Inuit and non-Inuit increased over this period of time. What is problematic is that the highest rate of unemployment is for the young people who are entering the labour market. Moreover, the data show that there has been no change in the percentage of Inuit moving from low-skilled occupations to more highly skilled jobs, with a concentration in tertiary industries—health and social services, trade and government services.

TABLE 10.3	Inuit Occupational Distribution by Sex (%) in Nunavut, 2001	
	Experienced Labour Force	
	Male	Female
Total	5 825	4 905
Management	12.7	7.6
Business, finance and admin.	7.5	23.3
Natural and applied sciences and health	6.6	6.8
Sales and service	22.2	30.8
Art, culture recreation	6.4	5.6
Social science, education, government	8.1	22.3
Trades, transport, equipment operators	31.7	1.8
Other/not stated	4.5	1.8

Sources: Statistics Canada, 2005; INAC, 2006; INAC, 2000; Champagne, Torjesen and Steiner, 2005; Statistics Canada, 2004.

As Inuit have become more involved in the wage economy, young people have redefined their involvement in subsistence activities. However, the change is not simple or straightforward. The cumulative changes have led to a reorientation of daily practices that has caused young Inuit to see subsistence activities not as desirable and valuable, but to see them as recreations and something to be enjoyed once other, more important demands—e.g., waged labour-force participation—are met (Stern, 2000). Young people see the town they live in as the "place they work and live" and the land as a "place to get away from it all." In addition, participation in the labour force acts as both a barrier and facilitator for individuals to engage in "subsistence activities." For example, the additional cash allows those who have high-status, high-paying jobs to purchase snowmobiles and other pieces of equipment that facilitate their "back to the land" activities. However, those who are not able to afford this kind of equipment are not able to participate in subsistence activities.

Urbanization

Nearly one-fourth of the Inuit population live in large southern urban areas. The numbers below provides the reader with some sense of the size of Inuit populations in urban areas of southern Canada and the North. If northern towns are added to the list, nearly 90 percent of the Inuit population live in non-rural areas. Today, in the five largest communities in Nunavut, with the exception of Iqaliut (which is the government centre for the Territory), over 80 percent of the population is Inuit (see Table 10.4).

Moreover, the number of Inuit in large urban centres in the South has grown significantly since this time with nearly 11 000 Inuit living in southern urban areas. Kishigami (1999) found that Inuit living in the South comprised three major groupings: students, workers, and unemployed. She also found that many residents of Montreal had moved from the North in order to escape alcohol and drug problems, sexual and physical violence, and other problems of human relations in a small town. In short, she found that individuals' decision to move to a southern urban centre was not mainly a function of urban resources and opportunities available to them, but was rather due to their desire to leave the North. Others, such as students once they completed their education, found they were able to expand their job opportunities and therefore postponed returning to the North. However,

TABLE 10.4	Inuit Populations in Various Communities, 2001		
South		**North**	
Toronto	1900	Iqaluit	3 010
Edmonton	850	Arviat	1 785
Montreal	800	Rankin Inlet	1 680
Ottawa-Hull	750	Baker Lake	1 405
Calgary	650	Kuujjuaq	1 540
Vancouver	600		
Winnipeg	550		

Statistics Canada, 2000, 2003, 2005, 2006; Inuit Tapiriit Kanatami, 2004.

none of the Inuit living in the urban centres were able to develop or create an Inuit urban culture and identity. The lack of a strong social network and the paucity of Inuit in any one locale prevents the development of Inuit organizations, the continuation of the Inuit language, and the maintenance of Inuit culture.

Housing

The housing stock in the North is aging and of poor quality. It is estimated that today the Inuit of the Arctic need 3000 new homes, but the federal government has projected budgets for only about 300 per year. This requires housing construction to fall back upon the income of Inuit and other sources. If the current population were to remain stable it would take a decade to provide the necessary housing units. However, by the end of the decade the population will have increased and older housing stock will have deteriorated even further. As a result, the housing crisis will worsen. The average number of persons per dwelling is about 5.4, with the number of rooms per dwelling at 4.3. The number of persons per dwelling is substantially higher than the Canadian average and suggests that crowding is the usual condition for Inuit families. Statistics Canada (2003) points out that over half of the Inuit in the North live in crowded conditions, and one-quarter live in homes requiring major repairs. Nevertheless, the existing housing for Inuit is relatively new, with 40 percent having been built within the last decade.[11] An additional 30 percent is less than 20 years old. Because most of the housing is located in urban settings, nearly two-thirds are linked to a municipal water system. However, about one-quarter of the current dwellings obtain their water directly from surface water—e.g., streams or lakes.

Education

At the end of World War II only four schools existed in the then Northwest Territories. Three were Catholic, and the other Anglican. When the federal government took over Northern education in 1947 it assumed that Inuit were illiterate and "backward" because they had not been exposed to the southern Canadian educational system and did not speak English or French. Thus, without evaluating the type of educational system that the North required, the entire southern educational structure was exported there. Two years later the government established a network of public schools for Inuit. However, because no southern non-Inuit teachers could speak Inuktitut (or any of the dialects), the sole language of instruction was English or French.

By 1951 a system of residential schools was established, with students from remote areas being relocated to schools for up to 10 months a year. While the government covered the cost of education, the schools were run by religious institutions. These residential schools isolated children from their parents, whose socialization efforts were limited to short visits by the children. Parental control was replaced by the religious fervour exhibited by the Catholic or Anglican teachers, who felt that students would do better once removed from the negative influences of home and parents.

Once communities grew to sufficient size, day schools were established. Nevertheless, the southern, Euro-Canadian curriculum in northern schools continued to be taught by non-Inuit, southern-trained teachers. It would not be until the 1960s that a curriculum was implemented that took into consideration Inuit language, culture, and values (Duffy, 1988). In 1970 administrative responsibility for northern schools was transferred to the government of the Northwest Territories. The Inuit Tapirisat's lobbying efforts were a major factor in the government's decision to change its educational methods in the Arctic. The Tapirisat proposed that courses be taught with a strong northern orientation, and the Inuit Cultural Institute was created to protect Inuit language and culture. In addition, the establishment of Nunavut and Aurora Arctic College has afforded the opportunity for Inuit students to obtain selected degrees while remaining in the North. As a result, many teachers in Inuit communities have bachelors and master's degrees in education and have taken on some administrative responsibility in the schools.

Table 10.5 reveals the level of formal education of Inuit for the years 1981 and 2001 in percentages. First of all it shows dramatic increases in the proportion of Inuit attending formal schooling since 1981. Comparing this data to that of non-Inuit, we find that over twice the number of Inuit have less than grade 9 education. However, with regards to having completed a trades program or completed college, Inuit are similar to non-Inuit. Finally the number having completed a university program is three times less than their non-Inuit counterpart.

Nevertheless, there has been and continues to be a high attrition rate of Inuit from the education system. Official data from Statistics Canada (2001) show that about one-third of Inuit children reach Grade 9, compared to over 80 percent for the Canadian population. Less than 25 percent graduate from high school (the overall Canadian rate is about 76 percent) and less than 2 percent go on to university. In the North, post-secondary institutions exist in Whitehorse, Yellowknife and Fort Smith that allow students to transfer to southern post-secondary educational institutions and continue their educational program to obtain a university degree. Today there are three post-secondary educational institutions in Nunavut—Iqaluit, Cambridge Bay, and Rankin Inlet. In other Nunavut communities, there are "community learning centres" that provide post-secondary courses. Focusing on the adult population[12] (ages 35–49), we find that 34 percent have less than a high school education. Twenty percent claim to have a secondary education and 16 percent claim some

TABLE 10.5	Highest Level of Education of Inuit Aged 15 and Over, Canada, 1981–2001 (in Percentages)	
	YEAR	
Level of Education	1981	2001
Less than grade 8	60.5	23.5
Some high school	20.1	29.3
High school certificate	3.2	7.3
Some post-secondary	6.3	15.6
Trades certificate	6.0	11.4
College graduation	2.2	9.7
University graduation	1.6	3.3

Source: Adapted from: Inuit Tapiriit Kanatami and Research and Analysis Directorate, *Gains Made by Inuit in Formal Education and School Attendance, 1981-2001*, Strategic Research and Analysis Directorate, Indian and Northern Affairs Canada, December, 2006; Statistics Canada, 2004, 2005.

post-secondary education, e.g., trades or college certificate. Just over 10 percent have a university certificate, diploma or degree.

When we look at the younger population (ages 5–14), we find that 99 percent are currently attending school, over three-quarters claiming to have an Aboriginal teacher. Eighty-one percent of the students say that their teachers use English in the classroom. However, nearly three-quarters also report that an Aboriginal language is also used in their classes.[13] Grades 1 through 3 in Nunavut and other Inuit communities are taught in Inuktitut, even for non-Inuit students in the class. This suggests that today's classrooms are bilingual, perhaps explaining why Inuktitut is still a thriving language (Sarkadi, 1992; Dorais and Krupnik, 2005). With regard to language, well over two-thirds of the Inuit population know and use it regularly. Furthermore, almost 70 percent of Inuit children claimed an ability to carry on a conversation in Inuktitut (see Figure 10.3).

However, less than one-quarter of these children report reading Aboriginal language newspapers, newsletters, or magazines. Three-quarters of the adults claim to speak Inuktitut.[14] Three-quarters of the Inuit population reported speaking Inuktitut in the home, while only one-third spoke it at work and only 10 percent in school. Two-thirds of the adults who claim to be Inuit are able to read Inuktitut, and nearly half of them claim to read Inuktitut newspapers and magazines. Sixty percent claim that they are able to write Inuktitut (Taqralik, 1984; Patrick, 2005).

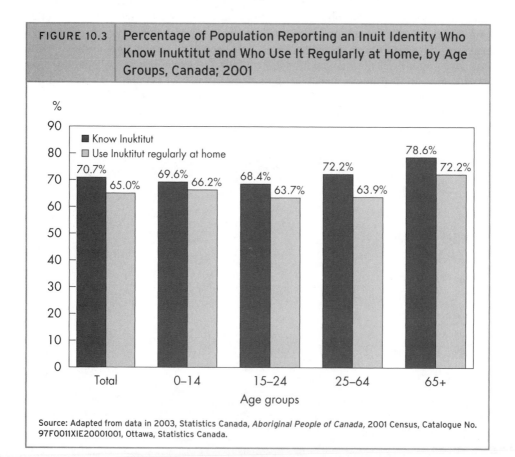

FIGURE 10.3 | Percentage of Population Reporting an Inuit Identity Who Know Inuktitut and Who Use It Regularly at Home, by Age Groups, Canada; 2001

Source: Adapted from data in 2003, Statistics Canada, *Aboriginal People of Canada*, 2001 Census, Catalogue No. 97F0011XIE20001001, Ottawa, Statistics Canada.

Health

Settlements with a population of over 200 usually have nursing stations, which are the backbone of the health care system of the North. They are staffed by registered nurses and are open 24 hours a day. Although health clinics have been established in the larger communities, the existence of hospitals in the North is not extensive. During the 1970s and 1980s the federal government carried out an evaluation of the efficiency and effectiveness of maintaining hospitals in the North. It concluded that, except in the largest urban areas of the North, the existence of hospitals was inefficient, ineffective, and posed both staffing and financial hardships. For example, it found that, while funds could be allocated to the construction of a hospital, staffing was most problematic. As such, even the best and most up-to-date equipment was useless if qualified staff were not in residence. In the end it was agreed that clinics would be the standard provision of health care in the North, although for serious medical cases patients would be airlifted to nearby northern hospitals or the nearest hospital in the South.[15] Nevertheless, many culturally relevant health services are provided in the existing hospitals—for example, in Iqaluit.

For the first half of the 20th century the most prevalent disease to afflict Inuit was tuberculosis. In 1944 the tuberculosis rate was 568 per 100 000. In an effort to deal with the disease the federal government promoted extensive relocation and regimentation of the Inuit population. Large Inuit communities were created in southern Canada through the establishment of TB sanatoriums, and it has been estimated that at one time the largest Inuit community was in Ontario. Today the rate is less than 50 cases per 100 000, but this is still considerably higher than the overall Canadian rate.

Another health issue for Inuit is the infant mortality rate. In 1958 the rate for Inuit was among the highest in the world, at 151 per 1000 live births (compared to 30 per 1000 for the rest of Canada). Again, due to improved health care, these figures have dropped dramatically over time. By 2004, infant mortality rates were 16 per 1000, still three times the national average.

Inuit health has been influenced by ecological, social, and nutritional changes. For example, creating urban zones in permafrost areas has created major environmental and health problems for the residents. Poor nutrition also has contributed to a general lowering of health of Inuit in all areas of the North. Increasing consumption of imported foods with little or no nutritional value has characterized the Inuit's current eating habits. Over time Inuit came to rely more and more upon imported foods of whose nutritional content they were not aware.[16] Thus, the standard of health for Inuit has steadily deteriorated. Moreover, nearly one-quarter of the adult Inuit population reported chronic health problems. In summary, while many economic strategies were developed to help the Inuit throughout the past half century, there has been little attempt to solve the nutritional problem facing Inuit people.

During the 1960s and 1970s, the death pattern and rate for Inuit changed dramatically. As tuberculosis decreased in importance, pneumonia became the leading cause of death. In the 1960s, pneumonia accounted for over one-fifth of the Inuit deaths. Today, "injuries, violence, and accidents" are the leading causes of death for Inuit. Today, the suicide rate in Nunavut is 132/100 000, while the Canadian average is 17.9. Drug and alcohol addictions also have become major problems facing Inuit people. In addition, new health hazards have appeared in the late 20th and early 21st centuries (Gombay, 2005). Sexually transmitted diseases like gonorrhoea and AIDS have attained near-crisis levels (Hobart, 1991).

As we assess the health of the Inuit people it is clear that several social and ecological factors have contributed to their decreasing quality of life, poor housing, nutrition, and poverty (Martin, 2005). The result is that the life expectancy of Inuit today is about 10 to 15 years less than that of a Canadian living in the South.

Law and Justice

As Canada began to impose its cultural and administrative structures on northerners, the implementation of southern law and justice prevailed. Today, most police services are provided by the RCMP with little input from Inuit residents. However, in some areas, such as Kativik, Quebec, a regional police force comprising many Inuit officers operates in Inuit communities (Burkhardt, 2004).

With regard to involvement in the justice system, we also find that many Inuit are serving sentences in federal and territorial prisons. Faulkner (1992) carried out a study of over 50 Inuit men and women currently serving time in correctional institutions. She found that, with few exceptions, the major cause for imprisonment was substance abuse. She also found that in most federal jails workers are not sensitive to the cultural needs of Inuit prisoners. Recent data confirms that this is still the case. Although many correctional personnel have obtained cross-cultural training, much of it is geared to the cultural needs of First Nations and not Inuit. In an attempt to deal with this concern, Corrections Canada is contracting out many of the activities dealing with Inuit inmates. Unfortunately, this means that it cannot control the quality of the work or the qualifications of the workers. Moreover, because the outsourced workers are not part of the Correctional Service of Canada, they are not eligible to participate in government "managing diversity" programs.

Federal officials also have placed some Inuit in provincial facilities in an attempt to match the cultural programs and the needs of Inuit inmates. This also means that Inuit are closer to home and have some contact with family and friends, which they do not have when removed from the community and placed in southern Canadian jails. However, these provincial facilities do not have long-term programs and appropriate counselling services. One exception is the new "healing house" about to be constructed in Kagluktuk. Nevertheless, this Catch-22 situation has yet to be resolved (Burkhardt, 2004).

ECONOMIC DEVELOPMENT

Under current arrangements, the North is completely dependent upon the federal government. With a current gross domestic product of barely $1 billion, and a territorial budget of $730 million, northern Canada remains heavily dependent upon Ottawa. Over 90 percent of territorial government revenue is derived from federal transfer payments. All natural resource royalty payments in the North flow directly to the south, and government spending still accounts for about two-thirds of the territory's economy.

When the federal government began to actively intervene in ongoing activities in the Northwest Territories during the 1950s, solutions to the economic plight of Inuit had a high priority. While co-ops in the rest of Canada were given lukewarm reception by the federal government, in the North they were supported and heavily subsidized. Although this was a departure from the usual stance taken by government it was felt that the end justified the means. The co-ops of the North were specifically ethnic and were not integrated into the mainstream co-op movement in Southern Canada. As such, they did not pose an economic threat to private industry. By 1966, 22 Arctic co-ops had been established, and by 1982 the annual level of business exceeded $30 million. Today there are over 40 active Inuit cooperatives, each belonging to one of two administrative bodies. There are 12 Arctic Quebec co-ops under the Montreal-based Fédération des Cooperatives du Nouveau-Québec, with the remainder being members of Arctic Co-operatives Limited (based in Winnipeg). Today the major activity of the co-ops has been in the production and marketing of handicrafts.

As noted above, co-ops were the federal government's economic structure of choice for integrating Inuit into Canadian society. But although there has been some success with these co-ops, particularly in the production of handicrafts, overall they have not allowed Inuit to integrate economically and have not provided a linkage with other Canadian economic institutions. The inability of co-ops to increase their membership and assets meant that Inuit were forced to look for new ways to develop sustainable economic ventures. But with no large amounts of money, little human capital relevant to the industrial economy, and limited backing by the federal government, this proved to be an impossible task. However, the settlement of comprehensive land claims has provided some hope as new forms of economic structures have emerged. When the new "development corporations" were established, their first act was to hire qualified individuals. Because co-ops had provided a training ground for Inuit, they were the first place to look. And with offerings of higher status and salaries, it was not difficult to produce "brain drain" in the co-op management. The impact of this action has been to further decrease the effectiveness of co-ops as independent economic institutions.

Most of these new development corporations have focused their efforts on mega-projects, requiring skilled workers and considerable "up-front, sunken costs." The end result has been the hiring of large numbers of non-Inuit and a reliance on capital from outside the region. For example, Makivik lost over $10 million in its first four years of operation. While it is making a small profit today, many of the subsidiary companies are losing money or have been terminated—e.g., Air Inuit and Kigiak Builders Inc. Nevertheless, other Inuit-owned-and-operated businesses are slowly developing into sustainable operations.

A recent federal report on the "economic health" of Arctic communities shows that only seven communities in the Northwest Territories were rated as being "developed," which means that they have good transportation systems, a significant private sector, and the potential to provide residents with jobs. Six other communities had some "potential," but the majority were classified as "underdeveloped" and with no real economic potential. However, when areas do have economic potential, Inuit involvement is challenged. For example, the discovery of copper, cobalt, and nickel in Voisey's Bay (50 kilometres north of Davis Inlet–Utshimassits) prompted the Inuit and Innu to more forcefully make their land claim case, since Voisey's Bay is within the currently contested land area. However, neither the federal nor provincial government has suggested that land rights might take precedence over outside exploitation of natural resources. In a recent move, the province of Newfoundland and Labrador has placed restrictions on the development of the potential nickel mine, and the developers have chosen to "shelve" their plans for the immediate future and move their development efforts to other areas in the world that are "more friendly" to the exploitation of natural resources.

Living in Arctic communities requires cash. And while new jobs have been created by the establishment of Nunavut, many Northerners do not wish to work for government or may not have the skills to participate. Many public service jobs created remain unfilled because of the local population's lack of skills to fill them. This means that other employment opportunities will need to be created. During the late 1980s and early 1990s, non-renewable resource development was touted as an alternative supply of work. However, mining has never employed more than 1.5 percent of the Native labour force in the Northwest Territories, and oil development has involved even fewer. Moreover, the boom and bust nature of such activities creates a volatile and transient labour force. For example, after drilling levels in the Arctic islands peaked at 37 wells in 1973, exploration declined sharply, eventually coming to a halt in 1987. Nevertheless, there is some evidence to suggest that part-time employment in the Arctic is preferred by Inuit, in that it allows them to participate in the traditional economy. Myers (2001) argues that the traditional economy is an important component of local life and he points out that, in the 1980s, the average of $11 000 (which today would equal $28 000) was an imputed value per Native household for country food and domestic production. He goes on to claim that more than 90 percent of Inuit households consume country food, and more than 70 percent hunt or fish. Today a boom is being contemplated once again. The major gas fields in the Mackenzie Delta area of the Northwest Territories and the proposed Mackenzie Pipeline are being touted as economic development projects that can involve local Aboriginal people. However, many note that the local people do not have the necessary skills to participate in long-term jobs associated with the development of the gas field and the pipeline.

In the early 21st century, the labour force showed that Arctic communities continued their participation in hunting, fishing, trapping, and producing crafts. In the Qikiqtaaluk communities, between 34 and 76 percent of the labour force is involved in traditional economies. On the other hand, small businesses are increasing in the North and Robinson, Dickerson and Pretes (1991) found that over half of the Northwest Territories' employment and 41 percent of the total payroll was made up of small businesses. Nevertheless, a combination of enterprises rooted in tradition (e.g., country food, commercial fishing, fur, leather, crafts, tourism) community-based developments (e.g., renewable resources) retail, wholesale, and non-renewable resource development will be necessary. The North remains significantly unexplored, but there is considerable evidence that it is a rich storehouse of oil, gas, gold, copper, zinc, uranium, diamonds and other minerals. In 2001, mining was the largest sectoral contributor to the gross domestic product (20%). In that year, $90 million worth of mineral exploration activity was under way in Nunavut. Towns such as Yellowknife and Inuvik clearly have developed markets in the retail and wholesale business sector and could expand their scope. With regard to other communities such as Kugluktuk, Cape Dorset, and Norman Wells, these communities could expand their roles as regional supply centres and expand the local range of goods and services. Other smaller communities have potential for developing their arts and crafts and other forms of human and natural resource development. For example, one in five individuals in the Nunavut region sold crafts in 2002. The Waddington auction house that sells Inuit art sold more than $1.2 million of Inuit art in 2002. Regardless of the type of development undertaken in the North, it will have to be based more on the Inuit lifestyle, resources, and values.

The traditional economy of the Inuit is no longer the main support structure for the development of an Arctic economy. The existing structures remain isolated from both the Canadian and the global industrialized economies. Even the new development corporations that have been created are marginal in their ability to become "engines" of growth in the Arctic. As a result, there is a clear ethnic stratification in the Arctic that segregates Inuit from non-Inuit southerners. This inequality is maintained through unequal access to jobs, services, and goods. Individual and structural discrimination has further divided the indigenous population from the remainder of the Arctic residents. For example, when the shrimp quota for Canada was increased because of new sources in the North, only 51 percent of the increase was allocated to northern companies, with the remainder being allocated to southern interests. These kind of structural inequalities make it difficult for local businesses such as the Pangrirung Fisheries (which employs 100 people and processes 1.5 million pounds of fish per year) to succeed.

Today there is recognition that development of the North up until now has been southern-driven, with only short-term benefits for northern residents. As a result, the traditional-based economy has survived and reaffirmed the Inuit cultural and social values. Nevertheless, there is acknowledgement that if the Inuit do not want to lose young people from the North to the South, they will need to develop and create community-based economic opportunities that meet the needs of northern residents. As such, there is agreement that four factors will need to be taken into consideration if Nunavut and other Inuit communities want to economically develop: physical capital (e.g., housing, commercial space, transportation, telecommunications), human capital (e.g., individual skill sets), natural capital (e.g., natural resources), and social and organization capital (e.g., community cohesion).

For example, Nunavut has a mixed economy that features both a land-based as well as a wage economy. These economies are not mutually exclusive, and most Inuit want to achieve a balance between both. Land-based activities represent more than economic activity—they are an integral part of the cultural and social processes of the Inuit way of life. The social relations underlying the production of food in the traditional economy are critical to the functioning of that economy, and the sharing of food within the household and through the extended family and community are major ways in which social relations are reinforced (Canada, 1996a:472).

Data from the Aboriginal Peoples Survey (2001) reveal that harvesting country food is an activity that is still actively practiced by the Inuit in all regions of the North. It shows that 7 in 10 Inuit adults harvested country food during 2000. In 40 percent of Inuit households in the Arctic, this food made up more than half of the meat and fish that was eaten. In another one-third of the households, about half of the meat and fish eaten was country food. In addition to the economic advantages of using country food (it is cheaper than store-bought foods), it also is higher in protein and lower in fat than most meats from southern Canada. Country foods are also rich in iron, calcium, omega-3 fatty acids, and other vitamins that are not prevalent in store-bought foods.

The utilization of "country foods" also supports Inuit culture, in that it involves the sharing of resources with roles and responsibilities for each member based on age, sex, and experience with the kinship affiliate. Tait (2006) points out that the sharing of food is an important Inuit tradition that serves to keep family and community ties strong. This tradition is alive and well in all regions across the North, as nearly all Inuit households shared harvested food with others outside of their home in the year 2000 (Burch, 2004). Today the size of the land-based economy is estimated at about $60M per year (Canadian Arctic Resources Committee, 2004). However, its contribution to the social fabric of Inuit society is invaluable and no value can be attributed. On the other hand, Nunavut's wage economy is estimated to be about $800M. Nevertheless, it is clear that Nunavut's four forms of capital will need to be developed if true development is to take place in the region.

In turn, Inuit values will need to be taken into consideration when developing a course for Inuit economic development. Values such as a collective approach to socio-economic development, e.g., the belief that economic opportunities should be shared among all communities, will need to be acknowledged. Other values influencing economic development include:

- Inuit having greater political and economic control of the area and its environment
- recognition of the value of Inuit knowledge and integrating it with other knowledge sources.
- the development of consensus building and consultation as the preferred manner in decision making
- focusing economic development at the community level
- focus on sustainable development activities.

While these values certainly characterize the working and aging population of the Inuit today, the question remains as to whether or not they are also central to values of Inuit youth. Finally, the role of the federal government in providing federal transfers to Nunavut has an important impact on the nature and pace of economic development of the region.

A TIME FOR CHANGE

As the Cold War intensified in the 1950s, the Distant Early Warning system was put in place throughout the Canadian Arctic.[17] These small, isolated military installations brought southerners to the Arctic on a permanent basis. Infrastructure had to be put in place in order to ensure that these installations could be accessed at any time. It also meant that existing communities in the North had to be modernized so that they could act as a secondary stage to access these installations. In short, the modern industrial economy began to impact upon the Arctic. At the same time, social programs were made available to Inuit.

By the early 1960s the federal government implemented a policy to develop the natural resources of the North. The government's "Roads for Resources" program, which gave direction to the development of the natural resources of the North, had introduced multinationals and their associated technology to the North. It was at this time that Inuit communities became more actively involved in policy and programs directed toward the North, even though they were not able to participate in the programs due to a lack of educational and technical skills (Jull, 1982).

The Inuit have been interested in integrating into the larger economic institutional structures of Canada and concerned with Aboriginal rights for some time, but it has only been in the past few years that they have been able to forcefully act on those beliefs. They have been facilitated by external and internal forces. For example, environmental concerns, linkages with other national indigenous groups, land settlements in Alaska and Greenland, and less demand for developing petroleum resources in the North have reduced southern intrusion into the Arctic, and have given Inuit an opportunity to organize and clearly articulate their concerns as well as their goals as Canadians. At the same time, the participation by Inuit in domestic governmental structures (both federal and territorial) has produced an awareness of Inuit concerns and helped them to develop political and economic strategies to deal with those issues.

The process of decolonization has begun for Inuit as self-government negotiations have taken place in all four Arctic regions: Inuvialuit (western Arctic), Nunavut (eastern Arctic), Nunavik (northern Quebec), and Nunatsiavut (northern Labrador and Newfoundland). Inuit have always argued that they do not want to achieve self-determination through racially segregated structures or secession. They consider themselves Canadian, yet they want an explicit recognition of the place of Inuit in Canadian society.

LAND CLAIMS

Aboriginal land claims are as old as Canada, and while many of the land claims were settled through treaty, there are virtually no treaty settlements involving the North.[18] A review of government documents clearly demonstrates that the federal government did not want to treat Inuit as they did Indians. Federal officials were adamant that Inuit were not Indians (although the Supreme Court decided differently in 1939) and they therefore refused to establish treaties with the Inuit. As a result, until the 1970s, most of the land in the Yukon and Northwest Territories was under contested ownership. The *Alaska Native Claims Settlement Act* (1971) was the first modern Aboriginal land settlement in North America and became the precursor to modern Aboriginal land claims in Canada. It both set the stage and served as a model for Canadian legal settlements. However, it should be made clear that the impetus for settling land claims was not generated by Inuit but by the federal government. The government's interest in settling land claims emerged out of the potential difficulties it foresaw in developing the natural resources of the North. Land claims were entered into because the government saw them as a legal obstacle that needed to be dealt with as quickly as possible if development was to move forward (Mitchell, 1996).

James Bay

The first major, modern-day land claims settlement occurred in 1975 with the James Bay Cree and Inuit of Quebec, who reside north of the 55th parallel. The agreement followed both the Alaska settlement and the *Calder* decision of the Supreme Court, which had recognized the existence of Aboriginal rights. It had not been until the James Bay Hydro development became an issue that anyone focused any concern on the local Aboriginal people. Government interest was piqued only once the Inuit and Indians objected to the development and obtained a court injunction against it. The end result, the James Bay and Northern Quebec Agreement (1975), dealt with the Aboriginal land claims and compensation. In addition, the settlement provided Aboriginal people (both Inuit and Indians) with hunting rights, land rights, and an acceptance of Aboriginal rights. The Inuit communities of this region became public municipal governments under Quebec's municipality legislation (Purich, 1992). The Kativik regional government in northern Quebec is the administrative structure now used to govern the region. This structure, like others advocated by Inuit, is not racially based. Because of their majority status the Inuit are able to control their regional government; however, their efforts are limited by their financial dependence on the federal government.[19]

Other organizational and administrative structures were also put in place. For example, under the James Bay Agreement the Makivik Corporation was created. Its role is to receive compensation and invest it in such a way that it will improve the quality of life of Inuit. The Kativik School Board was also established under the provisions of the James Bay Agreement.

Western Arctic

In the western Arctic the Inuvialuit[20] founded the Committee for Original People's Entitlement and formed an alliance with eastern Inuit. First put forward in 1976 by the Inuit

Tapirisat of Canada, a proposal for establishing Nunavut as a politically distinct federal territory extracted from the Northwest Territories was presented to the federal government. Later that year the proposal was withdrawn, and a new land claim was submitted a year later by the Committee for Original People's Entitlement, focusing only on the western Arctic. The resulting Inuvialuit Agreement was to become the second major land claims settlement reached in Canada since the federal land claims policy was put into effect in 1973. In 1984 the Inuvialuit Final Agreement was signed, providing a guarantee that Inuvialuit would not be treated any less favourably than any other group in the western Arctic. Under this agreement, the Inuvialuit surrendered their rights to 344 000 square kilometres of land. In return they were guaranteed title to 91 000 square kilometres and mineral rights in one-seventh of that zone. In addition, they received $152 million compensation payable over a 13-year period. Several wildlife-management structures were also put into place, along with an income support program (Alunik, 2003).

Labrador

As the Moravians entered the eastern coast of Labrador, they had been able to acquire land upon which to base their operations. Labrador Inuit subsequently tried, unsuccessfully, to get that land back for some time. In 1974 the Labrador Inuit Association outlined its land claims against the federal government. However, it would take more than 10 years before a comprehensive framework agreement to cover Labrador Inuit claims was initialled by the interested parties. By 1978 the federal government had accepted the claim by 3500 Inuit of Labrador. One year later the province of Newfoundland agreed to enter into the negotiations. It would not be until 1990, however, that the two governments signed a framework agreement outlining the scope, process, topics, and parameters for negotiation (Purich, 1992). It then took until 2005 before the Labrador Inuit Land claim agreement was ratified.

The Labrador Inuit Association, the regional organization that has spearheaded the struggle for recognition by the Inuit of Labrador, represents about 5000 people, and is recognized by the government of Canada and the province of Newfoundland and Labrador. As Haysom (1992) notes, the Labrador Inuit Association also has been influential outside the claims arena. Specifically, the association has sponsored at least nine other organizations that are influential in the provision of social, health, and economic benefits to Inuit—e.g., the Torngat Regional Housing Association, Labrador Inuit Health Commission, Labrador Inuit Development Corporation, and the Labrador Inuit Alcohol and Drug Abuse Program.

Inuit Corporate Structure

As we noted earlier, the economic development of the North and how it operates has been a concern for both northerners and government for some time. As a result, when governments have negotiated with Inuit people and land settlements were resolved, part of the agreements has been the creation of an overarching organization that will deal with the financial dimension. These corporate structures have been entrusted with ensuring that due diligence is given before development is undertaken, and that accountability is maintained for both the communities and the government. The following illustrates just one of these corporate structures (Inuvialuit) and the role it plays in the North.

In 1984 the federal government signed the Inuvialuit Final Agreement with the Committee for Original People's Entitlement, which represented the Inuvialuit of the western

Arctic. (See Figure 10.4 for the area encompassed under the agreement.) Under this agreement, the Inuvialuit relinquished their claim to lands in the western Arctic in exchange for legal title to selected lands, financial compensation, and hunting, fishing, and trapping rights (Keeping, 1989: 2). When the Inuvialuit Western Agreement was signed a political and corporate structure was also created. The Inuvialuit Regional Corporation (successor to the Committee for Original People's Entitlement) is controlled by the six communities in the region. A number of subsidiary corporations were also established—e.g., the Inuvialuit

FIGURE 10.4	Inuvialuit Settlement Region

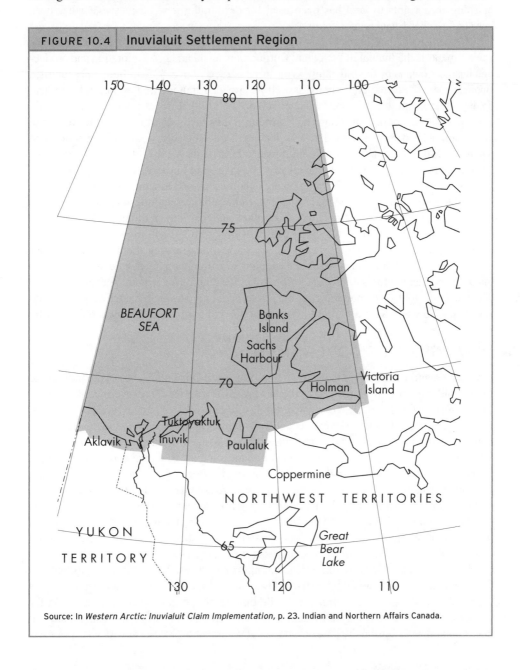

Source: In *Western Arctic: Inuvialuit Claim Implementation*, p. 23. Indian and Northern Affairs Canada.

Land Corporation, and Inuvialuit Development Corporation. The business activities of the Development Corporation are varied and extensive. They include ownership of an airline, a shipping company, a construction company (Koblunaq Construction), and the Inuvialuit Investment Corporation. The Development Corporation has not limited its investments to the northern region of Canada—e.g., Valgro Ltd. (industrial valve manufacturer for western Canada) and Riverside Park Developments Inc. (real estate developer on Vancouver Island). Moreover, most of the money received by the Inuvialuit as compensation for relinquishing their rights to land has been used for developing new businesses, or has been invested in other financial portfolios.[21]

The settlement has brought the Inuvialuit new and growing prosperity. One of the achievements is the Inuvialuit Petroleum Corporation, an oil and gas exploration and production business owned by the Inuvialuit. With current assets of over $35 million, it has returned financial benefits to the community as well as provided training and opportunity for academic achievement. It has interests in over 100 oil wells and nearly as many gas wells.

These new economic structures have produced jobs for Inuit who otherwise would not have been able to enter the modern-day labour force. However, a lack of education and technical skills has kept many of the Inuit from taking on these jobs. Professional positions such as lawyers and accountants have had to be given to non-Inuit, with the proviso that when Inuit became qualified they could take over these jobs (Duhaime, 1993).

As the Inuvialuit have tried to develop these new ethnic economic structures they have realized that they must develop links with other national and multinational companies. Thus, their primary activity today is to construct linkages that will provide them with the necessary capital and technology while at the same time allowing them to receive a fair return on their investment and keep the development within their scope of control. The Inuvialuit want their ventures to provide long-term opportunities for employment and training. Their overall goal is to nurture a more stable economy through recycling profits and wages, and to allow the Inuvialuit to contribute to, and gain from, the successful growth.

NEW FORMS OF GOVERNMENT

Until the creation of Nunavut (see the section "Nunavut, Our Land" below) the bulk of the Inuit population in Canada resided in the Northwest Territories. The government structure in the Northwest Territories consisted (and still consists) of three levels: territorial, regional, and local. Local governments generally represent communities and are elected by local residents. Regional councils are made up of municipal officials chosen by local councils. Thus, they are responsible to local government councils. Regional councils are unique to the Northwest Territories and are funded by the territorial government. Most regional governments being proposed by Aboriginal people are not interested in obtaining the "law-making" powers now held by the territorial legislative assembly. However, they are interested in obtaining more authority in running programs of the territorial government within their region. Without taking over ministerial responsibility, they want more program responsibility for setting policy and standards (Dickerson, 1993).

We also find the structure of government in the Northwest Territories is highly centralized[22] and at the same time non-partisan. Over the years, this has led to a citizenry that is highly alienated from its government. While discussions of devolution have gone on for decades, there is little concrete evidence that local and regional councils have obtained additional powers. During the past decade the government of the Northwest Territories has sent out conflicting messages. On the one hand it has suggested that local governments need to take on "prime public authority" over services such as sewage, sidewalks, and fire protection. But at the same time there has been no attempt by the government of the Northwest Territories to spell out a division of powers between it and the local councils. As a result, there has been no change in the status quo.

This condition was partially the reason for the Inuit population wanting to establish Nunavut. Moreover, the spatial distance between what is now Nunavut and Yellowknife is considerable, and Nunavut residents perceived their elected officials as not being interested in issues that impacted on them. If Inuit did not see the territorial government as legitimate, how were they to become integrated into Canadian society? Even though the government of the Northwest Territories has achieved some autonomy from the federal government, Inuit did not see the Northwest Territorial government as supporting their local and regional needs. There was a feeling that, as its actions become more pervasive, Inuit groups would be overwhelmed and lose any power to make decisions in their best interest. As such, Inuit felt that political legitimacy would come only after devolution, which will involve the creation of Nunavut (Dickerson, 1993).

The Quest for Self-Government

The question regarding the political structure of the North has been reviewed by the federal government many times in the past half-century. One of the first to investigate the issue of self-government was the Carrothers Commission struck in 1966. The Commission's report (1967) concluded that the Northwest Territories should be self-governing and that Yellowknife should be its capital. More recently the *Drury Report* once again addressed the issue of self-government and division of the Northwest Territories. While the report did not reject the idea of division, it suggested that Inuit land claims and setting land aside for Inuit was the priority issue. The question of self-government and division could come later. The Inuit Tapirisat of Canada rejected this conclusion.

Ten years later, the Inuit Tapirisat of Canada presented a case for settlement of its land claim along with the creation of Nunavut. In 1979 the Inuit Tapirisat of Canada adopted the contents of the document entitled *Political Development in Nunavut.* By that time a Territorial assembly had been put in place. The election that year brought about a change for the first time in the ethnic composition of the assembly, in that a majority of the members were now of Aboriginal ancestry (Duhaime, 1992).

As Inuit continued to press their concerns the federal government agreed to hold a plebiscite. In 1982 the first plebiscite for division of the North was held, with 56 percent of those casting their ballots in favour. It was then agreed that two forums be established to discuss the separation issue: the Nunavut Constitutional Forum (in the eastern Arctic) and the Western Constitutional Forum (in the western North). By 1984 Inuvialuit of the western Arctic independently signed an agreement with the federal government and settled their land claims. The activities of the Western Constitutional Forum were further supplanted by the Dene/Métis land claims negotiations. These negotiations continue, but no decision has been made regarding the fate of the western Mackenzie Valley area of the North.

Provincial governments have their own constitutional existence without a formal reporting relationship to the federal government. Most of the provincial government structures are set through either constitutions or conventions. However, this is not the case for the territorial governments. Much of the power they wield is not provided for by statute, but is in place due to discussions between political leaders in the North and the federal minister of Indian and Northern Affairs. In some cases, this is given formal recognition in letters of instruction, while in others it is instituted through unwritten understandings between the federal and territorial governments (Indian and Northern Affairs Canada, 1995).

Language and cultural differences between Inuit and other Canadians have led Inuit to feel that they will never be able to achieve cultural security unless they have their own government. The legacy of outside control is perhaps the single most important issue that Inuit are fighting against. While resistance to outsiders has not always been successful, Inuit have been remarkably resistant to assimilation. Today, as Sambo (1992) points out, there continues to be an unwavering determination to identify both self and community as indigenous, despite major social, economic, and political change.

Nunavut (Our Land)

The push for Nunavut began in the 1960s, when international demand for energy products, mining, and hydroelectric resources sparked a heightened interest in resource development. Canadians and other major resource users felt that new, stable sources of these commodities would need to be found if they were to ensure their access to these products. The North held vast amounts of these potential resources, and there was a rush to exploit them. As well, the Cold War was in full operation at this time and the Arctic and its strategic military importance did not escape notice.

By the 1970s, the *Alaska Native Claims Settlement Act* (1971) had been passed by Congress and set the framework for other settlements that would follow. The Act also demonstrated to Canadians that agreements could be made that would simultaneously address the concerns of government, private industry, and indigenous people, while allowing for the development of natural resources. The international Copenhagen Conference in 1971 was also influential in giving legitimacy to the claims of indigenous peoples. It should be noted that one year after the concept of Nunavut was first proposed in 1976, it was withdrawn because it was a concept that people in the Arctic could not understand. It did not express the realities of Inuit life and culture (Gombay, 2000). Dahl (1997) argues that the Aboriginal populations of the North exhibit a communitarian nationalism rather than regional nationalism, and their form of nationalism is not aligned with the politics of Canada. She goes on to argue that regional identities are superimposed on a people where no such identity has traditionally existed. As such, Inuit had a difficult time in attempting to accommodate self-government through public government.

Another global event having an impact on the claims laid by Inuit was the Danish parliament's agreement to grant home rule for Greenland (1979). This agreement is unique among modern settlements in that it was the first to provide for wide-ranging Aboriginal self-government. Moreover, this agreement made no provisions for monetary compensation, nor did it require the Aboriginal people to give up their ancestral indigenous rights.

Inuit involvement in constitutional reform has been well recognized in Canada since they first appeared before a special committee of the Senate and the House of Commons. Later they would be afforded observer status at the First Ministers' Conference on the Constitution. The Inuit Committee on National Issues was created in 1979 and, until it disbanded in 1987, this committee developed national positions on constitutional reform for the Inuit.

Through their various organizations (e.g., Inuit Tapirisat of Canada, the Nunavut Constitutional Forum, and the Tungavik Federation of Nunavut) the Inuit have struggled to achieve Inuit rights and the establishment of Nunavut.[23] The Inuit had pondered creating a Nunavut Territory out of the eastern half of the Northwest Territories for many years. It was first proposed in 1976,[24] supported through a referendum in the Northwest Territories in 1982, and eventually came into existence under the *Nunavut Act* (1993). This Act ensures their cultural survival through control of a non-racially based democratic government. To deal with the issue, the federal government created the Western Constitutional Forum and the Nunavut Constitutional Forum in order to discuss the issues with their respective constituents.

Fenge (1992) points out that the Inuit used every method available to them through the 1980s in order to achieve the creation of Nunavut. Distance between eastern communities and Yellowknife (capital of the Northwest Territories since 1967) was a prime argument presented to justify the existence of Nunavut. Other issues, such as the relative lack of east–west air traffic compared to north–south, revealed that the North was, in reality, divided into two separate entities. Minority rights and group rights were also cited as important factors in the need to create Nunavut. For Inuit, self-government does not mean independence or secession from Canada, but rather that communities have the right to govern their own affairs. The forums established were a particularly suitable method for facilitating claim negotiations, environmental and social impact assessments of oil and gas development in the Arctic, national constitutional discussions, and advocacy by the Nunavut Constitutional Forum (an Inuit-dominated organization established for the specific purpose of achieving Nunavut).

In 1983 the Nunavut Constitutional Forum presented a proposal for how the government of the new territory would operate. The 1983 document, *Building Nunavut,* was widely circulated among Inuit communities. By 1985 the revised version, *Building Nunavut: Today and Tomorrow,* was required reading for all Inuit. When the Iqaluit Agreement was signed two years later with the federal government, the principles within this document were agreed upon by both the Western and Nunavut Constitutional Forums. In 1987 the Western Constitutional Forum agreed on the splitting of the Northwest Territories. By 1990 an agreement in principle was signed between government and the Inuit, giving support to the creation of a division of the existing Northwest Territories.

In 1991 the federal government released a comprehensive package of proposals for the Arctic, called *Shaping Canada's Future Together.* Both the federal government and the Inuit (through the Inuit Tapirisat of Canada) conducted hearings across the country; the results of these consultations formed the Pangnirtung Accord, which was adopted unanimously by the Inuit Assembly on the Constitution. The Inuit outlined three of their major concerns in this accord. They wanted recognition of the inherent right of self-government, equal participation in the poliltical reform process, and recognition of Inuit as a distinct society with cultural and language rights. The Inuit Tapirisat of Canada presented a brief to the minister of Constitutional Affairs, entitled *Inuit in Canada: Striving for Equality,* which expanded upon the three fundamental objectives of the Pangnirtung Accord. In 1992 a non-binding vote was held, establishing a boundary line that would separate Nunavut from the remainder of the Northwest Territories. Fifty-four percent voted in favour of the proposal.

Nunavut was created out of the central and eastern part of the Northwest Territories (see Figure 10.2). This comprehensive realignment settled a long-standing land claim

covering 2 million square kilometres in the centre and eastern region of the Northwest Territories. An estimated 27 000 people (80 percent are Inuit[25]) live in this region. It is an area
in the eastern Arctic region of Canada that is larger than the Atlantic provinces and Quebec
combined, comprised of three regions; Kitikmeot, Kivalliq and Qikiqtaaluk.

The Nunavut Territory came into existence in 1999 through a political process that had
taken over one quarter-century. After years of negotiation, the federal government gave its
commitment to creating Nunavut and signed a political accord and land claims agreement
in 1992. One year later the *Nunavut Act* was signed and work on the details of how the new
government would operate began. Then in 1999, the Nunavut government was created and
given responsibility to operate as a territorial government. Budgets were allocated to the
new government and the transfer of power gave it authority to provide service delivery,
carry out economicand resource development, and enact legislation for the territory. The
agreement gives Inuit title to more than 350 000 square kilometres of land, including
nearly 40 000 square kilometres for which they have sole mineral rights. As with Indian
treaties, the Inuit agree to cede, release, and surrender all their Aboriginal rights and claims
to the land and water.[26]

Today, the residents of Nunavut are governed by a type of territorial government, with
the goal of eventually becoming a province. There are about 30 communities in the new
territory, most of which are Inuit, with the exception of Nanisivik (a mining community).
The size of these communities ranges from a population of 3000 (Iqaluit) to very small villages. As noted, the Inuit have title to 350 000 square kilometres and access to other lands.
Land cannot be sold except to the state. The agreement allows for land titles to be held in
two forms: fee simple *including* mineral rights, or fee simple *excluding* mineral rights.
Finally, access to and across Inuit-owned lands is granted only with the consent of Inuit.

Compensation of $1.14 billion is being paid over 14 years. Additional royalties from
natural resource development are paid to Inuit, a sharing of royalties that the government
receives from natural resource development on Crown land. Specifically, Inuit annually
receive 50 percent of the first $2 million of resource royalties received by government, and
5 percent of additional resource royalties within the newly created territory of Nunavut. In
addition, a $13-million training trust fund has been established. There are also specific
measures to increase Inuit employment within government in the Nunavut settlement
Aaea, and increased access to government contracts.

Nunavut has three official languages: Inuktitut, English, and French. In anticipation of
the split occurring, in mid-1990 the Inuit formed the Nunavut Wildlife Advisory Board in
opposition to the existing territorial Wildlife Advisory Board. The Nunavut Tungavik
Incorporation[27] will administer the land claim. This organization is responsible for making
sure that the terms of the Nunavut Political Accord signed by the federal government are
lived up to. Members of the organization meet in different Inuit villages to listen to the
wishes of the people and to make decisions on implementing the content of the Nunavut
Land Claims Agreement.

The Inuit also created a Nunavut Trust, an organization that receives the cash compensation under the land claims settlement. The Nunavut Agreement identifies five new institutions: a Nunavut Wildlife Management Board, a Nunavut Impact Review Board (which
screens project proposals to determine whether there is a need for a review of environmental,
social, or economic impacts), a Nunavut Planning Commission (which develops land use
plans and monitors compliance with land use plans), a Nunavut Water Board, and a Surface
Rights Tribunal. This last organization has jurisdiction across all of the pre-1999 Northwest

Territories, whereas the others are limited to Nunavut. An advisory group called the Nunavut Implementation Commission was established to advise the government on the setting up of the government. Like Quebec, Nunavut is to be a "distinct" society, although it is structured so as to operate like any province. Since 85 percent of the population are Inuit, it is highly unlikely that the elected government would represent anything other than Inuit needs and goals. However, Nunavut does not hold title to any land or non-renewable resources. The land is owned either by the Nunavut Tungavik Inc. or by the federal government.

Constitutionally, Nunavut has the same territorial powers afforded the Northwest Territories and Yukon. However, because of the Inuit majority, it is truly a form of Inuit self-government. As such, the Inuit will be in charge of education, health and social services, justice, and other social and economic programs. The legislative assembly (19 members) runs on a non-partisan basis and operates in a consensus style.

The dominant power structure in Nunavut is that of a coarchy (where all actors are in positions of power) (Legare, 1996). However, he also notes that this mode is unstable and can be easily broken if a higher political status actor (policy maker) tries to impose its own solutions to Inuit demands. The question now remains as to whether or not Inuit can change the power structure to that of a stratarchy (where most, but not all, actors are in authority), which would allow them to take on positions of authority while other actors, e.g., transnational companies, have less power.

Since the realization of self-government in Nunavut, the territorial government has been scaled back in terms of both funding and personnel. Ottawa reduced its financial commitment from $200 to $150 million for the creation of the new government. The new structure (called *Footprints 2*) has a smaller, more centralized, and less costly model of government than earlier planned. While the initial plan (*Footprints in New Snow*) called for 900 new jobs, it is now expected to have only 600, a majority being in the community of Iqaluit (the new capital of Nunavut). Nevertheless, the planned Nunavut government will have a premier, cabinet, legislature, and 10 ministries.

The Nunavut Agreement is not without its critics. Many believe that the Inuit gave away too much in return for the small amount of land, rights, and cash received. For example, the per capita cash payout is less than that received in the James Bay settlement. Others claim that there is no real power for the new territory. Still others feel that, since the Inuit owned all the land, they gave away much of what was really theirs to begin with. Moreover, there are many groups who opposed the creation of Nunavut. The Dene Nation vehemently opposed the proposed boundaries for Nunavut and called upon its members to vote against it. Likewise, First Nations from Keewatin and the northern regions of Saskatchewan and Manitoba, as well as the Assembly of First Nations, were urged to vote against the proposal. Non-Natives have also been critical of the creation of Nunavut. Howard and Widdowson (1999) argue that Nunavut is unviable because the communities within it were artificially developed by the federal government. The communities have no economic base, high living expenses, punishing transportation costs, no markets for their products, and a limited population base. In addition, what population there is has low education and lacks job skills. They conclude by arguing that "the function of the Nunavut government is to maintain Inuit culture in the Neolithic period, preserving it as a museum piece for the rest of the world to observe" and to pay for. (p.60)

The issue of the western boundary between Nunavut and the remainder of the Northwest Territories has long been contentious. During the early years the Western and Nunavut Constitutional Forums, along with the Constitutional Alliance, met to negotiate the exact boundaries. Later, the Tungavik Federation of Nunavut and the Dene/Métis Joint Negotiating Secretariat took over. After many years of negotiating, the two parties have not yet come to an agreement as to where the exact boundaries will be.

Residents of the "rump" Northwest Territories, and particularly those in the Mackenzie Valley, were given assurances that the federal government would provide additional funds to stabilize the level of services in the remainder of the Northwest Territories after the creation of Nunavut. Moreover, other residents of the Northwest Territories would not be asked to cover the cost of the establishment of Nunavut. A vote was taken over the boundary proposed by the proponents of Nunavut; it passed (56–44 percent). The closeness of the vote reflects a divisiveness that stems from ethnic origin. Many Inuit communities voted 90 percent to accept the proposed split, while 90 percent of many Dene communities were against it.

Other critics argue that, with 30 percent unemployment in the region, the Nunavut government will be unable to generate new jobs. Since most job creation activities are a result of the non-renewable resources, negotiations will have to take place with major transnational corporations who have economic power. Inuit are well aware that one of their biggest challenges is to find a way out of the economic dependency that has become a debilitating legacy of colonial relations (Kulchyski, 1994). Moreover, critics argue, since most of the initial funding for the government is from the federal government, the Nunavut legislature will not have any autonomy.

RESISTANCE: CONFRONTATION AND POLITICAL ACTIONS

Inuit did not historically view themselves as a distinct ethnic group. It was only through contact with outsiders that a clear demarcation between "us" and "them" emerged. Mitchell (1996) claims that the birth of the pan-Inuit movement occurred with the development of co-ops. She goes on to argue that the 1980 co-op conference was referred to as the Pan-Arctic Conference, and that the relationship between Inuit and other Canadians was the central issue discussed. It was agreed by Inuit that co-ops would best serve their goal of achieving both economic and cultural independence.

Over the years Inuit have learned from other Aboriginal groups that ethnic organizations could become powerful tools in achieving community goals. The Inuit Tapirisat of Canada (created in 1971) grew out of a meeting of Inuit leaders in Coppermine, and has become the major organization speaking on behalf of Inuit in Canada. One of its first actions was to begin the preparation of what would become the 1976 proposal, *Nunavut.* The Labrador Inuit Association was established in 1973 as an affiliate member of the Inuit Tapirisat of Canada. In 1979 the latter created the Inuit Committee on National Issues, which was given sole responsibility to advance the Inuit case in constitutional negotiations. The Inuit Committee on National Issues has been active since the 1980s, when it formally stated that Canada had not respected Inuit nation status and had failed to recognize the constitutional status of Inuit people. Later, the Canadian Inuit would join forces with other international Inuit/Eskimo groups (Inuit Circumpolar Conference) and engage in political activities germane to the Arctic region. In 1992 the Inuit Circumpolar Conference asserted that Inuit are a distinct indigenous people that transcend existing political boundaries.

Mitchell (1996) argues that Inuit have used non-confrontational techniques in dealing with the dominant society. The total domination by the South did not mean that Inuit simply accepted each new value and artefact as it was introduced. Both passive and active resistance has been exhibited over time. Back-to-the-land movements have been extensively used since the 1970s and have given Inuit the feeling of independence as well as lending credence to their traditional culture. Both elders and young Inuit have embraced this movement, which has also given legitimacy to the current land claims now being negotiated. Linked to this movement are the Inuit cultural associations that have sprung up over the past quarter-century. Language has been the focus of many of these associations, and is now viewed as an important indicator of cultural preservation. Other cultural associations (created in the 1970s) have taken on the larger task of revitalizing Inuit culture. For example, the Inuit Cultural Institute is obtaining knowledge from the elders in an attempt to preserve it as a basis for teaching new generations. The Inuit Tapirisat of Canada has created a Language Commission to standardize the two writing systems for Inuit: the roman orthography system developed by the Department of Indian and Northern Development and the syllabic system taught by the missionaries. Other organizations, such as the Torngasok Cultural Association in Labrador and the Avataq Cultural Institute (Northern Quebec), have similar objectives (Mitchell, 1996).

Other Inuit have taken on more direct confrontational strategies in dealing with social change. For example, in 1979 the Kitikmeot and Keewatin Inuit Association, along with other Aboriginal organizations, opposed the Polar Gas pipeline proposal. That same year the Inuit Tapirisat of Canada protested the International Whaling Commission's ban on beluga and narwhal hunting. More recently, the Quebec Inuit have presented a strong campaign for compensation for those Inuit who were forcibly relocated in the 1950s. However, on the whole, Inuit have not employed confrontational techniques. They have only reluctantly used them in an attempt to achieve their goals.

Inuit are using existing legitimate political organizations to express their concern about social change and the role that southern Canadians play in the Arctic. Throughout the North, Inuit have supported members of their community in becoming elected as members of the legislative assembly of the Northwest Territories, as members of parliament in Ottawa, or in their appointment to mainstream political bodies. Through participation in dominant, mainstream political organizations it is felt that Inuit can negotiate change and regulate intrusion by outsiders.

In the early 1970s Inuit from Alaska, Canada, and Greenland met in Copenhagen to discuss the back-to-the-land movement. This unity movement was first tested in 1975 when the Alaska Eskimo were asked to support the Inuvialuit fight against the Canadian government's decision to allow offshore drilling in the Beaufort Sea. In 1977 Canadian Inuit joined forces with other Aboriginal peoples from Alaska, Greenland, and Russia. This pan-Eskimo movement has sponsored a yearly Inuit Circumpolar Conference at which issues common to all are discussed. In 1983 the conference was accepted by the United Nations as a nongovernmental agency. It was also at this time that the conference joined with the World Council of Indigenous Peoples, which established the Alaska Native Review Commission and which in turn hired Justice Thomas Berger as the commissioner. Its overall goal is to establish some control over the development of Arctic policy—e.g., natural resources, land, and environment. However, as Hamilton (1984) points out, this is not a radical movement that uses political rhetoric or public demonstrations, but rather one that has carefully thought out the steps it will need to take if Inuit culture is to survive. Some have suggested that the Inuit's conciliatory stance is ineffective. Nevertheless, Inuit from around the world are now joining forces and developing linkages with other Aboriginal peoples who are realizing their mutual predicament.

The Inuit of today are caught in a complex web of institutional networks that hinders their attempts to overcome their marginality in Canadian society. First, they have been burdened with a history of exploitation and neglect. Second, the opportunities for economic development have not been extensive. Even marginal activities such as fur production have been devastated by European interest groups. Other forms of economic development— e.g., natural resource development—require large "up front" and "sunk" capital that Inuit communities are unable to raise. Third, the ecology of the area makes it difficult for Inuit to develop cohesive organizational structures. Until recently, communication links were so tenuous that most Inuit communities acted in isolation. Fourth, the colonialization of the Arctic by Euro-Canadian southerners has intruded into almost every institutional sphere of the Inuit.

The development of communication linkages among Inuit communities has provided the basis for organizational cohesion. Since television was introduced into the North in 1978 it has had both a positive and negative impact upon the culture of Inuit. It was not until 1982 that the Inuit Broadcasting Corporation aired its first program, and not until a decade later that it provided a dedicated channel. Its broadcasts are solely in Inuktitut and reach nearly 100 communities in the Northwest Territories, Yukon, Quebec, and Labrador.

Out of these linkages have come political and interest group organizations—e.g., the Inuit Tapirisat of Canada—which have provided the basis for political mobilization. As the organizations become more stable and influential, Inuit become better able to exert their sphere of influence upon the decisions that affect their lives. During the constitutional debate in 1992, Aboriginal people crashed the meeting at Harrington Lake. While the Inuit did not participate in this public display of confrontation, they did attempt to negotiate with other government (federal and provincial) officials to be included in the process.[28] Although the Inuit overwhelming supported the Charlottetown Accord, it was defeated in a national referendum.

Inuit of the North are facing the issue of modernity and identity like other colonialized peoples. Inuit are slowly being incorporated into the contemporary mainstream society of Canada. As Dorais (1997) points out, this inclusion brought with it the economic, political, and cultural institutions developed by Western capitalist societies. In many respects, these values and organizations do not reflect Aboriginal values and attitudes. The forces of modernity, such as delinking space and time, are evident in Inuit communities, and the intrusion of individualism and specialization are seen in the behaviour of individuals as well as communities. These changes have brought about major changes in the way communities are organized, the way Inuit think about themselves, and the identity of the group. How Inuit will creatively deal with these forces and still remain Inuit is a major task set before them.

SUMMARY

As the technocracy of the South invaded the Arctic, nothing was small or simple or readily apparent to the non-technical Inuit. Only experts from the South were capable of dealing with the large-scale public necessities. Within the Inuit communities, individual citizens were confronted by a bewildering bigness and complexity and had to defer on all matters to those who knew better. Indeed, it would have been a violation of Inuit reason to do otherwise. For years the technocracy of the Arctic grew without resistance, despite its failures. Moreover, those individuals working for the state did not see themselves as part of the political/industrial complex but rather as the conscientious managers of a social system that was inferior and needed to be replaced by a southern social structure.[29] It has only been recently that this view of reality has come to be challenged by the Inuit.

From their earliest contacts, Canadians have defined Inuit as marginal, both socially and economically. The federal government has relied upon its bureaucratic structure to develop strategies that would integrate Inuit into Canadian society. It promoted the Inuit traditional economy from the outset, believing that if Inuit were to remain in a relatively isolated condition it could avoid creating a dependent relationship and hence cost Canadian taxpayers less.

However, as the post-war period emerged, external events forced government officials to rethink this strategy. The new policy was to develop self-reliant Inuit who would become integrated into the capitalist mode of thought. Believing that the traditional economy could no longer support the Inuit, new settlements were created and smaller ones were expanded. As Tester and Kulchynski (1994) point out, bureaucrats wanted an infrastructure that would give Inuit a material security that had not been provided up to that time. In order to provide that security—e.g., housing, sanitation, and education, settlements had to be created that were accessible to southern Canada. A new public service was sent to the North, which included teachers, social workers, and service officers. This new occupational layer was the force that would bring Inuit into the 20th century. In short, this new cadre of public employees was instrumental in ensuring that Inuit would begin to define the world in terms of economic or material logic rather than through their old perspective which emphasized kinship relations.

The creation of the urban settlement was crucial in implementing and carrying out such a strategy. Once Inuit were placed within a village context the new institutional structure would dominate their lives. They would be subjected to new forms of education, social welfare, justice, and economic relations that would totally encapsulate their existence.

Inuit are no longer nomadic hunters and gatherers, and their communal way of life, which balanced competition and cooperation, is no longer operable. Most of the subsistence activities carried out in the past are now in serious jeopardy. Even such mundane activities as the production of handicrafts are being challenged by their mass production in southern Canada and elsewhere in the world. The production of furs through hunting and trapping has been curtailed by the lobbying forces of Europe. Only the industrial complex remains for Inuit to engage with. This process of incorporating capitalism, and the ideology that goes with it, is now unstoppable. As Mitchell (1996) points out, it is only belatedly and weakly that Inuit have resisted these forces.

As noted by many Northern researchers, subsistence activities by Inuit are no longer necessities of life. However, while not crucial to Inuit existence, they are considered important to them. Today the state, transnational corporations, Aboriginal organizations, and co-ops are the major employers of Inuit. The introduction of southern educational practices has allowed young Inuit to be socialized into the dominant ideology and serves to neutralize their resistance to it. Yet Inuit remain uneducated and unskilled for the workforce. Under the present conditions they are of no use to industry (or very limited in demand). Handicraft is only one of a few marketable products emerging out of the North.[30] While collective hunting and distribution of goods remain, to some extent, an integral part of the Inuit community, Inuit sharing practices have broken down with the introduction of cash into the economy. Moreover, welfare and other state-sponsored programs have also weakened the old "sharing" traditions. Mitchell (1996) claims that the notion of private property and individualism is now an entrenched value within Inuit culture.

Through land settlements and mega-agreements with the federal government, Inuit are creating new capitalist, industrial organizations. These corporations have created a cash economy, become major employers in the region, and are taking on a more political persuasion. Nevertheless, these new economic organizations are part of the larger transnational structure and must try to fit into a global network. Even though some linkages exist among Inuit organizations, external transnational organizations dominate these and set their agenda (Freeman, 1985).

The question remains as to how Inuit can become more self-sufficient and sustainable. How can they engage in productive activities within the North, using northern capital and spending that capital in the North? Some Inuit organizations have chosen to forge alliances with existing external transnational companies—for example, through joint ventures. Unfortunately, on the basis of previous experience, the Inuit development corporations will allow only a few Inuit to become wealthy while the remainder take on wage jobs. Already there has been the creation of an indigenous ruling class that is convinced of the positive value of integration into southern industrial forces. These individuals have taken on active and powerful roles within the Northwest Territories government. By involving these leaders in state politics, government has been able to control both the Inuit leaders and their constituents. Since most Inuit organizations and communication structures are funded by the federal government they must rely almost totally upon their support.

Southern Canadians, now seeing the influence of pan-Inuit groups, have become worried about the Inuit's potential power. For example, the sweeping powers that Inuit may wield over natural resource development mean that an ethnic regional group of less than 50 000 people could control oil and gas development regardless of the needs of the 30 million-plus southern Canadians. Some Canadians believe that Inuit have overstepped their boundaries of influence.

Inuit of today are well aware that they need an advanced education and social skills in order to integrate into the larger society while retaining their important cultural attributes. They also realize that if they are to survive as a people they will need to engage in more proactive strategies than they have utilized in the past. This means that more Inuit will need to become key players in the ongoing institutional structures of Arctic Canada. More Inuit will need to obtain the skills necessary to become community leaders and effectively network within the national and international sphere of power brokering. The early attempts by Inuit to adopt Western ways in the settlements were unsuccessful, and they became marginal people. Now they are trying to reverse this continuing trend of marginalization and exclusion. Their efforts have focused on self-government initiatives, promotion of Inuit culture, and the encouragement of sustainable development (Kuptana, 1992).

KEY TERMS

Inuit

Inuit cosmology

Inuivaluit

Alaska Native Claims Settlement Act

Nunavut

STUDY QUESTIONS

1. What impacts have Inuit experienced as a result of contact from southern Canadians?
2. What are the five tenets of Inuit culture?
3. How is Inuit health influenced by ecological, social and nutritional changes?
4. Discuss the ethnic stratification evident within the Arctic.
5. Explain why the federal government generated the settling of land claims within the North.
6. What are the three levels of government in the Northwest Territories? Discuss their relation to each other.
7. What is the *Nunavut Act* of 1993?

WEBLINKS

arcticcircle.uconn.edu

The Arctic Circle project examines northern Aboriginal peoples in a number of Arctic Circle countries. The project's site includes excellent information about Canada's Inuit and Cree peoples.

www.npc.nunavut.ca/eng/index.html

The Nunavut Planning Commission website includes an overview of the Nunavut land claim, discussion of the territory's government and political structure, and more.

www.stats.gov.nu.ca

This government of Nunavut website offers statistical information relating to the people of the Baffin, Keewatin, and Kitikmeot regions. Subject areas include Health, Economy, Justice, Education, Income, and Demography

NOTES

1. Inuit experiences with non-Inuit are different from those of Indians in Canada. For example, Inuit do not fall under the jurisdiction of Section 91(24) of the *Constitution Act, 1982* and thus are not considered, legally, as Indians. This means that the *Indian Act* is not applicable to Inuit.
2. After a time, the Hudson's Bay Company would be asked to act as a private agent for the government of Canada.
3. This group was also given the mandate to provide an education to Inuit.
4. The three parties agreed the Inuit were in need of "being civilized" even though they all had different interests. Missionaries were concerned with "wife lending" practices, the police were concerned that liquor was a problem and the fur traders were concerned about maintaining stability in the region. While the three groups did not agree on specifics, they did agree that steps had to be taken to assimilate the indigenous population.
5. The criteria for establishing sovereignty have changed over time. In the beginning, discovery or the issuance of Papal Bulls were considered sufficient for establishing sovereignty. However, by the 20th century, new criteria emerged.

6. The federal government has steadfastly argued that the relocation of Inuit was carried out on a humanitarian basis and was not intended to establish sovereignty. In fact, three separate reports have been commissioned by the federal government to address this issue. However, the work of Tester and Kulchynski (1994) throws considerable doubt on this argument. In the mid-1990s, after a decade-long campaign to force the federal government to accept its responsibility, 17 Inuit families finally reached a $10 million settlement.

7. Keeping Inuit "on the land" would not only reduce the financial commitment of the federal government but would also demonstrate Canada's sovereignty over the vast Arctic.

8. Nearly one-fourth of the adult population reported having received social assistance during the past year.

9. Census Canada found that 76.3 percent of total income of Inuit was from employment, 21.6 percent from government transfers, and 2.1 percent from other sources.

10. The overall participation rate in the labour force for Inuit was 57.2 percent in 1991, with an official unemployment rate of 25 percent.

11. In 1991 over half the dwellings required regular maintenance. One-quarter required minor repairs, while one-fifth of the current dwellings required major repairs.

12. If Inuit adults aged 50+ were included we would find that a majority of these individuals have no schooling or less than six years.

13. There are many different dialects spoken in the Arctic (Dorais, 1992).

14. About 2 percent of the adult population also reported being able to speak Cree and/or Montagnais–Naskapi.

15. The lack of a ground transportation infrastructure also influenced this decision.

16. The data show that in 1991, 87 percent of Inuit reported that they bought food to eat at home (excluding take-out). Forty percent claimed to have bought food from a restaurant or take-out.

17. This was the installation of a series of radar stations in the Arctic every four to five hundred kilometres, moving from the east to the west coast of Canada.

18. Treaty No. 11 is an exception and encompasses the Mackenzie Valley in the Northwest Territories. However, the terms of this treaty regarding land have never been implemented by the federal government.

19. The recent debate on Quebec secession has also produced tension between Inuit and Quebecers. In the 1996 referendum, Inuit were outspoken advocates of federalism and were almost unanimous in rejecting secession from Canada.

20. The Inuvialuit are descendants of Alaskan Eskimos. They live in the western Arctic.

21. Some dividends have been paid to elders in order to ensure that older Inuit will receive some short-term benefits from the agreement.

22. There is a belief by some government authorities that a more centralized system of constitutional authority is cheaper and more effective than a decentralized one (Government of Northwest Territories, 1990).

23. Pauktuutit (an Inuit women's association) clearly identified differences between Inuit and Qallunaat (persons with white faces) with regard to the use and priority placed upon formal institutions of government and written law (Moss, 1995).

24. It was actually the third version ("Political Development in Nunavut"), proposed by the Inuit Tapirisat in 1979, which became the starting point for an agreement in principle.

25. To be enrolled as an Inuit and benefit from the agreement, a person must be recognized as an Inuk under Inuit custom or Inuit law, and be associated with a community or the Nunavut Settlement Area. One must also be a Canadian citizen and benefit in only one Canadian land claim agreement.

26. This agreement fully protects any Aboriginal or treaty right of adjacent Native groups who use lands in Nunavut. There are also special provisions that assure that their hunting and land use rights can continue in areas where their interests overlap the settlement area.

27. This organization succeeded the Tungavik Federation of Nunavut as the stakeholder representing the interests of the Inuit people of Nunavut.

28. The role Inuit played in this public demonstration was relegated to that of the Assembly of First Nations. It has been suggested that the role of Inuit was downplayed because the three chief negotiators for the Inuit were women.

29. Individual bureaucrats placed in the North had (and continue to have) very high turnover rates, and as a result their capacity for a longitudinal perspective on issues is limited.

30. A considerable amount of natural resources are exported from the North, but few Inuit participate in these extractive industries and few Inuit directly benefit from the few industrial activities currently in operation in the Arctic.

Voices and Partners: Aboriginal Organizations in Canada

INTRODUCTION

The creation and sustenance of organizations involves the development of social capital and speaks to the importance of social networks, communication and sharing resources (Kay and Johnston, 2007). Social capital can also be seen as a cultural mechanism to establish and solidify boundaries of groups. However, social capital is less tangible than physical capital, in that it exists in the relations among individual human beings. It consists of the sharing of resources through networks of social relations along with the norms that are attached. It represents the willingness of individuals to work together and to engage in cooperative activities with others. In short, the concept has come to mean the willingness of individuals to create and sustain relationships through voluntary associations (Portes and Landolt, 1996).

As such, organizations are one of the keys to ethnic survival. Voluntary organizations produce a sense of community, solidarity and mutual obligation in order to support collective activities. In addition, they allow Aboriginal communities to develop economically, to enter the world of politics, to become an advocate for their goals and to develop social cohesion, solidarity and social integration amongst themselves. In dealing with the dominant society Aboriginal organizations play an important role in ensuring that their voices are heard, their needs understood and the achievement of those goals attained. Nevertheless, we will also show that, while broad social capital is easy to build in homogeneous communities, it is more difficult to develop and maintain in ethnically diverse settings. Individuals are more likely to trust others like themselves and less likely to trust those they perceive to be different (Uslaner, 2002). As we have pointed out in earlier chapters, there is a great deal of diversity of Aboriginal groups in urban centres and amongst various cultural groups across Canada that has posed major barriers in developing trust and multi-cultural voluntary associations.

For example, representation of indigenous knowledge as well as an indigenous worldview has come about through the efforts of Aboriginal organizations of many types. They have produced an awareness of the needs of Aboriginal people, including their need to be respected members of our society. The Aboriginal "movement," then, has had both a political and social impact on Canadian society. Aboriginal organizations have also instigated and supported legal challenges that have resolved conflicts and provided new opportunities for Aboriginal people. Many times they have been the centre of controversy in either the legal or the political field.

Unfortunately, little has been written about these organizations and the role they have played in the development of Canada. In the 19th and early 20th century several efforts were made by Aboriginal people to create regional and national political organizations (Whiteside, 1973b). The demise of many of these organizations was generally the result of suppression by the federal government (e.g., the *Indian Act, 1927* prohibited the political organization of Aboriginal people beyond local levels of government) and of the internal discord among Aboriginals themselves. These problems continue to plague Aboriginal organizations (Warry, 2007) in the 21st century.

The short-lived and ineffectual structure of many Aboriginal organizations has been the result of outside interference, mistakes made by Aboriginal leadership, and the inappropriateness of certain social structures within a larger social system. For example, the burgeoning number of Aboriginal organizations, all representing a myriad of goals and objectives, has prevented Aboriginal people from pursuing a cohesive and integrated set of objectives. Different tribal and linguistic groups have slowed the emergence of cohesive strategies, thereby limiting the extent to which they are able to develop their social capital.

The nature of the goals that the various organizations have set has also been problematic for Aboriginal people. Some groups have tried to pursue local objectives, while others have focused more on regional or national matters. Their goals have been political, social, religious, or economic, and this diffusion of focus has led to divisions among those pursuing the goals.

Early Aboriginal organizations were generally tied to specific concerns, such as particular land claims and unfulfilled treaty promises. These organizations had a single focus, were relatively simple in structure, and were limited to a particular area or group of Aboriginal people. Only since the mid-1950s have Aboriginal organizations become multifaceted, complex in structure, and representative of Aboriginal people from all across Canada (Patterson, 1972).

HISTORY OF ABORIGINAL ORGANIZATIONS

It has been suggested that the first Aboriginal association was established in about 1540, when the League of Iroquois was formed (Daugherty, 1982). This confederacy, composed of five Aboriginal groups (Seneca, Mohawk, Onondaga, Oneida, and Cayuga), had a governing council to decide on important issues that affected all the tribes. In addition, the council acted as an arbitrator for inter-tribal disputes. This organization did not, however, deal with intra-tribal affairs, leaving each tribe to deal with its own internal affairs.

With the emergence of the fur trade the League began to exert its influence beyond the confines of the Five Nations. Their strategic location, political cohesion, and alliance with the Dutch and English permitted them to both influence the activities of the fur trade (Daugherty, 1982) and act as middlemen in that trade. This action led to a series of wars with the French and eventually led the League to sign a treaty of neutrality with the French in 1701. This policy set the stage for positive relations between the Iroquois and the English after 1760 and, as a result, the League lost its key position as middleman in the fur trade. The encroachment of colonists and the success of the American Revolution brought about the final demise of the League.

In the late 1700s Joseph Brant (a Mohawk) tried to create a united Indian confederacy, but with little success. This interest was renewed by Tecumseh (a Shawnee), who also tried to organize the First Nations of the northwest into a united Indian Confederacy. In the War of 1812, however, he was killed fighting for a Native homeland and his planned alliance fell apart. During the next 75 years various First Nations leaders tried to unite Indians in an attempt to stop the westward and northward expansion of European civilization. Although great leaders such as Crowfoot, Piapot, Peguis, and Big Bear made serious attempts to develop various organizational structures that would be effective in safeguarding Aboriginal interests, all of them were unsuccessful.

It was not until 1870 that the first Aboriginal political organization in Canada was formed—the Grand General Indian Council of Ontario and Quebec. It was formed by both Iroquois and Ojibwa. Their major concern was with the government's implementation of Indian policy. A competing organization (League of Indians) was established in the late 19th century. The Council, faced with competition from the League coupled with a lack of operating funds, was forced to disband (Whiteside, 1980).

The League of Indians was based in the East, although its leaders thought of it as a national organization concerned with First Nations rights. After several conferences, the League of Indians in Western Canada emerged, never to unite with its Eastern counterpart. This League split in 1933, and two branches (Alberta and Saskatchewan) were created. The Alberta branch renamed itself the Indian Association of Alberta in 1939, and remains active in political causes today. While other organizations such as the Catholic Indian League (1962) and the Calgary Urban Treaty Indian Alliance (1972) have existed in Alberta, they have been very narrowly focused and short-lived.

The Saskatchewan branch phased itself out in 1942, but in 1946 two new provincial organizations (the Protective Association for Indians and the Union of Saskatchewan Indians) united to form the Union of Saskatchewan Indians. By the late 1950s this group had changed its name to the Federation of Saskatchewan Indians. The Federation has taken an active role in promoting the social, political, and economic goals of both registered and non-registered First Nations in Saskatchewan. Then, in 1970, the Saskatchewan Native Alliance was formed, and continues to be active today.

In British Columbia, the Nisga'a First Nation formed the Nisga'a Land Committee in the latter part of the 19th century. The genesis of this organization was their concern with land claims, in particular the claim that would culminate with the 1973 Supreme Court decision and the subsequent development of the government's land claims policy. By 1915 a supporting organization, the Allied Tribes of British Columbia, was created to lobby for land claims. It was short-lived, and by the 1920s it had been dismantled. In 1931 the Native Brotherhood of British Columbia began, and later amalgamated with the Pacific Coast Native Fishermen's Association, which gave it a broader base of both northern and southern coastal Indians. The Brotherhood, still in existence, did not focus on land claims; rather, it was more concerned about social and economic issues.[1]

The members of the Brotherhood were all Protestants; in 1943, a rival Catholic organization, the North American Indian Brotherhood, was also established in British Columbia. Although the two groups did not clash overtly, ill feeling and discord between them prevented either from accomplishing much. The government seized on the contradictions between the two groups and used them as an excuse to ignore all the requests from both of them.

By the 1940s First Nations from eastern and western Canada formed a new national organization, the Canadian Indian Brotherhood (later to be renamed the North American Indian Brotherhood). This organization had no religious bias and consisted solely of non-treaty Indians. In 1946 the Brotherhood attempted to form a coalition with treaty Indians from Saskatchewan. This proved fruitless, partly because of interference by Saskatchewan's CCF government. The NAIB remained active in national political affairs until it was phased out of existence in 1969. Aboriginal organizations in Manitoba did not emerge until the late 1940s, when the Manitoba Indian Brotherhood was formed. Since then, the MIB has been disbanded and a new organization (the Four Nations Confederacy) has been formed. Attempts to merge status and non-status organizations have, at times, been successful. Nevertheless, a definite division continues to persist throughout Canada among non-treaty First Nations, treaty First Nations, Inuit and Métis.

In 1944, attempts were made to establish the North American Indian Brotherhood. The rather loose structure of this organization collapsed in 1950 due to internal discord. In 1954 the National Indian Council was formed, and in 1961 it became the official organization for both status and non-status First Nations. By 1968 the NIC had split into two organizations: the National Indian Brotherhood for status First Nations, and the Canadian Métis Society for non-status Natives and Métis. In 1970 the Métis Society became the Native Council of Canada. Also in 1970 the National Indian Council, composed of middle-class, urban Aboriginals, formally dissolved; this was because of conflicts among its status, non-status and Métis members.

Organizations in Eastern Canada, particularly since 1960, have not been as vociferous or as organized as their Western counterparts, but they do have a long history. In 1840 missionaries helped the Ojibwa of Ontario to form the General Council of the Ojibwa Nations of Indians; in 1846 this was renamed the General Council of Indian Chiefs. Although the Council originally included only Christians, in 1882 it expanded its base and became the General Council of Ontario. This organization lasted until 1938 and was the beginning of the present Union of Ontario Indians. The Union of Ontario Indians was formed in 1946 and still actively concerns itself with contemporary Indian issues. Although Quebec's First Nations are today without a major provincial organization, the Indians of Quebec Association was active during the 1960s and 1970s. Finally, in the Maritime provinces few Aboriginal organizations have been formed. While the Grand General Indian Council was active for a few years in the early 1940s, it would not be until 1967 that the Union of New Brunswick Indians was formed. It deals with Indians in both New Brunswick and Prince Edward Island. In 1969 the Union of Nova Scotia Indians was also formed (IRIW, 1978).

Even though more than a quarter of the First Nations people in Canada live in Ontario, they have not seriously attempted to link up with other provincial or national Aboriginal organizations. The independence and aggressiveness of the Iroquois on the Six Nations Reserve have given them a unique position among First Nations in Canada.[2] This group was one of the first to develop agricultural practices and to establish semi-permanent villages. They were also advanced in their political structures, in that they developed powerful confederacies that had an impact on the region. This group became an important link in the trading networks that developed throughout the region. The pivotal role they have played historically has led them to preserve their traditions and culture, and this has placed them in direct conflict with the federal government. They have resisted the implementation of many policies of the government and have refused to be guided by the *Indian Act.* Other Aboriginal people, for example Métis in Eastern Canada, including those in Quebec, are considered non-Indians; as such, they are only nominally recognized by federal and provincial governments.

The emergence of a number of Aboriginal organizations since the late 1960s reflects the impact of two events. First was the ill-fated federal white paper on Aboriginal policy in 1969. This policy statement evoked a strong response from Aboriginal people all over the country and acted as a catalyst for Aboriginal cooperation, since it allowed First Nations to identify a clear-cut (at least from their perspective) event which plainly marked the federal government as "the enemy." Secondly, changes in funding meant that Aboriginal organizations were eligible for federal funds, and these funds could come from sources other than Indian Affairs. One example of the impact of the white paper was the creation of the Association of Iroquois and Allied Indians to represent various bands when dealing with different levels of government (Daugherty, 1982). The Union of B.C. Indian Chiefs was also formed during this time (1969) as a result of the fusion of the Indian Homemakers Association of B.C., the Southern Vancouver Island Tribal Federation, and the North American Indian Brotherhood.

Many other Aboriginal organizations have been created or changed over the past century. The Council of Yukon Indians is the result of a merger between the Yukon Native Brotherhood (representing status Indians) and the Yukon Association of Non-Status Indians. Others have undergone some changes in structure; for example, the Indian Brotherhood of the Northwest Territories has emerged as the Dene Nation. Finally, more locally or regionally based Aboriginal organizations have developed because of their dealings with various levels of government—for example, Grand Council Treaty No. 9 and Grand Council Treaty No. 3.

The Métis have also seen a proliferation of organizations. While the first Métis political organization was established in 1937 (Métis of Saskatchewan), until the 1960s it was the only provincial Métis organization. Then, in rapid succession, Métis associations were formed in Alberta, Manitoba, and British Columbia; the National Canadian Métis Society also emerged. Métis were then represented at both the provincial and federal levels. In 1970 the Métis of the western provinces met and formed a new organization—the Native Council of Canada. Its goal is to promote Aboriginal rights, land claims, and various social and economic policies. The Native Council of Canada represents a wide spectrum of Aboriginal people, including some status Indians, Eastern Canadian Métis, and Aboriginal people without status under the *Indian Act.* The Council claims to represent 1.2 million Aboriginal people, while the federal government estimates the number to be about 100 000. Even though the Council has a diverse constituency and does not have a legal basis such as the *Indian Act,* the federal government has agreed to recognize it as a lobbying group, and even provided it with a seat at the First Ministers' Conference in 1982. The Métis National Council, a new organization that split from the Native Council of Canada, was established in 1983, just before the first round of constitutional talks. Members of this new group felt that the Native Council of Canada did not reflect Métis aspirations for land and self-government.

After the split, the Native Council of Canada restyled itself the Congress of Aboriginal Peoples. Today the Métis National Council claims to represent only members of the Métis Nation. On the other hand, the Congress of Aboriginal Peoples represents anyone who claims "Métis status," including non-status Indians. The National Council has provincial affiliates in the three prairie provinces, although both organizations have provincial political affiliates in B.C. and Ontario. However, only the Congress has members who call themselves Métis in all the regions of Canada (Chartrand and Giokas, 2002). Today, we find that the Congress does not try to define the Métis people but rather views "Métis" as comprising a number of different groups and individuals. On the other hand, the National Council has tackled the definition of "Métis" and has clearly articulated its definition. Its membership consists of regional and provincial political representative organizations, not of Métis individuals. It includes organizations from across the country, although the specific organizations may change over time. This shifting membership of the National Council demonstrates the dynamic character of many Aboriginal organizations.

Inuit have also become politically involved during the past two decades. The national organization, the Inuit Tapirisat of Canada, was created in 1970. Its first headquarters were in Edmonton, but by 1972 the organization had been re-established in Ottawa. Its original goal was to preserve and promote Inuit culture as well as to negotiate land claims. But over the years it became evident that one single organization could not represent the diversity of Inuit. For this reason, six regional organizations emerged: representing the regions in the North as well as northern Quebec. The Tungavik Federation of Nunavut, an umbrella organization, was created to represent the Inuit organizations east of the Mackenzie Delta. It has been through the TFN that the issue of Inuit land claims has been discussed. This reveals the strategy of most Aboriginal groups to create different levels of organizations in order to best achieve their goals. It also reflects the complexity of Aboriginal organizations and the problems with adapting such a strategy. For example, the Northern Quebec Inuit Association (NQIA) was also formed to deal with both local and national issues. The Association established two headquarters—one in Fort Chimo, the other in Montreal. Finally, the splinter Inuit group, Tungavinga Nunamimi, emerged in response to the James Bay Settlement set forth by the NQIA; as a result of their refusal to ratify the agreement, three settlements near Povungnituk created their own organization.

During the 1960s the concern for equal and just distribution of political power, national income, and collective socio-economic provisions grew (Delmar, 1986; Jamieson, 1979). Despite legal and political changes that supported the ideology of equality, inequality between men and women in society remained. The international women's movement after the mid-1960s, therefore, focused on changing norms, values, and attitudes as they pertain to women's positions in society (Mitchell, 1986; Steinem, 1983). The movement not only provided new opportunities for women, but also redefined political issues, making them more pertinent to women in Canadian society (Smith et al., 1985). The women's movement had a significant impact on the awareness of Aboriginal women as well, and to a certain degree on the establishment of the Native Women's Association of Canada. It shaped a climate in which Aboriginal women could voice concerns and make them relevant to others (Fleming-Mathur, 1971; Krosenbrink-Gelissen, 1984b). The emergence of an Aboriginal women's movement in Canada during the 1960s had been largely unnoticed by non-Aboriginal people, as well as by Aboriginal men (Bonney, 1976; Jamieson, 1979). Although Aboriginal womens' contributions to the political scene were not taken seriously, the restructuring of the Assembly of First Nations in 2006 formalized their integration into the national organization by creating a women's council that is part of the formal Assembly of First Nations' structure.

Prior to the creation of contemporary Aboriginal associations there were many tribal organizations. These were closely tied to the religious and cultural components of tribal life and were directed inward, toward members of the group, rather than outward toward society as a whole. Few tribal organizations presently exist, and their role for Aboriginal people is more symbolic than instrumental; however, in some areas there has been a resurgence of tribal organizations, as in the case of pow-wows (Beaver, 1979).

Membership in the Aboriginal political organizations today has generally been determined by ascription: one is born into an organization, rather than choosing to join it. Legal factors also often determine membership; for example, membership in the National Indian Brotherhood was restricted to registered Indians. Table 11.1 illustrates the number of Aboriginal political associations that have been active since 1700. As the table shows, the total number of organizations has recently increased considerably, although many fewer still exist. In a recent study, Newhouse (2003) found approximately 600 Aboriginal organizations in Canada at the end of the 20th century. Half were small for-profit organizations while the other half were not-for-profit organizations mostly located in urban areas. In a recent study of Western Canada, there were over 300 non-business Aboriginal organizations found in six western Canadian cities, their focus ranging from education to child care to cultural support (Newhouse, 2003).

Table 11.2 illustrates the primary function of a number of voluntary associations active at some point between 1800 and 2003. Many of these organizations emerged in crisis situations to serve a specific need at a specific time; hence, many of them have been very short-lived. However, in addition to solving a specific problem, other Aboriginal organizations have expanded their roles. For example, in urban centres, many of these organizations offer relief from the frustrations felt by Aboriginal people who have recently left the reserve. Aboriginal people with similar backgrounds, values, and experiences can meet to discuss ways of adapting to urban life and to find solutions to specific individual problems (Canada, 1988).In 2005, the creation of the first Canadian off-reserve Grand Council of chiefs was created under the name of the Confederation of Aboriginal People of Canada. The purpose of creating such a Canadian sovereign Aboriginal government is that it will be able to support the different needs and interests of the off-reserve Aboriginal people of Canada. Once the by-laws were created they were sent to many Aboriginal territorial representatives interested in joining the new organization for final revisions. In 2006 the by-laws were approved and the first general founding assembly took place. The main goals of the organization are health, education and economic development, adapted specifically to the needs of the off-reserve Aboriginal people of Canada.

The contemporary organization structure has largely resulted from increased urbanization, the need to develop formal organizations to achieve goals and the changing role of advocacy groups in Canada. Although the organizations function within an urban context, their members are generally rural in orientation and are concerned with rural issues. Today's organizations are imbued with a sense of cultural nationalism, or what Smith (1981) calls "ethnic revival." The genesis of this lies partially in the emergence of Aboriginal intellectuals graduating from non-Aboriginal schools. These individuals were equipped to research and piece together an account of the past several centuries as seen from an Aboriginal perspective. And they were able to promote the historical legacy they discovered. This was reinforced when the National Indian Brotherhood reorganized itself under the

TABLE 11.1 | Major Aboriginal Political Voluntary Associations in Canada, by Date of Formation

	Prior to 1799	1800-99	1900-19	1920-29	1930-39	1940-49	1950-59	1960-69	1970-73	1974-80	1981-91	1992-97	TOTAL
National		2	1		2	1	1	4	5	2	2	0	20
Regional	2		1	4	1	1		1	1	4	3	2	20
National-Regional Total	2	2	2	4	3	2	1	5	6	6	5	2	40
Nfld.-Labrador								1	2	1	1	1	6
P.E.I.										1			1
New Brunswick								1	3	2	1	2	9
Nova Scotia						1		2	2	2	2	2	11
Quebec			1	2	1			3	5	3	3	1	17
Ontario		1	1	2	2	1	1	6	7	3	2	1	26
Manitoba					1	1		2	6	2	1	2	15
Saskatchewan				1	1	5	2	1	4	3	2	1	20
Alberta	1			1	2	1	1	4	3	3	3	3	22
B.C.	1		3	1	3	1	4	8	3	4	1	2	31
N.W.T.					1			3	3	4	1	3	15
Yukon								2	3	1	1	1	8
Provincial Total	4	4	5	7	7	12	9	33	41	26	18	21	183
Grand Total	8	9	9	15	13	16	11	43	54	38	28	23	262

Source: Don Whiteside, *Historical Development of Aboriginal Political Associations in Canada* (Ottawa: National Indian Brotherhood, 1973), 6. Additional data has been collected by the author since 1973.

TABLE 11.2	Reasons for the Formation of Aboriginal Canadian Associations by Time Periods							
	Specific: Treaty Rights, Land Rights, Social Issues		General Administrative Policies		Other General Protests		Total	
Year	No.	%	No.	%	No.	%	No.	%
I prior to 1849	4	100	–	–	–	–	4	100
II 1850-1939	10	31	19	59	3	9	32	100
III 1940-1965	4	14	18	62	7	24	29	100
IV 1966-1980	38	32	36	30	46	38	120	100
V 1981-1990	10	35	5	18	12	47	28	100
VI 1991-2003	12	34	6	8	17	58	35	100
Total	78	31	84	34	82	35	248	100

Note: For purposes of this analysis, all national, regional, and provincial associations were counted together. As a result, one could argue that nine "extra" provincial associations are included in the table (six in "specific protests," two in "administrative policies," and one in "general protests"). No cell, however, is changed by more than 3 percent because of the inclusion of associations that might be considered as "extras."

Source: Don Whiteside, *Historical Development of Aboriginal Political Associations in Canada* (Ottawa: National Indian Brotherhood, 1973), 10. Additional data has been collected by the author since 1973.

rubric of the Assembly of First Nations. In addition, in their efforts to achieve their goals, Aboriginal organizations are beginning to use new tactics, such as confrontation, protest and lobbying. Aboriginal people also are being taken seriously because they are (1) viewed as a threat to national security, and (2) now able to hire experts, including lawyers, who have an expertise in Canadian law as it pertains to Aboriginal rights. Finally, the new tactics being employed have generated a great deal of publicity—Aboriginal issues now receive media attention and have entered everyday discourse. The result has been some additional pressure brought to bear on government officials to make some concessions (Fleras, and Maaka, 2000).

ABORIGINAL ORGANIZATIONAL STRUCTURE: A TYPOLOGY

There are four broad categories of Aboriginal organizations: band, local, urban and pan-Aboriginal. Band organizations, which deal with the federal government, are based on historical precedents and have their authority vested in the *Indian Act*. Relations between Aboriginal people and government at this level are formal and regulated by the terms and conditions outlined in federal statutes. Local, urban and pan-Aboriginal organizations, in contrast, have no statutory basis for their dealings with the government. Nevertheless, these organizations have had extensive dealings with both government and non-government agencies over the years.

Local organizations in First Nations communities have emerged through specific efforts of individuals or groups living in a specific community, focusing on a specific issue. They are usually singular in focus, short lived and ineffective. Overall, these individual organizations pursue goals widely ranging from particular services to treaty rights to changes in federal Indian policy. In the 1960s two events occurred simultaneously that had a tremendous effect on these two types of Aboriginal organizations. First, new programs were introduced into the reserves, which also brought substantial funds to an otherwise poor constituency. Second, the urbanization of Aboriginals meant that for the first time a large number of Aboriginal people would not be effectively served by a band or local organization. This meant that urban Aboriginal people had to develop their own organizations. The original Aboriginal urban organizations focused on economic and social welfare goals. The central goal of these organizations was to change Aboriginal–non-Aboriginal relations to accommodate urban Aboriginal communities and their interests (Cornell, 1988; Cornell, 2000). The increase in the number of Aboriginal persons entering the urban areas resulted in a proliferation of organizations, reflecting the varied goals and objectives of each group. After a time of working at cross-purposes, some of the organizations began to carry out cooperative efforts. After several successful ventures, new pan-Aboriginal organizations began to emerge. More recently, the pan-Aboriginal organizations have attempted to reduce federal control and increase their own control over band and tribal affairs (Aggamaway-Pierre, 1983; Cairns, 2005).

Cornell (1988) has developed a typology of Aboriginal organizations that is based upon their goals; it illustrates and provides an understanding of the actions taken by them. The first distinction he makes is between reformative and transformative goals. A "reformative" organization focuses its efforts on changing the role of Aboriginal people without changing the structure of Aboriginal/non-Aboriginal relations. This approach is based on a belief that there must be a redistribution of social power/rewards to allow Aboriginal people their share, and that this can take place within the existing system. For example, they feel that more Aboriginal people should be hired by Indian Affairs, that more Aboriginal people should be in senior management positions, and that social services on the reserves need to be expanded. In summary, these organizations accept and endorse the existing structure of Canadian society and feel that only some changes are needed to make the existing system work better.

"Transformative" organizations agree that a redistribution of rewards and power needs to be undertaken, but not within the existing social structure. They feel that a fundamental change is required—for example, phasing out Indian Affairs, allowing Aboriginal people to establish their own legal system, reopening treaties. In summary, their goal is to change the existing structures that impinge upon Aboriginal people (Grand Council of the Crees, 1998).

The second distinction Cornell makes among Aboriginal organizations is the degree to which each is integrative or segregative. This distinction reflects the degree of acceptance or rejection of dominant institutions. Organizations with an integrative perspective accept the appropriateness of the dominant culture and thus promote the dominant institutions as the way of maximizing Aboriginal interests. As a result of their general acceptance of the dominant institutions, they also believe that Aboriginal communities should be built on this model.

On the other hand, Aboriginal organizations with a segregative ideology argue against accepting the dominant institutional structure as a role model. These organizations promote goals and objectives that are fundamentally anti-assimilationist. The relationship between these two variables is portrayed in Figure 11.1; they result in four basic types of Aboriginal organizations.

FIGURE 11.1	Types of Aboriginal Organizations		
		Aboriginal-White Relations	
		Reform	Transform
Orientation to institutions of dominant society	Integrate	1	2
	Segregate	3	4

Source: Based on S. Cornell, *The Return of the Native* (New York: Oxford, 1988), 154.

Reform-Integrate

Historically, organizations such as the National Indian Council and the Canadian Métis Society focused on helping Aboriginal people assimilate into the dominant society. More recently, friendship centres in large urban areas have been attempting to facilitate the adaptation and integration of Aboriginal people moving from reserves. Their goal is to integrate Aboriginal people into the dominant society with a minimum of stress. Friendship centres are designed to act both as drop-in centres and as counselling centres. Ideally, Aboriginal people who come to the city can use the facilities to help them adapt to urban life. However, a number of problems have plagued the centres since their formation. The federal government funds the centres only on a short-term, year-to-year basis; this prevents long-term planning and development. In addition, the amount of funding is not enough to allow the centres to play their role effectively and ease the process of urban adaptation (Minore and Hill, 1997).

Today the Métis Associations have taken a "reform-integrative" approach in that their goal is to right historical wrongs (through settling land claims and defining Aboriginal rights), but once this has occurred, they are prepared to accept the basic structure of Canadian society (Daniels, 1981; Flanagan, 1990). The Native Council of Canada's major interest was for individuals to be reinstated as Indians. No consideration was given to changing the status quo, although in recent days it would seem that the Métis National Council is moving toward being an integrative-transformative organization (Grand Council Treaty, n.d.).

Integrate-Transform

Today, the Métis are attempting to entrench their rights in the Constitution by (1) adding a preamble that would reflect their historical contribution to Canadian society; (2) creating a charter of Aboriginal rights to entrench the collective rights of Métis; and (3) introducing an amending formula to guarantee Aboriginal participation in future constitutional conferences and amendments They also are engaged in reviewing the existing federal and provincial legislation and policy that bear on Aboriginal issues. The short-lived United Treaty First Nations Council emerged because of their concern about the inability of AFN to deal with treaty issues. They were concerned that the provinces are now involved in treaty negotiations, which they feel should involve only the federal government.

Other Aboriginal organizations that would fit into this category are the Native Women's Association of Canada and the National Committee on Indian Rights for Indian

Women. Their early focus was on ending the discriminatory aspects of the *Indian Act*. In short, they wanted sexual equality. However, in pursuing this goal, it has found that First Nation males are as much the problem as the *Indian Act*. Thus, those women who support these movements find themselves dealing with male Aboriginal leaders as with Ottawa bureaucrats. A secondary goal is to provide a support base on which to develop Aboriginal women's self-confidence.

Segregate-Reform

In 1982, the Assembly of First Nations emerged as the primary national Aboriginal organization. It represents First Nations associations and has recently concentrated its efforts on constitutional issues and self-government. At the third Annual Assembly of First Nations held in Penticton, B.C. in 1982, a new structure for an Assembly of First Nations was formally adopted by the chiefs of provincial/territorial or regional associations. This new organization was deliberately established outside the corporate structure defined by Canadian law and was the culmination of two years' work by the Interim Council of Chiefs.

In adopting an organizational structure for the Assembly of First Nations, the chiefs were subject to a number of proposed amendments and additions. For example, provisions for an amendment clause, mechanisms for accountability, and a process for impeachment were included. These changes had been developed by a subcommittee for presentation to the next Assembly of First Nations for review and acceptance by the chiefs.

The Confederacy of Nations was mandated to formulate policy and oversee the direction of the executive and secretariat between sessions of the Assembly. There is no direct comparison between the Assembly of First Nations and any body within government or, likely, within traditional First Nations structures. The intention of the Assembly of First Nations is to represent the needs and wishes of the several First Nations.

The Assembly of First Nations was established by chiefs to respect the sovereignty of each individual First Nation It can be described as an organization involved in a process of transition from the statutory origins of the National Indian Brotherhood toward a national political institution that derives its existence and direction exclusively and entirely from the First Nations. In some respects, it remains an organization that has not completely divorced itself from its statutory foundations (Final Report to Assembly of First Nations, February 18, 1985, mimeo).

In 2003, the Assembly of First Nations Renewal Commission was formed to examine the purpose and structure of the Assembly of First Nations. It was felt that, now that the Assembly was more than 20 years old, it had not evolved in step with other First Nation communities. Moreover, with recent court decisions and land claims literally changing the landscape of Canada's First Nations, a huge contingent of First Nations peoples living in urban centres, and an increasingly young population, it was felt it needed to assess whether or not its structure and processes needed to change. After nearly two years, the commission tabled its report and in 2006 it was ratified by the Assembly. The commission took 18 months to complete its work, after having held consultations with individuals and organizations across Canada (Assembly of First Nations, 2005).

Figure 11.2 identifies the new structure of the Assembly of First Nations. Three groups inform the Assembly in addition to the regional chiefs. A circle of elders, a women's council and a youth council now support the general and special assemblies. However, while the

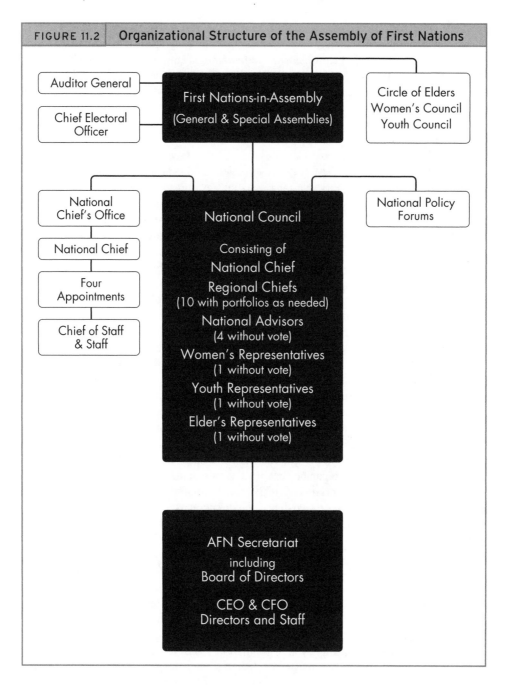

FIGURE 11.2   Organizational Structure of the Assembly of First Nations

Auditor General

Chief Electoral Officer

First Nations-in-Assembly
(General & Special Assemblies)

Circle of Elders
Women's Council
Youth Council

National Chief's Office

National Chief

Four Appointments

Chief of Staff & Staff

National Council

Consisting of
National Chief
Regional Chiefs
(10 with portfolios as needed)
National Advisors
(4 without vote)
Women's Representatives
(1 without vote)
Youth Representatives
(1 without vote)
Elder's Representatives
(1 without vote)

National Policy Forums

AFN Secretariat

including
Board of Directors

CEO & CFO
Directors and Staff

three groups have representation on the National Council, they do not have any voting rights. Only the national and regional chiefs are voting members of the council.

The circle of elders develops the rules and procedures of the Assembly for ratification by the entire Assembly. They are a resource for the Assembly of First Nations and its constituents. The elders are viewed as the custodians of the Assembly's rules and procedures, as they are for other traditional and customary laws. They have responsibility for the development, implementation, and maintenance of a redress system that provides mechanisms for impeachment, discipline, and loss of membership. The circle of elders also investigates and arbitrates any disputes within the Assembly. In addition, the elders select and present the speaker of the Assembly to the chiefs. They guide the speaker in the exercise of his/her duties and in seeking consensus of the Assembly. The women's council was created to give women a strong voice and allow them to participate in the Council activities. Finally the creation of a youth council came about as they recognized that new members of the community needed to have a voice in decisions made by the Council.

At the present time the ongoing political work of the Assembly is carried out by the Office of the National Chief. He represents the only body or person within the Assembly who can truly be held accountable by the chiefs. Between assemblies, the Confederacy of Nations tries to function as an executive committee and gives its own political mandates and direction to the Office of the National Chief.

Ten regional chiefs have portfolios as needed. They also provide a means of communication between the national chief, the Council and their regions. But in almost all cases, this function is secondary to their provincially or regionally held position, such as president of a provincial First Nation association. Finally, the new structure incorporates four national advisors (all without a vote) to provide the necessary expertise required when making decisions.

The national office has historically avoided running programs or providing services. At the same time, there is a desire to have the national office valued and respected within the First Nations communities. Therefore, a role must be identified for the national office—one that goes beyond support for the national executive on major political issues (which have already been fairly well defined).

Since its creation the AFN has established several committees, commissions, and portfolios to address the concerns and direction of the First Nations. Today the Assembly deals with a number of issues ranging from health and education to land rights, and has portfolios for regional chiefs to ensure these issues are dealt with. Resolutions are brought forward at both the general assembly and special assemblies to ensure that all members of the Assembly are informed of the issues and have the opportunity to discuss the resolution.

The AFN is the national organization that represents all First Nations in Canada. The chiefs meet annually to set national policy and direction through resolution. In addition, the members meet three to four times a year in a forum called the Confederacy of Nations which gives members a guide for future actions. Since the creation of the AFN, they have been active in the politics of Canada. The AFN met with the provincial premiers four times during the 1985–87 period to convince them that Aboriginal people had an inherent right to self-government. In the last meeting, most of the premiers were adamant that they did not, and only Ontario, Manitoba and New Brunswick were prepared to support the AFN position. Since that time, the AFN has been involved in the Meech Lake Accord of 1987, the Charlottetown Accord of 1992, the Free Trade Agreement with the United States and other legislative business. It works closely with other Aboriginal organizations and lobby groups.

Notwithstanding the opposition from many provincial premiers, the AFN takes the position that First Nations have the right to self-government, and that this prerogative exists as an inherent Aboriginal right that has never been surrendered, relinquished, or diminished by any formal treaty or agreement, nor by the Constitution, legislation, or policies of non-Indian governments in Canada. This right, although it exists, has yet to be exercised by the First Nations. Consequently, no contemporary national institutions exist as a derivative government of First Nations.

The AFN argues that any national institution established to represent or advance the interests of First Nations must reflect the sovereign jurisdiction of First Nations as the source of all that it does on behalf of the citizens of First Nations and, for that matter, on behalf of the governments of First Nations. Therefore, all powers, mandates, or responsibilities exercised on behalf of a First Nation are merely delegated, and the passage of time does not alter the delegated nature and quality of the power, mandate, or responsibility.

In conclusion, the Assembly of First Nations is an organization composed of members from varying backgrounds, cultures, histories, and philosophies. Out of respect for diversity and for the maintaining of solidarity, the Assembly of First Nations is trying to develop some basic principles of organization that are acceptable to all the First Nations.

As stated earlier, the growth of Aboriginal organizations and movements is helping Aboriginal peoples to retain their culture and identity, and is reinforcing links among them all over Canada. The pan-Aboriginal movement emphasizes the values and beliefs central to the culture of Canadian Aboriginal people, regardless of local band differences.[3] As such, the development of pan-Aboriginal organizations has been the first step in fostering a spirit of unity and brotherhood among Aboriginal people. This political activism also inspired a resurgent nationalism on the reserves, particularly in Eastern Canada. While some of the local or band goals were opposed to those of the pan-Aboriginal movement, all were united in opposing Indian Affairs and developing greater self-determination. (Hertzberg, 1971).

The emergence of pan-Aboriginal organizations has coincided with (although they are marginal to) the rise of conservation movements throughout North America. The leaders of pan-Aboriginal movements have extensive contacts with the larger society, while retaining a strong affiliation to an Aboriginal tribe. Members of these associations are generally bilingual, well-educated, and involved in typical Canadian occupations. The emphasis on Aboriginal values is all-pervasive, and extends into the decision-making process.

Although some Aboriginal and non-Aboriginal people see the reserve either as a prison or as a physical and psychological refuge, members of pan-Aboriginal organizations regard it as the basis for a viable community. They are not deterred by the fact that reserves are generally poverty-stricken, isolated, and lacking in essential services. Over the years Aboriginal people have tried to build a pan-Aboriginal movement, seeking to unite the various groups such as Métis, Inuit and non-status Indians.

Segregate-Transform

Broadly speaking, Red Power organizations address the problem of Aboriginal people's inability either to separate from or to integrate with the rest of Canada (Franklin, 1969). While Red Power has so far failed to present a clear-cut program, its most important focus seems to be on the control of reserve lands (Fidler, 1970; Jack, 1970). During the mid-1970s the American Indian Movement (AIM) gained some support in areas of Canada. AIM views itself as a grassroots organization in touch with the daily needs of Aboriginal people.

Red Power advocates attempt to unite a number of other moderate and militant groups into a network across Canada. Although there are many important differences, some of their major ideological themes have been derived from the Black Power movements in the

United States. In general, Red Power promotes self-supporting, self-directing, and commonly owned Aboriginal communities. Red Power members wish to create, develop, and carry out their own political, economic, and social programs. They also want to improve the Aboriginal's image on a personal level by changing both the negative stereotypes of Aboriginal people and their own negative thought patterns (Stewart, 1974).

Those pan-American Aboriginal organizations (who identify with South, Central, and North American Aboriginal people) who belong to the league of Nations are generally considered the most radical of the Red Power groups. The League is a very loose inter-tribal organization from which splinter groups, such as the National Alliance for Red Power (NARP), have emerged. Fewer and fewer militant youths are joining the League or one of its splinter groups (Lurie, 1971). League members rally around the central issue of treaty and Aboriginal rights. They argue that Aboriginal tribes must be viewed as nations, and they want any litigation between Aboriginal peoples and the Canadian government to be referred to the United Nations. While youth membership in the more militant groups is declining, membership in more moderate organizations continues to grow. As Lambertus (2004) points out, these members (from all age groups) are beginning to take a more strident position with regard to Aboriginal claims and rights. The recent blockade of rail lines in Ontario, the Caledonia blockade and the disruption of forestry activities in northern Saskatchewan all point to a more assertive style by Aboriginals.

Boldt argues that the pan-Aboriginal concept and the emergent political and cultural movement with which it is associated is serving to identify new boundaries and to create new overarching Indian loyalties at the national level. It is a movement to enhance a sense of commonality and group consciousness which goes beyond mere political organizations to include recognition of a shared history of oppression, cultural attitudes, common interests, and hopes for the future (1980c: 4).

No more than 3 to 5 percent of today's Aboriginal people can be considered Red Power advocates. However, this does not mean that militant organizations are not important. As research has shown, only a small percentage of a given population ever takes part in riots, revolutions, and urban guerrilla warfare. This small group, however, does need moral, economic, and physical support from the wider community—support that Aboriginal people seem increasingly willing to give to Red Power activists. It is not surprising that the RCMP has defined discontent among Aboriginal people as one of the most serious threats to Canadian unity.

Red Power supporters argue that violence is inevitable in the struggle to combat racism and achieve control over their lives. Although few non-Aboriginal people can agree, more and more Aboriginal people are beginning to do so. The activities of the Warrior Society at Oka and the supporting individuals who went to Oka or carried out militant activities elsewhere—e.g., the 1995 Gustafsen Lake standoff, Caledonia—suggest that while these organizations do not have a large membership, the potential number of recruits is high.

Other segregative-tranformative organizations adopt more contemporary forms of old traditional behaviours. The first of these is the pow-wow movement. The powwow is a planned inter-tribal affair usually held on neutral ground. There are dancing and social interactions, ritual healings, and serious discussions on the future of Aboriginal life. The young are encouraged to learn Aboriginal customs from their elders. It is hoped that, eventually, these pow-wows will build community solidarity among Aboriginal people everywhere.

As Corrigan (1970) points out, the pow-wow circuit acts as a communications network to promote the social and cultural integration of many Aboriginal groups. Other analysts, such as Howard (1951) and Lurie (1971), have also viewed the pow-wow as the current vehicle for achieving pan-Indianism. In an in-depth analysis, Dyck (1979) found that pow-wows constitute an autonomous achievement that summons a large community to celebrate the value and the excellence of Indianness in a manner that is both individually rewarding and collectively uncontroversial (p. 92–93). Furthermore, because pow-wows range over a large geographical area and provide continuity with the past, they can create a larger community out of various separate reserve communities.

Another form of segregative-transformative revitalization movement is the resurgence of prophet religions or religious pan-Indianism. Most Aboriginal religious movements have resisted assimilation efforts by the larger society. They have developed in the rural areas, and urge their followers to take up a style of life that is in harmony with nature. Humanity is viewed simply as one element of nature, which is always to be respected. A typical prophet religion was that led by Chief Robert Smallboy of Alberta.

There are other segregative-transformative organizations that do not take the conflict mode so characteristic of the Red Power organizations. Aboriginal people today are rediscovering their past and are attempting to sort out their identity. They are trying to develop a positive self-concept, and a group identity that can provide a reference point for them. They, like other minority groups, have developed myths that compensate for their subordinate status in Canadian society. These myths assert the moral superiority of Aboriginal people over other Canadians; for example, they depict Aboriginal people as living in harmony with nature, working to conserve the environment. These moral myths give Aboriginal people, oppressed for more than a century, a sense of positive self-esteem. In addition, the oppression experienced by them and their inability to fight back have produced a perpetual hostility in many of them. Moral superiority can also be one means of expressing their hostility (Fullwinder, 1969).

Aboriginal Dialogue: Our Place in Canadian Society

Because of the segregation and discrimination to which Aboriginal people are continually exposed, as well as their low position in the social and economic hierarchy of society, they are more or less suspended in a marginal position. As a result, within the Aboriginal communities a debate is taking place with regard to whether or not Aboriginal people should try to adapt to Canadian society. One sector of the community argues that the old traditional culture cannot provide Aboriginal people with the skills needed to survive in an urban industrial culture. Proponents of this view argue that Aboriginal culture has been assaulted by the dominant culture for so long and with such intensity that it cannot be salvaged. While the traditional cultural system may have been adaptive years ago, under today's conditions it no longer addresses the needs of Aboriginal people. It is useless, they argue, to continue to maintain a dying culture. Hence, their position is that Aboriginal people should take on the dominant industrial–urban culture and allow their traditional culture to fade into the past.

Other leaders argue that the dominant culture is not a moral one, nor is it relevant to their impoverished position in Canadian society. They feel that it cannot teach Aboriginal people how to cope with the kinds of situations that occur in their marginal position. This segment of the Aboriginal community argues that they must continue to develop their own culture and reject the dominant culture or any attempts to integrate (English, 1995).

The rejection of being dominated has been expressed by Aboriginal people in many different ways. Cornell (1988) identifies what he calls "lived" resistance movements in which Aboriginal communities tenaciously adhere to traditional Native values. These resistance movements are important in opposing social control efforts by the dominant group because they are not based on material interests but rather on a conceptualization of self and community. As a result, they challenge the values of the dominant society and of all of the assumptions held by those adhering to the dominant culture (Van Kirk, 1980).

These "passive" forms of resistance have given way, in more recent years, to more public forms of Aboriginal activism. The activist movement has resurged, and increasing extra-institutional actions have been carried out—mass protests, civil disobedience, land seizures, occupying buildings, and taking up arms. Such forms of activism ensure that the issue under consideration is given a public forum. However, equally important is the symbolism of such actions. Active engagement in overt conflict signifies a fundamental rejection of the formalized, institutional procedures provided for dealing with their grievance (Katznelson, 1976).

A third segment of the community takes a different approach. They point out that oppression over the past century has produced a unique culture—one under siege. As a result, Aboriginal people experience numerous personality conflicts, have reduced self-esteem, and seek relief in the overuse of defence mechanisms. They argue that Aboriginal people must be able to resolve their inner conflicts and conquer the inner self. Freedom from within is the first step that Aboriginal people must take if they are to resolve their conflicts and remove the self-hatred that characterizes Aboriginal behaviour today. The next step is to gain self-knowledge by coming to grips with reality through education (Venne, 1998).

However, it is a unique type of education that is advocated. To take on a dominant education would be to ignore the fact that it prepares Aboriginal people for a world that is denied to them—that it bears, in other words, little relation to the Aboriginal individual's future experiences. Such an education would be neither functional nor adaptive for most Aboriginal people. On the other hand, to engage only in traditional education would also be maladaptive in an urban-industrial society. Leaders speaking from this third position argue that Aboriginal people's education has to be in the context of their marginal position. Aboriginal education must thus be provided at two levels (NWAC, 1985a, 1985b).

This short review of the different types of Aboriginal organizations has demonstrated several points. All of these organizations have become important vehicles for meeting the needs of Aboriginal peoples. They have all provided forums for the understanding and discussion of Aboriginal issues. Each of these organizations has also had to adapt its structure and objectives to existing conditions or face quickly losing its membership. Clearly, the use of formal organizations among Aboriginal people is likely to increase. They have discovered that formal organizations carry a sense of legitimacy that can be very effective in persuading governments to act in the interest of Aboriginal people (Fine, 1989). In addition, it should be noted that many Aboriginal organizations have elements of more than one ideology. Some may have combined ideological perspectives as the best way to achieve the goals and objectives they have set forth.

How have Aboriginal organizations and social movements improved the quality of Aboriginal life? With the growth of various organizations and nationalist ideological movements, Aboriginal people are becoming more politically, socially, and economically aware. Formal organizations have allowed Aboriginal people to carry on discussions with the federal government on a legitimized basis, e.g., constitutional talks. In the past, the government could reject Aboriginal claims and recommendations on the grounds that they were speaking as individuals, and thus any advice or recommendations that were conflicting or inconsistent with the government's position could be ignored because they did not represent the demands of Aboriginal people as a whole. The creation of rational bureaucratic organizations reflects a collectively determined policy and allows for the presentation of cogent and coherent arguments on a variety of issues (Jamieson, 1978, 1979).

The impact of Aboriginal political organizations has been substantial, both on Aboriginal people and on government. These organizations have granted Aboriginal people input into the federal and provincial policies that affect them, thus providing them with instruments needed to bring about social change. But government also has found that dealing with an organization has many benefits. Because the bureaucracies within Aboriginal organizations are similar to those in government, both can now interact in an orderly, legitimate fashion. Government funding of most Aboriginal political organizations makes them more vulnerable to government control. As a consequence, Aboriginal leaders find themselves in the position of having to play by the government's rules in order to achieve their own goals—goals that may be at variance with those of the government. On the other hand, the government's power over Aboriginal organizations should not be overestimated. Governments also face a dilemma: without sufficient funds, Aboriginal organizations will not be able to negotiate; with sufficient funds, Aboriginal organizations will become too powerful (Krosenbrink-Gelissen, 1991). Weaver (1985) also notes that little evidence exists that demonstrates that the unequal power balance has compromised the positions held by national Aboriginal organizations on political issues.

LIMITS OF ABORIGINAL ORGANIZATIONS

The overall aim of many Aboriginal organizations is to gain input into the government decisions that affect them. In general, Aboriginal interest groups have found that appeals to members of parliament and provincial elected officials are ineffective, except as a last resort. Rather, they have learned to focus on the bureaucratic organizations that affect them most directly, whether at the federal, provincial, or municipal level. Aboriginal organizations can also influence government in other ways, such as through annual submissions to cabinet on aspects of federal policy. Local and provincial Aboriginal organizations may deal directly with the government at any level, or may channel their appeal through whatever nationwide organizations they possess (Tanner, 1983).

The impact of an Aboriginal organization varies in direct proportion to its resources. By resources we mean group assets such as high solidarity, well-structured organizations, and money, which can be directed toward social action that enhances the capacity of the group to achieve its goals. During the first half of the 20th century Aboriginal resources were extremely limited; however, since the 1960s they have markedly increased. The nature and extent of these resources have varied over time. Depending on the action taken by Aboriginal people, those resources utilized are built up and remain part of the total resources available to them in future. The relative importance of different types of resources may vary from time to time and from situation to situation. For example, economic resources are important, but they may be subordinate to political or legal resources under certain conditions. Furthermore, some resources (primarily economic) are portable, or transferable, while others have limited application, e.g., legal.

Cornell (1988) argues that a useful way to classify resources is by function. He identifies two types of resources: direct and mobilizational. Direct resources are those that directly influence the socio-political structure. Mobilization resources are those used in the process of bringing direct resources to bear on the issues under consideration.

One of the most common direct resources that organizations can use is the number of their members and/or supporters. However, because Aboriginal people are both dispersed and factionalized, they have been unable to convert this resource into a force. Commodities that are held by an organization may also be a direct resource. However, the commodity must be one desired by others. In the case of Aboriginal people, such commodities usually take the form of land, resources, or some other special right. Land and natural resources commanded by various Aboriginal organizations have been and continue to be valued bargaining resources. A third type of direct resource is the extent to which an organization has allied itself with other organizations, particularly those with power. Aboriginal organizations' success in the past has been the result of linkages with other non-Aboriginal organizations—e.g., religious organizations, human rights groups, and conservation groups. Some of these organizations have the aid of Aboriginal people as a primary purpose; others have related political agendas and find the alliance with Aboriginal people useful for obtaining their own goals and objectives, e.g., the Sierra Club.

As noted above, direct resources may not be useful if they are not mobilized. Having alliances, money, and land is of little use if you cannot mobilize them at the time you need to exert power. An example of an organization with good mobilization is the Native Women's Association of Canada. There are some 400 local chapters spread over Canada with no fewer than 100 000 members. These informal groups foster networks, facilitate communications, and provide Aboriginal women with an opportunity to develop organizational skills. These local groups are linked to the provincial and national offices; this affords quick communications and the ability to spread information quickly (NWAC, 1981).

What are the resources that allow organizations to mobilize and direct their activities? First, if an organization is to engage in sustained, focused activities, it must maintain a structured organization and retain relationships with other organizations. A major explanation for a group's failure or success seems to lie in its basic organizational structure. In Table 11.3, Pross (1975) delineates differences between two types of interest groups. Institutional interest groups can be placed at one end of a structural spectrum, and issue-oriented groups at the other.

Because of their lack of organizational structure, issue-oriented groups are generally less effective in pursuing and achieving their goals. Moreover, their goals are restricted to a narrow focus and can only be pursued one at a time. The highly structured institutional groups, however, are free to pursue a number of broadly defined issues simultaneously. Issue-oriented groups have a small membership and a minimal, usually volunteer, staff to handle communications. Institutional groups, meanwhile, can bring extensive financial and human resources to bear on a variety of issues. Clearly, the Aboriginal organizations that are more institutional in nature have a greater chance of achieving their goals. Institutional organizations can choose from a variety of persuasive techniques, such as advertising, and can cultivate long-term formal and informal relations with government officials and senior civil servants (Wuttunee, 1972).

An organization with a strong network forms a basis for recruiting. And a sharing of recruits among organizations leads in turn to a sharing of some of the same ideas. Thus, the linkages of the network are continually strengthened. An institutional type of organization is also in a position to distribute many more ideas than can an issue-oriented one. Organizations within a network also find that decision making is facilitated and that coordinated action is more possible.

The ability of a group of Aboriginal people to achieve their goals is also a function of the social cohesiveness of the organization to which they belong. The more central membership in an organization becomes to an individual's self-concept (identity), the greater the likelihood that the individual will act for the organization. The strength of the individual's identification with the organization also affects the nature and type of action he or she will take. Finally, leadership plays an important part in any organization's ability to carry out sustained social action. Any organization thus requires a pool of experienced, skilled individuals who are able to simultaneously deal with local community people as well as outsiders.

Certain factors associated with issue-oriented groups can reduce their effectiveness. For example, the emergence of divergent (or different) goals of various sub-interest groups leads to a decrease in ability to achieve goals as well as an increase in the amount of intergroup conflict. In addition, as the organization increases in scope and area, new sub-interest groups emerge—e.g., band affiliation, province, legal status, linguistics, and religion—that contribute to the multiple cleavages permeating Aboriginal organizations.

The internal leadership structure of an Aboriginal organization is also an important determinant of that organization's effectiveness in achieving its goals. Particularly important is the ability of Aboriginal leaders to exert strategic control over the goals and objectives of the organization. Organizational leaders must be adept at spanning boundaries at all times. They must monitor and control such factors as their clients' needs, funding opportunities, and reserve politics as they attempt to achieve their organization's goals. This requires leaders to be constantly vigilant in promoting their clients' interests, while at the same time maintaining their legitimacy in the eyes of external power groups (Howard, 1951).

As Pfeiffer and Salanchik (1978) point out, an organization survives when it is able to quickly adjust to external conditions and also cope with the environment in which it operates.

TABLE 11.3	The Organizational Structure of Interest Groups	
Institutional	**Issue-oriented**
Possess organizational continuity and cohesion.	Have limited organization and cohesion.
Are knowledgeable about government sectors that affect them.	Possess poor information about government.
Have a stable membership.	Have a fluid membership.
Have concrete and immediate operational objectives.	Show an inability to formulate long-term goals.
See credibility of the organization as important.	See goal achievement as important.

Sources: Adapted from P. Pross, ed., *Pressure Group Behaviour in Canadian Politics*, (Toronto, McGraw-Hill, 1975); P. Pross, "Pressure Groups: Talking Chameleons," in M. Whittington and G. Williams, eds., *Canadian Politics in the 1980s*, (Toronto: Methuen, 1981).

For example, Aboriginal organizational leaders invest considerable time and effort in dealing with and attempting to influence such external agencies as DIAND, the Department of Industry and various economic boards while also attending to the needs of their own constituents (Nielsen, 1991). The Native Women's Association of Canada was able to utilize the court rulings of the *Lavell* and *Bedard* cases as the basis for further lobbying efforts. They were able to identify "sex-equality" as the central issue of their organization and focus on that single goal (Cantryn, n.d.).

Nielsen and Silverman (1996) note that if an organization is dependent upon one or two sources for its resources then its task becomes even more difficult. An effort must be made to balance the relationships. Potential conflicts may arise in areas such as scope, priorities, and ideology. For example, funders of Aboriginal organizations may object to an organization expanding its services into areas that go beyond its usual range of activities. The funder may request that the organization withdraw that service (reduce its scope) or lose its funding. This may be more problematic if the constituency of the organization (Aboriginal people) is pressing the organization to continue its work in this area.

The organizational processes that have to be undertaken by Aboriginal organizations to survive are continuously in flux. Organizations with stable leadership and members are more likely to embark upon strategies that allow the organization to continue its existence. Oliver (1990) identifies several factors that push organizations into a "balancing" mode. Let us take each in turn.

Necessity comes into play when the organization must take an action in order to meet some legal or regulatory requirement. Non-compliance with this requirement will lead to negative sanctions against the organization—e.g., loss of funding. Thus, when government officials require Aboriginal organizations to comply with certain legal standards, the organizations must put themselves into a balancing mode. Reciprocity *motivates* an organization when it attempts to collaborate or coordinate its activities with those of another in the hope that there will be a mutually beneficial outcome. There is an anticipation that the benefits of establishing a partnership will outweigh the disadvantages. A third factor that makes it necessary for an organization's leadership to strive for balance is *efficiency*. All modern organizations are assessed in terms of their ratio of inputs to outputs. The cost–benefit ratios of Aboriginal organizations are continually being monitored. The establishment of a *stable* organization (resource flow and exchanges) is important if the Aboriginal organization is to remain in existence over time. Finally, the issue of *legitimacy* is significant to organization leaders. The image or reputation of the organization is important if it is to remain credible in the eyes of both its constituents and the broader society.

The evolution, survival, or phasing out of an organization is a function of both internal and external forces and how the organizational leadership deals with these forces. There is a need both to deal with the day-to-day issues and to attempt to predict where other organizations will be heading in the future. For if change is to take place and balance is to be achieved, the Aboriginal organization must integrate with, cooperate with, or support the goals and objectives evidenced by other organizations. If the disjunction between the Aboriginal organization and other organizations is too great, the Aboriginal organization will collapse for lack of support. Until recently, issue-oriented Aboriginal organizations have not attempted to achieve balance through cooperating with other organizations. They steadfastly retained their original goals and objectives and refused to change their strategies. The outcome has been a rapid demise of the organizations (Zlotkin, 1985).

As noted above, resources are not useful if they cannot be mobilized and brought to bear when needed. Aboriginal people have, in the past, mobilized some resources in the form of sporadic, incidental, collective action. However, this mobilization was not sustained and, within a short time, the organization was in disarray. Aboriginal people have lacked the structural organization necessary to carry out political action. An organizational structure, as noted by Cornell (1988), forms a basis for recruiting new members, linking members, and providing them with a vehicle to develop shared ideas and mutual respect. Thus, it helps develop a collective consciousness. Organizations also disseminate ideas that can be used to facilitate decisions and carry out concerted action.

To be sure, Aboriginal people have always had organizational structures. However, these structures were local (tribal) and focused around kinship. It has only been in recent years that pan-Indian and national Aboriginal organizations have emerged. Through this process various Aboriginal groups have become linked in their political action. However, while the organizational structures have emerged from the rural-based Aboriginal people, organizations are usually located in urban centres. Nor do they act on behalf of urban Aboriginal people.

Why haven't Aboriginal people become more involved in changing their lives? Why haven't they taken action in the past to provide themselves with the opportunities available to others? The answer seems to lie in their inability to amass the correct resources for the goals they want to achieve. As a rule, the greater the number and variety of resources held by a group, the greater their power. However, it is important to note that the importance of any resource is related to the issue being considered. As Cornell (1988) points out, not all resources are equally valuable, and their relative value depends on a variety of factors. For example, the size of a minority population is an important resource in a democracy because it will have more political influence than in a dictatorship. Legal skills are important if decisions are made by a judiciary but are not as important if they are made through a political process. Resources can also be assessed in terms of their convertibility, reusability, and applicability. For example, education is convertible into jobs, income, and power. It also can be used over and over and has a wide applicability to a number of situations. On the other hand, legal skills have a limited applicability but can be used over and over.

Aboriginal organizational efforts are all limited by a relatively small population size, a lack of access to power, and a dependency on the federal government for funding and resources. Although Aboriginal organizations have been able to bring some pressure to bear on private companies and local government agencies, their dependency on the federal government is still the most significant limitation to their activities (Taylor, 1983).

Strategies are developed by opposing groups to discredit potentially powerful organizations. One tactic involves forcing the resignation of controversial leaders through sanctions. While this may solve problems in the short term, such government actions unwittingly contribute to the growth of Aboriginal nationalism. Nonetheless, the federal government continues to exert control over Aboriginal organizations by a variety of means. It can offer or withhold information that is essential for effective planning and operations. It can also coopt the loyalties of Aboriginal leaders or define an organization as radical in order to reduce the chances of public and private financing and support. For example, in 1997 the federal and provincial government cut off all funding to the Indian Association of Alberta because of its political and lobbying efforts.

Communication

Curtailing the access to communications is an effective way to reduce the creation and sustainability of networks, the level of information, and the ability of groups to share information. Table 11.4 shows the distribution of various Aboriginal publications in the eight regions of Canada. In the early 1990s there were about 50 Aboriginal periodicals, compared to 37 in 1971. However, by the end of the millennium, the number of periodicals had dramatically increased. In addition, many single-issue magazines have been produced over the past five years. Today we also find an Aboriginal portal on the Internet that provides information and news with regard to Aboriginal issues (see "Weblinks" at the end of this chapter).

Aboriginal periodicals tend to be rural in orientation, although over half are published in cities. As Price (1972) points out, the growth of Aboriginal periodicals in a city reflects the increasing development of other institutions. Periodicals provide information to many Aboriginal people throughout Canada and reinforce Aboriginal values. Most Aboriginal periodicals aim to develop political awareness and Aboriginal identity, as well as to promote action on particular issues. The Aboriginal press still remains in its infancy and faces an uncertain future. Finances are the major problem, and as Raudsepp (1997) points out, most Aboriginal presses have a tribal, rural, and scattered readership. This means that they are unable to build up a viable advertising base. Few papers have a combined advertising and circulation revenue exceeding 40 percent of their budgets. So if the presses are to survive, government funding will need to continue.

In addition to written media, radio and television play an important role in providing Aboriginal people with both general information about Canadian society and specific information about Aboriginal issues. Minore and Hill (1997) analyze the impact of the Northern Aboriginal Broadcast Access Program, which facilitates the production of regional television shows by Aboriginal communication societies in northern areas of

TABLE 11.4	Aboriginal Periodicals by Province, 2004

	Percent
Atlantic	9
Quebec	21
Ontario	34
Manitoba	11
Saskatchewan	26
Alberta	15
British Columbia	34
Territories	15
Total number	165

Note: Some periodicals are unilingual (French, English, Aboriginal) while others have some combination of languages.

Source: Based on Price, *Native Studies*, 1978, p. 186; author has collected additional information since 1985.

seven provinces and in the territories. They demonstrate by case study how these programs have an empowering potential that is now being used by Aboriginal communities. Another example is the television channel, APTV, which provides national coverage on a number of issues of relevance to Aboriginal people. As the producers of these programs gain experience and skill, they will become a major force in the presentation of the Aboriginal voice of Canada. Finally we should note that the Internet is becoming an important purveyor of information. However, at the present time, there seems to be a large "digital divide" between Aboriginal and non-Aboriginal people with regard to access and use.

NATIVE ORGANIZATIONS: RESISTANCE AND RENEWAL

In 1969 the federal government provided a "solution" to the Aboriginal problem: *Statement of the Government of Canada on Policy*. In some respects, this white paper reflected the basic sentiments of the rest of Canada. It assumed that if Canadian Aboriginal people were to become fully integrated into Canadian society they would have to change radically. It argued that the separate legal status of Aboriginal people kept them from fully participating in the larger society. Therefore, the white paper proposed to repeal the *Indian Act,* do away with the legal status of Indians, and phase out DIAND (Indian Policy, 1969: 6).

Aboriginal organizations began their opposition to the white paper with formal briefs presented to the federal government. These presentations were separate but similar in content; they included the *Brown Paper* by British Columbia Aboriginal people, the *Red Paper (Citizens Plus)* by Alberta Aboriginal people, and *Wahbung* by Manitoba Aboriginal people. Even those Aboriginal people who did not submit formal briefs appeared to be in basic agreement with those who did. The coalition that resulted from the white paper was an important milestone in Aboriginal political organization. Aboriginal people had been unable to form strong coalitions against earlier bills, such as *Bill C-130* (1963), which provided for the disposition of Aboriginal claims.

The opponents of the white paper saw it as a disguised program of cultural extermination (Cardinal, 1969). Critics felt that Aboriginal people should remain legally, administratively, and socially separate if they so chose. The *Hawthorn Report* (1966–67), a sort of Royal Commission on the "Indian Problem," had just recommended that Aboriginal people be granted special status as "citizens plus" in order to ensure the preservation of their separate identity.[4]

In 1974, in response to the white paper, a joint committee of the National Indian Brotherhood (NIB) and Department of Indian and Northern Affairs was created. Although the composition of the joint committee was not what the NIB had called for, a special cabinet committee was created for the first time to deal specifically with Aboriginal concerns. The overall structure consisted of the NIB executive council and a number of federal cabinet ministers. The committee subsumed a joint subcommittee and a joint working group. However, in 1978 the NIB withdrew from the committee and the committee died a quiet death.

By the 1980s the federal government had decided not to implement the white paper. However, new issues began to emerge that required the attention of Aboriginal people. The debate prior to passage of the *Constitution Act, 1982* required extensive allocation of Aboriginal resources in order to ensure that their interests were protected. As a result of their vigilant action, several constitutional amendments were adopted that recognize Aboriginal and treaty rights. These changes recognize and affirm "existing Aboriginal rights" (Section 35.1), which then had to be defined. Legal and financial resources had to be devoted to ensuring that these rights would be properly defined and recognized. The subsequent First

Ministers' Conferences (1983 to 1987) on Aboriginal affairs also required detailed attention. The introduction of a comprehensive land claims policy (1981), which was subsequently revised in 1986, also meant that Aboriginal people had to broaden their resource allocations. The *Penner Report* (1983) was a major all-party parliamentary report on Indian self-government, and while it reflected favourably on First Nations' quest for self-government, it meant that Aboriginal people would have to promote and lobby Canadians to establish what those rights were.

During the mid-1980s the *Nielsen Report* was made public. This report narrowly defined the government's legal obligation toward Aboriginal people and identified ways in which DIAND could trim its budget. A major campaign was undertaken by Aboriginal organizations to inform Canadians as to the federal government's legal and moral responsibility toward them. Legal challenges emerged, and the Supreme Court of Canada upheld the federal government's fiduciary responsibilities (*Guerin* v. *Regina,* 1985).

At the same time, the federal government reversed its century-long policy on enfranchisement and passed *Bill C-31*. This amendment to the *Indian Act* removed sex discrimination, and allowed for the reinstatement of persons who had lost their Indian status. Furthermore, bands would be given greater control over who was a member. All of these changes required extensive actions on the part of Aboriginal organizations. (Ponting,1991).

There were many other activities entered into by Aboriginal organizations during the 1980s that continued on into the 1990s. The policy review on land and trusts for Indians provoked considerable reaction by Indians. Economic changes also forced Aboriginal people to establish priorities as government extended fewer resources to combat social and health issues. Changing educational benefits and shifting health responsibilities onto the bands were just two ways in which government action forced Aboriginal people to reallocate their meagre resources.

Aboriginal organizations were required to respond to all of the above initiatives in substantial and meaningful ways. It meant that resources had to be properly allocated and actions had to be monitored over long periods of time. Because of the scarcity of many resources (e.g., money and legal expertise), alliances had to be established. While these linkages enhanced the ability of Aboriginal people to achieve their goals, they also made the process more complex and intricate.

An unlikely independent ally emerged in the 1980s—the courts. Traditionally, the legal system took a very positivistic position in interpreting the law, which generally meant legal rulings against Aboriginal people. However, toward the end of the 1980s, court decisions began to support Aboriginal claims. The recognition of the Mi'kmaqs' and B.C. Indians' right to fish, the decision to hear the Manitoba Métis Federation's land claim, and the acknowledgement of Canada's fiduciary responsibility to Aboriginal peoples all gave both moral and legal support to the actions taken by them.

As a result of the actions taken by both the courts and Aboriginal organizations, there have been some federal and provincial policy changes regarding Aboriginal people. Other legal changes are being contemplated by the federal government as Aboriginal organizations continue their relentless pursuit of justice in the moral and legal arena. Aboriginal peoples will continue to make their presence known. They are afraid that otherwise they will be ignored and forgotten by the larger society and the government of Canada. Rather than let that happen, they will continue to unite their forces to achieve their rightful position in Canadian society.

CHANGE THROUGH CONFLICT

Conflict permeates all aspects of our lives—in our homes, at work, and in our linkages with the community. As Black (1998) points out, conflict arises when one individual behaves in a manner that is defined by another as inappropriate and necessitating a response. Thus, conflict is a relational concept and involves the interaction of at least two parties. While some conflict causes deep and long-lasting physical and emotional impacts, other forms of conflict can produce a positive result (Law Commission of Canada, 1999). Moreover, the duration of conflicts may differ, and their intensity can vary over time. This should alert the reader to the fact that conflict should not be seen as the other end of the continuum from order, nor should conflict always be viewed as harmful. Nevertheless, long-term conflict between groups within a society produces structural tensions that are difficult to change. Moreover, these conflicts can produce a context that becomes part of the culture of each group and defines future behaviour. How has conflict been managed? Aboriginal people have used the organizations they have created to challenge adversaries or those who seem to take advantage of the plight of Aboriginal people.

Conflict between Aboriginal and Euro-Canadian culture is not new; there have been numerous examples over time. While early conflict was widespread, it was sporadic and limited to the immediate locale. However, as we ended the 20th century, conflict became more endemic and widespread, and it has continued into the 21st century. For example, events occurring in British Columbia (e.g., forestry disruptions, highway blockades, park sit-ins) were quickly communicated across the country. Supporters from all over Canada have come to the aid of their "brothers and sisters" wherever they were engaged in conflict behaviour. Aboriginal peoples began to defend their way of life and reclaim resources they felt were theirs. Both political and legal negotiations were considered slow and cumbersome ways of solving problems (Richardson, 1993). Moreover, it seemed to Aboriginal people that the legal process was an inappropriate strategy to solve these conflict situations.

Resolving Conflicts: The Courts

When faced with resolving a conflict with Aboriginal people, the government has utilized the legal system. As such, courts have acted within a Euro-centric and positivistic model. Courts have operated on a logic that has not considered alternatives to existing principles and practices. For example, sentencing circles were not introduced until the 1980s. Medicine chests were considered to be small boxes containing local medicines and nothing more; any thought that they could be equated with health care premiums was unthinkable until recently. There have been some exceptions to the rule—e.g., the *Calder, Guerin,* and *Sparrow* decisions—but generally the courts have not been an ally of Aboriginal peoples. And as we have noted elsewhere, even when the courts do render decisions in favour of Aboriginal people, compensatory action by lower courts, governments, and private industries negates or limits the impact of these decisions. The 1988 *Eastmain* decision is characteristic of such court rulings.

In short, Aboriginal people generally have not looked to the courts to solve conflict situations involving them. Richardson (1993) points out that verdicts have shown themselves to be a function of how an individual judge views Aboriginal society. In short, court cases involving Aboriginal people seem to reflect the attitude and perspective that an individual judge has about Aboriginal society and individual Aboriginal persons, as well as his or her conception about history. The various decisions about Aboriginal peoples and their claims over the past 50 years defy any coherent logic and have failed to produce an integrated body of law on Aboriginal rights. Aboriginal people feel that Canadian law ignores any Aboriginal conception of the world and is completely based upon European models of explanation. It is unthinkable that Canadian law would ever give serious consideration to the view that no one can own land or that a consensus model of society could exist. These differences in ethos have been reflected in conflicts over the past century.

In some legal cases, the behaviour of the courts and government is simply unfathomable. For example, when the Cree in Alberta submitted a land caveat to freeze development in the area where they live, the provincial government refused to accept the caveat and referred the matter to the provincial supreme court. At the same time, the government retroactively changed the law so that the Cree would lose their case when it came before the court. In other cases, such as the *Delgamuukw et al.* v. *British Columbia* (1990), the Court not only rejected Aboriginal explanations about their society (as well as the explanations presented by expert witnesses such as anthropologists), but chastised them for wanting to continue a way of life that was different from the dominant Euro-Canadian culture. While this decision was appealed in 1993 and Aboriginal rights were once again accepted, the appeal court placed a narrow interpretation on their meaning.

From the perspective of the Aboriginal people, the courts have not listened to their concerns, have ignored their arguments, and have rendered decisions against their positions. At the same time, non-Aboriginal people view the courts as wielding too much influence in Aboriginal affairs and making decisions that do not reflect the will of the public. There is also a belief that the courts have tended to side with the Aboriginal people. These contrasting conceptions have emerged as the long-term conflicts between the two groups remain unresolved (Gamson, 1969).

COMPLIANCE IDEOLOGY

Each culture has its own system of shared values and beliefs that allows for its stable and efficient functioning. As such, each society has a collective orientation through which all members make decisions and resolve dilemmas. Members may not follow these orientations, but they are aware of the consequences if they do not. These orientations become embedded in the culture and take on moral and ethical values that govern people's behaviour. In other words, these rules inform people about what are appropriate goals and the appropriate ways in which these goals can be achieved. In short, the rules become guideposts that describe an individual's place in society, justify allegiance to that society, and prescribe the nature of participation in society (Wilson, 1992).

This compliance ideology (Wilson, 1992) serves its purpose by supporting the institutional arrangements and the behaviour of both individuals and organizations. Moreover, at the individual level, it allows people to carry out their behaviours with a minimum of transaction costs; i.e., each individual understands the rules of society as well as the consequences if they are violated. In the end, as Wilson (1992) points out, the compliance ideology provides an explanation and justification of the activities of institutions and individuals as well as their linkages. Laws are just one example of highly formalized compliance ideologies and are represented in highly codified forms. Other compliance ideologies may not be directly visible but represent the assumptions underlying most of our behaviour (Fletcher, 1992).

Aboriginal people older than 40 years of age have not been exposed to and socialized in the same compliance ideology as the younger generation. By and large they have remained outside mainstream Canadian culture, even though they have been exposed to the "new world order," and view the world very differently. Younger Aboriginal people have been exposed to the socializing efforts of mainstream society as well as to the compliance ideologies of their preceding generation; hence they have a bicultural orientation. But whatever their age, Aboriginal people are well aware of their inability to participate in the institutional spheres of mainstream society. Thus, there is a reluctance to "buy into" the mainstream compliance ideology.

Sources of Conflict

As we have noted elsewhere, there are many sources of conflict between Aboriginals and non-Aboriginals—e.g., religion, family life, and personal relations. However, one of the most important sources of conflict that has permeated Indian–non-Indian relations from the time of first contact has been that of land. From a European perspective, land is a central aspect of production in the triad of labour, capital, and land. Whereas Canadians believe that one cannot carry out economic activities unless all corners of the triad are available, Aboriginal people view land as a collective resource that is central to their identity (Armitage, 1995). The end result is that control over land continues to be of paramount importance for both parties—and lives have been lost from each side as the two groups attempt to grapple with the issue.

Armitage (1995) argues that in some respects the conflict over land is central to the relationship between Indians and non-Indians. Moreover, he argues that the relationship is defined on a racial basis and continues to remain a racial distinction. The continuous conflict over land has been frustrating for Aboriginal peoples and has been a major source of their anger and resentment toward non-Aboriginals. The clear demarcation between advantaged and disadvantaged is also always visible to Indians as they circulate among a non-Aboriginal population. Aboriginal people are clearly able to see that, while Canadians have prospered over the past half-century from economic development, they have not. They have been systematically excluded while other Canadians (native-born and immigrants) have been able to participate in the economic sphere that has enhanced their quality of life. Finally, the attitude of superiority (which manifests itself in the form of prejudice and discrimination) of non-Natives toward Natives is a continuous source of friction. Occasionally it takes the form of physical conflict. The question now remains whether or not this pent-up hostility will continue to be directed inward toward the self (self-hate), toward other members of the Aboriginal community (in-group hostility), or toward the non-Aboriginal community (overt confrontation). As Justice Greenberg noted when he was sentencing Ronald "Lasagna" Cross for actions at the Oka conflict:

> I am satisfied that he was not motivated by greed or reasons of personal gain. He acted out a deep anger, rage, desperation and a sense of hopelessness, all the result of the systematic discrimination and racism against his people over several centuries.

He went on,

> For years, decades, even centuries, the aboriginal people of this country have endured, at best, indifference, neglect and unfairness and, at worst, open hostility, contempt, discrimination and racism. (Imai, Logan, and Stein, 1993)

Over the past decade, conflict between Aboriginal and non-Aboriginal people has become a more common component of the interaction process. Examples, such as the Cardston blockade, the Oka resistance, the Gustafson confrontation and more recently the Caledonia conflict, confirm that Aboriginal peoples are not averse to engaging in overt physical conflict.

Government has dealt with Aboriginal people in ways that are to its advantage and not supportive of Aboriginal communities. The Royal Commission on Aboriginal Peoples (Canada, 1996d) grouped the relocation activities of government into two types: administrative and development. Administrative relocations were carried out to facilitate the operation of a government policy or to address the needs of Aboriginal people. For example, the Mi'kmaq of Nova Scotia were relocated to a central reserve in the 1940s in an attempt to reduce administrative costs (and to free up land for agricultural use by non-Aboriginal people). Twenty-five years later the GwaSala and Nakwaxdaxw Indians of British Columbia were relocated and amalgamated on a reserve in order to allow for more efficient delivery of government programs. At the same time the Innu of Labrador were moved to Davis Inlet, again for ease of government service delivery. After experiencing massive social problems for over nearly half a century, in 1994 the Innu agreed to a proposal to move from Davis Inlet to Little Sango Pond (back on the mainland), although a number of conditions still have to be met, including a long-term economic plan, site viability, and a formal ratification by Innu.

The second type of relocation also has a long tradition. Development relocation results from the implementation of an economic policy that involves tangible development activities—e.g., agriculture, hydro construction, or natural resource exploitation. The James Bay hydro development, which required thousands of Aboriginal people to relocate, is perhaps the best example. Phase 3 of the James Bay hydro development is now taking place and the Cree are much more involved in the development of the project. However, the massive oil/gas extraction activities as well as the logging efforts in the Lubicon Cree homeland in Alberta provides another example.

In either type of relocation, the movement of Aboriginal people has several consequences. First, the move severs people's relationships to the land and the immediate environs. Second, there is generally a loss of economic self-sufficiency. Third, there is generally a decline in health standards. Finally, the movement of people breaks bonds among them and produces changes in the social and political structures. (For a more detailed discussion of specific relocations, the reader should consult Volume 1—*Looking Forward, Looking Back*—of the Royal Commission on Aboriginal Peoples [Canada, 1996a.])

If a people are resentful of and feel hatred toward their colonizers, why do they not speak up? Why don't they do something? Why don't they initiate overt conflict? It should be noted that Aboriginal people do respond to actions that they feel are discriminatory or that impact negatively on their community. However, unless these reactions are exceptional, the media generally do not report on them. Because of this, it will look, at first blush, as if Aboriginal people are "doing nothing." Aboriginal people prefer (as a cultural attribute) to solve problems without resorting to direct confrontation or overt conflict. In other words, covert action may be the first step in dealing with a conflict situation. Their preference is to discuss the issue, evaluate a range of alternative solutions, and then attempt to achieve near consensus on the accepted solution. Sentencing circles are a good example of how this works (Linker, 1999). In the past, Aboriginal people used the courts as a primary way to solve conflict between Aboriginal and non-Aboriginal people in a variety of contexts—e.g., land rights, hunting rights, non-renewable resource development, and social customs. However, in almost every case, Aboriginal people found that they have lost their preferred solution to the problem. Moreover, the courts force the actors to take an adversarial position, a stance Aboriginal people prefer not to take. Finally, Aboriginal people have come to feel that there are no alternative solutions to their problems except to engage in direct confrontation such as blockades or sit-ins (Gibbins and Ponting, 1984; Slattery, 1985; Lambertus, 2004).

Aboriginal people have also begun to accept that conflict is an important element in the functioning of any society. While most people tend to see conflict as dysfunctional and detracting from the effective and efficient operation of society, it must be pointed out that conflict also has positive impacts. Aboriginal people have found that they can use conflict as a strategy to achieve their goals and objectives. For example, engaging in conflict forces the opposition parties to directly negotiate with the aggrieved parties. In doing so, dominant parties are forced to deal with the minorities as equals. In short, the dominant–subordinate relationship changes to one of equals. Second, the dominant party must communicate with the aggrieved party. Third, the nature of the complaint is made public and other interested parties may become involved in the negotiations. Finally, the dominant group may be forced to change its policies, attitudes, and behaviour toward the group initiating the conflict (Ponting and Symons, 1993).

SUMMARY

Most non-Aboriginal Canadians do not see the logic of First Nations holding the title of a "citizens plus" policy that grants special status to Aboriginal people, arguing instead that Aboriginals cannot be truly integrated into Canadian society unless special status is removed. Yet the two "founding nations" forced Aboriginals to assimilate and show deference to their cultural practices and products, and thus determined the formal, defining qualities of Canadian society—giving themselves, in effect, a special status of their own.

Removal of the legal status of Aboriginal people would not lessen discrimination against them. They would occupy the same depressed economic position as they do now, but without any group identification. They would become even more marginalized in Canadian society. Moreover, this marginality would not be wiped out in a generation; the stigma of Aboriginal birth is not only cultural, but physiological. Because intermarriage between Aboriginal and non-Aboriginal people is only slowly increasing in Canada, the marginal Aboriginal person will haunt Canadian society for many decades.[5]

Those who want to end the special status of Aboriginal people implicitly adhere to the myth of equality. This myth claims that, since everyone is equal, no one should be favoured or discriminated against. It is easy enough to stop the discrimination that favours Aboriginal people by eliminating economic incentives, affirmative action programs, educational advantages, and so on. However, out of political expediency and for other reasons, few efforts are made to stop discrimination against them. Aboriginal organizations have challenged this view and have used their collective powers to confront such a view.

In a nation that advocates cultural pluralism, suggestions that the unique status of First Nations be eliminated seems incongruous. Nevertheless, the idea continues to be supported (as evidenced by the *Nielsen Report*) as a response to the recent growth of Aboriginal political and economic organizations. There is a recognition by the political elite that if these organizations are allowed to control reserve policies and funds, they will become formidable pressure groups in the 21st century. The harsh sanctions imposed by the minister of Indian Affairs on the Indian Association of Alberta and the Assembly of First Nations reminds us all what Aboriginal organizations can expect if they continue to challenge the authority of Indian Affairs.

At present, more than $1 million per year is provided to Aboriginal organizations, with limited results. One problem is simply that Aboriginal people are still in the process of developing the skills that most Euro-Canadians take for granted. Far more serious, however, is the fact that many Aboriginal organizations can only take action with federal approval. Only then are the funds released. Moreover, the federal government seldom agrees with Aboriginal organizations on spending priorities. The government is constantly changing its long-range plans and shuffling its bureaucratic slots for allocating monies. Even when an allotment can be clearly perceived as unrealistic at the local level, it seldom can be changed. If INAC allocates several thousand dollars to be spent on a given project, then no amount of counter-argument by local Aboriginal organizations can divert this money into another project.

Political skills are vital to the survival of any group of people. In Canada, the cultural awakening of Aboriginal people has been preceded and outpaced by the growth of their political awareness. Aboriginal people are becoming increasingly sophisticated in their use of organizations to further their goals. This new knowledge will make itself felt more and more in Canada as we move into the 21st century.

KEY TERMS

pan-Aboriginal

Federation of Saskatchewan Indians

North American Indian Brotherhood

Native Council of Canada

Assembly of First Nations

Red Power

Native Women's Association of Canada

compliance ideology

STUDY QUESTIONS

1. What two events resulted in an increase of Indian organizations since the late 1960s?
2. Discuss the three categories of Aboriginal organizations.
3. Compare and contrast *reformative* and *transformative* perspectives.
4. What are *integrative* and *segregative* perspectives?
5. What impact(s) has the different types of Aboriginal organizations had?
6. Discuss how resources relate to the impact of an Aboriginal organization.
7. What are the two types of resources?
8. Discuss the *balancing mode*.
9. Discuss the importance of conflict for generating change.
10. What impact have the courts had upon the resolution of conflict?
11. Discuss *compliance ideology* and its relation to Aboriginal people within Canada.
12. How has Aboriginal people's viewpoint towards conflict changed throughout history?

WEBLINKS

www.aboriginalcanada.gc.ca/acp/site.nsf/en/index.html (Aboriginal Canada Portal)

This website provides links to over 40 provincial, regional, and national Aboriginal organizations, associations, councils, foundations, institutes, and cooperatives, all listed by name.

The websites of several of Canada's major national Aboriginal organizations include:

www.afn.ca

Assembly of First Nations

www.abo-peoples.org

Congress of Aboriginal Peoples

www.metisnation.ca

Métis National Council

www.nwac-hq.org

Native Women's Association of Canada

NOTES

1. For a more complete discussion of the history of British Columbia Aboriginal organizations, the reader should consult Drucker (1958).

2. The Six Nations community is attempting to separate politically from Canada. This may account for their lack of militancy.

3. The term "pan-Indian" is not used by Indians but was invented and is used now by social scientists.

4. See, for example, the work of S. Weaver, *The Hidden Agenda: Indian Policy and the Trudeau Government,* University of Waterloo, Waterloo ON, mimeo, 1980.

5. In 1961, the endogamous rate of Aboriginal marriages—Aboriginal persons marrying Aboriginal persons—was one of the highest in Canadian history. In fact, it increased from 91 percent in 1951 to over 93 percent in 1961. However, by 1971 the rate had decreased to 77 percent, and by 1981 a further decrease to 67 percent was evident.

chapter twelve

The Department of Indian and Northern Affairs Canada

INTRODUCTION

One of the most important challenges to government is to ensure stability and to manage change successfully, and the administration of Aboriginal affairs is no exception. The British Indian Department, the first department set up by the Crown in America, was established in 1755 to deal with Aboriginal issues. However, 1830 is considered the beginning of an ordered system of Aboriginal administration in Canada. Thirty years later, responsibility for Aboriginal affairs was transferred by the British government to the government of the province of Canada. At the time of Confederation, the *British North American Act,* now called the *Constitution Act, 1867,* gave the new Canadian federal government legislative authority over "Indians and lands reserved for Indians." In 1939 a Supreme Court decision allowed this bureau also to deal with Inuit affairs even though they were not considered Indians as defined by the *Indian Act.* Over the years, Aboriginal affairs have been under the control of many different government departments, such as Agriculture and Citizenship; it was not until the 1960s that the current structure was put in place.

The Department of Indian and Northern Affairs Canada (or INAC, sometimes referred to by its previous name, the Department of Indian Affairs and Northern Development, or DIAND) comprises a complex number of programs, sectors, branches, directorates, and secretariats. Within the department, the Indian and Inuit Affairs Program has four sectors that have been created to deal specifically with Aboriginal people. All of these organizations will be identified below to illustrate the size and complexity of the program. And, it should be noted at the outset, the size and complexity of the organization's structure have certain implicationsfor how it operates.

Furthermore, these branches, directorates, and secretariats are not the only federal agencies that deal with Aboriginal people. For example, the Secretary of State, Justice, Industry and the Medical Division all have units within their departments that have Aboriginal people as part of their mandate. In addition, there are many other branches of both the federal and provincial governments—e.g., Revenue Canada, Corporate Affairs—that deal with Aboriginal people. Hence, the scope and complexity of the structure of government involvement in Aboriginal life should be clear to the reader. The attendant problems of coordination and delivery are great indeed. It should come as no surprise, then, that there is a great deal of overlap, confusion, and tension among and between the many organizations that deal with Aboriginal people. Likewise, it should be clear that Aboriginal people find this complex web of uncoordinated organizations difficult to understand and to deal with. Finally, the utilitarianism of such a structure to its members should be clear. It is almost impossible to attribute blame to a specific individual or unit, and unsuccessful change cannot be clearly traced to any single unit. In short, accountability is not possible under such a structure—a point that the Auditor General's office has made for many years.

The Department of Indian and Northern Affairs Canada is responsible for all federal policy and programs concerning Canadian registered Indians and Inuit; it also administers the Northwest Territories, Nunavut and Yukon. It administers over 50 separate acts, encompassing every region in Canada.[1] The department's mission is to facilitate a better quality of life for First Nations, Inuit, and northerners. In doing so, the department collaborates with other federal departments and provincial and territorial governments, identifies both short-term and long-term goals, and then puts in place programs and services that ostensibly will improve the lives of Aboriginal people and increase their self-sufficiency.

The department's current strategic directions are based on the federal government's action plan outlined in the 1998 document *Gathering Strength—Canada's Aboriginal Action Plan*. The actions to be taken by the department are based on transforming relations with First Nations through supporting healthy and safe communities; closing socio-economic gaps; improving management of land, environment, water, and natural resources; and honouring responsibilities and commitments. Specific actions include fulfilling the obligations of the federal government arising from treaties, the *Indian Act*, and other legislation; negotiating settlements in respect of claims to Aboriginal rights; supporting the economic development of the North and protecting the northern environment, including Arctic seas. Its mandate also includes coordinating settlement implementation and continuing to promote self-reliance; establishing and implementing new funding arrangements with Aboriginal communities to facilitate their education; and assessing existing program delivery mechanisms and related organizational structures to establish Aboriginal control and community self-sufficiency.

Over a quarter-century ago the department decided to play a new role in the lives of Aboriginal people through "devolution" that would support Aboriginals in developing healthy, sustainable communities and in achieving their economic and social aspirations. This change to the role of an "enabler" and an advocate for initiatives launched by Aboriginal people has been difficult to implement and even more difficult for the department to accept. This new identity stands in stark contrast to the previously held role of controller and regulator of Aboriginal issues. As Weaver (1983) points out,

[I]n contrast to the historic role of DIAND as custodial administrator, new paradigm thinking proposes a smaller, more responsive and more development-oriented administrative role. Its job is to constructively support and advance First Nations political autonomy, and to service the negotiated agreements....(pp. 14–15)

The new paradigm adopted by the department is designed to achieve four goals that were identified after intensive meetings had gone on between the government and Aboriginal people. The four themes are self-government, economic development, quality of community life, and protection of the special relationship between the federal government and Aboriginal people. In an attempt to achieve these goals, the department shifted more decision making to First Nations communities; removed barriers to economic growth, and developed better housing, education, and social services in order to respond to local needs. Finally, it hopes to achieve better management of First Nations lands and monies and protect the special relationship that exists between the federal government and the Aboriginals of Canada. In short, the department is trying to strengthen Aboriginal governance, reduce the socio-economic gap, and encourage healthy communities.

Central to the above is the desire to have Aboriginals decide their own futures. The government's overriding stated objective is to nurture the socio-cultural and political development that will ultimately see Canada's first citizens realize their dreams. But this cannot be achieved without sound economic growth. Therefore, the federal government continues to contribute to economic development opportunities by bolstering Aboriginal participation in the educational system and commercially viable businesses and institutions.

As pointed out earlier, Indian and Northern Affairs is not the only organization that funds activities related to Aboriginal people. Nevertheless, the department has certain activities and outputs that directly impinge upon Aboriginal people, for which it is solely responsible, and this "operational circle" represents activities that the department has direct control over—e.g., funding, monitoring, policy. However, the department is equally cognizant that because many other agencies—e.g., Health Canada—also have Aboriginals as part of their mandate, it needs to develop partnerships with these organizations and engage in collaborative actions. These partnerships may be with other government departments/agencies, with First Nations, or with the private sector. Unfortunately this collaboration has not generally been successful, although there are some "best practices" that typify this type of thinking, e.g., Mushuau Innu Relocation Agreement, Labrador Innu Comprehensive Healing Strategy. Finally, the department has taken an even broader perspective in adopting a "global circle" of influence. This describes both the existing conditions that affect strategic outcomes and desirable changes in those conditions. Although these conditions are beyond the department's direct influence, they are still important to focus on as they may impact on First Nations in the long term.

INDIAN AND INUIT AFFAIRS PROGRAM

The Indian and Inuit Affairs Program traditionally has been highly centralized, with its headquarters in Ottawa. It is responsible for policy development, resource allocation, and planning for First Nations and Inuit through a variety of methods—for example, direct service delivery, grants, and loans. However, since the late 1970s, when a policy of devolution was introduced, the 10 regional offices—one in each territory, one for the Atlantic provinces, and one in each of the remaining provinces—have begun to develop their own programs. These programs emerge from the structures serving specific districts within each region (except in Manitoba). Thus, the districts have become influential, except in

Alberta, where control is retained in the regional office, and of course in Manitoba. The reader can already see the complexity of the operations.

The Indian and Inuit Affairs Program also supports Aboriginals in their quest to preserve and develop their culture. Support is channelled through three streams. First, financial assistance is given to bands, councils, or non-profit corporations that support Aboriginal heritage. Second, a cultural development program supports Aboriginal artists. Third, the community social services provide advice and guidance to band councils, their staff, and community service organizations.

The Indian and Inuit Affairs Program's policies, objectives, priorities, and programs are established by senior executives and then passed down and back up the bureaucratic ladder.[2] Budgets must be developed for each program and approved by Parliament. Most of the budget of the Indian and Northern Affairs Program (74 percent) is nondiscretionary; that is, it is set aside for specific items and is non-transferable. However, as the year proceeds, the Indian and Inuit Affairs Program often requests additional funds.

Today we find that about 17 percent of the total number of employees of the Indian and Inuit Affairs Program are Aboriginals. However, Aboriginal workers in the department have not yet gained access to policy-setting positions; only 4 percent of the Aboriginals employed by the Indian and Inuit Affairs Program are at the senior- and middle-management levels. The largest proportion—28 percent—is at the operational level, primarily involved in teaching. Less than 10 percent of its employees have been with the Indian and Inuit Affairs Program for more than 15 years and it is this group ("the old guard") that have almost total control over policy development and implementation.

THE COST OF THE DEPARTMENT OF INDIAN AND NORTHERN AFFAIRS

The government of Canada operates more than 100 programs that are directed in whole or in part toward Aboriginal people in Canada.[3] The direct cost of these programs is well in excess of $10 billion (see Table 12.1). The beneficiaries of these programs—Indians, Inuit, Métis, and status Indians—add up to almost one million people. However, as indicated in Table 12.1, Indian and Northern Affairs Canada is not the only federal agency that provides services for Aboriginals.

Twelve federal departments offer programs for Aboriginal Canadians. Table 12.2 identifies the federal expenditures for Aboriginals over the past two decades. It shows that the overall annual budget has increased from $703 million to over $8 billion. During this time, the yearly growth rate in expenditures has varied from 3.2 percent to over 20 percent, with an average annual growth rate of 5.7 percent. Nearly two-thirds of the total budget is covered by Indian and Northern Affairs, with Health and Welfare Canada being the second largest contributor.

In 1975 the federal expenditures on Aboriginal programs represented 2.1 percent of overall federal expenditures (excluding expenditures on public debt). By 2003, this had increased to 4.6 percent of the federal budget. Overall, federal spending during this time grew 8 percent, while spending on Aboriginals increased at about 11.2 percent annually. Since 2003 there has been a decrease in expenditures, so that by 2006, the increase was just over 6 percent (the budget was $6.3B), reflecting the government's cap on increases for Indian and Northern Affairs Canada.

Over the years the federal government has developed numerous programs for status Indians. Although we noted above that there are 12 major federal departments that deal with Aboriginals, nearly all federal expenditures flow through four main routes. **Quasi-statutory programs** receive 40 percent of the total budget. These programs are directed toward First Nations people living on reserves, and they reflect the legal obligations of Canada through the establishment of the *Indian Act, Constitution Act, 1982*, and other legal directives implemented over the past two centuries. **Basic services** (36 percent) include expenditures on schools, community infrastructures, health, housing, and local government. The third category of expenditures is **land claims.** As noted previously, while this program only made up 3 percent of the total budget a decade ago, it has increased substantially over the next decade as the backlog of claims is settled (15 percent). The fourth avenue is through **"discretionary" funds** that are allocated during the year on an "as needed" basis through supplementary estimates (e.g., relocation, safe drinking water, housing, residential schools settlements).

On a per capita basis the data show a steady increase over the past quarter century. In 1981, the per capita cost of operating Indian and Northern Affairs was $5 678. By 1993 it was well in excess of $12 000—a 54 percent increase, although it has subsequently decreased to just over $9300 in 2004, partially a result of the increase in Aboriginal people. As noted earlier, the Department of Indian and Northern Affairs covers two-thirds of all Aboriginal expenditures. The actual programs and services delivered to Aboriginal people vary by group and location. Some are provided directly by the Indian and Inuit Affairs Program, while others come from territorial governments that are, in turn, reimbursed for their

TABLE 12.1	Approximate Federal Expenditures for Aboriginal Peoples[1]							
	Expenditures by Department[2] ($ Millions)			Federal Departments				
Year	INAC	NHW	EIC	CMHC	ISTC	SS	Other	Total
1975-76	587	74	–	3	26	13	–	703
1980-81	1134	155	57	58	44	23	4	1475
1985-86	1990	341	159	156	15	53	22	2736
1990-91	3081	578	152	199	85	45	22	4162
1991-92	3412	639	200	240	79	62	42	4674
1992-93	3647	706	200	272	76	51	89	5041
2003-04	5471	1682	337	307	40	69	1905	9811
2004-05	5832	1705	417[3]	370	39	–	2406	10769

Note:
1. Federal departments and agencies that have Aboriginal programs include Indian and Northern Affairs Canada; Health and Welfare Canada; Employment and Immigration Canada; Canada Mortgage and Housing Corporation; Industry, Science and Technology Canada; Secretary of State; Solicitor General; Fisheries and Oceans; Public Service Commission; Justice; and National Defence. Data are from annual reports of the respective departments.
2. 1991-92 and 1992-93 figures are from Main Estimates. Figures include spending on Aboriginal employment equity programs, but do not include spending on programs available to all Canadians, such as Old Age Security and Unemployment Insurance. Data are from annual reports of respective departments.
3. This represents a combination of Health and Welfare as well as Human Resources and Skill Development.

costs. Aboriginals living on reserves deal directly with the federal government. On the other hand, off-reserve Aboriginals face a complicated pattern of eligibility for government services. The federal government takes the position that off-reserve Aboriginals should avail themselves of provincial services, while the provinces argue that registered Indians, no matter where they live, are a federal responsibility. Sometimes proof of residence is required, e.g., proof of having lived 12 months off the reserve, before provinces consider registered Indians eligible for provincial services.

TABLE 12.2	Budgets for Federal Programs Directed to Aboriginal Peoples (Millions)			
	1993-94	2003-04	% of INAC	% of Total
Indian and Northern Affairs Canada (INAC)				
Self-government	18.3	137	3	2
Claims	70.9	673	11	8
Economic Development	98	152	3	2
Lands, Revenues, and Trusts	140.3	119	2	1
Education	903.3	1431	23	16
Social Development	816.3	1194	19	13
Capital Facilities	665.1	1027	17	12
Band Management	269.4	377	6	4
Northern Affairs	572.4	133	2	2
Other	92.9	902	15	10
Subtotal	3647	6145	101	70
Other Government Departments/Agencies				
Health Canada	706.4	1682	-	19
Canadian Mortgage & Housing	271.8	307	-	3
Fisheries & Oceans	8.0	164	-	2
Solicitor General	44.7	84	-	1
Justice	9.7	13	-	-
National Defence	4.3	8	-	-
Secretary of State (Heritage)	51.3	69	-	1
Human Resources	200	337	-	4
Industry	76	40	-	-
Correctional Services	-	28	-	-
Indian Residential Schools and Resolution Canada	-	58	-	-
Natural Resources	-	17	-	-
Privy Council Office	-	15	-	-
Subtotal	1394.6	2820	-	30

FEDERAL EXPENDITURES: A COMPARISON

Courchene and Powell (1992) attempted to estimate the dollar value of federal spending on registered Indians living on the reserve. Overall, they found that on-reserve Indians received about $9300 per capita per year. If administrative costs were added to this figure, the value increased to $10 100. If we compare this value with the contemporary total provincial expenditures per capita, we find that the overall expenditure for all Canadians was $10 500, although this value varied by province, with a low of $9700 in Newfoundland and Labrador and a high of $11 700 in Nova Scotia. This suggests that on a per capita basis Indians were receiving expenditures similar to other Canadians. While the numbers have changed in the past decade, the analysis of data today reveals that a similar pattern exists.

However, Aboriginals argue that, because of their inferior position in Canadian society, the government needs to increase its expenditures to "catch up" for past inequities. For confirmation of this view, the recent Royal Commission on Aboriginal Peoples recommends that additional expenditures be allocated to Aboriginal people in order for them to shed their low socio-economic status.

There has been considerable criticism of Indian and Northern Affairs with regard to its administrative expenditures, which amount to $1100 per person. Overall, this adds an additional $81 million per year to the total budget. However, the percentage of Indian and Northern Affairs' budget that is allocated to administrative overhead has declined throughout the past two decades. For example, in 1985 the department's overhead was 6 percent of the total budget; by 2004 this had decreased to 3.1 percent. This reduction has come about through some loss of public employees, but much of it has occurred as a result of the process of devolution, in which departmental activities have been turned over to First Nations communities.

It should be noted that services provided to Aboriginals far exceed the federal government's constitutional and legislative responsibility. Many programs and services, e.g., housing, have been implemented as a strategy to lessen Aboriginal poverty and distress. While some programs have produced positive results, many have been dismal failures—both in the short and the long term.

In the early 1980s nearly 60 percent of the Indian and Inuit Affairs Program's expenditures were made through contribution arrangements to Indian bands or various Aboriginal organizations. In turn, these groups provided the specific services as outlined in the contract or agreement. As the new "devolution" policy was implemented, more and more of the budget was managed by First Nation communities. For example, by 2000, Ontario and Manitoba were each allocated about 18 percent of the budget. In addition, 32 percent was equally divided between B.C. and Saskatchewan. Alberta received about 5 percent. The remaining portion of the budget was equally split among the Atlantic region, headquarters, and the territories. On a per capita basis, Ontario and Alberta have the lowest Indian and Inuit Affairs Program expenditures. These low allocations reflect the relatively high rate of employment in Ontario and Alberta and the resource-rich bands in Alberta.

In addition to the allocation of funds, there have been major changes in the distribution of those funds. Since 1960 considerable shifts have occurred in the distribution of funds among operating expenses, capital costs, and expenditures for grants and contributions. In the early 1960s over half of the budget was used to meet operating expenses, while the rest was evenly split between the other two categories. In 1980–81, however, operating expenditures accounted for only 37 percent of the budget, while capital expenditures on additions and betterments had decreased to 4 percent. Expenditures on grants and contributions had increased substantially and made up nearly 60 percent of the total budget (Annual Report, DIAND, 1980–81). This reallocation continues and suggests a wide-scale transfer of the administrative costs of Indian and Inuit Affairs programs to provincial governments.

The actual spending patterns of the Indian and Inuit Affairs Program also have substantially changed in recent years. In the early 1960s approximately 45 percent of the budget was spent on education. By 1978 this had decreased to 39 percent and by 1990 it was further reduced to 33 percent. Today it represents 26 percent. Other activities funded by the Indian and Inuit Affairs Program also show changes in fiscal priorities. Community affairs accounted for about 43.1 percent of the budget in 1970 and 1978, but decreased to slightly more than half that level in 2000. Economic development, previously a low priority for the Indian and Inuit Affairs Program, ranging from between 6 and 9 percent of the total budget, has been identified as a high priority for Indian Affairs as we enter the 21st century. However, the data show that in the 2003–04 planning estimates, it only accounted for less than 3 percent. Indian Affairs argues that funding in other areas such as capital facilities and social development will lead to an increase in economic development. Moreover, they note that, with the introduction of new Aboriginal economic programs, private–public partnerships will result, with greater leveraging abilities and thus greater economic impact.

In 1967 the Indian and Inuit Affairs Program accounted for 1.06 percent of the government's total budget. This figure peaked at 1.74 percent in 1972–73 before it was reduced to 1.7 percent in 1980, and in 1987 it stood at about 1.6 percent. It has slowly increased since this time, so that by 2003 the federal expenditures on Aboriginal programs represented 4.1 percent of the federal budget. In 1965, the Indian and Inuit Affairs Program was allocated about one-half of the total Indian and Northern Affairs Canada budget. This proportion increased to nearly 75 percent in 1969 and today constitutes 83 percent of the total Indian and Northern Affairs Canada budget.

STRUCTURE OF THE DEPARTMENT OF INDIAN AND NORTHERN AFFAIRS CANADA

The structure of Indian and Northern Affairs is outlined in Figure 12.1, with approximately 75 percent of its employees delivering more than 500 distinct services in 10 regions across the country.

The organizational structure shows that there are ten major sectors in the department: Economic Development and Special Initiatives, Policy and Strategic Direction, Lands and Trust Services, Claims and Indian Government, Northern Affairs, Corporate Services, Socio-Economic Policy and Programming, Legal Services Support, Federal interlocutor and Office of the Corporate Secretariat. This structure shows that each sector of the department communicates directly to the deputy minister, while no formal linkages exist among the units. However, informal communication goes on among the various units on a routine basis in an attempt to keep each sector informed of other activities being carried out in the department.

The department administers the statutory requirements defined in the *Indian Act*, including the registration of Indian people, the deployment of reserve lands and other resources, and the regulation of band elections. It also attempts to ensure that the federal

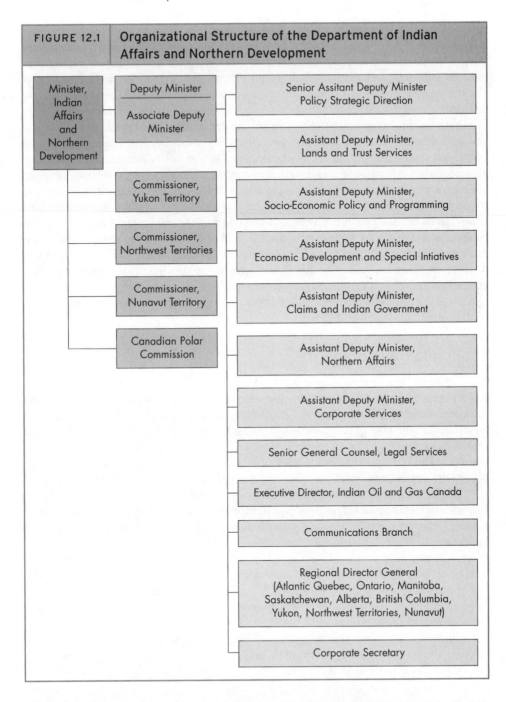

FIGURE 12.1 **Organizational Structure of the Department of Indian Affairs and Northern Development**

government's lawful obligations to registered Indians and Inuit under the *Indian Act* and the treaties are fulfilled. Overall, the department provides a wide range of services of a federal, provincial, and municipal nature to Aboriginal people. In meeting its responsibilities, the Indian and Inuit Affairs Program works closely with other federal departments and agencies such as Health Canada and Justice Canada. In keeping with the principle of self-development, the department attempts to assist and support Aboriginals in achieving their cultural, educational, and social aspirations. In addition, the agency tries to promote the economic and community development needs of Aboriginals and to ensure that Canada's constitutional and statutory obligations and responsibilities to Aboriginals are fulfilled.

There are three program/business lines in the department. The first deals with Indian and Inuit affairs, the second with northern affairs, and the third with administration. The Indian and Inuit Affairs Program, as discussed earlier, supports Aboriginals in achieving their economic, education, cultural, self-government, and community development needs and aspirations. It also helps to settle accepted Aboriginal claims through negotiations and to ensure fulfillment of Canada's constitutional and statutory obligations and responsibilities to Indian and Inuit people. The second program focuses on northern affairs. It will not be discussed in this book, save to note that the goal of this sector is to promote the political, economic, scientific, and social development of Canada's North. This of course means it assists northerners, including Aboriginal groups, to develop. The third component, administration, ensures that the bureaucracy established operates smoothly and efficiently to achieve the goals/objectives identified above. We now turn to a discussion of the major sectors within the department.

Economic Development

The Economic Development Sector is responsible for community planning, development, and access to resources. Two units (the Socio-Economic Policy Unit and the Programs and Economic Development and Special Initiatives Unit) have been created to deal with economic issues. The goal of this sector is to strengthen the economic base of First Nations communities, remove obstacles to economic development, and facilitate economic opportunities (see Figure 12.2). Most of the work of this sector is focused on developing and supporting the implementation of the Canadian Aboriginal Economic Development Strategy.

The government established the Canadian Aboriginal Economic Development Strategy, which is focused on helping Aboriginal peoples achieve their goal of economic self-reliance. This partnership among Indian and Northern Affairs, Industry, Science and Technology, and Employment and Immigration Canada has spent over $100 million over the past decade to ensure achievement of its goal. This approach is different from past attempts at providing economic development services directly to Aboriginal people. The new strategy offers support for Aboriginal economic development decision making, priority setting, and delivery of economic development services through community-based organizations and development.

In order to implement this program, the government has fostered linkages between Aboriginal communities, the private sector, and government (federal, provincial, and territorial) agencies in order to promote greater participation by Aboriginal people in the mainstream economy. The Canadian Aboriginal Economic Development Strategy comprises eight programs, e.g., Business Development, Joint Ventures, Skills Development. These economic programs have evolved over time but they are the major activities that the federal government has undertaken to create economic development on the reserves and to help individual Aboriginals integrate into the mainstream economy.

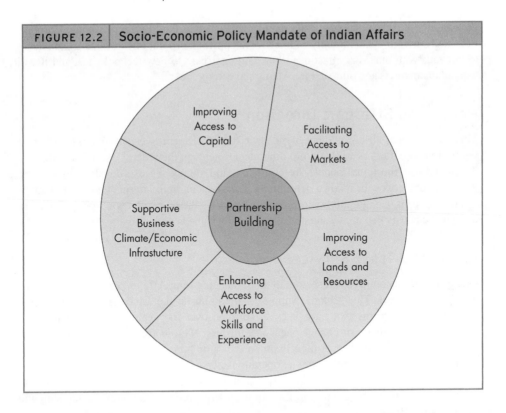

FIGURE 12.2 | Socio-Economic Policy Mandate of Indian Affairs

The overall strategy employed by this group is to develop an Aboriginal economic development program for the long term, which will be designed to support control by Aboriginal communities, i.e., community-based decision making, priority setting, and delivery of services. Indian and Northern Affairs' community economic planning and development program has been the key component of this strategy. This component is designed to assist Aboriginal people, through community economic development organizations, to create, maintain, or strengthen local organizational, advisory, and development capacity, which will help Aboriginal community members more clearly define and achieve their economic goals.

The Commercial Development program handles business development activities. Because of the creation of the Canada Aboriginal Economic Development Strategy, direct contributions to Aboriginal businesses have ceased. In 2001–02, the department budgeted nearly $140 million for economic development. An additional $900 million was set aside for capital facilities and maintenance. In addition to the above initiatives, Indian and Northern Affairs have created a number of other programs and strategies to enhance First Nations economic development. Programs such as the Resource Partnerships Program, Aboriginal Business Development Initiative, the Major Business Projects program, Procurement Strategy for Aboriginal Businesses, and the Aboriginal Fisheries Strategy Allocation Transfer Program are just a few that add support to the economic development thrust initiated by Indian Affairs. Others, for example, the Aboriginal Business Development Initiative, were launched in 1999 with $21 million designed to improve business development opportunities for Aboriginal communities. The Aboriginal Business Development Initiative strengthens the capacity of Aboriginal financial organizations (such as the Aboriginal Capital Corporations and Aboriginal Community Futures Development Corporations) to access capital and to network with other organizations, thus gaining access to new technologies, and it will expand the markets and outreach for Aboriginal entrepreneurs.

Policy and Strategic Direction

This unit oversees all of the other branches in the department to ensure that policies from within Indian Affairs as well as from other departments in the federal government that are developed for Aboriginal people are consistent and aligned. It also develops long-range goals and objectives for its own department. It carries out both internal and external environmental scans, e.g., population projections, to assess the political, legal, social, and technological changes that are taking place both within Canada and globally.

Lands and Trust Services

One of the more controversial sectors in the Indian and Inuit Affairs Program is the Lands and Trusts Services. This sector is supposed to administer the *Indian Act* and the Crown regulatory mechanisms that have been established over the years. It has recently been reshaped as a facilitator of change necessary for First Nations for them to take on greater responsibility and control over their lives. At the same time, it is a delivery agent of programs, services, and policies. From an operations perspective, it is divided into three interdependent branches that manage 21 business lines: the Registration, Revenues, and Band Governance Branch; the Lands and Environment Branch; and the Policy, Partnership and Coordination Branch.

The Registration, Revenues, and Band Governance Branch is responsible for elections, maintenance of Indian registration and lists, by-laws, Indian monies, estates, and transfer of control of membership, to mention just a few of their activities. The Indian registry administers about 3 million hectares of land and processes some 100 000 transactions per year, e.g., birth and death certificates. The trust fund managed over $3.4 billion in 2005, with revenues of $1.9 billion and disbursements of well over $1 billion. Recently this unit has come under scrutiny by the Federal Auditor General, who points out that First Nations are not getting the land they are entitled to. She notes, for example, that since 1994 only 12 percent of the land allocated to First Nations in Manitoba and Saskatchewan by the courts or through negotiation has actually been handed over to them.

The Lands and Environment Branch is responsible for First Nations land management initiatives, natural resources (forestry and minerals), land management, surveys, and land registration, as well as all forms of environmental protection and remediation activities. Over the past 10 years, this directorate has added 220 000 hectares of land to the total existing reserve land base in Canada (now at 2 846 000 hectares), an area roughly half the size of Nova Scotia. This branch also provides bands and Indian organizations with advisory, technical, and other support to deal with environmental problems.

Finally, the Policy, Partnership and Coordination Branch acts as a facilitator of change necessary for First Nations to assume greater responsibility and control over their lands and governance systems. It also acts as a catalyst for legislative reform and an agent for change and devolution.

It should be noted that these three branches maintain linkages with other federal and arm's-length organizations. In addition to the implementation of the Canada Aboriginal Economic Development Strategy, Lands and Trust Services also works in the area of Aboriginal taxation and in the administration of the *Indian Oil and Gas Act*. The Indian Oil and Gas Canada mandate is to identify, administer, and tender for permit or lease, Indian petroleum and natural gas rights on behalf of Indian bands. The Indian Taxation Advisory Board was created in the Economic Development Sector (as a result of *Bill C-115*, the 1988 amendment to the *Indian Act*) to consider new taxation bylaws. For example, the board granted bands broad powers to tax interests in Indian lands. The Indian Taxation Advisory Board, which used to be part of Indian Affairs, is now an arm's-length agency that deals with taxation-based issues in First Nations and maintains extensive linkages with the Lands and Trust Services. It also links with Indian Oil and Gas Canada to facilitate the development of fossil-fuel–based resource harvesting.

In its role of administering Indian land and money, this sector has been admonished over its role in administrating Indian funds. Recently the courts have awarded individuals and bands damages or other redress because Indian and Northern Affairs has not carried out proper administrative procedures. For example, in a landmark case, the Musquean band of British Columbia (*Guerin v. the Queen*, 1984) brought a breach of trust suit against the Crown. The federal government had not carried out the terms of a lease requested by the Indians and did not inform them of this breach. Almost a decade after the suit was launched, the Supreme Court ruled that a breach of trust had indeed occurred and found in favour of the First Nations community. This ruling overturned a federal Court of Appeal decision that had overturned the original judges' decision. The importance of the ruling lies in the judges' statement that the band had a "pre-existing right to its traditional lands" and that the Crown had "breached a fiduciary obligation to the band." This decision has forced the government to clarify its role when negotiating with third parties over Indian land, as well as to obtain informed consent from the band on whose behalf it is acting.

For nearly a decade, lawyer J. O"Reilly represented the Samson Cree in an attempt to take "Indian monies" out of the *Indian Act* control and give them to an independent trust for the use of First Nations. In 2005, the court ruled in favour of the transfer of all the Samson money (which had been held by the Federal government since 1892) to an independent trust, known as Kisoniyaminaw Heritage Trust. While the Federal government initially agreed with the decision, they appealed the decision in 2006 and it is now back before the courts.

Claims and Indian Government

This sector manages the negotiations, settlement, and implementation of land claims agreements, as well as special claims settlements and self-government arrangements. Within this sector, four branches have been created: Comprehensive Claims, Specific Claims, Implementation, and Self-government.

The Comprehensive Claims Branch represents Canada in all negotiations of comprehensive land claims with Aboriginal groups. This branch (also known as the modern-day treaties branch) has the responsibility to negotiate the settlement of land claims and to ensure that Aboriginal people are protected in the negotiated settlement. Its primary goal is to provide a clear and long-lasting definition of rights to lands and resources for Aboriginals and other Canadians. It is also responsible for ensuring that the settlement provides economic opportunities for Aboriginal groups, that the settlement respects the fundamental rights and freedoms of Canadians, and that the interests of the general public are respected.

Through the Specific Claims Branch, the Claims and Indian Government Sector undertakes the assessment of specific claims submitted by Indian bands and conducts negotiations on behalf of the government. The assessment process entails determining whether the federal government has breached legal obligations to a band and compensating the band if the government has breached this obligation.

The Indian Specific Claims Commission was created in 1985 to conduct an impartial inquiry when a First Nations claim is rejected by the minister of Indian and Northern Affairs Canada. It provides for mediation and facilitation services, if appropriate, in an attempt to resolve the dispute. In 2004, the commission worked on more than 60 inquiries and mediation efforts with a total budget of $6.3M. However, the government is not mandated to abide by the commission's ruling. In 2003 a new claims resolution centre was established although it has yet to come into force. As the centre takes on the role of resolving Aboriginal claims, the Indian Specific Claims Commission will be phased out of existence.

The Implementation Branch monitors and manages the implementation of comprehensive land claims and self-government agreements. This branch also provides policy support and expertise where specific claims agreements are being settled. This branch ensures that what the parties agreed to is in fact carried out. There are two steps to this process. The first is the development of an implementation plan, while the second phase is the monitoring and management of actual implementation activities. Today, the parties to a land claims and/or self-government agreement must negotiate a plan, which becomes an integral part of the overall agreement. This plan identifies what must be done to put the agreement into effect, who will be responsible for which implementation activity, and how and when these activities will be undertaken.

The fourth branch of the sector is Self-government. Self-government agreements identify arrangements for Aboriginal groups to govern their internal affairs and assume greater responsibility and control over the decision-making that affects their communities. Because Aboriginal groups have different needs, the federal government has recognized that there is no single model of self-government that will be used for all negotiations. As such, self-government arrangements will take many forms based on the diverse historical, cultural, political, and economic circumstances of the Aboriginal groups, regions, and communities involved.

Northern Affairs

The Northern Affairs sector assists the social, cultural, political, and economic development of the Yukon, Nunavut, and the Northwest Territories, and while not specifically directed toward Aboriginal people, it does place particular emphasis on the needs of northern Aboriginal peoples. The program operates directly, as well as indirectly, through the governments of the three territories. It also is responsible for the Polar Commission.

The Northern Affairs sector's activities, as they relate to Aboriginals, focus on the settlement of land claims, establishing cooperative mechanisms to support economic development, and the enhancement of Arctic sovereignty and circumpolar cooperation. The Constitutional Development and Strategic Planning Branch, Natural Resources and Economic Development Branch, and Comprehensive Claims Branch make up the focus of this program. The first branch's goal is to establish transfer programs resembling provincial

programs for territorial governments, thus encouraging the development of northern political institutions and diversification of the economy and reinforcing Canadians' sovereignty. The Natural Resources and Economic Development branch has a myriad of
functions, ranging from the Biological Division—which focuses on the management of
wildlife—to carrying out the responsibilities for the North American Air Defence Modernization Project.

Corporate Services and Legal Services focus on ensuring that operations within Indian
and Northern Affairs are carried out effectively, efficiently, and legally. In addition, Legal
Services Support oversees the various claims and grievances that are presented, as well as
ensuring that all contracts between Indians and the government of Canada are appropriate.

Federal Interlocutor for Métis and Non-Status Indians

A new role, quasi-independent of Indian and Northern Affairs Canada, has been created in
the Office of the Federal Interlocutor. While the activities of the agency are independent of
Indian and Northern Affairs Canada, the chair is the minister of Indian and Northern Affairs
Canada. The federal interlocutor works with Métis, non-status Indians and provincial governments to support capacity building within their organizations. Modest funding (in 2006
it was $29M) is provided to Aboriginal organizations such as the Métis National Council
and the Congress of Aboriginal Peoples. The office is also the director of the Urban Aboriginal strategy that deals with issues urban Aboriginal people face. Currently eight pilot projects in major urban centres across Canada are funded.

GOVERNMENT POLICY

Those who determine Indian and Inuit Affairs Program policies seldom, if ever, have direct
experience with Aboriginal issues. Policies are developed by Indian and Northern Affairs
Canada bureaucrats in headquarters (Ottawa) and amended by bureaucrats from other government areas that are likely to be affected by the policies. As Weaver (1980) points out in
her analysis of the 1969 white paper, the Privy Council Office, the Prime Minister's Office,
the Treasury Board, and the cabinet wield the most direct influence on federal policy concerning Aboriginal peoples. In the 1969s the Privy Council Office and Prime Minister's
Office were restructured to assert the primacy of the prime minister and Cabinet in setting
policy and monitoring programs. This restructuring has allowed the Privy Council Office,
Prime Minister's Office, and cabinet to maintain much closer control of Indian and Inuit
Affairs Program activities and to evaluate those activities in the context of other government
departments. The 1960s also saw a major restructuring of the system of standing committees in the House of Commons. This change has permitted members of Parliament to interact more directly with the staff of the Indian and Inuit Affairs Program and to expand their
roles through a process of open discussion (Weaver, 1980).

These two changes removed policy development and implementation from the total
control of particular departments and ensured that policies would be evaluated in the context of policies from other departments. Policy advisory councils were created to report to
the cabinet; in effect, these councils are one step above the cabinet in power. Information
from each department is now filtered through the Privy Council Office and Prime Minister's Office instead of passing directly from senior bureaucrats to cabinet ministers
(Cairns, 2005; Ponting and Gibbins, 1980).[4]

These changes have had a direct effect on organized attempts by Aboriginals to influence policy and program development. There is now another entire set of bureaucrats that must be lobbied. Moreover, they can only be lobbied by an intermediary and within the confines of committees with legitimate powers of inquiry (Pross, 1975). As a result, Aboriginal groups have reorganized their efforts to influence the politics that affect them. They have also found new ways to counter the increasing input of the Privy Council Office and Prime Minister's Office into general policy recommendations (Cairns, 2004; Prethus, 1974).

The federal government acknowledges a special relationship between itself and Aboriginal Canadians. It agrees that registered Indians and Inuit possess special rights, privileges, and entitlements, whether they live on or off the reserves. But, although the federal government acknowledges its responsibility to on- and off-reserve Aboriginals, it claims that they also should look to other levels of government for certain services. In addition, the federal government regards its responsibility for off-reserve services in a different light than that for on-reserve services. More specifically, under Section 91(24) of the *BNA Act* the government has accepted responsibility for on-reserve services in more program areas than for off-reserve services.

The federal government argues that as Aboriginals move off reserves they become citizens of a province; as such, they have a basic right to the same services provided by the province to all its other residents. Nevertheless, the federal government has a number of direct off-reserve support programs in such areas as housing and post-secondary education. In addition, it provides transfer and block payments to the provinces based on Aboriginal population figures under such programs as Established Program Financing and Equalization. These programs are intended to help provide the same services to Aboriginals as are provided to the general provincial population.

The federal government, then, maintains that each level of government has its respective responsibilities based on separate, distinct bonds with Aboriginal peoples. Aboriginals who live off reserves are residents of provinces and often contribute to provincial tax revenues; in addition, they have often provided indirectly many other resources now available to the provinces, and they are included in the calculation of transfer and block payments to the provinces. The provinces, on the other hand, take the position that registered Indians are a federal concern and not under the jurisdiction of provincial governments.

In early 1991 Ottawa decided to limit spending on social services for registered Indians. It decided that it would no longer pay social assistance to registered Indians for the first year after they leave a reserve. Provinces have reiterated their stance that "Indians and the welfare of Indians, whether it be on-reserve or off-reserve," is a responsibility of the federal government. Registered Indians likewise agree with the provinces' stand, and argue that the social services question is a federal responsibility and should not be transferred to the provinces.

DEVOLUTION

Indian and Inuit Affairs has been in the process of decentralization (decolonialization) since 1964. In 1969 the then Department of Indian Affairs and Northern Development simply stated in the white paper that Aboriginals were to become a provincial responsibility. This policy was rejected by Aboriginal organizations and provincial governments alike. In the mid-1970s a new policy emerged involving the transfer of federal responsibility to First Nations communities rather than to the provinces. At the same time, administrative responsibilities were being shifted from Ottawa to the regional and district offices of DIAND. As a result, First Nations gained greater involvement in the policy formations of the Indian and Northern Affairs Program (Ponting and Gibbins, 1980).

The devolution of responsibility for the delivery and management of services and programs from Indian and Northern Affairs to the direct control of First Nations began in earnest in the late 1970s. This process is taking place through a range of mechanisms—funding contributions, alternative funding arrangements, grants, and flexible transfer payments. For example, in 1993 there were 110 signed alternative funding arrangements with 198 bands, totalling nearly $400 million. Today this figure has nearly tripled. These alternative funding arrangements provide bands with the maximum level of authority available under existing legislation and policy. They also allow First Nations communities to redesign programs and re-allocate funds that meet community priorities.

From 1983 to 1993 the number of people working in the Indian and Inuit Program decreased by 42 percent. As a result of this strategy, Phase I of the Devolution Plan—which involves the transfers of community services such as social development and education—is complete.

The shift of responsibility to First Nations communities is taking place at three levels. First, funds for program management are being transferred from the Indian and Inuit Program to the direct control of the bands. This transfer began in 1968; by 1971, bands were managing about 14 percent of a $160 million budget and, by 1978–79, about 35 percent of a $659 million budget. Today they control over 70 percent of a budget exceeding $4 billion. Second, core funding grants are provided for the basic administrative costs of chiefs, councils, and band managers. In 1978–79, these grants represented 4 percent of the total DIAND budget; today this has nearly doubled to 7.5 percent. Third, band training and support services are supplied to encourage management skills and to provide technical support.

At present, the bands administer about 60 percent of the total capital and 80 percent of the school budgets. Approximately 90 percent of the bands are involved in the core funding program, but these figures show considerable regional disparity, e.g., Manitoba bands control a great deal of their operational expenditures, while the Yukon bands control very little. Overall, more than 80 percent of Indian and Inuit Affairs Program expenditures flow through Aboriginal governance structures. We also know that the number of full-time federal employees in the program has decreased by 51 percent, from nearly 4000 in 1987 to less than half that number today.

This policy of devolution was designed to promote the autonomy of Aboriginal communities and to support self-government. It marks a shift in federal policy from programs that promoted assimilation to those that encourage First Nations community government and cultural self-sufficiency. Band councils are increasingly responsible for financial allocations. However, although the Indian and Inuit Affairs Program is relinquishing specific control over expenditures, it still retains control of the overall allocation of funds and demands an accounting of funds spent. In effect, this policy has shifted critical attention away from the Indian and Inuit Affairs Program to the local chief, council, and manager.

This policy also has meant that Aboriginals must be fully involved in discussions on a broad range of program-related and political issues. With the new band autonomy, certain programs can no longer be implemented without first consulting Aboriginal peoples. Moreover, Aboriginal associations have been steadily putting pressure on the Indian and Inuit Affairs Program, requesting forums for discussion of a range of issues related to federal and provincial policies. Unfortunately, these consultations have not taken place. Or, in other cases, legitimately elected officials—e.g., Chiefs of the Assembly of First Nations—are bypassed, and discussions between Ottawa and individual members of the First Nations community are taking place.

Again, this attempt to provide a forum for Aboriginal participation reflects a shift in federal policy from a desire to assimilate Aboriginals toward an increasing emphasis on tribal government and Aboriginal governance. The tripartite (i.e., federal/provincial/Aboriginal) discussion partly arose from a belief by Indian Affairs personnel that Aboriginals had developed enough political leadership skills to articulate their needs. In addition, the provinces are willing to discuss priority issues set forth by Aboriginals, largely to avoid being excluded from any far-reaching negotiations that might take place elsewhere in Canada. However, despite promises to the contrary, First Nations are still effectively excluded from much of the negotiation process. Currently, much of the discussion between federal and provincial officials circumvents Aboriginal involvement through the use of personal communications, confidential documents, and so on.

In 1976 a new mega-policy was introduced by the minister of the then Department of Indian and Northern Development to promote "Indian identity within Canadian society." The definition and evolution of Aboriginal identity were to be treated as flexible and dynamic. In general, the policy continues to recognize Aboriginal status, treaty rights, and special privileges resulting from land claims settlements. Within Aboriginal band and reserve communities, local self-determination and control of Aboriginal affairs are encouraged. In addition, for the first time the policy noted that different needs, aspirations, and attitudes among Aboriginals in all parts of Canada rule out a single uniform strategy. As a result, the policy emphasizes joint participation in program development with organized Aboriginal leadership at all levels. Under the new policy, the federal government takes the initiative in defining the aims and general shape of strategies applied to Aboriginal issues. If the government chooses, this process can involve Aboriginal representatives at various levels. The major goal of the new policy is to transfer the administration of programs and resources to band governments. The rate of transfer is determined by the desire and ability of each to assume control of its own affairs, including the implementation of programs.

In today's environment, the government has tried to support strong, sustainable communities through such means as establishing government-to-government relations, as well as enhancing the First Nations communities's ability to establish proper governance structures. As an immediate activity, the department has tried to empower First Nations constituents to hold their governments to account by providing First Nations with the tools to implement modern, effective governance regimes and practices. This has been supported by a number of legislative governance packages that have been introduced over the past decade, e.g., the *First Nations Governance Act*, the *Specific Claims Resolution Act*, the *First Nations Fiscal and Statistical Management Act*, and the *First Nations Land Management Act*. It is hoped that these pieces of legislation will allow First Nations communities to engage in activities such as leadership selection, administration, financial management, land resource management, citizen redress, and organization support. At the same time, the federal government will be able to decrease its involvement in the day-to-day operations of First Nations communities. Therefore, the capacity of First Nations to achieve self-sufficiency and develop their own public service will be enhanced.

THE LATENT FUNCTIONS OF THE INDIAN AND INUIT AFFAIRS PROGRAM

Like many other organizations, the Indian and Inuit Affairs Program is a highly structured, rational system that espouses specific policies and pursues specific goals. It has defined Aboriginal welfare as its sole concern; overtly, all its activities are geared to improving that welfare. Also like other organizations, however, the Indian and Inuit Affairs Program pursues certain latent goals that are quite independent of its stated formal goals. As Perrow (1961) and several others have observed, organizations often exist not only to serve their stated goals but to serve other interests as well. In fact, some would even argue that the stated policy and goals of an organization largely function only to legitimize its existence. An organization makes its stated goals explicit through its formal policy statements. Its latent goal structure, however, becomes apparent only through an examination of the services that it provides for interest groups other than those it manifestly serves.

The organizations dealing with Aboriginal people all possess a number of latent functions. For the past century, the Indian and Inuit Affairs Program and its forerunners have stated that their primary manifest goal is the maximum participation by Aboriginals as equals in Canadian society. The latent goals of these organizations include such self-referential aims as cost-efficiency and freedom from conflict within their own structures. Another latent function is to provide resources for other organizations. Many other institutions make extensive use of the nearly $700 million and 2000 employees provided to the Indian and Inuit Affairs Program at public expense; examples range from Aboriginal organizations to educational institutions to businesses.

Although other latent functions could be documented here, none is so extensive as the latent attempt by federal administrators to control the lives of Aboriginals. Throughout its history, the major latent function of the various Aboriginal programs has been the regulation of Aboriginal behaviour. Aboriginal people have been lured to cities where their dependent status forces them to conform, or they have been segregated on reserves, concealed from the view of middle-class Canadians. They have been arbitrarily dispersed throughout cities or forcibly bused out of town, back to the reserve. Often the control of Aboriginals has been achieved through the behavioural requirements attached to various social services. For example, the off-reserve housing program requires applicants to have steady full-time jobs before they are eligible for loans.

Regardless of the technique, the result is that Aboriginals are manipulated and restricted in their actions. To be sure, some Aboriginals are helped in the process and many have obtained educational benefits, training, counselling, and money, but only after conforming to middle-class behavioural criteria. Thus, control is the central latent goal of the majority of organizations dealing with Aboriginal people.

The insistence of the federal government upon control over its Aboriginal wards has characterized federal government–Aboriginal relations since Confederation. As Whiteside (1980) points out,

> Perhaps we should recall the various measures the bureaucrats introduced during this period to ensure "orderly administration": (1) the development of a single piece of legislation in 1876, to govern all the Indian Nations, regardless of varying traditions and history; (2) the systematic destruction of tribal governments and replacement of them with band councils which were really an extension of the Department's [Indian Affairs'] structure; (3) the systematic attempt to destroy

Indian culture and the outlawing of Indian religious ceremonies; (4) the introduction of compulsory enfranchisement provisions to control bad Indians; (5) the systematic attempts to harness and discredit Indian leaders who attempt to develop or strengthen Indian political organization (p. 6).

On the reserve, the various federal programs are a "total" institution, in that they have a monopoly on the delivery of services to a captive clientele. Indian and Northern Affairs Canada is characterized by specialization, hierarchy, and regimentation, while its clients are relatively uneducated, unspecialized, and varied. By limiting the choices available to its Aboriginal clients, the Indian and Inuit Affairs Program shapes and standardizes Aboriginal behaviour at minimal cost and risk to itself.

The success of the Indian and Inuit Affairs Program is not assessed on the basis of the assistance it provides to Aboriginals but rather on the basis of how effectively it has kept Aboriginal behaviour under control. The brighter officials at the Indian and Inuit Affairs Program know perfectly well that they will not be fired, transferred, or demoted for failing to help Aboriginals receive decent education, find jobs, mend broken homes, and settle into life in the city. Rather, the officials' assessment will be based on the number of Aboriginals they handled, and at what cost per person. Programs that fail to meet their announced goals do not result in fired personnel or radical organizational changes. The upper management of the Indian and Inuit Affairs Program can simply blame failures on a need for organizational restructuring, a lack of adequately trained fieldworkers, a poorly allocated budget, and so on.

All this is not to suggest that the Indian and Inuit Affairs Program does not help Aboriginals. On the contrary, some Aboriginals get bursaries to go to university, some get loans to buy houses in the city, and others get vocational training. Nor is this analysis intended to suggest that Indian and Inuit Affairs Program officials deliberately neglect the needs of Aboriginal people. Rather, such neglect is the result of internal and structural forces that cause a reordering of goal priorities.

Internal forces acting upon the Indian and Inuit Affairs Program cause it to downplay its stated goal of improving the quality of Aboriginal life. First, government officials tend to become disproportionately concerned with the number of their employees, the size of their budgets, and the quantity, rather than the quality, of their programs. Because it is difficult, time-consuming, and speculative to assess the effectiveness of an organization, readily quantifiable criteria become the indicators of a successful program. Because these indicators measure cost efficiency rather than program effectiveness, they are simple to tabulate, highly visible, and extremely responsive to changes.

A second internal factor is the emphasis on stability within the Indian and Inuit Affairs Program. There is an implicit rule that conflict should not be evident in any federal department. If conflict does exist, it must remain an internal affair. The preoccupation of the Indian and Inuit Affairs Program with remaining conflict-free results, once again, in a downplaying of stated goals and objectives.

In all of the organizations that deal with Aboriginal issues, officials accept and promote the existing expectations, norms, and mores of a free-enterprise, class-based system. This places severe limitations on the programs offered to Aboriginal people. For example, not one organization has suggested that most of the Indian and Inuit Affairs Program's budget should be given directly to Aboriginal people or used to organize Aboriginals into an effective political force. Quite the contrary. One of the better-known attempts to organize Aboriginals politically in a Western urban centre resulted in the dissolution of one district office and substantial reassignment of personnel. A similar response ended the ill-fated Community Development Program, which was phased out within a few years of its inception.

Today's Aboriginal policy reflects the recent decisions of the courts as well as the recommendations of the Royal Commission on Aboriginal Peoples. Courts have become more intrusive in government–Aboriginal relations and have clearly identified the rights and responsibilities of government and Aboriginals. In addition, the royal commission identified key issues that needed to be addressed immediately if the mission of Indian and Northern Affairs is to be achieved. We now turn to a brief analysis of the royal commission.

THE ROYAL COMMISSION ON ABORIGINAL PEOPLES

The royal commission evolved out of the Oka crisis in 1990 and subsequent overt conflict that was erupting throughout the country as Aboriginals attempted to deal with legal and economic issues confronting them. The commission started in 1991 but it would take five years before it tabled a six-volume, 5000-page document on the status of Aboriginal people in Canada. After five years and nearly $60 million, the most expensive federal inquiry in Canadian history laid out a 20-year plan to deal with Aboriginals. The report is based on 177 days of hearings, with 3500 witnesses and some internally commissioned research. The report concludes that Canada can no longer allow Aboriginals to remain dependent on the nation.

The report begins by noting that Canada systematically denied First Nations their nation status, violated most agreements made with First Nations, and suppressed their culture and institutions. In short, the report claims that Canadians built a great liberal democracy, in part, through the dispossession of Aboriginal people. As a result, Aboriginals exist in conditions of poverty and social upheaval. A key approach is not to allocate more money but to address the fractured historical relationship between Aboriginals and Canada. The roots of injustice lie in history–and it is there that the key to regeneration of Aboriginal society and a new and better relationship with the rest of Canada can be found.

Report Recommendations

The commission was specific in its recommendations, and its major point was to encourage the federal government to move immediately and make major changes. The commission recognized that the relationship between First Nations and Canadian society needed to be restructured before positive outcomes could be achieved in social, economic and health dimensions of Aboriginal life. The Harvard project on American Indian Economic Development has produced evidence that shows that sustained development is linked to Aboriginal groups having the right and capacity to govern themselves. The key elements of the proposed restructuring included:

- **New Royal Proclamation** reiteration of Canada's affirmation of Aboriginal and treaty rights.
- **Recognition of First Nations** implementation of First Nation governments by the federal government, and recognition of these governments by the federal and all provincial governments
- **Administration** elimination of the current government structure, to be replaced by a minister of Aboriginal Relations and a minister of Indian and Inuit Services
- **Treaty Commission** establishment of a tribunal to deal with specific claims and all treaties.
- **Fiduciary Responsibility** clear financial responsibility and policies to support it

- **Land and Resource Distribution** development of a procedure by which First Nations would be ensured their fair share of the wealth of Canada
- **Healing Centres** develop an integrated service delivery structure for First Nations

The report recommends that, over the next 20 years, the federal government spend an additional $38 billion on Aboriginals. The report notes that documents reveal that $2.5 billion per year is now spent to offset Aboriginal poverty ($50 billion over 20 years). It notes that about $1 billion is spent annually on social assistance on reserves, where unemployment hovers around 80 percent and Aboriginal communities endure Third World living conditions. But it notes that lost productivity, lost income, and lost potential taxes bring the total economic cost of the unhealthy relationship with Aboriginals to over $7 billion, equivalent to 1 percent of Canada's gross domestic product ($140 billion over the 20-year period). The report also notes that, since over half of the Aboriginal population is under 25 years of age, if nothing is done the estimated cost for dealing with Aboriginals by the year 2016 will increase to $11 billion (see Table 12.3). The commission forecasts that if monies were now invested the result would be a huge saving by 2016. Table 12.3 shows the specific cost of maintaining the status quo, as well as how government finances would change if the strategy were implemented.

The report proposes that the federal government increase its spending for Aboriginals to $1.5 billion for the next seven years and to $2 billion for 13 years. The logic of such a recommendation is that within 10 years there will be a fall in the remedial costs and a rise in government revenues, as Aboriginal people become more productive and begin to make a

TABLE 12.3	Cost of the Status Quo		
		($ billions)	
		1996	2016
Cost to Aboriginal Peoples			
Earned income forgone		5.8	8.6
Income taxes forgone		-2.1	-3.1
Financial assistance from governments		-.8	-1.2
Net income loss of Aboriginal Peoples		**2.9**	**4.3**
Cost to Governments			
Expenditures on remedial programs		1.7	2.4
Financial assistance to Aboriginals		.8	1.2
Government revenue forgone		2.1	3.1
Total Cost to Governments		**4.6**	**6.7**
Total Cost of Status Quo		**7.5**	**11.0**

Note:
The cost of the status quo is shown in italics. Other figures show how this cost is distributed.
Most of the cost of forgone earned income ($5.8 billion in 1996) is borne by Aboriginal people in the form of lost income. The rest is borne by governments in the form of taxes forgone and various forms of assistance paid out. These costs to governments are not included in the amount given for "cost to Aboriginal people."

Source: "Table 2.12: Present and Future Annual Cost of the Status Quo ($ billions), Changes in Government Finances under the Strategy ($ millions)" from the Report of the Royal Commission on Aboriginal Peoples, Privy Council Office. Reproduced with the permission of the minister of Public Works and Government Services Canada, 2004.

TABLE 12.4	Projected Results of the Royal Commission's Strategy	
	Additional allocation in the year	
	2001	2016
	($ millions)	($ millions)
Structural Measures		
Tribunal and treaty commissions	50	50
Nation rebuilding	50	0
Nation governments	50	425
Land claims settlements	0	1000
Total for Structural Measures	**150**	**1475**
Social and Economic Measures		
Healing, education, youth, and culture	300	150
Health care	100	(450)
Social services	100	(425)
Justice	25	(325)
Economic Opportunities and Living Conditions		
Economic development	350	225
Income transfers	0	(250)
Housing and infrastructure	400	350
Human resource development	150	425
Total for Social and Economic Measures	**1425**	**(300)**
Government Revenue Gains	–	(1550)
Overall Total	**1575**	**(375)**

Note:
Positive entries (figures without parentheses) show the increase in spending by all governments needed to implement the strategy.
Reductions are shown by numbers in parentheses in the second column. These relate to amounts saved as a result of the strategy (that is, amounts that would be spent if the status quo were to continue) and to additional revenues collected by governments.
Figures are rounded to the nearest $25 million.

Source: "Table 2.12: Present and Future Annual Cost of the Status Quo ($ billions), Changes in Government Finances under the Strategy ($ millions)" from the Report of the Royal Commission on Aboriginal Peoples, Privy Council Office. Reproduced with the permission of the minister of Public Works and Government Services Canada, 2004.

net contribution to the economic development of Canada. For example, the expensive "front end" cost of addressing the housing crisis on reserves would cost nearly $3 billion. However, in 10 to 15 years the savings would be in excess of twice that value. The extra money would go toward building new health centres, stimulating the Aboriginal economy, upgrading the infrastructure on reserves, and dealing with crisis conditions now found in Aboriginal communities. Then a long-term program of training Aboriginals would be put in place. Later, monies would be used to settle land claims and to implement self-government.

Table 12.4 outlines the projected results of the royal commission's strategy.

Aboriginal Reaction

Aboriginal leaders were supportive of the commission's report and felt that for the first time in many years they had something to look forward to. However, they also noted that if this report were not taken seriously Canadians should be prepared to face some serious social and economic consequences. As Georges Erasmus (one of the members of the commission) noted, "If the reality is that once more people's hopes have been dashed, and that this was all for nothing, then what we say is that people will resort to other things." The president of the Métis National Council also strongly supported the commission's recognition of the Métis as an Aboriginal people who should have an adequate land base. In summary, most Aboriginal peoples responded favourably to the report and felt that positive outcomes would result.

The Assembly of First Nations, in its 10-year retrospective, noted than NONE of the above recommendations have been implemented. While there have been some increases in funding, it has been specific to targeted areas, e.g., water management, diabetes, sewage infrastructure. In these cases, caps of 3 percent on increases has been evident for the past 10 years. In the end, First Nations communities today continue to live in poverty, and an increasing gap in health, mortality and economic indicators is evident.

The assembly notes that, in their assessment of government action over the past decade, there has been no sustained investment in meeting the basic needs of First Nations communities. There have been no structural changes in the relationship between First Nations and the Canadian government, and the First Nations action plan proposed in accordance with the *Gathering Strength* policy (the government's formal policy response to the report of the royal commission) has never been pursued after changes in political leadership. The later Kelowna Summit agreement in 2005 was rejected when a new federal government took over. Of the 66 recommendations issued by the royal commission, the Assembly of First Nations' report card (2006) showed that only one recommendation received an "A" grade, three received a "B" grade and 12 were assigned a "C." The remaining 50 recommendations received a "D" or "F" grade, reflecting a clear lack of action on the key foundational recommendations of RCAP and a resultant lack of progress on key socio-economic indicators.

While some funds have been allocated to issues identified under the *Gathering Strength* policy, they have been inadequate. While other government agencies have been allocated an annual 6 percent increase, the government has placed a 2 percent increase for Aboriginal funding. This means that the lost funds to First Nations communities over the past decade has been over $10B. In the end, we find that in comparing the social development of communities, First Nations communities rank 76th out of 174 nations while non-Aboriginal communities rank 8th in the world.

In 2004, the Assembly of First Nations published a document titled *Federal Government Funding to First Nations: The Facts, the Myths, and the Way Forward*. In this document, the Assembly challenged the existing funding arrangements, the amount of funds allocated to First Nations and the myths that are being perpetuated about funds allocated to First Nations. They point out that even though INAC has a budget of over $10B per year, only two-thirds are allocated to INAC while the remaining one-third is allocated to other agencies to support Inuit, Métis and "non-status Indians" as well as for administration and bureaucracy at the federal or other levels of government and private sector organizations. In the end, the government of Canada provides about $7200 per First Nations person while it spends about $6000 on each of Canada's non-First Nations person. However, for non-First Nations people, an additional $2900 is provided to them by provincial and municipal governments. Figure 12.3 shows that both the core program as well as total spending of INAC over the past five years have decreased 13 percent and 3.5 percent respectively. These figures show that, while INAC claims to have increased their budget, the facts show a decrease, while expenditures for the general Canadian population has remained stable over this time.

There are some areas of expenditure for First Nations that exceed the per-capita non-Aboriginal person. For example, housing costs for First Nations reveals that the cost per person is $5.1 while only $1 is spent for non-First Nations. Other areas of core programming such as education, health care and social services also show a greater expenditure for First Nations than for non-Aboriginal people. These increased expenditures reflect the fact that most First Nations are in remote or northern areas where the cost of providing materials and service is much higher than in the south. Second, because of the demographic distribution of First Nations, e.g., higher number of youth, education costs will be higher. Finally, the history of neglect, displacement, and disenfranchisement has driven social costs higher for many First Nations.

Nearly all of the funds provided to First Nations are related to the provision of basic services such as health, education, roads, and potable water. The provision of these services by the federal government is intended to be comparable to what non-First Nations

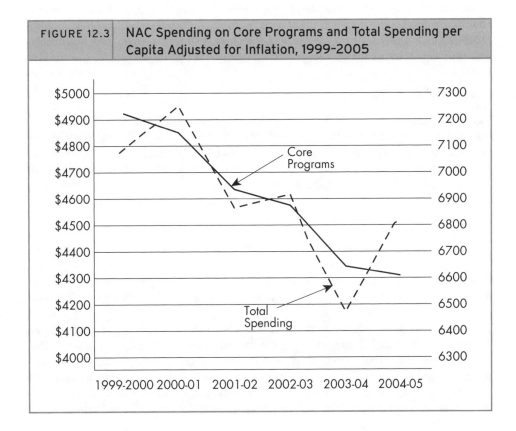

| FIGURE 12.3 | NAC Spending on Core Programs and Total Spending per Capita Adjusted for Inflation, 1999-2005 |

Canadians already receive from the three levels of government. The above figures show that First Nations people are not receiving comparable services (as outlined in the *Constitution Act, 1982*).

Additional funds are allocated to First Nations because of lawful obligations of the Crown in the form of claims, treaties and litigation. With regard to resolving these lawful obligations, the federal government has consistently taken a strategy (e.g., stall and delay resolution of claims, lengthy court battles) that costs First Nations and the Canadian public large sums of money and provides no benefits to either group. In fact, the 1998 *Report of the Joint First Nations-Canada Task Force on Specific Claims Policy Reform* recommended that other strategies be undertaken to reduce the time and cost for resolving these lawful obligations.

Canadians' Reaction

An Insight Canada survey in 1997 found that only 18 percent of Canadians believed that the royal commission was the best way to arrive at a solution for Aboriginal people. A majority of Canadians had more confidence in Aboriginals themselves or their organizations. The survey also noted that Canadian attitudes toward Aboriginals are hardening. Nearly 40 percent of Canadians believed Aboriginals have themselves to blame for their problems, and almost half of the poll respondents believed that Aboriginals had an equal or better standard of living than the average. Fifty-eight percent of Canadians are not convinced that adequate measures are in place to ensure that money received from the government is managed responsibly by Aboriginals. In the end, it would seem that Indian issues are losing their importance for most Canadians as other concerns—e.g., jobs, health care, and education—are becoming more important items on the political agenda.

Government Reaction

The initial response by the government to the royal commission was one of indifference and hostility. For some time, the federal government did not respond to the commission's report. The minister of Indian Affairs at the time noted that the report, because it was two years late in being submitted, had already been eclipsed by changes in the Department of Indian Affairs, and claimed that these changes had already addressed many of the issues raised in the report. Finally, the minister noted that he would find it impossible to approach his fellow cabinet ministers for additional monies in such a time of financial constraint. The prime minister also steered away from the report and, when invited to an all-chiefs conference at the time, declined to attend without offering an explanation. The federal government's sense of the negative political realities of providing more funding for Aboriginal communities, the lack of sensitivity or care for Aboriginal issues by the general population, and the emergence of other issues, all led to the downplaying of the commission's recommendations.

However, the federal government's formal reaction to the commission's report came on January 7, 1998, with the publication of the document *Gathering Strength—Canada's Aboriginal Action Plan*. This document, in tandem with another government document, *Sustainable Development Strategy*, outlines the goals of helping develop strong, healthy First Nations communities and setting up new relationships founded on mutual respect, with responsible, transparent, accountable, sustainable governance structures and institutions. It was an integrated, government-wide plan to address the major challenges facing Aboriginal people—structural reform of the federal government's Aboriginal programming to promote self-sufficiency and economic development, and the enhancement and strengthening of the capacity of Aboriginal governments and organizations to run accountable, responsive government systems. Some initial investments were made for "healing" and reconciliation, but these "one time" funds have since been exhausted and there has been no attempt to measure the impact of such a fund. However, the reader should be aware that the federal policy failed to endorse the national action plan recommended by the royal commission (Chartrand, 2002). Instead, the federal government has opted for its traditional strategy of trying for slow, incremental policy shifts. As Chartrand (2002) points out, the federal policy response seems to reflect the government's philosophy that incremental change is more politically manageable than the kind of fundamental change that was recommended by the royal commission.

In 2005, the last of a series of meetings between Aboriginal people and first ministers came to a close in Kelowna, B.C. In that last meeting, the first ministers and First Nations leaders agreed, through a document called "First Ministers and National Aboriginal Leaders Strengthening Relationships and Closing the Gap," to embark on a 10-year effort to close the gap in the quality of life that now exists between Aboriginal peoples and other Canadians. There was agreement that additional funds ($5.1B) for clean drinking water, health, education, and housing programs, as well as for economic development, would be made available over the next decade. However, in the spring of 2006, the newly elected Conservative government refused to honour the negotiations and rejected the agreement.

On the other hand, each year, the Department of Indian and Northern Affairs has outlined its goals and objectives, and has provided a listing of the strategies it has taken (and plans to take for the next year) to achieve these goals. In its annual reports, the department identifies targets and outcomes for each of the strategies and goals identified. For example, it was very clear in 1999 that it would be trying to enhance Aboriginal governance capacity. Other goals outlined by the federal government in 2000 have not been achieved at this time—e.g., to have 50 to 60 specific claims settled, and to conclude up to 18 comprehensive claim settlement agreements-in-principle and up to 17 final agreements by 2003. Nevertheless, the accountability framework adopted by Indian and Northern Affairs allows one to track its progress in achieving goals (or lack thereof) over time. It also allows one to match resource investment with goals to assess if the allocation is appropriate and sufficient.

SUMMARY

Throughout Canada's history little attention has been paid to developing an Aboriginal policy that has had major Aboriginal input. Moreover, funding of Aboriginal programs has always been short-term, a pilot project, or underfunded. Once it became clear that Aboriginal peoples would accept their fate peacefully, the government was allowed to ignore Aboriginal issues for more pressing concerns, such as building the railroad and encouraging European settlement. In the history of Aboriginal–European relations, government has acted on Aboriginal issues only when forced to. And when government has acted, it has invariably done so in non-Aboriginal interests. Recently, the courts have become a major force in ensuring that government change its perspective about Aboriginal issues. Judicial decisions since 1982, which form the basis of Aboriginal law in Canada, have grown increasingly more flexible and liberal in their interpretation of Aboriginal rights. As Isaac (2001) points out, restrictive, narrow views of these rights are being replaced by flexible and accommodating interpretations. These new interpretations have forced the federal government to make accommodations to existing programs and policies and to bring old attitudes and views about Aboriginal people into line with the courts' new decisions.

Our analysis of the Indian and Northern Affairs Program has shown that its programs have changed considerably over the years, failing to reflect any long-term, consistent policy. In general, however, the Indian and Northern Affairs Program has taken a wardship approach to Aboriginals. Its budget continues to grow in size, partly as a result of its expanded bureaucratic structure; other government departments have also increased their budgets to deal with Aboriginal issues, but to little effect. The federal government has tried to involve provincial governments in Aboriginal affairs, but it has not had much success except in the area of treaty/land claims. Provincial governments, with much different agendas and priorities, have rejected the idea that they become directly involved in Aboriginal issues. They resist such involvement on the grounds that this is not their responsibility, and that becoming involved would cause their commitments and their associated costs to snowball.

For their part, Aboriginals have found out over the years that the government of Canada does not always favour Aboriginal interests when making decisions. Moreover, government departments do not live up to what they seem to have promised; nor do they implement the policies/programs that are expected by Aboriginal people. As a result, over the years, Aboriginal people have tended to distrust government in general. In particular, they are suspicious of the participation of provincial governments, fearing a lessening of federal responsibility with an overall decrease in services. Aboriginal Canadians are convinced that the federal government must continue to honour its historical agreements with them, and that any transfer of these agreements is unlikely to be in their best interests. However, recently the federal government has undertaken a new strategy in approaching Aboriginal issues, by developing an Accountability Framework. This new strategy is designed to provide a clear articulation of the goals and objectives of Indian and Northern Affairs. Moreover, it should allow both Indian and Northern Affairs Canada and Aboriginals an opportunity to see if the goals are being achieved.

KEY TERMS

quasi-statutory programs
Canadian Aboriginal Economic Development Strategy

devolution
latent/manifest functions
total institution

status quo
core funding
social development

STUDY QUESTIONS

1. How does the Indian Affairs Program support Aboriginal people in their quest to preserve and develop their culture?
2. How has the federal government been shifting responsibility since the mid-1970s?
3. Discuss the goal of devolution.
4. What two internal factors can account for the Indian and Inuit Affairs Program downplaying its stated goal of improving the quality of Aboriginal life?

5. Describe the four key recommendation themes for which the Royal Commission stated political action was required.

6. How did Aboriginal communities react to the Royal Commission's report? How did their reaction compare to Non-Aboriginal and government reactions?

WEBLINKS

www.ainc-inac.gc.ca

This site will allow you to click on a number of additional sites that will give you information about the mandate, role, and responsibilities of the Department of Indian and Northern Affairs Canada. It will also provide answers to many questions that you might have about the department, Aboriginal people, and how the two interface.

www.inac-ainc.gc.ca/pr/leg/index_e.html

This site will provide you with a complete list of legislation that is administered by the Department of Indian and Northern Affairs Canada. It will allow you to examine the legislation that the department reviews and moderates each year.

http://www.tbs-sct.gc.ca/index_e.asp

This site will provide you with an evaluation of INAC by the auditor general of Canada. It will also give you information about the department's activities for the past year.

NOTES

1. Legislation under Indian and Northern Affairs responsibility includes a wide range of Acts such as: *Alberta Natural Resource Act, Arctic Waters Pollution Prevention Act, Cree-Naskapi (of Quebec) Act* and the *Indian Act.*

2. The following descriptions of Indian and Northern Affairs and the summary of each sub-department's scope and mandate have been taken from the department's website.

3. Much of the following discussion has been taken from the work of Ponting and Gibbins (1980).

4. Ponting and Gibbins (1980) indicate that "the resultant process is a complicated one which must be launched almost two years prior to the beginning (April 1) of the fiscal year for which the figures are being prepared."

chapter thirteen

Aboriginal Economic Development: Local and Global Opportunities

INTRODUCTION

The development model used in the previous chapters incorporates the basic tenets of three major theoretical perspectives: colonialism, political economy, and settler society. The basic assumptions of colonialism have been fully articulated in Chapter 1 (Cumming, 1967; Carstens, 1971; Patterson, 1972). However, a more explicit statement regarding the other two perspectives should be useful for the reader (Stasiulis and Yuval-Davis, 1995; Clement and Williams, 1989; Dickinson and Bolaria, 1992). Satzewich and Wotherspoon (1993) have described the political economy of Aboriginal peoples, noting that their changing material circumstances shape, and are shaped by, their life experiences. Underlying the political economy approach is the understanding that the historical and current political economy is a result of Canada's historical domination by European and American influences. Beginning with a resource-based staples economy, Canada entered the global economy with elements of technology showing through (Satzewich and Wotherspoon, 1993: 12). As Satzewich and Wotherspoon point out, at the centre of the political economy approach is the acceptance that people produce and reproduce the conditions for their existence. Their ability to do so (or change) is regulated by the conditions and context in which they find themselves. For example, ownership of property and resources significantly influences an individual's ability to engage in certain kinds of behaviour. Hence, it is important for social scientists to fully understand the historical and situational contexts in which groups of people find themselves as they participate in the political economy of any society. As such, it is imperative that the reader fully understand the position that Aboriginal people have held in Canadian society for the past two centuries.

382

The concept of "settler society" has been invoked to explain ethnic relations in colonial situations. These are societies that have been settled by Europeans, who have retained their political dominance over indigenous peoples. They are typified by colonialism where land, resources and labour are controlled by the European settlers (Stasiulis and Yuval-Davis, 1995; Alfred, 2005). Settler societies generally have established social boundaries between the indigenous population and the European settlers. These boundaries, defined by the settlers, determine the actions defined as legitimate and legal for all members of society. In most settler societies, the dominant culture reflects the "mother" country's values and culture, and is constantly reinforced through immigration and importation of "mother" country institutions, values, ideologies and economic practices. What worked in the mother country is reproduced in the colony.

These three perspectives have come to shape the explanation of why Aboriginal people have been excluded from the political and economic activities in today's society. Previously we have focused our discussion on the historical context in which Aboriginal–non-Aboriginal relationships emerged. However, to further explicate the contemporary scene, we need to investigate the political economy of Canadian society (Frank, 1967).

Since the turn of the 20th century, Aboriginal people have been unable to participate fully in the Canadian economy. Even before our economy moved to an agricultural base and then on to one of modern technology, Aboriginal people were restricted in their involvement and, as a result, fell further behind in their ability to integrate. Aboriginal people often still find themselves operating in a subsistence or welfare economy parallel to that of the more modern economy. In other words, there are two economies in our society. This dual system emerged over time as changes in institutional structures, technology, and industrial work practices took place. Aboriginal people were prevented from participating in the economy through a variety of policies and programs established by government. For example, Aboriginal people were prohibited from using resources in direct competition with non-Aboriginal users. Before the 20th century, Aboriginal people were not allowed to take homestead lands, as these lands were available only to immigrants. Aboriginal people were refused licences to act as commercial big-game hunting outfitters in areas where non-Aboriginal people had established commercial enterprises. And when inland commercial fisheries were created in the Canadian northwest, regulations were put in place so that Aboriginal people could not compete with non-Aboriginal people.

As Euro-Canadian society moved more quickly into an industrial–technological economy in the early 20th century, Aboriginal people found themselves without the skills and resources necessary to participate. As a result, two almost separate economies emerged: a modern, dynamic sector (industrially and technologically based) and a traditional, land-based subsistence sector. The former creates change, which in turn promotes further change, while the latter tends to resists change, may cling to traditional ways, and might see little need to adopt new technology except when it is expedient to do so (Wien, 1986). Aboriginal people have discovered that, without the necessary skills, they would only be able to participate at the fringes of the industrial economy.

Non-Aboriginal Canadians had a strategy in their relationship with Aboriginals prior to the patriation of the Constitution in 1982: the myth of equality (Willhelm, 1969). This myth's basic premise was that all humans were equal no matter how diverse they appeared to be. This, however, acted as a rationale for denying special privileges and affirmative action programs to various minority groups. The federal government's 1969 white paper, which recommended that reserves be terminated and special status revoked, exemplified this myth. Contemporary legislation continues to reflect this view of equality somewhat, though not as prominently. Proponents argue that the laws that express the equality of ethnic groups ought to be sufficient, regardless of the impact of centuries of entrenched discrimination.

An underlying assumption perhaps still held by many Canadians is that Natives contribute little economic product to the Canadian economy. In addition, non-Aboriginal people feel that the larger dominant economy supports the Aboriginal economy through governmental subsidies and through the creation of and payment for a variety of health, economic, and social services. For example, many people point out that governmental transfers provide between 80 and 100 percent of Aboriginal salaries and non-earned income. If Aboriginal communities did not receive government subsidies, their local economies would collapse.

However, as Salisbury (1986) pointed out, this perspective and its underlying assumption represents a fundamental misunderstanding of the relation between Aboriginal people and the federal government (and, indeed, the people of Canada). For example, the flow of money stems specifically from a "contract" agreed upon by the two parties (the fiduciary relation between the Crown and the Aboriginal peoples) and cannot be revised or amended unilaterally over time. The contents of the agreement were agreed to by both parties at the time of signing and were deemed to be in the best interests of both parties. The *Royal Proclamation* of 1763 is the best and earliest example of an agreement between the two parties that is still legally binding and recognized in the Canadian Constitution. Under this agreement, it was understood that, in return for the Aboriginal peoples' recognition of the sovereignty of the monarch, the monarch would protect them and preserve the Aboriginal way of life. While some specifics of the agreement have been modified (in favour of Euro-Canadians), the federal government has accepted the spirit of the original agreement struck with Aboriginal peoples. Hence, the "subsidization" of services to Aboriginal people has been and continues to be paid for by Aboriginal people through their original transferring of land and allegiance in 1763.

THE EVOLUTION OF ABORIGINAL DEVELOPMENT

As the settler economy developed, Aboriginal economies were disrupted and put in disarray. Some of the more isolated reserves were less affected than those close to urban centres, but as external controls gradually became institutionalized, further indigenous community disruption occurred. While government wanted Aboriginal people to enter agricultural pursuits, these efforts were not successful because government did not provide sufficient resources such as land and capital (Carter, 1990). In fact, there is considerable evidence that the federal government of the time (late 19th century and early 20th century) purposely undermined Aboriginal successes and efforts in agriculture (Miller, 2000). Thus, the transition from a traditional to a modern economy was very difficult for many Aboriginal people, and their participation was marginal. Continuous debates about who was responsible for Aboriginal people further reduced their ability to secure support. As the Royal Commission on Aboriginal Peoples commented, prior to the 1960s, Aboriginal economic development was not a priority for the federal government, and as time went on Aboriginal dependency on federal assistance grew.

After World War II Aboriginal people began to shed their passivity and to demand a much more active role in Canadian society (Miller, 2000). The government (both provincial and federal), having experienced the atrocities of the war, began to implement policies that would forever change its ideological position toward Aboriginal people. Human rights acts were passed, social assistance programs were put in place, and specific actions were taken regarding Aboriginal people—e.g., the *Indian Act* underwent its first major revision in almost a century. By the 1960s the federal government made public its report, *A Survey of the Contemporary Indians of Canada: Economic, Political, Educational Needs and Policies.* This report identified the poor quality of life experienced by Aboriginal people and concluded by suggesting extensive changes in government policy and programs. The government did act on the recommendation to set up programs for community development. (The most concrete program established was the Indian Revolving Fund, which at the time became the major vehicle for funding Aboriginal communities.) The strategy was to follow two stages. First, the community would define its own problems and devise ways to achieve its goals. Then, the community would be given resources to implement the program. While Phase One was implemented, Phase Two was never sufficiently funded, and by the late 1960s the concept of community development died.

After refusing to give local communities the necessary resources to achieve their goals, Indian Affairs implemented the National Indian Advisory Board. However, its ineffectiveness led to its abandonment in the 1970s. By this time the federal government had settled on a more traditional and orthodox plan for integrating Aboriginal people into the economy—modernization. The new approach embodied the principle of assimilation, yet it was hidden behind more opaque beliefs. Modernization meant that, if an individual wanted to enhance his or her quality of life, then he or she had to move from traditional beliefs, values, and behaviour to adopt more modern ones. This meant that science would be the basis for action, creative rationality would be the underlying mode of operation, and new ways of thinking would be embraced. There was (and continues to be) a belief that change and "progress" was inevitable and preferable. Furthermore, the direction of that change, along with its impact, could be controlled.

The federal government felt that Aboriginal people's traditional ways of life would have to end and a cultural replacement would have to be implemented. Specifically, individual values and goals needed to supersede those of groups or communities. Nevertheless, many Aboriginal groups rejected this approach. They began to suggest that economic integration of Aboriginal people would require more than the drive and motivation of each individual. They began to see the structure of our society as problematic in the poor quality of life for Aboriginal people. For example, the Métis Women's Association of Manitoba saw Aboriginal problems as a symptom of larger social and cultural problems, including patriarchy. It argued that, as long as development initiatives were handled solely by outsiders and men, the structural problems would remain.

The federal government, in its attempt to implement its modernization policy, then established the Indian Economic Development Fund. This fund continued the policy of funding only legal (registered; status) Indians. It provided direct loans, loan guarantees, and other forms of loans only to on-reserve projects. The National Indian Brotherhood publicly noted its objection to the way the fund was being operated by Ottawa. Aboriginal people felt that if economic development was to occur they must have control, and that this in turn implied political autonomy (P. Elias, 1991).

In the mid-1970s the federal government began to develop community and regional plans for Aboriginal economic development. A joint effort of the National Indian Brotherhood and DIAND produced its first report in 1976. Nevertheless, this report made it clear that Aboriginal people were not prepared to sacrifice their culture, land, or identity in order to develop economically. They wanted to develop in such a way that the two—development and culture—were complementary. Aboriginal people felt that local self-government could be the structure wherein both economic development and cultural maintenance could coexist. It was under these conditions that Aboriginal organizations became involved in economic development. As P. Elias (1991) pointed out, by the late 1970s models of change advocated a more multidisciplinary approach. Social and cultural issues became more important, and new models of socio-economic change sought to integrate them. The underlying assumption was that economic development included cultural revitalization as much as possible.

However, by the mid-1980s this integrated approach (which initially looked promising) had once again been set aside by Ottawa, and a more singular view of development took precedence—strict economic development. The earlier, multidisciplinary approach was ultimately abandoned by Aboriginal organizations as well, though more for practical reasons than ideological ones. Realizing how few resources they had, and the paucity of resources likely to be given to them by Ottawa, they believed that a multi-sector approach to development was doomed to failure. Nonetheless Aboriginal people realized that, if full endorsement of the new federal policy was not forthcoming, even fewer funds would be available.

By the mid-1980s Aboriginal organizations accepted economic development on a project-by-project basis as the major thrust of advancement. At the same time, however, they tried to develop new ideologies through different channels. The ideas of self-government, sovereignty, and Indian rights began to surface and were pursued through other Canadian institutions, especially the courts. Nevertheless, they had now accepted a blended (Aboriginal/non-Aboriginal) course of action through which they would pursue their economic development. Meanwhile, the federal government continued to view its own definition of development as the only acceptable one. The Indian Economic Development Fund (established in 1970) was later replaced by the Canadian Aboriginal Economic Development Strategy, and then in 1989 the Aboriginal Economic Development Strategy was created. Essentially all the development programs established over the years by the federal government have been explicitly economic and favour individual entrepreneurship and enterprise over any strategies based on community control (P. Elias, 1991, Armstrong, 1999).

In 1989 the federal government earmarked nearly $900 million (over five years) for Aboriginal economic development. It also suggested that more Aboriginal control would be given with respect to financial resources and decision-making. The design of the plan was such that Indian Affairs' role in program delivery would be phased out as local Aboriginal control took over. As Gadacz (1991) pointed out, DIAND's old focus on control, structure, rules, and procedures was to be replaced by collaboration, learning, networking, and innovation. In short, Indian Affairs would switch roles from a direct supplier of services to an assistant and facilitator for Aboriginal communities.

By the 1990s, funding policies once again began to change. An increased emphasis on providing training and education for all ages of Aboriginal people was the order of the day.

While community-based development became the overall paradigm used by government to encourage economic development in the 1960s (La Rusic, 1968), by the 1990s this perspective had disappeared and then again reappeared. However, its current appearance uses an integrated, holistic approach that combines such dimensions as governance, culture, spirituality and education. In short, the economic strategy of today is to strengthen Aboriginal culture as Aboriginal nations develop.

Today's philosophy recognizes that problems of economic development are not solvable by a single approach, and that control over policy and programs must reflect community desires, needs and control. There is also an understanding that Aboriginal economic development cannot take place in isolation from the rest of the country, its very context. However, given the shortage of land and resource allocation for Aboriginal communities, this approach also recognizes that economic development must be long term.

ABORIGINAL DEVELOPMENT: THEORETICAL UNDERPINNINGS

To break the pattern of colonization, Aboriginal people must incorporate both the notions of individual entrepreneurship and community ownership with the goal of controlling reserve economies (Dubois, 1940; Canada, 1996b). The problems facing Aboriginal people can be addressed through the implementation of strategies that involve both individual and community-based resource development. First, Aboriginal people must be provided access to training and employment opportunities. Furthermore, the delivery and control of these opportunities must reside within the Aboriginal community. Aboriginal communities that have followed this strategy have emerged with some success, however modest. For example, in the 1980s and 1990s the Meadow Lake Tribal Council focused on economic development and provided 450 jobs directly, and another 240 indirectly, through a mixture of Indian government, tribal council, and band community-based enterprises. These economic ventures were kick-started with a $1.5 million loan from the federal government. Six years after they received the loan the community returned tax revenues to both the federal and provincial governments that total more than seven times the original loan. In addition, it saved Canadians money, since over 200 people were removed from the welfare rolls.

A number of alternatives have been suggested as ways Aboriginal people could more fully integrate into the political economy of Canadian society. These recommendations and solutions for ending Aboriginal economic dependence have been around for a long time. For example, Heilbrun and Wellisz (1969) have suggested that the federal government provide funds for Aboriginal communities, as is done with the International Bank for Reconstruction and Development or the International Finance Corporation. These organizations make loans to underdeveloped countries based on long-term projects. These loans are not subject to an annual review, and thus financing is assured for five to seven years. Second, these projects can be reviewed and revised during the financing period so as to keep up with global changes. Finally, qualified staff would be attracted to projects because of the long-term stability and assured financing of the projects (Daugherty, 1978).

Koovos and Brown (1980) suggested that greater control over the goals and objectives of economic development, as well as its funding, needs to be placed within the Aboriginal community. Hatt (1969) agreed with MacGregor (1961), and stated that control over various projects must originate in the Aboriginal community and not simply be subject to its control. Hatt went on to argue that, if planning is not placed within the control of Aboriginal communities, the implementation of projects will not change the status quo.

Others, such as Sorenson and Wolfson (1969), suggested that, in addition to long-term financing of economic projects in Aboriginal communities, other structural rearrangements needed to be made. For example, they claim that the "unbalanced, single-industry" approach taken by government is unsustainable. In addition, they claimed that secondary and tertiary industries must be planned for Aboriginal communities (Deprez and Sigurdson, 1969, Banner, 2005).

By the late 1990s the Royal Commission on Aboriginal Peoples came forward with recommendations that integrate the above arguments into more current philosophy and beliefs about the abilities of Aboriginal peoples. For too long, Aboriginal people have been forced by the federal government to spend inordinate amounts of time and energy trying to pick out the "correct" project—one that would succeed, if only marginally. As Cornell and Kalt (1992) noted, instead of looking at the political and economic institutions and broader development strategies—e.g., sustainability—Aboriginal communities concerned themselves with picking a winner. As a result the degree of success was predictably low, with the amount of time and resources allotted to the decision process being neither efficient nor cost effective (IRIW, 1978).

Cornell and Kalt (1992) and the royal commission went on to say that economic development, at whatever level, is both complex and difficult. The specific situation and historical time period will profoundly influence the nature of the development, the extent of government support, and the probability of success of the project. For example, on the basis of many case studies they concluded that one of the most important factors in developing a successful economic project is to understand the political, economic and geographic environment of the Aboriginal community. They identify eight major considerations in assessing the level of success of any project:

1. the degree to which Aboriginal people have the ability to make decisions;
2. the extent to which the project fills a unique economic niche or opportunity;
3. the degree to which the Aboriginal community has access to financial capital on a long-term basis;
4. the distance from the Aboriginal community to the market;
5. the amount of natural resources available to the community;
6. the level of human capital;
7. the organizational structure of the Aboriginal community; and
8. the level of integration of the Aboriginal community with the dominant society.

As Peters (1968) stated long ago, new industries and the upgrading of Aboriginal skills are the key to economic development. The creation of new jobs for Aboriginal people would also boost reserve profits, upgrade individual income standards, and provide invaluable work experience for the development of Aboriginal leaders in community and business affairs.

Several basic assumptions (which the federal government had been slow to accept over the years) underline the need for community development and control. First, all people fundamentally desire to better themselves. When their attempts to do so are blocked, the social and psychological damage is considerable. Second, the major obstacle to improvement is a lack of such resources as funds, skills, equipment and education. Third, given resources and opportunity, people find their own effective ways to meet their needs and improve their lives. In the past, Aboriginal people had been forced to try to solve problems through the solutions provided for them by government agencies; procedures not part of the dominant capitalist culture were criticized and rejected. Fourth, a change in only one aspect of a group's behaviour seldom produces meaningful, lasting results. A simple influx of money does not solve very much given that the social behaviour of humanity has many facets; each component of behaviour stands in a relationship to other components. This interrelationship must be considered when any attempts at change are made (Belanger, 2006; Aberle, 1970).

Several structural changes need to take place. These changes will not happen overnight, nor will they occur without impact on Aboriginal people. The effects of industrialization on a population are well known and have been extensively documented. Industrialization has had a traumatic impact on people in virtually every society that has made the transition from agrarianism, let alone hunting-and-gathering. The disruptions of social relationships and related customs and practices are particularly severe. These disruptions were evident when Aboriginal peoples changed from a nomadic to a sedentary society. For example, the tipi, which was well suited for nomadic people, provided shelter for Prairie Indians. However, when stationary houses were introduced (because of reserve living), the system of sanitation did not change accordingly. As a result, stationary homes became a fertile breeding ground for tuberculosis and other infectious diseases. In short, the transition to an industrial economy and a more sedentary lifestyle has always exacted a great toll in human suffering and demoralization from the people going through it. Hence, it should not have been expected that Aboriginal people would somehow be exempt from this.

Nonetheless, it does not necessarily follow that Aboriginal people must experience the same level of disruption that others have had to undergo. Some structural changes could be introduced to bring about cultural and economic change with minimal impact. For example, movement into the city, a traditionally frustrating and tension-producing activity, can be facilitated through the proper institutional help (see Chapter 6). The removal of barriers to jobs can be implemented. The settlement of Aboriginal title and the integration of development plans can also be undertaken. In addition, development needs to proceed under local control—that is, only after plans have been developed that meet those local needs and priorities rather than those of the national government or multinational corporations. Finally, there must be more integration. Modern and traditional activities need to be developed together, rather than allowing one to develop at the expense of the other. The various institutional sectors of Aboriginal society also need to be "synchronized" with the dominant society. For example, educational needs have to be integrated with economic needs, and health-care facilities need to be related to the work world (Wien, 1986).

This structural approach to social change clearly requires an understanding of the institutional structures that influence Aboriginal life. Rather than focusing on the individual as the unit of analysis, such an approach examines the socio-economic role of internal Aboriginal institutions and their external relationships (Girvan, 1973). For too long, theorists have viewed Aboriginal–Euro-Canadian relations as an "Aboriginal problem" rather than as a "white problem," and have failed to take external factors into account (Skarlicki, n.d.).

Clearly, the "Aboriginal problem" has been created by the economic, cultural, and political structures of Canada, as much of this book has tried to explain. The position of Aboriginal people in Canada is certainly not the result of cultural isolation or particular psychological tendencies of Aboriginal people. Nor does individual racial and cultural discrimination provide a sufficient explanation for the historically low socio-economic position of Aboriginal people in Canada. While individual discrimination may have slowed socio-economic upward mobility, it has not eliminated it. Sunkel has shown that a totally marginal group is "deprived of all means of access to a source of income of reasonable level and stability" (1973: 141); clearly this is not the case for Aboriginal people in Canada.

The marginal position of Aboriginal people can only be explained when institutional and systemic discrimination against them are considered along with their limited sources of income and their lack of control over the means of production. The manner in which resources are deployed, whether human, capital, or technological, determines the level of employment, the extent of industrialization, and the distribution of income. As Mariategui (1934) pointed out in the early part of the last century, the roots of the Aboriginal problem are economic and lie in the system of land ownership. This clearly implies that the economy is not embedded in social relations, but rather that social relations are structures within society's economic institutions (Polanyi, 1974).

The federal government long argued against the creation of industries and jobs within reserves. It steadfastly holds that the reserve is basically a residential area and cannot be converted to industrial or commercial use. For example, Recommendation 3 of the *Hawthorn Report* (1966–67) stated:

> The main emphasis on economic development should be on education, vocational training, and techniques of mobility to enable Indians to take employment in wage and salaried jobs. Development of locally available resources should be viewed as playing a secondary role for those who do not choose to seek outside employment.

On the basis of the above, it is clear that not all Aboriginal communities will benefit equally over time with similar types of development. Any proposed development should be tailor-made for a community and implemented only when internal and external conditions are appropriate. Economic development for Aboriginal peoples also means that they must regain control over decisions, both at the planning and the operational stages. Moreover, this means that developmental policies and programs must be designed and delivered by Aboriginal institutions. As the Royal Commission on Aboriginal Peoples noted, instead of Aboriginal communities having to adjust to the criteria and procedures of distant bureaucracies, the process needs to be reversed. The communities need to define priorities and the instruments best suited to meet them. As such, the transformation of Aboriginal economies is a large-scale undertaking that will require resources as well as concerted, comprehensive effort over an extended period (Canada, 1996a).

COMMUNITY SOCIO-ECONOMIC DEVELOPMENT FROM A FIRST NATIONS PERSPECTIVE: A CASE STUDY

In mid-1989 representatives of both the federal government and First Nations gathered near Calgary for the announcement of a new initiative in the area of Aboriginal economic development.[1] The Canadian Aboriginal Economic Development Strategy (CAEDS) was considered an important advance in Aboriginal economic programming over past initiatives, such as the 1983 Native Economic Development Program (which expired in 1989) and various other ongoing Indian and Northern Affairs development and financing programs. It promised to provide Native peoples more flexibility, more money ($867 million over five years), and more control with respect to financial resources and decision making. The initiative also implied a definite change in the role of the federal government—particularly the Indian and Northern Affairs Department—which, according to the initiative's scenario, has to remove itself even more from any direct involvement in program delivery than in the past (Canada, 1989).

INAC's new role is to assist Indian/First Nations economic development organizations in developing and expanding the capacity to direct and deliver development programs and services themselves, things controlled in the past by INAC. The department's old focus on control, structure, rules and procedures will have to be replaced with an emphasis on collaboration, learning, networking, and innovation. CAEDS calls for INAC to change from being a direct supplier of services into an "assistant" for Aboriginal communities; the focus of economic development thus has to shift from being funder-oriented to being community-oriented.

For all intents and purposes the federal government's initiative has returned the responsibility for community economic development planning directly to the shoulders of Aboriginal communities. This initiative was taken partly in recognition of the fact that increased funding is not always a solution to what is not always necessarily a funding shortage. The initiative was also taken in view of the fact that economic development policies originating from outside Aboriginal communities have seldom made the best use of locally available human and natural resources (Hanson, 1985: 62).

In response to CAEDS and the slow transformation of INAC, Aboriginal communities have become increasingly involved in the process of "capacity-building" to plan and formulate their own strategies for economic development. According to Hanson (1985: 41), "the strategy and programs to serve the needs of the Indian people/Native people . . . is relatively simple because most, if not all, elements are already in place." This is not to suggest that their implementation is simple, but rather that the attitudes and interests are, if Hanson's optimism is justified (and notwithstanding significant internal divisions of interest and concerns), "in place." Hanson suggests that, more than anything else, the needs of Aboriginal peoples are "for [an] opportunity to revitalize and strengthen the social, cultural and economic aspects of a way of life which are at the very core of their continuing existence as a collectivity" (p. 49).

Put simply, there is a need to revitalize the Aboriginal community, rather than to integrate Aboriginal society into mainstream society or to further intensify its dependency. The related ideas of decolonization and alternative economic development—"reversing the theft of human history," as it were—have been thoroughly explored in relation to Aboriginal as well as rural-based communities over the past several years (Alfred, 2005; Watkins, 1977; Blishen et al., 1979; Hanson, 1985; Ponting, 1986; Ross and Usher, 1986; Robinson and Ghostkeeper, 1987, 1988; Usher, 1989). The consensus is that there is indeed something there to revitalize.

Notwithstanding INAC's slow devolution and its gradual withdrawal from what is perceived by some as its more traditional role, in late 1989 and early 1990 Indian and Northern Affairs Canada initiated the Development Indicators Project. One of the purposes of the DIP as envisioned by the department was to develop a particular type of socio-economic planning tool—the socio-economic development indicator—that would support, but not interfere with, First Nations communities' capacity and ability to manage their own development and, in the process, to revitalize the social and cultural foundations of community life.

The overall significance of development indicators for First Nations communities is threefold. First, it might be suggested that the cornerstone for self-government is the gathering, processing, and use of timely information on development trends and conditions. Second, given the globalization of the economy, the necessary openness of Aboriginal communities towards the rest of the world, and the complexity of the interrelationships between communities and their environments, there is a need for a more sophisticated information system that serves to assess the internal and external forces that impact on a community's and a people's well-being. Third, and finally, economic development is really human development; socio-economic development indicators should therefore be Aboriginal-value–based and should reflect a community's social and cultural life in a holistic sense.

The idea behind the Development Indicators Project was to produce a tool that First Nations communities could use in the process of managing their own socio-economic and cultural revitalization. Revitalization is defined in the dictionary as "to give new life or vigour to [something]," or to "revive [something]"; reference here can be made to the existing values, structures, organizations, and certain ways of doing things in the Aboriginal community. "Existing" might, optimistically, refer to traditional systems of governance, subsistence, dispute resolution, family and kinship life, spirituality, and so forth that might have survived contact with the external culture and efforts at acculturation. "Existing" might, more realistically, refer to the structures that historically have been imposed on Aboriginal peoples and that are the outcome of an adaptive process that has taken place since contact times.

In the course of Aboriginal–Euro-Canadian relations, traditional systems have been replaced with foreign, imposed ones, or they have been eroded to the point where they are in danger of being lost altogether. Aboriginal political structures, languages, and systems of religious beliefs and practices—including the family and kinship structure—have suffered oppression as well as transformations. Part of the revitalization process may involve reconstructing and reviving traditional ways of doing things, or at the very least, the process can involve gaining control over, modifying or imbuing existing imposed structures with a sense of local ownership and local values.

The key to successful revitalization/development lies in a unified (holistic) and dynamic approach that must take into account the social, cultural, political, and environmental/ecological aspects of Aboriginal community life—not just the "economic" aspect. One of the characteristics that distinguishes Aboriginal development from mainstream community development (as the concept is usually defined in the literature) is the equal significance of a non-market or subsistence orientation (Coffey and Polese, 1985; Hanson, 1985; Four Worlds Development Project, 1985; Robinson and Ghostkeeper, 1987, 1988; Usher, 1989). This unified approach thus includes local authority over economic decisions; the revival of traditional community structures; the creation of an economic mix that may include a combination of a subsistence, industrial, market, and retail orientation; cultural enrichment; and even the promotion of greater ecological harmony.

The idea of holistic development further includes all elements of human life that contribute to human welfare, such as nutrition, health, shelter, work and employment, the physical environment, and the socio-cultural environment. Participation in decision-making processes, a sense of human dignity, of belonging—anything pertaining to the "style" or pattern of development that is appropriate to Aboriginal people's values and circumstances—must likewise be part of a development strategy. In short, a holistic and unified approach to community development, or revitalization, calls for a renewed focus on people, not solely on the "product" or "project."

The rationale for generating Aboriginal-based socio-economic development indicators is based on the presumption that there are other kinds of development that are not based solely on the values and norms of an industrial society and on a market economy (see the essays in Watkins, 1977). There is a serious questioning of why an industrial and market-based economy that is the basis for development should entail environmental degradation, the squandering of non-renewable resources, the diminution of human dignity, and the alienation of the individual from social and cultural life among some of its consequences. Thomas Berger (1977, 1985), for example, has dealt in detail with the effects of industrial development on Aboriginal cultures with strong continuing ties to the land-based or bush economy. Berger (1977) argues that:

> It is self-deception to believe that large-scale industrial development would end unemployment and underemployment of Native people in the North. In the first place, we have always overestimated the extent to which Native people are unemployed and underemployed by under-stating their continued reliance on the land. Secondly, we have never fully recognized that industrial development has, in itself, contributed to social, economic, and geographic dislocation among Native people. (p. 123)

Despite the fact that Berger's arguments were developed in a northern Canadian context, they are nevertheless applicable to other regions of the country that are caught up in a hinterland/metropolis or a dominant/subordinate dependency relationship. Berger (1985) continued developing ideas for the promotion of regional diversification by talking about strengthening the renewable resource sector. In the promotion of traditional strengths, Berger (1985: 55) wrote that the economy of subsistence lies at the heart of Aboriginal culture and "enables the Native peoples to feel at one with their ancestors, at home in the present, confident of the future."

Community revitalization/development could, realistically, be considered in the context of both a hinterland economic adaptation and a so-called multi-sectoral approach. In place of the dependency that accompanies external cash transfers to local Aboriginal (and even non-Aboriginal) economies, for example, options for development should be balanced, pragmatic, and locally controlled. One flexible and adaptable option may be a revitalized domestic economy, involving home or local production and household self-reliance, in combination with occupations that are based on the rhythm of a seasonal lifestyle. Unfortunately, "mainstream" socio-economic development has always regarded these factors as barriers, yet it might be precisely this option that could be the most viable for many Aboriginal communities in the face of their continued marginalization from metropolitan centres and relative geographical (and social) isolation (Usher, 1989).

Another option, in combination with the previous one, might be a mixed and multi-sectoral economic base. Such an economic base might consist of mixing primary resource extraction, cultural industries, light manufacturing, and service industries into one sustainable economy. Such a "mixture" would include the features of a subsistence/bush economy as well as an industrial/market-based economy. Going further, Robinson and Ghostkeeper (1987, 1988) have argued that there may even be emerging structural parallels between a traditional bush economy and a post-industrial, or "next," economy (one that focuses on information and services). Features shared by both types of economy might be exploited by Aboriginal entrepreneurs, and become the basis for community development that does not have to depend upon specialization, competition, hierarchy, or environmental degradation for success and viability (Indian Minerals Directorate, 1981a, 1981b).

Given the kinds of economic development that Aboriginal communities might opt for, conventional socio-economic indicators based solely on an industrial and market model need to be revised or, as appropriate, applied in a different way. There is clearly an absence of a framework suited to Aboriginal community needs. A new one may need to be created that will be more effective in the context of Aboriginal community life and that would fit with development choices based on local concerns.

INAC's Development Indicators Project has a number of goals: (1) to identify and generate a list of Aboriginal-value–based indicators that could be used by First Nations peoples themselves to collect information on community life from a holistic perspective; (2) to test or validate this list of indicators in several communities (by way of workshops) in order to see if they adequately reflect the value systems of First Nations communities, as well as to look for consistent themes emerging across communities; and (3) to design a "template," or socio-economic indicator system, based on the findings that is meaningful to community members, and that could be used to describe a community's socio-economic profile. This template or indicator system would be used by economic development officers, band councillors, and others as a planning tool to gather and organize information that can support comprehensive community-based planning.

The process was begun, at the behest of INAC and with funding from INAC and other sources, when an organization in Edmonton called the First Nations Resource Council organized a symposium in the spring of 1990. Entitled "Socio-Economic/Quality of Life Indicators Symposium," the purpose was to talk about social and economic development from a quality of life perspective (First Nations Resource Council, 1990). The meeting was attended by Indian and Métis peoples, social scientists, community development practitioners, and several INAC officials. It was recognized by the participants that any sort of planning and development that is not imposed from the outside, but that comes from within, has ultimately to be guided by a people's values and vision of what they consider enabling (the strengths) and constraining (the weaknesses) in the community-building and development process.

The idea was to generate a list of community development indicators that could identify and somehow measure different aspects of a quality of life that would be meaningful in the context of First Nations communities. Efforts to measure community and First Nations development have often meant assessing social dependency or economic disparity. Symposium participants recognized that community development is an evolutionary, dynamic process that must be understood in both its quantitative and qualitative dimensions, something that "snapshot" statistics do not capture very well. The consensus that emerged from the meeting was that there is a need to extend measures of development beyond traditional (i.e., mainstream) indicators of disparity. As well, it was understood that the needs and specific requirements of any Aboriginal community mean that the tools traditionally used for monitoring community development may not suffice. Aboriginal development is a particular form of community development that requires its own unique framework of analysis and its own "social" or "development" indicators and set of measurement tools.

Social indicators are a combined, interpreted, and refined sets of statistics (Land, 1971; Land and Spilerman, 1975; Rossi and Gilmartin, 1980). This type of information can provide a glimpse of the "state" or condition of a community, region, country, etc., at a point in time (see Corporation for Enterprise Development, 1987; Lamontagne and Tremblay,

1989; Lane, 1989 for case studies of their application). Development indicators are statistics that measure socio-economic conditions and changes over time for various segments of a population, an entire community, a region or a country (White, Maxim, and Beavon, 2003). By socio-economic conditions is meant both the external ("objective," social, economic, physical) and the internal ("subjective," perceptual) contexts of human existence.

Indicators are also an important means by which information on the relative success or failure of individual development projects, programs, and policies can be gathered (Carley, 1981; Lane, 1989; Miles, 1985). The impact of development projects on the emotional, spiritual, and mental health of communities and their members can likewise be measured, assessed, and monitored by the use of socio-economic indicators (Banner, 2005; Kennedy et al., 1978). Thus, the information that is collected can be used to plan, influence, and inform the decision-making process with regard to development planning even on a national scale (UNESCO, 1981, 1984). Still, information on the overall process of community revitalization, or holistic development, and resulting changes (both positive and negative) in a people's emotional, spiritual, and mental well-being is by no means easy to collect (see Brodhead, 1990: 4–15 for a useful review of the literature and methodology of development indicator research).

From the point of view of Aboriginal communities, however, many existing "mainstream" or non-Aboriginal indicators fall short of being effective data-gathering tools. Mainstream indicators have often been developed in a predominantly urban and industrial context. Because they are externally created and imposed, they can be culturally biased. Quite often they are economic (disparity) indicators and so are very limited in their ability to help gather data related to the social, cultural, and spiritual aspects of community life. Many indicators may either not be valid in Aboriginal communities or may appeal to standards that are inappropriate (PJS Geach and Associates, 1985; White, Maxim and Beavon 2003). Blishen et al.'s (1979) early study on socio-economic impact modelling suggests it is essential to ensure that the relevant variables of a model of Aboriginal development are selected rather than some "alien" criteria. Indeed, data such as the number of libraries, television sets; or telephones per household; crime rates; social assistance recipients; suicides; infant mortalities; unemployment and education levels; etc. per unit population, give, at best, a one-dimensional view of life.

As desirable as it may be to increase or decrease these numbers, such "typical" indicators do not always allow for a holistic measure or assessment of individual and/or community quality of life. Not only is it necessary to use these numbers in different ways, but the reasons underlying the statistics and the behaviours should themselves be identified, since they are information that should become a part of a quality-of-life assessment. Thus, like "appropriate technology," appropriate revitalization–development indicators, i.e., those that are Aboriginal-value–based, should be identified and validated at the community level and should, ideally, reflect both the underlying value system and the holistic nature of a particular community's social and cultural life (Lithman, 1983).

There exists a mutually reinforcing set of relationships between development, values, and a people's quality of life, or wellness. A framework, for example, based on the Plains Indian "medicine wheel" (or sacred hoop) may be appropriate for developing indicators (see Figure 13.1). Four areas of personal and community life can be defined, corresponding to the four quadrants of the medicine wheel (First Nations Resource Council, 1990: vi–viii) (see Table 13.1). To be meaningful for community development, ways of "measuring" each of the four areas, or quadrants of the medicine wheel, must be found. It is apparent that all

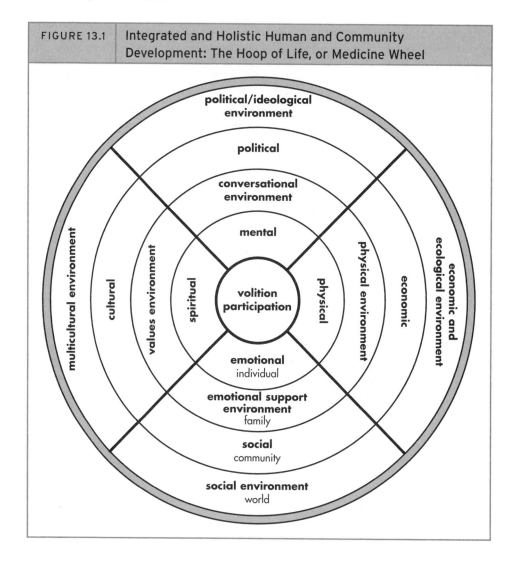

FIGURE 13.1 | Integrated and Holistic Human and Community Development: The Hoop of Life, or Medicine Wheel

of the four areas are very closely interrelated; it is unclear where one area ends and another begins (this, of course, highlights the holistic nature of the wheel and of life itself). While it was agreed that the four areas offered a holistic perspective of personal and community life, it was less clear—particularly in view of the extent of overlap between areas—which areas would yield the best kind of information that could be used in socio-economic planning and development. However, it is not at all clear that the data generated by any number of indicators are really a direct measure of something like "spirituality," "emotional well-being," or "self-determination." These areas (also referred to as "indices," in the parlance of indicator research) are very difficult to define, and it should be pointed out that indicators are by no means a replacement for definitions.

To begin to apply the framework, an important first step is to come up with some definitions of the four indices of personal and community life that correlate with the four

TABLE 13.1	Four Areas of Human and Community Development Derived from the Medicine Wheel Concept
Four Areas of Personal and Community Life	**Four Quadrants of Medicine Wheel**
Family Stability/Community Support	Mental/Political Potentialities
Psychological/Emotional Well-Being	Emotional/Social Potentialities
Cultural/Spirituality	Cultural/Spiritual Potentialities
Economy/Self-Determination	Physical/Economic Potentialities

quadrants of the "wheel." To ensure the validity of the indices, part of this crucial first step had to be the participation of First Nations communities and their members in the definition process itself. Accordingly, some of the definitions that were arrived at during workshops and discussions held in a number of First Nations communities in Alberta are shown in Table 13.2.

Many indicators were suggested that were thought to describe each of the four indices. They included the number of monogamous relationships, the levels of trust and sharing within and between families and community members, the number and kinds of clubs and associations, scholastic achievement levels, leisure activities, the number and kinds of cultural events, the extent and use of Indian languages, the role of elders, and so on. The difficulty that community participants faced, of course, was that any number of indicators they thought up seemed applicable across several indices, while at the same time the pool of indicators never seemed to be comprehensive enough. Thus, a more

TABLE 13.2	Community-Based Definitions of the Four Indices of Personal and Community Development	
Family Stability and Community Supports [Mental and Political]		**Culture/Spirituality [Cultural/Spiritual]**
Household integration		Pride in one's culture
Economic viability		Sense of identity
Member cohesion		Knowledge of tradition and of traditional values
Kinship loyalty		
Cross-kinship co-operation		
[Emotional/Social] Psychological/Emotional Well-being		**[Physical/Economic] Economic/Self-Determination**
General mental health		Control over one's own destiny and resources
Self-confidence		Creating/managing own opportunities
Self-esteem		Solving one's own problems
Positive self-image		Personal/community control

disciplined framework was still lacking whereby it would be possible to see how different aspects of social and community life would be affected—positively and negatively—by economic development. The question remained: What do designations like "the number of monogamous relationships" or "the extent and use of Indian languages" actually indicate or mean?

One of the outcomes of the community workshops was the proposal to identify a social indicator system that could be used to generate information to gauge the extent to which economic development either enhances and revitalizes each of the indices—e.g., family stability, or spirituality—or detracts from them. What is important, then, is not so much the variables or indicators that define the indices, but rather how an organized system of variables and accompanying indicators could be used to somehow evaluate or anticipate the impact of development projects, programs, practices, and policies on each of the four indices of personal and community life from the point of view of individuals and from the perspective of the community (see Figure 13.2).

FIGURE 13.2	A Proposed Social Indicator System

INDICES
Family Stability/Community Supports
Culture/Spirituality
Psychological/Emotional Well-Being
Economy/Self-Determination

↑

VARIABLES
Demographics
Social and Cultural Groups
Learning Opportunities
Work and Employment
Income and Wealth Distribution
Health, Safety, and Nutrition
Housing
Environment and Resources
Leisure, Culture, and Use of Time
Conflict and Dispute Resolution

↑

INDICATORS
List of indicators associated with each variable above

↑

DEVELOPMENT PROJECTS AND PROGRAMS

The logic of the proposed social indicator system would be as follows: How, as a result of an anticipated or actual economic development project or program, might family stability (one of four indices—the other three being emotional well-being, spirituality, and self-determination) be affected by accompanying changes in such variables as demographics, work and employment, housing, etc., as measured by such indicators as male/female life expectancy, the presence of volunteer organizations, unemployment rates, levels of formal education, traditional learning opportunities, role of elders, persons per household, etc.? The same could be asked about psychological/emotional well-being: What kind of an effect will changes in community demographics, income and wealth distribution, or in the environment (or any other variable), as a result of an anticipated or actual development project, have on a person's mental health, self-confidence, or self-esteem? Would economic development enhance these or detract from them, and if so, in what ways?

That socio-economic development will have an effect, in one way or another, on community demographics, the health and nutrition of community members, housing and so forth, is obvious. Ideally, it should be possible for an Aboriginal community to plan and control the kinds of changes it desires—e.g., those that are compatible with the values of its people—by monitoring or anticipating change in the particular indicators believed to have an effect on the four aspects of individual and community life—namely, family stability, emotional well-being, spirituality, and self-determination. Community members themselves will determine, in whatever ways are appropriate and by whatever process they agree upon, those variables and related indicators that they feel are best associated with promoting or contributing to the qualities they value most, such as family stability, emotional well-being, etc., in their own community setting. See Table 13.3 on the next page for examples of the indicators that could be associated with each of the socio-economic development variables specified in the previous table

As far as the indicators are concerned, they can be further disaggregated according to the kind of information that is sought and the use to which it might be put. Disaggregations can be as "coarse" or as "fine" in scale as circumstances allow or require. Age structure as an indicator within the variable "demographics," for example, can have as many or as few year-intervals as necessary. Household type (demographics), literacy rate (learning opportunities), types of employment (work and employment), etc., might be similarly disaggregated to fit local circumstances and to suit local needs. The number of indicators within each variable can of course be increased, decreased, prioritized, or left out, and new ones may be added according to the goals, priorities, and requirements of community members. Many of the indicators listed above were actually suggested by participants at the First Nations community workshops. Both non-Aboriginal as well as "traditional" data items were included. Mainstream, or non-Aboriginal, indicators can of course be interpreted according to Aboriginal values, and so need not be accepted without question—nor be rejected simply because they are non-Aboriginal.

The 10 variables were adapted in part from social reporting or accounting systems used in both the United Kingdom and the United States (Carley, 1981: 114–120). In those systems, variables (or areas of social concern) are referred to as "programmatic divisions." The information generated by both systems is strictly descriptive and there are no attempts to explain how or why the conditions described came about; an argument can be made that they are therefore, by definition, not really social indicators. Their primary usefulness, however, lies in their attempt to delineate areas of social life that are of concern to citizens, interest groups, business people, educators, and elected officials/policymakers. In providing

TABLE 13.3	Socio-economic Development Variables and Their Indicators
1. Demographics	male/female ratio
	age structure
	infant mortality
	male/female life expectancy
	death rate
	disability
	causes of death
	household type
2. Social and Cultural Groups	clubs and associations
	interest groups
	degree of involvement in group
	(cross-kinship) activities
	daycare
	volunteer groups for the elderly
	youth groups
	organized sports/games
3. Learning Opportunities	available education services
	level of mainstream education
	literacy rate
	school completion rate
	use of language
	role of elders
	availability of teachers
	mainstream vs. traditional learning
	availability of library/books
4. Work and Employment	types of wage employment
	seasonal vs. regular work
	locally-owned shops and businesses
	creating/managing own employment
	employment of community members
	unemployment rate
	unemployment spell
	kinds of subsistence work
5. Income and Wealth Distribution	income growth
	band taxation rate
	% social assistance recipients
	time spent on assistance

TABLE 13.3	Continued

	loans/assets ratio
	investment income per capita
	transfer payment (amount/kind)
	earned income levels
	barter system
6. Health, Safety, and Nutrition	violent crimes
	number of suicides
	alcohol abuse
	levels and causes of disability
	accidents and causes
	food/water quality
	number of smokers
	children fully immunized
	cases of cardiovascular disease
	cases of anxiety and depression
	prescription drug use
	incidence of hospitalizations
7. Housing	# of homeless families
	dwelling standards
	availability of water/electricity
	# of owners vs. renters
	# of persons per house/household
	# of housing starts and finishes
	$$ spent on housing/renovations
	inside/outside toilets
8. Environment and Resources	noise levels
	smells and odours
	levels of cleanliness
	sanitation facilities
	water quality
	waste management
9. Leisure, Culture, and Use of Time	use of language
	ceremonies and cultural events
	feelings of loneliness
	role of elders
	craft production for domestic use or for sale
	cultural/recreational facilities

(continued)

TABLE 13.3	Continued
10. Conflict and Dispute Resolution	violent crimes
	crime rate
	incidence of vandalism
	incidence of child/sexual abuse
	# of incarcerations
	kinds/levels of substance abuse
	police or peacekeepers
	dispute settlement forum or techniques
	traditional modes of discipline
	role of elders

descriptive statistics they therefore provide background information for a social indicator system. By this is meant a "group of social indicators organized around component parts of the social system" (Carley, 1981: 47). According to Carley, the term usually implies consideration of a number of the diverse parts, or domains, that make up individual as well as community well-being.

The key, then, is that any given social indicator system must have a determined structure for the information derived from this system to be of any use. Social indicator systems can be organized along a number of different lines (Miles, 1985: 114). For example, a system can be organized programmatically on the basis of geography (national, regional, local); institutional arrangements of society (housing, health services, law, transportation, education); agency, program, or service type (welfare, housing, employment, education); and even on the basis of an individual's life-cycle (learning, working, retirement). None of these are necessarily mutually exclusive, of course (Gerber, 1990).

One method of structuring a social indicator system is to work from the general to the specific—that is, to identify community or social goals, refine them to generate more specific objectives, and eventually to arrive at some indicators of the achievement of that goal. (Called the "goal-to-indicator" system [UNESCO, 1981, 1984; Carley, 1981: 54], this method was favoured by those community members who participated in the workshops). Here, there is an explicit internal logical consistency to the process of indicator development. The logical structure means that any particular indicator is related back to some goal or objective by the members of the community themselves. Making it "explicit" is clearly valuable for several reasons. First, it facilitates the building of some sort of causal models between goals and indicators. Secondly, and perhaps most importantly from the perspective of the Aboriginal community, it brings to the fore the value system of community members who themselves are actively structuring the system. It is a very good way of ensuring that the values of the community are articulated and reflected in the indicator system; it is also a good way of ensuring the participation of community members in this process.

It is suggested that the logical structure between the four indices, the ten variables, and their accompanying indicators as set out above qualifies as a social indicator system as defined by social indicator researchers—e.g., Rossi and Gilmartin, 1980. In contrast with existing socio-economic indicator models developed in the context of First Nations development planning, however—e.g., PJS Geach and Associates, 1985—the system advocated here is indeed "organized around component parts of the social system." Furthermore, a "goal-to-indicator" system can be used, based on the OECD model (Organization for Economic Co-operation and Development, 1973, 1974, 1976, 1982). The OECD, which comprises 24 Western (First World) member countries, developed a program intended to guide member governments in the preparation of social indicators. It was subsequently shown that the components of community well-being were similar across cultures as well as over time. Thus, the system of four indices and ten variables may be "universally" applicable across a range of communities dissimilar in economic prosperity, geography, and population size. Despite expected differences in the weighting and ordering of indicators within variables (reflecting different value orientations, priorities, etc.), the system of variables and indices themselves should therefore be applicable across different First Nations communities.

Despite some reservations about the applicability of the OECD model with respect to interpretation, comparability, and applicability in the context of Aboriginal development (Brodhead, 1990: 7), the authors of the OECD model make it clear that the identification and ranking of social concerns as well as their indicators has to be an ongoing process over time. What makes the structure of their model attractive is that the goal-to-indicator system has to be negotiated among the participants; this means that the selection of indicators reflects the participants' own value judgements on the components of individual and community well-being.

Thus, what would otherwise be a static exercise of collecting information now becomes an interactive as well as an interpretive process of collecting information with particular purposes in mind. One purpose may be to monitor and evaluate the effects of actual development projects on any number of variables (as reflected by their indicators) and, indirectly, on any of the four indices of personal and community life. How economic development may be perceived to affect family stability or spirituality, or, alternatively, how these may be enhanced by consciously choosing a particular development strategy, must necessarily be a process in which community members, the chief and council, and/or those responsible for economic development are involved.

It is clear from the current thrust of federal government policy making and band/tribal council development initiatives that the emphasis is increasingly being placed on self-reliance, self-government, and the use and development of local resources. On the one hand, INAC's openness towards the promotion of Aboriginal self-government may be seen as an implicit recognition of the need for a bottom-up approach to Aboriginal development. On the other hand, there is growing evidence that many First Nations communities are adopting a more entrepreneurial perspective on their common future. The creation, for example, of numerous Aboriginal-based development corporations and businesses is testimony to this trend—e.g., Canadian Indian Resource Corporation, 1990. Many communities, however, are still inclined to pursue more traditional paths of development.

An Aboriginal community's value system is part of the total resources of the community that must be considered during the actual course of economic revitalization and development. To generate a truly Aboriginal-value–based list of indicators requires the identification of those aspects of the community and community life which residents desire to maintain, enhance, or even remove. Validating a list of indicators provides an opportunity to ascertain how ready community residents are for changes, which changes

they feel are most desirable, urgent, or wholly unacceptable, and which values they anticipate might be compromised as a result of development.

This is not to suggest that a community's values be reduced to a checklist, but rather
that people need to identify and discuss them in order to help them determine their development priorities. Community development clearly rests on a strong value foundation, and
it must be a conscious, selective process. A development indicator system, while reflecting
the value judgments and cultural views of those persons who construct and interpret them,
is an essential tool. The system can be used to help collect and organize socio-economic
data (including the values) in communities; a system gives those data shape and coherence.
An indicator system, as a measure or description of community conditions in the broad
sense, can aid in improving a community's planning capacity by making available information that planners can use.

The formulation and assessment of the effectiveness of holistic development strategies
should be enhanced by the use of an indicator system described in this case study. Some
"baseline" data are necessary in order to detect the effects of changes brought about by
development in Aboriginal communities, and provide the foundation for helping the direction of that change. Indicators and an indicator system are a means of building this kind of
a data base. Indeed, an indicator system—such as the one described above or a modified
version of it—can be incorporated into more comprehensive First Nations development
studies. The indicator system described in the case study and the case study itself has been
utilized in a larger and more detailed study of First Nations socio-economic well-being
(Armstrong and Rogers, 1996).

ECONOMIC DEVELOPMENT STRATEGIES AND APPROACHES

We will now discuss several ways in which Aboriginal people could develop their natural
resource base: the concession, the joint venture, co-management, the service contract, the
management agreement, the community development corporation, and local producers'
cooperatives. Even though all these activities point to active participation by Aboriginal
people in development, the question of the extent of their involvement remains. How
deeply do the bands want to be involved, for instance, in projects where the risk factors
might be high?

The Concession   This has been the traditional strategy whereby Indians (through the
federal government) grant a company production rights. The company makes a direct
equity investment for the sole purpose of extracting a resource (Bankes, 1983). As Asante
(1979) pointed out, in many cases the concession amounts to a virtual assumption of sovereignty over the host country's or nation's resources by transnational corporations. Under
these conditions, the corporation asserts ownership not only of the fixed assets but also of
the natural resource itself (Bankes, 1983).

Under a concession agreement there is very little direct "up-front" cost for the band.
Nor are there any operating costs. In addition, these agreements are easy to administer,
since the need for supervision, auditing, and training is minimal. All of this is provided by
the company that agrees to exploit the resource. In short, the cost to the band is minimal,
but the return is also minimal. Aboriginal people have found that this type of agreement

does not encourage the training of local residents in order to assume jobs in the industry, thereby introducing them into the wage economy (Meadow Lake, 1989).

The Joint Venture This means that there are two (or more) parties that pool their money, technical expertise, and/or land in order to develop a project. There are two variations of this method. The first is one in which a separate legal entity is created that will be jointly owned by both parties, that is, the Aboriginal people and the development company. The second type does not involve the formation of a separate company, but instead the parties to the venture have a direct, undivided working interest in the project.

The joint venture type of agreement requires that Aboriginal people (1) already possess the technical expertise, and (2) have some "interest" that is considered valuable by the other party, such as land or mineral rights. There is both a direct and indirect cost involved with this type of development. The joint venture generally presents an opportunity for the local people to increase their control over the development. It can increase revenues for Aboriginal people and it allows for a flexible method of collecting revenues (Bankes, 1983; Asante, 1979).

The Co-management Partnership Partnerships involve two or more parties, whereby Aboriginal people would have a say in determining the rate and nature of development. Moreover, economic linkages with other organizations would have to be evaluated and "costed out" as to the benefits and costs for Aboriginal communities. Aboriginal people have generally opted for co-management strategies when renewable resources are involved. Ownership of the resources is not necessary, but all parties must recognize that each party has a legitimate interest in them. Aboriginal people use co-management strategies based on the belief that the orderly use of resources will facilitate the survival and health of their environment. Pinkerton (1989) has argued that Aboriginal people will continue to prefer co-management between themselves and non-Aboriginal people. There are several reasons for this preference:

1. Co-management creates cooperation among individual workers.
2. Co-management creates a commitment among local workers to share both the costs and benefits of their efforts toward enhancement and conservation.
3. Co-management creates a higher degree of organization and mutual commitment among Aboriginal workers, which translates into a better bargaining relationship with external agents.

Co-management arrangements represent a transfer of decision-making power to Aboriginal people, and are therefore difficult to negotiate with non-Aboriginal people. However, the view that Aboriginal people have a legitimate interest in natural resources is one that is slowly being recognized by government and business. The 1990 *Sparrow* decision by the Supreme Court, which noted that Aboriginal people have a legal and legitimate interest in renewable resources, went far in alerting government and businesses to accept this perspective and consider co-management initiatives.

The Service Contract Under agreements of this type the status of Aboriginal ownership over the natural resource is reaffirmed. Thus, rather than transferring the title of the resource (as in a concession) to the developing company, the band simply hires the corporation as a contractor or business partner to perform a specific task for a specified amount of money. The disadvantage in using this type of strategy is that bands must have a substantial cash flow in order to pay for the up-front cost of the development, which can be quite high. Both Zakariya (1976) and Bankes (1983) pointed out that under this type of agreement the band would have no internal control over the project, and there would be few opportunities for Aboriginal people to gain employment or technical and administrative skills. Also, the project would have to be carefully monitored by the band to ensure that its members got the maximum benefits from it. The advantage of such an arrangement is Aboriginal ownership and jurisdiction over the natural resource. In addition, other firms would supply the technology (and risk capital) to explore, develop and market the resources.

The Management Agreement This is a strategy whereby Aboriginal people purchase expertise for a specified period of time. The contracted consultants can either act as advisors while the Aboriginal management retains sole control of the company, or the Aboriginal people can choose to relinquish control to the consultants.

The Community Development Corporation A band or a First Nation can form a corporation and explore for minerals on its reserve. The corporation is granted permits and leases according to terms set by the federal government. These corporations are created to help plan and implement the business development goals of a community or region, and they can be involved either in risking capital or acting as an advisory body. A variation of this strategy is called a local producer's cartel, which involves the formation of a syndicate or trust that is able to take over a business venture from the original developer and carry on all negotiations with developers. In the mid-1960s, when 25 American Indian tribes created CERT (Council of Energy Resource Tribes) in order to control all mineral development on their reserves, they established a cartel.

Some bands and larger Aboriginal groups that have taken this course have chosen either to remain independent or to enter into joint ventures with other non-Aboriginal companies. Two major problems have beset those Aboriginal groups that have created corporations. First, the corporations tend to benefit from the development more than the band does, and may become more powerful than the band. This problem has been somewhat alleviated by making all members of the band (including newborns) members of the corporation. The second problem centres on the risk factor and the need for a considerable amount of money up front before the development starts. These difficulties are of course not insurmountable, as there have been numerous success stories throughout Canada. A notable one is Makivik Corporation, created in 1978 pursuant to the signing of the James Bay and Northern Québec Agreement (1975). The corporation, headquartered in Kuujjuaq (Nunavik, Quebec), has the mandate to implement the agreement, and to administer the funds accorded to the Inuit (see Box 13.1).

The Local Producers' Cooperative These are usually voluntary, non-profit societies incorporated to run a business. The members of the cooperative own shares of the business and have one vote at each general meeting. A board of directors is elected to operate the business and carry out day-to-day activities. In effect, a cooperative is a business owned by its customers.

Box 13.1	**Makivik Corporation**

As the main engine of Nunavik's economic development, Makivik negotiates agreements with private- and public-sector partners. This includes ongoing negotiations with Hydro-Québec on existing and proposed James Bay hydroelectric projects, and with the mining company Falconbridge Limited regarding the Raglan Nickel Mine project. Makivik, representing about 8500 Quebec Inuit, and operating offices in Quebec City, Montreal, and Ottawa, is also responsible for investing and managing funds obtained through these negotiations. Makivik is directly involved in economic development through its subsidiary companies, which include:

- Air Inuit: Nunavik's regional airline

- First Air: A major air carrier in Canada's eastern Arctic, with links to Greenland
- Seaku Fisheries: Exploits shrimp stocks and develops inshore projects with Inuit entrepreneurs
- Nunavik Arctic Foods Incorporated: Harvests and processes wild meats in four community processing centres and markets the products in Nunavik and southern markets

These companies create jobs (and training) for the residents of Nunavik as well as providing essential services at competitive rates. The corporation's portfolio size is in excess of $105 million and continues to grow.

Source: Information courtesy of Makivik Corporation, personal communication by R. Gadacz, 2003.

A history of the cooperatives shows that until the 1950s most of the Aboriginal trade in Canada (particularly in isolated regions) was carried out through the Hudson's Bay Company. In 1959 the government began to encourage and support a number of locally owned and operated cooperatives. This idea seemed to fit particularly well with one of the elements of Aboriginal culture—sharing. The first Aboriginal cooperatives were producer-oriented and involved such activities as art, crafts or fishing. Then consumer cooperatives emerged, where both importing and exporting activities were carried out. In many communities, cooperatives and other private enterprise businesses, such as the Hudson's Bay Company, exist side by side, selling and buying many of the same products.

In the past, Aboriginal cooperatives have encountered two major problems in their operations. First, they lacked skilled managers. Second, they found it difficult to engage in direct competition with integrated, multinational companies. Nevertheless, they have succeeded in providing employment for Aboriginal people. Today they are the largest employer of Aboriginal people in the North and elsewhere, and register annual sales in excess of $30 million. There are currently well over 50 co-ops nationwide, employing more than 600 people and generating between $10 and $20 million in income. However, an infusion of government monies is still required for some co-ops to survive; various government departments continue to contribute to the development of cooperatives. Much of this money is put towards training directors, managers, and staff. Additional federal monies are set aside to help with new production techniques and business marketing strategies.

Each of the strategies identified, including international ventures described in Box 13.2, point to the quest by Aboriginal people to gain control over their resources and to manage them. The variety of strategies reflects the differing situations in which Aboriginal people find themselves. The ultimate goal for Aboriginal people is to control their land and resources. Establishing the proper administrative structures is only the beginning. Once control has been established, structures have to be devised to manage economic development and to foster an enhancement of quality of life. This requires the necessary skills to operate businesses and to participate in what is already a global economy.

The most widely employed development strategy used by Aboriginal people has probably been the concession. However, the joint venture has also become a more attractive alternative, and has been encouraged by the federal government's involvement. The government has loaned money to Aboriginal companies and has guaranteed its backing. But since they allow for no control or ownership of the natural resources, it is unlikely that these joint ventures are a viable long-term economic strategy (Dyck and Waldram, 1993).

Each of the development strategies discussed above has benefits as well as costs. For this reason the type of agreement that an Aboriginal group might wish to make is ultimately determined by the group's goals. For example, if the Aboriginal group wanted to maintain a subsistence way of life, like the Cree of James Bay, and still allow development of natural resources, the concession type of agreement might be appropriate. On the other hand, if it wanted to become directly involved in a particular project, then a joint venture would seem more appropriate. For example, a joint venture called Shehtah Drilling was formed between Esso (50 percent), the Dene (25 percent), and the Métis (25 percent) development corporations in 1983 to conduct drilling and service-rig operations in the Northwest Territories.[2] The ATCO/EQUTAK drilling venture organized between Atco-Mustang Drilling and the Inuvialuit Development Corporation (with the assistance of Petro Canada); and the Beaufort Food Services, a joint venture between Beau-Tuk Marine and the Inuvialuit Development Corporation, are two other examples of joint ventures that have been relatively successful. Aboriginal international joint ventures of different kinds in this age of globalization and international capitalism are surely expected to increase in the decades to come (see Box 13.2).

Where successful agreements have been made to develop band natural resources, what do Aboriginal people do with their increased income? The number of cases is relatively small, but the Hobbema reserve in Alberta is one good example. There, the Samson Band's energy revenue exceeded $60 million even back in 1980. Besides appropriating one-half for individual band members, the band also built and operates a 283-hectare grain operation. But the band had also made investments beyond the agricultural domain. In the early 1980s, the Samson business manager bought the charter of the Edmonton Canadian Insurance Company for slightly more than $1 million. Other Samson Band investments now include rental properties in Edmonton, shares for subdivisions in three nearby towns, shares in a Vancouver condominium project, and shares in a housing development in Cold Lake, Alberta. Other oil-rich bands, like Samson, are also investing in land purchases, housing projects and banks. One band is trying to work out a deal with a consortium that is seeking a national pay-television licence.

Box 13.2	"Natives Talk Business in Nicaragua: Saskatchewan Group's Forestry Deal with Miskito Indians Reflects Entrepreneurial Trend"

By Erin Anderssen

The men from Meadow Lake Tribal Council motored down Nicaragua's Rio Coco in dugout canoes, stopping to talk business under the coconut trees in each community as they passed.

The group from Saskatchewan frequently spent the night, dining on fruits and beans, and sleeping on concrete. Often they would sit around a fire with the village elders and hear stories of children killing in war, and they would try to explain snow to people who have never known winter.

A few villages ahead, touching down in a helicopter, a group of Korean businessmen were making their pitch: Sell your trees to us, they'd promise, and we will build your village a baseball diamond.

The men from Meadow Lake promised nothing—except partnership. They made the same forestry-development offer to 72 Miskito Indian villages in the timber-rich land of Nicaragua's northern Atlantic coast. And not a single community said no.

"Those Koreans haven't moved a stick of wood for a year-and-a-half," Meadow Lake chief executive Ray Ahenakew said with a chuckle.

The Meadow Lake forestry venture reflects a growing trend among Canada's aboriginal entrepreneurs, who are starting to see bright opportunities beyond the border. They are encouraged by a more pragmatic native leadership—most marked in Phil Fontaine, national chief of the Assembly of First Nations—which pushes economic development as key to self-government.

"Revitalizing first-nation economies should not be restricted to Canada," Mr. Fontaine said. "We go where there are opportunities. And we see the benefits in doing business with our brothers and sisters in other parts of the world. We're taking a page out of the Team Canada trade missions."

And Ottawa is happy to help—trade officials feel that Canada is missing the boat on development projects funded by international financial institutions such as the World Bank. The country's native bands, the logic goes, are ideally suited to helping other indigenous people set up culturally sensitive schools, build houses and hospitals in remote communities and develop their natural resources.

Deals like the Meadow Lake project could get much easier come 2005, the target date for a gigantic free-trade agreement with 34 countries in the hemisphere dubbed the Free Trade Area of the Americas. Negotiations start this week in Chile on the treaty, which would open up new markets in Central and South America. Leaders at the Santiago summit will also discuss the issue of poverty among indigenous people, a topic pushed onto the agenda by Canada.

Despite the opportunities (there is even talk of creating an indigenous-to-indigenous trademark), there are few aboriginal companies as established as Meadow Lake, which runs a forestry operation in northern Saskatchewan worth $60-million a year. Only about 50 aboriginal companies in Canada are considered export-ready, and fewer than a dozen have made progress signing international deals.

Makivik Corp., a company owned by the Inuit of Northern Quebec, is working on a lobster deal with the Miskito in Nicaragua. The Saskatoon Tribal Council is developing a coffee-packaging partnership with communities in Guatemala.

To help native bands make international links, the federal government appointed Blaine Favel, then head of the Saskatchewan Federation of Indian Nations, to a new post as counsellor on international indigenous issues in January. Since taking the job, Mr. Favel has travelled to Central America to meet Mayan and Miskito Indian leaders. "The stories are the same," he said. "So there's a great affinity. And trust is a large part of business."

At the Meadow Lake Tribal Council, work is underway to sell the deal to the wary central government of Nicaragua. The plan is to set up a small sawmill among the Miskito Indians and harvest a portion of the pine forest, splitting the initial profits in half.

Eventually, the Miskito Indians can buy out Meadow Lake completely, equipped and trained to run their own operation. Buyers, encouraged by the unanimous endorsement from the communities involved, are already calling from Texas, Mr. Ahenakew said.

"It's a good feeling," he said about his connection with the Miskito Indians. "But it's also the smartest way to do business."

Source: *The Globe and Mail*, April 13, 1998, page A4. Reproduced with permission from *The Globe and Mail*.

DEVELOPMENT AND IDENTITY

La Violette (1961) argued that for any ethnic group to survive it must be able to assert control over its fate. Essentially, the struggle for survival is a struggle for identity. The group must view its past positively and maintain strong links with traditional customs and beliefs. It must also achieve political equality and look forward to a promising future. These processes can be set in motion only at the grass-roots level. If Aboriginal people are going to control their destiny, they must implement some form of community control immediately. Aboriginal communities are slowly becoming involved in the process of capacity building, which allows them to plan their own strategies for development. However, this development must revitalize and strengthen the social, cultural, and economic aspects of a way of life that is at the very core of being Aboriginal (Hanson, 1985). Over the years Aboriginal people have tried to develop community-based solutions to their economic plights.

Governments have encouraged Aboriginal people to develop small businesses on an individual basis. However, this could ensure non-Aboriginal control in two ways: first, non-Aboriginal society wins the loyalties of the Aboriginal businesspeople, who are potentially important community leaders; and second, the visible ownership of local business by Aboriginal people defuses anti–non-Aboriginal feelings and reduces the likelihood of violent demonstrations. The community becomes more stable, the leadership potential of non-Aboriginal–affiliated Aboriginal businesspeople is enhanced, and the non-Aboriginal domination of the community economy, though less direct, remains intact. In addition, discontent is defused through acceptable channels (Tabb, 1970). The strategy of individual entrepreneurship might not change the economic position of Aboriginal people substantially in the future.

Although community development must be encouraged, it must not be totally financed by the corporate sector of Canadian society. The federal government must not allow the corporate sector to interfere with or influence the development of Aboriginal communities, since economic development is not in the corporations' interests. So far, through close ties with the political elite, corporations have successfully blocked the federal financing that would permit Aboriginal development. For example, Saskatchewan First Nations hold $150 million in government-backed mortgages and pay almost $1 million a month to mortgage companies. If Aboriginal people started paying interest to their own institutions, the profit could be used to build up their own communities. If Aboriginal people were allowed to develop and control the reserves, they could eliminate corporate contracts for reserve projects and drain off the unskilled labour surplus for primary sector industries (Dyck, 1996).

If the corporate sector were allowed to initiate economic development on reserves, franchising would result. Under a franchise system, a corporation advances money to an individual Aboriginal person, who then manages a store that sells the corporation's product exclusively. The corporation also provides certain services and trains staff to ensure proper marketing techniques. In return for setting up the store, providing the loan, and training the staff, the company reaps several benefits, including a large percentage of the profits and access to the reserve and nearby communities. Franchising is an efficient and inexpensive way to guarantee non-Aboriginal corporate control of the reserve. Again, the presence of an Aboriginal staff defuses anti–non-Aboriginal sentiments and prevents the organization of a cohesive revolt. Moreover, the development of the reserve by outsiders allows for external control over the speed, extent, and nature of that development (Tabb, 1970: 58).

Although non-Aboriginal institutions are promoting individual entrepreneurship, many Aboriginal people have begun to recognize that the result of this policy will be continued subordination. Increasingly, cogent arguments like the following are put forward in support of Aboriginal community control and development:

> To accomplish this task, four sets of recommendations are proposed: (i) The establishment of economically viable reserves controlled by the Indians with sufficient natural resources to ensure adequate incomes for the residents. The key element in this recommendation is that the natural resources of expanded Indian lands should be firmly placed in the control of the community and its representative leaders. (ii) The establishment of an Indian corporation which can receive direct grants and long-term low-interest loans to promote economic development on the reserve, to improve and initiate village services, and to in other ways enable Indians to better utilize their natural and economic resources. (iii) A major revamping of the educational system so as to reduce discontinuities in learning, sustain effective ties with parents, strengthen the student's self-image as Indian, and maintain his self-esteem, as well as prepare him to be economically and socially competent in dealing with the institutions of the larger Canadian society. (iv) The establishment of an Indian social development program, funded by the federal and/or provincial governments, which can assist in providing the mechanism for the emergence of new Indian leaders, increase communication with other Indian and non-Indian groups, and promote local and regional community, social, and political infra-structures. (Chance, 1970: 33–35)

As the process of Aboriginal development intensifies and expands, a more holistic approach is necessary to achieve the basic minimum needs of the community. Residents need to have basic educational qualifications, access to adequate health care facilities, basic housing, and experience in the labour force. Once these minimum conditions have been achieved, the next approach to development must begin. Here, one central economic development project is pursued. The decision as to what development project should be pursued would be dependent on the history of the community, its location, and the resources and skills available within it. As these factors are brought together, the main project should lead to other forms of development spin-offs uniquely suited to the community.

But just as there are different kinds of development strategies, as outlined above, and a whole range of potential projects and activities, communities must remain alert to possible negative or unintended consequences. Even more, bands and communities must resist the temptation to "make a fast buck" by being drawn into "lucrative" enterprises in the name of "tradition" that are potentially damaging to their people and culture—as the community revitalization study earlier in this chapter emphasized. Economic benefits may come with social costs. An example readers may judge for themselves is the October 2006 official opening of the River Cree Resort and Casino on the Enoch reserve near Edmonton, Alberta. Touted as Alberta's first Native-run casino, it claims to be one of the largest employers of Aboriginal people in the province. The $178 million casino includes restaurants, bars, grills, two ice rinks (including an NHL-size hockey rink), and a nine-story, 255-room hotel with pool and fitness centre. The casino itself will have 600 slot machines and 40 gaming tables in the gaming rooms, with plans to double the number of slot machines in the future. The Enoch band's business partner is a corporation based in Las Vegas. The Alberta government made some rules about how First Nations spend the revenues: money will go towards addictions treatment, cultural events, elder and senior care, reserve infrastructure, community safety projects and life skills training.[3] Nevertheless, it has been noted that there has not been much research done on First Nations casinos in Canada. With the potential of problem gambling may come family, mental health and work problems—affecting Aboriginal people and non-Aboriginals alike (Belanger, 2006).

SUMMARY

Currently, Aboriginal people find themselves isolated from non-Aboriginal society and continue to be confronted by discrimination on a daily basis. To counter this position, they have embarked upon the long, arduous task of defining their group identity and clarifying their future goals. The growth of Aboriginal organizations shows that Aboriginal people have strengthened their political and cultural position. And, as Boldt (1980b) has shown, they are increasingly willing to engage in "extra-legal" politics:

> Enlightened Indian leaders reject White society's comfortable notions of slow and steady progress toward the achievement of basic human rights for their people and most are inclined not only to approve of extra-legal activity as a justifiable means for achieving their conception of the "good society," but are also willing to participate and, if necessary, suffer the consequences of such actions for their cause. (p. 33)

Aboriginal people have learned over time that externally directed conflict tends to enhance group solidarity. Group boundaries come into sharp focus as in-group members are differentiated from out-group members. As conflict emerges, the group is also forced to explicitly define its aims and goals. As grievances are defined, adversaries emerge and are identified. In the case of Aboriginal groups, the adversaries are non-Aboriginal: relations between the two become a zero-sum game.

In a zero-sum game one player always gains precisely what the other player loses, and vice versa. In other words, relations between the two sides are always competitive and antagonistic. Identification with one's "side" pervades the daily life of each group member. Each participant finds a particular role in the collective action and receives internal and social rewards for behaviour that reinforces group aims. Identification with the group grows, as do linkages with other members. As Pettigrew described:

> Recruits willingly and eagerly devote themselves to the group's goals. And they find themselves systematically rewarded [by the group]....They are expected to evince strong radical pride, to assert their full rights as citizens, to face jail and police brutality unhesitatingly for the cause. Note that these expected and rewarded actions all publicly commit the member to the group and its aim. (1964: 195–96)

And, as Himes stated, out of organized group conflict grows a strong group identity:

> In the interactive process of organized group conflict, self-involvement is the opposite side of the coin of overt action. Actors become absorbed by ego and emotion into the group and the group is projected through their actions. This linkage of individual and group in ego and action is the substance of identity. (1966: 10)

With the emergence of a strong pan-Aboriginal identity, the sense of alienation experienced by many has been dispelled by a new sense of significance and purpose. The personal ethnic identity of Aboriginal people is stronger now than it has been for many decades, as leaders of national and provincial Aboriginal organizations have successfully developed a national cohesiveness. As Pitts (1974) pointed out, ethnic identity is a social product, a result of actions and interpretations in a social context. Indeed, Brown (1935) argued long ago:

> A race conscious group... is a social unit struggling for status in society. It is thus a conflict group and race consciousness itself is a result of conflict. The race of the group, though not intrinsically significant, becomes an identifying symbol, serving to intensify the sense of solidarity. (p. 572)

Aboriginal identification is a mixture of internal dynamics and external pressures. At present, that identification is being translated into what Enloe (1981) called ethnic mobilization—the mobilization of an ethnic group's resources and manpower to better its position. Hopefully, non-Aboriginal Canada will no longer respond with such demobilization techniques as the white paper (1969) in order to remain in a controlling position. For, in response to such techniques, Aboriginal mobilization in turn would increase, and the accelerating spiral of conflict that could be set in motion would be counterproductive.

Aboriginal people are of course prepared to negotiate within the existing socio-legal system. In fact, both Aboriginal people as well as private industry and governments are prepared to negotiate within certain boundaries. The boundaries generally determine the status quo, and all parties are accustomed to operating within it. However, Aboriginal people continue to press for change, and, thus, pose demands that go beyond the status quo (Lightbody, 1969). As the critical point is approached in the negotiations, tension between the two negotiating parties emerges. Eventually, when Aboriginals force the issue beyond the critical point, tension changes to conflict. As Lightbody explained:

[B]eyond [this critical point] the state must realign its institutional structures about a new ethnic configuration by either physically attempting to suppress the dissident elements into grudging assimilation into the culture, or through accepting the creation of the new.... (1969: 334)

Willingness to move beyond the critical point by either party varies with time and conditions, although the history of negotiations is usually a good clue to whether or not conflict will emerge. For example, the Oldman River (Alberta) conflict, the Oka (Quebec) conflict, violence at Caledonia, and other Aboriginal–non-Aboriginal conflicts generally reflect a long history of Aboriginal peoples negotiating for social change that the other party is unwilling to accept. Constitutional talks and conferences since 1982 (over a quarter of a century ago!) show that the government is slow to change the status quo when it deals with First Nations and Aboriginal peoples as a whole. While it has been in favour of establishing conditions for a "distinct Quebec society" in the Constitution, the government has been very slow to give Aboriginal peoples similar consideration.

Even as we experience the first decade of the 21st century, more meaningful changes are still needed to enhance the political, socio-cultural and economic position of Aboriginal people in Canada. As Canadians, we would be poorer as a nation if Aboriginal leaders and youth abandoned the legal and political means to effect those changes, or to direct their frustration and helplessness inwards. It is clear that we have a collective responsibility to ensure the prosperity and self-determination of this land's first inhabitants.

KEY TERMS

settler society

Canadian Aboriginal
    Economic Development
    Strategy

revitalization

Development Indicators
    Project

medicine wheel

concession

joint venture

local producer's
    cooperative

STUDY QUESTIONS

1. Explain the term *settler society*.

2. How has non-Aboriginal Canadians' perception of Aboriginal people changed throughout Canadian history?

3. Define *modernization*.

4. What strategies have resulted in some success for Aboriginal communities? What factors can impact such successes?

5. Discuss the basic assumptions that underline the need for community development and control.

6. Describe the overall significance of development indicators for First Nation communities.

7. What is a *social indicator system*?

8. Briefly describe the different economic development strategies and approaches.

WEBLINKS

www.aboriginalcanada.gc.ca

The Aboriginal Canada Portal provides a link to the wider topic of economic development, with specific websites for business, finance, the resources sector, tourism, trade, employment and more—all by province. This site also has internal links to several government departments involved with Aboriginal development, including Human Resources Development Canada (HRDC), Industry Canada, Natural Resources Canada, and Indian and Northern Affairs. In turn, each department provides links to Aboriginal businesses, cooperatives (including case studies), entrepreneurs, resource guides, and more.

www.dfait-maeci.gc.ca/aboriginalplanet/business/directory2002-en.asp

This website of the Department of Foreign Affairs and International Trade features a unique directory of Aboriginal exporters, listing individual links to such areas as fashion design, music and theatre, forestry and mining, telecommunications technology, industrial products, and more.

NOTES

1. This case study is taken from Gadacz (1991), "Community Socio-Economic Development from a Plains Indian Perspective: A Proposed Social Indicator System and Planning Tool," *Native Studies Review*, Vol. 7 (1): 53–80. Used with permission.

2. The joint venture contract was worth $5 million. The majority of Shehtah drill crews are made up of skilled Aboriginal northerners (*Arctic Petroleum Operators' Association Review*, Vol. 6, 3, Winter 1983/84, Calgary, Alberta).

3. www.cbc.ca/news/story/2006/10/26/resort-opens.html, retrieved 11/24/2006; www.cbc.ca/canada/calgary/story/2006/10/20/expanded-rules.html, retrieved 11/24/2006.

Bibliography

Aberle, D. 1970 "A Plan for Navaho Economic Development." In *American Indians: Facts and Future, Toward Economic Development for Native American Communities*, Joint Economic Committee. New York: Arno Press.

Ablon, Joan 1965 " American Indian Relocation: Problems of Dependency and Management in the City." *Phylon*, 26 (Winter): 362–371.

Adams, Howard 1975 *Prison of Grass*. Toronto: New Press.

Adelson, N. 2005 "The Embodiment of Inequality Health Disparities in Aboriginal Canada," *Canadian Journal of Public Health*, 92: S45-S61.

Aggamaway-Pierre, M. 1983 Native Women and the State. In *Perspectives on Women in the 1980's*. J. Turner, and L. Emery (eds.), Winnipeg: University of Manitoba Press, pp. 66–73.

Ahenakew, D. 1985 "Aboriginal Title and Aboriginal Rights. The Impossible and Unnecessary Task of Identification and Definition." In *The Quest for Justice*, M. Boldt, J. Long, and L. Little Bear (eds.). Toronto: University of Toronto Press.

Alberta Federation of Métis Settlement Associations 1978 *The Métis People of Canada: A History*. Calgary: Gage Publishing.

Alberta, Government of 1991 *Report of the Task Force on the Criminal Justice System and Its Impact on the Indian and Métis People of Alberta*, Volume 1, Main Report, Edmonton.

Alfred, T. 2005 *Wasase: Indigenous Pathways of Action and Freedom*. Peterborough: Broadview Press.

Allan, D.J. 1943 "Indian Land Problems in Canada." In *The North American Indian Today*, C.T. Loram and T.F. McIlwraith (eds.). Toronto: University of Toronto Press.

Altman, J. and J. Nieuwenhuysen 1979 *The Economic Status of Australian Aborigines*. Cambridge: Cambridge University Press.

Alunik, I. 2003. *Across Time and Tundra: The Inuvialuit of the Western Arctic*. Vancouver: Raincoast Books.

Anand, S., S. Yusuf, R. Jacobs, A. Davis, Q. Yi et al. 2001 "Risk Factors, Atherosclerosis, and Cardiovascular Disease among Aboriginal People in Canada." *The Lancet*, 358: 1147–1152.

Anaya, S. James 2000 *Indigenous Peoples in International Law*. New York: Oxford University Press.

Anaya, S., R. Falk and D. Pharand 1995 *Canada's Fiduciary Obligation to Aboriginal Peoples in the Context of Accession to Sovereignty by Quebec*, Vol. 1. Ottawa: Minister of Supply and Services.

Anderson, T., B. Benson and T. Flanagan 2006 *Self-Determination*. Stanford CA: Stanford University Press.

Anderson, C. and C. Denis 2003 "Urban Natives and the Nation: Before and After the Royal Commission on Aboriginal Peoples." *Canadian Review of Sociology and Anthropology*, 40, 4: 373–390.

Andrist, Ralph 1964 *The Long Death*. New York: Macmillan.

Antonowicz, D. H. and R. Ross 1994 "Essential Components of Successful Rehabilitation Programs for Offenders." *International Journal of Offender Therapy and Comparative Criminology*, 38, 2: 97–104.

Armitage, A. 1995 *Comparing the Policy of Aboriginal Assimilation: Australia, Canada, and New Zealand*. Vancouver: University of British Columbia Press.

Armstrong, R. 1999 "Mapping the Conditions of First Nations Communities." *Canadian Social Trends*, Winter: 14–18.

Armstrong, Robin and Tim Rogers 1996 *A First Nations Typology: Patterns of Socio-Economic Well-Being*. Ottawa: Research and Analysis Directorate, Policy and Strategic Direction, Department of Indian Affairs and Northern Development.

Asante, S. 1979 "Restructuring Transnational Mineral Agreements." *American Journal of International Law*, 73, 3: 355–371.

Asch, Michael 1993 *Home and Native Land: Aboriginal Rights and the Canadian*

Constitution. Vancouver: University of British Columbia Press.

_____ **1997** *Aboriginal and Treaty Rights in Canada: Essays on Law, Equality, and Respect for Difference*. University of British Columbia Press: Vancouver.

Assembly of First Nations 1985 Final Report to Assembly of First Nations, February 18. Mimeo.

_____ **1990a** *Assembly of First Nations' Critique of Federal Government Land Claims Policy*, August 21, Summerstown, Ontario.

_____ **1990b** *Doublespeak of the 90s: A Comparison of Federal Government and First Nation Perception of Land Claims Process*. August, mimeo.

_____ **2005**. *A Treaty among Ourselves*. Ottawa: AFN Renewal Commission.

_____ **2006** *Royal Commission on Aboriginal People at 10 Years: A Report Card*, Ottawa: Assembly of First Nations.

_____ **2007** *Leadership Action Plan*. Ottawa.

Assembly of Manitoba Chiefs/Indian and Northern Affairs Canada 1994 *Towards First Nations Governments in Manitoba— Work Plan*. November 22, 1994.

Atleo, E. 2004 *Tsawalk*. Vancouver: University of British Columbia Press.

Auditor General 2004 *Report of the Auditor General*. Ottawa: House of Commons.

Bankes, N. 1983 *Resource Leasing Options and the Settlement of Aboriginal Claims*. Ottawa: Canadian Arctic Resources.

Banner 2005. *How the Indians Lost Their Land*. London: Belknap Press.

Barkwell, L. J. 1988 "Observations on Discrimination and Dehumanization in the Criminal Justice System." Paper presented to the *Aboriginal Justice Inquiry: Inquiry Proceedings*, December 15, 1988. Winnipeg: Four Seasons Reporting Services Ltd.

Barkwell, L., N. Chartrand, D. Gray, L. Longclaws, and R. Richard 1989 "Devalued People: The Status of the Métis in the Justice System," *The Canadian Journal of Native Studies*, 9.1, 121–150.

Barman, J., Y. Hebert, and D. McCaskill (eds.) 1987 *Indian Education in Canada*, Vol. II. Vancouver: University of British Columbia Press.

Barnhardt, R. 2001. *Domestication of the Ivory Tower Institutional Adaptation to Cultural Distance*. Unpublished paper.

Barsh, R. and J. Henderson 1982 "Aboriginal Rights, Treaty Rights and Human Rights: Tribe and Constitutional Renewal." *Journal of Canadian Studies*, 2 (1982): 55–81.

Bartlett, Richard 1980 *Indian Act of Canada*. Saskatoon: Native Law Centre, University of Saskatchewan.

_____ **1984** "Aboriginal Land Claims at Common Law." *Canadian Native Law Reporter*, 1: 1–63.

Bastien, B. 2004 *Blackfoot Ways of Knowing: The World View of Siksikaitsitapi*. Calgary: University of Calgary Press.

Battiste, M. and J. Barman (eds.) 1995 *First Nations Education in Canada: The Circle Unfolds*. Vancouver: University of British Columbia Press.

Beattie, K. 2005. "Adult Correctional Services in Canada, 2003/2004" *Juristat*. Canadian Centre for Justice Statistics. Ottawa: Statistics Canada.

_____ **2006**. "Adult Correctional Services in Canada, 2004/2005." *Juristat*, Canadian Centre for Justice Statistics, Catalogue no. 85-002-XIE, 26,5. Ottawa: Statistics Canada.

Beaver, J. 1979 *To Have What Is One's Own*. Ottawa: Department of Indian Affairs and Northern Development.

Belanger, Y. 2006. *Gambling with the Future*. Saskatoon: Purich Publishing.

Bell, C. 1991 "Who Are the Métis in Section 35(2)?" *Alberta Law Review*, 24 (2): 351–381.

_____ **1998** "New Directions in the Law of Aboriginal Rights," *Canadian Bar Review*, 77,1 & 2: 36–72.

_____ **2003** "Towards an Understanding of Metis Aboriginal Rights: Reflections on the Reasoning in R. vs. Powley." In *Aboriginal Rights Litigation*, J. Magnet and D. Dorey (eds.), Ch. 13. Markham, Ontario: Butterworths.

Bellfy, P. 2001 "Introduction: Aboriginal People: the Changing Face of Canada." *American Review of Canadian Studies*, 31,1/2, 11–13.

Bennett, G. 1978 "Aboriginal Title in the Common Law: A Stoney Path through Feudal Doctrine." *Buffalo Law Review*, 17: 601–623.

Bennett, J. and S. Rowley (eds) 2004 *Uqalurait: An Oral History of Nunavut*, Montreal: McGill-Queens University Press.

Berger, Thomas 1977 *Northern Frontier, Northern Homeland—The Report of the Mackenzie Valley Pipeline Inquiry*, Vol. 1. Ottawa: Minister of Supply and Services Canada.

_____ **1981** *Fragile Freedoms: Human Rights and Dissent in Canada*. Toronto: Clarke, Irwin and Co. Ltd.

_____ **1985** *Village Journey*. New York: Hill and Wang Co.

Black, D. 1998 *The Social Structure of Right and Wrong,* 1998. San Diego, California: Academic Press.

Blauner, Robert 1969 "Internal Colonialism and Ghetto Revolt." *Social Problems*, 16 (Spring): 393–408.

Blishen, B., F. Vallee, B. McFarlane and G. Rocher 1979 *Socio-Economic Impact Model for Northern Development,* Volumes 1 and 2. Department of Indian and Northern Affairs, Canada.

Blum, R. 2005 *Ghost Brothers.* Montreal: McGill-Queen's University Press.

Bobet, E. 1990 *The Inequalities in Health: A Comparison of Indian and Canadian Mortality Trends*. Ottawa: Health and Welfare Canada.

_____ **1997** *Diabetes among First Nations People.* Ottawa: Statistics Canada, Medical Services Branch, Health Canada.

Boe, R. 2000 Aboriginal Inmates: Demographic Trends and Projections. *Forum,*. 12 (1): 4–17.

Bol, M. (ed). 2003 *Stars Above, Earth Below.* Colorado: Roberts Rinehard.

Bolaria, S. 1979 "Self-Care and Lifestyles: Ideological and Policy Implications." In *Economy, Class and Social Reality,* J.A. Fry (ed.). Toronto: Butterworths, pp. 350–363.

Boldt, M. 1980a "Canadian Native Leadership: Context and Composition." *Canadian Ethnic Studies*, 12 (1): 15–33.

_____ **1980b** "Indian Leaders in Canada: Attitudes toward Extra-Legal Action." *Journal of Ethnic Studies*, 8 (1): 71–83.

_____ **1980c** "Canadian Native Indian Leadership: Context and Composition." *Canadian Ethnic Studies Journal,* 12 (1): 71–83.

_____ **1993** *Surviving as Indians: The Challenge of Self Government*. Toronto: University of Toronto Press.

Boldt, M., and J. Long 1983 *Tribal Traditions and the Canadian Charter of Rights and Freedoms*. Lethbridge AB: University of Lethbridge. Mimeo.

_____ **1985a** "Tribal Traditions and European–Western Political Ideologies: The Dilemma of Canada's Native Indians." In *The Quest for Justice*, M. Boldt, J. Long and L. Little Bear (eds.). Toronto: University of Toronto Press.

_____ **1985b** "Tribal Philosophies and the Canadian Charter of Rights and Freedoms." In *The Quest for Justice*, M. Boldt, J. Long and L. Little Bear (eds.). Toronto: University of Toronto Press.

Boldt, M., J.A. Long and L. Little Bear 1985 (eds.). *The Quest for Justice*. Toronto: University of Toronto Press.

Bonney, R. 1976 "The Role of Women in Indian Activism." In *The Western Canadian Journal of Anthropology*, 6 (3), 243–248.

Bonta, J.U., S. Lipinski, and M. Martin 1992 "The Characteristics of Aboriginal Recidivists." *Canadian Journal of Criminology*, 34 (3–4): 517–521.

Braithwaite, J. 1990 *Crime, Shame and Reintegration.* Cambridge: Cambridge University Press.

_____ **1993** "Shame and Modernity," *British Journal of Criminology,* 33 (1): 54–68.

Braroe, N. 1975 *Indian and White: Self–Image and Interaction in a Canadian Plains Community*. Stanford: Stanford University Press.

Brodhead, D. 1990 *Development Indicators in the Context of Aboriginal Development—An Overview.* Ottawa: Prepared for Indian and Northern Affairs Canada by E. T. Jackson and Associates Ltd.

Brody, Hugh 1971 *Indians on Skid Row: The Role of Alcohol and Community in the Adaptive Process of Indian and Urban Migrants*. Ottawa: Northern Science Research Group, Department of Indian Affairs and Northern Development. Information Canada.

_____ **1987** *Living Arctic*. Vancouver: Douglas and McIntyre.

_____ **2003**. *Inuits, Indiens, chasseurs-cueilleurs: les exiles de l'Eden*. Monaco: Editions du Rocher.

Brown, Dee 1971 *Bury My Heart at Wounded Knee*. New York: Holt, Rinehart and Winston.

Brown, J. 1980 *Stronger in Blood: Fur Trade Company Families in Indian Country.*

Vancouver, University of British Columbia Press.

Brown, J. and E. Vibert (eds.) 2003 *Reading beyond Words: Contexts for Native History.* Peterborough ON: Broadview Books.

Brown, W.C. 1935 "Racial Conflict among South African Natives." *American Journal of Sociology*, 40: 569–681.

Brownlie, R. 2006 "A Better Citizen than Lots of White Men: First Nations Enfranchisement," *Canadian Historical Review*, 87 (1): 29–52.

Brunnen, B. 2003 *Achieving Potential: Towards Improved Labour Market Outcomes for Aboriginal People*, Report # 19. Calgary: Canada West Foundation.

Brzozowski, J., A. Taylor-Butts and S. Johnson 2006 "Victimization and Offending among the Aboriginal Population in Canada." *Juristat*, 26 (3). Ottawa: Statistics Canada.

Buckley, H. 1992 *From Wooden Ploughs to Welfare.* Montreal and Kingston: McGill-Queens University Press.

Burch, E. 2004 "The Caribou Inuit." In B. Morrison and R. Wilson (eds), *Native Peoples.* Toronto: Oxford University Press, pp. 74–95.

Burkhardt, K. 2004 *Crime, Cultural Reintegration and Community Healing: Narratives of an Inuit Community.* Ph.D. dissertation, University of Windsor.

Cairns, Alan C. 2000 *Citizens Plus: Aboriginal People and the Canadian State.* Vancouver: University of British Columbia Press.

Cairns, A. 2005 *First Nations and the Canadian State.* Queens University, Institute of Intergovernmental Relations.

Cajete, G. 2000 *Native Science: Natural Laws of Interdependence.* Santa Fe, NM: Clear Light Publishers.

Calder, W. 1986 "The Provinces and Indian Self Government in the Constitutional Forum." In *Indian–Provincial Government Relationship*, M. Boldt, J. Long, and L. Little Bear (eds.). Lethbridge AB: University of Lethbridge.

Caldwell, G. 1967. *Indian Residential Schools.* Ottawa: Department of Indian Affairs and Northern Development.

Campbell, John and Alan Rew 1999 *Identity and Affect: Experiences of Identity in a Globalizing World.* London: Pluto Press.

Campbell, R. and L. Pal 1991 *The Real Worlds of Canadian Politics.* Peterborough ON: Broadview Press.

Canada, Government of 1966–70 *Annual Reports: 1966–67; 1968–69; 1969–70.* Department of Indian Affairs and Northern Development. Ottawa: Queen's Printer.

_____ **1969** *Statement of the Government of Canada on Policy, 1969* (White Paper). Ottawa: Queen's Printer.

_____ **1973** *Report of Task Force: Policing on Reserves.* Edmonton: Department of Indian and Northern Affairs.

_____ **1974** *Perspective Canada I.* Ottawa: Information Canada.

_____ **1977** *Perspective Canada II.* Ottawa: Statistics Canada, Supply and Services.

_____ **1978a** *A Recommended Plan for Evaluation in Indian Education.* Ottawa: IIAP, Department of Indian Affairs and Northern Development, Program Evaluation Branch.

_____ **1978b** *Evaluation of the RCMP Indian Special Constable Program (Option 3B).* Ottawa: IIAP, Evaluation Branch, Department of Indian Affairs and Northern Development, March 1978b.

_____ **1978c** *Indian Affairs and Northern Development Business Loan Fund: Indian Economic Development Direct Loan Order Policy and Guidelines.* Ottawa: Department of Indian Affairs and Northern Development, Loan Fund Division.

_____ **1979a** *Perspective Canada III.* Ottawa: Statistics Canada, Supply and Services.

_____ **1979b** *Social Assistance and Related Social Development Programs of the Department of Indian and Northern Affairs.* Ottawa: IIAP, Department of Indian Affairs and Northern Development.

_____ **1980** *Indian Conditions, A Survey.* Ottawa: Department of Indian Affairs and Northern Development.

_____ **1981** *In All Fairness: A Native Claims Policy.* Ottawa: Minister of Supply and Services.

_____ **1982** *Population, Repartition geographique—Terre-Neuve.* Recensement du Canada, 1981. Ottawa: Statistique Canada (Catalogue 93–901).

_____ **1983** *The Report of the House of Commons Special Committee on Indian Self-Government* (The Penner Report). Ottawa: Minister of Supply and Services Canada.

_____ **1984** *Response of the Government to the Report of the Special Committee on Indian Self-Government* (reply to the Penner Report). Ottawa.

_____ **1985a** *Living Treaties: Lasting Agreements*. Report of the Task Force to Review Comprehensive Claims Policy. Ottawa: DIAND.

_____ **1985b** *Indian and Native Programs*. A Study Team Report to the Task Force on Program Review. Ottawa: Minister of Supply and Services.

_____ **1988** *Census Metropolitan Areas, Dimensions*, Ottawa: Supply and Services.

_____ **1989** *The Canadian Aboriginal Economic Development Strategy*. Ottawa: Indian and Northern Affairs Canada.

_____ **1990** *Annual Report, 1989–90*, Department of Indian Affairs and Northern Development. Ottawa: Minister of Supply and Services.

_____ **1991** *Language, Tradition, Health, Lifestyle and Social Issues*. Ottawa: Statistics Canada (Catalogue 89-533), (1991): 52,102.

_____ **1996a** *Looking Forward, Looking Back. Royal Commission on Aboriginal Peoples*. Ottawa: Minister of Supply and Services.

_____ **1996b** *Restructuring the Relationship*. Royal Commission on Aboriginal Peoples. Ottawa: Minister of Supply and Services.

_____ **1996c** *Soliloquy and Dialogue: Overview of Major Trends in Public Policy relating to Aboriginal Peoples*. From the series "Public Policy and Aboriginal Peoples" 1965–1992, Volume 1. Royal Commission on Aboriginal Peoples, Canada Communication Group: Ottawa.

_____ **1996d** *Report of the Royal Commission on Aboriginal Peoples*, Ottawa: Canada Communications Group-Publishing.

_____ **1998** *Gathering Strength: Canada Aboriginal Action Plan*. Ottawa: Ministry of Supply and Services.

_____ **1999a** *From Restorative Justice to Transformative Justice*. Ottawa: Law Commission of Canada.

_____**1999b** *A Second Diagnostic on the Health of First Nations and Inuit People in Canada*, November. Ottawa: Health Canada.

_____**2000** *Diabetes Among First Nations People*. Ottawa: Statistics Canada, Medical Services Branch, Health Canada.

_____**2001** *Statistical Profile on the Health of First Nations in Canada*. Ottawa: Health Canada.

_____**2003** *Registered Indian Population by Sex and Residence 2002*. Ottawa: Indian Affairs and Northern Development, Public Works and Government Services Canada.

_____ **n.d.** *Indian Claims in Canada/Revendications des Indiens au Canada*. Toronto: Clarke, Irwin and Co. Ltd.

Canadian Arctic Resources Committee 2004 "An Inuit Response: Tungevik Federation of Nunavut." www.carac.org/pubs/v17no1/4.htm.

Canadian Indian Resource Corporation 1990 *Long Term Strategic Plan*. 34 pp.

Canadian Superintendent 1965 *The Education of Indian Children in Canada*. Toronto: Ryerson Press.

Cantryn, M. (n.d.) "Evaluation—Native Women's Program." Ottawa: Secretary of State.

Cardinal, H. 1969 *The Unjust Society*. Edmonton: Hurtig Publishers

_____ **1977** *The Rebirth of Canada's Indians*. Edmonton: Hurtig Publishers.

_____ **1979** "Native Women and the Indian Act." In *Two Nations, Many Cultures*, J. Elliott (ed.), pp. 44–50. Scarborough: Prentice Hall Canada.

_____ **1986** "Constitutional Change and the Treaty 8 Renovation." In *Indian–Provincial Relations*, M. Boldt, J.A. Long and L. Little Bear (eds.). Lethbridge: The University of Lethbridge.

Carley, M. 1981 *Social Measurement and Social Indicators: Issues of Policy and Theory*. London: George Allen and Unwin.

Carrothers Commission 1967 *Advisory Commission on the Development of Government in the Northwest Territories*. Ottawa: Minister of Supply and Services.

Carstens, P. 1991 *The Queen's People*, Toronto: University of Toronto Press.

Carter, S. 1990 *Lost Harvests*. Montreal and Kingston: McGill-Queen's University Press.

_____**1999** *Aboriginal People and Colonizers of Western Canada to 1900*. Toronto: University of Toronto Press.

Cassidy, F. and R. Bish 1989 *Indian Government: Its Meaning and Practice*. Halifax: Institute for Research on Public Policy.

Castellano, Marlene 1970 "Vocation or Identity: The Dilemma of Indian Youth." In *The Only*

Good Indian, Waubageshig (ed.). Toronto: New Press.

Cawsey, Justice R. 1991 *Justice on Trial*, Vol. 1, Report of the Task Force on the Criminal Justice System and its Impact on the Indian and Métis People of Alberta. Edmonton: Attorney General of Alberta.

Chance, Norman 1970 *Development Change among the Cree Indians of Quebec*. Ottawa: Summary Report, ARDA Project 34002 (Reprint 1970), Department of Regional Economic Expansion.

Chapman, L. 1972 *Women's Rights and Special Status for Indians: Some Implications of the* Lavell Case. Ottawa: Carleton University, n.p.

Charlebois, P. 1975 *The Life of Louis Riel.* Toronto: N.C. Press.

Chartier, C. 1988 *In the Best Interest of the Métis Child.* Saskatoon, Saskatchewan: Native Law Centre.

Chartrand, P. 1993 "Aboriginal Rights: The Dispossession of the Métis." *Osgoode Hall Law Journal*, 29: 425–467.

Chartrand, L. 1999/2000 "Are We Métis or Are We Indians? A Commentary on *R. v. Grumbo*," *Ottawa Law Review*, 31, 267–281.

Chartrand, P. (ed) 2002 *Who Are Canada's Aboriginal Peoples?* Saskatoon: Purich Publishing.

Chartrand, P. and S. Giokas 2002 "Defining 'The Metis People': The Hard Case of Canadian Aboriginal Law." In P. Chartrand (ed), *Who are Canada's Aboriginal Peoples?* Saskatoon, Purich Publishing, pp 157–186.

Cheda, S. 1977 "Indian Women: An Historical Example and a Contemporary View." In *Women in Canada,* M. Stephenson (ed.). Don Mills: General Publishing, pp. 195–208.

Chrétien, J. 1969 "Indian Policy... Where Does It Stand?" Speech at Empire Club, Toronto, October 16, 1969.

Churchill, W. 1999 *Struggle for the Land.* Winnipeg: Arbeiter Ring.

Clark, M. 1999 *Tuberculosis in First Nations Communities, 1999.* Ottawa: Minister of Health, Public Works and Government Services Canada.

Clark, T. 1994 Lonewolf *vs.* Hitchcock*: Treaty Rights and Indian Law at the End of the Nineteenth Century.* Lincoln: University of Nebraska Press.

Clatworthy, S. 1996 *The Migration and Mobility Patterns of Canada's Aboriginal Population*. Ottawa: Report for the Royal Commission on Aboriginal Peoples

_____ **2000** *Re-assessing the Population Impacts of Bill C-31.* Ottawa: Research and Analysis Directorate, Indian and Northern Affairs Canada.

_____ **2001** *Registered Indian Migration between On- and Off-Reserve Locations, 1986–1996.* Winnipeg: Four Directions Project Consultants.

_____ **2003** "Impacts of the 1985 Amendments to the Indian Act on First Nations Populations." In *Aboriginal Conditions: Research as a Foundation for Public Policy,* J. White, P. Maxim and D. Beavon (eds), Vancouver: University of British Columbia Press.

_____ **2004** "Registration and Membership: Implications for First Nations Communities," presentation at Congress, Winnipeg.

Clatworthy, S. and M. Cooke 2001 *Reasons for Registered Indian Migration.* Report prepared by Four Directions project consultants for the Research and Analysis Directorate. Ottawa: Department of Indian Affairs and Northern Development.

Clement, W. and G. Williams 1989 "Introduction." *The New Canadian Political Economy*, W. Clement and G. Williams (eds.). Kingston ON: McGill-Queen's University Press.

Coates, K. 1991 *Best Left as Indians: Native–White Relations in the Yukon Territory, 1840–1973.* Montreal: McGill-Queen's University Press.

_____ **2000** *The Marshall Decision and Native Rights.* Montreal and Kingston: McGill-Queen's University Press.

Coates, K. and W. Morrison 1986 "More Than a Matter of Blood: The Federal Government, The Churches and the Mixed Blood Populations of the Yukon and the Mackenzie River Valley, 1890–1950." In *1885 and After*, F. Barron and J. Waldham (eds.). Regina: Canadian Plains Research Centre (1986): 253–277.

Coffey, W. and M. Polese 1985 "Local Development: Conceptual Bases and Policy Implications." *Regional Studies* 19 (2): 85–93.

Cole, C. 1939 *Colbert and a Century of French Mercantilism.* 2 vols., New York: Columbia University Press.

Cook, Curtis and Juan Lindau (eds.) 2000 *Aboriginal Rights and Self-Government.* Montreal and Kingston: McGill-Queen's University Press.

Cooke, M. 2002 "The Effects of Personal Characteristics on Migration from Prairie Cities to First Nations." *Canadian Ethnic Studies*, 34 (2): 40–62.

Cornell, S. 1988 *The Return of the Native.* New York: Oxford University Press.

Cornell, S. 2000. Evidence presented to the Standing Committee on Aboriginal Affairs and Northern Development, June 6.

Cornell, S. 2005 "Indigenous Peoples, Poverty and Self-Determination in Australia, New Zealand, Canada and the United States." In *Indigenous Peoples and Poverty*, R. Eversole, J.A. Mcneish, and A. Cimadamore (eds). London: Zed Books, pp. 199–226.

Cornell, S. and J. Kalt 1992 "Reloading the Dice: Improving the Economic Development on American Indian Reservations." In *What Can Tribes Do? Structure and Institutions in American Indian Economic Development*, S. Cornell and J. Kalt (eds.). Los Angeles: American Indian Studies Center, University of California.

Corporation for Enterprise Development 1987 *Making the Grade: The Development Report Card for the States.* Washington, D.C.

Correctional Service Canada 1999 *Facts and Figures.* Ottawa: Aboriginal Initiatives Branch, Correctional Service Canada.

Corrigan, S. 1970 "The Plains Indian Pow-wow: Cultural Integration in Manitoba and Saskatchewan." *Anthropologica*, 12 (2): 253–271.

Courchene, T. and L. Powell 1992 *A First Nations Province.* Kingston ON: Queen's University Institute of Intergovernmental Relations.

Crowe, K. 1974 *A History of the Original Peoples of Northern Canada.* Arctic Institute of North America. Montreal: McGill-Queen's University Press.

Culhane, Dara 1998 *The Pleasure of the Crown: Anthropology, Law and First Nations.* Vancouver: Talonbooks.

Cultural Survival Quarterly *World Report on the Rights of Indigenous Peoples and Ethnic Minorities.* Cambridge, MA: Cultural Survival. [Volumes 1– to date]

Cumming, P. 1967 "Public Lands, Native Land Claims and Land Use." In *Canadian Public Land Use in Perspective*, J. Nelson, R. Scace, and R. Kouri (eds.). Proceedings of a symposium sponsored by the Social Science Research Council of Canada, Ottawa, (1967): 206–238.

_____ **1973a** "Our Land—Our People: Native Rights, North of 60." In *Arctic Alternatives*, D. Pimlott, K. Vincent and C. McKnight (eds.). Ottawa: Canadian Arctic Resources Committee.

_____ **1973b** "Native Rights and Law in an Age of Protest." *Alberta Law Review* (1973b): 230–245.

Cumming, P., and N. Mickenberg 1972 *Native Rights in Canada*, 2nd ed. Toronto: Indian–Eskimo Association of Canada.

Dahl, J. 1997 "Gender Parity in Nunavut." *Indigenous Affairs*, 3–4: 42–47.

Dalon, R. 1985 "An Alberta Perspective on Aboriginal Peoples and The Constitution." In *The Quest for Justice*, M. Boldt, J.A. Long, and L. Little Bear (eds.). Toronto: University of Toronto Press.

D'Anglure, B. 1984 "Inuit of Quebec." *Handbook of North American Indians*, vol. 5 *Arctic*, D. Damas (ed.). Washington: Smithsonian Institute, (1984): 476–507.

Daniel, R. 1980 *A History of Native Claims Processes in Canada, 1867–1979*. Ottawa: Research Branch, Department of Indian Affairs and Northern Development.

Daniels, H. 1981 *Native People and the Constitution of Canada*. Ottawa: Mutual Press.

Daughtery, W. 1978 *Discussion Report on Indian Taxation*. Ottawa: Department of Indian and Northern Affairs, Treaties and Historical Research Centre.

_____ **1982** *A Guide to Native Political Associations in Canada*. Treaties and Historical Research, Research Branch, Corporate Policy. Ottawa: Department of Indian and Northern Affairs.

Daugherty, Wayne and Dennis Magill 1980 *Indian Government under Indian Act Legislation, 1868–1951*. Ottawa: Research Branch, Department of Indian and Northern Affairs.

Davies, M. 1985 "Aspects of Aboriginal Rights in International Law." In *Aboriginal Peoples and the Law*, B. Morse (ed.). Ottawa: Carleton University Press, pp.16–47.

Deane, L., L. Morrissette, S. Bruyere, and J. Bosquet 2004. "Explorations in Urban Aboriginal Neighbourhood Development." *The Canadian Journal of Native Studies* 24 (2): 227–252.

Delgamuukw vs. Her Majesty the Queen in Right of the Province of British Columbia 1997 Supreme Court of Canada Decision, File No. 23799, December 11,.

Delisle, H. and J. Ekoe 1993 "Prevalence of Non-Insulin Dependent Diabetes Mellitus and Impaired Glucose Tolerance in Two Algonquin Communities in Quebec." *Canadian Medical Association Journal*, 149: 41–47.

Delmar, R. 1986 "What Is Feminism?" In *What Is Feminism?* J. Mitchell and A. Oakley (eds.). Oxford: Basil Blackwell, pp. 8–33.

Deloria, V. and C. Lytle 1984 *The Nations Within: The Past and Future of American Indian Sovereignty*. New York: Pantheon Books.

Denis, Claude 1997 *We Are Not You: First Nations and Canadian Modernity*. Peterborough ON: Broadview Press.

Denton, T. 1972 "Migration from a Canadian Indian Reserve." *Journal of Canadian Studies*, 7: 54–62.

Deprez, Paul and Glen Sigurdson 1969 *Economic Status of the Canadian Indian: A Re-Examination*. Winnipeg: Centre for Settlement Studies, University of Manitoba.

DIAND (Department of Indian Affairs and Northern Development) 1969 *Statement of the Government of Canada on Indian Policy*. Ottawa: Queen's Printer.

_____ **1978** *Native Claims: Policy, Processes and Perspectives*. Ottawa: Queen's Printer.

_____ **1980** *Indian Conditions. A Survey*. Ottawa: Minister of Supply and Services.

_____ **1980-81** *Annual Report*. Ottawa: Minister of Supply and Services.

_____ **1981** *In All Fairness: A Native Claims Policy*. Ottawa: Queen's Printer.

_____ **1982a** *Outstanding Business: A Native Claims Policy*. Ottawa: Minister of Supply and Services.

_____ **1982b** *James Bay and Northern Quebec Agreement Implementation Review*. Ottawa: Minister of Supply and Services.

_____ **1982c** *Strengthening Indian Band Government in Canada*. Ottawa: Minister of Indian Affairs and Northern Development. Ottawa, c. 1982c.

_____ **1982d** *An Optional System of Indian Band Government*. Ottawa: Minister of Indian Affairs and Northern Development. Ottawa, d, 1982d.

_____ **1982e** "The Legislation Proposals." *Annex I*. Ottawa: Minister of Supply and Services, c. 1982e.

_____ **1982f** "Financial Considerations—The Funding System." *Annex II*. Ottawa: Minister of Supply and Services, c. 1982f.

_____ **1982g** "Appendix VI: Pick up of Provincial Program Costs." Ottawa: Mimeographed, c. 1982g.

_____ **1982h** *The Alternative of Optional Indian Band Government Legislation*. Ottawa: Minister of Indian Affairs and Northern Development.

_____ **1984** House of Commons. *Indian Self-Government in Canada: Report of the Special Committee*, Ottawa.

_____ **1985** *Living Treaties: Lasting Agreements. Report of the Task Force to Review Comprehensive Claims Policy*. Ottawa: Department of Indian Affairs and Northern Development.

_____ **1986** *Coolican Report*. Ottawa: Department of Indian Affairs and Northern Development.

_____ **2006** *Registered Indian Population by Sex and Residence, 2005*. First Nations and Northern Statistics Section. Ottawa: Public Works and Government Services Canada.

Dickason, Olive 1992 *Canada's First Nations: A History of Founding Peoples from Earliest Times*. Norman: University of Oklahoma Press.

_____ **2002** *Canada's First Nations*. Don Mills, ON: Oxford University Press.

Dickerson, M. 1993 *Whose North?* Calgary and Vancouver: The Arctic Institute of North America and the University of British Columbia Press.

Dickinson, H. and B. Bolaria 1992 "Expansion and Survival: Canadian Sociology and the Development of the Canadian Nation." In *Handbook of Contemporary Developments in World Society*, 2nd ed., R. Mohan and D. Martindale (eds.). New York: Greenwood Press.

Dobbin, Murray 1981 *The One-And-A-Half Men: The Story of Jim Brady and Malcolm*

Norris, Métis Patriots of the 20th Century. Vancouver: New Star Books.

Dobyns, H. **1983**. *Their Number Become Thinned.* Knoxville: University of Tennessee Press.

Dockstator, M. **2005** "Aboriginal Representation of History and the Royal Commission on Aboriginal Peoples." In *Walking a Tightrope: Aboriginal People and Their Representation,* U. Lischke and D. McNab (eds). Waterloo ON: Wilfrid Laurier University Press.

Doerr, A.D. **1974** "Indian Policy." In *Issues in Canadian Public Policy,* G.S. Doern and V.S. Wilson (eds.). Toronto: Macmillan.

Dorais, Louis-Jacques **1992** "La situation linguistique dans l'Arctique." *Etudes/Inuit/Studies,* 16 (1–2): 237–255.

_____ **1997** *Quaqtaq: Modernity and Identity in an Inuit Community.* Toronto: University of Toronto Press.

Dorais J. and D. Kryupnik **2005**. "Comparing Academic and Aboriginal Definitions of Arctic Identities," *Polar Record,* 41 (216): 1–10.

Dosman, Edgar **1972** *Indians: The Urban Dilemma.* Toronto: McClelland and Stewart.

Driben, Paul **1975** *We Are Métis.* Ph.D. dissertation. Minneapolis: University of Minnesota.

_____**1983** "The Nature of Métis Claims." *The Canadian Journal of Native Studies,* 3 (1): 183–196.

Drucker, P. **1958** *The Native Brotherhoods: Modern Intertribal Organizations on the Northwest Coast.* Bureau of American Ethnology, 168. Washington DC: Smithsonian Institution.

Dubois, W. **1940** *Dusk of Dawn.* New York: Harcourt, Brace.

Duclos, N. **1990** "Lessons of Difference: Feminist Theory on Cultural Diversity." In *Buffalo Law Review,* 38 (2), 325–381.

Duff R. **1997** *The Indian History of British Columbia.* Revised ed. Victoria: Royal British Columbia Museum.

Duffy, R.Q. **1988** *The Road to Nunavut.* Kingston and Montreal: McGill-Queen's University Press.

Duhaime, G. **1992** "Le chasseur et le minotaure: Itineraire de l'autonomie politique au Nunavut," *Etudes/Inuit/Studies,* 16 (1–2): 149–177.

_____ **1993** *The Governing of Nunavut: Who Pays for What?* Universite Laval, Groupe d'etudes Inuit et circumpolaires.

Duhaime, G., E. Searles, P. Usher, H. Myers, and P. Frechette **2003** "Social Cohesion and Living Conditions in the Canadian Arctic: From Theory to Measurement," *Social Indicators Research,* 61: 1–23.

Dunning, R. **1972** "The Indian Situation: A Canadian Government Dilemma." *International Journal of Comparative Sociology,* 12 (June): 128–134.

_____ **1976** "Some Speculations on the Canadian Indian Socio-Political Reality." In *The Patterns of 'Amerindian' Identity,* Marc-Adelard Tremblay (ed.). Quebec: Les Presses de l'Université Laval.

Dupuis, R. and K. McNeil **1995** *Canada's Fiduciary Obligation to Aboriginal Peoples in the Context of Accession to Sovereignty by Quebec,* Vol. 2, Ottawa, Minister of Supply and Services.

Dybbroe, S. **1996** "Questions of Identity and Issues of Self-Determination." *Etudes/Inuit/Studies,* 20 (2): 39–53.

Dyck, Noel **1979** "Pow-wow and the Expression of Community in Western Canada." *Ethnos,* 1–2: 78–79.

_____ **1981** "The Politics of Special Status: Indian Associations and the Administration of Indian Affairs." In *Ethnicity and Politics in Canada,* J. Dahlie and T. Fernando (eds.). Agincourt ON: Methuen Publications.

_____ **1990** "Cultures, Communities and Claims: Anthropology and Native Studies in Canada." *Canadian Ethnic Studies,* 22 (3), 40–55.

_____ **1991** *What Is the Indian "Problem?* Memorial University of Newfoundland, Institute of Social and Economic Research.

_____ **1996** "Tutelage, Resistance and Co-optation in Canadian Indian Administration." *Canadian Review of Sociology and Anthropology,* 34 (3): 333–348.

Dyck, Noel and James Waldram **1993** *Anthropology, Public Policy and Native Peoples in Canada.* Montreal: McGill-Queen's University Press.

Eberts, M. **1985** "The Use of Litigation under the Canadian Charter of Rights and Freedoms as a Strategy for Achieving Change." In Nevitte, N. and A. Kornberg (eds.), *Minorities and the Canadian State.* Oakville ON: Mosaic Press, pp. 53–70.

Elias, D. **1976** "Indian Politics in the Canadian Political System." In *The Patterns of*

'Amerindian' Identity, Marc-Adelard Tremblay (ed.). Quebec: Les Presses de l'Université Laval (1976): 35–64.

Elias, P. 1991 *Development of Aboriginal People's Communities*. Toronto: York University, Captus Press.

Ellerby, L. 1995 "Community-Based Treatment of Aboriginal Sex Offenders: Facing Realities and Exploring Possibilities." *Forum on Corrections Research,* 6 (3): 23–25.

Elliott, D. 1971 *Minority Canadians: Native Peoples*. Scarborough, Ontario: Prentice Hall Canada.

_____ 1980 "Native People, Power and Politics." *Multiculturalism*, 3, 3 (1980): 10–74.

_____1991 "Aboriginal Title." In *Aboriginal Peoples and the Law*, B. Morse (ed.). Ottawa: Carleton University Press, pp. 48–121.

Englestad D. and J. Bird 1993 *Nation-To-Nation: Aboriginal Sovereignty and the Future of Canada.* Toronto: Anansi Press.

English, V. 1995 "Poverty and Native Women." In *Freedom within the Margins*, C. Pizanias and J. Frideres (eds.). Calgary: Detselig Enterprises, pp. 111–118.

Enloe, C. 1981 "The Growth of the State and Ethnic Mobilization: The American Experience." *Ethnic and Racial Studies,* 4 (2): 123–136.

Ens, Gerhard 1996 *Homeland to Hinterland: The Changing Worlds of the Red River Métis in the Nineteenth Century.* Toronto: University of Toronto Press.

Epprecht, N. 2000 "Programs for Aboriginal Offenders: A National Survey." *Forum,* 12 (1): 45–47.

Eschbach, K., K. Supple, and M. Snipp 1998 "Changes in Racial Identification and the Educational Attainment of American Indians, 1970–1990." *Demography,* 35 (1): 35–44.

Ewing Commission Report 1935 *Royal Commission on the Conditions of the Halfbreed Population of the Province of Alberta Report, 1935*. Sessional Paper No. 72.

Faulkner, C. 1992 "Inuit Offenders., In *Aboriginal Peoples and Canadian Criminal Justice*, by R. Silverman and M. Nielsen (eds.). Toronto: Butterworths.

Federation of Saskatchewan Indian Nations 1985 Memo from Chief Sol Sanderson re: Section 122 of the *BNA Act* and the Bilateral Process, Prince Albert, Saskatchewan.

Federation of Saskatchewan Indians 1977 *Indian Government: A Position Paper*. Prince Albert SK.

_____ 1978 *Off-Band Members in Saskatchewan*. Mimeographed. Saskatoon.

Fenge, T. 1992 "Political Development and Environmental Management in Northern Canada: The Case of the Nunavut Agreement." *Etudes/Inuit/Studies,* 16 (1–2): 115–141.

Fidler, Dick 1970 *Red Power in Canada*. Toronto: Vanguard Publications.

Fields, D. and W. Stanbury 1975 *The Economic Impact of the Public Sector upon the Indian of British Columbia*. Vancouver: University of British Columbia Press.

Fine, Sean 1989 "Near 1 in 4 Family Murders Among Natives, Study Says." *The Globe and Mail*, October 4. Toronto.

First Nations Centre National Aboriginal Health Organization 2004. *Preliminary Findings of the First Nations Regional Longitudinal Health Survey.* Ottawa: National Aboriginal Health Organization.

First Nations Resource Council 1990 *Socio-Economic/Quality of Life Indicators Symposium,* May 31 Report. 13 pps. Edmonton.

Fisher, A.D. 1969 "White Rites versus Indian Rights." *Transaction*, 7 (November) : 29–33.

Fisher, R. 1977 *Contact and Conflict: Indian–European Relations in British Columbia, 1774–1890*. Vancouver: University of British Columbia Press.

Flanagan, T. 1983a "The Case against Métis Aboriginal Rights." *Canadian Public Policy*, 9: 314–315.

_____ 1983b *Riel and the Rebellion: 1885 Reconsidered*. Saskatoon: Western Producer Prairie Books.

_____ 1985 "Métis Aboriginal Rights: Some Historical and Contemporary Problems." In *The Quest for Justice*, M. Boldt, J. Long and L. Little Bear (eds.). Toronto: University of Toronto Press.

_____ 1990 "The History of Métis Aboriginal Rights: Politics, Principle and Policy." *Canadian Journal of Law and Society*, 5, 71–94.

_____ 2000 *First Nations? Second Thoughts*. Montreal–Kingston: McGill-Queens University Press.

Fleming-Mathur, M. 1971 "Who Cares That a Woman's Work Is Never Done?" In *Indian Historian*, 4 (2), 11–15.

Fleras, A. and J. L. Elliott 1992 *The Nations Within: Aboriginal–State Relations in Canada, United States, and New Zealand.* Don Mills, ON: Oxford University Press.

Fleras, A. and R. Maaka 2000 "Reconstitutionalizing Indigeneity: Restoring the Sovereigns Within." *Canadian Review of Studies in Nationalism*, 27: 34–49.

Fletcher, C. 1992 *Altered States? Federalism, Sovereignty and Self Government, No. 22.* Australian National University, Federalism Research Centre.

Fontaine, P. 1998 "Aboriginal Peoples Making Giant Strides on Long Journey to Better Lives." *Canadian Speeches: Issues of the Day,* September, 32–34.

Fossett, R. 2001 *In Order to Live Untroubled: Inuit of the Central Arctic.* Winnipeg, University of Manitoba Press.

Foster, H. 1998–99 "Honouring the Queen: A Legal and Historical Perspective on the Nisga'a Treaty." *B.C. Studies,* 120: 5–11.

Foster, John E. 1976 "Mixed Bloods in Western Canada: An Ecological Approach" and "The Origins of the Mixed Bloods in the Canadian West." In *Essays on Western History*, Lewis H. Thomas (ed.). Edmonton: University of Alberta Press.

_____ **1978** "The Métis, the People and the Term." *Prairie Forum*, 3 (1 - Spring): 79–91.

Four Worlds Development Project 1985 *Towards the Year 2000.* Lethbridge AB: University of Lethbridge.

Francis, D. 1983 *A History of the Native Peoples of Quebec, 1760–1867.* Ottawa: Indian Affairs and Northern Development.

Frank, André Gunder 1967 *Capitalism and Underdevelopment in Latin America.* New York: Monthly Review Press.

Franklin, Raymond 1969 "The Political Economy of Black Power." *Social Problems*, 16 (Winter): 286–301.

Freeman, M. 1985 "Traditional and Contemporary Roles of Inuit Women." In *Association of Canadian Universities for Northern Studies, Social Science in the North: Communicating Northern Values.* Ottawa: ACUNS, pp. 57–60.

French, B.F. 1851 *Historical Collections of Louisiana.* Dublin: Arbers Annals.

Frideres, J.S. 1972 "Indians and Education: A Canadian Failure." *Manitoba Journal of Education*, 7 (June): 27–30.

_____ **1974** *Canada's Indians: Contemporary Conflicts.* Scarborough ON: Prentice Hall Canada.

_____ **1986** "Native Claims and Settlement in Yukon." In *Arduous Journey*, J.R. Ponting (ed.). Toronto: McClelland and Stewart: pp. 284–301.

Frideres, J. and B. Robertson 1994 "Aboriginals and the Criminal Justice System: Australia and Canada." *International Journal of Contemporary Sociology*, 31 (1): 1–27.

Frideres, J. and W. Reeves 1981 "Government Policy and Indian Urbanization: The Alberta Case." *Canadian Public Policy*, 7 (4): 584–595.

Frideres, J. and J. Ryan 1980 *Program Evaluation of the Calgary Native Outreach Office.* Unpublished report. Calgary: University of Calgary.

Fuchs, Estelle 1970 "Time to Redeem an Old Promise." *Saturday Review* (January 24): 53–58.

Fullwinder, S. 1969 *The Mind and Mood of Black America.* Homewood IL: Dorsey Press.

Furniss, E. 2000 *Victims of Benevolence,* Vancouver: Arsenal Pulp Press.

Gadacz, René 1991 "Community Socio-Economic Development from a Plains Indian Perspective: A Proposed Social Indicator System and Planning Tool." *Native Studies Review*, 7 (1): 53–80.

_____ **1999** "Aboriginal and Quebec Self-Determination under an MAI Regime." *Native Studies Review* 12 (2): 93–110.

_____ **2000** *The Canadian Encyclopedia 2000,* World Edition. Toronto: McClelland and Stewart.

Gadacz, René and N. McBlane 1999 "Aboriginal Peoples and National Rights Issues in Quebec." Special Issue of the *Native Studies Review,* 12 (2). University of Saskatchewan.

Gamson, W. 1969 *Power and Discontent.* Homewood IL: Dorsey Press.

_____ **1980** "The Development of Canadian Indian Communities: A Two-Dimensional Typology Reflecting Strategies of Adaptation to the Modern World." *The Canadian Review of Sociology and Anthropology*, 16 (4): 126–134.

George, M., S. Loh, R. Verma and E. Shin 2001 *Population Projections for Canada, Provinces and Territories, 2000-2026.* Ottawa: Statistics Canada.

Gerber, L. 1977 "Community Characteristics and Out-Migration from Indian Communities: Regional Trends." Paper presented at Department of Indian Affairs and Northern Development, Ottawa, November 9, 1977.

_____ **1980** "The Development of Canadian Indian Communities: A Two-Dimensional Typology Reflecting Strategies of Adaptation to the Modern World." *The Canadian Review of Sociology and Anthropology,*16, (4): 126–134.

_____ **1990** "Multiple Jeopardy: A Socio-Economic Comparison of Men and Women among the Indian, Métis and Inuit Peoples of Canada." *Canadian Ethnic Studies*, 22 (3), 69–84.

Gibbins, R. 1986a "Canadian Indians and the Canadian Constitution: A Difficult Passage toward an Uncertain Destination." In *Arduous Journey*, J.R. Ponting (ed.). Toronto: McClelland and Stewart.

_____ **1986b** "Citizenship, Political and Intergovernmental Problems with Indian Self Government." In *Arduous Journey*, J.R. Ponting (ed.). Toronto: McClelland and Stewart.

Gibbins, R. and J.R. Ponting 1984 "Prairie Canadians' Orientations towards Indians." *Prairie Forum*, 2 (1): 57–81.

_____ **1986** "An Assessment of the Probable Impact of Aboriginal Self Government in Canada." In *The Politics of Gender, Ethnicity and Language in Canada*, A. Cairns and C. Williams (eds.). Vol. 34. Research Studies of the Royal Commission on the Economic Union and Development Prospects for Canada. Toronto: University of Toronto Press.

Gibson, D. 2002 "When Is a Métis an Indian? Some Consequences of Federal Constitutional Jurisdiction over Métis." In *Who are Canada's Aboriginal Peoples?* P. Chartrand (ed). Saskatoon: Purich Publishing, pp. 258–268.

Gibson, G. 1998–99 "Comments on the Draft Nisga'a Treaty." *B.C. Studies,* 120: 55–72.

Giokas, J. and P. Chartrand 2002 "Who Are the Métis? A Review of the Law and Policy." In *Who are Canada's Aboriginal People?* P.

Chartrand (ed.). Saskatoon: Purich Publishing.

Giokas, J. and R. Groves 2002 "Collective and Individual Recognition in Canada." In *Who are Canada's Aboriginal People?* P. Chartrand (ed.). Saskatoon: Purich Publishing, pp. 41–82

Girvan, N. 1973 "The Development of Dependency Economics in the Caribbean and Latin America." *Social and Economic Studies*, 22: 1–33.

Gombay, N. 2000 "The Politics of Culture: Gender Parity in the Legislative Assembly of Nunavut." *Etudes/Inuit/Studies*, 24 (1): 125–148.

_____ **2005.** "Shifting Identities in a Shifting World: Food, Place, Community and the Politics of Scale in an Inuit Settlement. " *Environment and Planning Society and Space*, 23 (3): 415–433.

Grand Council of the Crees 1998 *Never Without Consent: James Bay Crees' Stand against Forcible Inclusion into an Independent Quebec.*

Grand Council Treaty No. 9 n.d. *A Declaration by the Ojibway–Crees Nation of Treaty No. 9 to the People of Canada.*

Grant, A. 1996 *No End of Grief: Indian Residential Schools in Canada.* Winnipeg: Pemmican Publications.

Green, C., J. Blanchard, A. Wajda, N. Depew, C. Cooke, L. Brazeau, S. Martel and C. Menard 1997 "Projecting Future Diabetes Prevalence in Manitoba First Nations," 4th International Conference on Diabetes and Aboriginal People, San Diego.

Green, L. 1983 "Aboriginal Peoples, International Law and the Canadian Charter of Rights and Freedoms." *The Canadian Bar Review*, 61, 339–353.

Green, R. and K. Healy 2003 *Tough on Kids: Rethinking Approaches to Youth Justice.* Saskatoon: Purich Publishers.

Groves, R. and B. Morse 2004 "Constituting Aboriginal Collectivities: Avoiding New Peoples 'In Between,'" *Saskatchewan Law Review*, 67(1), 257–300.

Guillemin, J. 1975 *Urban Renegades—The Cultural Strategy of American Indians.* New York: Columbia University Press.

Hagan, J. 1974 "Criminal Justice and Native People: A Study of Incarceration in a Canadian Province." *Canadian Review of*

Sociology and Anthropology. Special issue (August): 220–236.

Hall, T. 1991 "Aboriginal Futures—Awakening Our Imagination." *Canadian Dimension,* July/August, 15–17.

Halvorson, K. 2005 *Indian Residential School Abuse Claims.* Toronto: Thomson Carswell.

Hamilton, E. 1984 "Rosing Wins Second Term—Arctic Policy Delayed." *Inuit Today*, Special edition. Iqaluit: Inuit Circumpolar Conference, (February): 6–7.

Hampton, E. 1993. "Toward a Redefinition of American Indian/Alaskan Native Education." *Canadian Journal of Native Education,* 20 (2): 14–23.

Hann R. and W. Harman 1993 "Predicting Release Risk for Aboriginal Penitentiary Inmates." Corrections Branch, Ministry of Solicitor General, User Report, 1993-21.

Hanselmann, C. 2001 *Urban Aboriginal People in Western Canada: Realities and Policies.* Calgary: Canada West Foundation.

_____ 2002. *Uncommon Sense: Promising Practices in Urban Aboriginal Policy-Making and Programming.* Calgary: Canada West Foundation.

Hanselmann, C. and R. Gibbins 2002 *Another Voice Is Needed: Intergovernmentalism in the Urban Aboriginal Context.* Paper presented at the Reconfiguring Aboriginal–State Relations in Canada Conference, Queens University, November.

Hanson, B., 1985 *Dual Realities—Dual Strategies: The Future Paths of the Aboriginal People's Development.* Saskatoon, privately printed.

Harper, A. 1947 "Canadian Indian Administration: The Treaty System." *America Indigena*, 7 (2): 129–140.

Harris, C. 2002 *Making Native Space: Colonialism, Resistance and Reserves in British Columbia.* Vancouver: University of British Columbia Press.

Harris, S., J. Gittelsohn, A. Hanley, A. Barnie, T. Woleer, J. Gao, A. Logan, and B. Zinman 1997 "The Prevalence of NIDDM and Associated Risk Factors in Native Canadians." *Diabetes Care*, 20: 185–187.

Harris, S., B. Zinman, A. Hanley, J. Gittelsohn, R. Hegele, P. Connely, B. Shah and J. Hux 2002 "The Impact of Diabetes on Cardiovascular Risk Factors and Outcomes in a Native Canadian Population." *Diabetes Research and Clinical Practice*, 55 : 165–173.

Harrison, G.S. 1972 "The Alaska Native Claims Settlement Act: 1971." *Arctic*, 25 (3): 232–233.

Harvey, S. 1996 "Two Models to Sovereignty: A Comparative History of the Mashantucket Pequot Tribal Nation and the Navajo Nation." *American Indian Culture and Research Journal*, 20 (1): 147–194.

Hatt, Fred K. 1969 "The Métis and Community Development in Northeastern Alberta." In *Perspectives on Regions and Regionalism and Other Papers*, B.Y. Card (ed.). Edmonton: University of Alberta, pp. 111–119.

_____ 1972 "The Canadian Métis: Recent Interpretations." *Canadian Ethnic Studies*, 3 (1): 23–26.

_____ 1982 "On Hold: A Review of *In All Fairness: A Native Claims Policy.*" *The Canadian Journal of Native Studies*, 2 (2): 352–355.

_____ 1983 "The Northwest Scrip Commissions as Federal Policy—Some Initial Findings." *The Canadian Journal of Native Studies*, 3 (1): 117–130.

Hawkes, D. 1985 *Aboriginal Self-Government.* Kingston, Ontario: Queen's University, Institute of Intergovernmental Relations.

Hawley, D. 1990 *1990 Indian Act*, Toronto: Carswell.

Hawthorn, H.B. 1966–67 *A Survey of the Contemporary Indians of Canada* ("Hawthorn Report"), 2 Vols. Indian Affairs Branch. Ottawa: Queen's Printer. Excerpts reproduced by permission of Information Canada.

Haysom, V. 1992 "The Struggle for Recognition: Labrador Inuit Negotiations for Land Rights and Self-Government." *Etudes/Inuit/Studies*, 16 (1–2): 179–197.

Health Canada 2000. Diabetes *Among Aboriginal People in Canada: The Evidence.* Ottawa: Minister of Public Works and Government Services Canada.

Health Canada 2003 *Health Policy Research Bulletin*, 1, 5.

Hedican, E. 1991 "On the Ethno-Politics of Canadian Native Leadership and Identity." *Ethnic Groups*, 9: 1–15.

_____ 1995 *Applied Anthropology in Canada: Understanding Aboriginal Issues.* Toronto: University of Toronto Press.

Heilbrun, James and Stanislaw Wellisz 1969 "An Economic Program for the Ghetto." In *Urban Riots*, Robert Conner (ed.). New York: Random House.

Helm, J. 2000 *The People of Denendeh*. Montreal: McGill-Queen's University Press.

Henderson, J., M. Benson and I. Findlay 2000 *Aboriginal Tenure in the Constitution of Canada*. Scarborough ON: Carswell.

Henderson, J.Y. 1985 "The Doctrine of Aboriginal Rights in Western Legal Tradition." In *The Quest for Justice*, M. Boldt, J. Long and L. Little Bear (eds.). Toronto: University of Toronto Press.

Henderson, W. 1983 "Canadian Legal and Judicial Philosophies on the Doctrine of Aboriginal Rights." In *Aboriginal Rights: Toward an Understanding*, J. Long, M. Boldt and L. Little Bear, (eds.). Lethbridge, Alberta: University of Lethbridge.

Henderson, W.B. 1978 *Land Tenure in Indian Reserves*. Ottawa: DIAND.

_____ **1980** "Canada's Indian Reserves: The Usufruct in Our Constitution." *Ottawa Law Review*, 12: 160–187.

Hendrick, D., M. Martin and P. Greenberg 2003 *Conditional Sentencing in Canada: A Statistical Profile 1997-2000*. Ottawa: Statistics Canada, Canadian Centre for Justice Statistics.

Hertzberg, Hazel 1971 *Search for an American Indian Identity: Modern Pan-Indian Movements*. Syracuse, NY: Syracuse University Press.

Himes, J. 1966 "The Functions of Racial Conflict." *Social Forces*, 45: 1–10.

Hirschmann, Alberta 1971 *The Strategy of Economic Development*. New Haven: Yale University Press.

Hobart, C. 1991 "The Impact of Resource Development on the Health of Native People in the Northwest Territories." *Readings in Aboriginal Studies, Human Services*, Vol. 1, S. Corrigan (ed.). Brandon MB: Bearpaw Publishing, pp. 82–100.

Hodgins, B., S. Heard and J. Milloy 1992 *Co-Existence? Studies in Ontario–First Nations Relations*. Peterborough ON: Frost Centre for Canadian Heritage and Development Studies, Trent University.

Holmes, J. 1987 *Bill C-31, Equality or Disparity? The Effects of the New Indian Act on Native Women*. Ottawa: Canadian Advisory Council on the Status of Women.

Honigman, John 1967 *Personality in Culture*. New York: Harper and Row.

House of Commons 1982 Minutes of Proceedings and Evidence of the Sub-Committee on Indian Women and the *Indian Act*, Issue No. 2, Ottawa: Minister of Supply and Services Canada.

Howard, A. and F. Widdowson 1999. "The Disaster of Nunavut," *Policy Options*, July/August, 58–61.

Howard, J. 1951 "Notes on the Dakota Grass Dance." *Southwestern Journal of Anthropology*, 7: 82–85.

Howard, John Kinsey 1952 *Strange Empire*. Toronto: Swan Publishing Co. Ltd.

Hull, J. 2005 *Aboriginal Post-Secondary Education and Labour Market Outcomes, Canada, 2001*. Ottawa: Research and Analysis Directorate, INAC.

_____ **2006** *Aboriginal Women: A Profile from the 2001 Census*. Ottawa: Indian and Northern Affairs Canada.

Hunt, George 1940 *The Wars of the Iroquois: A Study in Intertribal Trade Relations*. Madison: University of Wisconsin Press.

Hutchins, P., C. Hilling, and D. Schulze 1999 "The Aboriginal Right to Self-Government and the Canadian Constitution: The Ghost in the Machine." *U.C.B. Law Review*, 29 (2): 251–287.

Hylton, John 1981 "The Native Offender in Saskatchewan, Some Implications for Crime Prevention Planning." In *Selected Papers of the Canadian Congress for the Prevention of Crime*. Winnipeg: Canadian Association for the Prevention of Crime.

Hylton, John (ed.) 1994 *Aboriginal Self-Government in Canada: Current Trends and Issues*. Saskatoon: Purich Publishers.

Imai, Shin 1999 Indian Act *and Aboriginal Constitutional Provisions*. Scarborough ON: Carswell.

Imai, Shin and Donna Hawley 1995 *The Annotated Indian Act*. Toronto: Carswell.

Imai, S., K. Logan, and G. Stein 1993 *Aboriginal Law Handbook*. Toronto: Carswell.

Indian and Northern Affairs Canada 1977 *Arctic Women's Workshop*. Ottawa: DIAND.

_____ **1982** *The Elimination of Sex Discrimination from the Indian Act*. Ottawa: DIAND.

_____ **1983** *A Demographic Profile of Registered Indian Women.* Ottawa: DIAND.

_____ **1984** *Western Arctic Claim Agreement (Inuvialuit Final Agreement).* Ottawa: Minister of Supply and Services.

_____ **1988** *Basic Departmental Data.* Ottawa: Minister of Supply and Services.

_____ **1990** *Basic Departmental Data.* Ottawa: Minister of Supply and Services.

_____ **1993** *Basic Departmental Data.* Ottawa: Minister of Supply and Services.

_____ **2000** *Registered Indian Population Projections, 1998-2008.* Ottawa: Minister of Supply and Services.

_____ **2002a** *Basic Departmental Data.* Ottawa: Minister of Supply and Services.

_____ **2002b** *Highlights of Aboriginal Conditions 1981-2001, Part 1, Demographic Trends.* Ottawa: Minister of Supply and Services.

_____ **2003** *Basic Departmental Data.* Ottawa: Minister of Supply and Services.

_____ **2006** *Aboriginal People in Canada.* Ottawa: Strategic Research and Analysis Directorate, Ministry of Industry.

Indian Association of Alberta 1971 *The Native People.* Edmonton.

Indian Claims Commission 1975 *Indian Claims in Canada: An Essay and Bibliography.* Ottawa: Supply and Services.

_____ **2005** *Charting the Claim Inquiry Process: How the ICC's System Works* 10 (4).

Indian Minerals Directorate 1981a Personal Communication, Reserves and Trust Branch, Department of Indian and Northern Development, Ottawa.

_____ **1981b** Minerals Inventory, Reserve and Trust Branch, Department of Indian and Northern Development, Ottawa.

Indian Rights for Indian Women (IRIW), n.d. Alberta Committee, The Arbitrary Enfranchisement of Indian Women, Edmonton: IRIW.

_____ **1978** Research Workshop: Resolutions, Edmonton, IRIW, n.p.

_____ **1979** A Study on the Emotional Impact of Arbitrary Enfranchisement on Native Women and on Their Families in Canada, Edmonton: IRIW.

Innis, Harold A. 1970 *The Fur Trade in Canada.* Toronto and Buffalo: University of Toronto Press.

Inuit Tapiriit Kanataim 2006 *Determining the Inuit Population.* Ottawa: INAC.

Isaac, T. 1995 *Aboriginal Law: Cases, Materials, and Commentary.* Saskatoon: Purich Publishing.

_____ **2001** *Aboriginal Law: Cases, Materials, and Commentary* (2nd edition). Saskatoon: Purich Publishing.

_____ **2004** *Aboriginal Law: Cases, Materials, and Commentary* (3rd edition). Saskatoon: Purich Publishing.

Iverson, P. 1990 "Plains Indians and Australian Aborigines in the Twentieth Century." In *The Struggle for the Land*, P. Olson (ed.). Lincoln NB: University of Nebraska Press, pp. 171–188.

Jack, Henry 1970 "Native Alliance for Red Power." In *The Only Good Indian*, Waubageshig (ed.). Toronto: New Press.

Jackson, M. 1992 "In Search of the Pathways to Justice: Alternative Dispute Resolution in Aboriginal Communities." *U.B.C. Law Review,* 26: 139–152.

Jaenen, C. 1986 "French Sovereignty and Native Nationhood during the French Regime." Native Studies Review, 2: 83–113.

Jamieson, K. 1978 *Indian Women and the Law in Canada: A Citizens Minus.* Ottawa: Minister of Supply and Services Canada.

_____ **1979** "Multiple Jeopardy: The Evolution of a Native Women's Movement." *Atlantis* (part 2), 4 (2), 157–178.

Jantzen, L. 2003 "Reporting Métis in Urban Centres on the 1996 Census." *Canadian Ethnic Studies*, 35 (1): 149–170.

Jarvis, G. and T. Heaton 1989 "Language Shift among Those of Aboriginal Mother Tongue in Canada." *Canadian Studies in Population*, 16 (1), 25–42.

Jefferson, C. 1978 *Conquest by Law.* Solicitor General Canada. Ottawa: Supply and Services Canada.

Jenness, Diamond n.d. *The Indian Background of Canadian History.* Bulletin No. 86, Anthropological Series No. 21. Ottawa: Department of Mines and Resources.

_____ **1967** *Indians of Canada*, 7th ed. Ottawa: Queen's Printer.

Jhappan, C. Radha 1990 "Indian Symbolic Politics: The Double-Edged Sword of Publicity." *Canadian Ethnic Studies*, 22 (3), 19–39.

Johnston, J. 1997 *Aboriginal Offender Survey: Case Files and Interview Sample*. Ottawa: Correctional Service Canada.

Johnson, S. 1976 *Migrating Native Peoples Program*. Ottawa: National Association of Friendship Centres.

_____ **2003** "Custodial Remand in Canada, 1986/87–2000/01," *Juristat*, 25 (2), Ottawa: Statistics Canada, Canadian Centre for Justice Statistics.

_____ **2005** "Returning to Correctional Services after Release: A Profile of Aboriginal and non-Aboriginal Adults Involved in Saskatchewan Corrections from 1999/00 to 2003/04." *Juristat*, Canadian Centre for Justice Statistics, Cat. No. 85-002-XIE. 25.2. Ottawa: Statistics Canada.

Joseph, S. 1991 "Assimilation Tools: Then and Now." In *In Celebration of Our Survival*, D. Jensen and C. Brooks (eds.). Vancouver: University of British Columbia Press, pp. 65–79.

Jull, Peter 1982 "Nunavut." *Northern Perspectives*, 10, 2.

Junger-Tas, J. 1994 "Alternative Sanctions: Myth and Reality." *European Journal of Criminal Policy and Research*, Consistency in Sentencing Issue, Kugler Publication, 2 (1): 44–66.

Kardiner, Abraham and Lionel Ovesey 1951 *The Mark of Oppression*. New York: W.W. Norton.

Katznelson, I. 1976 "The Crisis of the Capitalist City: Urban Politics and Social Control." In *Theoretical Perspectives in Urban Politics*, W. Hawley and M. Lipsky (eds.). Englewood Cliffs: Prentice Hall.

Kay, F. and R. Johnston 2007 *Social Capital, Diversity and the Welfare State*. Vancouver: University of British Columbia Press.

Kaye, L. 1981 "I Think I'm Indian . . . But Others Aren't Sure." *Ontario Indian*, 4 (5), 8 and 34.

Keeping, J. 1989 *The Inuvialuit Final Agreement*. Calgary: The Canadian Institute of Resources Law, University of Calgary.

Kennedy, L., H. Northcott, and C. Kinzel 1978 "Subjective Evaluation of Well-Being: Problems and Prospects." *Social Indicators Research* 5: 457–474.

Kennedy, Raymond 1945 The Colonial Crisis and the Future." In *The Science of Man in the World Crisis*. Ralph Linton (ed.). New York: Columbia University Press.

Kerr, S. 1975 *Women's Rights and Two National Native Organizations: The Native Council of Canada and the National Indian Brotherhood*. Ottawa: Carleton University, n.p.

King, Cecil 1972 "Sociological Implications of the Jeannette Corbiere Lavell Case." *The Northian*, 8 (March): 44–45.

Kishigami, N. 1999 "Why do Inuit Move to Montreal? A Research Note on Urban Inuit." *Etudes/Inuit/Studies*, 23 (1): 221–227.

Knight, Rolf 1978 *Indians at Work. An Informal History of Native Indian Labour in British Columbia, 1858–1930*. Vancouver: New Star Books.

Koovos, A. and E. Brown 1980 "The Implications of the International Energy Markets for Indian Resources." *The Journal of Energy and Development*, 5: 252–257.

Kreager, P. 1997 "Population and Identity." In *Anthropological Demography: Toward a New Synthesis*, D. Kertzer and T. Fricke (eds.). Chicago: University of Chicago Press.

Krosenbrink-Gelissen, L. 1983 *Native Women of Manitoba, Canada: Feminism or Ethnicity?* Nijmegen, the Netherlands: Catholic University of Nijmegen, n.p.

_____ **1984a** "De Canadese Indian Act en de gevolgen daarvan voor Indiaanse vrouwen." In *De Kiva*, 21 (3), 44–45.

_____ **1984b** *No Indian Women, No Indian Nation: Canadian Native Women in Search of Their Identity*. Nijmegen: the Netherlands: Catholic University of Nijmegen, n.p.

_____ **1989** "The Métis National Council: Continuity and Change among the Canadian Métis." *Native American Studies*, 3 (1), 33–41.

_____ **1991** *Sexual Equality as an Aboriginal Right*. Saarbrucken, Germany: Verlagbreitenbach.

Kulchyski, P. (ed.) 1994 *Unjust Relations: Aboriginal Rights in Canadian Courts*. Toronto: Oxford University Press.

_____ **2005** *Like the Sound of a Drum*. Winnipeg: University of Manitoba Press.

Kuptana, R. 1992 "The Canadian Inuit and the Renewal of Canada." *Etudes/Inuit/Studies*, 16 (1–2): 39–42.

Lachance-Brulotte, Ginette 1984 "La nuptialité des Indiens du Canada." In *Les populations amerindiennes et inuit du Canada, Aperçu* *démographique,* L. Normandeau et V. Piche (eds.). Montréal: Les Presses de l'Université de Montréal.

Laing, A. 1967 *Indians and the Law.* Ottawa: Queen's Printer.

Lambertus, Sandra 2004 *Wartime Images, Peacetime Wounds: The Media and the Gustafsen Lake Standoff.* Vancouver: University of British Columbia Press.

Lamontagne, F. and C. Tremblay 1989 *Development Indices: A Quebec Regional Comparison.* Local Development Paper No. 14, Economic Council of Canada. 70 pp.

Land, K. 1971 "On the Definition of Social Indicators." *The American Sociologist* 6: 322–325.

Land, K. and S. Spilerman 1975 *Social Indicator Models.* New York: Russell Sage Foundation.

Lane, B. 1989 *Canadian Healthy Communities Project: A Conceptual Model for Winnipeg.* Health and the Community 1. Winnipeg: Institute of Urban Studies.

LaPrairie, C. 1996 *Examining Aboriginal Corrections in Canada.* Solicitor General of Canada. Ottawa: Supply and Services Canada.

_____ 1998 "The 'New' Justice: Some Implications for Aboriginal Communities." *Canadian Journal of Criminology,* 40: 60–78.

_____ 2002 "Aboriginal Over-Representation in the Criminal Justice System: A Tale of Nine Cities." *Canadian Journal of Criminology,* 44 (2): 181–208.

LaPrairie, Carol and J. Roberts 1997 "Circle Sentencing, Restorative Justice and the Role of the Community." *Canadian Journal of Criminology,* 34: 40–52.

La Rusic, Ignatius 1968 *Hunter to Proletarian.* Research paper for Cree Development Change Project.

Laselva, S. 1998–99 "Aboriginal Self-Government and the Foundations of Canadian Nationhood." *B.C. Studies,* 120: 41–55.

Laslett, P. 1963 "The Face-to-Face Society." In *Philosophy, Politics and Society,* P. Laslett (ed.). Oxford: Basil Blackwell.

La Violette, F.E. 1961 *The Struggle for Survival.* Toronto: University of Toronto Press.

Law Commission of Canada 1999 *Urban Aboriginal Governance in Canada.* Ottawa: Minister of public Works and Government Services.

Legare, A. 1996 "The Process Leading to a Land Claims Agreement and Its Implementation: The Case of Nunavut Land Claims Settlement." *Canadian Journal of Native Studies,* 16 (1): 139–163.

Leonard, D. 1995 "Indigenous Nature of Water." *The DLA Financial,* 2 (3): 15–27.

Lerat, H. with L. Ungar 2005 *Treaty Promises, Indian Reality.* Saskatoon: Purich Publishing.

Leslie, J. and R. Maguire 1978 *The Historical Development of the Indian Act, Treaties, and Historical Research Centres.* Ottawa: Department of Indian Affairs and Northern Development, PRE Group.

Levesque, C. 2003 "The Presence of Aboriginal Peoples in Quebec's Cities: Multiple Movements, Diverse Issues." In *Not Strangers in These Parts,* D. Newhouse and E. Peters (eds.). Ottawa: Policy Research Institute, pp. 23–34.

Levine, S. 1970 "The Survival of Indian Identity." In *The American Indian Today,* S. Levine and N. Lurie (eds.). Hardmondsworth, UK: Pelican.

Lightbody, J. 1969 "A Note on the Theory of Nationalism as a Function of Ethnic Demands." *Canadian Journal of Political Science,* 2: 327–337.

Lindesmith, A. and S. Strauss 1968 *Social Psychology.* New York: Holt, Rinehart and Winston.

Linker, M. 1999 "Sentencing Circles and the Dilemma of Difference." *Criminal Law Quarterly,* 42 (1): 116–128.

Lithman, I. 1983 *The Practice of Underdevelopment and the Theory of Development. The Canadian Indian Case.* Stockholm: Department of Social Anthropology, University of Stockholm.

Little Bear, L. 2000. "Jagged Worldviews Colliding." In *Reclaiming Indigenous Voice and Vision,* M. Baaataaatise (ed). Vancouver: University of British Columbia Press.

Loh, S. and M.V. George 2003 "Estimating the Fertility Level of Registered Indians in Canada." *Canadian Studies in Population,* 31 (2), 117–135.

Long, J.A., M. Boldt, and L. Little Bear 1982 "Federal Indian Policy and Indian Self-Government in Canada: An Analysis of a Current Proposal." *Canadian Public Policy,* 8 (2): 189–199.

_____ 1983 (eds.). *Aboriginal Rights: Toward an Understanding*. Lethbridge AB: Law Foundation.

Longboat, D. 1987 "First Nations Control of Education: The Path to Our Survival as Nations." In *Indian Education in Canada*, Vol. 2, J. Barman, Y. Hebert and D. McCaskill (eds.). Vancouver: University of British Columbia Press.

Lower, A. 1957 *Colony to Nation: A History of Canada*. Toronto: Longman, Green.

Lu, Chang-Mei and Mathurin Emerson 1973 *Projections démographiques des Territoires du Nord-Ouest jusqu'en 1981*. Ottawa: Affaires Indiennes et du Nord, au nord du 60.

Lurie, N. 1971 "The Contemporary American Indian Scene." In *North American Indians in Historical Perspective*, E. Leacock and N. Lurie (eds.). New York: Random House Inc.

Lussier, A. 1979 *Louis Riel and the Métis: Riel Mini Conference Papers*. Winnipeg: Pemmican Publishers.

_____ 1984 *The Métis and Non-Status Indians 1967–1984, and the Métis and the Indians 1960–1984*. Ottawa: Treaties and Historical Research Centre, Department of Indian Affairs and Northern Development.

Lussier, Antoine S. and D. Bruce Sealey (eds.) 1978 *The Other Natives—Les Métis*. Winnipeg: Manitoba Métis Federation Press.

Lyon, N. 1985 "Constitutional Issues in Native Law." In *Aboriginal Peoples and the Law*, B. Morse (ed.). Ottawa: Carleton University Press.

MacGregor R. 1961 *Racial and Ethnic Relations in America*. Boston: Allyn and Bacon.

Macklem, Patrick 2001 *Indigenous Differences and the Constitution of Canada*. Toronto: University of Toronto Press.

Mainville, Robert 2001 *An Overview of Aboriginal and Treaty Rights and Compensation for Their Breach*. Saskatoon: Purich Publishers.

Malatest and Associates 2004. *Aboriginal Peoples and Post-Secondary Education*. Montreal: Canada Millennium Scholarship Foundation.

Mallea, R. 1994 *Aboriginal Law: Apartheid in Canada*. Brandon MB: Bearpaw Publishing.

Malloy, J. 2001 "Double Identities: Aboriginal Policy Agencies in Ontario and British Columbia." *Canadian Journal of Political Science*, 34 (1): 131–155.

Manitoba Métis Federation Justice Committee 1989 *Research and Analysis of the Impact of the Justice System on the Métis: Report to the Aboriginal Justice Inquiry*, November 22, 1989. Winnipeg: Manitoba Métis Federation Inc.

Manuel, G. and M. Poslums 1974 *The Fourth World: An Indian Reality*. Toronto: Collier-Macmillan Canada.

Mariategui, J.C. 1934 *Siete ensayos de interpretación de la sealidad peruana*, 2nd ed. Lima: Editorial Librariá Peruana.

Martens, P., D. Sanderson and L. Jebamani 2005 "Mortality Comparisons of First Nations to all Other Manitobans." *Canadian Journal of Public Health*, 96 (January/February), S33-57.

Martin, S. 2005 *Determinants of Well-Being in Inupiat and Yuplit Eskimos: Do Communities Matter?* Ph.D. dissertation, University of Texas at Dallas.

Marule, M.S. 1977 "The Canadian Government's Termination Policy: From 1969 to the Present Day." In *One Century Later*, J. Getty and D. Smith (eds.). Vancouver: University of British Columbia Press.

Mata, F. 1997. *Intergenerational Transmission of Education and Socio-Economic Status: A Look at Immigrants, Visible Minorities and Aboriginals*. Multicultural Branch, Department of Canadian Heritage.

Mathias, Chief Joe and G. Yabsley 1991 "Conspiracy of Legislation: The Suppression of Indian Rights in Canada." In *In Celebration of Our Survival*, D. Jensen and C. Brooks (eds.). Vancouver: University of British Columbia Press, pp. 34–47.

Maxim, P. and J. White 2003 "Toward an Index of Community Capacity: Predicting Community Potential for Successful Program Transfer." In *Aboriginal Conditions*, J. White, P. Maxim and D. Beavon (eds.). Vancouver: University of British Columbia Press, pp. 248–263.

Maxim, P,, J. White, P. Whitehead and D. Beavon 2000. *Patterns of Urban Residential Settlement among Canada's First Nations Communities*, Paper No. 00-8. London: Population Studies Centre, University of Western Ontario.

Maybury-Lewis, David 1997 *Indigenous Peoples, Ethnic Groups, and the State. Cultural Survival Studies in Ethnicity and Change*, Vol. 1. Boston: Allyn and Bacon.

McCaskill, D. 1981 "The Urbanization of Indians in Winnipeg, Toronto, Edmonton, and Vancouver: A Comparative Analysis." *Culture,* 1: 82–89.

_____ **1985** *Patterns of Criminality and Corrections among Native Offenders in Manitoba: A Longitudinal Analysis.* Ottawa: Correctional Service Canada.

McCaslin W. (ed.) 2005 *Justice as Healing Indigenous Ways.* St. Paul MN: Living Justice Press.

McCullum, H. and K. McCullum 1975 *This Land Is Not for Sale.* Toronto: Anglican Book Centre.

McGhee, R. 1996 *Ancient People of the Arctic.* Vancouver: University of British Columbia Press.

McInnis, E. 1959 *Canada: A Political and Social History.* New York: Holt, Rinehart and Winston.

McMahon, D. and F. Martin 1995 *Aboriginal Self-Government: Legal and Constitutional Issues.* Ottawa: Minister of Supply and Services.

McNab, David 1999 *Circles of Time: Aboriginal Land Rights and Resistance in Ontario.* Waterloo: Wilfred Laurier University Press.

Meadow Lake Tribal Council 1989 *A Position Paper on Indian Labour Force Development,* submitted to the Canadian Labour Market and Productivity Centre, October.

Meadows, M. 1981 *Adaptation to Urban Life by Native Women.* Calgary: University of Calgary Department of Sociology.

Melville, B. 1981 *Indian Reserves and Indian Treaty Problems in Northeastern B.C.* Vancouver: B.C. Hydro and Power Authority.

Mendelson, M. 2006 "Improving Primary and Secondary Education on Reserves in Canada." *Caledon Commentary,* October, 1–7.

Mendelson, M. and K. Battle 1999 *Aboriginal People in Canada's Labour Market.* Ottawa: Caledon Institute of Social Policy, June.

Mendes, E. and P. Bendin n.d. "The New Canadian Charter of Rights and International Law and Aboriginal Self-Determination: A Proposal for a New Direction." Saskatoon SK: mimeograph.

Métis National Council 1983 *A Brief to the Standing Senate Committee on Legal and Constitutional Affairs* September 8. Ottawa.

_____ **1984** *The Métis Natives.* Toronto: Métis National Council.

Métis and Non-Status Indian Crime and Justice Commission 1977 *Report.* Serpent River Reserve, Cutler ON: Woodland Studio.

Mickenberg, Neil 1971 "Aboriginal Rights in Canada and the United States." *Osgoode Hall Law Journal,* 9: 154.

Miles, I. 1985 *Social Indicators for Human Development.* London: Frances Pinter (Publishers).

Miller, J.R. 1991 *Sweet Promises.* Toronto: University of Toronto Press.

_____ **2000** *Skyscrapers Hide the Heavens: A History of Indian–White Relations in Canada.* Toronto: University of Toronto Press.

Minore, J. and M. Hill 1997 "Native Language Broadcasting: An Experiment in Empowerment." In *The Mass Media and Canadian Diversity,* S. Nancoo and R. Nancoo (eds.). Mississauga: Canadian Educators' Press, pp. 162–186.

Mitchell, J. 1986 "Reflections on Twenty Years of Feminism." In *What Is Feminism?* Mitchell, J. and A. Oakley (eds.). Oxford: Basil Blackwell, pp. 34–48.

Mitchell, M. 1996 *From Talking Chiefs to a Native Corporate Elite.* Montreal and Kingston: McGill-Queen's University Press.

Moore, R. 1978 *The Historical Development of the Indian Act.* Draft manuscript. Ottawa: Department of Indian Affairs and Northern Development.

Morris, Alexander 1880 *The Treaties of Canada with the Indians of Manitoba and the North West Territories.* Toronto: Belfords, Clark.

Morrison, Bruce and C. Roderick Wilson (eds.) 1986 *Native Peoples: The Canadian Experience.* Toronto: McClelland & Stewart.

Morrison, Bruce and Rod Wilson 1995 *Native Peoples: The Canadian Experience.* Toronto: McClelland & Stewart.

_____ **2004** *Native Peoples: The Canadian Experience.* Toronto: McClelland & Stewart.

Morse, B. (ed.) 1991 *Aboriginal Peoples and the Law: Indian, Métis and Inuit Rights in Canada.* Ottawa: Carleton University Press.

_____ **1999** "The Inherent Right of Aboriginal Governance." In *Aboriginal Self-Government in Canada,* J. Hylton (ed.). Saskatoon: Purich Publishers.

Morton, W.L. 1963 *The Kingdom of Canada: A General History from Earliest Times.* Toronto: McClelland and Stewart.

Moss, W. 1995 "Inuit Perspectives on Treaty Rights and Governance Issues." *Aboriginal Self-Government*, P. Macklem, D. Reaume and M. Levin (eds.). Ottawa: Royal Commission on Aboriginal Peoples: pp. 55–139.

Moss, W. and P. Niemczak 1991 *Aboriginal Land Claims Issues*. Ottawa: Library of Parliament.

Motiuk, L. and M. Nafekh 2000 "Aboriginal Offenders in Federal Corrections: A Profile." *Forum*, 12 (1): 10–14.

Mount Pleasant-Jette, M. 1993 *Creating a Climate of Confidence: Providing Services within Aboriginal Communities*. In National Round Table on Economic Issues and Resources. Ottawa: Royal Commission on Aboriginal Peoples, April 27.

Murphy, M. 2001 "Culture and the Courts: A New Direction in Canadian Jurisprudence on Aboriginal Rights?" *Canadian Journal of Political Science*, 34 (1): 109–129.

Murray, G. to J. Kempt 1834 "Correspondence and Other Papers Relating to Aboriginal Tribes in British Possessions." January 25, 1830, *British Parliamentary Papers*, No. 617, 88.

Myers, H. 2001 "Options for Appropriate Development in Nunavut Communities." *Etudes/Inuit/Studies*, 24 (1): 25–40.

Nadeau, Ron 1979 *Indian Local Government*. Ottawa: Department of Indian Affairs and Northern Development. Policy Research and Evaluation.

Nagler, Mark 1971 *Indians in the City*. Ottawa: Canadian Research Centre for Anthropology, St. Paul University.

Neils, Elaine 1971 *Reservations to City*. Chicago: University of Chicago Press.

Neilsen, Marianne O. 1990 "Canadian Correctional Policy and Native Inmates: The Control of Social Dynamite." *Canadian Ethnic Studies*, 22 (3), 110–121.

Newhouse, D. 2003 "The Invisible Infrastructure: Urban Aboriginal Institutions and Organizations." In *Not Strangers in these Parts: Urban Aboriginal Peoples*, D. Newhouse and E. Peters (eds.). Ottawa: Policy Research Institute, pp. 243–254.

Newhouse, D. and E. Peters (eds.) 2003 *Not Strangers in These Parts: Urban Aboriginal Peoples*. Ottawa: Policy Research Initiative.

Nichols, R. 1998 *Indians in the United States and Canada*. Lincoln NB and London ON: University of Nebraska Press.

Nielsen, M. 1991 "Balance and Strategy: Native Criminal Justice Organizations, Native Communities and the Canadian State." Kingston ON: Paper presented at the Annual Meeting of the Canadian Sociology and Anthropology Association.

Nielsen, M. and R. Silverman (eds.) 1996 *Native Americans, Crime and Justice*. Boulder CO: Westview Press.

Niezen, Ronald 1998 *Defending the Land: Sovereignty and Forest Life in James Bay Cree Society*. Boston: Allyn and Bacon.

Norris, M.J. 1998 "Canada's Aboriginal Languages." *Canadian Social Trends*, Winter, 8–16.

_____ **2000**. "Aboriginal Peoples in Canada: Demographic and Linguistic Perspectives." In *Visions of the Heart: Canadian Aboriginal Issues*, D. Long and O. Dickason (eds.). Toronto: Harcourt Brace Canada.

Norris, M., D. Beavon, E. Guimond and M. Cooke 2001 *Migration and Residential Mobility of Canada's Aboriginal Groups*. Ottawa: Indian and Northern Affairs Canada.

Norris, M.J., M. Cooke, and S. Clatworthy 2004 "Aboriginal Mobility and Migration Patterns and Policy Implications." In *Population Mobility and Indigenous Peoples in Australasia and North America*, J. Taylor and M. Bell (eds.), London: Routledge Press.

Norris, M.J. and L. Jantzen 2003 "Aboriginal Languages in Canada's Urban Areas." In *Not Strangers in These Parts*, D. Newhouse and E. Peters (eds.). Ottawa: Policy Research Initiative, pp. 93–118.

Nuffield, Joan 1998 *Issues in Urban Corrections for Aboriginal People*. Ottawa: Ministry of the Solicitor General.

Nuttall R. 1982 "The Development of Indian Boards of Health in Alberta." *Canadian Journal of Public Health,* 73: 300–303.

Native Women's Association of Canada (NWAC) "Statement by NWAC on Native Women's Rights." In *Women and the Constitution in Canada*. A. Doerr and M. Carrier (eds.) Ottawa: Canadian Advisory Council on the Status of Women 1981 pp. 64–73.

_____ **1985a** *First Nation Citizenship: A Discussion Paper*. Ottawa: NWAC.

_____ **1985b** *A Voice of Many Nations: Native Women*. Ottawa: NWAC.

O'Callaghan, E. (ed.) 1856–57 *Documents Relative to the Colonial History of the*

State of New York: 1856–1857. Albany NY.

O'Donnell, V. and H. Tait 2004. "Well-being of the Non-Reserve Aboriginal Population." *Canadian Social Trends*, Spring, 19–23.

Office of the Correctional Investigator 2005-2006 *Annual Report of the Office of the Correctional Investigator of Canada.* Ottawa.

Oliver, C. 1990 "Determinants of Interorganizational Relationships: Integrative and Future Directions." *Academy of Management Review*, 15 (2), pp. 241–265.

Olofsson, E. 2004. *In Search of a Fulfilling Identity in a Modern World: Narratives of Indigenous Identities in Sweden and Canada.* Ph.D. dissertation, Uppsala Universitet.

O'Meara, S. and D. West 1996 *From Our Eyes: Learning from Indigenous Peoples.* Toronto: Garamond Press.

ONWA 1983 *Nations within a Nation: An Aboriginal Right?* A Report of the Conference Proceedings, November 12, 13 and 14, 1982. Thunder Bay: ONWA.

Organization for Economic Co-Operation and Development (OECD) 1973 *List of Social Concerns Common to Most OECD Countries.* The OECD Social Indicator Development Program, 1. Paris.

_____ 1974 *Subjective Elements of Well-Being.* The OECD Social Indicator Development Program, 2. Paris.

_____ 1976 *Measuring Social Well-Being.* The OECD Social Indicator Development Program, 3. Paris.

_____ 1982 *The OECD List of Social Indicators.* The OECD Social Development Program, 5. Paris.

Paquette, Lyne and Jeannine Perreault 1984 "Un demi-million d'Indiens inscrits au Canada en l'an 2000?" *Cahiers québécois de démographie*, 13 (1): 101–115.

Pask, R. and J. Scott 1971 "Learning Strategies and Individual Competence." *International Journal of Man–Machine Studies*, 4: 217–253.

Paton, R. 1982 *New Policies and Old Organizations: Can Indian Affairs Change?* Centre for Policy and Program Assessment, School of Public Administration. Ottawa: Carleton University.

Patrick, D. 2005. "Language Rights in Indigenous Communities: The Case of the Inuit of Northern Quebec." *Journal of Sociolinguistics*, 9 (3): 369–389.

Patterson, E. Palmer 1972 *The Canadian Indians: A History Since 1500.* Toronto: Collier-Macmillan Canada.

Paul, P. 1990 *Bill C-31: The Trojan Horse: An Analysis of the Social, Economic and Political Reaction of First Nation People as a Result of Bill C-31.* Thesis, University of New Brunswick.

Peeling, A. and P. Chartrand 2004 "Exploring the Origins of Métis Rights of Self-Government in the Context of s. 35, *Constitution Act*, 1982" *Saskatchewan Law Review*, 67 (1): 339–357.

Pelletier, Emile 1974 *A Social History of the Manitoba Métis.* Winnipeg: Manitoba Métis Federation Press.

_____ 1975 *Exploitation of Métis Lands.* Winnipeg: Manitoba Métis Federation Press.

Pelletier, W. 1970 *Two Articles.* Toronto: Neewin Publishing.

Pennekeok, F. 1976 "The Anglican Church and the Disintegration of Red River Society, 1818–1870." In *The West and the Nation*, C. Berger and R. Cook (eds.). Toronto: McClelland and Stewart.

Penner, K., 1983 *Indian Self-Government in Canada: Report of the Special Committee* (The Penner Report). Ottawa: Minister of Supply and Services.

Perreault, Jeannine, Lyne Paquette, and M.V. George 1985 *Projections de la population indienne inscrite, 1982–1996.* Ottawa: Affaires indiennes et du Nord Canada.

Perrow, C. 1961 "Goals in Complex Organizations." *American Sociological Review*, 26: 854–865.

Perry, Richard 1996 *From Time Immemorial: Indigenous Peoples and State Systems.* Austin: University of Texas Press.

Peters, E. 1987 *Aboriginal Self Government Arrangements in Canada: An Overview.* Kingston ON: Queen's University, Institute of Intergovernmental Relations.

_____ 2000. "Aboriginal Peoples in Urban Areas." In *Visions of the Heart: Contemporary Aboriginal Issues*, D. Long and O. Dickason (eds.). Toronto: Harcourt Brace, 238–333.

_____ 2001 "Developing Federal Policy for First Nations People in Urban Areas." *Canadian Journal of Native Studies*, 21 (1): 57–96.

_____ 2002 "Our City Indians: Negotiating the Meaning of First Nations Urbanization in

Canada, 1945–1975." *Historical Geography*, 30: 69–84.

Peters, E., M. Rosenberg, and G. Halseth **1989** "The Ontario Métis: A People without an Identity." Mimeographed.

Peters, Omar **1968** "Canada's Indians and Eskimos and Human Rights." Paper presented to the Thinkers' Conference on Cultural Rights. Mimeographed.

Peterson, Jacqueline and Jennifer S.H. Brown (eds.) **1985** *The New Peoples: Being and Becoming Métis in North America*. Winnipeg: University of Manitoba Press.

Pettigrew, T. **1964** *A Profile of the Negro American*. Princeton: D. Van Nostrand Co.

Pfeiffer, J. and G. Salanchik **1978** *The External Control of Organizations: A Resource Dependence Perspective*. New York: Harper and Row.

Piche, Victor and M.V. George **1973** "Estimates of Vital Rates for the Canadian Indians, 1960–1970." *Demography*, 10: 367–382.

Pinkerton, E. **1989** *Co-operative Management of Local Fisheries: New Directions for Improved Management and Community Development*, Vancouver: University of British Columbia Press.

Pitts, J. **1974** "The Study of Race Consciousness: Comments on New Directions." *American Journal of Sociology*, 80: 665–687.

PJS Geach and Associates **1985** *Band Planning Handbook on the Use of Socio-Economic Indicators*. Prepared for Department of Indian Affairs and Northern Development, B.C. Region.

Plain, F. **1985** "A Treaty on the Rights of the Aboriginal Peoples of the Continent of North America." In *The Quest for Justice*, M. Boldt, J. Long, and L. Little Bear (eds.). Toronto: University of Toronto Press.

Polanyi, Karl **1974** *The Great Transformation*. Boston: Beacon Press.

Ponting, J.R. **1986** *Arduous Journey: Canadian Indians and Decolonization*. Toronto: McClelland and Stewart.

_____ **1987** *Profiles of Public Opinion on Canadian Natives and Native Issues: Special Status and Self Government*. Calgary: Research Unit for Public Policy Studies, University of Calgary.

_____ **1991** "An Indian Policy for Canada in the 21st Century." In *Canada on the Threshold of the 21st Century*, C. Remie and J. Lacroix (eds.). Amsterdam: John Benjamins.

_____ **1997** *First Nations in Canada: Perspectives on Opportunity, Empowerment, and Self-Determination*. Toronto: McGraw-Hill Ryerson.

Ponting, J.R. and R. Gibbins **1980** *Out of Irrelevance: A Socio-Political Introduction to Indian Affairs of Canada*. Toronto: Butterworth and Co. (Canada.)

Ponting, J. Rick and G. Symons **1993** "Environmental Geo-Politics and the New World Order: Grande Baleine, the Crees and Hydro-Quebec." Paper presented at the International Conference "Geopolitics of the Environment and the New World Order: Limits, Conficts, Insecurity?" Chantilly, France, January 5–9.

Portes, A. and P. Landolt **1996** "The Downside of Social Capital." *The American Prospect*, 16: 18–21.

Postl, B. **2005** *British Columbia First Nations Schools Funding Analysis: 2003-04 School Year*. Report submitted to Indian and Northern Affairs Canada.

Prentice, J. and J. Bellegarde. **2001** *Report to the House of Commons Standing Committee on Aboriginal Affairs*, Indian Claims Commission Annual Report 1999-2000, Ottawa.

Prethus, R. **1974** *Elites in Policy Process*. London: Cambridge University Press.

Price, J. **1972** "U.S. and Canadian Indian Periodicals." *Canadian Review of Sociology and Anthropology*, 9 (May): 150–162.

_____ **1978** *Native Studies*. Toronto: McGraw Hill Ryerson.

_____ **1979** *Indians of Canada: Cultural Dynamics*. Scarborough ON: Prentice Hall Canada.

_____ **1981** "The Viability of Indian Languages in Canada." *Canadian Journal of Native Studies*, 1 (2): 349–361.

Price, R. (ed.) **1979** *The Spirit of the Alberta Indian Treaties*. Montreal: Institute for Research on Public Policy.

Priest, G. **1984** *Aboriginal Languages in Canada*. Ottawa: Minister of Supply and Services.

Pross, P. (ed.) **1975** *Pressure Group Behaviour in Canadian Politics*. Scarborough ON: McGraw-Hill Ryerson.

_____ **1981** "Pressure Groups: Talking Chameleons." In M. Whittington and G. Williams (eds.), *Canadian Politics in the 1980s*. Toronto: Methuen.

Purich, D. **1988** *The Métis*. Toronto: James Lorimer.

_____ **1992** *The Inuit and Their Land*. Toronto: James Lorimer.

QED Information Systems, 2004 *Funding for First Nations Schools: A Comparison of INAC and Provincial Funding Regimes in Saskatchewan.* Report submitted to Indian and Northern Affairs Canada.

Quan, N. and S. Trevethan 2000 *Police-Reported Aboriginal Crime in Saskatchewan.* Cat. No. 85F0031-XIE, Canadian Centre for Justice Statistics. Ottawa: Statistics Canada.

Ram, Ball 2004 "New Estimates of Aboriginal Fertility, 1966–71 to 1996–2001." *Canadian Studies in Population,* 31 (2), 179–196.

Ram, Ball and A. Romaniuc 1984 *Fertility Projections of Registered Indians.* Ottawa: Statistique Canada (in edit.).

Raudsepp, E. 1997 "Emergent Media: The Native Press in Canada." In *The Mass Media and Canadian Diversity,* S. Nancoo and R. Nancoo (eds.). Mississauga: Canadian Educators' Press, pp. 187–206.

Raunet, D. 1984 *Without Surrender without Consent.* Vancouver: Douglas & McIntyre.

Rawson B. 1988 "Federal Perspectives on Indian–Provincial Relations." In *Governments in Conflict?* J.A. Long and Menno Boldt (eds.). Toronto: University of Toronto Press, pp. 147–154.

Ray, Arthur J. 1974 *Indians in the Fur Trade.* Toronto and Buffalo: University of Toronto Press.

_____ **1996** *I Have Lived Here Since the World Began.* Toronto: Key Porter Books.

Reeves, W. and J. Frideres 1981 "Government Policy and Indian Urbanization: The Alberta Case." *Canadian Public Policy,* 7 (4 (Autumn)): 584–595.

Reitano, J. 2004 "Youth Custody and Community Services in Canada 2002/3." *Juristat,* 24 (9), 20.

Report of the Affairs of the Indians in Canada 1844 "History of the Relations between the Government and the Indians." *Journals,* Section 1. Ottawa: Queen's Printer.

Reynolds, J. 2005 *A Breach of Duty.* Saskatoon: Purich Publishers.

Richardson, B. 1972 *James Bay.* San Francisco: Sierra Club.

_____ **1993** *People of Terra Nullius.* Vancouver: Douglas & McIntyre.

Rieber, J. 1977 *Fundamental Concerns Regarding Indian Local Government: A Discussion Paper of Potential Problem and Research Areas.* Ottawa: Department of Indian Affairs and Northern Development.

Robertson, Eleanor 1988 *Native Women in Conflict with the Law.* Winnipeg: unpublished.

Robinson, M., M. Dickerson, and M. Pretes 1991 "Sustainable Development in Small Northern Communities: A Micro Perspective." In *Old Pathways and New Directions: Towards a Sustainable Future.* Calgary: Arctic Institute of North America.

Robinson, M. and E. Ghostkeeper 1987 "Native and Local Economies: A Consideration of Economic Evolution and the Next Economy." *Arctic,* 40 (2): 138–144.

_____ **1988** "Implementing the Next Economy in a Unified Context: A Case Study of the Paddle Prairie Mall Corporation." *Arctic,* 41 (3): 173–182.

Rohen, D. 1967 *The Quest for Self-Determination.* New York: Yale University Press.

Romaniuc, A. 2003 "Aboriginal Population of Canada: Growth Dynamics under Conditions of Encounter of Civilizations." *Canadian Studies in Population,* 30(1): 75–115.

Romaniuc, A. and V. Piche 1972 "Natality Estimates for the Canadian Indians by Stable Population Models, 1900–1969." *The Canadian Review of Sociology and Anthropology,* 9 (1): 1–20.

Roosens, E. 1986 *Micronationalisme: een antropologie van het etnische reveil.* Leuven, Belgium: Uitgeverij Acco.

Ross, Alexander 1972 *The Red River Settlement.* Edmonton: Hurtig.

Ross, D. and P. Usher 1986 *From the Roots Up: Economic Development as if Community Mattered.* Toronto: James Lorimer.

Rossi, R. and K. Gilmartin 1980 *The Handbook of Social Indicators.* New York: Garland Press.

Roth, L. 2005 *Something New in the Air.* Montreal: McGill-Queen's University Press.

Rotman, Leonard I. 1996 *Parallel Paths: Fiduciary Doctrine and the Crown–Native Relationship in Canada.* Toronto: University of Toronto Press.

_____ **1997** "Symposium on Aboriginal Legal Issues." Special Issue of *Alberta Law Review,* 36 (1). University of Alberta.

Russell, D. 2000 *A People's Dream: Aboriginal Self-Government in Canada.* Vancouver: University of British Columbia Press.

Ryan, J. 1978 *Wall of Words: The Betrayal of the Urban Indian*. Toronto: Peter Martin Associates.

Salisbury, R. 1986 *A Homeland for the Cree*. Kingston and Montreal: McGill-Queen's University Press.

Sambo, D. 1992 "Indigenous Human Rights: The Role of Inuit at the United Nations Working Group on Indigenous Peoples." *Etudes/Inuit/Studies*, 16 (1–2): 27–32.

Sanders, D. 1983a "The Rights of the Aboriginal Peoples of Canada." *Canadian Bar Review*, 6 (1): 314–338.

_____ **1983b** "Prior Claims: Aboriginal People in the Constitution of Canada." In *Canada and the New Constitution: The Unfinished Business*, S. Beck and I. Bernier (eds.). Montreal: Institute for Research on Public Policy.

_____ **1983c** "The Indian Lobby." In *And No One Cheered*, K. Banting and R. Simeon (eds.). Toronto: Methuen.

_____ **1985a** "The Indian Lobby and the Canadian Constitution, 1978–1982." In *Indigenous Peoples and the Nation-State: 'Fourth World' Politics in Canada, Australia and Norway*, N. Dyck (ed.). St. John's: Memorial University of Newfoundland, Institute of Social and Economic Research, pp. 151–189.

_____ **1985b** "Aboriginal Rights: The Search for Recognition in International Law." In *The Quest for Justice*, M. Boldt, J. Long, and L. Little Bear (eds.). Toronto: University of Toronto Press.

_____ **1990** "The Supreme Court of Canada and the 'Legal and Political Struggle' Over Indigenous Rights." *Canadian Ethnic Studies*, 22 (3): 122–129.

Sarkadi, L. 1992 "Nunavut: Carving Out a New Territory in the North." *Calgary Herald*, January 4, A5.

Satzewich V. and T. Wotherspoon 1993 *First Nations: Race, Class and Gender Relations*. Scarborough ON: Nelson Canada.

Sawchuk, Joe 1978 *The Métis of Manitoba: Reformulation of an Ethnic Identity*. Toronto: Peter Martin Associates.

_____ **1998** *The Dynamics of Native Politics: The Alberta Métis Experience*. Saskatoon: Purich Publishing.

Sawchuk, J., P. Sawchuk and T. Ferguson 1981 *Métis Land Rights in Alberta: A Political History*. Edmonton: The Métis Association of Alberta.

Schmeiser, D. 1974 *The Native Offender and the Law*. Ottawa: Information Canada.

Schouls, T. 2004 *Shifting Boundaries: Aboriginal Identity, Pluralist Theory, and the Politics of Self Government*. Vancouver: University of British Columbia Press.

Schwartz, B. 1986 *First Principle: Constitutional Reform with Respect to the Aboriginal Peoples of Canada, 1982–84*. Kingston: Institute of Intergovernmental Relations, Queen's University.

Sealey, D. Bruce 1975 "One Plus One Equals One." In *The Other Natives: The Métis*. Antoine S. Lussier and D. Bruce Sealey (eds.). Winnipeg: Manitoba Métis Federation Press.

Sealey, D. Bruce and Antoine S. Lussier 1975 *The Métis—Canada's Forgotten People*. Winnipeg: Manitoba Métis Federation Press.

Shea, I.G. 1879 *Charlevoix's History of New France*. New York: Colonial Documents, Vol. 2, 1879.

Shewell, H. 2004 *"Enough to Keep Them Alive": Indian Social Welfare in Canada, 1873–1965*. Toronto: University of Toronto Press.

Shkilnyk, A. 1985 *A Poison Stronger Than Love: The Destruction of an Ojibwa Community*. New Haven CT and London: Yale University Press.

Siggner, A. 1980 "A Socio-demographic Profile of Indians in Canada." In *Out of Irrelevance*, J.R. Ponting and R. Gibbins (eds.). Toronto: Butterworth (Canada).

_____ **1986** "The Socio-demographic Conditions of Registered Indians." *Canadian Social Trends*, (Winter): 2–9.

_____ **1998** *Aboriginal Population Characteristics: Fifteen Years of Data, What Have We Learned?* Research paper #15. Calgary: The University of Calgary.

_____ **2001** *Profile of the Urban Aboriginal Population, Canada, 1996*. Ottawa.

_____ **2003a** "Urban Aboriginal Populations: An Update Using the 2001 Census Results." In *Not Strangers in These Parts: Urban Aboriginal Peoples*, D. Newhouse and E. Peters (eds.). Ottawa: Policy Research Initiative.

_____ **2003b** "Impact of 'Ethnic Mobility' on Socio-economic Conditions of Aboriginal Peoples." *Canadian Studies in Population*, 31 (2): 137–158.

Siggner, A. and R. Costa 2005 *Aboriginal Conditions in Census Metropolitan Areas, 1981-2001.* Ottawa: Indian and Northern Affairs Canada.

Siggner, A. and C. Locatelli 1980 *Regional Population Projections by Age, Sex, and Residence for Canada's Registered Indian Population, 1976–1991.* Ottawa: Research Branch, Department of Indian Affairs and Northern Development.

Silman, J. 1987 *Enough Is Enough: Aboriginal Women Speak Out.* Toronto: The Women's Press.

Silver, J. and K. Mallett 2002 *Aboriginal Education in Winnipeg Inner City High Schools.* Winnipeg Inner-City Research Alliance, Canadian Centre for Policy Alternatives, Manitoba.

Silver, J., D. Klyne and F. Simard 2003 *Aboriginal Learners in Selected Adult Learning Centres in Manitoba.* Canadian Centre for Policy Alternatives, Manitoba.

Skarlicki, D. n.d. *Socio-Economic Planning Model: Tools for Native Community Economic Planning.* Edmonton: First Nations Resource Council.

Skea, W. 1993–94 "The Canadian Newspaper Industry's Portrayal of the Oka Crisis." *Native Studies Review,* 9 (1): 15–31.

Slattery, B. 1985 "The Hidden Constitution: Aboriginal Rights in Canada." In *The Quest for Justice,* M. Boldt, J. Long, and L. Little Bear (eds.). Toronto: University of Toronto Press.

Smith, A. 1981 *The Ethnic Revival.* New York: Cambridge University Press.

Smith, J., A. Kornberg and B. Rushing 1985 "The Changing Political Situation of Women in Canada." In *Minorities and the Canadian State,* N. Nevitte and A. Kornberg (eds.). Oakville ON: Mosaic Press, pp. 221–238.

Smylie, J. 2001. "Health Issues Affecting Aboriginal Peoples." *Journal of the Society of Obstetricians and Gynaecologists of Canada,* 99: 54–68.

Solicitor General of Canada 1985 *Native and Non-Native Admissions to Federal, Provincial and Territorial Correctional Institutions.* Ottawa: Solicitor General of Canada.

_____ **1989** *Task Force on Aboriginal Peoples in Federal Corrections: Final Report.* Ottawa: Solicitor General of Canada.

Sorenson, Gary and Murray Wolfson 1969 "Black Economic Independence: Some Preliminary Thoughts." *The Annals of Regional Science,* 3 (December): 168–178.

Special Senate Committee Hearing on Poverty 1970 *Proceedings,* Vols. 13–14. Ottawa: Supply and Services Canada.

Speck, D. C. 1989 "The Indian Health Transfer Policy: A Step in the Right Direction, A Revenge of the Hidden Policy?" *Native Studies Review,* 5 (1), 187–214.

Stanbury, R., and J. Fields 1975 *Success and Failure: Indians in Urban Society.* Vancouver: University of British Columbia Press.

Stanley, George 1952 "The Indian Background of Canadian History." *Canadian Historical Association Annual Report.* Canadian Historical Society.

_____ **1961** *The Birth of Western Canada: A History of the Riel Rebellions.* New York: Longman, Green.

Starblanket, N. 1979 *On the Rights of Indian Women and Children Under the Indian Act.* Ottawa: NIB.

Stasiulis, D. and N. Yuval-Davis (eds.) 1995 *Unsettling Settler Societies,* Vol. 11. London: Sage Publications.

Statistics Canada 1986 *Canadian Metropolitan Areas.* Dimensions Series. Ottawa.

_____ **2001a** *Aboriginal Peoples Survey.* Ottawa: Indian and Northern Affairs Canada

_____ **2001b** *Aboriginal Peoples of Canada: Demographic Profile.* Ottawa: Ministry of Industry.

_____ **2003** *Aboriginal Peoples Survey.* Ottawa.

_____ **2004** *Aboriginal Network,* Winter. Ottawa.

_____ **2005.** *Projections of the Aboriginal Populations, Canada, Provinces and Territories: 2001-2017.* Ottawa: Ministry of Industry.

Steinem, G. 1983 "Perspectives on Women in the 1980s: The Baird Poskanzer Memorial Lecture." In *Perspectives on Women in the 1980s,* J. Turner and L. Emery (eds.). Winnipeg: University of Manitoba Press, pp. 14–27.

Stern, P. 2000 "Subsistence: Work and Leisure." *Etudes/Inuit/Studies,* 24 (1): 9–24.

Sterritt, N. 1998–99 "The Nisga'a Treaty: Competing Claims Ignored!" *B.C. Studies,* 120: 73–98.

Stewart, Walter 1974 "Red Power." In *Canada's Indians: Contemporary Conflicts,* J.S. Frideres (ed.). Scarborough ON: Prentice Hall Canada.

Stymeist, David H. 1975 *Ethnics and Indians: Social Relations in a Northwestern*

Ontario Town. Toronto: Peter Martin Associates.

Sunkel, Oswaldo 1973 "Transitional Capitalism and National Disintegration in Latin America." *Social and Economic Studies,* 22: 132–176.

Surtees, R.J. 1969 "The Development of an Indian Reserve Policy in Canada." *Ontario History,* LCI, 2 (June): 87–98.

Swain, H. 1988 "Comprehensive Claims." *Transition,* 1 (6 (December)): 7–9.

Tabb, William 1970 *The Political Economy of the Black Ghetto.* New York: W.W. Norton.

Tait, H. 2006 *Harvesting and Community Well-being among Inuit in the Canadian Arctic.* Ottawa: Ministry of Industry, Statistics Canada.

Tanner, A. (ed.) 1983 *The Politics of Indianness.* St. John's NF: Institute of Social and Economic Research, Memorial University of Newfoundland.

Taqralik 1984 *Native Women's Association Offers Help to Inuit Women.* Mimeograph.

Taylor, J. 1983 "An Historical Introduction to Métis Claims in Canada." *The Canadian Journal of Native Studies,* 3: 151–181.

Taylor, J. and M. Bell (eds.) 2004 *Population Mobility and Indigenous People in Australasia and North America.* London: Routledge.

Tennant, P. 1984 "Indian Self Government: Progress or Stalemate." *Canadian Public Policy,* 10 (2): 211–215.

Tester, F. and P. Kulchyski 1994 *Tammarniit: Inuit Relocation in the Eastern Arctic, 1939-63.* Vancouver: University of British Columbia Press.

Thom, B. 2001 "Aboriginal Rights and Title in Canada after *Delgamuukw*: Part I and II," *Native Studies Review,* 14 (2): 1–42.

Thomas, D.H. 1972 "Western Shoshoni Ecology Settlement Patterns and Beyond." In *Great Basin Cultural Ecology: A Symposium,* D.D. Fowler (ed.). Desert Research Institute, Publications in the Social Sciences, 8.

Thomas, Robert K. 1985 "Afterward." In *The New Peoples: Being and Becoming Métis in North America,* Jacqueline Peterson and Jennifer S.H. Brown (eds.). Winnipeg: University of Manitoba Press: 243–251.

Thompson, M. 2004 "Adult Criminal Court Statistics, 2003/04," *Juristat,* 24 (12). Ottawa: Statistics Canada, Canadian Centre for Justice Statistics.

Thompson, R. 1982 "Aboriginal Title and Mining Legislation in the Northwest Territories." *Studies in Aboriginal Rights No. 6.* Saskatoon: University of Saskatchewan Native Law Centre.

Thornton, R. 1986 *We Shall Live Again,* Cambridge: Cambridge University Press.

Titley, B. 1983 "W.M. Graham: Indian Agent Extraordinaire." *Prairie Forum,* 8: 26–28.

_____ **1986** *A Narrow Vision.* Vancouver: University of British Columbia Press.

Tjepkema, M. 2001 "The Health of the Off-Reserve Aboriginal Population." *Supplement to Health Reports,* vol. 13. Ottawa: Statistics Canada, Cat. No. 82-003.

Tobias, J. 1976 "Protection, Civilization, Assimilation: An Outline of Canada's Indian Policy." *Western Canadian Journal of Anthropology,* 6 (2): 13–30.

Todd, R. 2000–2001 "Between the Land and the City: Aboriginal Agency, Culture and Governance in Urban Areas." *The London Journal of Canadian Studies,* 16: 48–66.

Treaty 7 Elders and Tribal Council 1996 *The True Spirit and Original Intent of Treaty.* Montreal and Kingston: McGill-Queen's University Press.

Trigger, B. 1965 "The Jesuits and the Fur Trade." *Ethnohistory,* 12 (Winter): 30–53.

_____ **1985** *Natives and Newcomers.* Kingston and Montreal: McGill-Queen's University Press.

Trovato, F. 2001 "Aboriginal Mortality in Canada, the United States and New Zealand." *Journal of Biosocial Science,* 33 (1): 67–86.

Trudel, Marcel and Genevieve Jain 1970 "Canadian History Textbooks." *Studies of the Royal Commission on Bilingualism and Biculturalism,* No. 5. Ottawa: Queen's Printer.

Turcotte, M. and J. Zhao 2004 "Well-being of off-Reserve Aboriginal Children." *Canadian Social Trends,* Winter, 22–27.

Turpel, Mary 1990 "Aboriginal Peoples and the Canadian Charter: Interpretive Monopolies, Cultural Differences." *Canadian Human Rights Year Book,* 1989–90. Ottawa: University of Ottawa, Human Rights Research and Education Centre, pp. 3–45.

Two-Axe Early, M., Z. Keywan, and H. Potrebenko 1981 "Ethnicity and Femininity as Determinants of Life Experience." *Canadian Ethnic Studies,* 13 (1), 37–42.

Uchendu, U. 1970 "The Passing of Tribal Man: A West African Experience." In *The Passing of Tribal Man in Africa,* P. Gutlaind (ed.). Leiden, the Netherlands: E.J. Brill, pp. 51–56.

Umorzurike, U. 1972 *Self-Determination in International Law*. Hamden CT: Anchor Books.

United Nations Educational, Scientific and Cultural Organization (UNESCO) 1981 "Socio-Economic Indicators for Planning: Methodological Aspects and Selected Examples." *Socio-Economic Studies* 2. Paris.

_____ 1984 "Applicability of Indicators of Socio-Economic Change for Development Planning." *Socio-Economic Studies* 7. Paris.

Usher, P. 1989 *Towards a Strategy for Supporting the Domestic Economy of the Northwest Territories*. Ottawa.

Usher, P., G. Duhaime, and E. Searles 2003. "The Household as an Economic Unit in Arctic Aboriginal Communities and its Measurement by Means of a Comprehensive Survey." *Social Indicators Research*, 61: 175–202.

Uslaner, E. 2002 *The Moral Foundations of Trust*. Cambridge: Cambridge University Press.

Vanderburgh, R. 1968 *The Canadian Indians in Ontario's School Texts: A Study of Social Studies Textbooks, Grades 1 through 8*. Report prepared for the University Women's Club of Port Credit, ON.

Vandergoot, M. 2006 *Justice for Young Offenders*. Saskatoon: Purich Publishers.

Van Kirk, Sylvia 1980 *Many Tender Ties*. Winnipeg: Watson, Dwyer Publishing.

Venne, Sharon Helen 1998 *Our Elders Understand Our Rights: Evolving International Law Regarding Indigenous Peoples*. Penticton BC: Theytus Books.

Verma, Ravi and Pierre Gauvin 2004 "Abridged Life Tables for Registered Indians in Canada." *Canadian Studies in Population* 31 (2): 197–235.

Vick-Westgate, A. 2002 *Nunavik*. Calgary: University of Calgary Press.

Waddell, Jack and O.M. Watson 1971 *The American Indian in Urban Society*. Boston: Little, Brown.

Walker, James 1971 "The Indians in Canadian Historical Writing." Paper delivered at Canadian Historical Association meetings.

Walters, D., J. White and P. Maxim 2004 "Does Postsecondary Education Benefit Aboriginal Canadians? An Examination of Earnings and Employment Outcomes for Recent Aboriginal Graduates," *Canadian Public Policy/Analyse de politiques*, 30 (3): 283–301.

Warry, W. 2007 *Ending Denial*. Peterborough, ON: Broadview Press.

Waters, A. (ed.) 2004 *American Indian Thought*. Malden,MA: Blackwell Publishing.

Watkins, M. 1977 *Dene Nation: The Colony Within*. Toronto: University of Toronto Press.

Watson, G. 1979 "On Getting Nothing Back: Managing the Meaning of Ethnicity in Canada's Northwest Territories." *Ethnos*, 1–2: 99–118.

_____ 1981 "The Reification of Ethnicity and Its Political Consequences in the North." *Canadian Review of Sociology and Anthropology*, 18 (40): 453–469.

Waubageshig 1970 *The Only Good Indian*. Toronto: New Press.

Weaver, S. 1978 *Indian Women, Marriage and Legal Status*. Waterloo, ON: University of Waterloo, n.p.

_____ 1980 *The Hidden Agenda: Indian Policy and the Trudeau Government*. Waterloo, ON: University of Waterloo, mimeo.

_____ 1981 *Making Canadian Indian Policy: The Hidden Agenda 1968–1970*. Toronto: University of Toronto Press.

_____ 1983 "Federal Difficulties with Aboriginal Rights Demands." In *Aboriginal Rights: Towards an Understanding*, J.A. Long, M. Boldt, and L. Little Bear (eds.). Lethbridge, AB: University of Lethbridge.

_____ 1984 "A Commentary on the Penner Report." *Canadian Public Policy*, 10 (2): 215–221.

_____ 1985 "Political Representivity and Indigenous Minorities in Canada and Australia." In *Indigenous Peoples and the Nation State: 'Fourth World' Politics in Canada, Australia and Norway*, N. Dyck (ed.). St. John's: Memorial University of Newfoundland.

_____ 1986 "Indian Policy in the New Conservative Government, Part II: The Nielsen Task Force in the Context of Recent Policy Initiatives." *Native Studies Review*, 2 (2): 1–47.

Weitz, J. 1971 *Cultural Change and Field Dependence in Two Native Canadian Linguistic Families*. Unpublished Ph.D. dissertation, University of Ottawa, 1971.

Welsh, A. 2000 "Aboriginal Offenders and Full Parole: A Profile." *Forum*, 12 (1): 61–64.

Wertman, P. 1983 "Planning and Development after the James Bay Agreement." *Canadian Journal of Native Studies*, 2 (3): 48–56.

Wherrett, J. and D. Brown 1994 *Models of Aboriginal Government in Urban Areas*,

Policy and Strategic Direction. Ottawa: Department of Indian Affairs and Northern Development.

White, Jerry P., Paul Maxim and Dan Beavon 2003 *Aboriginal Conditions: Research as a Foundation for Public Policy*. Vancouver: University of British Columbia Press.

Whitehead, S., B. Henning, J. Johnston and A. Devlin 1996 *Developing an Injury Morbidity and Mortality Profile in the Sioux Lookout Zone: 1992–1995*. Ottawa: Canadian Hospitals Injury Reporting and Prevention Program.

Whiteside, D. 1972 *A Good Blanket Has Four Corners: An Initial Comparison of the Colonial Administration of Aboriginals in Canada and the United States*. Paper presented at the Western Association of Sociology and Anthropology, Calgary.

_____ **1973a** *Historical Development of Aboriginal Political Associations in Canada*. Ottawa: National Indian Brotherhood.

_____ **1973b** *Historical Development of Aboriginal Associations in Canada: Documentation*. Ottawa: National Indian Brotherhood.

_____ **1980** *Bullets, Bibles, Bureaucrats, and Businessmen: Indian Administration in Upper Canada, 1746–1980*. Address to the Indian Historical Conference, Walpole Island Reserve, November 15, 1980.

Wien, F. 1986 *Rebuilding the Economic Base of Indian Communities: The Micmac in Nova Scotia*. Montreal: Institute for Research on Public Policy.

Wildsmith, B. 1985 "Pre Confederation Treaties." In *Aboriginal Peoples and the Law*, B. Morse (ed.). Ottawa: Carleton University Press, pp.122–271.

Wilkes, R. 2004 "First Nation Politics: Deprivation, Resources and Participation in Collection Action," *Sociological Inquiry*, 74 (4): 570–589.

Wilkins 1999 ". . . But We Need the Eggs: The Royal Commission, the Charter of Rights and the Inherent Right of Aboriginal Self-Government." *University of Toronto Law Journal*, 44 (1): 53–121.

Willhelm, Sidney M. 1969 "Red Man, Black Man, and White America: The Constitutional Approach to Genocide." *Catalyst*, 4 (Spring): 3–4.

Wilson, Richard W. 1992 *Compliance Ideologies: Rethinking Political Culture*. Cambridge: Cambridge University Press.

Wong, D. 2002 *Cities at the Crossroads: Addressing Intergovernmental Structures for Western Canada's Cities*. Calgary: August, Canada West Foundation.

Wood, D. and C. Griffiths 2000 "Patterns of Aboriginal Crime." In *Crime in Canadian Society*. Toronto: Harcourt Brace Canada.

Woodward, J. 1989 *Native Law*. Toronto: Carswell.

Wotherspoon, T. 2003 "Prospects for a New Middle Class among Urban Aboriginal People." In *Not Strangers in These Parts*, D. Newhouse and E. Peters (eds.). Ottawa: Policy Research Institute, pp. 147–166.

Wright, C. 1995 "Diversions are a Bright Light." *Native Issues Monthly*, special issue, 61–63.

Wright, R. 2003 *Stolen Continents*. Toronto: Penguin Canada.

Wuttunee, W. 1972 *Ruffled Feathers*. Calgary: Bell Books.

Young, K. 1984 "Indian Health Services in Canada: A Sociohistorical Perspective." *Social Science and Medicine*, 18 (3), 257–264.

Young, T. J. O'Neill and B. Elias 1999 *Chronic Diseases, First Nations and Inuit Regional Health Survey*. First Nations and Inuit Regional Health Survey, National Steering Committee. Ottawa.

Young, T., J. O'Neill and B. Elias, J. Readin, and G. McDonald 1998 (First National and Inuit Regional Health Survey National Steering Committees and Technical Committees), "Chronic Diseases Among Aboriginal People in Canada." Conference of the National Aboriginal Information and Research. Ottawa.

Zakariya, H. 1976 "New Directions in the Search for and Development of Petroleum Resources in the Developing Countries." *Vanderbilt Journal of Transnational Law*, 9 (Summer): 545–577.

Zlotkin, N. 1983 *Unfinished Business: Aboriginal Peoples and the 1983 Constitutional Conference*. Kingston ON: Institute of Intergovernmental Relations, Queen's University.

_____ **1985** "Post-Confederation Treaties." In *Aboriginal Peoples and the Law*, B. Morse (ed.). Ottawa: Carleton University Press.

Index